T0211706

Lecture Notes in Business Information Processing 378

More information about this series at http://www.springer.com/series/7911

Joaquim Filipe · Michał Śmiałek ·
Alexander Brodsky · Slimane Hammoudi (Eds.)

Enterprise Information Systems

21st International Conference, ICEIS 2019
Heraklion, Crete, Greece, May 3–5, 2019
Revised Selected Papers

 Springer

Editors
Joaquim Filipe
INSTICC and Polytechnic Institute
of Setúbal
Setúbal, Portugal

Alexander Brodsky
George Mason University
Fairfax, VA, USA

Michał Śmiałek
Warsaw University of Technology
Warsaw, Poland

Slimane Hammoudi
MODESTE/ESEO
Angers, France

ISSN 1865-1348 ISSN 1865-1356 (electronic)
Lecture Notes in Business Information Processing
ISBN 978-3-030-40782-7 ISBN 978-3-030-40783-4 (eBook)
https://doi.org/10.1007/978-3-030-40783-4

This Springer imprint is published by the registered company Springer Nature Switzerland AG
The registered company address is: Gewerbestrasse 11, 6330 Cham, Switzerland

Preface

The present book includes extended and revised versions of a set of selected papers from the 21st International Conference on Enterprise Information Systems (ICEIS 2019), held in Heraklion-Crete, Greece, during May 3–5, 2019.

ICEIS 2019 received 205 paper submissions from 51 countries, of which 13% were included in this book. The papers were selected by the event chairs and their selection was based on a number of criteria that included classifications and comments provided by Program Committee members, the session chairs' assessment, and also the program chairs' global view of all the papers included in the technical program. The authors of selected papers were then invited to submit revised and extended versions of their papers having at least 30% innovative material.

The purpose of ICEIS 2019 was to bring together researchers, engineers, and practitioners interested in advances and business applications of information systems. Six simultaneous tracks were held, covering different aspects of enterprise information systems applications, including enterprise database technology, systems integration, artificial intelligence, decision support systems, information systems analysis and specification, internet computing, electronic commerce, human factors, and enterprise architecture.

We are confident that the papers included in this book will strongly contribute to the understanding of some current research trends in enterprise information systems. Such systems require diverse approaches to answer challenges of contemporary enterprises. Thus, this book covers diverse but complementary areas such as: data science and databases, ontologies, social networks, knowledge management, software development, human-computer interaction, and multimedia.

We would like to thank all the authors for their contributions and the reviewers for their hard work which helped to ensure the quality of this publication.

May 2019

Joaquim Filipe
Michał Śmiałek
Alexander Brodsky
Slimane Hammoudi

Organization

Conference Co-chairs

Alexander Brodsky   George Mason University, USA
Slimane Hammoudi   ESEO, ERIS, France

Program Co-chairs

Joaquim Filipe   Polytechnic Institute of Setúbal, INSTICC, Portugal
Michal Smialek   Warsaw University of Technology, Poland

Program Committee

Amna Abidi	Altran Research, France
Nevena Ackovska	Ss. Cyril and Methodius University, Macedonia
Adeel Ahmad	Laboratoire d'Informatique Signal et Image de la Côte d'Opale, France
Zahid Akhtar	University of Memphis, USA
Emel Aktas	Cranfield University, UK
Patrick Albers	ESEO, France
Javier Albusac	Escuela Superior de Informática, Universidad de Castilla-La Mancha, Spain
Eduardo Alchieri	Universidade de Brasília, Brazil
Mohammad Al-Shamri	Ibb University, Yemen
Luis Álvarez Sabucedo	University of Vigo, Spain
Omar Alvarez-Xochihua	Universidad Autónoma de Baja California, Mexico
Rachid Anane	Coventry University, UK
Leandro Antonelli	LIFIA, Universidad Nacional de La Plata, Argentina
Marco Antonio Casanova	Pontificia Universidade Católica do Rio de Janeiro, Brazil
Josephina Antoniou	Uclan Cyprus, Cyprus
Olatz Arbelaitz Gallego	Universidad del País Vasco (UPV/EHU), Spain
Lerina Aversano	University of Sannio, Italy
Oscar Avila	Universidad de los Andes, Colombia
Tamara Babaian	Bentley University, USA
José Banares Bañares	Universidad de Zaragoza, Spain
Cecilia Baranauskas	State University of Campinas (Unicamp), Brazil
Ken Barker	University of Calgary, Canada
Reza Barkhi	Virginia Tech, USA
Jean-Paul Barthes	Université de Technologie de Compiègne, France
Imen Ben Fradj	Research Laboratory in Technologies of Information and Communication and Electrical, Tunisia

François Bergeron	TELUQ-Université du Québec, Canada
Edward Bernroider	Vienna University of Economics and Business, Austria
Ana Bertoletti De Marchi	Universidade de Passo Fundo, Brazil
Ilia Bider	DSV, Stockholm University, Sweden
Frederique Biennier	INSA Lyon, France
Sandro Bimonte	IRSTEA, France
Carlos Blanco Bueno	University of Cantabria, Spain
Tales Bogoni	Universidade do Estado de Mato Grosso, Brazil
Boyan Bontchev	Sofia University St. Kliment Ohridski, Bulgaria
Gabriela Bosetti	LIRIS, Université de Lyon, France
Zita Bošnjak	University of Novi Sad, Serbia
Jean-Louis Boulanger	CERTIFER, France
Andrés Boza	Universitat Politècnica de València, Spain
Maria-Eugenia Cabello-Espinosa	University of Colima, Mexico
David Cabrero Souto	University of A Coruña, Spain
Luis Camarinha-Matos	New University of Lisbon, Portugal
Manuel Capel-Tuñón	University of Granada, Spain
João Luís Cardoso de Moraes	Federal University of São Carlos, Brazil
Glauco Carneiro	Universidade Salvador (UNIFACS), Brazil
Angélica Caro	University of Bio-Bio, Chile
Diego Carvalho	Federal Centre of Engineering Studies and Technological Education, Brazil
Nunzio Casalino	Università Luiss Guido Carli, Italy
Laura M. Castro	University of A Coruña, Spain
Salvatore Cavalieri	University of Catania, Italy
Luca Cernuzzi	Universidad Católica Nuestra Señora de la Asunción, Paraguay
Chen Chen	Mercy College, USA
Max Chevalier	UMR 5505, France
Nan-Hsing Chiu	Chien Hsin University of Science and Technology, Taiwan, China
William Chu	Tunghai University, Taiwan, China
Betim Cico	Epoka University, Albania
Daniela Claro	Universidade Federal da Bahia (UFBA), Brazil
Pedro Coelho	State University of Rio de Janeiro, Brazil
Cesar Collazos	Universidad del Cauca, Colombia
Antonio Corral	University of Almeria, Spain
Mariela Cortés	State University of Ceará, Brazil
Jean-Valère Cossu	My Local Influence (MYLI), France
Henrique Cota de Freitas	Pontifícia Universidade Católica de Minas Gerais, Brazil
Karl Cox	University of Brighton, UK
Sharon Cox	Birmingham City University, UK
Broderick Crawford	Pontificia Universidad Catolica de Valparaiso, Chile

Beata Czarnacka-Chrobot	Warsaw School of Economics, Poland
Hennie Daniels	University of Tilburg, The Netherlands
José de Almeida Amazonas	Escola Politécnica of the University of São Paulo, Spain
Vincenzo Deufemia	University of Salerno, Italy
Kamil Dimililer	Near East University, Cyprus
Aleksandar Dimov	Sofia University St. Kliment Ohridski, Bulgaria
Dulce Domingos	Universidade de Lisboa, LASIGE, Portugal
César Domínguez	Universidad de La Rioja, Spain
António Dourado	University of Coimbra, Portugal
Helena Dudycz	Wroclaw University of Economics, Poland
Sophie Ebersold	IRIT, France
Hans-Dieter Ehrich	Technische Universitaet Braunschweig, Germany
Monika Eisenbardt	University of Economics in Katowice, Poland
Zineb El Akkaoui	The National Institute of Posts and Telecommunications, Morocco
Fabrício Enembreck	Pontifical Catholic University of Paraná, Brazil
Marcelo Fantinato	University of São Paulo, Brazil
João Faria	FEUP, Portugal
Fausto Fasano	University of Molise, Italy
Edilson Ferneda	Universidade Catolica de Brasíla, Brazil
Maria Ferreira	Universidade Portucalense, Portugal
Paulo Ferreira	INESC-ID, IST, Portugal
Luis Ferreira Pires	University of Twente, The Netherlands
Jiri Feuerlicht	Prague University of Economics, Czech Republic
Gustavo Figueroa	Instituto Nacional de Electricidad y Energías Limpias, Mexico
Sonja Filiposka	Ss. Cyril and Methodius University, Macedonia
Adriano Fiorese	Santa Catarina State University (UDESC), Brazil
Sergio Firmenich	Universidad Nacional de La Plata, Argentina
Francesco Folino	ICAR-CNR, Italy
Kevin Foltz	IDA, USA
Anna Formica	CNR-IASI, Italy
Rita Francese	Università degli Studi di Salerno, Italy
Ana Fred	Instituto de Telecomunicações and Instituto Superior Técnico, University of Lisbon, Portugal
Lixin Fu	University of North Carolina at Greensboro, USA
Luiz Gadelha Junior	National Laboratory for Scientific Computing, Brazil
Leonid Galchynsky	NTUU KPI, Ukraine
Cristian García Bauza	UNCPBA-PLADEMA-CONICET, Argentina
Mouzhi Ge	Masaryk University, Czech Republic
Manuel Gómez Olmedo	University of Granada, Spain
Amr Goneid	The American University in Cairo, Egypt
Pascual Gonzalez	Universidad de Castilla-La Mancha, Spain
Feliz Gouveia	University Fernando Pessoa, Portugal, and CEREM, Spain

Virginie Govaere	INRS, France
Janis Grabis	Riga Technical University, Latvia
Rogéria Gratão de Souza	São Paulo State University (UNESP), Brazil
Luca Greco	University of Salerno, Italy
Wieslawa Gryncewicz	Wroclaw University of Economics, Poland
Hatim Hafiddi	INPT, Morocco
Karin Harbusch	Universität Koblenz-Landau, Germany
Celso Hirata	Instituto Tecnológico de Aeronáutica, Brazil
Wladyslaw Homenda	Warsaw University of Technology, Poland
Wei-Chiang Hong	Jiangsu Normal University, China
Miguel J. Hornos	University of Granada, Spain
Fu-Shiung Hsieh	Chaoyang University of Technology, Taiwan, China
Kai-I Huang	Tunghai University, Taiwan, China
Miroslav Hudec	University of Economics in Bratislava, Slovakia
Nantia Iakovidou	Aristotle University, Greece
George Ioannidis	University of Patras, Greece
Arturo Jaime	Universidad de La Rioja, Spain
Kai Jakobs	RWTH Aachen University, Germany
Agnieszka Jastrzebska	Warsaw University of Technology, Poland
Yichuan Jiang	Southeast University, China
Luis Jiménez Linares	Universidad de Castilla-La Mancha, Spain
Hermann Kaindl	TU Wien, Austria
Olga Kalimullina	The Bonch-Bruevich St. Petersburg State University of Telecommunications, Russia
Christos Kalloniatis	University of the Aegean, Greece
Kalinka Kaloyanova	Soa University St. Kliment Ohridski, Bulgaria
Roland Kaschek	CSB-System AG, Germany
Dimitrios Katsaros	University of Thessaly, Greece
Nina Khairova	NTUU KPI, Ukraine
Andrea Kienle	University of Applied Sciences Dortmund, Germany
Yoney Kirsal Ever	Near East University, Cyprus
Angeliki Kitsiou	University of the Aegean, Greece
Alexander Knapp	Universität Augsburg, Germany
Fotios Kokkoras	University of Thessaly, Greece
Christophe Kolski	Université Polytechnique des Hauts-de-France, France
Natalija Kozmina	University of Latvia, Latvia
Burra Kumar	Xiamen University Malaysia Campus, Malaysia
Rob Kusters	Open Universiteit, The Netherlands
Jan Kwiatkowski	Wroclaw University of Science and Technology, Poland
Maria Lambrou	University of the Aegean, Greece
Ramon Lawrence	University of British Columbia Okanagan Campus, Canada
Jintae Lee	Leeds School of Business at University of Colorado Boulder, USA

Claus Pahl	Free University of Bozen-Bolzano, Italy
Malgorzata Pankowska	University of Economics in Katowice, Poland
Eric Pardede	La Trobe University, Australia
Rafael Parpinelli	Universidade do Estado de Santa Catarina, Brazil
Silvia Parusheva	University of Economics Varna, Bulgaria
Ignazio Passero	Kineton, Italy
Maria Penadés Gramaje	Universitat Politècnica de València, Spain
Taoxin Peng	Edinburgh Napier University, UK
Dana Petcu	West University of Timisoara, Romania
Matus Pleva	Technical University of Kosice, Slovakia
Placide Poba-Nzaou	Université du Québec à Montréal, Canada
Valentina Poggioni	University of Perugia, Italy
Fiona Polack	Keele University, UK
Alexandra Pomares-Quimbaya	Pontificia Universidad Javeriana, Colombia
Luigi Pontieri	CNR, Italy
Filipe Portela	Centro ALGORITMI, University of Minho, Portugal
Naveen Prakash	IIITD, India
Daniele Radicioni	University of Turin, Italy
T. Ramayah	Universiti Sains Malaysia, Malaysia
Pedro Ramos	Instituto Superior das Ciências do Trabalho e da Empresa, Portugal
Carlos Arturo Ray-Mundo Ibañez	Universidad Peruana de Ciencias Aplicadas (UPC), Peru
Francisco Regateiro	Instituto Superior Técnico, Portugal
Ulrich Reimer	University of Applied Sciences St. Gallen, Switzerland
Nuno Ribeiro	Universidade Fernando Pessoa, Portugal
Ricardo Ribeiro	ISCTE-IUL, INESC-ID, Portugal
Michele Risi	University of Salerno, Italy
Sonja Ristic	University of Novi Sad, Serbia
Jose Rivero	LIFIA, Universidad Nacional de La Plata, Argentina
Carlos Roberto Valêncio	São Paulo State University, Brazil
Leonardo Rocha	Federal University of São João Del Rei, Brazil
Alfonso Rodriguez	University of Bio-Bio, Chile
Daniel Rodriguez	University of Alcalá, Spain
Jose Raul Romero	University of Cordoba, Spain
Michael Rosemann	Queensland University of Technology, Australia
Gustavo Rossi	LIFIA, Argentina
Artur Rot	Wroclaw University of Economics, Poland
Ounsa Roudiès	Ecole Mohammadia d'Ingénieurs (EMI), Morocco
Mohamed Roushdy	Ain Shams University, Egypt
Antonio Juan Rubio-Montero	CIEMAT, Universidad Complutense de Madrid, Spain
Francisco Ruiz	Universidad de Castilla-La Mancha, Spain
Boong Ryoo	Texas A&M University, USA
Rafael Sachetto	Federal University of São João Del Rei, Brazil

Belen Vela Sanchez	Rey Juan Carlos University, Spain
Gizelle Vianna	UFRRJ, Brazil
Melina Vidoni	RMIT University, Australia
M. A. Vila	University of Granada, Spain
Gualtiero Volpe	Università degli Studi di Genova, Italy
Vasiliki Vrana	International Hellenic University, Greece
Boris Vrdoljak	University of Zagreb, Croatia
Dariusz Wawrzyniak	Wroclaw University of Economics, Poland
Hans Weigand	Tilburg University, The Netherlands
Janusz Wielki	Opole University of Technology, Poland
Adam Wójtowicz	Poznan University of Economics and Business, Poland
Mudasser Wyne	National University, USA
Qishan Yang	Dublin City University, Ireland
Muhammed Younas	Oxford Brookes University, UK
Geraldo Zafalon	São Paulo State University, Brazil
Luciana Zaina	UFSCar, Brazil
Brahmi Zaki	RIADI, Tunisia
Jinyu Zhang	Nanjing University, China
Yifeng Zhou	Southeast University, China
Eugenio Zimeo	University of Sannio, Italy

Additional Reviewers

Hércules Antônio do Prado	Universidade Católica de Brasília, Brazil
Loredana Caruccio	University of Salerno, Italy
Andre Cordeiro	State University of Maringa, Brazil
Zineb Lamghari	LRIT, Morocco
Ricardo Pérez-Castillo	ITSI, Universidad de Castilla-La Mancha, Spain
Santiago Sánchez	Universidad de Castilla-La Mancha, Spain
Igor Santos	CEFET/RJ, Brazil

Invited Speakers

Danny Menasce	George Mason University, USA
Marie-Christine Rousset	Université Grenoble Alpes and Institut Universitaire de France, France
Mike Papazoglou	Tilburg University, The Netherlands
Manlio Del Giudice	University of Rome Link Campus, Italy

Contents

Enterprise Security with Endpoint Agents

Kevin Foltz[(✉)] and William R. Simpson

Institute for Defense Analyses, Alexandria, VA 22311, USA
{kfoltz,rsimpson}@ida.org

Abstract. Enterprise security is complicated by the use of mobile devices. These devices roam outside the protections of the enterprise core network. They operate closer to threats while simultaneously being farther from the enterprise, which makes compromise more likely and response more difficult. This paper describes an approach using software agents installed on endpoint devices to maintain security of these devices and their associated enterprise. These agents monitor local activity, prevent harmful behavior, allow remote management, and report back to the enterprise. The challenge in this environment is the security of the agents and their communication with the enterprise. This work presents an agent architecture that operates within a high-security Enterprise Level Security (ELS) architecture that preserves end-to-end integrity, encryption, and accountability. This architecture uses secure hardware for sensitive key operations and device attestation. Software agents leverage this hardware security to provide services consistent with the ELS framework. Additional agents leverage this baseline security to provide additional features and functions. This enables an enterprise to manage and secure all endpoint device agents and their communications with other enterprise services.

Keywords: Enterprise · Software agent · System design · Confidentiality · Integrity · Application security · Security · End-to-End encryption · Mobile device management · Host based security

1 Introduction

Defense of an enterprise and its information against external attacks has moved from the central network to the edge devices. Network monitoring provides a centralized approach where all communications can be intercepted, recorded, and analyzed for malicious intent and modified as needed. However, this is complicated by current threats and operational practices.

Network monitoring can provide important insights about lower layer resources and communications but, with widespread encrypted hypertext transfer protocol secure (HTTPS) and similar protocols, it does not have access to the higher layer content. Web application firewalls (WAFs) attempt to bridge this gap by decrypting content for the server, analyzing and modifying it for security, and passing the clean content to the server. The WAF may even open files and execute code to determine if certain content presents a danger to the receiver. This approach catches many attacks that network monitoring

© Springer Nature Switzerland AG 2020
J. Filipe et al. (Eds.): ICEIS 2019, LNBIP 378, pp. 1–16, 2020.
https://doi.org/10.1007/978-3-030-40783-4_1

and pattern-based detection miss, but it breaks the end-to-end security model, introduces latency in communications, and does not stop all attacks.

Widespread encrypted HTTPS traffic requires a network scanner to act as a central point of decryption. This can be accomplished by sharing server private keys with network appliances on the wire, but such an approach violates end-to-end security by breaking every secure connection within the enterprise. In addition, these network appliances provide central points of attack that enable access to all traffic and allow an attacker to impersonate any entity within the enterprise. Such a network-based approach has critical security flaws.

Moving the defense to the edge of the network offers several advantages. There is no need to break end-to-end secure connections. There is no central point of attack that can compromise all connections and impersonate any entity. The defense tools can operate at the endpoint to detect malicious behavior as it happens and directly respond instead of trying to predict it before it happens based on network traffic and then trying to respond remotely after the damage is done.

The edge defense model does have some drawbacks. The distributed nature of the defense introduces the challenge of coordination and correlation of data. End-to-end security requires new approaches to decrypt data for analysis. Also, software agents at the endpoints, which are often lightweight applications, must perform secure operations and initiate secure communication channels.

Endpoint agent architecture design has seen some work with varying goals. (Wang et al. 2003) describe an agent architecture that preserves battery life of mobile devices. (Assink 2016) describes the potential benefits of using agents for Internet of Things (IoT) applications. (Berkovits et al. 1998) and (Varadharajan and Foster 2003) examine security of agents that migrate between different hosts. (Liu and Wang 2003) describe a secure agent architecture for sensor networks. (Šimo et al. 2009) describe a secure agent architecture for mobile agents with similar security goals. However, its agents operate with their own software-based private keys, so the agent code itself must be carefully protected.

There is a lot of work in the area of mobile agent computing, where agents move from device to device. However, our interest is in monitoring the device itself using agents, not doing computations that move agents across devices.

This paper presents a method for enabling distributed endpoint-based defense while preserving end-to-end integrity, encryption, and authentication of communications across the enterprise. This agent architecture extends (Foltz and Simpson 2019), and it is part of a larger effort to secure information sharing for the United States Air Force (Foltz and Simpson 2017).

2 Enterprise Level Security Baseline

This work uses as a starting point the Enterprise Level Security (ELS) model. ELS is designed for high assurance information systems subject to constant sophisticated attacks (Trias et al. 2016). It then addresses the challenge of integrating endpoint device agents into such an architecture while adhering to and working with the existing ELS concepts, components, and protocols. This section provides an overview of ELS and the integration challenges for agent-based security.

2.1 ELS Overview

The core of ELS is identity management and access control. The goal is to uniquely identify every entity in the enterprise, human and non-human, and use these identities with strong authentication methods to initiate communication. For interactions where data or services are requested, access is determined by data providers using rules based on attributes stored in an Enterprise Attribute System (EAS).

The data owner or service provider is part of the enterprise and is responsible for setting access rules. This preserves some degree of autonomy for the data owners and supports scalability through its distributed architecture. These rules are compared against attributes collected from across the enterprise to compute which entities have access to which resources. This information is provided on-demand to requesters in the form of a secure access token. Requesters must authenticate to the token server to receive an access token, and this token is time-limited and tied to the requester's identity and the target resource.

Requesters then authenticate to the target resource and provide the token for access. The token is checked for validity using a server handler. This handler code is provided by the enterprise to all entities using access controls, and it parses the token and conducts security checks in a standardized way. A token that is valid and contains the proper identity and access information provides a requester access to data or services at the provider.

2.2 ELS Design and Implementation

ELS starts with high level goals and design philosophies, which are successively refined into specific methods and implementation details for the core security functions (Foltz and Simpson 2016b). Some of the highest level tenets include the following:

- The enemy is present: We cannot assume that any defense or boundary will keep attackers out of our systems. We must assume that any component can be compromised and plan accordingly. This drives the approach of a distributed architecture instead of a centralized approach.
- Simplicity: Complexity is the enemy of security, and the simpler a security function is, the easier it is to implement correctly and securely.
- Extensibility: A point solution may be effective now, but enterprises change over time, and we need to plan for this change in our initial design. Although this may contradict simplicity at times, it actually makes things simpler in the longer term by forcing us to find solutions that match the level of abstraction of the problems instead of over-constraining our solutions.

These tenets guide the development of basic concepts for ELS design. These include a number of items related to identity:

- Authentication is implemented by a verifiable identity claims-based process. This is required to address the tenet that the enemy is present, and serves to distinguish valid entities from attackers.

- The verification of identity is by proof of ownership of the private key associated with an identity claim. This elaborates on the authentication process by requiring cryptographic key operations to verify identity.
- Active entities act on their own behalf. This prevents the many vulnerabilities associated with impersonation and proxies, and provides a baseline for non-repudiation and strong attribution to assist forensics and accountability.

These concepts are further refined into specific requirements. For identity, each entity is issued an X.509 certificate that is tied to a public/private key pair. The distinguished name (DN) in the certificate is used as a unique identifier for each entity in the enterprise. These X.509 certificates are signed by a certificate authority (CA) that is part of a public key infrastructure (PKI). This PKI includes root CAs, issuing CAs, online certificate status protocol (OCSP) responders for validity checks, and certificate revocation lists (CRLs) for offline use. All entities are vetted thoroughly before they are assigned a certificate and key pair. All private keys are stored in hardware to prevent duplication and to provide accountability.

Communication uses transport layer security (TLS) with HTTPS as well as other protocols that integrate TLS, such as secure lightweight directory access protocol (LDAPS). The PKI credentials are used within TLS to provide a secure, authenticated communication channel for entities within the enterprise. The use of TLS is restricted further by security concerns. For example, the zero-round-trip-time handshakes of TLS v1.3 are generally not permitted, and cipher suites are carefully selected for desired security properties.

Access to resources is generally provided by a token from a security token server (STS). This access token is formatted according to the security assertion markup language (SAML) version 2.0. This provides fields for the identity, attribute values, validity time window, target resource, and digital signature. It also provides the option for encryption of tokens, as well as other security options. The SAML standard allows many options, but the tokens allowed in ELS are restricted to access tokens of a particular form, which differs from many non-ELS implementations where SAML tokens are used primarily for single sign-on (SSO). These restrictions prevent attacks such as SAML wrapping that exploit the wide degree of freedom available in the standard. This is consistent with the tenets of simplicity and extensibility by using only what we need while conforming to a broader standard that permits later changes.

The standards mentioned here, including PKI, TLS, and SAML, are not fundamental to the ELS concepts, but they are the currently adopted implementation choices, so integration with ELS must use these particular choices in addition to conforming to the overall architectural goals.

2.3 Agent Security Challenges

The ELS model starts with the premise that security is between authenticated active endpoints. However, in reality endpoints are one of the most vulnerable areas of any information system. As a result, ELS requires strong guarantees that the endpoints have not been compromised. For example, a stolen smart card credential compromises an individual, but such a problem is often quickly reported by the person who lost the credential.

A compromised device can monitor user activity and act as the user surreptitiously over long periods of time with no obvious signs to the user. A systematic approach is required to monitor devices for such compromise and malicious behavior. An agent is placed on the device for this purpose.

In addition, the ELS infrastructure includes other types of agents, such as logging and monitoring agents and endpoint device management agents.

The primary challenges for agents in a secure environment are as follows:

- Establishing secure agent communication with external entities.
- Tying agent communication to its host device.

The first challenge requires that all endpoints use the same ELS methods to communicate whether they are a person, server, or other active entity in the enterprise. The agent, as the initiator of communication with a central server, gateway, or collection system, qualifies as such an active entity. It must be secured at a level comparable to a user with a hardware-based PKI credential or a server with a key pair stored in hardware. This is challenging because agents operate differently than normal users, servers, or other active entities.

The second challenge relates to the separate methods of authenticating endpoint requesters and the devices themselves. Users, for example, can use smart cards, and servers can use hardware security modules (HSMs) to authenticate from different underlying hardware platforms or even virtual machines. However, hardware authentication must be through a different means, as it must be tied to the hardware platform itself. The challenge for an agent is to tie the agent to its digital identity, and then tie its digital identity to a hardware-based device identity.

3 Endpoint Agent Architecture Security Fundamentals

This section establishes the baseline conditions for secure agents. This relies on agents that communicate security information between the device and central servers. The following section builds on this baseline to provide additional agents with additional functionality.

3.1 Endpoint Device Agents

With the move from desktops and laptops to mobile devices like phones and tablets, the edge of the enterprise has changed. Gone are the days where employees log in from an enterprise machine on an enterprise network in an enterprise building. Current users can come from personal mobile devices in public spaces through a commercial cellular network. This motivates our first use case of endpoint device management. These endpoints may be mobile devices or more traditional laptops, desktops, and servers. Agents for device management must have a software component for the agent code, but they must also leverage a hardware key store on the device. Unlike standard ELS authentication, where the keys are tied only to the user or other entity using the device, agent authentication must be tied to the user and the device hardware.

Such an agent need not and should not have any embedded security information for authentication, because such information could be easily duplicated or extracted. The agent is similar to a web browser on a desktop. The browser does not itself authenticate to servers. It provides the means for a user to authenticate and request or provide content. The agent is similar in nature. It relies on existing device keys and certificates to authenticate and communicate securely. The source of the agent keys must be the device hardware rather than a portable or external key store, because such agents speak for the device itself and not for some other entity like a person or server that can migrate from device to device. The agent provides the communication channel for the device hardware to communicate security information.

This introduces some complications. First, the agent is a piece of software that is separate from its hardware-based keys. Hence, any agent, real or malicious, that gains access to the real agent's keys can act as that real agent. There are a number of attacks possible between a software instance and the hardware keys it uses. This is similar to the challenge of securing keys in the cloud, which has a similar key and software separation issue. The agent, and endpoint security in general, must rely on the device to monitor itself, including the software on it, because the agent cannot be trusted by itself.

Secure key storage and use (SKSU) on a device, such as a TPM, has the capability to perform attestations, and such an attestation is required to ensure that the device is running the proper agent and other software. The attestation is a report that lists the state of hardware and software on the device and provides a signature using a key associated with the particular SKSU module on the device. The SKSU hardware module serves as the root of trust for all device-based communications, as indicated in Fig. 1 (Foltz and Simpson 2019). The SKSU must itself be trusted as a starting point. From there, security for the device and its software functionality can be provided using attestation reports.

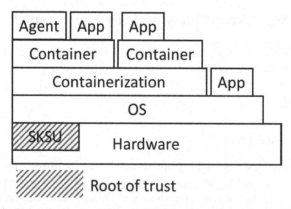

Fig. 1. Using the hardware based SKSU as a root of trust for the device.

The attestation report must cover the hardware, operating system, any virtualization or containerization, and the applications and agents installed on the device. For an agent to communicate securely, it must first produce an attestation report that shows that the device is running as intended at the current time with no malicious entities or configuration modifications. Typically, this is implemented as a white list of approved software.

The agent invokes the TPM to produce an attestation report with the required parameters. The TPM is an implementation detail that is not important, and it can cause its own problems. The goal is not a separate module that does key operations, but instead an integrated key management capability that is part of the device hardware. For example, a TPM that can easily be removed from a device is not an effective SKSU. Such a hardware element could be placed into a different device that is valid, and a fake hardware element could replace it in the original device. Whenever needed, the TPM output can be captured from the valid device and provided by a compromised device through the fake TPM. This allows the compromised device to look like it is still in a valid configuration. The key problem here is the ability to separate the keys from the device. The keys must be embedded in the device hardware in a way that makes it difficult to extract.

In Fig. 2 (Foltz and Simpson 2019), the elements contained within the attestation report are highlighted. They include the full set of components that can affect the agent, which is running as an app in a container in this case. In this case, the containerization and containers are trusted to isolate the apps within their containers sufficiently well that any other apps or containers are allowed to operate on the device. Other apps outside the container need not be validated, and other containers need not be validated. This might be the case for a phone with separate work and personal spaces. However, if the containerization or containers had known vulnerabilities or insufficient protections and isolation capabilities, then the attestation report would have to include the other components as well. In general, the attestation report must include all elements of the device and its software that could negatively affect the agent's ability to securely communicate with an external entity. This includes modification of the agent as well as attacks that leverage the valid agent's ability to authenticate to external entities.

The trust starts at the bottom with hardware and works its way up the stack. The SKSU validates that the device hardware is operating correctly. It then validates that the operating system is correct. This may include such checks as whether the OS is "rooted," which version is installed, and whether the software is installed properly, such as checking a hash of the executable against a known value. The containerization and applications, including the agent itself, can then be validated in a similar manner.

With a trusted SKSU, and a valid agent running with other valid applications in a valid container in a valid containerization method on a valid operating system on valid hardware, a high degree of trust can be established in the agent functionality. In particular, there is a high degree of trust that a private key operation for the agent was actually initiated by the agent itself. This is required, because there is no external method, such as a PIN or biometric information, to validate the agent's request at the SKSU. The SKSU, in combination with the full validated software stack, is required to secure the private key use by the agent. Without such validation it may be possible for another entity to use the key, which would prevent proper authentication of the agent to the central server.

The agent, with its attestation report, communicates with the external entity, which is often an aggregation point for many device agents. After authentication, the agent may send a SAML token to the external endpoint for access, in accordance with standard ELS rules for access. A simpler alternative is to have the agent use identity-based authentication. In this case, the server maintains an access control list (ACL) of the known deployed device agents. This reduces the need for a SAML token but eliminates the efficiency that ELS provides for managing access control rules for large groups.

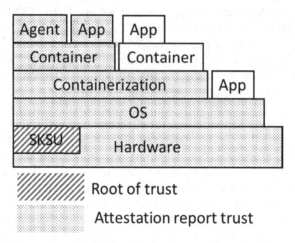

Fig. 2. Extending trust to other hardware and software using a trusted attestation report.

The external entity must be configured to expect and then validate an attestation report for an agent request. The agent's credential is stored on the TPM or other SKSU module. Such a credential alone is not sufficient for ELS authentication, because rogue software may have compromised the device and used the agent key. To secure against this attack, the attestation report validates that the proper software is installed and running at the time of the communication with the agent.

The SKSU module itself may be compromised, which would allow an attacker to generate valid attestation reports for a compromised device. This is addressed by choosing hardware devices that protect against such attacks. Such hardware is becoming a standard part of mobile phones, and keys generated on such devices are very difficult to extract (Apple 2018; Trusted Computing Group 2016).

The full secure communication sequence from agent to external entity is shown in Fig. 3 (Foltz and Simpson 2019). The steps are as follows:

(1) The agent requests an attestation report from the SKSU module.
(2) The SKSU module validates the hardware.
(3) The SKSU module validates the operating system version, configuration, and hash.
(4) The SKSU module validates the containerization mechanism or other isolation mechanism(s), if applicable.
(5) The SKSU module validates the container or other isolation unit where the agent is located, if applicable.
(6) The SKSU validates other applications in the same container as the agent.

(7) The SKSU validates the agent itself.

(8) The SKSU provides the attestation report to the agent.

(9) The agent initiates a secure connection to the external entity and validates the external entity credentials.

(10) The external entity requests authentication of the agent.

(11) The agent requests a private key operation for the agent key stored in the SKSU.

(12) The SKSU returns the results of the private key operation.

(13) The agent uses the private key operation to authenticate to the external entity and provides the attestation report through the secure connection.

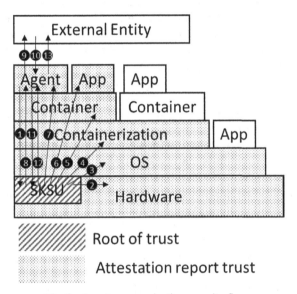

Fig. 3. Agent communication security flows.

The external entity must validate that the attestation report has a valid signature from a trusted source and that the items listed for the device conform to a valid configuration of the device. At this point, the agent has successfully authenticated to the external entity using the device key in the SKSU and by leveraging the SKSU and its internal key as a root of trust.

The external entity may then request an access token, or it may check the identity of the agent against an ACL for authorization. This process proceeds similar to normal ELS SAML requests. The only difference is that authentication to the token server also uses the flows above to use the SKSU and its attestation report for authentication.

The actions described in this section are often integrated with a mobile device manager (MDM) or unified endpoint manager (UEM). Such a system includes a central control panel and agents that reside on each endpoint device. The agents communicate with the MDM or UEM control panel and either provide data from the device or apply commands to the device. The agents leverage operating system interfaces to apply remote operations to the device. These may or may not require user acceptance or confirmation.

4 Endpoint Functionality Agents

This section discusses the agents on the endpoints that provide additional functionality. These leverage the security provided by the basic management agents in Sect. 3 and include added functionality through additional agents. Unlike the agents that help to secure the device, the agents in this section rely on that security and build on it.

4.1 Monitoring Agents

With the end-to-end security of ELS it is not possible to directly monitor the content of communication between endpoints. This information must be collected from the endpoints using agents. These monitoring agents operate on servers as well as user devices. The monitoring agents watch for potentially malicious inputs and outputs, much like a network-based monitoring system does. However, the monitoring agents only process a single device's communications. This can help performance by distributing the load across all enterprise devices. With this distributed approach, the endpoints must share some data with a central entity to enable cross-device correlations. The agent is responsible for communicating with the central aggregator and sending relevant data periodically or upon request. The agent also responds to configuration changes pushed from the central aggregator in response to changing monitoring needs. Such communications may be sent using the endpoint device management agents.

The monitoring agents process security sensitive information related to device, operating system, or application anomalies and compromises, and they initiate the transmission of this as active entities, so they must be authenticated much like the endpoint device management agents. The monitoring agent keys are stored in the TPM and used to initiate TLS connections to central servers. The agent authenticates using its key, which is coupled to an endpoint device management agent's attestation report that certifies the operational state of the device. Because monitoring agents and endpoint device management agents are both part of the standard ELS infrastructure, such attestation reports can be shared among the backend servers through a standard interface.

With a TPM attestation report from the endpoint device management system, the device's state is established as "clean." Such a clean device can then be trusted to authenticate and provide proper information from all of the agents covered by the attestation report, including the monitoring agent. The monitoring agent then provides further information about potentially malicious activity on the device itself. This information can include details of malicious operating system configuration changes, such as rooting, or malicious or anomalous application activities, such as accessing or requesting resources that are restricted.

4.2 Log Aggregation Agents

Log aggregation agents periodically assemble the relevant log content from the device, which may include monitoring logs, browser history, key usage, location history, network utilization rates, or other information as configured by the enterprise. They then send this information to an aggregator, which may further aggregate it at the enterprise level. The log information from a single device is packaged as a signed message that can be passed through multiple aggregators without loss of security properties. The intermediate aggregators are not active entities because they do not modify the data packages. They only provide performance benefits, such as load balancing or aggregation of data packets.

Log records can come directly from the hardware. These are often handled and made available through the operating system. To ensure the log content was generated by the hardware itself, an attestation report is a natural security measure. This log attestation report is simply a digital signature that only the hardware can generate. Log records can also come from the operating system, which is often tightly coupled with a SKSU module—again, the attestation report is a natural choice for security.

Application-layer logging is more challenging. The application may not have direct control of the log files it generates. The operating system may interfere with the log file management, make log files available to other applications, or directly modify log files. The operating system could also act on behalf of the application when requesting logging related activities. Again, the attestation report for the software on the device provides a method to secure against a modified or compromised operating system. The system attestation report combined with the log attestation report provides the needed security for transferring the log record to the central aggregator.

The log aggregator has a unique position. It is a passive entity with respect to the content of the log records. These are signed by the log aggregation agents on individual devices, so such content cannot be modified by the aggregator. However, the aggregator does have an important active role to play in validating the integrity of the signature. The aggregator must validate the attestation report for the device that signed the log record. A bad attestation report implies that the signature cannot be trusted, and the log aggregator is the point where this is checked. The log aggregator signs valid log records and refuses to sign invalid log records. The aggregator serves as an active entity in providing its own validation but a passive entity with respect to the signed log record content. Each log record is treated as a blob with no internal structure. This permits the use of encryption on log records without affecting the aggregators.

The central aggregator need not be a central point of failure for log record security. Confidentiality is difficult to provide due to the nature of the aggregator, but integrity is often more important for log-related applications. The signatures from the device-based keys and certificates, combined with a validation of their attestation reports, provides a high level of integrity for such records. For aggregation functions, it may be necessary to strip the signatures and use the raw data for further processing. In this case, there is no direct method to validate the processed data, but because all original data is signed, it is possible to independently validate such computations. Thus, the central aggregator is a single point of aggregation, but it is not a single point of integrity vulnerability due to the device signatures for individual records.

4.3 Service Desk Agents

Another type of agent is installed for the enterprise service desk. Such an agent provides remote access and capabilities for a service desk person or automated service. The service desk agent provides a higher degree of access than other agents. The service desk operators often need to explore and experiment in order to troubleshoot an issue, which requires privileged access to many functions on the device. The service desk agent, as a highly capable agent, introduces a potentially dangerous interface into the device and a tempting target of attack.

The security goals are slightly different for the service desk agents than for other agents. For other agents, the goal is strong validation of what comes out of the agents. Log records must be validated, and monitoring information must be accurate. Even attestation reports themselves must be protected. Although it is not feasible to modify the contents of an attestation report, blocking its transmission or invalidating the signature on a report with valid data could cause confusion or incorrect behavior.

For the service desk agent, the goal is strong validation of what goes into the device. It is important to prevent intruders from using the service desk agent as an attack vector into the machine. A command to reconfigure the device, if not properly validated, could put the device into an insecure state. Although such a change should be detected by the next attestation report, there is a window of opportunity for an attacker to have remote access to a device. Other agents must provide security in order for external entities to accept them and provide services. The service desk agent must strongly validate all incoming requests in order to protect the device's hardware, software, and data from malicious external entities.

The attestation reports collected by the endpoint device management system identify devices that are out of compliance. Agents will not be able to authenticate to external servers under these conditions, just as for any other agent on the compromised device. However, a service desk agent on an out-of-compliance device can potentially open the door for attackers, so a stronger response is required. Instead of just denying the service desk agent external access, the agent must be locked down or disabled until the device is brought into compliance. In order to shorten the window of opportunity for an attacker, periodic heartbeat messages can be employed by the endpoint device management agent.

The security for a service desk agent-based attack has two levels. The first is the ability of the mobile device management agent to lock the device until it comes into compliance. This could be a simple as preventing network communications, which forces a user to return the device for physical inspection and fixes. It could also remotely reset the device to factory settings. This is a very flexible and targeted response.

In situations where the attack quickly compromises the service desk agent and then the endpoint management agent, or in cases where the endpoint management agent is targeted in order to open up service desk agent interfaces, such a response is inadequate. In this case, the second level of security is the requirement by enterprise external resources of a valid attestation report from the device. After such a compromise, the attacker may control the device, but it will not be able to connect it to any other enterprise resources. This effectively isolates the device from the enterprise. This response is blunter and less effective at preventing data loss. It serves as a back-up when it is not possible to stop an attack from compromising the device. This aligns with the tenet that the enemy is among us, and the general assumption that no element is completely safe, and we must operate even when things fail.

4.4 Import and Mediation Agents

Import agents are used to refresh data in reference stores and mediate their content for compatibility with other information. The agents pull data through a guard for integrity and accuracy checking. Guarded and filtered inputs are aggregated. Because numerous errors and inconsistencies may exist, the guard checks for formatting errors, discrepancies between data bases, incorrect or missing data, illogical data, and other undesirable conditions. Handling of discrepancies from sources depends upon the nature of the discrepancy, and corrections may be required before the data can be imported.

Import and mediation agents handle sensitive personal data that is used across the enterprise for security decisions, so they also have special responses beyond a normal agent. Any attestation report anomaly related to the import and mediation agent must lead to failure of authentication and disabling of these agents, much like the service desk agents. However, the data managed by these agents must also be rolled back to a prior known good state, because data modifications made from an import and mediation agent on a non-compliant device could have widespread lasting effects on the entire enterprise.

4.5 Self-help Agents

Self-help agents are provided on the standard desktop and provide the user with a tool to examine configuration and software conflicts. They also allow support personnel at the enterprise service desk to take over the desktop or device for diagnosis and repair of common software problems. This agent combines the capabilities of the endpoint device management agent, service desk agent, and monitoring agent. It is more common on desktops and laptops than mobile devices, but the capability can apply to any endpoint device.

Security of self-help agents has different goals and threats for different activities. Providing a user information from a static file requires very little associated security. In many cases, this may be enough to solve a problem. In other cases, the self-help agent scans the device, operating system, applications, or configurations in order to make an assessment and suggest remediation options. Because this agent has access to potentially sensitive system information, it must be included in the attestation report generated by the endpoint device management agent. This ensures that the self-help agent has not been corrupted to provide sensitive data to an unauthorized entity.

A self-help agent that not only assesses a situation but also takes action to correct it often has privileged device access. The attestation report that validates the self-help agent can also provide protection against malicious modifications by validating the self-help agent software. When the self-help agent allows remote administration of the device, it must include the protections provided by the service desk agent. This includes strong authentication of all incoming requests before taking corresponding actions on the device.

4.6 Embedded Agents

The embedded agent is for middleware, such as Java, .NET, or messaging systems, and it monitors the performance associated with application resources. This is a low level agent that is specific to its middleware. It provides information about the middleware that an application uses. This is above the layer of the operating system and below the layer of the application. It may be important for diagnosing middleware issues that do not show up in the application or operating system. For example, an application could be running slowly but only using 40% of the available CPU despite having multiple threads. An embedded Java agent could resolve whether the Java virtual machine is limiting the CPU resources to the application or the OS is limiting the Java virtual machine.

The embedded agent should be configured to provide performance, connectivity, and anomaly data to the log file for its associated middleware. It is unaware of some of the events transpiring within the application that is built on the middleware. It can be configured to provide alerts to users or administrators. The native device's alerting system can be used for user alerts, but administrator alerts rely on approaches similar to the monitoring agent and log agent. It may be possible to integrate the embedded agent with monitoring and logging agents.

4.7 Other Agents

The preceding descriptions of agents focused on enterprise agents. These are installed on devices as part of normal enterprise operations in order to conform to enterprise rules for security and functionality. In addition, there may be other application specific agents that are desired for subgroups of the enterprise or individuals within the enterprise. These may or may not have enterprise approval or support.

Such agents can operate like the monitoring or logging agents. They ultimately rely on device hardware key storage, the operating system, and the MDM system to bootstrap the security of their communications. They require an attestation report, a hardware-based authentication key, and possibly an access token, much like any other active entity in the enterprise.

The response to an attestation report showing an out-of-compliance device depends on the function of the agent. In many cases, the response is to prevent such agents from authenticating to external servers. This is a simple and effective way to prevent the device from providing bad data or invoking sensitive enterprise services. In other cases, a honeypot approach could provide more information about the anomaly. For example, a simple bit flip in a data item would invalidate a digital signature, but it might be caused by inconsistent hardware, a software bug, or other mistakes instead of malicious activity. By accepting and recording such attestation reports in a honeypot, it is possible to perform forensics that might help to resolve mistakes while also blocking malicious activity. In addition, if it does end up being malicious, the normal systems are protected, and forensics can focus on the attack mechanics to better stop future attacks.

5   Conclusions

Moving from a centralized network-based security model to a distributed endpoint-based model provides many benefits for the current enterprise information sharing network dominated by mobile devices. However, the endpoint-based model requires careful planning to preserve existing security properties within an enterprise while adding additional functionality.

This paper explores the use of agents within the ELS model. ELS adheres to high level design principles, which are further refined to concepts and requirements. The use of agents is designed to adhere to the design principles, concepts, and requirements to provide their functionality. The first agent must establish that the device is clean. This endpoint management agent ties directly with the operating system and hardware components. It collects attestation reports, generated by trusted device hardware, and provides them to the enterprise while adhering to ELS rules for communication. The agent software itself cannot be guaranteed to be genuine, so the software agent's role is only to request and provide the attestation report, which is a self-validating record based on the SKSU signature.

Other agents leverage the fact that the device is secure to provide their functionality. Building on this secure base, they can provide additional data, perform computations, or enable remote access to device functions. Using such an approach, the end-to-end security between all active endpoints is preserved, and network-based monitoring is performed on the devices.

This provides a way to extend the enterprise footprint onto mobile devices outside the enterprise while maintaining security comparable to internal networks.

This work is part of a body of work for high-assurance enterprise computing using web services (Foltz and Simpson 2016a, c; Simpson and Foltz 2016).

6 Extensions

Other tools or applications that use agents may use the same process to provide secure device-based communication. For example, in addition to an MDM, it is possible to use a mobile application manager (MAM) from a different vendor. The MAM has a lower level of control than the MDM due to the restricted operating system interfaces. However, it would use the same basic communication methods with external servers and internal operating system components and hardware elements.

Many mobile device applications have tight ties to external servers and serve mainly as a user interface to web APIs. Such applications function much like agents because they are lightweight and communicate with a central server. As such, the architecture described in this paper also serves as a blueprint for such applications.

References

Apple. iOS Security, iOS 12.1, November 2018. https://www.apple.com/business/site/docs/iOS_Security_Guide.pdf

Assink, A.: The Potential of Agent Architectures (2016). https://dzone.com/articles/the-potential-of-agent-architectures

Berkovits, S., Guttman, J.D., Swarup, V.: Authentication for mobile agents. In: Vigna, G. (ed.) Mobile Agents and Security. LNCS, vol. 1419, pp. 114–136. Springer, Heidelberg (1998). https://doi.org/10.1007/3-540-68671-1_7

Foltz, K., Simpson, W.: Secure endpoint device agent architecture. In: Proceedings of 21st International Conference on Enterprise Information Systems (ICEIS 2019), Heraklion, Greece, 3–5 May 2019

Foltz, K., Simpson, W.: Enterprise level security with homomorphic encryption. In: Proceedings of 19th International Conference on Enterprise Information Systems (ICEIS 2017), Porto, Portugal, 26–29 April 2017

Foltz, K., Simpson, W.R.: The virtual application data center. In: Proceedings of Information Security Solutions Europe (ISSE 2016), Paris, France (2016a)

Foltz, K., Simpson, W.R.: Enterprise level security – basic security model. In: Proceedings of the 7th International Multi-Conference on Complexity, Informatics, and Cybernetics: (IMCIC 2016). Orlando, FL (2016b)

Foltz, K., Simpson, W.R.: Federation for a secure enterprise. In: Proceedings of the Twenty-first International Command and Control Research and Technology Symposium (ICCRTS 2016). London, UK (2016c)

Liu, Z., Wang, Y.: A secure agent architecture for sensor networks. In: Proceedings of the International Conference on Artificial Intelligence, IC-AI 2003, Las Vegas, Nevada 2003

Šimo, B., Balogh, Z., Habala, O., Budinská, I., Hluchý, L.: Architecture of the Secure Agent Infrastructure for Management of Crisis Situations. Institute of Informatics, Slovak Academy of Sciences, Dúbravská cesta 9, 845 07 Bratislava, Slovakia (2009) http://www.secricom.eu/images/articles/UISAV_simo_final.pdf

Simpson, W.R.: Enterprise Level Security – Securing Information Systems in an Uncertain World, p. 397. CRC Press, Boca Raton (2016)

Trias, E.D., et al.: Enterprise level security. In: Proceedings of the 35th MILCOM Conference, pp. 31–36 (2016). https://doi.org/10.1109/milcom.2016.7795297. http://ieeexplore.ieee.org/document/7795297/

Trusted Computing Group. TPM 2.0 Library Specification, 29 September 2016. https://trustedcomputinggroup.org/resource/tpm-library-specification/

Varadharajan, V., Foster, D.: A security architecture for mobile agent based applications. World Wide Web **6**, 93 (2003). https://doi.org/10.1023/A:1022360516731

Wang, A.I., Sørensen, C.-F., Indal, E.: A Mobile Agent Architecture for Heterogeneous Devices. Department of Computer and Information Science, Norwegian University of Science and Technology, N-7491 Trondheim, Norway (2003). https://pdfs.semanticscholar.org/874b/20fbd73f5c598c8032db0c6c9e5708bc7cec.pdf?_ga=2.107853322.929957899.1544120432-1559163387.1544120432

Self-managed Computer Systems: Foundations and Examples

Daniel A. Menascé[✉]

George Mason University, Fairfax, VA 22030, USA
menasce@gmu.edu
http://www.cs.gmu.edu/faculty/menasce.html

Abstract. The traditional approach to managing complex computer systems is to use a cadre of skilled IT professionals who use monitoring tools in order to detect when problems arise. They are then able to use their skills and experience to determine what actions should be taken to solve the problems. This approach is no longer viable for highly complex, networked computer information systems that have numerous configuration knobs, and operate in environments that vary with time at a very high rate. In this case, one cannot expect that design-time configurations will make the system operate optimally at run-time. For that reason, complex systems need to manage themselves using controllers that make the systems self-configuring, self-optimizing, self-healing, and self-protecting. This paper provides a formalism to describe self-managed systems and discusses concrete examples that illustrate how these properties are enforced by controllers in a variety of domains including cloud computing, fog/cloud computing, Internet datacenters, distributed software systems, and secure database systems.

Keywords: Autonomic computing · Self-managed systems · Utility functions

1 Introduction

The traditional approach to managing complex computer systems is to use a cadre of skilled IT professionals who use monitoring tools in order to detect when problems arise. They are then able to use their experience to determine what actions should be taken to solve the problems. This approach is no longer viable for networked computer systems composed of a very large number of interconnected servers, have many software layers that may include services developed by many different vendors, are composed of hundreds of thousands of lines of code, and are user-facing. The complexity described above is compounded by the fact that the workload intensity of these complex systems varies in rapid and hard-to-predict ways.

For the above reasons, it is virtually impossible for human beings to change the configuration settings of a complex computer system in near real-time in

© Springer Nature Switzerland AG 2020
J. Filipe et al. (Eds.): ICEIS 2019, LNBIP 378, pp. 17–36, 2020.
https://doi.org/10.1007/978-3-030-40783-4_2

order to steer the system to an optimal or near optimal operating point that meets user-established Quality of Service (QoS) goals. Recognizing this, IBM introduced the concept of *autonomic computing*, as a sub-discipline of computer science that deals with systems that are self-configuring, self-optimizing, self-healing, and self-protecting [15]. Autonomic computing systems are also referred to as *self-managed* systems.

Self-managed systems have stringent QoS requirements in terms of response time, throughput, availability, energy consumption, and security. The values of the metrics above depend on the current settings of the configuration knobs. Additionally, there are *tradeoffs* between these metrics. For example, the throughput of a database server is a function of its maximum number of database connections. However, contention for processing and I/O resources increases with the number of database connections. As a result, the average response time increases with resource contention. As another example, a system's security increases as stronger encryption algorithms are used. However, these stronger algorithms imply in added CPU processing time and increased response time. As yet another example, current microprocessors allow for the CPU clock frequency to be adjusted by software. Lower clock frequencies reduce energy consumption but increase response time.

This paper is an extended version of the conference paper [21]. The rest of this paper is organized as follows. Section 2 describes the fundamentals of self-managed systems and provides a concrete example based on automatically allocating CPU shares to virtual machines. Section 3 discusses how an autonomic controller can be used to provide elasticity to cloud providers allowing them to cope with workload surges by dynamically varying the number of servers offered to users. Section 4 provides an example of how an autonomic controller can deal with tradeoffs between security and response time by dynamically varying the security policies of an Intrusion Detection and Prevention Systems (IDPS). The next section discusses how an autonomic controller can dynamically control the voltage and frequency of a CPU in order to meet performance requirements with the least possible energy consumption. Section 6 provides a list of other examples of self-managed systems. Finally, Sect. 7 discusses some concluding remarks.

2   Fundamentals of Self-managed Systems

This section discusses the basics of self-managed systems aka *autonomic computing* systems, a term coined by IBM [15] more than a decade ago. Additionally, this section provides a simple example to illustrate the notation and formalism presented here.

2.1   Self-managed Systems

The term autonomic computing was inspired by the central autonomic nervous system, which unconsciously regulates bodily functions such as the heart and respiratory rate, digestion, and others, based on high-level goals. For example,

if you arrive at an airport late for your flight, you will run to the gate, more
adrenaline will be secreted into your bloodstream, your heart rate will acceler-
ate, and your lungs will breath at a higher rate; all of this without you being
conscious. But, you have a high-level goal that is driving all of it: catch your
flight.

Figure 1 illustrates the basic components of a self-managed system. The system to be controlled is subject to a *workload* that consists of the sets of all inputs
to the system (e.g., requests, transactions, web requests, and service requests).
The *output metrics* of the system are associated with the QoS delivered by the
system when processing the inputs.

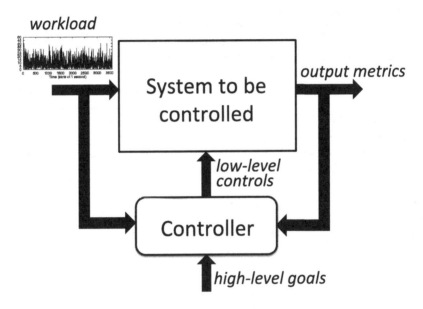

Fig. 1. Basic components of a self-managed system (From [21]).

Figure 1 also depicts a controller that *monitors* the system input, i.e., the
workload, its output metrics, and compares the measured output metrics with
high-level goals established by the system stakeholders. Examples of high-level
goals are: (a) 95% of web requests have a response time less than or equal to
0.8 s; (b) the average search engine throughput is at least 4,600 queries/sec; (c)
the availability of the e-mail portal is greater than or equal to 99.98%; and (d)
the percentage of phishing e-mails filtered by the e-mail portal is greater than
or equal to 90%. The controller reacts to deviations from the high-level goals
established by the stakeholders and automatically derives a *plan* to change the
system's configuration by acting on low-level controls in a way that improves
the system's QoS and makes it compliant, if the system resources permit, with
the high-level goals.

Self-managed systems work along the following dimensions: (a) *Self-configuring*: The system automatically decides how to best configure itself when new components or services become available or when existing ones are decommissioned. (b) *Self-optimizing*: The system attempts to optimize the value of its QoS metrics (e.g., minimizing response time, maximizing throughput and availability). (c) *Self-healing*: The system has to automatically recover from failures. This requires that the root causes of failures be determined and that recovery plans be devised to restore the system to an adequate operational state. In addition, the system has to predict the occurrence of failures and prevent their manifestation. (d) *Self-protecting*: The system has to be able to detect and prevent security attacks, even zero-day attacks, i.e., attacks that target publicly known but still unpatched vulnerabilities.

Optimizing a system for the four dimensions above may be challenging because there are tradeoffs among them. For example, it may be necessary to add several cryptographic-based defenses to improve a system's security. However, these defenses have a computational cost and increase the response time and decrease the throughput [17]. As another example, one may increase the reliability of a system, and therefore improve its self-healing capabilities, by using redundant services with diverse implementations. However, this approach tends to increase response time.

In addition, there usually are constraints in terms of cost and/or energy consumption associated with this optimization problem, which has to be solved in near real-time to cope with the rapid variations of the workload. This problem is a multi-objective optimization problem [24]. In order to deal with the tradeoffs, it is common to use *utility* functions for each metric of interest and then combine them into a *global utility* function to be optimized.

2.2   Utility Functions

A utility function indicates how useful a system is with respect to a given metric. Utility functions are normalized (in our case in the [0, 1] range) with 1 indicating the highest level of usefulness and 0 the lowest. A utility is a dimensionless quantity. For example, if the metric is response time, the utility function of the response time decreases as the response time increases, and approaches 1 as the response time decreases and approaches zero. As another example, a utility function of availability increases as the availability increases.

We assume here that all utility functions are *consistent*, i.e., they increase or decrease in the right direction according to the metric. So, a utility function that increases as the response increases is not consistent. Figure 2 shows two examples of utility functions in the shape of sigmoid functions. The top part of the figure shows three different utility functions of execution time with different shape factors (α) but with the same service level goal ($\beta = 65.0$), which is the inflection point of the curve. The bottom part of Fig. 2 shows three different availability utility functions. The inflection point is the same for all of them, i.e., 0.99.

The controller of Fig. 1 typically awakes at regular time intervals, called *controller intervals* of duration denoted as Δ. Then, the controller (a) verifies all the *monitoring* data collected during the past controller interval(s), (b) *analyzes* how the measured output metrics compare with the high-level goals, (c) generates, if necessary, a *plan* to change the configuration controls to bring the system in line with the high-level goals, and (d) *executes* the plan by sending commands to the system. The plan is generated based on *knowledge* of *models* of the system behavior, which will guide the generation of new configuration parameters as explained in what follows. The paradigm described above is called MAPE-K, which stands for **M**onitor, **A**nalyze, **P**lan, and **E**xecute based on **K**nowledge [15]. Figure 3 shows the details of the elements of an autonomic controller and the MAPE-K loop.

2.3 Formal Definition of an Autonomic Controller

We formalize here the operation of an autonomic controller (just controller heretofore). To that end we define the following notation.

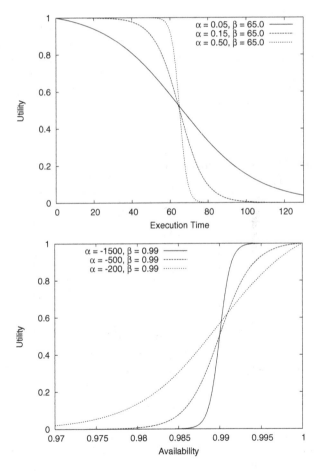

Fig. 2. Top: examples of utility functions for execution time. Bottom: examples of utility functions for availability. All examples are sigmoid functions. (From [21]).

- K: number of configuration knobs (low level controls in Fig. 1) the controller is able to change.
- $\mathbf{C}(t) = (C_1(t), \cdots, C_K(t))$: vector of values of the K configuration knobs at time t.
- $\mathcal{C}$: set of all possible vectors $\mathbf{C}(t)$.
- $\mathbf{W}(t)$: workload intensity at time t. This is usually the workload intensity in the last controller interval(s) but could also be the predicted workload for the next controller interval.
- $S(t) = (\mathbf{C}(t), \mathbf{W}(t))$: system state at time t, which consists of the system configuration and the workload at time t.
- m: number of output metrics monitored by the controller.
- $\mathcal{D}_i$: domain of metric i ($i = 1, \cdots, m$).
- $x_i(t) \in \mathcal{D}_i$: value of metric i ($i = 1, \cdots, m$) at time t.
- $g_i(S(t))$: function used to compute (i.e., estimate) the value of metric i when the system is at state $S(t)$. So, $x_i(t) = g_i(S(t)) = g_i((\mathbf{C}(t), \mathbf{W}(t))$. The function $g_i()$ represents a *model* of the system being controlled. This function can be obtained by solving an analytic model or can be learned from previous observations. In virtually all cases of interest, the functions $g_i()$ are non-linear.
- $U_i(x_i) \in [0, 1]$: utility function for metric i. This is a function of the values of metric i.
- $U_g(x_1, \cdots, x_m) = f(U_1(x_1), \cdots, U_m(x_m))$: global utility function, which is a function of all individual utility functions.

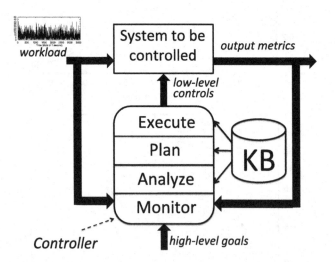

Fig. 3. An autonomic controller and the MAPE-K loop. KB = Knowledge Base.

The functions $U_i()$, $i = 1, \cdots, m$ and $U_g()$ are the high-level goals and are determined by the stakeholders.

At any time instant t at which the controller wakes up, it selects values for the configuration parameters that will be in place from time t to time $t + \Delta$; when the controller wakes up again at time $t + \Delta$ it makes another selection of parameters.

Because the global utility function is a function of the values of the metrics (i.e., $U_g(x_1, \cdots, x_m)$) and because each value x_i is a function $g_i(S(t)) = g_i((\mathbf{C}(t), \mathbf{W}(t))$ of the system parameters, the controller needs to find a configuration vector $\mathbf{C}^*(t)$ that maximizes the global utility function. More precisely,

$$\mathbf{C}^*(t) = \text{argmax}_{\forall\ \mathbf{C}(t) \in \mathcal{C}} \{ f(U_1(g_1((\mathbf{C}(t), \mathbf{W}(t)))), \cdots, U_m(g_m((\mathbf{C}(t), \mathbf{W}(t))))) \}. \tag{1}$$

In many cases, we may want to add constraints such as a cost constraint: $Cost(\mathbf{C}(t)) \leq \text{CostMax}$.

It should be noted that complex computer systems have a large number of configuration knobs and the number of possible values of each is usually large. Therefore, we have a combinatorial explosion in the cardinality of $\mathcal{C}$, which is of the order of $\prod_{k=1}^{K} \mid C_k(t) \mid$, where $\mid C_k(t) \mid$ is the number of possible values of configuration knob k.

Additionally, the solution of the optimization problem stated above has to be obtained in near-real time. For this reason, we often resort to the use of combinatorial search techniques such as hill-climbing, beam-search, simulated annealing, and evolutionary computation to find a near-optimal solution in near real-time [11].

Most designers of autonomic controllers use global utility functions as the function to be optimized. Another approach, presented in [12] uses the optimal multi-dimensional utility vectors on a Pareto front identifying the scalarization weights that makes each utility vector better than all other optimal utility vectors. Exact solvers may be used if they are able to solve the optimization problem in a timely manner so that it can be used for control purposes.

2.4   VM CPU Shares Mapping Example

In order to illustrate the formalism above consider the following scenario. A physical machine runs K virtual machines (VM). Each virtual machine k ($k = 1, \cdots .K$) is allocated a share $C_k(t)$ of the physical CPU at time t, where $\sum_{k=1}^{K} C_k(t) = 1$. An example of CPU shares allocation can be found in VMware's vSphere 4.1 Resource Allocation Shares capability. So, the vector of values of the K configuration knobs at time t is $\mathbf{C}(t)$. The workload intensity at time t is $\mathbf{W}(t) = \{ \mathcal{W}_1(t), \cdots, \mathcal{W}_K(t) \}$ where $\mathcal{W}_k(t), k = 1, \cdots, K$ is the average arrival rate of requests to VM k at time t. Thus, the system state at time t is $S(t) = (\mathbf{C}(t), \mathbf{W}(t))$. The example in this section illustrates a controller that dynamically changes at each controller interval the CPU shares allocated to each VM in order to maximize a global utility function defined as a function of the utility function of each of the K VMs (see below).

Let the average CPU time of requests at VM k be denoted as D_k when VM k is allocated 100% of the CPU. Thus, the average CPU time of requests at VM k is $D_k/C_k(t)$ when VM k is allocated a share $C_k(t)$ of the CPU. Assuming for simplicity that the workload is CPU bound, the average response time $R_k(t)$ of requests submitted to VM k is given by Eq. (2) using well-known queuing theory results [22].

$$g_k(S(t)) = R_k(t) = \frac{D_k/C_k(t)}{1 - \mathcal{W}_k(t)D_k/C_k(t)}. \tag{2}$$

Note that $D_k/C_k(t)$ does not include any contention for the virtual CPU at VM k while $R_k(t)$ is the sum of $D_k/C_k(t)$ with the contention for the use of the virtual CPU at VM k. Assume that the utility function $U_k(R_k(t))$ assigned by the stakeholders to VM k is the sigmoid function given by Eq. (3).

$$U_k(R_k(t)) = \frac{1 + e^{\alpha_k \cdot \beta_k}}{e^{\alpha_k \cdot \beta_k}} \frac{e^{\alpha_k(\beta_k - R_k(t))}}{1 + e^{\alpha_k(\beta_k - R_k(t))}} \tag{3}$$

where $R_k(t)$ is given by Eq. (2). Note that $U_k(R_k(t)) = 1$ when $R_k(t) = 0$ and $\lim_{R_k(t) \to \infty} U_k(R_k(t)) = 0$.

Equation (4) shows an example of a global utility function as a weighted average of the utility functions of all VMs. The weights w_k are such that $\sum_{k=1}^{K} w_k = 1$.

$$U_g(\mathbf{C}(t), \mathbf{W}(t)) = \sum_{k=1}^{K} w_k U_k(R_k(t)). \tag{4}$$

The autonomic controller will then wake up at every Δ seconds and compute an allocation of CPU shares to the K VMs that achieves an optimal (i.e., maximum) or near-optimal value of the global utility $U_g(\mathbf{C}(t), \mathbf{W}(t))$.

Figure 4 shows four consecutive time instants at which the controller wakes up. There are two workloads in this case (solid blue and dashed red in the figure) indicated by the average value of the arrival rate of request in each controller interval of duration Δ. The bottom part of the figure shows how the allocation of CPU shares to the two VMs varies due to the variation of the workload in the previous interval. For example, at time $t + \Delta$ the controller assigns 70% of the CPU to VM1 and 30% to VM2. However, during the next controller interval, the workload submitted to VM2 surpasses that of VM1 and the allocation of CPU shares changes to 25% to VM1 and 75% to VM2. During the subsequent controller interval, the workload submitted to VM1 exceeds that of VM2 and the controller allocates 80% of the CPU to VM1 and the remaining 20% to VM2.

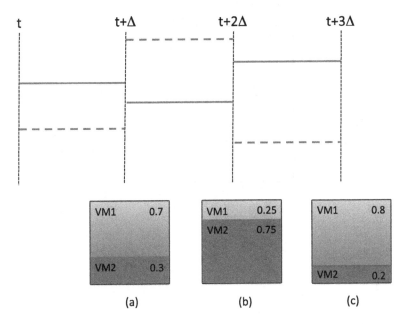

Fig. 4. Example of VM CPU allocation variation every Δ time units. There are two different workloads (solid blue and dashed red). (Color figure online)

3 Taming Workload Surges

Most user-facing systems such as Web sites, social network sites, and cloud providers suffer from the phenomenon of *workload surges* (aka flash crowds), i.e., periods of relatively short duration during which the arrival rate (measured in arriving requests per second) exceeds the system's capacity (measured in the maximum number of requests per second that can be processed). The ratio between the average arrival rate of requests and the system's capacity is called *traffic intensity* and is typically denoted by ρ in the queuing literature [22]. A queuing system is in steady-state when $\rho < 1$.

The top of Fig. 5 illustrates an example of a workload intensity surge from traces publicly made available by Google. As the figure illustrates, the surge occurs in the interval between 600 s and 1,500 s, during which time the workload intensity increased by a 4.5 factor: from an average of 0.2 req/sec to 0.9 req/sec. The peak of the surge occurred at time equal to 1,200 s. The middle curve of Fig. 5 shows that the response time increased from its pre-surge value of 10 s to a peak value of 375 s, i.e., a 37.5-fold increase. Additionally, the peak response time caused by the surge occurred at 1,600 s, i.e., 300 s after the peak of the surge occurred.

The bottom part of Fig. 5 shows various curves obtained by using an elasticity controller that employs an analytic model to predict the response time of a multiserver queue under surge conditions (i.e., when $\rho > 1$) [31]. This model establishes a relationship between the maximum desirable response time, the traffic intensity, and parameters that determine the geometry of the surge (the red curve in the

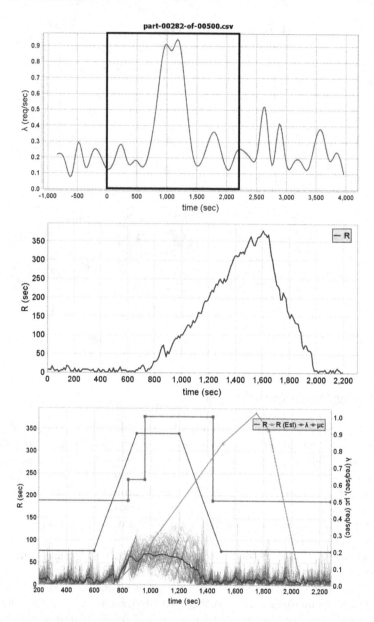

Fig. 5. **(a) Top** – Example of a trapezoidal workload surge from Google's cluster-usage trace file, part-00282-of-00500.csv; workload surge period: 600–1,500 s; average arrival rate before and after surge: 0.2 req/sec; maximum arrival rate during surge: 0.9 req/sec; **(b) Middle** – System's response time for the duration corresponding to the black highlighted box from the top figure; **(c) Bottom** – Red curve: approximated trapezoidal workload; Green curve: total server capacity; Cyan curve: Estimated response time curve based on the red curve; Blue curve: Response time with the controller averaged over 100 independent runs using the Google trace workload in part (a) above. See [31]. (Color figure online)

bottom figure is a trapezoidal approximation of the surge in the top figure). The cyan curve is a predicted response time curve based on the trapezoidal approximation and is obtained from the analytic model.

The autonomic controller monitors the traffic intensity ρ at regular intervals and detects when it exceeds 1. At this point it uses the analytic model to compute the minimum number of servers needed to bring down the response time. Every time the controller wakes up and notices that $\rho > 1$ it adjusts the number of needed servers. The green step curve in the bottom of Fig. 5 shows that the system capacity increased twice during the surge and that the response time (blue curve at the bottom of Fig. 5) reached at most 50 s instead of 375 s without the controller.

4   Autonomic Intrusion Detection Prevention Systems

As indicated in Sect. 2, the properties of self-managed systems include self-optimizing and *self-protecting*. In this section, we present an example of a work [3] that discusses the design, implementation, and use of an autonomic controller to dynamically adjust the security policies of an Intrusion Detection Prevention System (IDPS).

There are two types of IDPSs: data-centric and syntax-centric. The former type inspects the data coming from a backend database to a client and determines if the security policies of the IDPS allow the requesting user to receive the data. The latter, inspects the syntax of SQL requests and determines if the security policies of the IDPS allow the requesting user to submit that request to the backend database. Because no single IDPS is able to cover all types of attacks, many systems use several data-centric and several syntax-centric IDPSs.

So, an incoming request will have to be processed by several syntax-centric IDPSs of different types and an outgoing response will have to be handled by several different data-centric IDPSs. While this process increases the security of a system, it may severely degrade its performance.

For example, when a system is under a high workload, it might be acceptable to modify the security policies to relax some of the security requirements temporarily to meet increasing demands. Additionally, since in most situations, different system stakeholders view priorities differently, the relaxation in security requirements should ideally be based on predefined stakeholder preferences and risks.

We designed an autonomic controller that dynamically changes the system security policies in a way that maximizes a utility function that is the combination of two utility functions: one for performance and another for security [3]. The former is a function of the predicted response time and the latter is a function of the detection rate and false positive rate. Users are classified into *roles* and security policies are associated with the different roles. A security policy for a *role* r is defined as a vector $\boldsymbol{\rho}_r = (\epsilon_{r,1}, \cdots, \epsilon_{r,i}, \cdots, \epsilon_{r,M})$ where $\epsilon_{r,i} = 0$ if IDPS i $(i = 1, \cdots, M)$ is not used for requests of role r and equal to 1 otherwise.

Figure 6 illustrates the results of experiments conducted with the controller in a TPC-W e-commerce site [19]. The x-axis for all graphs is time measured in controller intervals (i.e., the time during which the controller sleeps).

The graph in Fig. 6(a) illustrates the variation of the workload intensity measured in number of requests received by the system over time. As it can be seen, the workload is very bursty and varies widely (between 50 req/sec and 140 req/sec). The high workload peaks cause response time spikes that violate the Service Level Agreements (SLA) of 1 s for access to the home page and 3 s for search requests as illustrated in Fig. 6(b). Figure 6(c) shows three global utility curves. The top curve is obtained when the controller is enabled and shows that the utility is kept at around 0.8 despite the variations in the workload. The middle curve is obtained when the controller is disabled and the security policy is pre-configured and does not change dynamically; in this case the global utility is about 0.6. Finally, the bottom curve is obtained when a full security policy (i.e., one in which all IDPSs are enabled for all roles) is used. In this case, a very low global utility of around 0.48 is observed.

Thus, as Fig. 6 shows, the autonomic controller is able to maintain the global utility at a level 67% higher than when all IDPSs are enabled by reducing the security policies when the workload goes through periods of high intensity.

5 Autonomic Energy-Performance Control

Power consumption at modern data centers is now a significant component of the total cost of ownership. Exact numbers are difficult to obtain because companies such as Google, Microsoft, and Amazon do not reveal exactly how much energy their data centers consume. However, some estimates reveal that Google uses enough energy to continously power 200,000 homes [20].

Most modern CPUs provide Dynamic Voltage and Frequency Scaling (DVFS), which allows the processor to operate at different levels of voltage and clock frequency values. Because a processor's dynamic power is proportional to the product of the square of its voltage by its clock rate, it is possible to control the power consumed by a processor by dynamically varying the clock frequency. However, lower clock frequencies imply in worse performance and higher clock rates improve the processor's performance at the cost of higher power consumption. Therefore, it would be ideal to dynamically vary a processor's clock rate so that as the workload intensity increases, the clock rate is increased to meet response time SLAs. And, as the workload intensity decreases the clock frequency should be decreased to the lowest value that would maintain the desired SLA so as to conserve energy.

Many microprocessors allow for states in which a different voltage-frequency pair is allowed. For example, the Intel Pentium M processor supports the following six voltage-frequency pairs: (1.484 V, 1.6 GHz), (1.420 V, 1.4 GHz), (1.276 V, 1.2 GHz), (1.164 V, 1.0 GHz), (1.036 V, 800 MHz), and (0.956 V, 600 MHz) [14]. As indicated above, microprocessors with DVFS offer a discrete set of voltage-frequency pairs.

We designed and experimented with an autonomic DVFS controller that dynamically adjusts the voltage-frequency pair of the CPU to the lowest value that meets a user-defined response time SLA [20].

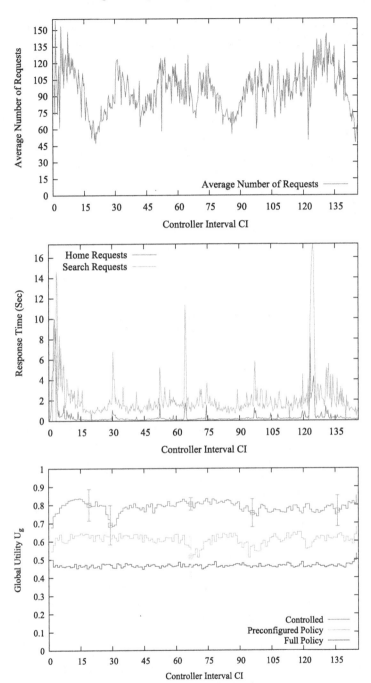

Fig. 6. Experiment results (see [3]): (a) **Top:** Workload variation, (b) **Middle:** Response time for Home and Search page requests without the controller, (c) **Bottom:** Three global utility values: with the controller, for a fixed pre-configured policy, and for a full security policy.

Figure 7 illustrates an example of the variation of the average arrival rate (λ) of requests over time. As it can be seen, the workload intensity varies widely between 0.01 tps and 0.61 tps.

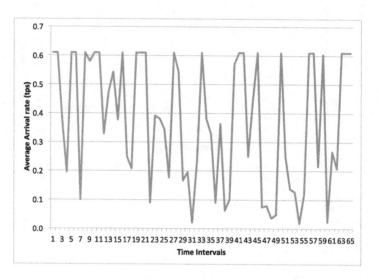

Fig. 7. Average transaction arrival rate (in tps) vs. time intervals. (see [20]).

The DVFS autonomic controller is able to react to these variations as shown in Fig. 8 that shows three different curves. The x-axis follows the same time intervals as in Fig. 7 but the scale on that axis is labelled with the values of λ over the interval. The solid blue curve shows the variation of the *relative power consumption* that results from the variation of the voltage and CPU clock frequencies. We define relative power consumption as the ratio between the power consumed by the processor for a given pair of voltage and frequency values and the lowest power consumed by the processor, which happens when the lowest voltage and frequencies are used.

As can be seen, the shape of the relative power curve follows closely the variation of the workload intensity. Higher workload intensities require higher CPU clock frequencies and voltage levels and therefore higher relative power consumption. The dashed curve of Fig. 8 shows the variation of the average response time over time. The first observation is that the average response time never exceeds its SLA of 4 s. The response time, given that the I/O service demand is fixed throughout the experiment, is a function of the arrival rate λ and the CPU clock frequency during the time interval. This curve and the dotted line (i.e., the CPU residence time) in the same figure clearly show how the autonomic DVFS controller does its job.

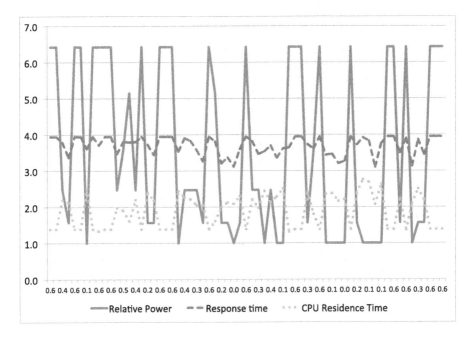

Fig. 8. Solid blue line: Relative power vs. time intervals; **Dashed red line:** Average response time (in sec) vs. time intervals; **Dotted green line:** CPU residence time (in sec) vs. time intervals; Time intervals are labelled with their arrival rate values (in tps). See [20]. (Color figure online)

Other work on autonomic power-performance control can be found in [4, 13, 16, 26, 33, 34].

6   Other Examples of Self-managed Systems

Self-managed systems have been used in a wide variety of systems in addition to the examples discussed above. This section provides several additional examples.

6.1   Autonomic Fog Computing

In [28, 29], the authors discuss a controller for fog/cloud computing environments that dynamically determines the portion of a transaction that should be processed at a fog server vs. at a cloud server. The controller deals with tradeoffs between local processing (less wide area network time but higher local congestion) and remote processing (more wide area network traffic but use of more powerful servers and therefore less remote congestion). The controller was validated with data obtained from several IoT traces [30].

6.2   Autonomic Resource Allocation in Cloud Computing

The authors in [2], discuss the design and evaluation of an autonomic controller that dynamically allocates and re-allocates communicating virtual machines (VM) in a hierarchical cloud datacenter. Communication latency varies if VMs are colocated in the same server, same rack, same cluster, or same datacenter. The controller employs user-specified information about communication strength among requested VMs in order to determine a near-optimal allocation. Another approach was described in [32] in which the authors present a novel, autonomic, Adaptive Bin Packing (ABP) algorithm for autonomic resource allocation in the cloud.

6.3   Autonomic Checkpointing

The authors in [5] show how one can dynamically control the checkpointing frequency of processes in a distributed system so as to balance execution time and availability tradeoffs. The more often a checkpoint is taken the less time a process is available for useful computation. On the other hand, less frequent checkpoints incur in more work to be redone in case of failures, which extends process execution time.

6.4   Autonomic Moving Target Defenses

The work in [8] presents analytic models of Moving Target Defense (MTD) systems with reconfiguration limits. MTDs are security mechanisms that periodically reconfigure a system's resources to reduce the time an attacker has to learn about a system's characteristics. When the reconfiguration rate is high, the system security is improved at the expense of reduced performance and lower availability [37]. To control availability and performance, one can vary the maximum number of resources that can be in the process of being reconfigured simultaneously. The authors of [8] developed a controller that dynamically varies the maximum number of resources being reconfigured and the reconfiguration rate in order to maximize a utility function of performance, availability, and security.

6.5   Autonomic Distributed Software Systems

The Distributed Adaptation and REcovery (DARE) framework designed at Mason [1] uses a distributed MAPE-K loop to dynamically adapt large decentralized software systems in the presence of failures. The Self-Architecting Service-Oriented Software SYstem (SASSY) project [18], also developed at Mason, allows for the architecture of an SOA system to be automatically derived from a visual-activity based specification of the application. The resulting architecture maximizes a user-specified utility function of execution time, availability, and security. Additionally, run-time re-architecting takes place automatically when services fail or the performance of existing services degrades. Other examples of autonomic software adaptation can be found in [9,25,35,36,38].

6.6   Autonomic Smart Manufacturing

In [23] the authors describe how autonomic computing can be used to dynamically control the throughput and energy consumption of smart manufacturing processes. They use a queuing network model of the manufacturing system to predict the throughput and energy consumption of a car production system.

6.7   Autonomic Multi-tiered Web Sites

The authors in [10] presented the detailed design of an autonomic load balancer (LB) for multi-tiered Web sites. They assumed that customers can be categorized into distinct classes (gold, silver, and bronze) according to their business value to the site. The autonomic LB is able to dynamically change its request redirection policy as well as its resource allocation policy, which determines the allocation of servers to server clusters, in a way that maximizes a business-oriented utility function.

6.8   Autonomic Datacenters

In [6,7], the authors presented a self-managed method to assign applications to servers of a data center. As the workload intensity of the applications varies over time, the number of servers allocated to them is dynamically changed by an autonomic controller in order to maximize a utility function of the application's response time and throughput.

7   Concluding Remarks

Most modern information systems are very complex due to their scale and resource heterogeneity, consist of layered software architectures, are subject to variable and hard-to-predict workloads, and use services that may fail and have their performance degraded at run-time. Thus, complex information systems typically operate in ways not foreseen at design time.

Additionally, these software systems have a large number of configuration parameters. A few examples of parameters include: web server (e.g., HTTP keep alive, connection timeout, logging location, resource indexing, maximum size of the thread pool), application server (e.g., accept count, minimum and maximum number of threads), database server (e.g., fill factor, maximum number of worker threads, minimum amount of memory per query, working set size, number of user connections), TCP (e.g., timeout, maximum receiver window size, maximum segment size).

Some parameters have a discrete set of values (e.g., maximum number of worker threads, number of user connections) and others can have any real value within a given interval (e.g., TCP timeout, DB page fill factor). In the latter case, the parameter values in a continuous range have to be discretized in order for combinatorial search methods to be used. The authors in [27] discussed a method for evaluating the impact of software configuration parameters on a system's performance.

As discussed in this paper, it is next to impossible for human beings to continuously track the changes in the environment in which a system operates in order to make a timely determination of the best set of configuration parameters necessary to move the system to an operating point that meets user expectations. For that reason, complex systems have to be self-managed.

A useful framework to reason about self-managed systems is the **M**onitor **A**nalyze **P**lan and **E**xecute based on **K**nowledge (MAPE-K) loop described by IBM [15]. This loop is continuously executed by an autonomic controller that (1) monitors a managed system's inputs and outputs, (2) analyzes if the outputs have violated user-defined Service Level Objectives usually specified in the form of utility function, (3) plans adaptation actions that optimize the utility function, and (4) executes the plan. All four steps are based on a knowledge repository of models that can be used to predict future system states and corresponding values of the utility function based on a set of actions to be taken by the controller.

Many adaptive systems determine how they should evolve based on their recent past history. However, as indicated in [39], one can take a proactive adaptation approach that uses adaptive forecasting methods in order to anticipate future states of a system and determine the best actions based on predicted future states.

Acknowledgements. I would like to thank my former Ph.D. students whose work is referenced here: Arwa Aldhalaan, Firas Alomari, Noor Bajunaid, Mohamed Bennani, Warren Connell, John Ewing, Mohan Krishnamoorthy, Uma Tadakamlla, and Venkat Tadakamalla.

References

1. Albassam, E., Porter, J., Gomaa, H., Menascé, D.A.: DARE: a distributed adaptation and failure recovery framework for software systems. In: 2017 IEEE International Conference on Autonomic Computing (ICAC), pp. 203–208 (2017)
2. Aldhalaan, A., Menascé, D.A.: Autonomic allocation of communicating virtual machines in hierarchical cloud data centers. In: 2014 International Conference on Cloud and Autonomic Computing, pp. 161–171 (2014)
3. Alomari, F.B., Menascé, D.A.: Self-protecting and self-optimizing database systems: implementation and experimental evaluation. In: Proceedings of the 2013 ACM Cloud and Autonomic Computing Conference, CAC 2013, pp. 18:1–18:10, New York, NY, USA. ACM (2013)
4. Arnaboldi, M., Brondolin, R., Santambrogio, M.D.: Hyppo: hybrid performance-aware power-capping orchestrator. In: 2018 IEEE International Conference on Autonomic Computing (ICAC), pp. 71–80 (2018)
5. Bajunaid, N., Menascé, D.A.: Efficient modeling and optimizing of checkpointing in concurrent component-based software systems. J. Syst. Softw. **139**, 1–13 (2018)
6. Bennani, M., Menascé, D.: Resource allocation for autonomic data centers using analytic performance models. In: Proceedings of International Conference on Automatic Computing, ICAC 2005, pp. 229–240, Washington, DC, USA. IEEE Computer Society (2005)

7. Bennani, M.N., Menasce, D.A.: Assessing the robustness of self-managing computer systems under highly variable workloads. In: International Conference on Autonomic Computing, 2004, Proceedings, pp. 62–69 (2004)
8. Connell, W., Menasce, D.A., Albanese, M.: Performance modeling of moving target defenses with reconfiguration limits. IEEE Trans. Dependable Secure Comput. (2018). https://doi.org/10.1109/TDSC.2018.2882825
9. Esfahani, N., Yuan, E., Canavera, K.R., Malek, S.: Inferring software component interaction dependencies for adaptation support. ACM Trans. Auton. Adapt. Syst. **10**(4), 26:1–26:32 (2016)
10. Ewing, J., Menascé, D.A.: Business-oriented autonomic load balancing for multi-tiered web sites. In: Proceedings of the International Symposium on Modeling, Analysis and Simulation of Computer and Telecommunication Systems, MASCOTS. IEEE (2009)
11. Ewing, J.M., Menascé, D.A.: A meta-controller method for improving run-time self-architecting in SOA systems. In: Proceedings of the 5th ACM/SPEC International Conference on Performance Engineering, ICPE 2014, pp. 173–184. ACM, New York (2014)
12. Horn, G., Rozanska, M.: Affine scalarization of two-dimensional utility using the Pareto front. In: 2019 IEEE International Conference on Autonomic Computing (ICAC), pp. 147–156 (2019)
13. Imes, C., Zhang, H., Zhao, K., Hoffmann, H.: Copper: soft real-time application performance using hardware power capping. In: 2019 IEEE International Conference on Autonomic Computing (ICAC), pp. 31–41 (2019)
14. Intel. Enhanced Intel speedstep technology for the Intel Pentium M processor (2004)
15. Kephart, J.O., Chess, D.M.: The vision of autonomic computing. IEEE Comput. **36**(1), 41–50 (2003)
16. Krzywda, J., Ali-Eldin, A., Wadbro, E., Ostberg, P., Elmroth, E.: Alpaca: aaplication performance aware server power capping. In: 2018 IEEE International Conference on Autonomic Computing (ICAC), pp. 41–50 (2018)
17. Menascé, D.: Security performance. IEEE Internet Comput. **7**(3), 84–87 (2003)
18. Menascé, D., Gomaa, H., Malek, S., Sousa, J.: SASSY: a framework for self-architecting service-oriented systems. IEEE Softw. **28**, 78–85 (2011)
19. Menasce, D.A.: TPC-W: a benchmark for e-commerce. IEEE Internet Comput. **6**(3), 83–87 (2002)
20. Menascé, D.A.: Modeling the tradeoffs between system performance and CPU power consumption. In: Proceedings of the International Conference on Computer Measurement Group, CMG (2015)
21. Menascé, D.A.: Taming complexity with self-managed systems. In: 21st International Conference on Enterprise Information Systems (ICEIS), vol. 1, pp. 5–13 (2019)
22. Menascé, D.A., Almeida, V.A.F., Dowdy, L.W.: Performance by Design: Computer Capacity Planning by Example. Prentice Hall, Upper Saddle River (2004)
23. Menascé, D.A., Krishnamoorthy, M., Brodsky, A.: Autonomic smart manufacturing. J. Decis. Syst. **24**(2), 206–224 (2015)
24. Miettinen, K.: Nonlinear Multiobjective Optimization. Springer, New York (1999). https://doi.org/10.1007/978-1-4615-5563-6
25. Pfannemueller, M., Krupitzer, C., Weckesser, M., Becker, C.: A dynamic software product line approach for adaptation planning in autonomic computing systems. In: 2017 IEEE International Conference on Autonomic Computing (ICAC), pp. 247–254 (2017)

26. Schmitt, N., Iffländer, L., Bauer, A., Kounev, S.: Online power consumption estimation for functions in cloud applications. In: 2019 IEEE International Conference on Autonomic Computing (ICAC), pp. 63–72 (2019)
27. Sopitkamol, M., Menascé, D.A.: A method for evaluating the impact of software configuration parameters on e-commerce sites. In: Proceedings of the 5th International Workshop on Software and Performance, WOSP 2005, pp. 53–64. ACM, New York (2005)
28. Tadakamalla, U., Menascé, D.: FogQN: an analytic model for fog/cloud computing. In: Proceedings of the 1st Workshop on Managed Fog-to-Cloud (mF2C), pp. 307–313 (2018)
29. Tadakamalla, U., Menascé, D.: Autonomic resource management using analytic models for fog/cloud computing. In: IEEE International Conference on Fog Computing (ICFC 2019), pp. 69–79 (2019a)
30. Tadakamalla, U., Menascé, D.: Characterization of IoT Workloads, pp. 1–15 (2019b)
31. Tadakamalla, V., Menascé, D.A.: Model-driven elasticity control for multi-server queues under traffic surges in cloud environments. In: 2018 International Conference on Autonomic Computing (ICAC), pp. 157–162. IEEE (2018)
32. Tantawi, A.N., Steinder, M.: Autonomic cloud placement of mixed workload: an adaptive bin packing algorithm. In: 2019 IEEE International Conference on Autonomic Computing (ICAC), pp. 187–193 (2019)
33. Tesfatsion, S.K., Wadbro, E., Tordsson, J.: Perfgreen: performance and energy aware resource provisioning for heterogeneous clouds. In: 2018 IEEE International Conference on. Autonomic Computing (ICAC), pp. 81–90 (2018)
34. von Kistowski, J., Deffner, M., Kounev, S.: Run-time prediction of power consumption for component deployments. In: 2018 IEEE International Conference on Autonomic Computing (ICAC), pp. 151–156 (2018)
35. Weyns, D., Malek, S., Andersson, J.: Forms: unifying reference model for formal specification of distributed self-adaptive systems. ACM Trans. Auton. Adapt. Syst. **7**(1), 8:1–8:61 (2012)
36. Yuan, E., Esfahani, N., Malek, S.: A systematic survey of self-protecting software systems. ACM Trans. Auton. Adapt. Syst. **8**(4), 17:1–17:41 (2014)
37. Zangeneh, V., Shajari, M.: A cost-sensitive move selection strategy for moving target defense. Comput. Secur. **75**, 72–91 (2018)
38. Zoghi, P., Shtern, M., Litoiu, M., Ghanbari, H.: Designing adaptive applications deployed on cloud environments. ACM Trans. Auton. Adapt. Syst. **10**(4), 25:1–25:26 (2016)
39. Zuefle, M., Bauer, A., Lesch, V., Krupitzer, C., Herbst, N., Kounev, S., Curtef, V.: Autonomic forecasting method selection: examination and ways ahead. In: 2019 IEEE International Conference on Autonomic Computing (ICAC), pp. 167–176 (2019)

A Hybrid Algorithm for the Unrelated Parallel Machine Scheduling Problem

Marcelo Ferreira Rego[1,2(✉)] and Marcone Jamilson Freitas Souza[1]

[1] Programa de Pós-Graduação em Ciência da Computação,
Universidade Federal de Ouro Preto (UFOP),
Ouro Preto, Minas Gerais 35.400-000, Brazil
`marcone@ufop.edu.br`
[2] Universidade Federal dos Vales do Jequitinhonha e Mucuri (UFVJM),
Diamantina 39.100-000, Brazil
`marcelofr@ufvjm.edu.br`

Abstract. This work proposes a hybrid algorithm for the unrelated parallel machine scheduling problem with sequence-dependent setup times, aiming to minimize the makespan. The proposed algorithm, named Enhanced Smart General Variable Neighborhood Search (e-SGVNS), combines heuristic and exact optimization strategies to explore the solution space of the problem. The exact strategy works like a local search and consists of applying a mathematical programming formulation based on the time-dependent traveling salesman problem to obtain the optimal solution to the sequencing problem on each machine. In turn, the heuristic strategy explores neighborhoods based on swap and insertion moves. The computational results, performed in benchmark instances from literature, showed that e-SGVNS is competitive when compared to state-of-the-art algorithms.

Keywords: Unrelated parallel machine scheduling · Makespan · VNS · Metaheuristic · Mixed integer linear programming

1 Introduction

The Unrelated Parallel Machine Scheduling Problem with Setup Times (UPMSP-ST) consists of scheduling a set N of n independent jobs on a set M of m unrelated parallel machines. Each job $j \in N$ must be processed exactly once by only one machine $i \in M$, and requires a processing time p_{ij}. Each machine can process only one job at a time. In addition, job execution requires a setup time S_{ijk}, which depends on the machine i and the sequence in which jobs j and k will be processed. The objective is to minimize the makespan.

The study of the UPMSP-ST is relevant due to its theoretical and practical importance. From a theoretical point of view, it attracts the interest of researchers because it is NP-hard, since it is a generalization of the Parallel Machine Scheduling Problem with Identical Machines [1]. In practical, it is found in a large number of industries, such as the textile industry [2]. According to

© Springer Nature Switzerland AG 2020
J. Filipe et al. (Eds.): ICEIS 2019, LNBIP 378, pp. 37–56, 2020.
https://doi.org/10.1007/978-3-030-40783-4_3

Avalos-Rosales et al. [3], in a lot of situations where there are different production capacities, the setup time of machine depends on the previous job to be processed [4]. This situation is also found in the manufacture of chemical products, where the reactors must be cleaned between the handling of two mixtures; however, the time required for cleaning depends on the jobs that were previously completed [5].

In this work, a hybrid algorithm, named e-SGVNS, is proposed. It is an improvement of the SGVNS algorithm from Rego and Souza [6]. It is based on the General Variable Neighborhood Search – GVNS [7] and explores the solution space through five strategies: swap of jobs in the same machine; insertion of job on the same machine; swap of jobs between machines; insertion of jobs on different machines; and an application of a mathematical programming formulation based on the time-dependent traveling salesman problem to get the optimal solution to the sequencing problem on each machine. The first four strategies are used as shaking mechanism, while the last three are applied as local search through the Variable Neighborhood Descent. Unlike SGVNS, the proposed algorithm limits the increase of perturbation level. In addition, it applies MILP to all machines whose completion time is equal to makespan and not just to a single machine that meets this condition. This algorithm has been shown to be competitive when compared to state-of-the-art algorithms.

The remainder of this paper is organized as follows: Sect. 2 gives a brief review of the literature. In Sect. 3, a mathematical programming formulation for the problem is presented. In Sect. 4, the proposed algorithm is detailed. The results are presented in Sect. 6, while in Sect. 7 the work is concluded.

2 Related Work

Santos et al. [8] implemented four different stochastic local search (SLS) methods for the UPMSP-ST. The algorithms explore six different neighborhoods. The computational results show that the SLS algorithms produce good results, outperforming the current best algorithms for the UPMSP-ST. They updated 901 best-known solutions from 1000 instances used for testing.

Arnaout [9] introduced and applied a Worm Optimization (WO) algorithm for the UPMSP-ST. The WO algorithm is based on the behaviors of the worm, which is a nematode with only 302 neurons. The WO algorithm was compared to tabu search (TS), ant colony optimization (ACO), restrictive simulated annealing (RSA), genetic algorithm (GA), and ABC/HABC. The experiments showed the superiority of WO, followed by HABC, ABC, RSA, GALA, ACO, and TS last.

Arnaout et al. [10] proposed a two-stage Ant Colony Optimization algorithm (ACOII) for the UPMSP-ST. This algorithm is an enhancement of the ACOI algorithm that was introduced in [11]. An extensive set of experiments was performed to verify the quality of the method. The results proved the superiority of the ACOII in relation to the other algorithms with which it was compared.

Tran et al. [5] introduced a new mathematical formulation for the UPMSP-ST. This formulation provides dual bounds that are more efficient to find the optimum solution. The computational experiments showed that it is possible to solve larger instances than it was possible to solve with other previously existing formulations.

A variant of the Large Neighborhood Search metaheuristic, using Learning Automata to adapt the probabilities of using removal and insertion heuristics and methods, named LA-ALNS, is presented by Cota et al. [12] for the UPMSP-ST. The algorithm was used to solve instances of up to 150 jobs and 10 machines. The LA-ALNS was compared with three other algorithms and the results show that the developed method performs best in 88% of the instances. In addition, statistical tests indicated that LA-ALNS is better than the other algorithms found in the literature.

The UPMSP-ST was also approached by Fanjul-Peyro and Ruiz [13]. Seven algorithms were proposed: IG, NSP, VIR, IG+, NSP+, VIR+ and NVST-IG+. The first three are the base algorithms. The following three are improved versions of these latest algorithms. Finally, the last algorithm is a combination of the best ideas from previous algorithms. These methods are mainly composed of a solution initialization, a Variable Neighborhood Descent – VND method [7] and a solution modification procedure. Tests were performed with 1400 instances and it was showed that the results were statistically better than the algorithms previously considered state-of-the-art, which were, [14,15].

A Genetic Algorithm was proposed by Vallada and Ruiz [16] for the UPMSP-ST. The algorithm includes a fast local search and a new crossover operator. Furthermore, the work also provides a mixed integer linear programming model for the problem. After several statistical analyzes, the authors concluded that their method provides better results for small instances and, especially, for large instances, when compared with other methods of the literature at the time [17,18].

Rego and Souza [6] proposed the SGVNS algorithm for treating the UPMSP-ST. It explores the solution space by three strategies of local search: insertion of jobs in different machines, swap of jobs between machines and an application of a mixed integer linear programming formulation to obtain optimum scheduling on each machine. The SGVNS algorithm was tested in 810 instances and compared to four other literature methods (ACOII, AIRP and LA-ALNS). SGVNS had better performance when executed in small instances. The results of LA-ALNS and ACOII were significantly better than the results of SGVNS algorithm. Even so, SGVNS was superior in 5 groups of instances and able to find best results in 79 of the 810 instances.

3 Mathematical Formulation

This section provides a Mixed Integer Linear Programming (MILP) formulation for the unrelated parallel machine scheduling problem with sequence-dependent setup times with the objective of minimizing the makespan. This formulation was proposed by Tran et al. [5].

In order to introduce this MILP, the parameters and decision variables are defined and shown in Table 1.

The objective function is given by Eq. (1):

$$\min C_{\max}, \tag{1}$$

and the constraints are given by Eqs. (2)–(10):

$$\sum_{i \in M} \sum_{\substack{j \in N \cup \{0\}, \\ j \neq k}} X_{ijk} = 1 \qquad \forall k \in N \tag{2}$$

$$\sum_{i \in M} \sum_{\substack{k \in N \cup \{0\}, \\ j \neq k}} X_{ijk} = 1 \qquad \forall j \in N \tag{3}$$

$$\sum_{\substack{k \in N \cup \{0\}, \\ k \neq j}} X_{ijk} = \sum_{\substack{h \in N \cup \{0\}, \\ h \neq j}} X_{ihj} \qquad \forall j \in N, \forall i \in M \tag{4}$$

$$C_k \geqslant C_j + S_{ijk} + p_{ik} - V(1 - x_{ijk}) \qquad \forall j \in N \cup \{0\}, \forall k \in N, j \neq k, \forall i \in M \tag{5}$$

$$\sum_{j \in N} X_{i0j} \leqslant 1 \qquad \forall i \in M \tag{6}$$

$$C_0 = 0 \tag{7}$$

$$\sum_{\substack{j \in N \cup \{0\}, \, k \in N \\ j \neq k}} (S_{ijk} + p_{ik}) X_{ijk} = O_i, \qquad \forall i \in M, \tag{8}$$

$$O_i \leqslant C_{\max}, \qquad \forall i \in M, \tag{9}$$

$$X_{ijk} \in \{0, 1\} \qquad \forall j \in N \cup \{0\}, \forall k \in N, j \neq k, \forall i \in M, \tag{10}$$

$$C_j \geq 0 \qquad \forall j \in N \tag{11}$$

$$O_i \geq 0 \qquad \forall i \in M \tag{12}$$

$$C_{\max} \geq 0 \tag{13}$$

Equation (1) defines the objective function of the problem, which is to minimize the maximum completion time or makespan. Eqs. (2)–(10) define the constraints of the model. The constraint set (2) ensures that each job is assigned to exactly one machine and has exactly one predecessor job. Constraints (3) define

Table 1. Parameters and decision variables of Tran et al. [5] model.

Name	Description	Type
V	A very large constant	Parameter
N	Set of jobs	
M	Set of machines	
p_{jk}	Processing time of job j on machine i	
S_{ijk}	Setup time required for processing job $k \in N$ immediately after job $j \in N$ on machine $i \in M$	
X_{ijk}	Equal to 1, if job j immediately precedes job k on machine i and 0, otherwise	Decision variable
C_j	Completion time of job j	
O_i	Completion time of last job in machine i	
$C_{\max}$	Maximum completion time	

that every job has exactly one successor job. Each constraint (4) establishes that if a job j is scheduled on a machine i, then a predecessor job h and a successor job k must exist in the same machine. Constraints (5) ensure a right processing order. Basically, if a job k is assigned to a machine i immediately after job j, that is, if $X_{ijk} = 1$, the completion time C_k of this job k) must be greater than or equal to the completion time C_j of job j, added to setup time between jobs j and k and the processing time p_{ik} of k on machine i. If $X_{ijk} = 0$, then a sufficiently high value V makes this constraint redundant. With constraint set (6) we define at most one job is scheduled as the first job on each machine. Constraints (7) establish that the completion time of the dummy job is zero. Constraints (8) compute, for each machine, the time it finishes processing its last job. Constraints (9) define the maximum completion time. Constraints (10)–(13) define the domain of the decision variables.

4   The Enhanced Smart GVNS Algorithm

The algorithm presented in this work, named e-SGVNS, is a is an improvement of the SGVNS algorithm from Rego and Souza [6]. In turn, SGVNS is a variant of the General Variable Neighborhood Search (GVNS) metaheuristic [7].

This metaheuristic performs systematic neighborhood exchanges to explore the solution space of the problem. It uses the Variable Neighborhood Descent procedure – VND [19], described in Sect. 4.4 as the local search procedure, and it has a perturbation phase in order to not get stuck in local optima, which is described in Sect. 4.2.

The perturbation phase of e-SGVNS depends of the perturbation level of the algorithm. This level is always increased when a certain number of VND applications occur without producing improvement in the current solution. The e-SGVNS was implemented according to the Algorithm 1:

Algorithm 1. e-SGVNS.

    input : stopping criterion, $MaxP$, $MaxSameLevelP$, $\mathcal{N}$
1 $s_0 \leftarrow Initial\ Solution()$;
2 $ItSameLevelP \leftarrow 1$;
3 $p \leftarrow 2$;
4 $s \leftarrow VND(s_0, \mathcal{N})$;
5 **while** (stopping criterion was not satisfied) **do**
6 | $s' \leftarrow Shaking(s, p)$;
7 | $s'' \leftarrow VND(s', \mathcal{N})$;
8 | **if** $(f(s'') < f(s))$ **then**
9 | $s \leftarrow s''$;
10 | $p \leftarrow 2$;
11 | $ItSameLevelP \leftarrow 1$;
12 | **end**
13 | **else**
14 | $ItSameLevelP \leftarrow ItSameLevelP + 1$;
15 | **if** $(ItSameLevelP > MaxSameLevelP)$ **then**
16 | $p \leftarrow p + 1$;
17 | $ItSameLevelP \leftarrow 1$;
18 | **if** $p > MaxP$ **then**
19 | | $p \leftarrow 2$;
20 | **end**
21 | **end**
22 | **end**
23 **end**
24 **return** s ;

Algorithm 1 has the following inputs: (1) the stopping criterion, which in our case was the CPU timeout t, described in Sect. 5.2; (2) $MaxP$, maximum level of perturbation; (3) $MaxSameLevelP$, the maximum number of iterations without improvement in $f(s)$ with the same perturbation level; (4) the set $\mathcal{N}$ of neighborhoods. In line 1, the solution s is initialized from the solution obtained by the procedure defined in Sect. 4.1. In line 6, a random neighbor s' is generated from a perturbation performed according to the procedure defined in Sect. 4.2. The loop from lines 5–23 is repeated while the stopping criterion is not satisfied. In line 7, a local search on s' using the neighborhood structures described in Sect. 4.3 is performed. It stops when it finds the first solution that is better than s or when the whole neighborhood has been explored. The solution returned by this local search is attributed to s'' if its value is better than the current solution. Otherwise, the procedure continues to exploit from a new neighborhood structure.

4.1   Initial Solution

An initial solution to the problem is constructed according to Algorithm 2.

Algorithm 2. Initial Solution.

---

    input : M, N

1 **foreach** $k \in N$ **do**

2 | Find the machine i and the position j for the job k that produces the lowest cost for the objective function;

3 | Insert job k in position j on machine i;

4 **end**

Algorithm 2 gets as input the sets M and N of machines and jobs, respectively. At each iteration, it looks for position j on a machine i to insert the job k into scheduling, it always chooses the position that gives the smallest increase in the objective function according to Eq. (1). The previously described steps are repeated for all jobs, so the procedure ends when all jobs are already allocated on some machine.

4.2 Shaking

The shaking procedure is an important phase of a VNS-based algorithm. It is applied to not limit the local search to the same region of the solution space of the problem, and consequently explore other solutions. The shaking procedure implemented increases progressively the level of perturbation in a solution when it is stuck in a local optimum.

The shaking procedure consists of applying to the current solution p moves chosen among the following: (1) change of execution order of two jobs on the same machine; (2) change of execution order of two jobs belonging to different machines; (3) insertion of a job from a machine into another position of the same machine and (4) insertion of a job from one machine into a position of another machine.

It works as follows: p independent moves are applied consecutively on the current solution s, generating an intermediate solution s'. This solution s' is, then, refined by the VND local search method (line 7 of the Algorithm 1). The level of perturbation p increases after a certain number of attempts to explore the neighborhood without improvement in the current solution. This limit is controlled by the variable Max. When p increases, then p random moves (chosen from those mentioned above) are applied to the current solution. Whenever there is an improvement in the current solution, the perturbation returns to its initial level, $p = 2$.

The operation of each type of perturbation is detailed below:

Swap on the Same Machine. This operation consists in randomly choosing two jobs j_1 and j_2 that are, respectively, in the positions x and y of a machine i, and allocate j_1 in the position y and j_2 in the position x of the same machine i.

Swap between Different Machines. This perturbation consists in randomly choosing a job j_1 that is in the position x on a machine i_1 and another job j_2 that is in the position y of the machine i_2. Then, job j_1 is allocated to machine i_2 in position y, and job j_2 is allocated to machine i_1 in position x.

Insertion on the Same Machine. It starts with the random choice of a job j_1 that is initially in the position x of the machine i. Then, a random choice of another position y of the same machine is made. Finally, job j_1 is removed from position x and inserted into position y of machine i.

Insertion between Different Machines. It consists of a random choice of a job j_1 that is in the position x of the machine i_1 and a random choice of position y of the machine i_2. Then, the job j_1 is removed from machine i_1 and inserted into position y of machine i_2.

4.3   Neighborhoods

We used three neighborhood structures to explore the solution space of the problem, and they are described below.

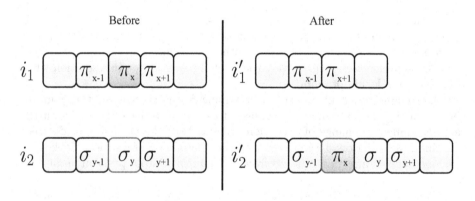

Fig. 1. Insertion move between machines i_1 and i_2.

$\mathcal{N}_1$: **Insertion between Machines.** Let π and σ be two schedules, where $\pi = (\pi_1, \pi_2, \ldots, \pi_t)$ is performed on machine i_1 and $\sigma = (\sigma_1, \sigma_2, \ldots, \sigma_r)$ on machine i_2. In these schedules, t and r represent the number of jobs on machines i_1 and i_2, respectively. In this neighborhood, each job $\pi_x \in \pi$ is removed from machine i_1 and added to machine i_2 at position $y \in \{1, \cdots, r\}$. The set of insertion moves of jobs of a machine i_1 in every possible positions of another machine i_2 defines the neighborhood $\mathcal{N}_1(\pi, \sigma)$, which is composed by $t \times (r + 1)$ neighbors.

Figure 1 illustrates an insertion move of a job π_x of a machine i_1 in the position y of the machine i_2. The right side of this figure shows the result of applying this move.

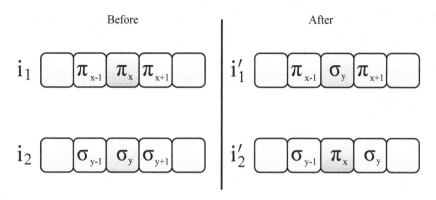

Fig. 2. Swap move between machines i_1 and i_2.

$\mathcal{N}_2$: **Swap Move between Machines.** Let π and σ be two schedules as described above. Let also be two jobs $\pi_x \in \pi$ and $\sigma_y \in \sigma$. The swap move between machines consists in swapping these jobs between these schedules, that is, to move the job π_x to the position y of the machine i_2 and the job σ_y to the position x of the machine i_1. The set of swap moves between machines i_1 and i_2 defines the neighborhood $\mathcal{N}_2(\pi, \sigma)$, formed by $t \times r$ neighbors.

Figure 2 illustrates the swap between two jobs π_x and σ_y, which are initially allocated to machines i_1 and i_2, respectively. After the swap move, the job σ_y is allocated to machine i'_1 and job π_x to machine i'_2.

$\mathcal{N}_3$: **Scheduling by Mathematical Programming.** In this local search, the objective is to determine the best scheduling of the jobs in each machine by applying a MILP formulation. For this, the time-dependent traveling salesman problem (TDTSP) formulation of Bigras et al. [20] was adapted, where the distance between the cities i and j is represented by the sum of the processing time of job i and the setup time between jobs i and j. In addition, a dummy job 0 was added to allow the creation of a Hamiltonian cycle, where 0 represents the first and the last job.

So, the MILP formulation is solved for the sequencing problem in each machine in which the completion time is equal to the makespan. If there is an improvement in the current solution, the local search method returns to the first neighborhood ($\mathcal{N}_1$). If there is no improvement in the current machine and there is another machine whose completion time is equal to the makespan, then the model is applied to this machine. If there is no improvement by applying this formulation, then the exploration in this neighborhood $\mathcal{N}_3$ is ended.

In order to introduce this MILP, the parameters and decision variables are defined and shown in Table 2. The other parameters used by the model are described in Table 1.

Then, the mathematical formulation used as local search strategy in each machine i is given by Eqs. (14)–(18).

Table 2. Parameters and decision variables based on the Bigras et al. [20] model.

Name	Description	Type
N_i	Set of jobs in machine i	Parameter
δ	Any subset of N_i	
Y_{jk}	Equal to 1, if job k is processed directly after job j and equal to 0, otherwise	Decision variable
$C_{\max}^i$	Maximum completion time on machine i	

Objective function:

$$\min C_{\max}^i, \tag{14}$$

Subject to:

$$\sum_{\substack{j \in N_i \cup \{0\}, \\ j \neq k}} Y_{jk} = 1 \qquad \forall k \in N_i \tag{15}$$

$$\sum_{\substack{k \in N_i \cup \{0\}, \\ j \neq k}} Y_{jk} = 1 \qquad \forall j \in N_i \tag{16}$$

$$\sum_{\substack{j \in N_i \cup \{0\} \\ j \neq k}} \sum_{k \in N_i} (S_{ijk} + p_{ik}) Y_{jk} = C_{\max}^i \tag{17}$$

$$\sum_{j \in \delta} \sum_{k \notin \delta} Y_{jk} \geq 1 \qquad \forall \delta \subset N_i, \delta \neq \emptyset \tag{18}$$

$$Y_{jk} \in \{0,1\} \qquad \forall j \in \{0\} \cup N_i, \, \forall k \in \{0\} \cup N_i, j \neq k \tag{19}$$

$$C_{\max}^i \geq 0 \tag{20}$$

Equation (14) defines the objective function, which is to minimize the completion time of the machine i. Equations (15)–(18) define the constraints for the sub-model. Constraints (15) ensure that every job k has exactly one predecessor job, and the predecessor job of the first job is the dummy job 0. Constraints (3) ensure that each job k has a successor job, and the successor of the last job is the dummy job 0. Constraints (17) compute the completion time on the machine i. Constraints (18) ensure that there is no subcycle, therefore, any subset $\delta \in N_i$ of jobs must have at least one link with another subset complementary to δ, that is, $N_i \setminus \delta$. This strategy is similar to the subtour elimination constraints for the traveling salesman problem, proposed by Bigras et al. [20]. Constraints (19) and (20) define the domain of the decision variables.

The mathematical model has a constraint for each subset of jobs. Thus, in cases where the scheduling problem has many subsets of jobs, the model will demand a high computational cost. For this reason, the set of constraints (18) was initially disregarded from the model. However, the relaxed model can produce an invalid solution, that is, a solution containing one or more subcycles. If this happens, a new set of constraints for each subcycle is added to the mathematical model to be solved again. In this new set of constraints (18), the set δ is formed by the group of jobs belonging to the subcycle. This process is repeated until a valid solution is found.

For illustrating this situation, consider the matrix below that represents the values of the decision variables for a problem of one machine with five jobs (Table 3).

Table 3. Example of an invalid solution.

Y	0	1	2	3	4	5
0	0	0	0	0	0	1
1	0	0	1	0	0	0
2	0	1	0	0	0	0
3	1	0	0	0	0	0
4	0	0	0	1	0	0
5	0	0	0	0	1	0

Consider that if $Y_{jk} = 1$ then job j immediately precedes job k, and that the first job of the sequence is preceded by the dummy job 0. Then, we have the following subcycles: $\delta_1 = \{5, 4, 3\}$ and $\delta_2 = \{1, 2\}$. This solution is invalid since there should be a single scheduling involving all jobs and not two as can be observed. Figure 3 illustrated this situation:

Thus, a new constraint must be added for any solution that has a subcycle, since this situation does not obey Eq. (18).

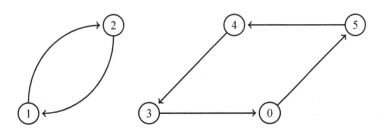

Fig. 3. Representation of an invalid solution.

4.4 Local Search

The local search of our algorithm is done by a VND procedure, that uses the three neighborhood structures $\mathcal{N}_1$, $\mathcal{N}_2$ and $\mathcal{N}_3$ defined in Sect. 4.3. Its pseudocode is presented in Algorithm 3.

Algorithm 3. VND.

	input : s, $\mathcal{N}$
1	$k \leftarrow 1$;
2	**while** $(k \leq 3)$ **do**
3	$\quad$ $s'' \leftarrow BestNeighbor(s, \mathcal{N}_k)$;
4	$\quad$ **if** $(f(s'') < f(s))$ **then**
5	$\quad\quad$ $s \leftarrow s''$;
6	$\quad\quad$ $k \leftarrow 1$;
7	$\quad$ **end**
8	$\quad$ **else**
9	$\quad\quad$ $k \leftarrow k + 1$;
10	$\quad$ **end**
11	**end**
12	**return** s ;

Thus, the VND returns a local optimum in relation to all three neighborhoods $\mathcal{N}_1$, $\mathcal{N}_2$ and $\mathcal{N}_3$.

5 Computational Experiments

The Smart GVNS algorithm was coded in C++ language and the tests were performed on a microcomputer with the following configurations: Intel (R) Core (TM) i7 processor with clock frequency 2.4 GHz, 8 GB of RAM and with a 64-bit Ubuntu operating system installed. The mathematical heuristic, used as local search, was implemented using the Gurobi API [21] for the C++ language.

The proposed algorithm was tested in three sets of instances available by Rabadi et al. [18]: Balanced, Process Domain, and Setup Domain. Each set is formed by 18 groups of instances, and each group contains 15 instances, totaling 810 instances. In the first set, the processing time and the setup time are balanced. In the second, the processing time is dominant in relation to the setup time and in the third, the setup time is dominant in relation to the processing time.

5.1 Parameter Tuning

The implementation of the e-SGVNS algorithm requires the calibration of two parameters: *MaxP* and *MaxSameLevelP*, which are defined in Algorithm 1.

The Irace package [22] was used to tune the values of these parameters. Irace is an algorithm implemented in R that implements an iterative procedure having as main objective to find the most appropriate configurations for an optimization algorithm, considering a set of instances of the problem.

We tested the following values for the two parameters of the e-SGVNS: $MaxP$ and $MaxSameLevelP \in \{3, 4, 5, 6, 7, 8, 9, 10, 11, 12\}$. The best configurations returned by Irace were $MaxP = 5$ and $MaxSameLevelP = 12$.

5.2 Stopping Criterion

As stopping criterion of the e-SGVNS algorithm and for a fair comparison, the average execution time of ACOII by Arnaout et al. [10] was used. Their time was divided by 2.0 because our computer is approximately 2.0 times faster[1] than the computer used in [10] according to PassMark [23]. Cota et al. [12] also used the same stopping criterion to report the results of LA-ALNS algorithms (Table 4).

Table 4. Time limit for e-SGVNS Algorithm in minutes (the same of SGVNS).

Jobs	Machines		
	8	10	12
80	2.78	2.78	2.86
100	4.97	5.13	5.13
120	6.88	7.09	7.09

The WO algorithm used a time limit different from others. Thus, it is compared only with respect to its results and not to its efficiency.

6 Results

Tables 5, 6 and 7 compare the results of the proposed e-SGVNS algorithm with those of ACOII reported by Arnout et al. [10], LA-ALNS reported by Cota et al. [12], WO described by Arnaout [9] and SGVNS by Rego and Souza [6] in relation to the average Relative Percent Deviation (RPD) in each group of 15 instances. For each instance l, the RPD is calculated by:

$$RPD_l = \frac{f_l^{alg} - f_l^{\star}}{f_l^{\star}} \times 100 \qquad (21)$$

where f_l^{alg} is the value of the objective function for the algorithm alg in relation to the instance l, while $f_l^{\star}$ represents the Lower Bound (LB) for the l-th instance reported by Al-Salem [24].

---

[1] https://www.cpubenchmark.net/compare/Intel-i7-870-vs-Intel-Pentium-4-3. 00GHz/832vs1074.

Table 5. Average RPD in Balanced instances.

m	n	ACOII	LA-ALNS	SGVNS	WO	e-SGVNS
2	80	1.24	1.8	1.49	1.41	**1.21**
	100	1.08	1.51	1.33	1.35	**0.94**
	120	0.92	1.36	1.16	1.06	**0.79**
4	80	3.97	3.54	4.53	3.83	**3.29**
	100	3.54	2.96	4.22	3.4	**2.91**
	120	3	2.75	3.73	3.1	**2.41**
6	80	7.09	**5.64**	7.27	5.89	5.88
	100	5.58	**4.25**	6.27	4.86	4.57
	120	4.52	**3.73**	5.84	4.52	3.87
8	80	7.41	**5.59**	8.04	6.0	6.41
	100	8.11	**5.85**	8.62	6.67	7.0
	120	5.7	**4.35**	6.74	5.24	4.9
10	80	8.14	**6.79**	9.26	6.96	7.72
	100	8.15	**5.54**	8.38	6.35	6.58
	120	6.99	**4.01**	8.05	6.13	5.88
12	80	11.97	–	13.82	**10.39**	11.07
	100	12.18	–	13.71	**11.18**	11.47
	120	7.6	–	9.03	**6.82**	7.02

Table 6. Average RPD in the Process Domain instances.

m	n	ACOII	LA-ALNS	SGVNS	WO	e-SGVNS
2	80	0.80	1.14	0.91	0.90	**0.71**
	100	1.65	0.95	0.80	1.16	**0.63**
	120	1.49	0.83	0.66	1.01	**0.46**
4	80	2.50	2.16	2.79	2.25	**2.02**
	100	2.07	**1.70**	2.26	1.98	1.74
	120	2.14	1.88	2.24	1.98	**1.56**
6	80	5.48	5.33	6.07	**5.24**	5.33
	100	4.07	**3.00**	4.35	3.35	3.24
	120	2.97	2.36	3.09	2.52	**2.32**
8	80	4.44	–	4.81	**3.50**	3.66
	100	6.52	–	6.71	5.40	**5.29**
	120	3.69	–	3.92	**2.91**	2.97
10	80	4.44	3.79	5.48	**3.70**	4.27
	100	4.91	**3.26**	4.97	3.56	3.93
	120	4.55	**3.19**	4.52	3.47	3.56
12	80	9.07	–	10.16	**7.92**	8.57
	100	10.36	–	11.09	**9.50**	9.86
	120	4.64	–	5.05	**3.71**	4.21

Table 7. Average RPD in the Setup Domain instances.

m	n	ACOII	LA-ALNS	SGVNS	WO	e-SGVNS
2	80	0.77	1.06	0.83	0.87	**0.66**
	100	1.43	0.90	0.74	1.07	**0.59**
	120	1.37	0.85	0.70	1.04	**0.50**
4	80	2.49	1.96	2.64	2.22	**1.86**
	100	2.16	1.84	2.36	2.04	**1.67**
	120	1.90	1.61	2.09	1.82	**1.50**
6	80	5.64	5.18	6.00	**5.01**	5.39
	100	4.12	**2.99**	4.73	3.31	3.22
	120	2.82	2.41	3.35	2.52	**2.35**
8	80	4.74	**3.30**	4.71	3.49	3.53
	100	6.54	**5.05**	6.72	5.32	5.43
	120	3.78	**2.59**	4.11	2.96	2.88
10	80	4.67	**3.90**	5.76	4.00	4.54
	100	4.77	**3.17**	4.98	3.43	3.66
	120	4.28	**3.22**	4.60	3.58	3.42
12	80	8.84	–	10.24	**7.85**	8.73
	100	9.95	–	16.42	**9.81**	9.91
	120	4.25	–	5.21	**3.58**	3.90

In these tables, the first and second columns represent the number of machines and jobs, respectively. In the subsequent columns are the average RPD for ACOII, LA-ALNS, SGVNS, WO and e-SGVNS algorithms, respectively.

According to Tables 5, 6 and 7, the LA-ALNS algorithm was superior in 20 groups of instances, while the WO algorithm was superior in 14 groups of instances and the e-SGVNS algorithm was superior in 20 groups of instances. The results from SGVNS and ACOII algorithms were outperformed in all instance sets. Considering the presented results, it is possible to affirm that the LA-ALNS algorithm obtained the best average results, even though it was not applied to all the instances made available in [18].

The proposed algorithm presented a value for RPD less than 0 in instances with two machines. If we consider instances with 4 machines, the RPD was always less than 2, while for instances with up to 8 machines, the RPD was always less than 3. For the other instances, the RPD was always less than 4. These results indicate that the proposed method obtained a better performance in instances with fewer machines, in which the solution space is smaller. In other cases, the method has lower performance, given the high computational cost of the mathematical heuristic, which is used as one of the local search operators.

6.1 Statistical Analysis

A hypothesis test was performed to verify if the differences between the results presented by the algorithms are statistically significant. Therefore, the following hypothesis test was used:

$$\begin{cases} H_0 : \mu_1 = \mu_2 = \mu_3 = \mu_4 = \mu_5 \\ H_1 : \exists i, j \mid \mu_i \neq \mu_j \end{cases}$$

in which μ_1, μ_2 and μ_3 are the average RPDs for ACOII, LA-ALNS, SGVNS, WO and e-SGVNS, respectively.

An exploratory analysis of the data was performed in order to better understand the data of the samples before the application of the statistical test.

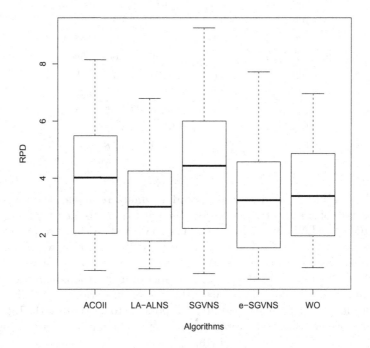

Fig. 4. Boxplot of the results.

Figure 4 shows the boxplot plot containing the sample distribution of the RPD values for the collected samples:

Before performing the hypothesis test, it is necessary to decide between test types, parametric or non-parametric. Generally, parametric tests are more powerful; however, they require three assumptions:

1. Normality: every sample must originate from a population with normal distribution,

2. Independence: the samples shall be independent of each other,
3. Homoscedasticity: every sample must have a population of constant variance.

The Shapiro-Wilk normality test was applied to the samples and its results are shown in Table 8:

Table 8. Shapiro-Wilk normality test.

Algorithm	p-value
ACO II	0.04632
LA-ALNS	0.06239
SGVNS	0.09066
e-SGVNS	0.0737
WO	0.0365

Considering a significance level of 0.05, the results presented above indicate that the samples of the ACOII and WO algorithms come from populations with normal distribution, since the p-values presented are lower than the level of significance. However, the test does not present evidence that the LA-ALNS, SGVNS and e-SGVNS algorithm samples come from a normal population.

Therefore, it was decided to use the Pairwise Wilcoxon test, which calculates pairwise comparisons between group levels with corrections for multiple testing.

The Pairwise Wilcoxon test for the samples of the average results of the ICOII, LA-ALNS, SGVNS, WO and e-SGVNS algorithms are presented in Table 9. In this comparison, we excluded instance sets in which Cota et al. [12] did not report the results of LA-ALNS algorithm.

Table 9. Pairwise comparisons using Wilcoxon test in all algorithms.

	ACOII	e-SGVNS	LA-ALNS	SGVNS
e-SGVNS	1.70×10^{-7}	–	–	–
LA-ALNS	6.70×10^{-6}	1	–	–
SGVNS	8.6×10^{-4}	1.70×10^{-7}	7.70×10^{-8}	–
WO	5.90×10^{-6}	0.2819	2.4×10^{-4}	5.70×10^{-6}

According to Table 9, the observed differences are statistically significant for all algorithm pairs, except to (e-SGNVS, LA-ALNS) and (e-SGNVS, WO).

Table 10 displays the Pairwise Wilcoxon test considering the average RPD of algorithms that were tested in all instances.

Considering that this p-value is much lower than 0.05, then the null hypothesis of equality between the means is rejected and it is concluded that there is evidence that at least two populations have different distribution functions.

Table 10. Pairwise comparisons using Wilcoxon test in all instances.

	ACOII	e-SGVNS	SGVNS
e-SGVNS	1.00×10^{-9}	–	–
SGVNS	2.60×10^{-6}	1.00×10^{-9}	–
WO	2.10×10^{-8}	1	1.60×10^{-8}

As can be seen in Table 9, there is a statistically significant difference between the e-SGVNS algorithm and the SGVNS, ACOII algorithms.

7   Conclusions

This work dealt with the unrelated parallel machine scheduling problem with sequence-dependent setup times, aiming to minimize the makespan.

Since it is NP-hard, a hybrid heuristic algorithm was developed. The proposed algorithm, named Enhanced Smart General Variable Neighborhood Search (e-SGVNS), combines heuristic and exact optimization strategies to explore the solution space of the problem. The exact strategy works as local search and consists of applying a mathematical programming formulation based on the time-dependent traveling salesman problem to get the optimal solution to the sequencing problem on each machine. In turn, the heuristic strategy, in turn, explores neighborhoods based on swap and insertion moves.

The e-SGVNS was tested in benchmark instances from literature and its results were compared to four other literature methods (ACOII, LA-ALNS, SGVNS and WO).

The statistical analysis of the average results produced by the algorithms proved that e-SGVNS is statistically better than the SGVNS and ACOII algorithms. On the other hand, there is no statistical evidence of significant difference among the average results of the e-SGVNS, LA-ALNS and WO algorithms.

Overall, the e-SGVNS algorithm performed best on small instances, with up to 4 machines and up to 120 jobs, regardless of instance type.

As future work, we intend to test other mathematical programming formulations to perform the exact local search as, for instance, to apply a mixed integer linear programming formulation that considers two machines instead of a single one.

Acknowledgments. The authors gratefully thank *Coordenação de Aperfeiçoamento de Pessoal de Nível Superior* (CAPES) - Finance Code 001, *Fundação de Amparo à Pesquisa do Estado de Minas Gerais* (FAPEMIG, grant PPM/CEX/FAPEMIG/676-17), *Conselho Nacional de Desenvolvimento Científico e Tecnológico* (CNPq, grant 307915/2016-6), *Universidade Federal de Ouro Preto* (UFOP) and *Universidade Federal dos Vales do Jequitinhonha e Mucuri* (UFVJM) for supporting this research. The authors also thank the anonymous reviewers for their valuable comments.

skos:majorMatch [25], which support the subsequent construction of the dataset explained in Sect. 3.3.

3.3 Dataset

NETHIC currently makes use of a dataset of 57,304 text documents, taken from Wikipedia. Wikipedia was chosen for this research because it provides an extensive general-purpose knowledge archive that is regularly updated, as well as being easily accessible on the Internet via its HTTP APIs. As mentioned earlier, the

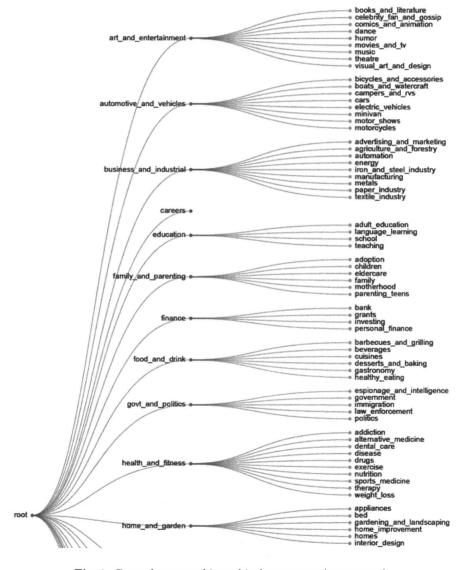

Fig. 1. General-purpose hierarchical taxonomy (upper part).

taxonomy defined as NETHIC's core knowledge model is used to provide the connections between the various classes and the Wikipedia knowledge graph. The first step of this process lies in downloading the entire library of categories from Wikipedia and storing them in a graph structure. These categories are used to group pages by related topics, and are used mostly to find and navigate articles related to a particular subject[1, 2].

Starting from the `Category:Main_topic_classifications` category, the list of sub-categories and documents belonging to that category is recursively

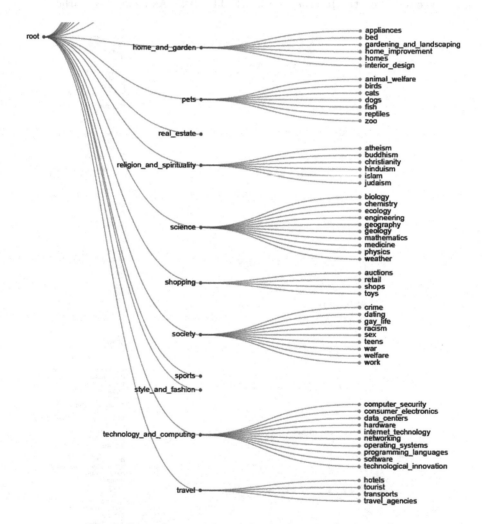

Fig. 2. General-purpose hierarchical taxonomy (lower part).

[1] https://www.wikidata.org/wiki/Q2945159.

[2] https://en.wikipedia.org/wiki/Help:Category.

retrieved by using the available APIs. This first step results in a graph containing 1.5 million nodes linked together with a subclassing relationship.

The next step of this process involves the computation of the feature vectors, by using the category and sub-category names and, when available, their short description, for each of the nodes in the graph via a word embedding approach. Nodes and vectors are cached locally and the edges are weighted as follows.

Given an edge $e(u, v)$ and the respective vectors V_u and V_v, the weight w_e is:

$$w_e = inverse\_cosine\_similarity(V_u, V_v)$$

This allows NETHIC to have a weighted graph based on the semantic value of Wikipedia's categories, here referred to as *Wikipedia Category Graph*. The subsequent step of the process starts from the *leaf* categories of NETHIC's taxonomy and proceeds by navigating and collecting documents from Wikipedia's categories following the shortest semantic path, until the desired amount of documents are collected. The collected documents are then stored in a structure of folders and sub-folders that follows the structure of NETHIC's taxonomy, where the intermediate folders are formed by using a balanced amount of documents coming from each *leaf* category folder.

3.4   Document Embedding

In the latest years, very important results has been achieved regarding text representation to solve many NLP problems. One of the most renowned solution is a word embedding model, called Word2Vec and proposed by Google [18]. A direct update of this model performs the embedding of sentences or entire documents, and is known as Doc2Vec [15], which is useful to transform sentences or documents into corresponding n-dimensional vectors. This transformation is pivotal since it provides the possibility to work with documents without facing the high dimensionality problem commonly present when a bag-of-words approach is used for text representation. Another advantage for this type of word and document representation lies in the semantic similarity as explained by the authors in their studies. A generic application consists of comparing similar words or document vectors through a cosine similarity metric, in order to evaluate how close two items are in the semantic space. NETHIC uses a Doc2Vec model, trained with an English Wikipedia corpus, following two different strategies. In the first strategy, BOW features are replaced with Doc2Vec vectors, used as features for NETHIC's corpus, in order to verify if sufficiently good results could be obtained with less information. In the second strategy, the BOW functionality is merged with Doc2Vec, so that it may be possible to use the occurrences of words in conjunction with the semantic meaning of the documents.

4   NETHIC's Methodological and Technological Framework

This section reprises and extends NETHIC's framework with respect to the earlier discussion in [6] in terms of its architecture, pre-processing and training mechanisms and algorithms used, underlining the improvements over its earlier version.

4.1 Architecture

The main components of NETHIC's current architecture are artificial neural networks, a hierarchical taxonomy, dictionaries and a Doc2Vec pre-trained model. Figure 3 shows these components and graphically represents the structure and NETHIC's whole process. The latter starts with a text elaboration, by using dictionaries and a document embedding instance to vectorize the input documents, and goes on by relying upon a hierarchical neural networks model to find the main leaf categories to be used as classification labels for the given documents.

4.2 Reasons for a Hierarchical Neural Network Model

In NETHIC, as initially clarified in [6], a neural network hierarchy is employed for several reasons. In fact, in order to classify a document whose main topic is, for instance, *kitchens*, it is sensible to use a neural network that is trained only on texts whose focus is on interior decoration and house supplies, instead of a more heterogeneous or too general artificial neural network.

This avoids the presence of unnecessary words and reduces the noise on the classification process. In NETHIC, for each taxonomy concept, with the exception of the leaf concepts, one neural network is trained and a dictionary of words is built. In the upper levels, the neural networks trained are characterized by a somewhat horizontal view, splitting documents according to general, wide concepts like Economy, Religion, Science and Sports, whereas in the deeper levels the networks tend to assume a more vertical separation and classify the documents according to a more specific category that is a descendant of the general concept (for example, Sports), *e.g. Basketball, Combat Sports, Golf, Soccer, Swimming, Tennis, Volleyball...*

Thus, the classification function used in the neural networks, located at different levels in the hierarchy, is trained with a vocabulary and a set of words, having a varied logical structure and granularity. The upper levels are trained with generic words, which are alike to general "concepts", and the vocabulary used does not include the complete glossary of words associated with the context. When reaching the deeper levels, instead, there is a progressively extensive need to discriminate between semantically-close concepts.

Therefore, the glossary used in the training process contains more specific words, since the classification process, in order to be as effective as possible, has the need to learn additional knowledge on the given area of interest. That is why an iterative approach is followed, particularly suited to artificial neural network-based methods, by descending to the more specific, deeper levels of the classification.

This allows NETHIC to prevent the occurrence of semantic errors when dealing with words belonging to different conceptual areas (like the word *tree*

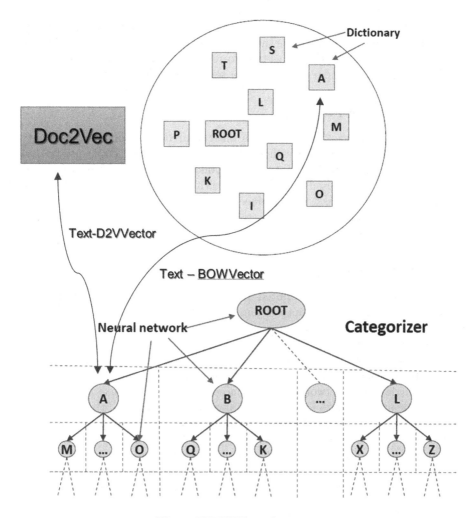

Fig. 3. NETHIC's architecture.

(that represents a plant in the natural world, a component of a ship or a data-representation structure in computer engineering). This sometimes forces the process, when it tries to classify more generic documents, to stop the iteration earlier before it reaches the deepest levels.

In order to understand the potential offered by this approach, let us consider another example where a given document talks about *advertising and marketing*. By taking a look at the taxonomy shown in Figs. 1 and 2, there are many concepts semantically close to the given category such as *personal finance*, *shops* and *movies and tv*, each belonging to different paths. In a scenario where a single neural network is used on 117 different classes, it can be easy to get irrelevant results and low scores due to using the same words in different contexts and with different meanings. In order to face these issues, a hierarchical approach comes thus in handy to decompose the main problem into many sub-classification problems, all of them working together to reduce the noise due to the context by considering trained neural networks on semantically distant concepts.

4.3   Classification Process

The classification process starts with an unstructured text/document as input.

Initially, the *root* category's dictionary and a Doc2Vec (D2V) pre-trained model is used to transform text into a corresponding vectorized form. After that, a BOW+Doc2Vec composed vector is passed as input to *root's Neural Network* to perform the prediction task. As explained in Sect. 4.6, the first relevant categories are chosen to continue with the next steps, considering appropriate dictionaries and neural networks.

4.4   Data Pre-processing

The pre-processing step is required to transform the unstructured datasets explained in Sect. 3.3 in order to obtain a useful and structured version of the data. Before delving deeper into the pre-processing step, it is noteworthy to say that the initial corpus has been split into two balanced corpora with a ratio of 95% - 5%. The first corpus, named *Corpus-A* and containing 54.439 documents (about 465 for each leaf category), has been used for the training and validation tasks on single neural networks. The second corpus, called *Corpus-B*, containing 2843 documents (about 25 for each leaf category), has been used throughout the entire validation of the hierarchical model. As known in literature as well as in commercial environments, an ETL (Extraction, Transformation and Loading) process represents a key point for data collection and feature extraction tasks. In this work, three kinds of transformations, explained below, are used in order to build a sufficient number of datasets to check and identify the best features to be used.

The details of the first transformation can be found in [6]; it produces BOW-based datasets that will be referred to as *Datasets_BOW* from now on. Dictionaries used in the hierarchical validation step are saved in order to transform the validation corpus by considering the same words already used to train the neural networks.

A second transformation used the Doc2Vec model to convert documents into suitable vectors of 300 dimensions. Unlike the first transformation, the built datasets called *Datasets_D2V* consume a really slight portion of memory and there is no need to store dictionaries for the subsequent validation phase.

Finally, the two abovementioned transformations in order to use both features type. In this case the datasets obtained called *Datasets_D2V-BOW* are far too large to be kept in memory, just like the BOW-based datasets. The resulting vectors will be in this case the concatenation of the BOW and D2V vectors, thus dictionaries are saved here as well.

For each of these transformations, 18 datasets are built.

The next subsection describes how three corresponding models of neural networks, each for one of the three transformations, have been trained and compared.

4.5 Training

As mentioned in the previous subsection, the training phase carried out by using *Corpus-A* has been performed three times, one for each transformation (and thus for each group of datasets). In this subsection, firstly the generic method used to train the single neural networks will be explained, and then the different models will be compared in order to find the best features to be used for the classification problem.

According to the best practices for training artificial intelligence models, a cross-validation was executed to check for potential overfitting/underfitting, by using the k-fold and "leave one out approach" [30]. By resorting to this technique, an initial, balanced splitting of the datasets has been necessary to compute the training and testing in "leave one out". Starting from this assumption, for any single dataset two sub-datasets have been built, with 90% and 10% proportions, respectively. For example, considering a theoretical category X and a corresponding BOW dataset saved as *Dataset_BOW_X*, a splitting is made in order to obtain *Dataset_BOW_X_Training_CV* and *Dataset_BOW_X_Validation_LOO*. The following pseudocode describes how the training phase was performed.

Algorithm 1. Training using Cross-Validation and Test in One Shot.

1: **procedure** TRAINING
2:     **for** *middle Taxonomy's Category* **X do**
3:         *Dataset_X_Training_CV* ←*Dataset_X*
4:         *Dataset_X_Validation_LOO* ←*Dataset_X*
5:         *CV_accuracy* ←*0*
6:         **for** *each folds combinations (4,1) from Dataset_X_Training_CV* **do**
7:             *current_CV_model_X* ←training(4_ folds)
8:             *current_CV_accuracy_X* ←model.validation(1_fold)
9:             *CV_accuracy* ←*CV_accuracy + current_CV_accuracy_X*
10:        *CV_accuracy* ←*CV_accuracy : 5*
11:        *model_X* ←training(*Dataset_X_Training_CV*)
12:        *model_accuracy_X* ←model.validation(*Dataset_X_Validation_LOO*)
13:        **save(model_X)**

Basically, any category used to realize the hierarchical model covers all the steps described in Algorithm 1, and for each of them, a cross-validation has been performed in order to evaluate the potential presence of underfitting and overfitting. After making sure that none of these problems had arisen, it was possible to train the neural network using *Dataset_X_Training_CV* subsequently validated with *Dataset_X_Validation_LOO*. This algorithm has been executed on the three groups of datasets previously described, obtaining neural networks for each of the features considered, that is to say BOW, Doc2Vec and BOW-Doc2Vec. The three tables showed in Figs. 4, 5 and 6, respectively, contain Cross-Validation Accuracy, Training Accuracy, Test Accuracy, Precision, Recall and F1-score metrics for each of the trained models. As shown, the best accuracies are obtained with the combined model that uses BOW and D2V features together. The worst performance was obtained by using the model trained on D2V features only: this means that for this kind of complex classification, document embedding by itself is not a good choice to represent documents, but it can nevertheless be useful to improve the accuracy of the BOW model, as seen in the results obtained. By considering the BOW and BOW-D2V accuracy values, there is an improvement of about 2% for most categories, and an improvement of about 1% for the *root* category: this is especially important, because in the hierarchical model it represents the heaviest category for the correct construction of the classification paths. Cross-validation results show that there are no overfitting and underfitting issues exactly as expected. Training and test accuracies show that all the trained models learn well and are able to generalize with data never seen before. Precision, Recall and F1-Score show that the trained models are able to obtain a good accuracy for all of the labels, and in general they do not confuse among classes that are semantically close to one another.

4.6 Algorithm to Build Paths

The algorithm used to build paths has not undergone significant modifications from the one described in [6]. For each returned path, the average between all the single scores for each of the corresponding categories is computed.

For instance, given the following path: $P = C_1/C_2/C_3$ with its respective scores SC_1, SC_2 and SC_2, its corresponding total score S_P is the average of the single scores. The system keeps considering categories until the probabilities returned by the current neural networks reach a threshold that is initially set as 0.7. If after the first classification a good current tolerance is obtained, this will consequently lead to a reasonable classification; otherwise, if such a value is low, it means that there are paths with a low score. In this case, a second classification iteration is run by considering the paths with a lower score value. In general, this algorithm allows the system to select the highest-level categories and concepts when the textual content examined contains only generic terms, whereas it is possible to select more detailed and low-level categories and concepts by examining texts that are very specific, technical or focused on a certain topic.

BOW

Category	Cross Validation	Training Accuracy	Test Accuracy	F1-Score	Precision	Recall
pets	0.86	0.96	0.84	0.85	0.85	0.85
automotive and vehicles	0.81	0.96	0.81	0.80	0.84	0.78
govt and politics	0.80	0.97	0.77	0.77	0.77	0.77
home and garden	0.84	0.97	0.80	0.81	0.82	0.81
education	0.79	0.97	0.80	0.79	0.80	0.78
family and parenting	0.78	0.97	0.81	0.79	0.81	0.78
technology and computing	0.73	0.95	0.74	0.74	0.74	0.74
food and drink	0.80	0.96	0.83	0.83	0.83	0.83
society	0.79	0.97	0.75	0.75	0.76	0.76
root	0.73	0.97	0.73	0.73	0.73	0.73
science	0.82	0.97	0.82	0.83	0.83	0.83
health and fitness	0.79	0.95	0.77	0.77	0.77	0.78
religion and spirituality	0.87	0.98	0.86	0.86	0.86	0.86
art and entertainment	0.83	0.98	0.83	0.83	0.83	0.83
business and industrial	0.85	0.97	0.83	0.82	0.82	0.83
travel	0.89	0.97	0.89	0.74	0.94	0.70
finance	0.84	0.97	0.88	0.78	0.90	0.75
shopping	0.87	0.97	0.89	0.89	0.89	0.89

Fig. 4. Single ANN's scores with BOW dataset.

5 Experimentation of NETHIC's Extended Method and Comparison with the Earlier Method

In this section the results of the new experimentation carried out after the introduction of the combined BOW+Doc2Vec document embedding mechanism is reported and compared with the earlier version of NETHIC (with only the BOW mechanism). The focus here is on the pie charts and confusion matrices that show how integrating the Doc2Vec model for feature extraction is a sound approach combined with the earlier BOW-based method. For the purposes of such a comparison, the terms "NETHIC" and "NETHIC-2" will be used to differentiate between NETHIC's original approach and the extended one, respectively. The last part of this section discusses a couple of practical examples to conclude the analysis.

Doc2vec

Category	Cross Validation	Training Accuracy	Test Accuracy	F1-Score	Precision	Recall
pets	0.81	0.86	0.81	0.81	0.81	0.81
automotive and vehicles	0.73	0.79	0.75	0.64	0.64	0.66
govt and politics	0.74	0.78	0.72	0.72	0.72	0.72
home and garden	0.78	0.83	0.76	0.77	0.78	0.77
education	0.67	0.69	0.64	0.57	0.64	0.59
family and parenting	0.68	0.73	0.67	0.64	0.65	0.64
technology and computing	0.63	0.69	0.63	0.62	0.62	0.63
food and drink	0.70	0.76	0.72	0.72	0.72	0.72
society	0.69	0.75	0.66	0.66	0.66	0.66
root	0.62	0.68	0.65	0.64	0.65	0.65
science	0.75	0.79	0.77	0.77	0.77	0.78
health and fitness	0.72	0.77	0.74	0.74	0.75	0.75
religion and spirituality	0.62	0.71	0.63	0.63	0.63	0.64
art and entertainment	0.72	0.76	0.74	0.74	0.75	0.74
business and industrial	0.78	0.82	0.77	0.77	0.77	0.77
travel	0.84	0.89	0.88	0.65	0.69	0.63
finance	0.74	0.78	0.76	0.58	0.56	0.59
shopping	0.80	0.83	0.78	0.78	0.78	0.78

Fig. 5. Single ANN's scores with Doc2Vec dataset.

5.1 Comparison Between NETHIC and NETHIC-2

As explained in [6], to evaluate the tool's accuracy the first three categories returned by the algorithm to build paths detailed in Sect. 4.6 are considered. This choice is meaningful because when many classes—some of them semantically close to one another—are used for text classification, a single assigned class may not be the only and optimal solution. For this comparison *Corpus_B*, which contains 2843 documents (about 25 for each leaf category), has been used to test both methods.

Clearly, dictionaries are used step-by-step for each different path in order to build the correct BOW vector to be merged with the unchanged Doc2Vec vector (which stays the same for every document to be classified), in order to keep the coherence with the currently analyzed category. The pie charts in Fig. 7 emphasize the improvement obtained with the extended method, which is able to correctly classify ∼60 documents more than the earlier approach. The improvement observed during the training phase is the same as in this evaluation, and therefore confirms an overall improvement of 2%.

Doc2vec-BOW

Category	Cross Validation	Training Accuracy	Test Accuracy	F1-Score	Precision	Recall
pets	0.86	0.96	0.85	0.86	0.85	0.86
automotive and vehicles	0.82	0.96	0.82	0.79	0.84	0.77
govt and politics	0.80	0.97	0.78	0.78	0.78	0.78
home and garden	0.86	0.97	0.82	0.83	0.84	0.83
education	0.79	0.97	0.83	0.82	0.83	0.82
family and parenting	0.78	0.97	0.80	0.77	0.78	0.77
technology and computing	0.73	0.95	0.74	0.74	0.74	0.74
food and drink	0.81	0.96	0.84	0.84	0.84	0.84
society	0.80	0.97	0.75	0.75	0.75	0.76
root	0.74	0.97	0.74	0.73	0.74	0.73
science	0.83	0.97	0.84	0.84	0.84	0.84
health and fitness	0.80	0.95	0.78	0.78	0.78	0.79
religion and spirituality	0.87	0.98	0.85	0.85	0.85	0.85
art and entertainment	0.83	0.98	0.84	0.84	0.84	0.84
business and industrial	0.86	0.97	0.83	0.83	0.83	0.83
travel	0.90	0.95	0.88	0.65	0.68	0.65
finance	0.85	0.97	0.86	0.72	0.89	0.71
shopping	0.87	0.97	0.88	0.88	0.88	0.88

Fig. 6. Single ANN's scores with BOW+Doc2Vec dataset.

The following confusion matrix shows the methods' accuracy for the first hierarchical level in order to understand the improvement for the root neural network. The diagonal values for the matrix in both Figs. 8 and 9 represents the correct classifications and make the matrix almost diagonal. The best performance for the *Science* category is obtained by NETHIC-2 with about 8 more documents that with the earlier method had been lost. In general, improvements over NETHIC's previous method can be seen in *Art and Entertainment*, which is now less confused with other categories, in *Society*, which is now less confused with *Family_and_parenting*, and in *Health_and_fitness*, previously more confused with a lot of other categories containing similar contents like *Society, Sport and Food_and_drink*. In computational terms there are no relevant differences, since the addition of a 300-sized Doc2Vec vector does not change the order of magnitude of the feature vectors to be used for the training and classification steps.

5.2 Examples

Last but not least, practical classification examples are reported by showing two different Wikipedia documents. In the first example, a document that talks

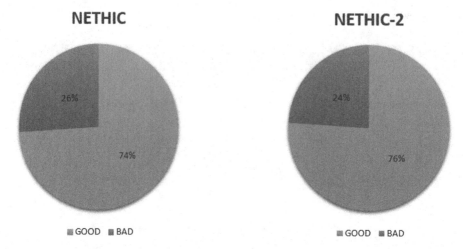

Fig. 7. Classification accuracy of the initial (leftmost chart) and the extended method (rightmost chart).

about a specific mineral called "Bukovskyite", and was labeled in *Corpus_B* as *Iron_and_steel_industry*, has been classified correctly as *business_and_industrial-/iron_and_steel_industry/*, as well as *science/geology/* that is correct for obvious reasons. In the second example a document talking about food-related problems has been classified. As shown, the classifier returned categories including the correct label *food_and_drink/healthy_eating/* as the second choice, which may be considered a good result, but also contains a more relevant category for such a document like *health_and_fitness/addiction/*, which constitutes a surprising achievement.

Iron_and_steel_industry Wikipedia Document. *Bukovskyite (also known as "clay of Kutná Hora") is an iron arsenate sulfate mineral which forms nodules with a reniform (kidney-shaped) surface. Under a microscope, these nodules appear as a collection of minute needles similar to gypsum. Some can be seen with the naked eye and occur inside the nodules. Bukovskyite was first described from pit heaps from the Middle Ages, where sulfate ores had been mined at Kank, north of Kutná Hora in Bohemia, Czech Republic, and other old deposits in the vicinity. Only recently defined and acknowledged, it was approved by the IMA in 1969. Bukovskyite was collected a long time ago from the overgrown pit heaps by the inhabitants of Kutná Hora. It was used for poisoning field mice and other field vermin. This poisonous clay, known also by the place name as "clay of Kutná Hora", was widely known and it was considered to be arsenic (arsenic trioxide).*

Classification Results

– **Label** = *business_and_industrial/iron_and_steel_industry/* **Score** = 0.68
– **Label** = *science/geology/* **Score** = 0.53

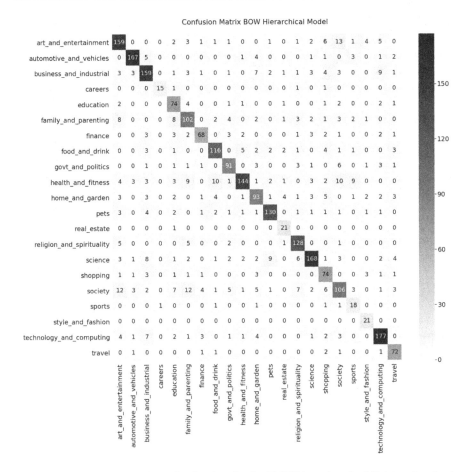

Fig. 8. NETHIC's original results (with only the BOW-based embedding mechanism).

Healthy Eating Wikipedia Document. *Overeaters Anonymous (OA) is a twelve-step program for people with problems related to food including, but not limited to, compulsive overeaters, those with binge eating disorder, bulimics and anorexics. Anyone with a problematic relationship with food is welcomed, as OA's Third Tradition states that the only requirement for memberships is a desire to stop eating compulsively. OA was founded by Rozanne S. and two other women in January 1960. The organizations headquarters, or World Service Office, is located in Rio Rancho, New Mexico. Overeaters Anonymous estimates its membership at over 60,000 people in about 6,500 groups meeting in over 75 countries. OA has developed its own literature specifically for those who eat compulsively but also uses the Alcoholics Anonymous books Alcoholics Anonymous and Twelve Steps and Twelve Traditions. The First Step of OA begins with the admission of powerlessness over food; the next eleven steps are intended to bring members physical, emotional, and spiritual healing.*

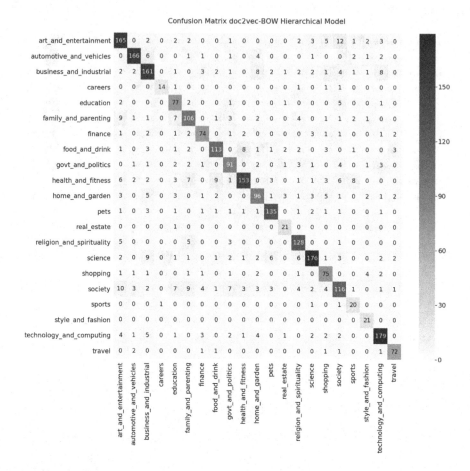

Fig. 9. NETHIC's results with the introduction of the combined BOW+Doc2Vec embedding mechanism.

Classification Results

- **Label** = *health_and_fitness/addiction/* **Score** = 0.64
- **Label** = *food_and_drink/healthy_eating/* **Score** = 0.38
- **Label** = *food_and_drink/gastronomy/* **Score** = 0.26

5.3 Technical Configuration for the Experimentation

The hardware configuration employed for the reported experimentation includes the following systems: one Intel i7-6700HQ CPU with 16 GB DDR3 RAM, one Intel i7-7700 CPU with 32 GB DDR3 RAM and Sandisk Ultra SSD, and one Intel i7-8550U CPU with 32 GB DDR4 RAM and Samsung Pro SSD. The classifier used in NETHIC has been written in Python and exploits the *scikit-learn*,

CountVectorizer and *Multi-layer Perceptron (MLP)* libraries to create the feature vectors and the artificial neural networks themselves. For the Doc2Vec pre-trained model, the *Gensim* library has been used. Persistence and loading of the networks is done via the *pickle* library.

6   Discussion and Conclusion

This work reported and extended the discussion on NETHIC, a software tool implementing a classification method for textual documents relying upon hierarchical taxonomies, artificial neural networks and a document embedding mechanism.

The earlier research discussed in [6] proved the combination of artificial neural networks and hierarchical taxonomies to be effective for tackling the classification problem, displaying an overall solid performance together with relevant characteristics of scalability and modularity.

With respect to the initial version of NETHIC, the current tool now takes advantage of a state-of-art Natural Language Processing technique like Doc2Vec, and the results achieved with the introduction of such an embedding technique, in combination with the earlier used bag-of-words, have demonstrated that with a slight increase in the dimensional space it is possible to obtain better results in the classification of documents and texts.

In this regard, the experimentation reported in this work showed that the improvements obtained with respect of NETHIC's original method via the combination of the BOW and Doc2Vec embedding mechanisms encourages their combined usage so that more information can be considered by NETHIC's neural networks in order for it to understand and choose the correct categories for classification. Taken individually, the BOW mechanism proved to be sufficiently solid (as seen in [6]), whereas it may not be advisable to use Doc2Vec by itself, probably because semantically-close categories, like the leaves of a given intermediate category, are difficult to be told apart without considering the words used.

Future work may explore the possibilities of integrating and/or extending other state-of-the art methods like BERT [8] that are currently heading towards ever newer and future-envisioning frontiers.

References

1. Atzeni, P., Polticelli, F., Toti, D.: An automatic identification and resolution system for protein-related abbreviations in scientific papers. In: Pizzuti, C., Ritchie, M.D., Giacobini, M. (eds.) EvoBIO 2011. LNCS, vol. 6623, pp. 171–176. Springer, Heidelberg (2011). https://doi.org/10.1007/978-3-642-20389-3_18
2. Atzeni, P., Polticelli, F., Toti, D.: Experimentation of an automatic resolution method for protein abbreviations in full-text papers. In: 2011 ACM Conference on Bioinformatics, Computational Biology and Biomedicine, BCB 2011, pp. 465–467 (2011). https://doi.org/10.1145/2147805.2147871

3. Atzeni, P., Polticelli, F., Toti, D.: A framework for semi-automatic identification, disambiguation and storage of protein-related abbreviations in scientific literature. In: Proceedings - International Conference on Data Engineering, pp. 59–61 (2011). https://doi.org/10.1109/ICDEW.2011.5767646

4. Bird, S., Klein, E., Loper, E.: Natural Language Processing with Python - Analyzing Text with the Natural Language Toolkit. O'Reilly, Sebastopol (2009)

5. Buda, M., Maki, A., Mazurowski, M.A.: A systematic study of the class imbalance problem in convolutional neural networks. CoRR abs/1710.05381 (2017). http://arxiv.org/abs/1710.05381

6. Ciapetti, A., Florio, R.D., Lomasto, L., Miscione, G., Ruggiero, G., Toti, D.: NETHIC: a system for automatic text classification using neural networks and hierarchical taxonomies. In: ICEIS 2019 - Proceedings of the 21st International Conference on Enterprise Information Systems, pp. 284–294 (2019). https://doi.org/10.5220/0007709702960306

7. Dalal, M.K., Zaveri, M.: Automatic text classification: a technical review. Int. J. Comput. Appl. **28** (2011)

8. Devlin, J., Chang, M., Lee, K., Toutanova, K.: BERT: pre-training of deep bidirectional transformers for language understanding. CoRR abs/1810.04805 (2018). http://arxiv.org/abs/1810.04805

9. Forman, G.: An extensive empirical study of feature selection metrics for text classification. J. Mach. Learn. Res. **3**, 1289–1305 (2003)

10. Ha, J.W., Pyo, H., Kim, J.: Large-scale item categorization in e-commerce using multiple recurrent neural networks. In: Proceedings of the 22nd ACM SIGKDD International Conference on Knowledge Discovery and Data Mining, KDD 2016, pp. 107–115. ACM, New York (2016). https://doi.org/10.1145/2939672.2939678

11. Hermundstad, A., Brown, K., Bassett, D., Carlson, J.: Learning, memory, and the role of neural network architecture. PLoS Comput. Biol. **7**, e1002063 (2011)

12. Kalchbrenner, N., Grefenstette, E., Blunsom, P.: A convolutional neural network for modelling sentences. In: Proceedings of the 52nd Annual Meeting of the Association for Computational Linguistics (Volume 1: Long Papers), pp. 655–665. Association for Computational Linguistics, Baltimore, June 2014. http://www.aclweb.org/anthology/P14-1062

13. Kim, Y.: Convolutional neural networks for sentence classification. In: Proceedings of the 2014 Conference on Empirical Methods in Natural Language Processing, EMNLP 2014, Doha, Qatar, 25–29 October 2014, A meeting of SIGDAT, a Special Interest Group of the ACL, pp. 1746–1751 (2014). http://aclweb.org/anthology/D/D14/D14-1181.pdf

14. Koppel, M., Winter, Y.: Determining if two documents are written by the same author. J. Assoc. Inf. Sci. Technol. **65**, 178–187 (2014)

15. Le, Q., Mikolov, T.: Distributed representations of sentences and documents. In: Proceedings of the 31st International Conference on International Conference on Machine Learning - Volume 32, ICML 2014, pp. II-1188–II-1196 (2014). http://dl.acm.org/citation.cfm?id=3044805.3045025. JMLR.org

16. Lewis, D.D., Ringuette, M.: A comparison of two learning algorithms for text categorization. In: Third Annual Symposium on Document Analysis and Information Retrieval, pp. 81–93 (1994)

17. McCallum, A., Nigam, K.: A comparison of event models for Naive Bayes text classification. In: Learning for Text Categorization: Papers from the 1998 AAAI Workshop, pp. 41–48 (1998). http://www.kamalnigam.com/papers/multinomial-aaaiws98.pdf

18. Mikolov, T., Sutskever, I., Chen, K., Corrado, G., Dean, J.: Distributed representations of words and phrases and their compositionality. In: Proceedings of the 26th International Conference on Neural Information Processing Systems - Volume 2, NIPS 2013, pp. 3111–3119. Curran Associates Inc. (2013). http://dl.acm.org/citation.cfm?id=2999792.2999959
19. Sebastiani, F.: Machine learning in automated text categorization. ACM Comput. Surv. **34**, 1–47 (2002)
20. Shen, D., Ruvini, J.D., Mukherjee, R., Sundaresan, N.: A study of smoothing algorithms for item categorization on e-commerce sites. Neurocomputing **92**, 54–60 (2012). https://doi.org/10.1016/j.neucom.2011.08.035
21. Silla Jr., C.N., Freitas, A.A.: A survey of hierarchical classification across different application domains. Data Min. Knowl. Discov. **22**(1–2), 31–72 (2011). https://doi.org/10.1007/s10618-010-0175-9
22. Toti, D., Atzeni, P., Polticelli, F.: Automatic protein abbreviations discovery and resolution from full-text scientific papers: the PRAISED framework. Bio Algorithms Med Syst. **8** (2012). https://doi.org/10.2478/bams-2012-0002
23. Toti, D., Rinelli, M.: On the road to speed-reading and fast learning with CONCEPTUM. In: Proceedings - 2016 International Conference on Intelligent Networking and Collaborative Systems, IEEE INCoS 2016, pp. 357–361 (2016). https://doi.org/10.1109/INCoS.2016.30
24. Vidhya, K., Aghila, G.: A survey of Naive Bayes machine learning approach in text document classification. Int. J. Comput. Sci. Inf. Secur. **7**, 206–211 (2010)
25. W3C: Skos - simple knowledge organization system reference (2009). https://www.w3.org/TR/2009/REC-skos-reference-20090818/
26. W3C: RDF resource description framework (2014). http://www.w3.org/RDF/
27. Wang, L., Zhao, X.: Improved K-NN classification algorithm research in text categorization. In: Proceedings of the 2nd International Conference on Consumer Electronics, Communications and Networks (CECNet), pp. 1848–1852 (2012)
28. Wang, S., Manning, C.: Baselines and bigrams: simple, good sentiment and topic classification. In: Proceedings of the 50th Annual Meeting of the ACL: Short Papers, vol. 2, pp. 90–94. ACL (2012)
29. Wetzker, R., et al.: Tailoring taxonomies for efficient text categorization and expert finding. In: 2008 IEEE/WIC/ACM International Conference on Web Intelligence and Intelligent Agent Technology, vol. 3, pp. 459–462, December 2008
30. Wong, T.T.: Performance evaluation of classification algorithms by k-fold and leave-one-out cross validation. Pattern Recogn. **48**(9), 2839–2846 (2015). https://doi.org/10.1016/j.patcog.2015.03.009
31. Zhang, Y., Roller, S., Wallace, B.C.: MGNC-CNN: a simple approach to exploiting multiple word embeddings for sentence classification. In: Proceedings of the 2016 Conference of the North American Chapter of the Association for Computational Linguistics: Human Language Technologies, pp. 1522–1527. Association for Computational Linguistics, San Diego, June 2016. https://doi.org/10.18653/v1/N16-1178
32. Zhang, Y., Wallace, B.: A sensitivity analysis of (and practitioners' guide to) convolutional neural networks for sentence classification. In: Proceedings of the Eighth International Joint Conference on Natural Language Processing (Volume 1: Long Papers), pp. 253–263. Asian Federation of Natural Language Processing, Taipei, November 2017. https://www.aclweb.org/anthology/I17-1026
33. Zhou, Z.H., Liu, X.Y.: Training cost-sensitive neural networks with methods addressing the class imbalance problem. IEEE Trans. Knowl. Data Eng. **18**(1), 63–77 (2006). https://doi.org/10.1109/TKDE.2006.17

An Iterated Local Search-Based Algorithm to Support Cell Nuclei Detection in Pap Smears Test

Débora N. Diniz[1]([⊠])(iD), Marcone J. F. Souza[1](iD), Claudia M. Carneiro[2](iD),
Daniela M. Ushizima[3](iD), Fátima N. S. de Medeiros[4](iD),
Paulo H. C. Oliveira[1](iD), and Andrea G. C. Bianchi[1](iD)

[1] Institute of Exact Sciences and Biological, Graduate Program in Computer Science,
Federal University of Ouro Preto, Ouro Preto, Brazil
debnasser@gmail.com, paulocalaes@gmail.com,
{marcone,andrea}@ufop.edu.br
[2] Biological Sciences Research Center, Graduate Program in Biotechnology,
Federal University of Ouro Preto, Ouro Preto, Brazil
carneirocm@ufop.edu.br
[3] Berkeley Institute for Data Science, University of California and Lawrence Berkeley
National Laboratory, Berkeley, CA, USA
dani.lbnl@gmail.com
[4] Teleinformatics Engineering Department, Federal University of Ceará,
Fortaleza, Brazil
fsombra@ufc.br

Abstract. The focus of this work is on the detection of nuclei in synthetic images of cervical cells. Finding nuclei is an important step in building a computational method to help cytopathologists identify cell changes from Pap smears. The method developed in this work combines both the Multi-Start and the Iterated Local Search metaheuristics and uses the features of a region to identify a nucleus. It aims to improve the assertiveness of the screening and reduce the professional workload. The *irace* package was used to automatically calibrate all parameter values of the method. The proposed approach was compared with other methods in the literature according to recall, precision, and F1 metrics using the ISBI Overlapping Cytology Image Segmentation Challenge database (2014). The results show that the proposed method has the second-best values of F1 and recall, while the accuracy is still high.

Keywords: Nuclei segmentation · Cervical cells · Simple linear iterative clustering · Density-based spatial clustering of applications with noise · Iterated Local Search · Multi-Start · Metaheuristic · Pap smear images analysis

1 Introduction

According to the World Health Organization (WHO) and the Pan American Health Organization (PAHO), cervical cancer is the fourth most common cancer

© Springer Nature Switzerland AG 2020
J. Filipe et al. (Eds.): ICEIS 2019, LNBIP 378, pp. 78–96, 2020.
https://doi.org/10.1007/978-3-030-40783-4_5

in women, accounting for 7.5% of deaths in females in 2018 (about 570,000 cases). Also, an estimate indicates that over 311,000 deaths from this cancer occur each year, of which over 85% occur in less developed regions of the world.

This estimate is made based on the fact that in these countries the symptoms are the source for disease detection. However, the symptoms only appear when the disease is already advanced, reducing the chance of cure. Besides that, in underdeveloped countries, treatment options may also be more precarious. In contrast, early detection and treatment (commonly done in developed countries) can prevent up to 80% of cervical cancer cases.

WHO and PAHO also claim that adequate screening and treatment programs could reduce the high worldwide cervical-cancer mortality rate. One way to find out about the disease in its early stages is to make a preventive test, the Pap smear. The conventional and most inexpensive way to perform this test starts by collecting cellular samples from the inner and outer surface of the cervix, which are placed on a glass slide, called a cytological smear and sent for analysis by laboratories specialized in cytopathology.

The challenge of slide analysis is the complexity of the images, the number of images (one slide is around 15000), and the small number of professionals able to perform it. Thus, an aid tool can contribute to this screening.

Moreover, as presented by Amaral et al. [1], despite the extensive use of the screening since the 1980s, it has a high rate of false-negative results (from 2 to 62%). As this rate is directly related to the challenges mentioned above, an aid tool would contribute to an improvement in the assertiveness of the tests.

The first development step of this tool is the detection and segmentation of the nuclei present in the images obtained from the slide. This is a crucial step because when nuclei are altered, the morphological and textural features of the nucleus vary considerably [14,19]. For example, the nuclei can have a more massive nucleus or irregular chromatin condensation.

The idea of this work is to propose and study methods to detect and segment cervical nuclei in order to obtain one step for the construction of an aid tool for Pap smear.

The structure of the article's remainder follows as described: Sect. 2 presents the problem description along with the database used in tests and the explanation of some metrics applied. Section 3 discusses the techniques used in the literature to deal with the same problem. Section 4 preprocessing steps applied in the database images. Section 5 details a heuristic approach, based on the Iterated Local Search metaheuristic, focused on solving the nuclei detection. The computational experiments are discussed in Sect. 6. Finally, Sect. 7 exposes conclusions and a future work.

2   Problem Description

The problem approached in this article is a challenge proposal made by the International Symposium on Biomedical Imaging (ISBI) in 2014. It was called the *Overlapping Cervical Cytology Image Segmentation Challenge* [9,10].

This challenge provides a database that has 945 synthetic images divided into training (45 images) and testing (900 ones) groups. All of them were generated from real images obtained from a Pap smears test, but only have normal nuclei.

The images are 512 pixels wide and 512 pixels high (512 × 512), in grayscale. The images present different number of cells, which range from one to ten, and the overlapping levels of cells also vary differently. An example of the information presented in the database is shown in Fig. 1, in which (a) has the synthetic image example and (b) has its corresponding ground truth.

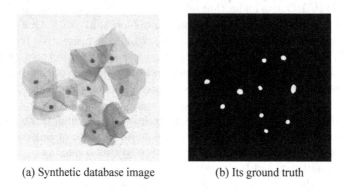

(a) Synthetic database image   (b) Its ground truth

Fig. 1. Example of database information.

The goal of this challenge is to segment nuclei and cytoplasms independently. Our will be adopted exclusively for the detection and segmentation of the nucleus following the idea supported by a number of researchers, such as Moshavegh et al. and Samsudin et al. [14,19], who understand that only this information is sufficient to detect lesions since the morphological features and nuclei texture variations vary significantly when altered.

For example, suppose that the algorithm used to detect the nuclei in Fig. 1(a) obtained the result shown in Fig. 2.

Fig. 2. Example of result obtained. (Color figure online)

Assuming that the green nuclei were the ones detected by the algorithm, we can verify that:

- 1 incorrect nucleus was found (marked with red box) - false positive (FP);
- 7 correct nuclei were found (those with no marks) - true positive (TP);
- 3 nuclei were not found (marked with yellow box) - false negative (FN).

With these values, it is possible to calculate the quality of the detection performed. For this, we use the metrics defined by Manning and Schutze [11], that are shown in Eqs. 1, 2 and 3 and calculates the precision, recall and F1, respectively.

$$precision = \frac{TP}{TP + FP} \tag{1}$$

$$recall = \frac{TP}{TP + FN} \tag{2}$$

$$F1 = 2 \times \frac{precision \times recall}{precision + recall} \tag{3}$$

in which TP is the number of true positives, FP the number of false positives, and FN the number of false negatives.

Thus, using the Eqs. 1 and 2 it is possible to see that for this example we would have an accuracy of $0.875 = 7/(7+1)$ and a recall of $0.700 = 7/(7+3)$. These precision and recall values will be used to measure the assertiveness of the solution found. Recall measures the number of nuclei detected, while precision measures the number of nuclei detected that are actually nuclei. Finally, F1 measures the harmonic mean between precision and recall. In this example, $F1 = 0.778 = 2 \times (0.875 \times 0.7)/(0.875 + 0.7)$.

As a computer cannot give a diagnosis, cytopathologists will have to analyze the result of the proposed method. The purpose of using a support algorithm is to minimize the number of images that professionals need to analyze. Also, all nuclei must be detected, as a failure to detect a nucleus can lead to a misdiagnosis.

The desired scenario would be one that all nuclei present in the image are found without finding other nuclei incorrectly. In this case, precision and recall would be 100%. However, this is rare due to complexities, such as overlap and noise.

This makes it evident that it is desirable to have a 100% recall as it will guarantee the detection of all nuclei, even if it also detects FP. In this case, the cytopathologists would still have all the necessary information to give the diagnosis. The importance of high precision is because it determines reductions in the professionals' work. Therefore, the focus of this work is to find a high recall in the proposed method.

3   Related Work

The problem of cell and nucleus segmentation is already addressed by different techniques.

Ren and Malik [17] proposed the concept of superpixel for image segmentation, which has become widely used. Superpixel is a group of pixels that are grouped by having similar colors or gray levels. Song et al. [20] use superpixel as a grouping stage to generate the superpixels that were used to train a Convolutional Neural Network (CNN) to classify as background, cytoplasm, or nucleus. Ushizima et al. [23] estimate cell mass as initial preprocessing and use superpixels to detect nuclei. Diniz et al. [4] used superpixels as preprocessing to detect possible nuclei. As the presented works had good results for the segmentation of nuclei, this work will also use this concept.

As Song et al. [20], other works also used CNN to perform nuclei segmentation. Xing et al. [24] presented CNN to generate a probability map to obtain initial cell contours using an iterative region merge approach. Braz and Lotufo [2] proposed an approach in which after training, the network layers that were fully connected are converted into convolutional layers to not limit the size of images to be classified.

Another widely adopted technique is the Support Vector Machine (SVM). Mariarputham and Stephen [12] used some types of SVM and neural networks for texture-based classification. Tareef et al. [22] use SVM based on distinctive local features and guided deformation to segment the image into nuclei, cells, and background.

Nosrati and Hamarneh [15] combined the Maximally Stable Extremal Region (MSER) and Random Forest (RF) methods to detect nuclei, while Saha et al. [18] introduced a Circular Shape Function (CSF) that determines a shape constraint on the regions considered to improve the nuclei segmentation using Fuzzy C-Means Clustering (FCM).

Table 1. Related work.

Authors	Method	Database
Song et al. [20]	Superpixel, CNN	Database from the Sixth People's Hospital of Shenzhen
Ushizima et al. [23]	Superpixel	ISBI 2014 Challenge
Diniz et al. [4]	Superpixel, ILS	ISBI 2014 Challenge
Nosrati and Hamarneh [15]	MSER, RF	ISBI 2014 Challenge
Mariarputham and Stephen [12]	SVM, Neural networks	Database from Herlev University Hospital, Denmark
Xing et al. [24]	CNN	Base with brain tumor, NET and breast cancer images
Saha et al. [18]	CSF, FCM	ISBI 2014 Challenge
Tareef et al. [22]	SVM, DRLSE	ISBI 2014 Challenge
Braz and Lotufo [2]	CNN	ISBI 2014 Challenge

Table 1 summarizes the most relevant methods from literature to nuclei and cell detection as well as the database used for testing them.

The proposed method is the same as the one adopted by Diniz et al. [4], except that, is discussed what features should be considered, and a design of experiments to calibrate the parameters is produced. All works that used the same database as ours (challenge of ISBI 2014) are used for comparison.

4 Preprocessing Phase

The proposed method has a preprocessing step that first uses an algorithm called Simple Linear Iterative Clustering (SLIC) [6] to generate superpixels by clustering pixels based on their color similarity and proximity. So, SLIC receives the original image (Fig. 3a) as input and returns an image of generated superpixels (Fig. 3b).

Once the method obtained an image of generated superpixels, the next step is to group similar superpixels. For that purpose, the DBSCAN algorithm [5], which cluster similar superpixels according to their density, is used. Thus, DBSCAN receives as input the SLIC output (Fig. 3b) and returns an image of generated superpixels (Fig. 3c).

 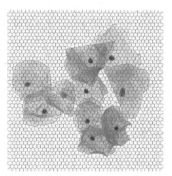

(a) Original Image   (b) Superpixels generated by SLIC

(c) Superpixels clustered by DBSCAN

Fig. 3. Steps of preprocessing images.

Each superpixel generated by DBSCAN (shown in Fig. 3c) is considered as a nucleus candidate. Hence, the metaheuristic is going to analyze each one to perform the nuclei detection.

During the preprocessing stage, it was necessary to define the values of four SLIC and DBSCAN parameters:

- $kSlic$, the number of desired superpixels in SLIC;
- $mSlic$, the weighting factor between color and spatial differences in SLIC;
- $seRadiusSlic$, the cluster size threshold in SLIC;
- $EDbscan$, the threshold that controls which superpixels should be clustered in DBSCAN.

These values were obtained using the training database and will be shown in the experiments section.

5 Iterated Local Search

The Iterated Local Search method (ILS) [7,21] explores the solution space through perturbations in local optimum. An important point in this algorithm is that these perturbations should be strong enough to prevent the algorithm from being trapped in a local optimum and, consequently, explore different solutions, but sufficiently weak to prevent random restarts.

Algorithm 1. ILS.

Input: $F_1(.)$, $ILSMax$

1 $s_0 \leftarrow$ Initial Solution
2 $s \leftarrow LocalSearch(s_0)$
3 $iter \leftarrow 0$
4 $bestIter \leftarrow iter$
5 $p \leftarrow 1$
6 **while** $iter - bestIter < ILSMax$ **do**
7     $iter \leftarrow iter + 1$
8     $s' \leftarrow Perturbation(s, p)$
9     $s'' \leftarrow LocalSearch(s')$
10   **if** $F_1(s'') > F_1(s)$ **then**
11       $s \leftarrow s''$
12       $bestIter \leftarrow iter$
13       $p \leftarrow 1$
14   **else**
15       $p \leftarrow p + 1$
16   **end**
17 **end**
18 **return** s

Algorithm 1 presents the pseudo-code of the ILS method. The algorithm starts in line 1 with an initial solution s_0. In line 2, this solution is refined by a local search method, falling in a local optimum s. Then, the algorithm goes through a loop and, in order to avoid getting stuck in a local optimum, in line 8 the current solution s is disturbed, generating an intermediate solution s'. A new local search is made into s' in line 9, resulting in a solution s''. Then, a conditional if-clause is analyzed in line 4. If the solution s'' is better than s according to the cost function, then s'' becomes the new current solution and the perturbation level is restarted; otherwise, the perturbation level is incremented. entire loop repeats until it reaches the maximum number of iterations (*ILSMax*) without improvements in the solution. The method ends up returning to solution s.

The remainder of this section is organized as follows: Subsect. 5.1 points to the representation of a solution; Subsect. 5.2 contains the construction of an initial solution and discusses the need for a good initial solution to quickly improve results; Subsect. 5.3 defines the adopted neighborhood structure. Finally, Subsect. 5.4 explains how a solution is evaluated.

5.1   Solution Representation

This method considers that each cluster returned by DBSCAN is a nucleus candidate. Besides that, some of its important features must be analyzed. So, a vector with t positions represents a solution s of the problem, in which t is the number of considered features.

An example solution s is shown below. In this example, the method is going to analyze the values of $t = 3$ features for each nucleus candidate: the minimum circularity, the maximum intensity, and the maximum area. As we can see, the solution shows that the circularity of the candidate has to be bigger than 0.5, the intensity less than 70 and the area less than 120 for it to be considered a nucleus.

$$s = \langle 0.50, 70, 120 \rangle.$$

5.2   Initial Solution

The proposed method constructs an initial solution to the problem by picking up values randomly for each parameter. The only restriction in this method is to respect the limits listed in Table 2.

Table 2. Value limits defined for each feature.

Parameters	Value	
	Minimum	Maximum
Minimum circularity	0.48	0.71
Maximum intensity	57	178
Minimum area	100	284

These limits were set using the training database. At first, it analyzes the values according to the parameters of all nuclei present in the training base. For example, the area value of all nuclei is registered. Thus, the smallest value obtained is set as the minimum allowed area. Also, it would be necessary to determine the value of the largest minimum area. It is defined that this value would be the reference value (minimum area) increased by 20%.

ILS-based algorithms usually need a good initial solution for getting good results quickly. However, since the proposed initial solution is produced entirely randomly it is not possible to guarantee quality assurance in the generated solution. In order to solve it, two possibilities have been tested to improve the quality of the initial solution. The first one is the implementation of the Multi-Start ILS algorithm (MS-ILS). The second possibility analyzed was the construction of multiple initial solutions, and the ILS algorithm initial solution simply becomes the best one.

A Multi-Start [13] algorithm is a metaheuristic that consists of repeating the generation of random solutions, followed by their refinement through a local search heuristic. The best solution found during the iterative procedure is the one returned by the algorithm.

In this article, the MS-ILS was applied according to Algorithm 2. As we can see, in line 1, a solution is built and refined by ILS. This solution is attributed to s^* because it is the best one found so far. Next, the algorithm goes into looping in which a new solution s is constructed and refined by ILS (line 3). If this solution s is better than s^*, then s becomes the best solution found so far (line 5). The loop repeats until the method reaches the defined number of restarts ($nStart$).

Thus, analyze these strategies to deal with the importance of good initial solutions to improve results quickly, it is necessary to calibrate two parameters:

Algorithm 2. MS-ILS.

Input: $ILSMax, nStart$

1   $s^* \leftarrow ILS(ILSMax)$
2 **for** $i \leftarrow 2$ to $nStart$ **do**
3     $s \leftarrow ILS(ILSMax)$
4   **if** $f(s) > f(s^*)$ **then**
5       $s^* \leftarrow s$
6   **end**
7 **end**
8 **return** s^*

- $nStart$, which is the number of MS-ILS restarts;
- $nSolRand$, which corresponds to the number of randomly generated initial solutions for choosing the best one among them.

5.3   Neighborhood Definition

In order to explore the solution space, the ILS uses a move of incrementing or decrementing a value of a solution position, i.e., the value of one of its features. Features with decimal values have a step value r_{dec} and integer ones have a step value up to r_{int}. For example, if $r_{int} = 3$, then the step could be of 1, 2, or 3 units. On the other hand, if $r_{dec} = 0.01$, then the step is 0.01. In both situations the step can be positive or negative, respecting the limits established in Table 2. Thus, the solution s with one decimal feature and two integer ones has $2 \times (1 + 2 \times r_{int}) = 14$ neighbors.

The following is an example in which the third position of the solution s is an integer value and thus has the step r_{int}. Assuming that $r_{int} = 3$ and it was chosen that the position would be decremented by a step size equal to 2, then a neighbor s' of the s solution is generated as shown below:

$$s = \langle 0.50, 70, \mathbf{120} \rangle,$$
$$s' = \langle 0.50, 70, \mathbf{118} \rangle.$$

This neighborhood was the only one implemented because with this move it is possible to explore all the problem-solution space using local search methods.

5.4   Solution Evaluation

The method solution evaluation must analyze the nuclei candidate according to solution s. In this case, each nucleus candidate must have its features compared with the acceptable limits of s. Algorithm 3 is an example of this analysis using the solution s of Sect. 5.1. This algorithm returns TRUE or FALSE, if the candidate is a nucleus or not, respectively.

For example, suppose that the method needs to define whether a candidate with *circularity* = 0.73, *intensity* = 52 and *area* = 95 is a nucleus or not, considering the solution s shown below:

$$s = \langle 0.50, 70, 120 \rangle.$$

In line 1 of Algorithm 3, the method compares if $0.73 \geq 0.50$. If it is true, the method compares if $52 \leq 70$ in line 2. Again, if it is true, the method checks if $95 \leq 120$ in line 3. Finally, if the check is true, the candidate is considered a nucleus.

For another example, suppose that the method needs to classify a candidate with *circularity* = 0.48, *intensity* = 64 and *area* = 107, considering the same solution s above. In Algorithm 3, the method compares if $0.48 \geq 0.50$ in line 1. Since this is not true, the candidate is classified as non nucleus.

At the end of Algorithm 3, the method selected only the candidates classified as nuclei. Suppose that the method returned a mask image, called X, with two selected nuclei shown in Fig. 4(a), it will then have to be compared with the corresponding ground truth, called Y, shown in Fig. 4(b).

Algorithm 3. Analysis of a nucleus candidate.

Input: *candidate, s*

1 **if** *circularity*(*candidate*) $\geq s_0$ **then**
2   **if** *intensity*(*candidate*) $\leq s_1$ **then**
3   **if** *area*(*candidate*) $\geq s_2$ **then**
4 | **return** TRUE
5   **end**
6   **end**
7 **end**
8 **return** FALSE

First of all, if the mask X or the ground truth Y has more than one nucleus, it is split into new images $X_1, \cdots, X_a$ and $Y_1, \cdots, Y_b$ in which a and b are the number of nuclei in X and Y, respectively. Each new image contains only one of its nucleus. Figures 4(c) and (d) show an example of this procedure.

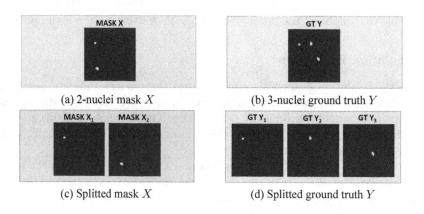

(a) 2-nuclei mask X (b) 3-nuclei ground truth Y

(c) Splitted mask X (d) Splitted ground truth Y

Fig. 4. Splitting n-nuclei images into its corresponding single-nucleus images.

In sequence, each single-nucleus image of mask X, Fig. 4(c), is compared with each ones of the ground truth Y, Fig. 4(d), as shown in Fig. 5.

The metric used for the comparison is the Similarity Coefficient Dice [3], calculated by Eq. 4. The coefficient is a statistical metric used to compare the similarity between two samples and return a real value between 0 and 1. The proposed method uses 0.6 as the threshold to define the match of two images [5].

$$Dice(X_i, Y_j) = \frac{2|X_i \cap Y_j|}{|X_i| + |Y_j|}. \tag{4}$$

As we can see in Fig. 5, a nucleus was found correctly because mask X_1 matches with ground truth Y_1 (TP = 1). Moreover, mask X_1 did not match

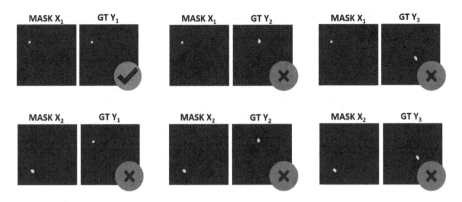

Fig. 5. Comparison between mask and ground truth single-nucleus images.

with ground truth, so the method found a false positive (FN = 1). Finally, the method did not find the nuclei presented by ground truths Y_2 and Y_3 (FP = 2). When these values have been set, it is possible to define the quality of the detection performed (explained in the Sect. 2).

6   Computational Experiments

MATLAB and Python were the languages used to implement the preprocessing phase (Sect. 4) and the heuristic approach (Sect. 5). The experiments were performed on Windows 10 (64-bits), in a machine with Intel Core i7-8700, a 3.20 GHz processor, and 16 GB RAM.

After executing the experiments, precision (*prec*), recall (*rec*) and F_1 measurements were used to determine the quality of the nuclei detection performed, according to Eqs. 1, 2 and 3, as presented in Sect. 2.

Following this section, Subsects. 6.1 and 6.2 present and discuss the experiments done in processing and via MS-ILS, respectively. Subsection 6.3 performs a comparison considering the literature methods and the proposed one.

6.1   Preprocessing

As presented in Sect. 4, it was necessary to define the values of four SLIC and DBSCAN parameters: *kSlic*, *mSlic*, *seRadiusSlic* and *EDbscan*.

For that, an exhaustive search was performed to verify which parameter value combinations are the ones that imply that the best nucleus detection will be found. The exhaustive search was made because the time to test all combinations is acceptable considering the parameters' values presented in Table 3.

In all images of the training base, there are 270 nuclei. The exhaustive search found six best parameter value combinations, in which each one detects 269 of these nuclei. These combinations are presented in Table 4. As all combinations found are equivalent, the values of *kSlic* = 2000, *mSlic* = 10, *seRadiusSlic* = 1.5 and *EDbscan* = 7 were randomly chosen to be used in the other tests.

Table 3. Values for each parameter in the exhaustive search.

Parameter	Values
kSlic	500, 1000, 1500, 2000, 2500, 3000
mSlic	5, 10, 15, 20, 25, 30, 35, 40
seRadiusSlic	0, 1, 1.5
EDbscan	5, 6, 7, 8, 9, 10

Table 4. Best parameter combinations returned by the exhausted search.

kSlic	mSlic	seRadiusSlic	EDbscan
2000	10	1.5	7
2000	25	1	6
2000	25	1	7
2500	5	1.5	7
2500	10	1.5	6
2500	10	1.5	7

6.2   MS-ILS

This subsection presents the experiments related to the heuristic approach via MS-ILS. The calibration of all parameters made in this section uses the *irace* package [8]. The *irace* package is a method that determines, given a set of problem instances, the best combination of values for the parameters of an optimization algorithm. Besides that, each experiment was executed 30 times and its best and average values were registered.

Initially, the solution of the proposed method considered five parameters (namely CIA), based on the proposal of Oliveira et al. [16]: minimum circularity, maximum circularity, maximum intensity, minimum area, and maximum area. So, $t = 5$.

At first, to perform the experiments, it would be necessary to define the value of five other parameters: the maximum number of ILS iterations (*ILSMax*, presented in Algorithm 1); the step values for decimal and integer parameters (r_{dec} and r_{int}, defined in Subsect. 5.3); the number of initial solutions and restarts (*nSolRand* and *nStart*, presented in Subsect. 5.2). As explained before, these parameter values were determined using the *irace* method. Table 5 lists the values that *irace* considered when setting each of the parameters.

The best values returned by *irace* were: $ILSMAX = 20$, $r_{dec} = 0.05$, $r_{int} = 5$, $nSolRand = 1$ and $nStart = 5$. These values were those used in tests, and the results obtained over 30 runs were the following:

- Precision average: 0.955 (ranging from 0.949 to 0.967);
- Recall average: 0.801 (ranging from 0.740 to 0.895);
- F1 average: 0.870 (ranging from 0.832 to 0.926).

Table 5. Values considered by irace for each parameter to be calibrated.

ILSMax	3, 5, 10, 15, 20, 25, 30, 35, 40, 45, 50, 100, 150, 200, 250, 300
r_{dec}	0.001, 0.003, 0.005, 0.01, 0.03, 0.05, 0.1, 0.2, 0.3
r_{int}	1, 3, 5, 7, 9
nSolRand	1, 3, 5, 7, 9
nStart	1, 3, 5, 7, 9, 11, 13, 15, 17

As already explained in Sect. 2, the recall measure is the most important regarding the problem considered. The best solution considering the recall is shown below; it also has a precision of 0.959, recall of 0.895, and F1 of 0.926.

$$s^\star = \langle 0.66, 1.62, 150, 111, 681 \rangle$$

Following, three hypotheses were analyzed: (1) only three parameters are sufficient for classification; (2) only two parameters are sufficient for classification; (3) the addition of a new parameter may improve the classification. Finally, it presents a summarized comparison of the experiments' results.

Hypothesis 1. In the following, the working hypothesis is that the maximum values of circularity and area in the training base were not representative of the test base, which limited the MS-ILS performance. So, a new experiment using $t = 3$ was done.

The *irace* package was used with the same values presented in Table 5, in order to calibrate the method parameter values and verify the hypothesis raised. The best values returned by *irace* were: *ILSMax* = 50, r_{dec} = 0.05, r_{int} = 1, *nSolRand* = 1 and *nStart* = 15. Over the 30 test runs the MS-ILS method got:

- Precision average: 0.961 (ranging to 0.959 to 0.961);
- Recall average: 0.939;
- F1 average: 0.946.

The best solution found in relation to recall has a precision of 0.961, recall of 0.939 and F1 of 0.946, and is given by:

$$s^\star = \langle 0.66, 152, 111 \rangle.$$

With this, it was possible to verify that the raised hypothesis that the maximum values of the circularity and area of the training base were not representative of the test base was correct.

Hypothesis 2. Another hypothesis is that only two of the three parameters would be sufficient for classification. Therefore, the two-by-two combination of CIA parameters was analyzed using $t = 2$ and the irace package, with the values from Table 5, to calibrate the MS-ILS parameter values. The best values returned by irace for each combination performed are presented in Table 6.

Table 6. Irace best values for CIA parameters combinations two-by-two.

Parameter combination	$ILSMax$	r_{dec}	r_{int}	$nSolRand$	$nStart$
Circularity and Intensity (CI)	40	0.05	9	5	9
Circularity and Area (CA)	40	0.05	9	5	9
Intensity and Area (IA)	20	0.01	3	1	7

Besides, Table 7 presents the average results obtained over the 30 runs of each combination.

Table 7. Results of combination two-by-two.

Combination	Precision	Recall	F1	Best values
CI	0.897	0.776	0.832	C = 120, I = 0.71
CA	0.943	0.908	0.925	C = 114.5, A = 0.71
IA	0.933	0.920	0.926	I = 133, A = 111

Therefore, as no solutions found with this hypothesis obtained better results than previous ones, it was possible to verify that the hypothesis raised is not valid.

Hypothesis 3. Finally, the last hypothesis analyzed is that the addition of one more parameter, in this case the eccentricity, could favor the classification. So, the experiment is run with $t = 4$. Again *irace* was used, with values from Table 5, to calibrate the MS-ILS parameter values, and the best ones returned were: $ILSMax = 300$, $r_{dec} = 0.01$, $r_{int} = 3$, $nSolRand = 7$, $nStart = 15$. Over the 30 test runs we got:

- Precision average: 0.943 (ranging from 0.941 to 0.959);
- Recall average: 0.902 (ranging from 0.896 to 0.905);
- F1 average: 0.923 (ranging from 0.921 to 0.927).

The best solution found with respect to recall was a precision of 0.941, recall of 0.905 and F1 of 0.922, and is given by:

$$s^\star = \langle 0.66, 132, 110, 0.83 \rangle.$$

Therefore, as the solution found did not obtain better results than previous ones, so adding the eccentricity parameter derived no benefits, invalidating the hypothesis raised.

In summary, Table 8 presents the best results obtained in all experiments with the MS-ILS method. It is possible to see that the strategy of using only three CIA parameters (minimum circularity, maximum intensity, and minimum area) was the best considering precision, recall, and F1 metrics.

Table 8. MS-ILS experiments' results.

Parameters	Precision	Recall	F1
CIA (5)	0.959	0.895	0.926
CIA (3)	**0.961**	**0.939**	**0.946**
CI	0.897	0.776	0.832
CA	0.943	0.908	0.925
IA	0.933	0.920	0.926
CIA + excentricity	0.941	0.905	0.922

6.3 Comparison Among Literature Methods

The MS-ILS investigation analyzed which features (attributes) would be relevant to the classification. First of all, the proposed method considered five features of CIA attributes. Sequentially, three hypotheses to be analyzed were raised: (1) containing only three CIA attributes; (2) combining two-by-two of the three CIA attributes; (3) adding eccentricity to the three CIA attributes. The best strategy found for the database used was the one raised by the hypothesis 2, and the best solution found is as follows:

$$s^{\star} = \langle 0.66, 152, 111 \rangle.$$

As we can see, to be considered a nucleus, the minimum circularity of a cluster should be 0.66, the maximum intensity set to 152, and the minimum area equal to 111. This solution had a precision of 0.961, recall of 0.939, and F1 of 0.946.

Table 9 presents the precision and recall values obtained by the proposed approach and other literature methods.

Table 9. Comparison among methods for nuclei detection.

Method	F1	Precision	Recall
Tareef et al. [22]	0.964	0.990	0.940
Proposed	**0.946**	**0.961**	**0.939**
Diniz et al. [4]	0.929	0.985	0.879
Lu et al. [10]	0.928	0.977	0.883
Ushizima et al. [23]	0.926	0.959	0.895
Braz and Lotufo [2]	0.923	0.929	0.917
Saha et al. [18]	0.916	0.918	0.915
Nosrati and Hamarneh [15]	0.898	0.903	0.893

As can be seen from Table 9, the proposed MS-ILS approach obtained the second best F1 and recall values, as well as having a high accuracy when compared to the other methods.

7   Conclusions

This article presents an ILS-based method to detect nuclei in cervical cell images. The main objective is to simulate the analysis of cytopathologists. For that purpose, the method considers that the nuclei features are sufficient to detect lesions since the morphological features and nuclei texture variations vary significantly when altered.

The Overlapping Cervical Cytology Image Segmentation Challenge (ISBI 2014) proposed the database used in the experiments. The metrics used to compare this method with those in the literature were F1, precision, and recall.

In the heuristic approach, it was made an investigation about what features (attributes) would be relevant to the classification considering circularity, intensity, area, and eccentricity.

The best solution found by the proposed method analyzes each image in relation to the minimum circularity, maximum intensity, and minimum area values of a cluster. When compared with other literature methods, it showed the second-best values of F1 and recall, while the accuracy is still high.

The recall is known to be related to the number of nuclei found. Therefore, recall of Pap smears must be as close as possible because failure to detect an injury may influence prognosis. On the other hand, as a computer cannot give a diagnosis, the detected images also are analyzed by a pathologist posteriorly. Thus, the importance of high accuracy is because it represents the workload reduction.

Finally, as a future work, it is suggested that experiments using real images be performed.

Acknowledgements. This study was financed in part by the *Coordenação de Aperfeiçoamento de Pessoal de Nível Superior* - Brazil (CAPES) - Finance Code 001. The authors thank CAPES, *Fundação de Amparo à Pesquisa do Estado de Minas Gerais* (FAPEMIG, grants PPM/CEX/FAPEMIG/676-17 and PPSUS-FAPEMIG/APQ-03740-17), *Conselho Nacional de Desenvolvimento Científico e Tecnológico* (CNPq, grant 307915/2016-6), *Universidade Federal de Ouro Preto* (UFOP), the Moore-Sloan Foundation, and Office of Science, of the U.S. Department of Energy under Contract No. DE-AC02-05CH11231 for also supporting this research. Any opinion, findings, and conclusions or recommendations expressed in this material are those of the authors and do not necessarily reflect the views of the Department of Energy or the University of California.

References

1. Amaral, R.G., et al.: Influência da adequabilidade da amostra sobre a detecção das lesões precursoras do câncer cervical. Revista Brasileira de Ginecologia e Obstetrícia **30**, 556–560 (2008)

2. Braz, E.F., Lotufo, R.A.: Nuclei detection using deep learning. In: Anais do XXXV Simpósio Brasileiro de Telecomunicações e Processamento de Sinais, São Pedro, Brasil, pp. 1059–1063 (2017)
3. Dice, L.R.: Measures of the amount of ecologic association between species. Ecology **26**(3), 297–302 (1945)
4. Diniz, D., et al.: An iterated local search algorithm for cell nuclei detection from pap smear images. In: Proceedings of the 21st International Conference on Enterprise Information Systems, pp. 319–327. INSTICC, SciTePress, Setubal (2019)
5. Gençtav, A., Aksoy, S., Önder, S.: Unsupervised segmentation and classification of cervical cell images. Pattern Recogn. **45**(12), 4151–4168 (2012)
6. Kovesi, P.D.: MATLAB and octave functions for computer vision and image processing (2000). https://www.peterkovesi.com/matlabfns/. Accessed 20 Sept 2018
7. Lourenço, H.R., Martin, O.C., Stützle, T.: Iterated local search: framework and applications. In: Gendreau, M., Potvin, J.Y. (eds.) International Series in Operations Research & Management Science, vol. 146, pp. 363–397. Springer, Boston (2010). https://doi.org/10.1007/978-1-4419-1665-5_12
8. López-Ibáñez, M., Dubois-Lacoste, J., Cáceres, L.P., Birattari, M., Stützle, T.: The irace package: iterated racing for automatic algorithm configuration. Oper. Res. Perspect. **3**, 43–58 (2016)
9. Lu, Z., et al.: Evaluation of three algorithms for the segmentation of overlapping cervical cells. IEEE J. Biomed. Health Inform. **21**(2), 441–450 (2017)
10. Lu, Z., Carneiro, G., Bradley, A.P.: An improved joint optimization of multiple level set functions for the segmentation of overlapping cervical cells. IEEE Trans. Image Process. **24**(4), 1261–1272 (2015)
11. Manning, C.D., Schütze, H.: Foundations of Statistical Natural Language Processing. MIT Press, Cambridge (1999)
12. Mariarputham, E.J., Stephen, A.: Nominated texture based cervical cancer classification. Comput. Math. Methods Med. **2015**, 10 (2015)
13. Martí, R., Resende, M.G.C., Ribeiro, C.C.: Multi-start methods for combinatorial optimization. Eur. J. Oper. Res. **226**(1), 1–8 (2013)
14. Moshavegh, R., Bejnordi, B.E., Mehnert, A., Sujathan, K., Malm, P., Bengtsson, E.: Automated segmentation of free-lying cell nuclei in pap smears for malignancy-associated change analysis. In: Engineering in Medicine and Biology Society, pp. 5372–5375. IEEE, San Diego (2012)
15. Nosrati, M.S., Hamarneh, G.: A variational approach for overlapping cell segmentation. In: ISBI Overlapping Cervical Cytology Image Segmentation Challenge, pp. 1–2 (2014)
16. Oliveira, P.H.C., et al.: A multi-objective approach for calibration and detection of cervical cells nuclei. In: 2017 IEEE Congress on Evolutionary Computation (CEC), pp. 2321–2327 (2017)
17. Ren, X., Malik, J.: Learning a classification model for segmentation. In: Proceedings Ninth IEEE International Conference on Computer Vision, Nice, França, pp. 10–17. IEEE (2003)
18. Saha, R., Bajger, M., Lee, G.: Spatial shape constrained fuzzy c-means (FCM) clustering for nucleus segmentation in pap smear images. In: Proceedings of the International Conference on Digital Image Computing: Techniques and Applications (DICTA), Gold Coast, Australia, pp. 1–8. IEEE (2016)
19. Samsudin, N.A., Mustapha, A., Arbaiy, N., Hamid, I.R.A.: Extended local mean-based nonparametric classifier for cervical cancer screening. In: Herawan, T., Ghazali, R., Nawi, N.M., Deris, M.M. (eds.) SCDM 2016. AISC, vol. 549, pp. 386–395. Springer, Cham (2017). https://doi.org/10.1007/978-3-319-51281-5_39

20. Song, Y., et al.: A deep learning based framework for accurate segmentation of cervical cytoplasm and nuclei. In: Engineering in Medicine and Biology Society (EMBC), Chicago, USA, pp. 2903–2906. IEEE (2014)
21. Stützle, T.: Local search algorithms for combinatorial problems: analysis, improvements, and new applications. Tese de doutorado, Darmstadt University of Technology, Germany (1998)
22. Tareef, A., et al.: Automatic segmentation of overlapping cervical smear cells based on local distinctive features and guided shape deformation. Neurocomputing **221**, 94–107 (2017)
23. Ushizima, D., Bianchi, A., Carneiro, C.: Segmentation of subcellular compartments combining superpixel representation with voronoi diagrams. In: Proceedings of the International Symposium on Biomedical Imaging, Beijing, China. Elsevier (2014)
24. Xing, F., Xie, Y., Yang, L.: An automatic learning-based framework for robust nucleus segmentation. IEEE Trans. Med. Imaging **35**(2), 550–566 (2015)

A Generic Architectural Framework for Machine Learning on Data Streams

Christoph Augenstein[1]($\boxtimes$), Theo Zschörnig[2], Norman Spangenberg[1], Robert Wehlitz[2], and Bogdan Franczyk[1,3]

[1] Leipzig University,
Information Systems Institute, Grimmaische Strasse 12, Leipzig, Germany
{augenstein,spangenberg,franczyk}@wifa.uni-leipzig.de
[2] Institute for Applied Informatics (InfAI),
Leipzig University, Goerdelerring 9, Leipzig, Germany
{zschoernig,wehlitz}@infai.org
[3] Wroclaw University of Economics, ul. Komandorska 118/120, Wroclaw, Poland

Abstract. In the past years, the importance of processing data streams increased with the emergence of new technologies and application domains. The Internet of Things provides many examples in which processing and analyzing data streams are critical success factors. With the growing amount of data, the usage of machine learning (ML) algorithms has become an essential part of data analysis. However, the high volume and velocity of data presents new challenges, which need to be addressed, e.g. frequent model changes, concept drift or insufficient time to train models. From our point of view, these challenges cannot be tackled alone by using an algorithm-centric approach, i.e. to focus solely on finding appropriate algorithms, and neglecting the structure of the overall processing system.

Therefore, we propose a generic architectural framework, which describes common components and their interactions with each other in order to apply ML technologies to streaming data. Furthermore, we implement essential components in two real-world use cases to highlight the feasibility of our approach.

Keywords: Machine learning · Architecture · Internet of Things

1 Introduction

A major challenge for companies nowadays is to gain useful insights into their business data. In recent years, machine learning (ML) has become an important cornerstone in addressing this challenge. In this regard, many state of the art ML algorithms and methodologies are available, which require vast amounts of well-prepared data in order to produce high quality results. The resulting costs of preprocessing and analyzing data dramatically increase with growing volume. This is especially true for processing streaming data, which are, seemingly, indefinitely incoming data, as witnessed in Internet of Things (IoT) use cases. In general, prior to building data processing pipelines for ML on streaming data, it is necessary to define:

.

© Springer Nature Switzerland AG 2020
J. Filipe et al. (Eds.): ICEIS 2019, LNBIP 378, pp. 97–114, 2020.
https://doi.org/10.1007/978-3-030-40783-4_6

- What is the learning strategy (e.g. online learning, local learning or transfer learning)?
- What is to be learned (e.g. classification, regression or visualization)?
- How to learn it (e.g. supervised, unsupervised or reinforcement)?

Answering these questions is the first step in preparing ML-based data analytics on data streams and should be done taking into account the available data. The next step is to design and implement an appropriate system architecture for building and running the planned processing pipelines. A few years ago, architectural frameworks for end-to-end data stream processing based on ML were wanted. The first end-to-end frameworks were provided by companies, such as Nvidia and Google, based on their own ML solutions. Though the development and operation of ML processing pipelines got cheaper, easier and faster, the dependency on providers increased which possibly lead to vendor lock-in effects. This is the case if, for instance, requirements on a system architecture change over time due to additional use cases and the used framework cannot cope with that. Against this background, it seems reasonable to provide a generic architectural framework, describing fundamental components and their interactions, which may be scaled across multiple different uses cases, and is not bound to a specific type of data. In our previous work [3], we sketched out a proposal for such a generic architectural framework. In this paper, we describe how this framework was utilized in order to fit the requirements of two IoT use cases, which differ in the way of data preprocessing as well as in the used ML algorithms for streaming analytics.

The first use case is about predicting the consumption of electrical appliances based on ML in a home energy management scenario. The objective is to provide end users with information on how their historical and current consumption behavior affects future expected electricity costs. In this use case, the overall electricity consumption of household appliances is digitally measured by smart meters, which are connected to the Internet for remote reading. The consumption data arrive as streams (every 15 min), which are processed by a cloud-based analytics platform. Electricity consumption is predicted on a daily, monthly and yearly basis, multiplied with a price per kWh and visualized by a dashboard application. In this regard, the analytics platform has to handle a large amount of small problems (i.e. processing meter readings of one household) which, depending on the number of platform users respective households, results in the need for big data processing capabilities.

The second use case is about analyzing network traffic data in order to build a network intrusion detection system (IDS). In this use case, the resulting system has to deal with identifying abnormal network traffic to prevent attacks, such as denial of service or the hijacking of clients or servers. According to the Oxford dictionary, anomalies are deviations from what is regarded as normal, or more specifically, describe events or measurements that are extraordinary, whether they are exceptional or not [29]. In data mining, the term describes data objects that are not compliant with the general behavior or model of the data [15]. The IDS use case has to cope with a vast amount of high dimensional data aligned with multiple attack vectors (e.g. denial of service variants, SQL injections, cross-site scripting or infiltration attacks). Aside from signature- or rule-based approaches, anomaly-based approaches are commonly used for IDS. In the latter, patterns for normal traffic are defined in order to be able to identify unusual network traffic. This allows a reaction to new attack vectors that are yet unknown but requires intense work on the data and a multidimensional analysis.

In these two, and in many other, use cases, streaming data are essential to meet higher demands on the availability of up-to-date information. However, they are accompanied with additional challenges related to real-time data processing. In this context, the relevance and contribution of this work for information systems research is the description of a generic architectural framework for ML on streaming data, which provides the fundamental basis for designing and implementing detailed system architectures in a broad range of different (IoT) use cases.

The remainder of this paper is structured as follows: In Sect. 2, we present general challenges in the field of ML resulting from high volume and high speed of data. In Sect. 3, we list specific ML challenges related to streaming data and outline existing architectural solutions. In Sect. 4, we introduce our generic architectural framework for ML on streaming data. In Sect. 5, we demonstrate how to implement different instances of the architectural framework according to the needs of two specific use cases. The paper concludes in Sect. 6 with a summary and an outlook on future research.

2 Data-Driven Challenges in ML

As stated in the introduction, vast amounts of data are necessary to produce high quality results with state of the art ML algorithms. Compared to the human brain, specifically cognition, current ML algorithms are not capable of learning from just a few examples. Instead, thousands of (labeled) examples have to be provided in order to successfully train ML models. These training data may have heterogeneous real-life sources, e.g. customers of a company or IoT devices, which has an impact on the complexity of analytics scenarios. In this regard, the number of features that have to be incorporated into the analysis also influences data processing. Especially in IoT use cases, data is often provided as a stream of, potentially, indefinite length. Since the value of these data perished quickly, real-time analytics are often a requirement. Therefore, processing data as fast as or faster than the input velocity of the data into the system is important. So called streaming applications allow for a low latency between the arrival of data and the storage, processing, analysis and presentation of the results [7]. However, such applications focus primarily on the throughput of data and do not address specific analysis challenges like [13, 17]:

- Data has potentially infinite size, thus only a brief summary may be extracted and stored. In addition, the memory usage for processing huge streams of data is challenging since storing such data is very costly and timely not possible. Thus, to a certain extent, datasets are unknown prior to processing.
- There is no control over the order of arriving data points of a data stream. Processing data streams, where data points are not in the order of their generation, may affect the processing of new items and the results of the analysis, e.g. the shape of clusters or distribution of values over time. In this context, distribution of data is unknown and may vary over time.

- Dealing with multidimensional data streams leads to high computation costs, hence, it should be attempted to reduce costs by using effective techniques that cut the multi-dimensionality of streaming data. Thus, there are no guarantees that observed features are statistically independent.
- A straightforward training, testing and prediction approach can produce unexpected results if new data is not used to adapt the model but only to predict. Therefore, it is important to take into consideration that models are usually suspect to change and have to be continually monitored and adapted.

Applications dealing with data streams have to cope with these challenges and thus have to be suitably designed. However, aside from a (potentially) high volume and a high velocity of incoming data, there are also characteristics like veracity or variety that need to be addressed. These characteristics and more are known as the "V's of big data".

Although, there is a large number of "V's" (e.g. [45], with up to 51 described in [18]) we focus on the four characteristics listed above because they lead to the most important challenges in data handling. With regard to streaming data and ML, the volume characteristic encompasses the size of datasets, the number of variables or features, the correlation of data, computational complexity or bias. The term "variety" describes not only the structural variation of a dataset and of corresponding data types, but also the variety in what it represents, i.e. its semantic interpretation [16] and sources. The velocity dimension of big data not only refers to the speed at which data are ingested into a system, but also the rate at which they have to be analyzed [12]. Finally, veracity of big data refers not only to the reliability of the data forming a dataset, but also, to the inherent unreliability of data sources [11]. Table 1 summarizes findings from literature [24, 45, 51] and shows specific challenges for ML.

In [2] we found that existing approaches, regarding data stream processing in conjunction with ML, were mostly designed to cope with volume-related problems because the increasing high volume of data was, and still is, one of the most important issues, analytics architectures have to address. In contrast, variety- and veracity-related problems remained open. A reason for this may be the fact that specific challenges of these characteristics are closely related to preprocessing steps and not to the application of algorithms themselves. Regarding our generic architecture framework, we consider these facts and assign characteristic challenges to either architectural or procedural aspects. The former hereby describes solutions, which encompass components, and interfaces whereas the latter focuses on using these components in (automated) pipelines and work-flows. Hence, from an architectural point of view the four big data characteristics can be broken down to:

1. Architectural problems like scalability, parallelizing, hardware requirements or choice of appropriate algorithms (volume, velocity) and
2. Procedural problems like domain analysis, building preprocessing pipelines (variety, veracity).

The objective of our work is to overcome these challenges by providing architectural guidelines and recommendations on what is necessary to cope with them. Focusing on building end-to-end pipelines, we propose a generic architectural framework, which

Table 1. Big data characteristics & ML-challenges (cf. [2]).

Characteristic	Machine learning challenges
Volume	
Processing performance	Increase of complexity (time, space)
Curse of modularity	Need for parallel or iterative processing of data (space)
Class imbalance	Sampling techniques can lead to corrupted data (space, distribution)
Curse of dimensionality	Decrease of effectivity and reliability with increase of number of variables (space, accuracy)
Feature engineering	Extracting correct features leads to increasing costs when volume of data grows (space, selectivity)
Non-linearity	Identification of nonlinearity is a challenge itself
Bonferonni's principle	Inferring multiple hypotheses on the same data requires statistically precise actions (significance)
Variance & bias	Generalization failures and overfitting is more likely with increasing data volume (space, accuracy)
Variety	
Data locality	Having all data in a local storage can neither be guaranteed nor provided
Data heterogeneity	Syntax & semantics: increasing costs with increasing volume Statistics: uniform distribution across multiple data sources is unlikely
Dirty & noisy data	Increase of costs for data cleaning, handling missing data and outlier detection
Velocity	
Data availability/streaming	A train, test and predict approach is not applicable for stream data; models are suspect to changes
Real-time/streaming	Need to reduce time to train models dramatically
Concept drift	Models are suspect to changes; a prior good result may get worse in future
Independent & identically distributed random variables	Statistically independent variables cannot be guaranteed for the overall population
Veracity	
Data provenance	Increase of costs for collecting and administering metadata to be used to configure ML-techniques
Data uncertainty	Reliability of data or missing model validation makes interpretation of results questionable
Dirty & noisy data	Increase of costs for missing or misleading labels or for poor data quality

supports the handling of data streams in ML application scenarios. In contrast to already established concepts, such as lambda [19] or kappa [21] architectures, we explicitly do not want to determine each piece of functionality in advance in order to preserve flexibility.

3 Background

The IoT uses cases we refer to in this paper (cf. Sect. 5) vary in terms of application domain, amount and speed of data ingestion, used algorithms as well as the purpose of data analysis. However, their main similarity is the need to analyze potentially indefinite streams of data. IoT is one of the major areas, in which big data plays a dominant role, given that millions of IoT devices are continuously generating and consuming a large volume of data. However, resource scarcity is one of the major issues associated with IoT devices, as they do not have the capabilities of collecting, storing, analyzing, and sharing big data in (real) time. Thus, new solutions are required in order to effectively conjoin IoT and big data technologies [50]. With this in mind, this section presents the current state of the art approaches in the fields of handling large data streams, ML approaches for streaming data and of associated architectural solutions.

3.1 ML Challenges on Data Streams

ML techniques are widely used by practitioners and researchers alike, but there are many requirements in terms of data quality in order to apply them. Depending on the specific approach, like supervised, unsupervised or reinforcement learning, requirements may vary. Some need a historical database with labeled data; most of them are batch-oriented, some cannot cope with categorical data or some are restricted to data with only linear relationships in between. Artificial neural networks (ANN) outperform other ML approaches in several fashions. For instance, perceptrons, a simple type of ANN, are capable of identifying non-linear relationships in a dataset [38]. Deeper nets or deep learning (DL) approaches respectively, i.e. nets that have many hidden layers, are even more powerful [23], but used to be impractical. The availability of powerful graphics hardware, with their ability to perform fast matrix multiplications, is a technological advancement that brought many theoretical approaches and especially DL into practice. However, the training of ANN's is typically done batch-oriented.

We found many approaches in literature focusing on streaming data from a finance, social media or IoT perspective. An overview is given, for instance, by the work of [13]. Most identified approaches are labeling or rather classification approaches. For instance, [20, 28, 36, 49] and [26] focus on the concept drift characteristic and thus cope with the challenges of unknown datasets and distributions. [28, 49] and [26] use a hoeffding tree as a part of their solutions, which is a special kind of decision tree. These trees assume that the distribution within the dataset does not change over time. Hence, the concept drift and especially varying distributions are not addressed entirely. [27] provide a fixed training set of labels (i.e. classes) but are aware that classes can vanish, arise or change over time. This way, they provide a solution for an efficient model update. In contrast, [36] and [33] use a sliding window based approach, which addresses the distribution problem.

[42] and [47] additionally face the problem of real time prediction or classification, but are the only approaches dealing with real time data and thus explicitly include frequent model updates in their solutions. Similar, [20] state that real time or at least answering in a reasonable time is critical for a production environment but has to deal with limited resources. Therefore, they especially focus on decision optimizing to provide results given their restrictions.

3.2 Architectural Solutions for ML Challenges

Against this background, we also reviewed architectural solutions and how they address the challenges, which arise from the usage of ML algorithms. Such solutions especially dealing with streaming data and ML can be found in different domains of the IoT. In this regard, we focused on how streaming data was handled, including the process of data ingestion, preprocessing and model building. A first example can be given by [30] who provide a detailed reference architecture. Further approaches are provided by [22] regarding condition-based maintenance in cyber-physical systems or in [5] who describe a general architecture. Another domain of the IoT are smart cities. [1] provide an architectural approach, which is able to ingest data streams from different sources and provide city traffic predictions in real-time using ML algorithms. Another approach addressing city traffic is presented by [37], who use Apache Spark Streaming together with ML and graphics processing units to analyze traffic video footage. A domain-independent solution is described by [39] who provide an architecture to deploy ML processing on data streams at the edge level of the network. Linking technologies for processing streaming data and ML is also an integral part of activity discovery and recognition in smart home scenarios. In this area, online activity recognition, i.e. the real-time recognition of human activities based on streaming sensor data, is of particular importance. In [9] a smart home system is described that uses both online activity recognition and activity discovery based on a client-server architecture. The authors aim at using this architecture to facilitate the scalability, maintainability and extensibility of their system. The authors use a support vector machine (SVM) for online activity recognition and a greedy algorithm for activity discovery. In addition, [34] present a smart home platform based on Microsoft Azure. The platform uses deep learning methods to support different applications from the smart home area. Among other things, online activity recognition is supported. The authors also list the most important requirements they considered when designing their platform (robustness, interoperability, security and costs).

In this paper, we do not provide a reference architecture but one that is reusable for multiple different use cases and application areas. In this regard, we make recommendations and give advice, which components are necessary to build end-to-end pipelines for processing and analyzing data. Likewise [4] provide an overview of best practices and architectural recommendations and [43] provide a solution for continuous integration & development (CI/CD) with microservices, which is also part of the cross-cutting elements of our proposed solution. Many comparable approaches often also adopt the microservice paradigm as a cornerstone of their architecture. In this context, [10] describe microservice-based architecture for an end-to-end IoT platform. Similar to our presented

IoT use cases [46] created cyber-physical microservices, which are reusable in many settings in manufacturing and industry. There are also approaches like [6], who compare microservices with service-oriented architectures and also emphasize the possibility of independent deployments.

To sum up, the research fields we introduced in this section are currently investigated intensively. On the one side, there is the need for solutions applying ML-algorithms on data streams and on the other side, there are approaches that tackle this need by constructing architectural solutions. However, a holistic approach that is capable of providing a more generic solution is yet not available. Due to this situation, we present the first steps in this direction beginning with the next section.

4   Architectural Framework

In general, architectures provide a set of components and define the relationships between them. While our proposal follows the same procedure, it describes its components at a rather high level. Still, it describes necessary components for end-to-end pipelines and their relationships.

The architecture depicted in Fig. 1 provides an overview of the necessary components designed to deal with processing and analyzing data streams. The foundation of the development of this proposal derived from the observation that different use cases in stream processing and ML presented us with similar procedural and architectural challenges. Thus, the intention of this work was to extract common components and if possible common workflows for data handling in streaming environments.

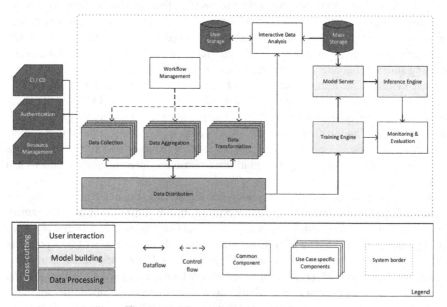

Fig. 1. Architectural framework (cf. [3]).

Additionally, in order to provide an approach similar to the ones found in software engineering, where more or less strict rules are applied to develop software, we wanted to offer architectural best practices and a standardized set of necessary components. For this reason, we included components that do not directly affect data processing or analyses but are necessary in order to build such components. Applying the separation of concerns paradigm [31] we extracted four building blocks:

1. Cross-cutting concerns are necessary to support the development, management, monitoring and maintenance of all components (continuous integration/continuous development), provide secure access to the system (authentication), offer storage for user-specific and use case-specific data and allow for an abstraction of the underlying hardware and system resources (resource management).
2. User interaction concerns involve components, at which users interact with the system. Especially, this concerns the monitoring of ML training phases and evaluation of prediction quality of the trained algorithms. Aside from that, the module for interactive data analysis allows users to gain insights on small subsets of their data in order to allow for experimenting with algorithms and thus for evaluating (hyper-)parameters prior to training. Finally, the workflow management components enable users to develop and manage data processing pipelines based on available processing components.
3. Data (pre-)processing concerns include components, which help to prepare raw data in a way that they can be fed into the selected algorithms. For instance, these are components to load data from disk or interface with external sources (collection), components that integrate data from various sources, handle null values, etc. (aggregation) and components that provide transformations (e.g. format conversions, decoding, cropping or augmentations) on (raw) data. The distribution component acts as a middleware and is responsible for ingesting data into other processing and model building components. In particular, the data distribution is responsible for handling data streams within the system and as such is a special kind of collection component.
4. Model building concerns include components that are responsible for the training environment, for versioning and providing trained models as well as for performing inference based on the selected models. The three components model training, model management and model inference provide frameworks for training algorithms and storing the resulting models, for selecting and updating these models as well as for applying models on incoming data.

Each component addresses a specific piece of functionality, which have to be adapted and applied based on a specific use case pipeline. In addition, data collection, aggregation and transformation functionalities have to be designed individually for every use case along its specific requirements. In principal, there is no predefined order for using the components but basically data enters the system either by pushing or pulling it from its sources. The data then passes through a variety of preprocessing steps before it is ingested into mass storage and injected into the training engine. Trained algorithms are then checked into the model server or directly passed to the inference engine to generate insights based on the data. Almost all components are designed to be independent from each other, i.e. the only way they are able to interact is by pushing respectively pulling data into/from the distribution component and the mass storage. The workflow management is the only component that is allowed to directly interact with the processing components. To enforce independency, we suggest the use of the microservice or SOA paradigm and to package all functionality into distinct services with a common interface.

The main purpose for developing such an architectural framework is to process raw input data into high quality information in a constant manner in different contexts. It provides blueprints for specific components and demonstrates how to organize these components with the help of a focal distribution component responsible for delivering data to the components and representing a single point of truth. We are aware, that this is a very simplified description, which does not reflect the complexity within specific use cases. Because of this, the next section highlights that transferring our proposed solution to real-world use cases may lead to more sophisticated instantiations of the framework. However, it provides a first guideline towards designing architectures for ML processing on streaming data and their necessary components as well as illustrating an idea concerning the interaction and hierarchy between these components. Typical architectures that can be implemented using such a configuration are kappa and lambda architectures whereas the lambda version additionally utilizes a distinct batch layer for storing data.

5   Use Cases

The IoT consists of a large variety of different sensors, tags and actuators. These IoT devices can be found in various domains, which are industrial, commercial or consumer-driven in nature. The main purpose of them is to provide insights into their usage and their surroundings as well as remote and automated control. In this regard, the application of ML algorithms to gain insights into their generated data seems promising to further enhance the usefulness of IoT devices [25] in areas such as smart energy or smart city. Another major consideration in terms of processing IoT data is the linked big data challenges. While the number of IoT connected devices has been 22 billion in 2018, it is estimated that this number will grow to 38.6 billion in 2025 [44]. Smart devices continuously emit data, which can be described as data streams. Additionally, the data emitted is heterogeneous concerning its structure and semantics, which may also change. IoT data are therefore time series, which are perishable and their value for generating information decreases over time, thus generating the need for real-time data analytics. With regard to the aforementioned characteristics of big data as described in Sect. 2, it becomes evident that data processing tasks, originating in the IoT, are big data problems in terms of volume, velocity, variety and veracity and may be addressed using the proposed architectural concept introduced in the previous section.

Since IoT technologies are used in different domains of industry and business, the requirements and challenges of architectures used for data processing are manifold. The problem spaces described in Sect. 1 vary in terms of domain, data structure, amount and velocity of data and purpose of the analysis. Nevertheless, the proposed architectural framework is generic and can be applied to both use cases. In this section, we demonstrate this application to real-world problems. More specific, we introduce two use cases from the areas of the IoT, respectively electricity consumption prediction and network intrusion detection, to highlight the adaptability and usefulness of the proposed architectural framework. Both use cases are described in detail as well as their specific challenges with regard to the application of ML in big data environments. Furthermore, the different instantiations are described in terms of their configuration and extension in order to show the real-world feasibility of the architectural framework. In order to highlight the different ways on how to utilize our proposed framework, the electricity consumption prediction use case was implemented using a kappa architecture, while the IDS use case deployed a lambda architecture.

5.1 Electricity Consumption Prediction

Consumer-centric IoT domains, such as smart home, need to be able to handle a multitude of different analytics scenarios per consumer, which may include only a small number of IoT devices, but are still different in terms of their configuration, device types used, etc. While the resulting analytics problems are not big data problems per se, the processing resources, e.g. in smart home scenarios, are usually cloud-based. Therefore, a large amount of small problems results in the need for big data processing capabilities. A typical analytics scenario is the prediction of the electricity consumption of households over a period. Consumption data is generated by smart meters, with differing types being used in different households. This might be data on the current consumption level or the consumption up until this moment. The data, which varies in terms of its structure and semantics, is sent to smart home platform providers. Providers are responsible for predicting the customers' energy consumption according to a requested time frame, which may be the end of the day, month or year. Furthermore, platform providers may include further data sources, e.g. weather, environmental, census or additional sensor data, into the ML training process to make the prediction models more accurate. An increasing number of customers is tantamount to the need to train and apply an increasing number of ML models, which are different from each other. Moreover, the consumption profiles of different consumers are inherently different, thus limiting the utilization of a general model for different consumers.

We used the proposed framework, as described in Sect. 4, to implement an approach based on the kappa architecture concept to tackle the aforementioned problem (cf. Fig. 2). The central component of the resulting architecture is a streaming platform, which handles data collection and distribution. Specifically, this is achieved using Apache Kafka and its software ecosystem in order to ingest data from different IoT data sources and distribute the data within the architecture. In addition, all ingested data streams are stored in the log data store Apache Kafka offers. It stores all incoming messages in sequential order using topics and partitions to organize the data. It is especially useful for time-series data, as observed in IoT use cases. Besides, data may be pushed to a serving database, which, in our scenario, is implemented using InfluxDB, thus allowing ad hoc queries on the data. Together, both components are used for mass storage of data.

In the adopted architecture, the orchestration platform provides the capabilities to develop manage and deploy analytics pipelines based on predefined analytics operators. In terms of the proposed framework, it is used as the workflow management component without any further changes. The orchestration platform comprises several microservices to allow for the orchestration of analytics operators, which are written in Java and use an

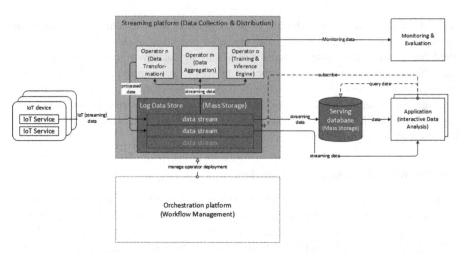

Fig. 2. Kappa instance of the architectural framework.

external library to integrate with the platform as described in [52, 53]. For ML use cases in smart home environments, operators are utilized to provide data transformation and aggregation capabilities and may be recomposed according to the different requirements of individual analytics scenarios. In this use case, we utilized a dataset of 945 smart meters, which we gathered in previous research. The data structure differs between smart meters, thus we implemented a preprocessing pipeline to normalize all data using analytics operators. This pipeline also distributes coherent data into the partition of the underlying topic. In this regard, the number of partitions determines the maximum number of parallel processing threads.

Following the kappa architecture approach, we used online ML algorithms, which incrementally evolve the ML model over time and at the same infer knowledge from the streaming data. More specifically, we used the adaptive random forest regressor, which is part of the MOA library[1] and described in [14]. Its main advantage is that the processing time does not increase with growing data sets. In order to allow for online ML in the architecture, we have implemented a new analytics operator, which predicts the electricity consumption of individual households. With regard to the proposed framework, this operator is a combined training and inference engine. Additionally, the current model state is saved in the operator. We scaled this operator according to the number of partitions of the topic, in which the data was located after preprocessing. Monitoring the individual model quality was done by an additional service, which has access to all analytics operators. In between each (pre-)processing step, streaming data is pushed back into Apache Kafka. For further usage, e.g. by interactive data analysis applications, the data is also be pushed to the serving database.

---

[1] https://github.com/Waikato/moa/.

5.2 Network Intrusion Detection

The second use case describes the detection of abnormal behavior and threats in network traffic by using network intrusion detection systems. IDS analyze network traffic in order to identify attacks. Typically, they consist of three essential parts, namely sensors, analytics and reporting. Depending on the specific infrastructure, sensors and analytics can be placed on each node in the network or on a specialized node. In many IoT use cases, the latter is favored due to limited resources on the individual nodes [41]. As already stated in the introduction, IDS can be based on rules, signatures or like in our case on detection of anomalies. Often, IDS use a hybrid approach with fixed rules for known attacks and an anomaly detection for yet unknown attacks. Attack vectors can differ depending on the specific network nodes and may include denial of service (DOS), sniffing components, altering sensor information but also attacks to serving components like SQL injections or brute force infiltration. Purpose of IDS is to ensure security, privacy and prevention of data loss of the specific devices. In this use case, we extract network data by using a network sniffer like wireshark, a tool that senses on the network and captures raw network traffic in PCAP (packet capture) format. Depending on the size of the network or the amount of nodes, the resulting data has a size of about a few GB per day because PCAP includes data from a multitude of protocols starting with layer two up to layer seven of the ISO/OSI model. To be able to identify a variety of attack vectors, all these protocol data have to be incorporated into the anomaly detection and thus we need to store and preprocess the data prior to train an ML algorithm. To develop an anomaly-based IDS, we use a special recurrent ANN, namely an LSTM (Long-Short term memories) that is capable of processing sequences of data. Therefore, we need to create sequences of the PCAP data and feed them to the LSTM. In contrast to the other use case, we thus use a database to store raw data as well as preprocessed sequences.

By utilizing the described framework of Sect. 4, we implemented an IDS, based on a lambda architecture, that is able to learn from historical, labeled datasets and is capable of real time classification (inferencing) on incoming network data streams (cf. Fig. 3). For an initial setup, we use a refined public dataset called CICIDS2017[2] (cf. [40]) because of its clean structure. It contains five days of PCAP data of simulated network traffic and threats. To train the LSTM with real data, a PCAP data stream generated by sniffing network interfaces of IoT devices is fed into the data distribution part of the architecture, also realized with Apache Kafka. Based on this data, the following components are implemented to realize a real-time classification approach for IDS. Source to develop this IDS is the work presented in [35].

The batch layer of our lambda architecture consists of an HDFS where we store historical data (raw data as well as sequences). Focal point of distribution is the Kafka broker, i.e. input or output of each processing step is a topic in Kafka. The data preprocessing tasks are realized with a processing pipeline. It includes a data transformation component for data preprocessing, which loads persisted data, extracts necessary features and generates new features for analysis. These preprocessing tasks are implemented in Python. A further step partitions PCAP data in time windows. This time-framed data is then led through a component that generates bidirectional network flows [8] and generates a variety of network traffic features.

---

[2] https://www.unb.ca/cic/datasets/ids-2017.html.

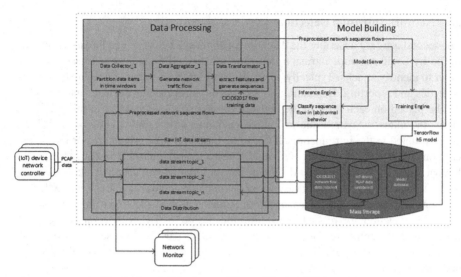

Fig. 3. Lambda instance of the architectural framework.

Having performed the necessary preprocessing steps, the model building component is responsible for training and providing the intended ML model. The LSTM, responsible to learn normal network traffic patterns is modeled with Keras and Tensorflow respectively. This approach uses different sequence models of various features as part of preprocessing tasks. The LSTM consists of an embedding layer, two bidirectional LSTM layers and two fully-connected dense layers. For the classification of incoming PCAP data streams, the preprocessed IoT network data has to be aligned with the trained model. The instantiated inference engine loads the model and produces predictions based on the data to be classified. The result of this classification is pushed to Kafka broker and can be consumed from monitoring or reporting components.

6 Summary and Conclusion

In this paper, we proposed an architectural framework for use cases driven by data streams and application of ML-algorithms. Therefore, we illustrated challenges to cope with when applying ML-algorithms to high volume and fast data. We then presented existing solutions that either tackle algorithmic challenges or provide architectural approaches. The main contribution of this paper is a generic architectural solution for building end-to-end pipelines for processing data streams using ML technologies. Consequently, our proposed solution has a distribution component as its focal point. We also addressed aspects, which are not directly involved in data processing or analyzing but are needed to design and implement all necessary components. Therefore, we differentiate between architectural and procedural aspects and group corresponding components. In order to demonstrate the applicability of our proposed solution, we subsequently presented two implemented use cases and provided a mapping of the architectural framework onto their implemented components.

In [3] we described how we wanted to evaluate the architectural framework. This is still an ongoing work and the strategy is twofold. We follow the principles of design science research artefact evaluation [32, 48] and, furthermore, conduct technical experiments to evaluate the performance in addition to more formative evaluation methods. Compared to [3] we already implemented the IDS use case as described in the previous section. Besides, we were able to map a further use case from the consumer-centric IoT domain. The reason for this is to identify potential consequences for further streaming-based ML use cases, e.g. to derive additional components as architectural building blocks. In contrast to the original paper, we draw attention to the challenges resulting from processing data streams because we wanted to provide a more in-depth view on specific components of the architectural framework. Many of the use cases we have seen so far were based on data streams why we chose the distribution component as the focal point of our framework and hence we laid out the specific problems we encountered and found in literature respectively. Dependent on the specific use case the necessary steps to train a model and how the training itself can be achieved vary. We provided the two use cases to demonstrate that models may either be trained and updated directly on the data stream or data need to be stored and be further processed to gain a trainable representation. Hence, specific challenges to be addressed vary with the use case; for instance because of continuous model updates, the concept drift is easier to handle in the first use case than in the second. In both cases we still have to cope e.g. with volume- or veracity-related challenges in general.

The novelty of this approach lies in a holistic view on the overall processing of data beginning with pushing or pulling it from source and ending with a common representation being fed into ML-based algorithms. In contrast to approaches for specific use cases, we additionally want to suggest considering non-algorithmic aspects in order to develop end-to-end pipelines. Though this might seem to be only a software engineering problem it often affects the overall approach and having developed a generic solution to process and analyze data enables us quickly to adapt our approach to a broad range of use cases and data respectively.

Future work will address two important parts, namely automatic generation of components and dealing with training phase of algorithms in the context of data streams. With a generation of components (cf. CI/CD) and in particular implemented models it shall be possible to explore data in the interactive data analysis prior to directly generate a training component that is fed into the training engine. The training phase of models in the context of data streams may lead to different challenges. Concept drift is currently the most investigated challenge but probably also the one, which can be tackled by just adapting existing techniques. To handle variable distributions and statistically dependent variables in data is more challenging and might require development of new techniques. Frequent model updates are also still a challenge, especially, if real time requirements come into play. Using neural nets as ML-algorithm, we are still confronted with the drawbacks of (big) data streams. A major question arises from the problems of continuous model updates. Updates usually force (re-)training of the underlying model, which might not be applicable at all hours, so the question remains how to adapt to fast changing data, in particular when applying neural nets.

Acknowledgements. The work presented in this paper is partly funded by the European Regional Development Fund (ERDF), the European Social Fund (ESF) and the Free State of Saxony (Sächsische Aufbaubank - SAB).

References

1. Akbar, A., Khan, A., Carrez, F., et al.: Predictive analytics for complex IoT data streams. IEEE Internet Things J. **4**(5), 1571–1582 (2017). https://doi.org/10.1109/JIOT.2017.2712672
2. Augenstein, C., Spangenberg, N., Franczyk, B.: Applying machine learning to big data streams: an overview of challenges. In: IEEE 4th International Conference on Soft Computing and Machine Intelligence (lSCMI 2017), pp. 25–29 (2017)
3. Augenstein, C., Spangenberg, N., Franczyk, B.: An architectural blueprint for a multi-purpose anomaly detection on data streams. In: Filipe, J. (ed.) Proceedings of the 21st International Conference on Enterprise Information Systems ICEIS 2019, vol. 2, pp. 470–476. SciTePress (2019)
4. Carrasco, A., van Bladel, B., Demeyer, S.: Migrating towards microservices: migration and architecture smells. In: Ouni, A., Kessentini, M., Cinnéide, M.Ó. (eds.) Proceedings of the 2nd International Workshop on Refactoring - IWoR 2018, pp. 1–6. ACM Press, New York (2018)
5. Caselli, M., Zambon, E., Kargl, F.: Sequence-aware intrusion detection in industrial control systems. In: Proceedings of the 1st ACM Workshop on Cyber-Physical System Security (2015)
6. Cerny, T., Donahoo, M.J., Trnka, M.: Contextual understanding of microservice architecture. SIGAPP Appl. Comput. Rev. **17**(4), 29–45 (2018). https://doi.org/10.1145/3183628.3183631
7. Chang, W.L., Boyd, D.: NIST Big Data Interoperability Framework, volume 6, reference architecture version 2 (2018). https://doi.org/10.6028/nist.sp.1500-6r1
8. CICFlowMeter: CICFlowmeter - network traffic Bi-flow generator and analyzer for anomaly detection (2019). https://github.com/ISCX/CICFlowMeter
9. Cook, D.J., Crandall, A.S., Thomas, B.L., et al.: CASAS: a smart home in a box. Computer (Long Beach Calif.) **46**(7) (2013). https://doi.org/10.1109/mc.2012.328
10. Datta, S.K., Bonnet, C.: Next-generation, data centric and end-to-end IoT architecture based on microservices. In: IEEE International Conference on Consumer Electronics, pp. 206–212. IEEE (2018)
11. Dundar, M., Krishnapuram, B., Bi, J., et al.: Learning classifiers when the training data is not IID. In: Proceedings of the 20th International Joint Conference on Artificial Intelligence, pp. 756–761. Morgan Kaufmann Publishers Inc., Hyderabad (2007)
12. Fan, J., Han, F., Liu, H.: Challenges of Big Data analysis. Nat. Sci. Rev. **1**(2), 293–314 (2014). https://doi.org/10.1093/nsr/nwt032
13. Gama, J., Sebastião, R., Rodrigues, P.P.: On evaluating stream learning algorithms. Mach. Learn. **90**(3), 317–346 (2013). https://doi.org/10.1007/s10994-012-5320-9
14. Gomes, H.M., Bifet, A., Read, J., et al.: Adaptive random forests for evolving data stream classification. Mach. Learn. **106**(9–10), 1469–1495 (2017). https://doi.org/10.1007/s10994-017-5642-8
15. Han, J., Pei, J., Kamber, M.: Data mining: Concepts and Techniques. Elsevier, Amsterdam (2011)
16. Jagadish, H.V., Gehrke, J., Labrinidis, A., et al.: Big data and its technical challenges. Commun. ACM **57**(7), 86–94 (2014). https://doi.org/10.1145/2611567
17. Khamassi, I., Sayed-Mouchaweh, M., Hammami, M., et al.: Discussion and review on evolving data streams and concept drift adapting. Evol. Syst. **9**(1), 1–23 (2018)

18. Khan, N., Naim, A., Hussain, M., et al.: The 51 V's of big data: survey, technologies, characteristics, opportunities, issues and challenges. In: COINS 2019 Proceedings of the International Conference on Omni-Layer Intelligent Systems (2019). https://doi.org/10.1145/3312614.3312623

19. Kiran, M., Murphy, P., Monga, I., et al.: Lambda architecture for cost-effective batch and speed big data processing. In: Ho, H. (ed.) Proceedings, 2015 IEEE International Conference on Big Data, Santa Clara, CA, USA, 29 October–01 November 2015, pp. 2785–2792. IEEE, Piscataway (2015)

20. Krawczyk, B., Minku, L.L., Gama, J., et al.: Ensemble learning for data stream analysis. A survey. Inf. Fusion **37**, 132–156 (2017). https://doi.org/10.1016/j.inffus.2017.02.004

21. Kreps, J.: Questioning the Lambda Architecture. The Lambda Architecture has its merits, but alternatives are worth exploring (2014). https://www.oreilly.com/ideas/questioning-the-lambda-architecture. Accessed 29 Jan 2019

22. Larrinaga, F., Fernandez, J., Zugasti, E., et al.: Implementation of a reference architecture for cyber physical systems to support condition based maintenance. In: 5th International Conference on Control, Decision and Information Technologies, pp. 773–778 (2018)

23. LeCun, Y., Bengio, Y., Hinton, G.: Deep learning. Nature **521**(7553), 436–444 (2015). https://doi.org/10.1038/nature14539

24. L'Heureux, A., Grolinger, K., Elyamany, H.F., et al.: Machine learning with big data. Challenges and approaches. IEEE Access **5**, 7776–7797 (2017). https://doi.org/10.1109/access.2017.2696365

25. Mahdavinejad, M.S., Rezvan, M., Barekatain, M., et al.: Machine learning for internet of things data analysis: a survey. Digit. Commun. Netw. **4**(3), 161–175 (2018). https://doi.org/10.1016/j.dcan.2017.10.002

26. Marrón, D., Read, J., Bifet, A., et al.: Data stream classification using random feature functions and novel method combinations. J. Syst. Softw. **127**, 195–204 (2017). https://doi.org/10.1016/j.jss.2016.06.009

27. Mu, X., Ting, K.M., Zhou, Z.-H.: Classification under streaming emerging new classes. A solution using completely-random trees. IEEE Trans. Knowl. Data Eng. **29**(8), 1605–1618 (2017). https://doi.org/10.1109/TKDE.2017.2691702

28. Osojnik, A., Panov, P., Džeroski, S.: Multi-label classification via multi-target regression on data streams. Mach. Learn. **106**(6), 745–770 (2017). https://doi.org/10.1007/s10994-016-5613-5

29. Oxford Dictionaries: anomaly (2019). https://en.oxforddictionaries.com/definition/anomaly. Accessed 23 Jan 2019

30. Papazoglou, M., van den Heuvel, W.-J., Mascolo, J.: Reference architecture and knowledge-based structures for smart manufacturing networks. IEEE Softw. **32**, 61–69 (2015)

31. Parnas, D.L.: On the criteria to be used in decomposing systems into modules. Commun. ACM **15**(12), 1053–1058 (1972). https://doi.org/10.1145/361598.361623

32. Peffers, K., Rothenberger, M., Tuunanen, T., Vaezi, R.: Design science research evaluation. In: Peffers, K., Rothenberger, M., Kuechler, B. (eds.) DESRIST 2012. LNCS, vol. 7286, pp. 398–410. Springer, Heidelberg (2012). https://doi.org/10.1007/978-3-642-29863-9_29

33. Polyzotis, N., Roy, S., Whang, S.E., et al.: Data management challenges in production machine learning. In: Chirkova, R., Yang, J., Suciu, D., et al. (eds.) Proceedings of the 2017 ACM International Conference on Management of Data - SIGMOD 2017, pp. 1723–1726. ACM Press, New York (2017)

34. Popa, D., Pop, F., Serbanescu, C., et al.: Deep learning model for home automation and energy reduction in a smart home environment platform. Neural Comput. Appl. **31**(5), 1317–1337 (2019). https://doi.org/10.1007/s00521-018-3724-6

35. Radford, B.J., Richardson, B.D., Davis, S.E.: Sequence Aggregation Rules for Anomaly Detection in Computer Network Traffic. CoRR abs/1805.03735 (2018)

36. Ramírez-Gallego, S., Krawczyk, B., García, S., et al.: A survey on data preprocessing for data stream mining. Current status and future directions. Neurocomputing **239**, 39–57 (2017). https://doi.org/10.1016/j.neucom.2017.01.078
37. Rathore, M.M., Son, H., Ahmad, A., et al.: Real-time big data stream processing using GPU with spark over Hadoop ecosystem. Int. J. Parallel Program. **46**(3), 630–646 (2018)
38. Sadegh, N.: A perceptron network for functional identification and control of nonlinear systems. IEEE Trans. Neural Netw. **4**(6), 982–988 (1993). https://doi.org/10.1109/72.286893
39. Serra, J., Sanabria-Russo, L., Pubill, D., et al.: Scalable and flexible IoT data analytics: when machine learning meets SDN and virtualization. In: 2018 IEEE 23rd International Workshop on Computer Aided Modeling and Design of Communication Links and Networks (CAMAD), 17–19 September 2018, pp. 1–6. IEEE, Piscataway (2018)
40. Sharafaldin, I., Lashkari, A.H., Ghorbani, A.A.: Toward generating a new intrusion detection dataset and intrusion traffic characterization. In: ICISSP, pp. 108–116 (2018)
41. Singla, A., Sharma, A.: Physical access system security of IoT devices using machine learning techniques. SSRN J. (2019). https://doi.org/10.2139/ssrn.3356785
42. Smailović, J., Grčar, M., Lavrač, N., et al.: Stream-based active learning for sentiment analysis in the financial domain. Inf. Sci. **285**, 181–203 (2014). https://doi.org/10.1016/j.ins.2014.04.034
43. Steffens, A., Lichter, H., Döring, J.S.: Designing a next-generation continuous software delivery system: concepts and architecture. In: 2018 IEEE 4th International Workshop on Rapid Continuous Software Engineering, pp. 1–7 (2018)
44. Strategy Analytics: Internet of Things Now Numbers 22 Billion Devices but Where is the Revenue? (2019). https://news.strategyanalytics.com/press-release/iot-ecosystem/strategy-analytics-internet-things-now-numbers-22-billion-devices-where. Accessed 30 Oct 2019
45. Suthaharan, S.: Big data classification Problems and challenges in network intrusion prediction with machine learning. SIGMETRICS Perform. Eval. Rev. **41**(4), 70–73 (2014). https://doi.org/10.1145/2627534.2627557
46. Thramboulidis, K., Vachtsevanou, D.C., Solanos, A.: Cyber-physical microservices: an IoT-based framework for manufacturing systems. In: IEEE Industrial Cyber-Physical Systems (ICPS). ITMO University, Saint Petersburg, Saint Petersburg, Russia, 15–18 May 2018, pp. 232–239. IEEE (2018)
47. Valsamis, A., Tserpes, K., Zissis, D., et al.: Employing traditional machine learning algorithms for big data streams analysis. The case of object trajectory prediction. J. Syst. Softw. **127**, 249–257 (2017). https://doi.org/10.1016/j.jss.2016.06.016
48. Venable, J., Pries-Heje, J., Baskerville, R.: FEDS: a framework for evaluation in design science research. Eur. J. Inf. Syst. **25**(1), 77–89 (2016)
49. Xu, S., Wang, J.: Dynamic extreme learning machine for data stream classification. Neurocomputing **238**, 433–449 (2017). https://doi.org/10.1016/j.neucom.2016.12.078
50. Younas, M.: Research challenges of big data. Serv. Oriented Comput. Appl. **13**(2), 105–107 (2019). https://doi.org/10.1007/s11761-019-00265-x
51. Zhou, L., Pan, S., Wang, J., et al.: Machine learning on big data. Opportunities and challenges. Neurocomputing **237**, 350–361 (2017). https://doi.org/10.1016/j.neucom.2017.01.026
52. Zschörnig, T., Wehlitz, R., Franczyk, B.: A personal analytics platform for the Internet of Things. Implementing Kappa architecture with microservice-based stream processing. In: Proceedings of the 19th International Conference on Enterprise Information Systems, pp. 733–738. SCITEPRESS - Science and Technology Publications (2017)
53. Zschörnig, T., Wehlitz, R., Rößner, I., et al.: SEPL: An IoT platform for value-added services in the energy domain - architectural concept and software prototype. In: Proceedings of the 20th International Conference on Enterprise Information Systems, pp. 593–600. SCITEPRESS - Science and Technology Publications (2018)

Usage of Smart Contracts with FCG for Dynamic Robot Coalition Formation in Precision Farming

Alexander Smirnov[1], Leonid Sheremetov[2] (ID), and Nikolay Teslya[1]([✉]) (ID)

[1] SPIIRAS, 14th Line 39, St. Petersburg, Russia
{smir,teslya}@iias.spb.su
[2] Mexican Petroleum Institute, Eje Central Lázaro Cárdenas Norte, 152 Mexico City, Mexico
sher@imp.mx

Abstract. In solving the problems of precision farming, an important place has the organization of joint work of robots for processing the field. The paper presents an approach to the dynamic formation of a coalition for solving the problem of precision farming, based on the use of fuzzy cooperative games in determining the structure of the coalition. To collect the initial data and save the result of the calculation of the game, a cyberphysical space is used, built based on the "blackboard" and blockchain technologies. Their use allows to combine the advantages of the concept of the Internet of Things for collecting information from sensors of agricultural robots and the immutability of data blocks to save the results of the calculation of the game in a competitive environment. To ensure the dynamic change of the coalition, smart contracts are used over the blockchain technology. Contracts contain the rules for calculating a fuzzy cooperative game and the rules for changing the composition of the coalition. As a result, the proposed approach provides the dynamic formation of a coalition with the trust of all participants and the ability to collect and disseminate information from robot sensors in a common trusted information space. To implement the blockchain and smart contract, the approach proposes to use the Hyperledger Fabric platform.

Keywords: Fuzzy logic · Coalition · Coalition game · Smart contract · Robot dynamic · Precision farming

1 Introduction

The growth of the Earth's population in the conditions of limited areas of fertile land for food production requires the search for a more efficient organization of agriculture. One of the main directions in this area is the concept of precision farming, the essence of which is the precise control of the parts of a field for growing a crop that most closely matches the part. Given the development of robotics, sensors, and the use of remote sensing of the earth, the solution to this problem can be automated to a very high degree. At the same time, to solve this problem, it is necessary to organize the joint work of many robotic devices that perform the tasks of periodically examining the geological, chemical,

© Springer Nature Switzerland AG 2020
J. Filipe et al. (Eds.): ICEIS 2019, LNBIP 378, pp. 115–133, 2020.
https://doi.org/10.1007/978-3-030-40783-4_7

physical and biological properties of field sites, performing operations to change some of these properties, by irrigation, fertilizing, processing, and other actions.

Among the existing models for the interaction of robots, the coalition collaboration model is most suitable for solving the problem of precision farming. This is explained by the fact that swarm and flock models are based on fairly simple rules that do not take into account or weakly take into account the difference in the functionality of robots, the dynamics of the external environment, and the long-term planning of their own actions. The coalition model, in turn, provides a complex interaction of robots based on the assessment of the gain in achieving the final goal. The implementation of the distribution model of the gain and the description of the actions required to obtain it allows the robots to form coalitions that best meet the requirements of the task, plan the order of their own actions and make decisions in case of unforeseen impacts, for example, in the case of precision farming, when com changing weather conditions or plant disease. In detail, coalition formation models are considered in the work [1].

The previous work by the authors proposes to use the model of fuzzy coalition games to evaluate the winnings of an individual robot and the entire coalition [2]. This model provides the possibility of calculating a coalition based on the estimates of each robot separately about the expected reward and a general assessment of the coalition's effectiveness.

To store the rules of the game, competencies and requirements of robots, as well as information about the current state of coalition and task distribution between robots, it is proposed to use blockchain technology and its extension with smart contracts. Smart contracts as a computerized protocol for storing and carrying out contractual clauses via blockchain become a useful tool used in many industries [3, 4]. In the previous work [2] it was proposed to use two types of smart contracts: first one for storing the rules of a coalition formation, and second one for adjusting the composition of the coalition in order to reflect environment changes. Both types of rules are defined using the theory of fuzzy sets. The contract source code, as well as the current state of the problem solution, is stored in a blockchain-based distributed ledger. This allows providing a trusted information source for robots to store and searching information about stage of task solving and current coalition state. Since the data in any block is linked with other existing blocks by calculating Merkle Tree hash, none of them can be changed without recalculating hashes of other blocks. It makes possible to provide unchangeable process logs by which one can trace the history of operations and, if necessary, find a weak point, to enhance the effectiveness of future coalitions.

Compared to the earlier work by the authors [2], this work presents a detailed description of the problem of precision farming. The process of robots' interaction during the dynamic formation of a coalition is analyzed in detail. The principle of choosing a platform for organizing the blockchain is presented, it is justified, from the point of view of the solution architecture, the use of the Hyperledger platform.

The rest of the paper is organized as follows. Related work about robot coalitions types, concept of fuzzy coalition games and using blockchain for robot coalition organization is revised in the following section. The precision agriculture problem for robot coalition is presented in Sect. 3. A fuzzy cooperative game (FCG) model with core is described in detail in Sect. 4. In Sect. 5, criteria of dynamic robot coalition formation for precision agriculture are analyzed. Section 6 provide information about implementation of smart contracts and frameworks for robots' negotiation during coalition formation.

2   Related Work

2.1   Robot Coalition Formation

There are a lot of existing models of robots' joint work such as swarms, flocks, and coalitions that differ by the freedom of single participant. The swarm model is based on the biological model of ant colony where all members have uniform rules for making decisions about their own actions in the current situation. The rules are quite simple and consistent, which guarantees the coherence of the swarm in solving the common problem. The exchange of information between the swarm participants is minimal [5].

A flock model is similar to a swarm model and differs from it by the presence of a basic hierarchy in which the main participant and his subordinates can be distinguished. The main flow of information is distributed from the higher-level participant to the lower-level, while simple rules of interaction between the lower-level participants allow them to effectively organize joint work on the tasks of the main participant.

In contrast to robots in swarms or flocks where they are limited in actions by strong rules and actions of nearest neighbors, robots in coalitions calculate their next steps based on the common goal reaching according to the current coalition state and set of alternatives provided by norms of coalition [6]. Existing models of task solving in coalition claim that a robot can receive a reward for the successful problem solving according to its contribution. The independency of robots makes it urgent to develop an approach to coalition formation and interaction organization between robots that allows making joint decision during joint solution of the problem the coalition is faced to.

There are many subject areas that require the use of a coalition of robots to solve a complex problem, including industrial cyberphysical systems, precision farming, and remote or local explore of space objects. Complex tasks in each area can be decomposed to small simple tasks (for instance in precision farming it is needed to scan the relief, check the soil composition, select and put plant or seed in the soil, water it) that are solved by single robots [7]. To form a coalition, robots provide their competences and select tasks that they can perform.

Robots are equipped with different hardware and software as well as expect different levels of reward. Therefore, it is important to consider the heterogeneity and provide common model to consensus reaching during task decomposition and resolution. Each robot is an independent agent with own competencies and goals, which he aims to achieve after the problem solving. In this case, the coalition can be considered as a union of agents with their own interests, which through the negotiation make a decision on a joint solution of the problem and the distribution of the reward.

Most of the approaches to coalition formation are characterized by the exponential nature of the computations and communications complexity. To transition from hyper-exponential and exponential complexity to polynomial, the following parameters are usually limited: the number of agents in one coalition, the number of coalitions, and the rationality of agents [8]. In this case, the additional complexity is caused by the inability to accurately estimate the size of the gain, which introduces fuzziness into the formulation of the problem.

2.2 Fuzzy Cooperative Games

The cooperative nature of modern robotic complexes causes necessity of considering them within the context of cooperative game theory in order to model and understand their cooperative behavior. The main questions of coalition formation are as follows: what coalitions will be formed, how the common winning will be distributed among them and if the obtained coalition structure is stable. Once coalitions are formed and they have a feasible set of payoffs available to its members, the question is the identification of final payoffs awarded to each player. That is, given a collection of feasible sets of payoffs, one for each coalition, can one predict or recommend a payoff (or set of payoffs) to be awarded to each player?

The payoff distribution should guarantee the stability of the coalition structure when no one player has an intention to leave a coalition because of the expectation to increase its payoff. The benefit distribution among the coalition members has proved to be fuzzy, uncertain, and ambiguous [9]. Using the theory of fuzzy cooperative games (FCGs), the uncertainty is processed by means of the introduction of a fuzzy benefit concept through the bargaining process to the conclusion about the corresponding fuzzy distribution of individual benefits among the coalition members [10].

The predictions or recommendations of payment distribution are embodied in different solution concepts. According to [11], cooperative games are divided into two classes based on the way a solution of the game is obtained: games with a solution set and games with a single solution. Games with core considered in this paper, belong to the former class and represent a mechanism for analyzing the possible set of stable outcomes of cooperative games with transferable utilities [12]. The concept of a core is attractive since it tends to maximize the sum of coalition utilities in the particular coalition structure. Such imputations are called C-stable. The core of a game with respect to a given coalition structure is defined as a set of such imputations that prevent the players from forming small coalitions by paying off all the subsets an amount, which is at least as much they would get if they form a coalition (we proceed with a formal definition of a core in the following section). Thus, the core of a game is a set of imputations which are stable.

The drawbacks of the core is that, on the one hand, the computational complexity of finding the optimal structure is high since for the game with n players at least $2^n - 1$ of the total $n^{\frac{n}{2}}$ coalition structures should be tested. On the other hand, for particular classes of the game a core can be empty. Because of these problems, using the C-stable coalition structures was quite unpopular in practical applications [6] and only recently has attracted more attention of the researchers, when the concept of fuzzy cooperative games with core was introduced [13, 14]. For realistic applications like collaborative work of groups of robots, additive environments and the absence of the restrictions on the type of membership functions should be considered [15].

For practical applications of FCGs, one of the key problems is the management of the coalition formation and payoff distribution tasks. In our previous work, a negotiation algorithm has been developed [18]. In this paper, we propose a novel approach using blockchain technology.

2.3 Blockchain in Robot Coalition Organization

Since robot coalitions are characterized by dynamic nature it is required to implement a changes in coalition composition by adding new of removing existing robots, according to changes of the problem being solved [16]. New robots should be quickly familiarized with the current state of the problem solution and provide description of own competences to help to solve the problem. At the same time, the rest part of coalition should operate without any changes as it was defined in their schedule. This problem is usually solved by using external knowledge repositories for storing the history of interaction between coalition members. Such knowledge can be stored in centralized or decentralized knowledge bases. Centralized knowledge base usually provides single access point for connecting robots to the data network. Decentralized knowledge base allows to organize a distributed network without any single access point in which the knowledge base is distributed among all participants with a share of the backup, which makes the general information space more resistant to the disconnection of one or more nodes.

Regarding the organization of robots' interaction, the blockchain is mostly used as immutable storage for information exchange and platform for smart contracts. Information stored in the blockchain could contain records about task and consumables distribution [17, 18], smart contracts and reward transactions [19], as well as global knowledge about coalition previous actions [20]. In combination with cooperative games blockchain technology can provide more trust for communication between robots, due to the storing information about transactions in immutable log that are verified by every coalition participant. In contrary to existing approaches, blockchain does not require central authority that provide trust for all nodes. All nodes negotiate with each other coming to consensus with one of possible mechanisms: Proof of Work, Proof of Stake, or practical byzantine fault tolerance [21]. The blockchain is used to provide safe and trustiness logging of robots' task distribution and rewarding for task solving.

It is also noted that the combination of the peer-to-peer network and the cryptographic algorithms used in blockchain technology allow for a negotiation process and consensus building without the presence of any controlling authorities. The distributed nature of the blockchain is proposed to be used in swarm robotics to store global knowledge about swarm actions [20]. At the same time, due to blockchain, the security of the transmitted data is ensured (garbage data can affect the achievement of a common goal), distributed decision making (creating a distributed voting system for the solution), separation of robots behavior (switching between behavior patterns depending on the role in the swarm), the emergence of new business models using the swarm. In addition, the availability of a distributed transaction ledger allows new robots to join the swarm and gain all the knowledge they have gained prior to the moment of inclusion by downloading and analyzing the transaction history.

3   Precision Farming Case with Robot Coalition

In this section, an example of solving the problems of precision farming by coalition of robots is considered. The problem is stated as follows (see Fig. 1). There is a field with various geological and ecological characteristics of soils, suitable for growing several types of crops that require different growth conditions. The field is processed by several robots equipped with devices for plowing, loosening, planting, watering, fertilizing and harvesting crops.

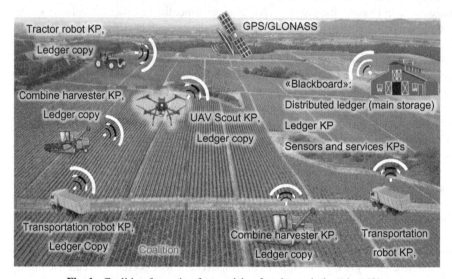

Fig. 1. Coalition formation for precision farming task (based on [2]).

In the set of robots, the following types can be distinguished, according to the main tasks to be solved: combine harvesters, the list of tasks of which includes planting and harvesting, studying the composition of the soil; a transport robot that carries out the movement of seed and finished crop, as well as fertilizers between the combine harvester and the warehouse; a robot scout (wheeled or UAV) that perform periodic field reconnaissance to measure light characteristics, wind direction and strength, soil moisture, and plant status. Each robot is equipped with a set of sensors and actuators that allow exploring the soil structure, light and humidity conditions ant take a picture in each sector of the field. Based on the explored data a map of the field is built, where the current conditions are bound with the coordinates from GPS/GLONASS satellites. Crops are selected for each sector based on the sector conditions that are the most favorable in terms of yield, as well as technologies are selected for their care of planted agriculture. The technology of caring for each type of crop requires the use of robots that are capable of carrying out specific operations for the culture chosen, while some robots are capable of performing operations on several technologies, or the technologies can have common steps being solved by the same type of robots. Storing of the history of fieldwork and crops can help both in subsequent decision-making and in drawing up special reporting on the production cycle, which is increasingly required by the laws of developed countries. In addition, the history of growing process can be shared with customers to provide insight information about a process and help customers to get food based on the quality of farming process. This, as well as the requirement of storing the history of fieldwork requires the presence of a repository, in which the history of actions and the results of field processing will be recorded.

Robots are interacting through the cyberphysical framework presented on Fig. 2. The framework is based on the smart cyberphysical space created by extending of smart space concept (based on the "blackboard") with distributed ledger based on blockchain [22, 23]. This combination provides the ability to organize basic interaction of robots in the physical and cyber (virtual) spaces with storing history of each robot actions sequence in immutable blockchain structure. The interaction includes solo and joint manipulations with physical objects, information exchange about the current state of robots and objects for planning further joint actions during the coalition formation.

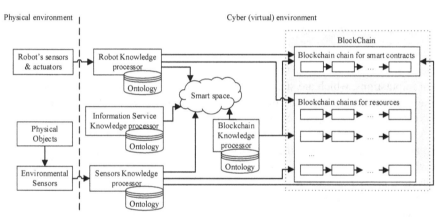

Fig. 2. Cyberphysical framework with blockchain support [2].

One of the typical coalitional tasks for precision agriculture is the field exploration where different types of robots are engaged. The overall task of the study is divided between them into subtasks, according to the available competences of the robots. In this case, task division is performed using the cooperative game model for the dynamic coalition formation. Within the framework of this model, individual robots interact with each other, putting forward their competencies and requirements based on which the selection of coalition participants is being carried out and their effectiveness in solving the assigned task is estimated. The process of coalition formation is presented with the sequence diagram on Fig. 3.

4   Fuzzy Cooperative Game Model with Core

A generalized model of a fuzzy cooperative game (FCG) with core was proposed in [15, 24, 25]. As shown in [15], the concept of a core is attractive since it tends to maximize

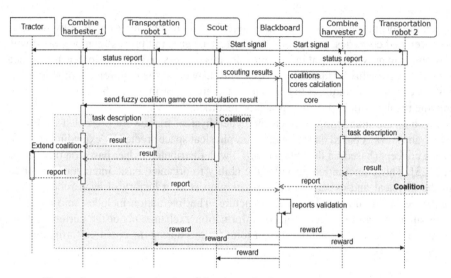

Fig. 3. Sequence diagram of coalition formation in precision agriculture task.

the sum of coalition utilities in the particular coalition structure. The core of a game is a set of imputations, which are stable. The proposed model helped solving the problems of the computational complexity of finding the optimal structure and of the empty core, which enabled its use in practical applications of selecting robots in coalitions.

A FCG is defined as a pair $(Robot, w)$, where $Robot$ is nonempty and finite set of players, subsets of $Robot$ joining together to fulfil some task T_i are called coalitions K, and w is called a characteristic function of the game, being $w : 2^n \to \Re^+$ a mapping connecting every coalition $K \subset Robot$ with a fuzzy quantity $w(K) \in \Re^+$, with a membership function $\mu_K : R \to [0, 1]$. A modal value of $w(K)$ corresponds to the characteristic function of the crisp game $v(K)$: $\max \mu_K(w(K)) = \mu_K(v(K))$. For an empty coalition $w(\emptyset) = 0$. A fuzzy core for the game $(Robot, w)$ with the imputation $X = (x_{ij})_{i \in I, j \in Robot} \in \Re^+$ is a fuzzy subset C_F of $\Re^+$:

$$C_F = \left\{ x_{ij} \in \Re^+ : vf = \left(w(Robot), \sum_{\substack{i \in I, \\ j \in Robot}} x_{ij} \varphi_{ij} \right), \right.$$

$$\left. \min_{\substack{K_i \in k \\ j \in Robot}} \left(vf = \left(\sum_{j \in K_i} x_{ij} \varphi_{ij}, w(K_i) \right) \right) \right\} \tag{1}$$

where x_{ij} is the fuzzy payment of a robot j participating in a coalition i, $i = 1, 2, \ldots, I$, $j = 1, 2, \ldots, N$, $\bar{k} = [K_1, K_2, \ldots, K_I]$ is the ordered structure of effective coalitions; φ is a fuzzy partial order relation with a membership function $vf =: R \times R \to [0, 1]$, and φ_{ij} is a binary variable such that:

$$\varphi_{ij} = \begin{cases} 1, if\ robot\ j\ participates\ in\ a\ coalition\ i; \\ 0, otherwise. \end{cases} \tag{2}$$

This variable can be considered as a result of some robot's strategy on joining a coalition.

A fuzzy partial order relation is defined as follows (for more details see [26]). Let a, b be fuzzy numbers with membership functions μ_a and μ_b respectively, then the possibility of partial order $a\phi = b$ is defined as $v\phi = (a, b) \in [0, 1]$ as follows:

$$v\phi = (a, b) = \sup_{\substack{x,y \in R \\ x \geq y}} (\min(\mu_a(x), \mu_b(y))) \tag{3}$$

The core C_F is the set of possible distributions of the total payment achievable by the coalitions, and none of coalitions can offer to its members more than they can obtain accepting some imputation from the core. The first argument of the core C_F indicates that the payments for the grand coalition are less than the characteristic function of the game. The second argument reflects the property of group rationality of the players, that there is no other payoff vector, which yields more to each player. The membership function $\mu_{C_F} : R \to [0, 1]$, is defined as:

$$\mu_{C_F}(x) = \min \left\{ vf = \left(w(Robot), \sum_{\substack{i \in I \\ j \in Robot}} x_{ij}\varphi_{ij} \right), \right.$$
$$\left. \min_{\substack{K_i \in k \\ j \in Robot}} \left(vf = \left(\sum_{j \in K_i} x_{ij}\varphi_{ij}, w(K_i) \right) \right) \right\} \tag{4}$$

With the possibility that a non-empty core C_F of the game $(Robot, w)$ exists:

$$\gamma_{C_F}(Robot, w) = \sup\left(\mu_{C_F}(x) : x \in \mathfrak{R}^n \right) \tag{5}$$

The solution of a cooperative game is a coalition configuration (S, x) which consists of (i) a partition S of $Robot$, the so-called coalition structure, and (ii) an efficient payoff distribution x which assigns each robot in Robot its payoff out of the utility of the coalition it is member of in a given coalition structure S. A coalition configuration (S, x) is called stable if no robot has an incentive to leave its coalition in S due to its assigned payoff xi.

It was proved that the fuzzy set of coalition structures forming the game core represents a subset of the fuzzy set formed by the structure of effective coalitions. In turn, this inference allows us to specify the upper possibility bound for the core, which is a very important condition for the process of solution searching, because in this case, the presence of a solution that meets the efficiency condition may serve as the signal to terminate the search algorithm [25].

The game purpose is to generate an effective structure of robot coalitions for executing some task. In turn, the generated structure of robot coalitions represents the optimal configuration of the grand coalition.

Individual robots use the technique of nonlinear fuzzy regression to estimate the parameters of utility functions for their payments [27]. A "coalition robot" is enabled for constructing membership functions (MF) of coalitions and generating the game core (fuzzy-number generator). The algorithm of fuzzy number summation for obtaining coalition membership functions represents an important element of the model. The sum operation is based on Zadeh extension principle [26] for fuzzy numbers a and b (which are convex sets normalized in R):

$$\mu_{a(*)b}(Z) = \sup_{z=x*y} \min(\mu_a(x), \mu_b(y)) \tag{6}$$

where * can designate the sum ⊕ or the product • of fuzzy numbers. Each fuzzy set is decomposed into two segments, a non-decreasing and non-increasing one. The operation * is performed for every group of n segments (one segment for each fuzzy set) that belong to the same class (non-decreasing or non-increasing one). Thus, a fuzzy set is generated for every group of n segments. The summation result is derived as superposition of these sets, which gives the membership function as the sum of n fuzzy numbers.

5   Criteria for Dynamic Robot Coalition Formation

Joint problem solving requires a well-coordinated interaction of the participants' actions during the coalition formation. Regardless of the coalition model used, coalition formation process can be considered as three types of interrelated actions:

- Generation of a coalition structure. The structure includes a subset of robots that will jointly interact to coordinate their activities on problem solving;
- Solving the problem of optimization of each coalition; union of agents' competencies for effective problem solving. On this stage, the task is dividing to the subtasks and robots are assigned to each subtask based on the benefit it can bring to coalition. The benefit is estimated based on the functions, winning expectations and efficiency of robot;
- Profit sharing between agents.

If the actions presented above are performed before problem solving, a static coalition formation is considered. The structure of static coalitions does not change over the time. Such a situation is typical for environments with quite low dynamic. At the time of optimization of the coalition, in parallel to coalition structure also a plan for solving the problem is calculated as well as all possible deviations from the plan. The deviations can be predicted due to the known patterns or equations of situation development. In case of a deviation, for example, due to the failure of one of the coalition members, the correction of the plan is carried out by the forces of the last coalition members taking into account the changed conditions in order to return to the original plan with minimal losses. This approach is quite rough due to the situation that coalition will fail in case of unpredicted deviation happens or a set of deviations will be accumulated and coalition cannot fix all of them based only on pre-calculated actions.

A more complex, but flexible case of a coalition formation is the dynamic formation. In this case, during the optimization, an initial plan of problem solving is formed same as for the static coalition. However, in case of deviation from the plan, a return is made by changing the structure of the coalition, for example, by adding a new participant or reassigning and rescheduling subtasks. To do this, the rules for the formation of the coalition should describe actions for extraordinary situations, as well as the overall benefit of the coalition, so the plan of action is dynamically recalculated considering the context of the task has changed.

One of the following parameters can be used to evaluate the coalition efficiency:

- Minimizing the energy spent. Since all robots are autonomous it means that they used electrical or fuel power (or both) to move and perform any kind of actions. Therefore, the solution of each task or sub-task can be estimated by the energy (charge of the battery of fuel level) $E_k(T_i)$ of the robot k that is spent to solve it by using own competencies:

$$E_k(T_i) = \sum_j f_{T_i}\left(b_j^k\right) \cdot \varphi(T_i, k, j) \tag{7}$$

The exact amount of energy spent on solving the problem is not possible to estimate precisely due to the influence of a large number of external and internal factors. However, based on average data over the similar problems, it is possible to obtain an approximate estimation, which, however, introduces fuzziness into the final decision to form a coalition. In this case, the robots are interested in spending minimum energy with the maximum efficiency. The coalition efficiency can be estimated as relation of the number of solved problems to the total energy expended:

$$v\left(K_{T_i}\right) = Payoff(T_i) - \min_{K_i \in k} \sum_{j \in K_i} E_j(T_i) \tag{8}$$

- Robot uptime can serve as an analogue of the estimated energy expended. Robots are consisting of a great amount of parts and units and each of them has the probability of failure, which increases as the operation proceeds. Solution of each task requires a certain time of unit operation. Thus, the estimation of failure probability is the ratio of the time difference between the time of the node work and the average uptime of this type of robot units: $P_{C_i} = \frac{T_{c_i}^w - T_{c_i}^m}{T_{c_i}^{avg}}$, where P_{C_i} – failure probability of unit c_i by robot r_j, $T_{c_i}^w$ – total work duration of the unit c_i, $T_{c_i}^m$ – last maintenance time point. The probability of entire robot failure is evaluated according to the maximum probability of nodes failure $P_r = \max_i P_{c_i}$. An estimation of this probability is also approximate and bring fuzziness in solution of coalition game. The efficiency criterion in this case will be the maximum duration of the coalition's overall work to the next maintenance, which requires such a distribution of tasks among the participants, so that the probability of coalition member failure will be minimal.
- Maximizing the coalition benefit. For example, in relation to precision farming, the coalition's benefit is the cumulative crop of all cultures on the field. This requires coordinated and timely interaction of all robots in a dynamic coalition. The value of the solution of the problem decreases with the passage of time: the longer the task is postponed, the less benefit it can provide. For example, untimely watering due to the lack of robots in a coalition with a enough supply of water can cause the death of a crop, which will reduce the potential benefit. Thus, the choice of coalition participants and the distribution of tasks among them should be carried out in such a way as to minimize downtime and, accordingly, to maximize the overall benefit of the coalition.

6 Implementation of a Fuzzy Cooperative Game Over Smart Contracts

In this section, the implementation of the rules of the coalition game is proposed by means of smart contracts that describe the interaction of robots during the coalition formation. This is enabled by the ability of smart contracts within the scope of blockchain technology to describe complex algorithms by using the Turing-complete programming language. Examples include Solidity for the Ethereum platform [28] or GoLang and JavaScript for Hyperledger Fabric [29]. To date, many platforms for blockchain organization have been developed, a comparison of the main ones is presented in Table 1.

Table 1. Overview of existing blockchain platforms.

Platform	Permissions	Consensus protocol	Smart contract (language)	Performance (trans/sec, tps)
Bitcoin [30]	Public	Proof-of-Work	Partly	Up to 7
Ethereum [28]	Public & private	Proof-of-Work	Yes (Solidity)	15–25
Corda [31]	Public	PBFT, PoET	Yes (Java)	170
HyperLedger (Fabric, Burrow) [29]	Public & private	Pluggable (PBFT, PoET)	Yes (Go, Java, Python)	3500
Symbiont [21]	Private	BFT	Yes (Python)	~80000
Kadena	Public & private	PBFT, SmartBF	Partly (Pact lang.)	7000
Quorum (ETH, enterprise)	Private	FBA	Yes (Solidity)	35–130
HydraChain (ETH)	Private	Proof-of-Work	Yes (Python)	15–25
Exonum [32]	Private	FBA, PBFT	Yes, Rust	5000

To use the blockchain for storing the results of a coalition game and organizing interaction between robots in precision farming, several requirements must be observed. The platform used should support the organization of public and private blockchain structures. Since the consistency of the data exchanged by robots is important when solving the problem of precision farming, the consensus algorithm used should correctly handle disconnection or coupling of some nodes (presented by robots). To store the core of the coalition and the particular tasks of robots, the ability to describe any algorithm in a smart contract is required. For this, the language used to describe the contract must be Turing-complete, that is, provide the ability to describe algorithms of any complexity. And the last requirement is the speed of transaction processing for the rapid dissemination of verified data between coalition members, which will ensure the speed of decision-making in a critical situation. Table 1 provides a comparison of the main platforms according to the requirements presented above.

Table 1 also shows that the Hyperledger Fabric platform meets the most presented requirements. Its detailed description and adaptation to the tasks of precision farming will be presented later in Sect. 6.2.

6.1 Smart Contract Theory

The idea of smart contract was proposed in 1994 by Nick Szabo. He had defined smart contract as "a set of promises, specified in digital form, including protocols within which the parties perform on these promises." [33] The example of resource exchange is presented on Fig. 4.

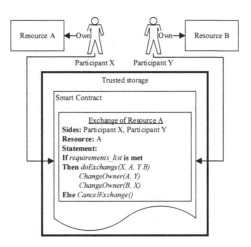

Fig. 4. Smart contract usage example [2].

In scope of the current level of information systems, smart contracts are viewed as decentralized applications that are available to all sides of the contract through the cloud of in decentralized way, for instance, blockchain. Due to the use of Turing-complete language for contract description, it is possible to implement rather complex algorithms. At the same time, it is mandatory to have conditions under which the contract must be executed as well as the list of actions assigned to the submitted conditions. All conditions of a smart contract must be described in a strong mathematical way and provide clear execution logic. In this regard, the first smart contracts in the blockchain are created to formalize the simplest relationships and consist of a small number of conditions.

To be valid and trusted smart contracts have to be signed by all sides with their private key [34] and sent as a transaction to be written to in the cloud or decentralized storage. After signing by all contract sides, the smart contract comes into force. To ensure the automated performance of contract obligations, an environment of existence is required that allows fully automated execution of contracts. This means that smart contracts can only exist within an environment that has unrestricted access to executable code of smart contract objects. Having unimpeded access to the objects of the contract, the smart contract monitors the specified conditions of achievement or violation of the points and makes independent decisions based on the programmed conditions. Thus, the main principle of a smart contract is the complete automation and reliability of the performance of contractual relations between participants.

6.2 Smart Contracts for Robot Coalition Formation

Figure 5 shows the scheme of interaction of robots in the coalition by means of a blockchain. It is proposed to use two kinds of chains in the blockchain network system for robot interaction: (i) for storing resources and (ii) for storing contracts. All system resources including consumables, energy, reward, which are represented by tokens, are stored in the resources chains. In the chain with contracts, the rules of cooperative game are stored, which are used by the robot's coordinators during the coalition forming and the distribution of tasks. The first contracts in the chain of contracts are rules for processing tasks and assigning coalition core. New task is formed with a program interface outside a coalition by problem manager, or by the cores of another coalition in case of obtaining a new context that cannot be processed by the existing coalition. New tasks are stored in the contract chain of the blockchain, from where they become available for all coalition cores. Tasks contain a formalized description of the goal, the initial parameters and the amount of reward for the solution.

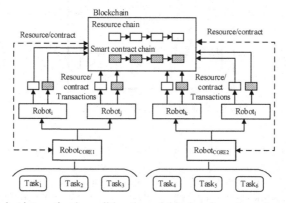

Fig. 5. Robot interaction in coalition through blockchain and smart contracts [2].

The robot coordinator selects robots guided by contracts that describe their competencies and reward expectations, as well as the rules of the cooperative game, defined for the subject area to which the task belongs. If the robot can participate in several coalitions, each robot coordinator calculates the cooperative game core and win for each of the coalitions, as well as the availability of sufficient resources for the robot successful work. If there are enough resources for robot's operations, it can participate in several coalitions. Otherwise, the robot is assigned to a coalition for which it can bring the highest benefit. The reward for the successful solution of the problem is distributed among the coalition members based on the reward rules for the cooperative game, described in the code of the relevant contract.

The blockchain network for the case study has been implemented based on the Hyperledger Fabric platform that is provided by community of software and hardware companies leading by IBM [29]. The platform provides possibilities of wide range configurations: changing of a core database for transactions and block storing, changing of consensus mechanisms, and changing signature algorithms for peers' interaction with blockchain. For the case study presented in the paper, the default configuration has been used that includes Byzantine Fault Tolerate consensus mechanism based on BFT-SMaRT core [35], Apache CouchDB as a database and an internal solution for peer certification. This configuration provides processing of more than 3500 transactions per second with latency of hundred milliseconds.

The choice of the Hyperledger Fabric platform is also justified by the peculiarities of its architecture, which makes it easy to adapt the coalition structure obtained when calculating the coalition game into the platform structure (see Fig. 6). The main elements of the architecture are nodes, divided into three levels: "Client", "Peer", "Orderer". Client level corresponds to robots whose main task is to conduct reconnaissance and send data, or to perform operations and report on their performance. In precision farming, such robots can be individual harvester combine tools, scouts, and transport robots. Above them, in terms of level, are devices that collect information and execute the code of contracts – "Peer" that can be presented by control block of harvester combine. Their main task is to collect information from the lower level, process it using smart contracts and transfer it to the upper level, in which information will be disseminated and stored. The upper level – "Orderer" - corresponds to the "Blackboard" device in the robot interaction scheme on Fig. 2. Its task is to store information in the appropriate block chain, to ensure the coordination and distribution of the new block between other Orderers or between Peers.

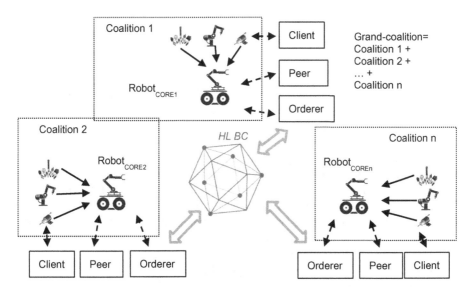

Fig. 6. Model of robot interaction through Hyperledger Fabric blockchain platform.

The Hyperledger Fabric platform also provides possibility to create smart contracts called chaincodes (program code that describes interaction between resources) using Go or Java programming languages. The chaincodes are running in isolated containers of core peers of Hyperledger based on the Docker technology stack. Each chaincode contains rules for cooperative fuzzy game that used for coalition participants negotiation. The example of chaincode for core calculation is presented at listing 1.

Listing 1. Example of a chaincode for coalition core calculation [2].

```
var robots []Robot // Robot list
var tasks []Task      // Tasks to be solved
var core []FCG // Fuzzy coalition core
var coreMaxGain FGC   // Core with max gain
func coreCalc(stub shim.ChaincodeStubInterface, args []string)
(string, error) {
    robots[i], tasks[j] = args[i], args[j]
    core = FCGCalculation(robots, tasks) //according to equa-
    tion(2)
    for c in core {
      if c.gain > coreMaxGain.gain
        coreMaxGain = c
      }
      for rob in robots{
      // bind task for robot according to formula (1)
      stub.PutState(rob, c.getTask(rob)) // Estimate and fix
      processing time
      stub.PutState(c.getTask(rob), CalcProcTime(rob))
    }
  }
}
```

7 Conclusions

Solving the problems of precision farming requires the development of a new approaches, which provide the dynamic formation of a coalition of robots for processing fields taking into account the current situation. This paper presents an approach based on the use of fuzzy coalition games and blockchain technology.

The main difference of the presented approach is the integration of the mathematical apparatus of the fuzzy coalition game and the trusted information space based on the "blackboard" and blockchain technologies. Their combination ensured that the results of the coalition game are preserved in an unchanged form, which is important in the case of the interaction of competing agents, which are robots in the coalition. Competition arises because robots, in addition to interest in achieving common goals, pursue their own interest, which consists in obtaining the maximum individual gain.

Fuzziness in the presented approach serves as the fundamental component of realistic cooperation models when there exist fuzzy expectations of player and coalition benefits. When an effective solution is found, individual benefits for players (the agreement efficiency) increase, as well as the capability of the coalition to find an effective and stable agreement. The blockchain model allows to avoid the synchronization problem, which is critical for distributed negotiation algorithms with large robot populations.

The integration of fuzzy coalition games with smart contracts can make coalition formation more transparent and to smooth out the operations of the tasks. The use of Internet of Things (IoT) concept with the blockchain, provides continuous tracking of food, from warehouses to manufacturers and enables verification at each stage of the precision agriculture task solving. If any stakeholder fails to meet the terms of the contract, for instance if a robot did not perform some operation on time, it would be clear for every party to see and new coalitions can be arranged dynamically.

The future work is aimed in developing smart contracts for participants changing in coalition. The changing process will be based on the negotiation between coalition core and robots outside the coalition that can perform task instead of failed coalition members.

Acknowledgements. The present research was supported by the projects funded through grants # 17-29-07073, of the Russian Foundation for Basic Research. The part of research is supported by the program №7 "New developments in the areas of energy, mechanics and robotics" of the Russian Academy of Sciences.

References

1. Mouradian, C., Sahoo, J., Glitho, R.H., Morrow, M.J., Polakos, P.A.: A coalition formation algorithm for Multi-Robot Task Allocation in large-scale natural disasters. In: 2017 13th International Wireless Communications and Mobile Computing Conference (IWCMC). IEEE, pp. 1909–1914 (2017)

2. Smirnov, A., Sheremetov, L., Teslya, N.: Fuzzy cooperative games usage in smart contracts for dynamic robot coalition formation: approach and use case description. In: ICEIS 2019 - Proceedings of the 21st International Conference on Enterprise Information Systems, pp. 349–358 (2019)

3. Cong, L.W., He, Z., Zheng, J.: Blockchain disruption and smart contracts. SSRN Electron. J. **48** (2017). https://doi.org/10.2139/ssrn.2985764

4. Delmolino, K., Arnett, M., Kosba, A., Miller, A., Shi, E.: Step by step towards creating a safe smart contract: lessons and insights from a cryptocurrency lab. In: Clark, J., Meiklejohn, S., Ryan, P.Y.A., Wallach, D., Brenner, M., Rohloff, K. (eds.) FC 2016. LNCS, vol. 9604, pp. 79–94. Springer, Heidelberg (2016). https://doi.org/10.1007/978-3-662-53357-4_6

5. Ordaz-Rivas, E., Rodríguez-Liñán, A., Torres-Treviño, L.: Collaboration of robot swarms with a relation of individuals with prey-predator type. Smart Technology, pp. 121–132. Lecture Notes of the Institute for Computer Sciences, Social Informatics and Telecommunications Engineering (2018)

6. Klusch, M., Gerber, A.: Dynamic coalition formation among rational agents. IEEE Intell. Syst. **17**, 42–47 (2002). https://doi.org/10.1109/MIS.2002.1005630

7. Kardos, C., Kovács, A., Váncza, J.: Decomposition approach to optimal feature-based assembly planning. CIRP Ann. **66**, 417–420 (2017). https://doi.org/10.1016/j.cirp.2017.04.002

8. Jennings, N.R., Faratin, P., Lomuscio, A.R., Parsons, S., Wooldridge, M., Sierra, C.: Automated negotiation: prospects, methods and challenges. Group Decis. Negot. **10**, 199–215 (2001). https://doi.org/10.1023/A:1008746126376

9. Hosam, H., Khaldoun, Z.: Planning coalition formation under uncertainty: auction approach. In: Proceedings - 2006 International Conference on Information and Communication Technologies: From Theory to Applications, ICTTA 2006, pp. 3013–3017. IEEE (2006)
10. Aubin, J.-P.: Cooperative Fuzzy Games. Math. Oper. Res. **6**, 1–13 (1981). https://doi.org/10.1287/moor.6.1.1
11. Kahan, J.P., Rapoport, A.: Theories of Coalition Formation. Lawrence Erlbaum Associates, Inc., Hillsdale (1984)
12. Gillies, D.B.: Some theorems on n-person games. Princeton University (1953)
13. Mareš, M.: Fuzzy Cooperative Games. Physica-Verlag HD, Heidelberg (2001). https://doi.org/10.1007/978-3-7908-1820-8
14. Shen, P., Gao, J.: Coalitional game with fuzzy payoffs and credibilistic core. Soft. Comput. **15**, 781–786 (2010). https://doi.org/10.1007/s00500-010-0632-9
15. Smirnov, A.V., Sheremetov, L.B.: Models of coalition formation among cooperative agents: the current state and prospects of research. Sci. Tech. Inf. Process. **39**, 283–292 (2012). https://doi.org/10.3103/S014768821205005X
16. Bayram, H., Bozma, H.I.: Coalition formation games for dynamic multirobot tasks. Int. J. Rob. Res. **35**, 514–527 (2015). https://doi.org/10.1177/0278364915595707
17. Verma, D., Desai, N., Preece, A., Taylor, I.: A block chain based architecture for asset management in coalition operations. In: Pham, T., Kolodny, M.A. (eds.) Proceedings of the SPIE 10190, Ground/Air Multisensor Interoperability, Integration, and Networking for Persistent ISR VIII, p. 101900Y (2017)
18. Dorri, A., Kanhere, S.S., Jurdak, R.: Towards an optimized BlockChain for IoT. In: Proceedings of the Second International Conference on Internet-of-Things Des Implement - IoTDI 2017, pp. 173–178 (2017). https://doi.org/10.1145/3054977.3055003
19. Zhang, Y., Wen, J.: The IoT electric business model: using blockchain technology for the internet of things. Peer-to-Peer Netw. Appl. **10**, 983–994 (2017). https://doi.org/10.1007/s12083-016-0456-1
20. Ferrer, E.C.: The blockchain: a new framework for robotic swarm systems. Adv. Intell. Syst. Comput. **881**, 1037–1058 (2019). https://doi.org/10.1007/978-3-030-02683-7_77
21. Cachin, C., Vukolić, M.: Blockchain Consensus Protocols in the Wild, 24 (2017). https://doi.org/10.4230/LIPIcs.DISC.2017.1
22. Teslya, N., Ryabchikov, I.: Blockchain-based platform architecture for industrial IoT. In: Conference of Open Innovation Association, FRUCT (2018)
23. Smirnov, A., Kashevnik, A., Ponomarev, A., Shilov, N.: Context-aware decision support in socio-cyberphysical systems: from smart space-based applications to human-computer cloud services. In: Demazeau, Y., Davidsson, P., Bajo, J., Vale, Z. (eds.) PAAMS 2017. LNCS (LNAI), vol. 10349, pp. 3–15. Springer, Cham (2017). https://doi.org/10.1007/978-3-319-59930-4_1
24. Sheremetov, L.B., Smirnov, A.V.: A fuzzy cooperative game model for configuration management for open supply networks. Contrib. Game Theory Manag. **4**, 433–446 (2011)
25. Sheremetov, L.B.: A model of fuzzy coalition games in problems of configuring open supply networks. J. Comput. Syst. Sci. Int. **48**, 765–778 (2009). https://doi.org/10.1134/S1064230709050116
26. Zadeh, L.A.: Similarity relations and fuzzy orderings. Inf. Sci. (Ny) **3**, 177–200 (1971). https://doi.org/10.1016/S0020-0255(71)80005-1
27. Haekwan, L., Tanaka, H.: Fuzzy approximations with non-symmetric fuzzy parameters in fuzzy regression analysis. J. Oper. Res. Soc. Jpn. **42**, 98–112 (1999)
28. Buterin, V.: A next-generation smart contract and decentralized application platform. Ethurum 1–36 (2014). https://doi.org/10.5663/aps.v1i1.10138
29. Androulaki, E., et al.: Hyperledger fabric. In: Proceedings of the Thirteenth EuroSys Conference on - EuroSys 2018, pp 1–15. ACM Press, New York (2018)

30. Nakamoto, S.: Bitcoin: a peer-to-peer electronic cash system. WwwBitcoinOrg 9 (2008). https://doi.org/10.1007/s10838-008-9062-0
31. Brown, R.G., Carlyle, J., Grigg, I., Hearn, M.: Corda : an introduction 1–15 (2016). https://doi.org/10.13140/RG.2.2.30487.37284
32. What is Exonum - Exonum Documentation (2018). https://exonum.com/doc/get-started/what-is-exonum/. Accessed 1 Mar 2018
33. Szabo, N.: Smart contracts: building blocks for digital markets copyright. In: alamut.com (1996). http://www.fon.hum.uva.nl/rob/Courses/InformationInSpeech/CDROM/Literature/LOTwinterschool2006/szabo.best.vwh.net/smart_contracts_2.html. Accessed 16 Sep 2017
34. Goldreich, O.: Foundations of cryptography, 1st edn. Cambridge University Press, Cambridge (2006)
35. Bessani, A., Sousa, J., Vukolić, M.: A byzantine fault-tolerant ordering service for the hyperledger fabric blockchain platform. In: Proceedings of the 1st Workshop on Scalable and Resilient Infrastructures for Distributed Ledgers - SERIAL 2017, pp. 1–10. ACM Press, New York (2017)

Business Layer: An Enterprise Approach for Workflow Engine and Record Management Systems Integration

João Pires, André Vasconcelos$^{(\boxtimes)}$ (iD), and José Borbinha (iD)

INESC-ID, Instituto Superior Técnico, Avenida Rovisco Pais 1, Lisbon, Portugal
joaopires_94@hotmail.com,
{andre.vasconcelos,jlb}@tecnico.ulisboa.pt

Abstract. Records management systems support organization in reaching business benefits when properly aligned with business processes. This paper frames records management in business process management by identifying the role records management plays in business. This research proposes Business Layer a solution that replaces a records management system workflow module by an open source solution, composed of an enterprise service bus and two workflow engines, whose capabilities are accessed through a single API. The business layer acts as the back end for the workflow module and allows it to communicate to several workflow engines through a single REST API. The API is develop in the WSO2 Enterprise Integrator ESB profile, where for each identified functionality, message transformation and forwarding integration flows are produced. The results show that the business layer is a flexible and scalable solution to the workflow modules. This paper supports that Records Management enables the automation of the document management, along with the management, monitoring and preservation of documents, increasing the efficiency of business activities.

Keywords: System integration · Records management · Business process management · Workflow · Enterprise service bus · REST API

1 Introduction

Document management is the way an organization stores, generates and monitors its documents. This information (existing in organizations, regardless of whether it is structured or unstructured) needs to be preserved through processes that allow the information to retain its probative value, through the recording of actions applied to stored documents and their correct management. Organizations need to ensure the preservation of documents during the period during which, according to regulations, it needs to be preserved. Document management implies practices such as the use of systems that support processes related to document management, called document management systems, which in themselves do not translate into the application of document management, requiring additional mechanisms such as the record of the activities performed in organizations.

© Springer Nature Switzerland AG 2020
J. Filipe et al. (Eds.): ICEIS 2019, LNBIP 378, pp. 134–153, 2020.
https://doi.org/10.1007/978-3-030-40783-4_8

The information and documents used and produced in organizations are associated with the various business activities that are carried out. Therefore it is necessary for organizations that apply document management to their business. Document management can assist business activities in the right way, i.e., framing document management in the business in a way that produces the most value. Thus, the implementation of a document management system, together with the definition of the desired document management and the business process analysis can increase the efficiency of the business activities.

The application of a document management system can lead to benefits such as dematerialization of paper documents, reduce of costs of searching, storing, and producing records, which is expected to increase the overall efficiency of business processes, mainly in relation to the automation of document processing work. Thus, proper implementation of document management can bring huge benefits to organizations, but it can also result in inefficiencies, returnless costs and missed opportunities if it is poorly implemented or if it is not aligned with the organization business processes.

In order to get the full benefits of records management organizations must develop several practices, including requirement specification, classification tables definition, and the implementation of records management systems that support records management processes.

Although Records management systems' implementation is an important step towards records management, other information, organizational, application, and strategic concerns must be addressed.

Thus, this paper frames records management in business process management, in order to identify the role of records management applied to the business processes. This paper contributes in the efficiency increasing of records management and business processes management by identifying the role that records management plays in business.

In order to frame records management regarding business process management.

There must be an identification to the benefits that come from an optimal interaction between records management and business.

This framing includes the development of a records management system, through the identification of requirements, system components and interaction with other systems. This research also pruposes a workflow module inside of a specific system, that supports the automatization records management tasks. The solution described in this paper is the back end of the workflow module in a records management system.

This paper also presents the key issues in the implementation of a records management system. In this research the role that records management plays regarding other business components, mainly business processes, is identified, allowing for the correct framing of records management regarding business process management.

After the introduction to the problem and the concept of records management and the benefits that come to an organization form applying it properly, in Sect. 2, the topics of business process management, records management, workflow and integration of systems are detailed. In Sect. 3 the solution to address the problems of developing RMS presented through the proposal of an architecture, functionalities, message behavior and finally through the development of a back end workflow module: the business layer. To identify benefits of the use of the proposed business layer, evaluate its functionality and consider if the problems presented were solved, in Sect. 4, including the development of a prototype to which tests were made, and the analysis of the results regarding the business layer are mentioned and the implementation of records management system are discussed. Finally, in Sect. 5, the main conclusions of the research are presented along with the future work.

2 Background

2.1 Business Process Management

Business process management (BPM), according to The Object Management Group [1], defined as "a method of efficiently aligning an organization with the wants and needs of clients". Dumas et al. [2] defines a business process as "a chain related events, activities and decisions that lead to a raise of value to an organization or for its clients. One or more actors participate in these processes and they also possess resources and artefacts associated" (Fig. 1).

Dumas et al. [2] refers to BPM as a continuous cycle of improvement, with the following phases:

- Process identification: development of an organization's process architecture;
- Process discovery: processes are documented as one or more models (As-is model);
- Process analysis: each process is evaluated regarding problem identification and impact and effort to solve each problem;
- Process redesign: changes are made to processes and result in a new process model (To-be model);
- Process implementation: processes are implemented, regarding changes in the organization's culture and technology to support new processes;
- Process monitoring and controlling: data gathering from the execution of processes is used to identify new problems, giving birth to a new iteration of the cycle.

To model business processes, the most important notation used is the Business process modelling notation (BPMN), being an easy to use graphical modelling notation, which produces easy to understand processes [1]. Along with this notation, also

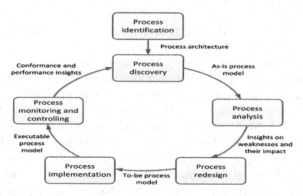

Fig. 1. Business Process Management continuous cycle of improvement [2].

other notations that complement the use of BPMN, such as Case management modelling notation (CMMN), which supports case management, Decision modelling notation (DMMN), which provides support regarding decision making and XPDL, which "provides a standard mechanism for defining and executing business processes, allowing interoperability" [3].

Process Identification. In the process identification stage (of the Process Management cycle [2]) the process are identified according to the purpose of the modeling. Therefore, the same tasks, developed by the same actors may be modeled as different processes, according to the concerns. Consider, for instance, the process of *painting a car*, performed in the factory, and in the greenhouse by a mechanic, and a painter – see Fig. 2.

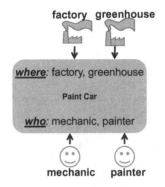

Fig. 2. Paint car business process.

The paint car business process may be decomposed into different business processes according to the concerns of the stakeholders. For instance if the concern is on managing spaces, manage people, or both, different modeling scenarios will be developed – see Fig. 3.

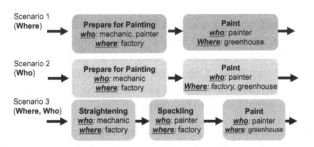

Fig. 3. Decomposition of "Paint car", under "Where", "Who", and "Where, Who" Concerns.

Several other business process identification criteria may be used considering different concerns including Management, Audit, Optimization, Automation, Competence/Skills, quality, cost, among others.

2.2   Records Management

"Records management has the goal of providing efficient and systematic control over the production, reception, maintenance, utilization and destination of records, including the processes to constitute and maintain evidence and information about activities and transactions" [4]. Records management, as referred by [4], includes the application of several practices regarding documentation, including simple ones such as ordering and development of classification tables and more advanced ones such as the implementation of a records management system. Standards such as MoReq 2010, ISO 15489:2016 and ISO/PDTR 21965 are guidelines that support the development of records management in an organization, including the structure and processes a records management system should possess regarding the management of information stored [5] (Fig. 4).

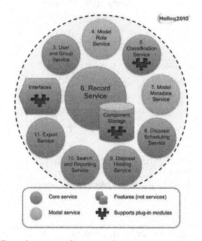

Fig. 4. Modular Requirements for records management systems (MoReq) [5].

Implementation of Records Management in Organizations. APDSI [6] identifies obstacles to the correct implementation of a records management system in organizations, such as the lack of interoperability and loss of business process due to focus only on document procedures. APDSI [6] also proposes guidelines that would lead to a correct implementation of records management, such as analysis of the organization's reality and processes, formation of users and proper selection of information systems that follow requirements based on standards such as MoReq 2010 [5] but that also adjust to the records management desired to be applied.

GfiDoc. "GfiDoc is and innovative solution in total alignment with the European standard MoReq (Model Requirements for the Management of Electronic Records) and with new digital tendencies. It ensures an integrated and complete capture, registry and management of all document's life cycle. GfiDoc is characterized by its functional richness, simplicity and ergonomic utilization or administration. It provides a robust integration layer, allowing the aggregation of documental evidence from other business applications, while also providing workflows." [7].

GfiDoc provides workflows through its workflow module, that uses the system K2, mainly through its framework SmartObjects, which allows for GfiDoc to possess an interface managed by K2 in its workflow module. The workflows present in GfiDoc's are called document-centric workflows, which Marchetti et al. defines as "the automation and administration of particular document procedures" [8]. Many records management systems possess workflow modules, which are workflow management systems that hold these workflows, that possess only activities regarding the management of records stored in the records management systems such as GfiDoc.

2.3   Enterprise Service Bus

Zdun [9] refers that the use of an enterprise services bus as a mediator for communicating applications, on top of SOA, allows these to communicate by using adaptors regardless of the communication protocols supported, because of the capabilities over messages that an enterprise service bus possesses. In this way, applications that only support REST protocols (being the most used nowadays) can communicate with an application that only supports SOAP protocols, due to the utilization of an enterprise service bus, that mediates the messages.

An example of an enterprise service bus is WSO2 Enterprise Integrator, an open source solution, which possesses an enterprise service bus as a main component, illustrated in Fig. 5. It also possesses other profiles to better the integration experience, such as a Message broker profile that provides queueing and message storage capabilities to the enterprise service bus profile.

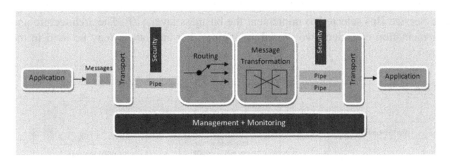

Fig. 5.   Enterprise service bus profile architecture of WSO2 Enterprise Integrator [10].

3   Business Layer: The Proposed Solution

Business processes and records management have a relevant contribution in organization efficiency levels. Thus, the alignment among records management systems and organization business processes are central for the organization success.

A records management system should comply to the requirements and structure proposed by standards such as MoReq 2010, which identified additional services such as a workflow module for enabling the optimization of tasks related to document handling. This module would also support the automation of activities of business processes. For this reason, the requirements and architecture definition is required for a functional workflow module as a component of a records management system.

This research was applied to GfiDoc, a records management system referred in Sect. 2.2. This application supports the records management framing in the business process management context. In this research a workflow module was replaced that used the system K2 and its framework, SmartObjects and presented two problems that needed to be solved regarding the module.

Firstly, flexibility is central challenge. Since the workflow module functionality depends on K2, the GFIDoc solution was not able to use any workflow engines to support GfiDoc's workflow module. Therefore, besides the full dependence of on vendor (vendor lock-in), GFIDoc did not have effective control in its module interface, since the actions are received and processed by K2 (through SmartObjects).

Secondly, the overall cost of the solution was a major problem, since K2 requires the acquisition of a paid license contributing to increase considerably the total cost of ownership of the solution.

This section describes the architecture of the solution proposed for replacing the GfiDoc's workflow module. The solution proposed is based on an enterprise service bus that supports the communication, through a REST API, to other workflow modules. The enterprise service bus is expected to replace the K2 system and its SmartObjects ensuring workflow management support.

The solution proposed is named "business layer" and is presented in Fig. 6. Business layer is supported by an Enterprise Service Bus that receives messages, transforms and redirects them among workflow engines. WSO2 Enterprise Integrator is the Enterprise Service Bus selected to implement the business layer [10]. The architecture and implementation considers two workflow engines, but any others may be used in the future.

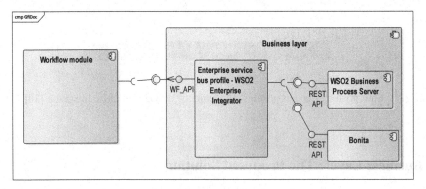

Fig. 6. Architecture of the proposed solution [11].

The decision to use two different workflow engines ensures that there won't be a point-to-point communication between the enterprise service bus and a specific workflow engine. Two open source systems were considered for the business layer: Bonita Community edition and WSO2 Business Process Server.

In order to the business layer supports a workflow module and to provide correctly workflow management capabilities, the following functionalities are defined:

- List workflows;
- Generate instance of a workflow;
- Give task to a user;
- Complete task;
- Cancel a workflow instance;
- Suspend/Active the instantiation from a specific workflow.

Additionally, there are four more functionalities, which consists of events that are triggered when the following actions occur in the workflow engines:

- When a workflow instance is created;
- When a new pending task appears;
- When a task is completed;
- When a workflow instance ends.

In these four cases, the workflow engine sends a message directly to the workflow module (GfiDoc) notifying about the event that occurred, along with the information related to the workflow/task in question so that GfiDoc can store the information about the event. In the case of the other functionalities, the message is sent from GfiDoc

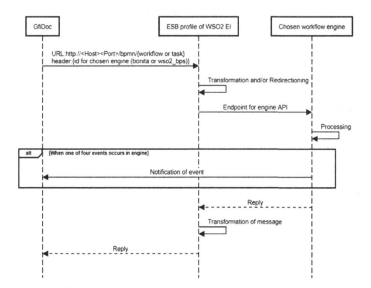

Fig. 7. Messages of GfiDoc with business layer [11].

asking for an action to be performed to the business layer. The message is treated by the enterprise service bus, which transforms and redirects it as needed, sending the message to the API of the chosen engine, as shown in Fig. 7.

3.1 Data Model and Interface

In order to record data regarding the workflow and task in GFIDoc, changes were done in the data model. Therefore Workflow and Task entities were added in the existing data model – see Fig. 8. Workflows and tasks metadata are recorded in the attributes of each information entity.

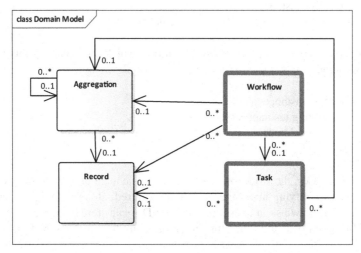

Fig. 8. Entities added to the data model (with thicker and red border) and their relations [11]. (Color figure online)

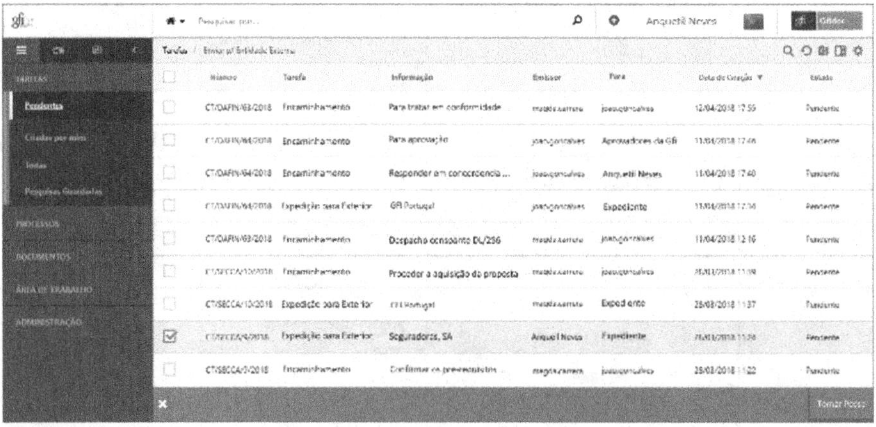

Fig. 9. New interface showing pending workflows [11].

Being able to store information essential for the workflow module, a user interface was also developed in GfiDoc. This interface, completely controlled by GfiDoc, is not dependent of any other system like the last one, which belonged to K2. This interface presented in Fig. 9 shows a list of pending workflows to instantiate.

3.2 Business Layer

Requirements. The business layer requirements, regarding the support GFIDoc workflow module, are summarized in Table 1. The requirements were identified by GFIDoc users as major issues that must be addressed.

Table 1. Detailed requirements of the business layer [11].

Requirement	Description
REquation 1	Allow the modelling of workflows using tools compatible with the notation BPMN 2.0
REquation 2	Process workflow autonomously and deliver results to GfiDoc
REquation 3	Present the state of a workflow graphically
REquation 4	Maintain independence of specific workflow engine
REquation 5	Allow the use of more than one workflow engine simultaneously

The comparison, in Table 2, of the requirements and the technologies that allow to perform them, show that, using the business layer, all requirements are fulfilled. Even though neither one of the two engines used can fulfil requirements 3 and 4, the enterprise service bus introduces capabilities that fulfil them and show the business layer can support GfiDoc's workflow engine.

Table 2. Detailed requirements of the business layer [11].

Requirement	Bonita	WSO2 business process server	Business layer (ESB and engines)
REquation 1	Yes	Yes	Yes
REquation 2	Yes	Yes	Yes
REquation 3	No	Yes	Yes
REquation 4	No	No	Yes
REquation 5	No	No	Yes

Enterprise Service Bus Profile of WSO2 Enterprise Integrator. According to the functionalities requested for the business layer, a service was defined, resulting in the development of a REST API that is the API that receives messages from GfiDoc. In the API there are the resources workflow and task, to better explain where each functionality are applied. For example, for the actions "Give task to a user", "Complete task" and "Suspend/Active the instantiation from a specific workflow", the services are accessible through the URL http://<Host> <Port>/bpmn/task, the HTTP method POST, the header "software" indicating the engine desired (with value "bonita" or "wso2_bps") and with a field, in the body, named "action" that has the value of "claim", "complete" and "suspend/activate", respectively. For a service to be applied on the workflow resource, for example the action "Cancel a workflow instance", the URL is http://<Host> <Port>/bpmn/task.

The integration flows in the enterprise service bus, that indicate the steps through which the message goes through until it is sent to a workflow engine, were develop using the tool WSO2 Developer Studio, that allows a graphical modelling of the integration flows, that are translated in run time to an XML that describes the API. For each functionality of the first six for the business layer, an integration flow was developed, given that the other four, regarding events, are done by each of the workflow engines. In each integration flow, the redirection to the desired workflow engines is enabled by a mediator called switch mediator, that chooses a path of the flow to take depending on the value of the header that chooses the workflow engine. Figure 10 shows the integration flow for the functionality "Generate instance of a workflow", where there are three branches because, regarding whether a workflow needs variables or not to be instantiated, the message format differs.

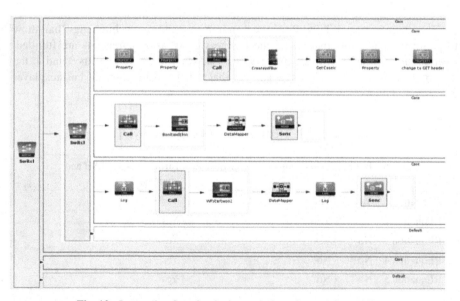

Fig. 10. Integration flow for the instantiation of a workflow [11].

Bonita. We use Bonita as a workflow engine, in the business layer, since its REST API can already receive messages from the enterprise service bus used.

The first workflow modelled in the workflow engines is a simple workflow, composed of two events, a start event and an end event, and one task named "Send message" that receives two variables "remetent" and "message". This ad-hoc workflow is meant to simulate the sending of a message to a certain user and is modelled in BPMN 2.0.

For the sending of messages, since the use of listeners and events are not available in the open source version of Bonita (Community edition), a connector called REST connector was used, that allows, for each of the 4 events defined, sending of a REST message to a URL (being this URL specified as the one to GfiDoc). The message to send, for each event of each task/workflow, is written in Groovy.

WSO2 Business Process Server. Following the same development as in Bonita, a workflow identical to the ad-hoc workflow modelled in Bonita was modelled to be uploaded to the WSO2 Business Process Server, by creating an Activiti project with the workflow in BPMN 2.0, as shown in Fig. 11. Since, in this case, we can use listeners and events, written in *Java*, these just have to be associated with the workflow and its task, associating a different event to each of the four events, because the data sent to GfiDoc in the case of each of the four events differs from one another. In Fig. 11, besides the workflow modelled, there are also represented the associations for the two events regarding workflows, where we associate the event "start" for the event of when a workflow instance is created and "end" for when a workflow instance ends.

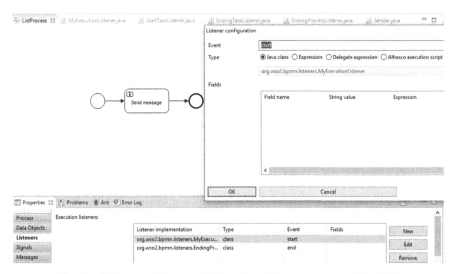

Fig. 11. Ad-hoc workflow modelled, and workflow events associated [11].

4 Results and Discussion

The proposed solution was assessed, firstly at the integration between the business layer and GfiDoc's module. Performance and scalability is assessed by injecting messages from users simultaneously. After it is evaluated if the business layer supports the back end of a workflow module in a records management system.

Thus, after demonstrating the business layer solution, assessing the solution qualities (including throughput, cost and flexibility) the problems identified in Sect. 3 are discussed, and the additional benefits of the proposes solution are described.

4.1 Demonstration

A prototype was developed to evaluate if the business layer can act as a back end for GfiDoc's workflow module. As presented in Fig. 12, the prototype uses a HTTP server to receive messages from the engines in the business layer regarding events and uses a REST client, Postman, to send messages to the business layer REST API (WF_API).

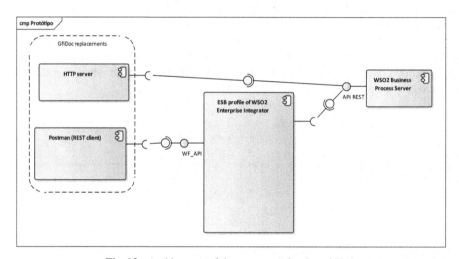

Fig. 12. Architecture of the prototype developed [11].

The test of the prototype was developed according to [12], by sending simultaneous messages to simulate an increasing number of simultaneous users and calculating the throughput value for each set of messages sent and processed by the engine of the business layer. By comparing the throughput obtained and its growing rate, these shows if the system is a good workflow management system compatible with the notation BPMN 2.0. The message chosen to be the same sent in all messages is for the instantiation of a workflow, given it requires processing from the system. The sequence of messages that will happen for each message sent in the test is the same as the one illustrated in Fig. 13.

As a comparing measure, the tests performed on the business layer were also performed with a point to point communication between the REST client (Postman) and WSO2 Business Process Server. The only difference in this case is that messages, instead

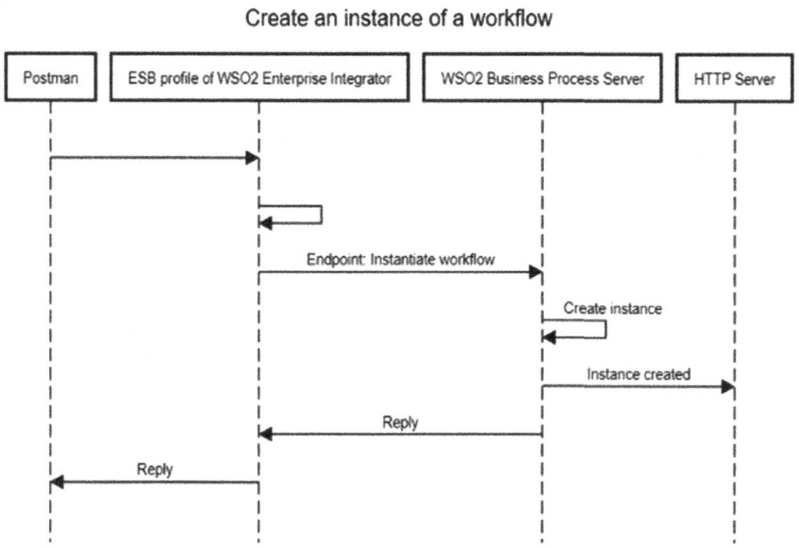

Create an instance of a workflow

Fig. 13. Sequence of each message performed in the test [11].

of being treated by the enterprise service bus, go directly to WSO2 Business Process Server. This way not only the functionality of the business layer is evaluated, but also if the use of the enterprise service bus as a mediator of the messages is beneficial or not to support the business layer and GfiDoc.

4.2 Results

Throughput. The results of the tests performed using Jmeter are illustrated in Fig. 14, which shows that the business layer is an acceptable workflow management system and can support GfiDoc's workflow module. Also, the use of an enterprise service bus is beneficial and guarantees a scalable solution. The throughput values obtained show that, when using an enterprise service bus, the throughput values are always higher than when there is a point-to-point communication with the workflow engine.

The values shown regarding throughput could be even greater if more profiles of WSO2 Enterprise Integrator would be used, given that the queueing capabilities are much greater when also using the Message broker profile. Also, the API and integration flows developed lack optimizations regarding performance, given that they intend to show most of all the functionality of the business layer.

Adding to these results, latency was tested, which results are presented in Fig. 15, showing that the messages processed with the help of the enterprise service bus are in average faster than in the other test case, that proves the use of the business layer for GfiDoc's workflow module.

Price. Since the business layer is, for now, only composed of open source systems, the use of this system comparing to the use of a proprietary system like K2 presents less

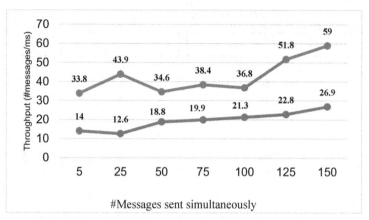

Fig. 14. Values of throughput for the test cases of using an enterprise service bus (blue) and only using and workflow engine (red) [11]. (Color figure online)

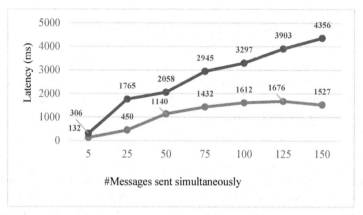

Fig. 15. Values of latency for the test cases of using an enterprise service bus (blue) and only using and workflow engine (red) [11]. (Color figure online)

costs. Therefore, cost wise, the use of the business layer in GfiDoc's workflow module presents a cheaper solution than its predecessor.

Regarding the cost of development, the business layer possesses a high development time to implement a workflow module, given the low amount and quality of support that exists regarding open source technology, relying mostly on user forums or on paid support packages, that still are cheaper than the acquisition of most proprietary systems such as K2.

Furthermore, because the business layer is composed of open source systems, according to [13], it also possesses the following benefits:

- "Test before buying";
- "Lower cost to start";
- "More simplistic and easier to understand";
- "No mishmash";
- "Availability of the source code and the right to modify it";
- "Right to redistribute modifications and improvements to the code".

Additionally, given that many cloud services vendors charge based on CPU usage, the use of the enterprise service bus profile of WSO2 Enterprise Integrator, which is an XML that describes all the API and can be uploaded to the server, is a lightweight solution to deploy in the cloud.

Flexibility. Regarding the challenges referred in Sect. 3 about the use of K2 preventing other workflow engines from being used, the business layer does not suffer from this problem, allowing several workflow engines to be implemented in the layer and to even be used simultaneously.

To add another workflow engine to the business layer, the integration flow, after analysis of the engine's available functionalities and REST API, needs to be developed and all endpoints added. Additionally, in the workflow engine, there needs to be a way to send messages to GfiDoc in the referred events, whether by using listeners like in WSO2 Business Process Server or a *REST connector* like in Bonita. Having done this, with the adding of another possible value for the header of the message for the selection of this workflow engine, it can be used by GfiDoc's workflow module.

4.3 Main Contributions

Through the proposal and development of the business layer, the workflow module of GfiDoc is now a more flexible and cheaper solution. The development of an open source solution that allows the communication with several workflows' engines and the use of their capabilities through a single REST API, being also a scalable and lightweight solution, is an attractive solution for a back end of a workflow module. Using a workflow module in a records management system, the task regarding records management are automatized, and human error in records processing are reduced.

The simultaneous use of several workflow engines is not advised, but can be useful in exceptional cases, such as when a migration of processes from an engine to another occurs.

By using a records management system aligned with an organization's business processes and culture, the usage of documents and the efficiency of business activities are optimized. This also allows the automatic generation of records to act as evidence for the execution of these activities, having in mind that the perseverance and management of all records stored, according to records management standards such as MoReq 2010.

4.4 Discussion

In this section we analyse how a records management system, such as GfiDoc, and the workflow module developed in Sect. 3 should be implemented in an organization.

Since organization's activities have as main focus the business and the generation of value, the focus on records of the records management systems show that these cannot be a central platform for a business. Instead, records management systems, along with other practices of records management must act as support for the business, mainly for the business processes. These business processes are orchestrators of activities that have the objective of producing value for the organization and the records management systems need to be able to generate records that prove these executions and support activities that utilize records stored in the system.

Does this mean that workflows are not necessary? [14] refers that workflow are meant to automatize only manual tasks and business processes are composed of manual tasks and service calls to other systems, like workflow management systems. Furthermore, Ruh and Gold-Bernstein [14] also refer that workflow management focus on the optimization of processes, while business process management focus on a continuous improvement lifecycle. Therefore, to perform complex calls, made by business processes, to certain systems such as records management systems, workflow modules can be used to automatize these workflows.

This way, the implementation of records management in an organization needs to be aligned with the existing business processes and how these are managed, while also having in mind the culture and reality of the organization, for optimal benefits to be achieved.

Obstacles to the Implementation of Records Management. Although the benefits of the application of records management in organizations that include the implementation of a records management system such as GfiDoc, according to [6], only 74% of organizations interviewed in Portugal possess records management systems implemented, and not all possess integration with business processes. In order to analyse why records management systems are not implemented in every organization, along with their workflow modules such as the one developed in Sect. 3, which introduces an open source and flexible solution to increase business efficiency, the main obstacles identified that lead to an incorrect or inexistent integration of records management and business process management are described in the following subsections.

Wrong Idea of Records Management. Records management and its benefits are not totally acknowledged by organizations; the benefits of the management of information are but the ones regarding the increase of business efficiency when integrated with the business are not. Also, records management is not only about acquiring a records management system, because it requires other practices to be applied such as the development of classification tables, control access lists and analysis of the business processes. By only implementing a records management system and not integrating with any other systems and practices because they are not seen as essential components to the business, some organizations undervalue records management, seeing it as a cost to comply with regulations and not as an investment to achieve benefits for the business.

Using the architecture proposed in this paper, the organization can possess a records management system with a set of workflows that increase the efficiency of the business and benefits from applying records management. As shown in Sect. 5, the business layer supports the workflow module and can provide an increase in efficiency for the organization's business.

Business Process with Low Maturity. In a Portuguese public administration organization, the records management system is used as a main platform and is not integrated with its business processes because these do not present a maturity level high enough to support be business, leading to a greater focus of records management and loss of context in the business when executing workflows. Having acknowledge this, the organization has not been able to optimize its business process due to a strong resistance to change, which along with the limited interoperability that its records management system possesses with other systems, leads to the use of paper documents.

Regardless of the benefits that can come from implementing a records management system such as GfiDoc, with a workflow module that introduces flexibility and cost reduction to an organization, if the business processes cannot support records management practices, there are going to be inefficiencies. The organization will still benefit from using the records management system, which will store its documents and increase the automation of workflows, but optimal benefits from aligning these with business processes cannot be achieved. Additionally, there is the danger of loss of business context and incorrect modelling of the workflows, given that most of the workflows in the workflow module are modelled by the organization and these workflows can present the same problem that for the business processes, which is a low maturity level, that leads to an inefficient records management performed by the records management system.

Framing Records Management. Having in mind that records management is a business component that supports an organization's business processes, these processes need to be adjusted to the desired records management, implying the identification of problems and new modelling of business processes by an organization. These processes, according to the business process management cycle referred in Sect. 2.1, are executed and data is gathered from this execution to identify possible improvements to the processes.

Furthermore, [15] refers that, when defining the architecture of an organization, records management must accounted for. This way, we conclude that records management is present in all phases of the business process management lifecycle, as a support business rather than an independent area of an organization's business.

5 Conclusions

Records management in organizations, through the application of practices such as the use of capabilities in document management systems, ensures benefits such as the dematerialization of paper documents, the preservation of the organization's memory business process optimization, increased efficiency in terms of time and workload reduction, and document-centric workflows.

In this paper, the workflow module of the GfiDoc document management system was presented, which initially used K2 system technology as a workflow management engine and wanted to develop a back end for the cheapest and most flexible workflow module.

In order to support the workflow module, the Business Layer solution is proposed in this paper. This solution uses an enterprise service bus and one or more business process management system engines, and may be added further if desired by client organizations.

GFIDoc Workflow module was replaced by business layer, an open source, scalable and flexible solution. This solution was defining considering the requirements and architectural components of a records management system. Business layer supports the integration to different workflow engine through a common REST API, besides acting as a back end of GfiDoc's workflow module.

An API was developed in the WSO2 Enterprise Integrator ESB profile, where for each identified functionality, message transformation and forwarding integration flows were produced for each of the execution engines analyzed. In order to report events to GfiDoc, in each business layer management business process management system, Bonita and WSO2 Business Process Server, REST connectors and event-associated listener classes were implemented.

During this research several common problems in records management system implementation were identified and assessed allowing the identification of the role that records management play in the organizations. Therefore this research frames records management in business process management supporting the conclusion that records management is a central asset for business process management, which optimizes the usage of records and the generation of records that act as evidence for the actions done in the business.

Thus, Record Management is correctly applied when aligned with business processes and considers the constraints of organizations. Participating in all phases of the BPM cycle, document management is a business-critical and supportive area that must be taken into account in the business process management cycle, enabling the automation of the document management, along with ensuring the management, monitoring and preservation capabilities of all documents, as well as increasing the efficiency of business activities.

Acknowledgements. The authors express their gratitude to Gfi Portugal, mainly João Portugal and Anquetil Neves for all the help and for the opportunity provided in making the research for this paper.

This work was supported by national funds through Fundação para a Ciência e a Tecnologia (FCT) with reference UID/CEC/50021/2019 and by the European Commission program H2020 under the grant agreement 822404 (project QualiChain).

References

1. Object Management Group (OMG): Business Process Model and Notation (BPMN) (Version 2.0.2). Object Management Group, Needham (2013)
2. Dumas, M., La Rosa, M., Mendling, J., Reijers, H.: Fundamentals of Business Process Management, 1st edn. Springer, Heidelberg (2013). https://doi.org/10.1007/978-3-642-33143-5
3. White, S.: XPDL and BPMN. SeeBeyond, Monrovia (2017)

4. Direção-Geral de Arquivos (DGARQ): Recomendações para a produção de: Planos de Preservação Digital (Recommendations for the production of: Digital Preservation Plans). Lisbon, November 25th, 2011 (2011)
5. DLM Forum Foundation: Modular Requirements for Records System(MOREQ) 2010, version 1.1 (2011). ISBN 978-92-79-18519-9, https://doi.org/10.2792/2045
6. Associação para a Promoção e Desenvolvimento da Sociedade da Informação (APDSI): O Estado da Arte na Gestão Documental em Portugal (State of art of Records management in Portugal). Lisbon (2016)
7. Microsoft: GfiDoc (2017). https://www.microsoft.com/pt-pt/azurebizcenter/GfiDoc.aspx. Accessed 15 Nov 2017
8. Marchetti, A., Tesconi, M., Minutoli, S.: XFlow: an XML-based document-centric workflow. In: Ngu, Anne H.H., Kitsuregawa, M., Neuhold, Erich J., Chung, J.-Y., Sheng, Quan Z. (eds.) WISE 2005. LNCS, vol. 3806, pp. 290–303. Springer, Heidelberg (2005). https://doi.org/10.1007/11581062_22
9. Zdun, U., Hentrich, C., van der Aalst, W.M.P.: A survey of patterns for service-oriented architectures. Int. J. Internet Protoc. Technol. 1(3), 132–143 (2006). https://doi.org/10.1504/IJIPT.2006.009739
10. WSO2: WSO2 Enterprise Integrator: Overview (2018). https://docs.wso2.com/display/EI630/Overview. Accessed 8 Aug 2018
11. Pires, J., Vasconcelos, A., Borbinha, J.: Business process support in the context of records management. In: 21st International Conference on Enterprise Information Systems (ICEIS 2019), Crete, Greece (2009)
12. Ferme, V., Ivanchikj, A., Pautasso, C.: A framework for benchmarking BPMN 2.0 workflow management systems. In: Motahari-Nezhad, H.R., Recker, J., Weidlich, M. (eds.) BPM 2015. LNCS, vol. 9253, pp. 251–259. Springer, Cham (2015). https://doi.org/10.1007/978-3-319-23063-4_18
13. Das, R., Patra, M., Misro, A.: OPEN SOURCE SOA FOR E-GOVERNANCE. In: 7th International Conference on E-Governance ICEG 2010: Indian Institute of Management, Bangalore (IIMB) (2010)
14. Ruh, W., Gold-Bernstein, B.: Enterprise Integration: The Essential Guide to Integration Solutions. Addison-Wesley Professional, Boston (2004)
15. International Organization for Standardization (ISO): ISO 15489-1:2016 – Information and Documentation – Records Management – Part 1. International Organization for Standardization (2016)

CPS-PMBOK: How to Better Manage Cyber-Physical System Development Projects

Filipe E. S. P. Palma[1], Marcelo Fantinato[1(✉)], Laura Rafferty[2],
and Patrick C. K. Hung[2]

[1] School of Arts, Sciences and Humanities, University of São Paulo, São Paulo, Brazil
{fpalma,m.fantinato}@usp.br
[2] Faculty of Business and IT, Ontario Tech University, Oshawa, Canada
{laura.rafferty,patrick.hung}@uoit.ca

Abstract. We propose specific practices for managing Cyber-Physical Systems (CPS) development projects. Our approach is named CPS-PMBOK as it is based on the Project Management Institute's PMBOK body of knowledge. CPS-PMBOK is focused on the integration, scope, human resource and stakeholder knowledge areas; which were chosen considering some particularities of CPS, such as multidisciplinary team and high innovative aspect. The proposed approach was assessed with managers and developers of a R&D organization, who identified that the proposed practices can improve several aspects related to CPS projects.

Keywords: Project management · Scope · Human resources · Stakeholders cyber-physical systems · PMBOK

1 Introduction

Cyber-physical Systems (CPS) are computational systems that interact with the physical world. The need to reproduce and understand the real world led to the creation of this new technological system field [31,36]. Merging areas from embedded systems, mechanical engineering, software, among others [19], CPS gained remarkable advances in science, such as medical surgery, autonomous vehicles, energy harvesting and smart buildings [30]. CPS-related projects tend to be large, complex and groundbreaking, with innovative technologies [3,31,36]. They are often proof of concept-related projects, with new technologies being tested. CPS can be related to research and development due to the natural complexity of the environment in which CPS interacts. A usual CPS feature is multidisciplinary, which requires good team communication skills as CPS development merges computing and physical world concepts. A recurring issue in CPS projects is the misunderstanding caused by the large number of concepts involved. The collaboration among practitioners from different areas is also necessary [3,19].

© Springer Nature Switzerland AG 2020
J. Filipe et al. (Eds.): ICEIS 2019, LNBIP 378, pp. 154–181, 2020.
https://doi.org/10.1007/978-3-030-40783-4_9

Project management practices aim to enhance the probability of success in a product or service development [21]. Success depends on the project goals, organization and industry but the priority may vary such as: finishing on schedule, meeting an agreed scope, achieving satisfactory quality or finishing in a given budget. Project management consists of controlling its development and providing all the resources necessary for its execution, which are usually assigned to a project manager. Project management is useful for many industries in many applications, such as medicine, civil engineering, software development, advertising campaigns and event organization. The Project Management Institute (PMI) gathers best practices in the so called Project Management Body of Knowledge (PMBOK) [29], which shows tools and techniques for a better management considering experts' knowledge. PMBOK organize the best practices through 10 knowledge areas: integration, scope, time, cost, quality, human resource, communications, risk, procurement, and stakeholder.

Considering the particularities of CPS projects and the need to properly manage them to reach their goals according to the success factors established, this paper addresses specific practices for better managing CPS projects. These specific practices are proposed as a PMBOK extension, called CPS-PMBOK. CPS-PMBOK is focused on the integration, scope, human resource and stakeholder knowledge areas. These four areas were chosen considering a systematic literature review conducted to identify the main CPS challenges. Thus, we expected to improve both team communication skills and understanding of the project activities. The proposed practices are based on approaches previously presented in literature as well as the authors' background. We consider that a well-managed CPS project may increase physical world comprehension, modeling and interaction, enhancing the technological advances.

This paper details a preliminary version of CPS-PMBOK presented in [25] and comprises background concepts, related work, research method, description and assessment of CPS-PMBOK, and conclusion.

2 Background

2.1 Cyber-Physical Systems

The expression *Cyber-Physical Systems* (CPS) was coined in 2006 by Helen Gill at the National Science Foundation (NSF) Workshop on CPSs [9] to describe a new generation of engineered systems capable of high performance in information, computing, communication and control. Some examples of such systems are: smart power grids, in which the power line health and consumption can be monitored at distance all the time; online and robotic medical surgeries; and autonomous vehicles, as trains, cars, drones or Unmanned Aerial Vehicles (UAV).

CPS represents a new way of interaction based on both full understanding of physical phenomena and environmental behaviors as well as exchanging of contextualized information between the computing world and the physical world, in the same way as people interact with each other at the internet [31].

Previously, computer components were bigger, more expensive and the communication (wireless or not) capacity was limited, whereas the physical world was only witnessed by the computing world. While the computing world includes all types of computing platforms, able to process and provide information for people or other technological components; the physical world includes physical phenomena and processes that can be found in the environment.

From the computing side, the following devices can be found: Unix-based computers, micro-controllers, microprocessors, embedded systems, signal acquisition hardware, Digital Signs Processors (DSP), Programmable Logic Controller (PLC), Field-Programmable Gate Arrays (FPGA) etc. From the physical side, the following physical phenomena can be found: temperature, electrical current and voltage, atmospheric pressure, motion (velocity and direction), lighting, radio-frequency, sound, time etc. Physical processes are a combination of some physical phenomena in a certain context, such as: room temperature, which changes over the time considering the number of people in the room; airplane pressure, which changes according to the flight altitude; and the current provided by an electrical engine, which is proportional to its load.

To bring together both worlds, sensors and actuators allow interaction as intermediate elements. Sensors may be any hardware device able to transform a physical phenomenon (such as: light, electrical current, humidity, gravity etc.) into electrical signs or some other computer-readable sign. Sensors are the bridge connecting the physical and computing worlds. Actuators are specific hardware devices responsible to send processed information to other sensors or hardware, stimulating the environment. Actuators are able to generate electrical signs, sound, radio-frequency, indirect motion or any other physical phenomena to stimulate elements in a physical process [20]. This interaction consists of computers reading and controlling the physical world, through cycles of feedback reading, and the control adaptation through computing for the next interaction [18].

Figure 1 illustrates a generic CPS architecture comprised of the physical plant, the platforms and the network fabric. The *physical plant* represents the physical world, including physical phenomena and processes as well as human operators [20]. The physical world is the more challenging, unexpected and still unknown element. It is composed of all physical processes and phenomena which the computing platform will interact with, such as: electricity, wind, solar energy, human behavior, among others. The physical world is often linked to mathematical modeling and simulation, which allows interpretation of real world data dealing with discrete data. The *platforms* represent the computing world, including computers and operating systems as well as sensors and actuators as interfaces to the physical world. The computing platform means all hardware able to process and store data, working in a similar architecture to a personal computer, but with some specific features of communication. These features include signs reading through digital or analog inputs and outputs, such as the programmable logic controllers. Many options are available nowadays with the Internet of Things (IoT). The *network fabric* represents the mechanisms for computers to communicate, such as wireless networks or industrial protocols and buses, and can be

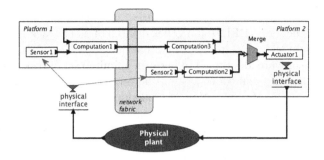

Fig. 1. Illustrative example of a generic CPS architecture [20].

considered also part of the computing world. Many CPS show network elements, since several computing platforms may communicate reliably.

CPS are addressable through a multidisciplinary view, since they are a confluence of embedded, real-time, distributed sensors and control systems. This requires a diversity of experts working together from different areas, such as: civil engineering, mechanical engineering, biomedical engineering, electrical engineering, control engineering, software engineering, chemical engineering, network engineering, computer science, human interaction, learning theory, material science, signal processing and biology [3,18,20,31,36].

Issues related to reliability, safety, robustness, security and quality of services are highly relevant since wrong actuation or misinterpretation of signs in a physical world may cause accidents. There are still open technical challenges, as preventing cyber-attacks in non-Unix systems [18,31,36]. In order to properly address CPS, computing and networking abstractions need to be redesigned, seeing that, in the physical world, time can define the required computing approach, and concurrency is intrinsic [18]. Moreover, network components should be remodeled to fit the new technologies of computing platforms [36]. As many industrial CPS are designed to decoupling the control system design from hardware/software implementation details, the trend of creating new models of abstraction and architectures can be seen [3]. In terms of technological challenges regarding the development of CPS, mobile device integration as well as distributed sensors and actuators can be mentioned [36]. On the other hand, in terms of methodological issues, items such as architecture patterns, composition of protocols, and new modeling languages and tools can be mentioned [31].

There are many possible areas for potential application of CPS, such as: advanced automotive systems (including autonomous vehicles), agriculture, avionics and airplanes, critical infrastructure control, defense systems, robotics, electric vehicles, energy harvesting, environmental control, health-care, instrumentation, intelligent buildings, medical devices and systems (including medical prostheses), mobile devices, power generation, real-time systems, space vehicles, traffic control, among others [3,18,20,31,36]. Moreover, some existing technological devices can acquire these CPS features, such as: cognitive radio, Radio Frequency Identification (RFID) and other devices of asset tracking [18].

CPS are closely related to embedded systems [20], which are specific hardware running specific software, developed to perform a limited set of tasks with limited resources. Some specific embedded systems became conceptually similar to CPS, given that some areas of application of embedded systems started to demand more increased features and networked devices, besides the need for interaction with physical environment, which are found in CPS [18]. Besides embedded systems, other terms can be seen as very similar, part of or even equal to CPS, such as: automation and control systems, system of systems, IoT and sensors networks. However, CPS have been recently more widely used, since it shows a wider context, including these previously mentioned applications and concepts.

2.2 Project Management Practices

A project is a temporary effort to reach a specific goal (usually to create a new product or service) taking some time, cost and requirements constraints. Goals and constraints may vary according to organizations' environmental factors and policies. For the PMI, a project is a temporary endeavor undertaken to create a unique result and it comes to an end when the goals are reached or it is impossible to reach them [29], which should be managed to be successfully finished.

Project management means to apply knowledge, skills, tools and techniques over the development of a product or a service to assure the achievements of the project's requirements [29]. Project management is also defined as a process of definition, planning, monitoring, controlling and delivering projects [1]. The PMI keeps a base of knowledge called Project Management Body of Knowledge (PMBOK) that shows a set of best practices to be used in project management. These best practices have been collected from experts in project management in different areas. Similarly, the Association for Project Management (APM) also keeps its set of project management best practices called APM Body of Knowledge. Nevertheless, PMBOK is probably the set of best practices most used by project managers and academic researchers worldwide.

Some constraints project management practices should be concerned are related to scope, quality, schedule, budget, resources and risks; but limited to them. All these constraints are dependently interrelated, i.e., if one changes, at least some other one is affected [29]. For example, PMBOK states that if the schedule of a project is shortened, the budget needs to be increased to allocate additional resources; or if the scope changes, the risks may have changed as well, creating new risks or changing the severity or probability of the existing ones. The project's goals must satisfy three fundamental criteria: timely completion, completion within budgeted cost and compliance of quality requirements [22].

The project success criteria, or *Critical Success Factors* (CSF), may vary according to the organization approach. The goals established for the project define which criteria must be satisfied as project success criteria. All the goals proposed for some project must be satisfied so that a project can be considered

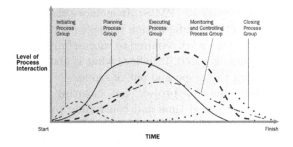

Fig. 2. Process groups interactions in a project or a project phase [29].

completed. However, a project can be considered successful, if at least the primary goals were achieved when secondary goals are unfeasible. For example, a project in civil engineering must be finished on time for the inauguration day, even if there are paintings not finished yet. In this case, cost and part of the scope had to be sacrificed to satisfy the time constraint, and these other goals may be satisfied later [22]. Another possible success factor, mainly in CPS projects, refers to safety, for which a system or application can only be used if does not provide any harm risky to users. Security can also be part of the success factors in CPS projects as a cyber-attack may cause huge consequences [2]. In such cases, if a project is finished on time, but its safety or security features are not properly satisfied, it can be considered completed but not successful. In general terms, PMBOK defines project success criteria as completing the project within realistic and feasible constraints of scope, time, cost, quality, resources and risk.

PMBOK is composed by 47 suggested processes. Each process represents a set of activities that should be executed to reach some specified project stage. A process is characterized by its inputs and outputs, and tools and techniques used for its execution [29]. The suggested processes may be adapted according to the project needs or organizational environment. The set of suggested processes is organized orthogonally in five *process groups'* and ten *knowledge areas.*

The five process groups are: initiating (2 processes), planning (24 processes), executing (8 processes), monitoring and controlling (11 processes) and closing (2 processes). These groups organize the processes in terms of main shared purposes, distributed over time. Although these groups represent time organization, they are not mutually excluding. Overlapping occur as illustrated in Fig. 2.

The ten knowledge areas are: integration (6 processes), scope (6 processes), time (7 processes), cost (4 processes), quality (3 processes), human resource (4 processes), communications (3 processes), risk (6 processes), procurement (4 processes) and stakeholders (4 processes). These knowledge areas organize the processes considering their conceptual objectives and in terms of specialized tasks to be executed and responsibilities, summarized below:

1. **Integration:** identifying, defining, combining and coordinating all the processes and activities. This knowledge area basically organizes and prepares all the processes of the other nine knowledge areas. It includes the use of a Project

Management Information Systems (PMIS). It includes the change management planning and may also include configuration management practices.

2. **Scope:** ensuring that all the work required to successfully complete the project was predicted and is being executed. It defines what is and what is not included in the project, i.e., within the scope and out of scope.

3. **Time:** managing the time of a project, i.e., ensuring the project activities will be completed in the planned time and controlling the possible delays and advances so that the project still remains feasible. The planning and definition of the milestones, if used, are made in the context of this knowledge area.

4. **Cost:** managing the approved or authorized budget to be executed. The amount of available funds depends on the origins of the project and the organizations involved. In order to conduct the project within the given budget, the costs of the project need to be properly managed, which consists of planning, estimating and controlling the costs as the activities are completed, the results are delivered, and, although rare, the approved budget changes.

5. **Quality:** ensuring that the project and product requirements are satisfied and validated; the quality criteria may depend on organizational policies and the project nature. It is directly related to the results delivered to its customers and the customers' satisfaction regarding the project. Quality is also related to overcoming the stakeholders' expectation about the overall project progress.

6. **Human Resource:** organizing, managing and leading the project team, which is comprised of all people with assigned roles and responsibilities for completing activities. The team members may have varied skills, according to their roles in the project. The members' participation time also vary and may be either full-time or part-time. The inclusion of all team members in project planning and decision making is beneficial because this improves motivation and commitment, besides to add the experience of the team members in the planning process.

7. **Communications:** ensuring that all the project information is properly shared with different stakeholders and stored. Its goal is to create effective communication methods so that the diverse stakeholders, including the project team members, may understand each other. The differences in terms of cultural, technical and organizational background are the primary sources of misunderstanding that can provide risks to the project progress and overall quality, and can be avoided by properly managing communication.

8. **Risk:** planning, identifying, analyzing and controlling the project risks to increase the impact of positive events and decrease the impact of negative events. The risks are any event that can change the project status, performance, quality, acceptance or results. The event can be unexpected or foreseen but controlled. Risks can be indeed positive events that improve indicators related to some result, cost or time or positively affect any other knowledge area.

9. **Procurement:** purchasing or acquiring products, services or any results from outside the project team. It involves legal treatment of official artifacts such as agreements, contracts and non-disclosure agreements. It includes supplier management to provide a reliable relationship network among organizations.

10. **Stakeholders:** identifying the stakeholders, analyzing their expectations and potential impacts on the project, and developing appropriate strategies for effectively engaging them. The stakeholders represent all the parts interested in the project success or failure, including people, groups or organizations which could positively or negatively impact or be impacted by the project. The engagement of the stakeholders in project decisions and execution is essential for their satisfaction, and should be managed as a major goal of the project, through continuous communication and the understanding of their needs and expectations.

3   Related Work and Research Method

Although PMBOK is a general-purpose guide, specific application areas, including CPS projects, may benefit from adapted or focused project management practices, which can better drive project activities and prevent common weaknesses [21]. Some approaches emphasize knowledge areas improvement or depict specific application area practices, while others focus on organizational differences. Some authors propose, for example, new techniques for stakeholder management in civil engineering projects and in clinical research environments [26,38]. Considering organizational structures differences, some works address concerns on stakeholders, scope, human resources and communications, for globally distributed projects [6,10]. Others propose entire revisions of PMBOK processes, knowledge areas or other project management approach adaptations, but still in a general way. One example extends the PMBOK knowledge areas creating the new *project sustainability management*, dealing with reuse of lessons learned and standardization of project management practices within an organization [32]. This author also proposes to add portfolio context in project stakeholder management and quality standard plan in project quality management.

Our PMBOK extension focused on CPS projects relies on the results of a systematic literature review, conducted to link PMBOK's knowledge areas and the CPS development. We looked for literature works proposed to address specific CPS project management issues. To carry out the systematic review, we used various technical CPS-related terms to embrace as many primary studies as possible, such as: embedded systems, system of systems, sensors network, IoT, and automation and control. These terms are used for different levels of interactions but still useful for our purpose: embedded systems and system of systems commonly refer only to hardware and software interaction, without including physical phenomena; sensor networks and IoT are usually related to informative and data collection applications; and automation and control is widely used in industrial applications in general not associated with an information system.

The primary studies obtained were analyzed to find which knowledge areas were subject of study. A relevance score was applied based on the number of times that keywords related to each knowledge area were mentioned. Scope, human resource and stakeholder were the knowledge areas with more issues studied. These results do not mean that the remaining knowledge areas are not important, but that the current project management practices are probably enough to properly manage them in the CPS context. Considering the outcomes of this systematic review, our work proposes project management practices, focused on the CPS context for the scope, human resource and stakeholder knowledge areas. We also propose a generic practice related to the integration knowledge area.

These practices are suggested to address the project scope management in CPS projects: application of international standards, estimations based on use case points and hardware points, software and frameworks for requirements analysis, specific modeling languages for requirements elicitation and system architecture visualization, requirements review through peer reviewing and Scrum boards, development of design models, specific development approaches, meetings with live demonstrations, analysis-driven design, lists of requirements, model-driven design and new process models for scope management and project development [4,7,8,11–15,17,23,24,27,28,33–35,37,39,42,43].

As for the project human resource, the following practices are suggested to address this knowledge area in CPS projects: acquisition of a multidisciplinary and expert team; definition of specific key-roles usually needed for the team members; distribution of tasks considering the team members' profile and expertise; statistical estimation and classification of familiarity of team members, according their profiles and requirements; training in specific development methods, such as goal-driven, model-driven and extreme programming; and skill based human resource management [5,11–13,23,24,27,33,37,41–43].

Finally, these practices are suggested to address project stakeholders in CPS projects: identification of stakeholders and assignment of tasks following systematic algorithms and norms, assignment of stakeholders within the organization, involvement of stakeholders during the transition between development phases, face-to-face meetings, workshop meetings and specific stakeholders management approaches such as the evolutionary development and the constructive SoS integration model [11,13,23,24,28,33,37,40,42,43].

We further analyzed all the practices related to scope, human resource and stakeholder management that were found in the primary studies identified during the systematic review. We compared these project management practices with the best practices existing in PMBOK. As a result, we found both practices still not covered by PMBOK and practices covered but with suggested specializations. Following an empirical approach, we refined this list of practices considering the authors' practical experience in CPS projects. More specifically, the final practices chosen are those most frequently found in the primary studies as well as aligned with the primary insights of the authors of this work. Finally, such chosen practices were also assessed by experts in a CPS-related R&D company, including managers and developers, who presented some final suggestions to produced the last list of chosen practices to compose CPS-PMBOK.

4   The CPS-PMBOK Approach

This approach proposes appropriate practices for managing CPS projects. Our main goal is improving both team communication skills and understanding of the project activities when addressing CPS projects. The Cyber-Physical Systems – Project Management Body of Knowledge (CPS-PMBOK) approach proposes practices based on PMI's PMBOK, but oriented to the specific context of CPS projects. Agile methods indirectly influence the practices since agile practices are also commonly related to the issues addressed here. One of the main characteristics of CPS-PMBOK is the adequate treatment of concerns with hardware beyond software as well as teams composed of very different technical profiles.

CPS-PMBOK comprises the original PMBOK best practices plus extensions to address CPS projects. The extensions address four PMBOK's knowledge areas: integration management, scope management, human resource management and stakeholder management. For each extended knowledge area, one or more practices are proposed, as follows: integration: *characterization model* output artifact; scope: *pre-elaborated list of requirements* technique, *review requirements* process, *process simulation* technique; human resource: *specialized team division* technique and *cross-training* technique; and stakeholder: *build technical trust* technique and *dynamic follow-up strategies* technique.

Figure 3 shows an overview of CPS-PMBOK based on PMBOK. From the 47 processes suggested by PMBOK version 5, seven of them are receiving some suggestion to better cover CPS projects. Two types of suggestions have been made: inclusion of a new output for some process and inclusion of a new tool/technique for some process. Moreover, one additional whole process has been suggested. The processes involved in the suggestions made are highlighted in bold and italics font. Next subsections show the details of such suggested items.

4.1   Project Integration Management

First proposed practice, the characterization model should be used a brainstorm driving, to equalize the comprehension and familiarization with the system to be developed. This artifact is proposed to be produced as an output of the develop project chart process, which is part of the initiating process group. Figure 4 shows the proposed characterization model output artifact, highlighted in **bold**, within the develop project charter process, following the graphic pattern used in PMBOK to show its processes. This output should be used as input by all processes that use the project charter also as input, i.e.: plan scope management, collect requirements, define scope, plan schedule management, plan cost management, plan risk management, and plan stakeholder management.

Figure 5 shows a characterization model example. For each proposed characteristic, the participants of the brainstorming fill the characterization model choosing between low, moderate and high. This may provide estimates regarding project size, complexity and technical challenges besides to discussions among the project team members. These characteristics are divided in two sections: CPS environment and CPS complexity. Our example of CPS characterization model shows some characteristics usually found in CPS projects.

The CPS environment represents the variables show in the CPS to be developed, such as how much: limited tasks are required, communication with known

Knowledge Areas	Project Management Process Groups				
	Initiating Process Group	Planning Process Group	Executing Process Group	Monit. and Control. Process Group	Closing Process Group
4. Project Integration Management	*4.1 Develop Project Charter (*1)*	4.2 Develop Project Management Plan	4.3 Direct and Manage Project Work	4.4 Monitor and Control Project Work 4.5 Perform Integrated Charge Control	4.6 Close Project or Phase
5. Project Scope Management		5.1 Plan Scope Management *5.2 Collect Requirements (*2)* 5.3 Define Scope 5.4 Create WBS		5.5 Validate Scope 5.6 Control Scope *5.7 Review Requirements (*3)*	
6. Project Time Management		6.1 Plan Schedule Management 6.2 Define Activities 6.3 Sequence Activities 6.4 Estimate Activity Resources 6.5 Estimate Activity Durations 6.6 Develop Schedule		6.7 Control Schedule	
7. Project Cost Management		7.1 Plan Cost Management 7.2 Estimate Costs 7.3 Determine Budget		7.4 Control Costs	
8. Project Quality Management		8.1 Plan Quality Management	8.2 Perform Quality Assurance	8.3 Control Quality	
9. Project Human Resource Management		*9.1 Plan Human Resource Management (*2)*	*9.2 Acquire Project Team (*2)* *9.3 Develop Project Team (*2)* 9.4 Manage Project Team		
10. Project Communications Management		10.1 Plan Communications Management	10.2 Manage Communications	10.3 Control Communications	
11. Project Risk Management		11.1 Plan Risk Management 11.2 Identify Risks 11.3 Perform Qualitative Risk Analysis 11.4 Perform Quantitative Risk Analysis 11.5 Plan Risk Responses		11.6 Control Risks	
12. Project Procurement Management		12.1 Plan Procurement Management	12.2 Conduct Procurements	12.3 Control Procurements	12.4 Close Procurements
13. Project Stakeholder Management	13.1 Identify Stakeholders	13.2 Plan Stakeholder Management	*13.3 Manage Stakeholder Engagement (*2)*	*13.4 Control Stakeholder Engagement (*2)*	

Legend:
*1: inclusion of a new suggested output
*2: inclusion of a new suggested tool/technique
*3: inclusion of a new suggested process

Fig. 3. CPS-PMBOK overview, adapted from PMI [29].

group of devices, interaction with known group of people and industrial standards or norms should be followed. The higher the score assigned for each characteristic, the better defined and surrounded by formalized processes is the CPS environment. The opposite means that the CPS environment can be chaotic and unpredictable, which may define project management strategies, adequate teams to work on the project or budget adjustments, for example.

The CPS complexity relies on specific technological areas: mechanical structures, network, sensors, actuators, data storage, user interaction, legacy systems integration and power energy system. The complexity characterization is made by choosing how relevant is the integration of the CPS with each technology. For each, a specific technical team may be required to estimate such complexity. Like

Fig. 4. Proposed *characterization model* artifact in the *develop prj charter* process [25].

CPS characterization model			
CPS environment	**Low**	**Moderate**	**High**
• Limited tasks			
• Communication with known group of devices			
• Interaction with known group of people			
• Following industrial standards or norms			
CPS complexity	**Low**	**Moderate**	**High**
• Mechanical structures			
• Network			
• Sensors			
• Actuators			
• Data storage			
• User interaction			
• Integration with legacy systems			
• Power energy system			

Fig. 5. Example of a CPS projects' characterization model [25].

the environment characterization, depending on the CPS complexity in terms of different technologies, different project management decisions may be taken.

We do not intend to define a fixed CPS characterization model, with fixed characteristics. Instead, Fig. 5 proposes a basic example which may be adapted for each organization or team, based on lessons learned, project goals and area of application considering the CPS concepts. Moreover, we expect that the list of characteristics evolves considering the team's experience on past projects.

4.2   Project Scope Management

In terms of project scope management, some processes show special challenges for CPS projects due to their highly innovative and dynamic aspects [3,18,20,30,36]. In addition, the high complexity involved for modeling the physical world and its phenomena is another challenge source. Such innovative and complex requirements result in ever-changing requirements mainly due to: realignment of the stakeholders' conception, understanding of further issues, rise of new technologies, adaptation of unstructured processes, and finding of new physical phenomena. In this innovative scenario, a late discovery of new requirements is inevitable mainly when considering an exploratory development method as required and adopted by many organizations [13]. CPS project managers and team should be able to constantly look for new requirements, bringing up changes in scope as soon as possible. Besides contributing to a proper system specification, a partnership-based approach, involving an outsourced organization, also allows to proper address ever-changing requirements when its participation is needed.

As a result of this scenario and needs, two practices are proposed to the project scope management, as showed in this section: pre-elaborated lists of requirements technique and review requirements process.

Pre-elaborated Lists of Requirements Technique. To support requirements gathering, CPS-PMBOK includes a tool/technique called pre-elaborated lists of requirements. The purpose of such lists is to create reusable assets through gathering common requirements found in CPS projects. This technique is proposed to be used within the collect requirements process, which is part of the planning process group. Figure 6 shows the proposed pre-elaborated requirements lists technique, highlighted in **bold**, within the collect requirements process.

Pre-elaborated requirements lists help collect requirements which should be used to estimate project size and avoid missing requirements. It contains topics of possible requirements so the project manager or project team can fill with weights, points or simple tags signaling the existence of some requirement, such as a checklist. These topics may be divided in domains related to those technical areas previously described in the characterization model (cf. Fig. 5).

Figure 7 shows an example of a pre-elaborated list of software requirements for an initial collection of CPS requirements. This list shows a subject of high level of abstraction (*Requirements topic* column) and a corresponding technical question for each topic (*Technical issue* column) to be answered as a support for the collect requirements process. This technique is based the hardware points technique, proposed to estimate hardware assembly and development cost [39].

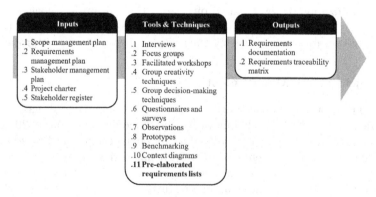

Fig. 6. Proposed *pre-elaborated rqmts lists* technique in the *collect rqmts* process [25].

CPS software requirements checking	
Requirements topic	**Technical issues**
• Automation level	How much human intervention is required?
• Processing load	How complex is the processing of data collected?
• Data storage	What is the size of the data type addressed?
	Which technology is used to store results?
• Graphical interface	How should the graphical interface look like?
• Running time	How long should the system remain in operation?
• Parameters insertion	Should it be possible to register new parameters?
• Remote access	Should it be necessary to provide web visualization or operation?

Fig. 7. Example of a pre-elaborated requirements list [25].

Fig. 8. *Review requirements* process: inputs, tools and techniques, and outputs [25].

Review Requirements Process. CPS development may result in unexpected results and consequently dynamic requirements [13]. Accordingly, the innovative aspect of CPS demands many scope revisions and redefinition. By understanding that such scope revisions and redefinitions are highly common in CPS projects, one of our specific practices is proposing an additional process to the scope management knowledge area – review requirements – as part of the monitoring and controlling process group. Figure 8 shows the proposed review requirements process, including its inputs, tools and techniques, and outputs.

The review requirements process aims to advance requirements reviews, bringing up the changes as soon as possible, so it can be timely addressed. This process results in change requests similarly to the PMBOK's control scope process. The difference is that, in CPS-PMBOK, review requirements is a creation-focused process, considering less the known requirements and revisiting the highest definitions of the project looking for new requirements whereas, in PMBOK, the control scope process focuses on ensuring the accomplishment of the defined scope and, when needed, the appropriate processing of changes are made.

This new process follows principles of agile methodologies. Its purpose is to predict requirements changes enabling the project team to react in real time and according to the resources available. Moreover, this additional process aims to reduce the impacts of requirements constantly changing.

PMBOK's techniques to collect requirements are used, as meetings, surveys and interviews. CPS-PMBOK additionally includes the process simulation technique in support of the review requirements process. It consists of tests and validation of the various stages of development, according to the features becoming ready to use. Simulation tools to predict environment or conditions such as mechanical simulation, radiation diagrams and thermal dissipation are useful in the review requirements process and are part of the process simulation technique. Other tools to isolate part of the CPS, to validate models or equipment, such as hardware in the loop and software in the loop may be also used.

Figure 9 shows the data flow diagram for the review requirements process. One can see the interaction among the review requirements process and the other PMBOK processes, including the scope management's collect requirements process. Again, we do not intend to define a fixed pre-elaborated requirements list, with fixed requirements topics and corresponding technical issues. In Fig. 9, we are only illustrating a basic example which may be adapted for each organization or team, based on lessons learned, project goals and area of application considering the CPS concepts. This example, for instance, refers only to software requirements, but other types of requirements should be covered as well.

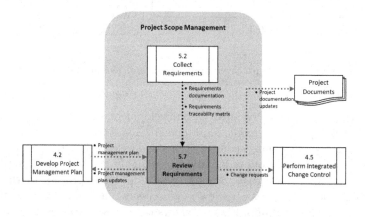

Fig. 9. Data flow diagram for the *review requirements* process.

4.3   Project Human Resource Management

Considering the multidisciplinary of CPS projects, the human resources which may be part of a project team can be from very different areas of specialization, what increases the challenge of managing relationships and technical communication [41]. In a practical example, a project to develop a smart power grid system may include professionals from electrical supply, hardware design, telecommunication and software development. Professionals from electrical supply and software may be not familiar with hardware technologies whereas telecommunication professionals and hardware designers come from a very different school, where software is usually not object of study. These different academic approaches applied in a same product or project may cause misunderstanding among team members, influencing requirements understanding and even task priorities.

As a result, two additional techniques are proposed in CPS-PMBOK for human resource management: specialized team division and cross-training.

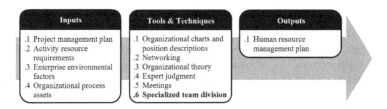

Fig. 10. Proposed *specialized team division* techn. in the *plan HR mgmt* process [25].

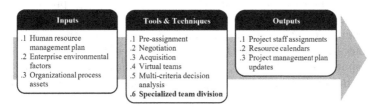

Fig. 11. Proposed *specialized team division* techn. in the *acquire prj team* process [25].

Specialized Team Division Technique. The specialized team division technique is proposed to improve the development performance and avoid inappropriate assignment of tasks. According to this technique, the project team should be split into sub-teams considering different application areas or project deliverables. Some works found in literature for CPS projects were used as a basis to propose this technique, including: the application of team division based on academic profiles, such as electrical engineering, computer engineering and information technology [12] and other main applications visualized in [16, 30, 36].

This technique is to be used within two processes: plan human resource management process (of the planning process group) and acquire project team process (of the executing process group). Figures 10 and 11 show the proposed specialized team division technique, highlighted in **bold**, within both processes.

We propose an initial suggestion for a specialized team division considering the context of CPS projects and taking into account the proposed CPS characterization model in terms of CPS complexity. According to our suggestion, the sub-teams for a CPS projects could be: *mechanical design team*, responsible for physical structures and mechanical packing; *hardware design team*, responsible for processing platforms, sensors and actuators specification; *electrical design team*, responsible for electrical project and drawings, besides power energy design; *network design team*, responsible for communication protocols and technologies specification; *information system development team*, responsible for software development; and *other specialized teams*, power bank development team, human-computer interface team, antenna design team, specific sensors team etc.

Other specialized team divisions can be based on the context of the system application. An alternative division is based on deliverables or partial results of the project, assigning a focused team for each logical deliverable part of the developed CPS system. As an example, considering an autonomous meteorological information collector, which involves drone development allied with weather sensing and statistical software for forecasting, a specialized team division based on deliverables could be: *mechanical structure*, mixing mechanical and hardware design profiles, responsible for structure and engines design and development; *flight system*, composed of mechanical and hardware design profiles and possibly a theoretical flight expert, responsible for designing and developing the propellers and orientation sensors; *power energy system*, composed of electrical design profiles plus chemists for battery technologies experts; *communications system*, responsible for delivering the radio communication system for remote control and data collection; *embedded software*, composed by software engineers with a focus on reliable embedded software design and development, responsible for delivering the main drone software, which controls the engines, reads sensors, communicates with radios and also has some autonomous routines for emergencies; and *weather data system*, composed by statistical experts on weather sensors allied with some electrical and hardware design professionals, responsible for specifying appropriate sensors to be used and for interpreting their results.

A specialized team division may be used to support organizational breakdown structures or resource breakdown structures. It may include varied departments or even external organizations, depending on the project needs.

Cross-training Technique. Cross-training is a practice briefly depicted in PMBOK to reduce impact when a team member leaves the project. It consists in allocating more than one resource to one task execution. For CPS projects, we propose that the cross-training should be always used to enable some team members acting as a communication bridge between different sub-teams by allocating a team member from a given area to perform a task of some other area. This technique is proposed to be used within the develop project team process, which is part of the planning process group. Figure 12 shows the proposed cross-training technique, highlighted in **bold**, within the develop project team process.

Considering the cross-training technique, a software engineer, for instance, may sporadically follow a mechanical engineer's work with the purposed of understanding and even positively contributing with potential ideas and insights emerged from another outlook. Cross-training can be used as a facilitator in the identification and development of multidisciplinary practitioners.

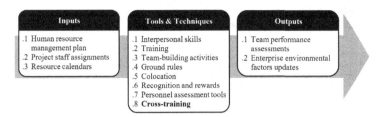

Fig. 12. Proposed *cross-training technique* in the *develop project team* process [25].

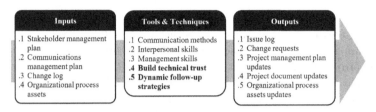

Fig. 13. Proposed *build technical trust* techn. in the *manage stkh engmt* process [25].

4.4   Project Stakeholder Management

Project stakeholders in CPS projects are usually highly technical or very close to the system's final users. This occurs mainly in joint projects of research with universities, where the stakeholders are researchers and students. Another occurrence is in industrial projects to improve production performance, where many stakeholders are production leaders experts in many technologies of the area [3, 30].

Due to the diverse and complex nature of CPS project stakeholders, we understand that specific techniques should be applied to properly address this profile to guarantee that the best results are achieved. Consequently, two additional techniques are proposed in CPS-PMBOK for stakeholder management: build technical trust technique and dynamic follow-up strategies technique.

Build Technical Trust Technique. CPS projects tend to involve academic researchers or experts to support the development of the CPS physical elements. They represent technical stakeholders with knowledge of both the application and engineering areas. PMBOK describes a practice of trust building for stakeholder engagement management, by showing them that company, project team and manager are able to accomplish project's requirements in time and cost.

Accordingly, building technical trust between stakeholders and the project team is also necessary in CPS projects. In this context, CPS-PMBOK proposes a specialization of the trust building, adding the technical aspect to this practice. The build technical trust technique is proposed to be used within the manage stakeholder engagement process, which is part of the executing process group. Figure 13 shows the proposed build technical trust technique, highlighted in **bold**, within the manage stakeholder engagement process.

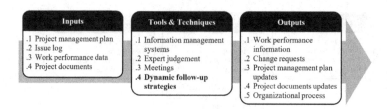

Inputs	Tools & Techniques	Outputs
.1 Project management plan .2 Issue log .3 Work performance data .4 Project documents	.1 Information management systems .2 Expert judgement .3 Meetings **.4 Dynamic follow-up strategies**	.1 Work performance information .2 Change requests .3 Project management plan updates .4 Project documents updates .5 Organizational process

Fig. 14. Proposed *build technical trust and dynamic follow-up strategies* techniques in the *control stakeholder engagement* process [25].

Building technical trust means to pass technical confidence regarding project accomplishment conditions, considering the team and project manager. Accordingly, the project team should get close to the stakeholders, mainly in situations in which the stakeholders are highly technical. For CPS-PMBOK, an internal expert or an external consultant should be put in charge of following up the project management activities allowing more technical stakeholders to be more comfortable with the project progress. This person has the role of translating technical stakeholders concerns. The technical trust may improve stakeholders' satisfaction due to their proximity and understanding of technical issues. Besides that, the developers may feel more comfortable as well, due to the understanding of terms and concerns provided by a expert or consultant.

Dynamic Follow-Up Strategies Technique. As observed in the outcomes of the systematic review conducted for this project, some authors identified that the proposed practices for communication with stakeholders may be not enough to keep stakeholders properly updated in a CPS project. Some approaches found in literature to improve communication with CPS projects' stakeholders are: face-to-face meetings to update the project status to stakeholders [13], stakeholders' participation in every last weekly follow-up meeting of development iterations [33] and weekly workshops for system demonstrating, to update stakeholders [28]. Most of these approaches are based on agile methods, which has the communication with stakeholders as one of their most important concerns.

To meet different levels of demand and satisfaction of stakeholders, we propose for CPS-PMBOK the dynamic follow-up strategies technique, based on practices found in literature. This technique should be used within two processes: manage stakeholder engagement process (of the executing process group) and control stakeholder engagement process (of the monitoring and controlling process group). Figures 13 and 14 show the proposed dynamic follow-up strategies technique, highlighted in **bold**, within both the manage stakeholder engagement process and the control stakeholder engagement process, respectively.

The project manager should adapt the follow-up strategy to enhance stakeholder engagement and reach their expectations. The following suggested strategies are proposed here: *(1)* during the project initiation and planning stages, which involve, for example, discovering of requirements and stakeholders, understanding of highly engaged stakeholders, and understanding of stakeholders' application area: regular face-to-face meetings should be adopted as follow-up strategy; *(2)* during the project execution and monitoring stages, which involve, for example, resolution of requirements conflicts and alignment between technical demands from stakeholders and project documents: only sporadic participation of stakeholders could be included during planning and technical meetings; and *(3)* during the closing stage, which involves, resource scarcity, time re-planning and stakeholder staff updating: the stakeholders should be able to follow up on the final results through workshops with live CPS demonstrations.

5   Assessment of the CPS-PMBOK Approach

To assess CPS-PMBOK, we conducted a qualitative empirical analysis considering the experience of practitioners working in an R&D organization. This organization was chosen because one of the researchers authoring this paper works there and several CPS projects are developed there. We consulted two types of practitioners: six managers and four developers. We conducted the assessment in two phases: an in-person interview and an online survey, showed as follows.

5.1   In-Person Interviews

For the in-person interviews, we firstly showed to these practitioners the proposed practices. For each practitioner type, we showed a specific description. For managers, we explained that CPS-PMBOK is a PMBOK-based approach to enhance CPS project success likelihood through project management concepts focused on CPS development. For developers, we emphasized that CPS-PMBOK should be applied by project managers with collaboration of technical personnel, to obtain better conditions. During the approach presentation, we discussed, with the practitioners, issues raised in CPS projects that they have previously experienced, now considering the practices proposed in CPS-PMBOK. Our purpose with this assessment phase was to raise critical analysis regarding the CPS-PMBOK benefits and feasibility. We conducted this assessment individually, i.e., a practitioner at a time. We were not able to conduct a group assessment due to the non-availability of common hours by the involved practitioners, especially from those at managerial level. Nevertheless, we developed a non-structured roadmap to increase the chances of spontaneous feedback.

In terms of results from the in-person interviews, we could collect feedback from the practitioners, which allowed us to align the understanding of CPS project concepts. However, while we asked the practitioners to assess the proposed approach in a generic way, some feedback seems to be strictly related to the organization where the assessment was conducted. Moreover, some developers showed knowledge about project management and hence some of their opinions are more related to managerial rather than technical aspects.

Table 1 summarizes the most relevant opinions. Different types of opinions have been recorded, including praise, criticism and suggestions. In some cases, we concluded that CPS-PMBOK and the proposed practices have not been properly

Table 1. Feedback from in-person interviews [25].

Feedback for integration mgmt practices (CPS characterization model)	From
− *Life-threatening* should be added as a characteristic in the environment section	Man
− The characterization model obtained can support project planning activities such as estimating time or cost	Man
− Available time, team and budget may influence the CPS characterization	Man
− Something similar to the CPS characterization model could be proposed to specifically characterize the project team	Man
− The model's characteristics could be weighted considering profile and expertise	Man
− The characterization model may inhibit creativity and innovation	Man
− The levels *low, moderate* and *high* should be better defined	Dev
− *Intelligence over data* should be added as a characteristic in the complexity section	Dev
− *Hazardousness* (and possibly related industrial standards and norms) should be added as a characteristic in the model's environment section	Dev
− *Unknown* should be added to complement the low, moderate and high levels	Dev
Feedback for scope management practices	From
− A list of rqmts should be provided when considering an exposed environment	Man
− Both proposed practices (the pre-elaborated lists of requirements technique and the review requirements process) should be more connected to each other	Man
− The review requirements process should be formally associated to the risk management knowledge area (cf. Fig. 9) since both are closely related	Man
− Assuming fixed requirements, for the pre-elaborated lists of requirements, is very risky when considering different contexts of project success	Dev
− The process simulation technique, proposed for the review requirements process, should be better integrated with other processes	Dev
− The pre-elaborated lists of requirements should allow to define the project team	Dev
Feedback for human resource management practices	From
− The cross-training technique can be very useful as a parallel approach when the technologies involved are still quite unknown	Man
− An architect role should be considered in a specialized team division; this architect would integrate all sub-teams involved	Man
− The cross-training technique should work only if all sub-teams practice it	Dev
− An integration role is missing as part of a specialized team division; all sub-team leaders should formally act as an integrator	Dev
Feedback for stakeholder management practices	From
− The workshop dynamic follow-up strategy may be useful to show what is being achieved and hence avoid the need for changes	Man
− The building technical trust technique can be useful to bring confidence also into the project team and not only with the stakeholders	Man
− The building technical trust technique can be also useful to translate technical concerns and terms to the project team	Man
− The dynamic follow-up strategies technique should also be suggested as a technique to the scope management processes	Man
− The building technical trust technique can be enriched by providing access to the developed software's source code for technical stakeholders	Dev
− Preparing for a follow-up workshop may be very costly considering its potential results as return	Dev

Table 2. Online survey responses [25].

KA	Proposed practice	Managers			Developers		
		Eff.	TC	AU	Eff.	TC	AU
Integ.	CPS characterization model output artifact	4.0	33%	83%	4.3	50%	75%
Scope	Review requirements process	4.0	83%	83%	4.5	0%	75%
	Pre-elaborated lists of requirements technique	4.3	17%	67%	3.8	75%	50%
HR	Cross-training technique	4.2	50%	50%	4.5	75%	75%
	Specialized team divisions technique	4.3	50%	17%	4.3	75%	75%
Stkh	Building technical trust technique	4.3	33%	50%	4.5	50%	0%
	Dynamic follow-up strategies technique	4.2	83%	67%	3.8	25%	0%
Average		4.2	50%	60%	4.2	50%	50%

- Eff (Effectiveness): general perceived effectiveness rate of each proposed practice to the corresponding knowledge area (between 1 and 5).
- TC (Team Communication): percentage of practitioners who consider that the corresponding practice contributes specifically to *team communication*.
- AU (Activities' Understanding): percentage of practitioners who consider that the corresponding practice contributes specifically to project *activities' understanding*.

showed since the raised criticism or suggestions are related to something indeed addressed by our approach. A large part of the suggestions is related to possible extensions of the proposed items. Such extensions or adaptations are in fact what we expect to be done by practitioners with specific needs.

5.2 Online Survey

For the online survey, we elaborated a structured questionnaire. This questionnaire aimed to gather the practitioners' opinions regarding the potential effectiveness and relevance of each proposed practice. For each assessed practice, the practitioners were expected to consider the corresponding knowledge area to inform their opinions. We elaborated the questions and possible responses considering a five-points Likert-type scale. For each question, we chose standard five-level responses to represent the perceived effectiveness of each practice to its corresponding knowledge area. The used responses are: totally disagree, partially disagree, neutral, partially agree and totally disagree. Moreover, the practitioners were asked to inform if they perceived each proposed practice as relevant to two specific needs: *(i)* team communication and *(ii)* project understanding. These two additional questions were included to assess the proposed approach to our main goals when proposing such practices. Lastly, we also used a question with free-response style to allow the practitioners to show general comments about CPS-PMBOK and the proposed practices.

Table 2 shows the results of the online survey from the perspective of managers and developers. We assigned sequential integers to the categorical responses. We followed this procedure to allow the calculation of an average among the different responses to obtain an overview of the practitioners' opinions, representing an average response. The following weights were considered for the practitioners' opinions about the approach effectiveness: totally disagree (1), partially disagree (2), neutral (3), partially agree (4) and totally disagree (5). For contribution to the team communication and activities' understanding needs, each practitioner should only inform *yes* or *no*.

In terms of the proposed practices' effectiveness, both managers and developers reported a common general perception with high assessment rates. For both practitioner groups, the practices together received an average result of 4.2, which shows a general response slightly higher than *partially agree*. There were only some small differences between both practitioner groups. For example, managers' general opinions vary from 4.0 to 4.3 while developers' general opinions vary from 3.8 to 4.5. Both groups reported the building technical trust technique with the highest effectiveness. On the other hand, managers reported the review requirements process with the lowest effectiveness while developers reported this same proposed practice with the highest effectiveness. Either way, the rating differences attributed to them are very small.

In terms of contribution of the proposed practices to team communication and activities' understanding, both managers and developers reported a common general perception with lower values in this case. For almost all assessed cases, an average of 50% of the proposed practices were reported as contributing to both specific needs considered. Specifically for activities' understanding, managers related the contribution of an average of 60% of the proposed practices. Some notable differences are identified within each practitioner group: some practices contribute more to team communication than to activities' understanding (as the specialized team divisions technique, considering the managers' opinions) while for some other practices the opposite is noticed (as the review requirements process, considering the developers' opinions). Other differences are identified between both groups: managers reported that the dynamic follow-up strategies technique highly contributes to both team communication and activities' understanding whereas developers reported the same practice with a low contribution to both specific needs. The opposite was reported for the specialized team divisions technique. On the other hand, both managers and developers agree that the cross-training technique shows a good contribution for both needs.

5.3   Discussion of Results

In this section, we discuss some of the most important results obtained with both assessments conducted with managers and developers. We could observe some convergences and divergences between the managers' and developers' opinions. We analyzed some divergences to understand their motivations.

From the managers' point of view, they perceived the review requirements process as one of the most contributors to team communication, which was not expected by us (considering the online survey, cf. Table 2). Although not initially expected, managers should have taken into account that reviewing requirements requires collective cooperation, mainly considering the proposed process simulation technique. Review requirements was also considered as one of the most contributors to activities' understanding, which is naturally understandable. Nevertheless, the review requirements process is contradictorily one of the two worst rated by managers in terms of general effectiveness. This contradiction probably occurs due to the risk of losing the project control seeing that, if not properly managed, the requirements review can make the project scope infinite. This conclusion is corroborated by one of the managers' feedback (cf. Table 1) that states: *The review requirements process should be formally associated to the risk management area since both are closely related.*

The developers did not perceived any contribution from the review requirements process to team communication, exactly the opposite of the managers' view (considering the online survey, cf. Table 2). In fact, there is no feedback from developers considering the in-person interviews (cf. Table 1), which shows they really do not see any importance for this practice. Another divergence, considering the online survey, is for the activities' understanding aspect, for which the managers saw an important contribution of the dynamic follow-up strategies technique whereas the developers did not perceive any contribution of it for this aspect. Moreover, the developers raised some cost issues related to his technique, considering the in-person interviews (cf. Table 1). On the another hand, developers showed more importance for the practices suggested to the human resource management when comparing to the managers' opinions about these practices.

Overall, there is no consensus as to what suggested practices may contribute most to team communication. For managers, review requirements process and dynamic follow-up strategies technique can do this, whereas for developers, pre-elaborated lists of requirements technique, cross-training technique and specialized team division technique can do it. The other two practices (CPS characterization model output artifact and building technical trust technique) were not well rated for both managers and developers. In terms of contribution to activities' understanding, there was some convergences between both groups. For example, both consider that CPS characterization model output artifact and review requirements process are the most important for this aspect, although they diverge in terms of importance for the other practices considering this aspect.

For the organization where the assessment was conducted, the assessment process per se allowed to reconsider its own practices. The assessment allowed to know technical team members skills and professional possibilities. Some legislative concerns showed up, not addressed in CPS-PMBOK, such as privacy and flight rules for drones, and metering regulation in power grid communication systems. The extinction of some professions in industry automation was also highlighted. Specific human resource issues appeared in discussions, which may depend on country and organization developing the CPS system, such as availability or suitability of professionals. Nevertheless, despite the differences among countries, very specific profile resources may be a problem for every organization in any country, such as a physicist specialized in light propagation, for example.

One suggestion given by the developers group was to provide a way to keep every person involved in the project, by using a wiki, for example. This technique can be aggregated to specialized team division, assigning the updating tasks to a specific support team. The role of an architect or integrator appeared twice in feedback: one from managers and other from developers group. But in the developers context, it was suggested that the leader for each team could do this role. Since the goal is to get together all information about current development in one person, this can create another need: an integrator of the leaders. The most wise strategy would be the assignment of the architect or integrator role to one person who gather skills of leadership, technical experience, impartiality and a good understanding of the project. If it was not possible to find this profile of professional, then the creation of an integration team may be necessary.

As predicted by other authors, social issues seemed to influence the assessment: some managers showed more interest in taking part of this research project, understanding the academic context, whereas other managers faced it as a work assessment, questioning the need to review their methods. Some raised issues led to concerns related to relevant subjects for CPS research, which are not the focus of this research, such as: types of project life-cycles, software development methods, and project funding strategies. Since the organization in case is both industry and research-driven, issues related to project final goals showed up, such as any project to creating a product, methods or an art study for wider R&D projects. These issues show that particular refinements of CPS-PMBOK or other approaches may be necessary according to the final project goal, which connects to the success definition, as cited by one of the managers. Although these points can also be specific for each organization or country, it is relevant for the CPS-PMBOK application, mainly in scope and human resource management, since some requirements and team members can never change due to legal requirements in case of R&D projects funded by the government, for example.

6   Conclusion

This work aimed to propose a set of project management practices target specifically to CPS development projects in an approach called CPS-PMBOK. We based the proposed approach on PMI's PMBOK best practices and focused it on the following knowledge areas: integration, scope, human resource and stakeholder management. We chose these four knowledge areas due to the results obtained from a systematic literature review conducted specifically to this context. The systematic review aimed to correlate CPS development and project management practices to list the most recurrent project management practices in the CPS context. Besides the addressed knowledge areas, we also based CPS-PMBOK on the following requirements for CPS projects: multidisciplinary teams, high level of innovation and very unpredictable requirements. Considering these specific needs, our main goal was to improve both team communication skills and understanding of the project activities.

As assessment, CPS-PMBOK was showed to six managers and four developers in an R&D organization to assess its potential benefits, feasibility and effectiveness as well as collect feedback for future improvements. Both managers and developers were very excited about applying CPS-PMBOK to the organization and found it particularly audacious and innovative, mainly considering some characteristics imported from agile methodologies. Overall, CPS-PMBOK met the expectations of managers to be in close contact with the CPS domain, considering variables such as hardware development, multidisciplinary teams, and how to represent physical world issues through project management practices. Considering developers, CPS-PMBOK also met their expectations to allow for the representation of technical issues to improve understanding of CPS-related project activities and provides sharing-based knowledge to all team members, following the need for a multidisciplinary team.

The collected feedback allows us to improve the CPS-PMBOK considering a series of opportunities. Nonetheless, some suggested improvements should be considered as the natural extensions or adaptations that each group of practitioners may perform to their specific needs. Our challenge is to be able to evolve the proposed practices, including proposing new ones, considering two needs that can be seen as antagonistic ones: for one hand, being specific to the CPS project domain; but, for the other hand, being not too specific to allow adjustments as required for specific contexts and organizations.

References

1. APM: APM Body of knowledge. Association for Project Management, 6 edn. (2012)
2. Axelrod, C.W.: Managing the risks of cyber-physical systems. In: Systems, Applications and Technology Conference, pp. 1–6 (2013)
3. Baheti, R., Gill, H.: Cyber-physical systems. Impact Control Technol. **12**, 161–166 (2011)
4. Berger, C., Rumpe, B.: Supporting agile change management by scenario-based regression simulation. IEEE Trans. Intell. Transp. Syst. **11**(2), 504–509 (2010)
5. Chen, Y.M., Wei, C.W.: Multiagent approach to solve project team work allocation problems. Int. J. Prod. Res. **47**(13), 3453–3470 (2009)
6. Deshpande, S., Beecham, S., Richardson, I.: Using the PMBOK guide to frame GSD coordination strategies. In: International Conference on Global Software Engineering, pp. 188–196 (2013)
7. Faschang, M., Kupzog, F., Widl, E., Rohjans, S., Lehnhoff, S.: Requirements for real-time hardware integration into cyber-physical energy system simulation. In: Workshop on Modeling and Simulation of Cyber-Physical Energy System, pp. 1–6 (2015)
8. Garay, J.R., Kofuji, S.T.: Architecture for sensor networks in cyber-physical system. In: IEEE Latin-American Conference on Communications, pp. 1–6 (2010)
9. Gill, H.: National science foundation workshop on cyber-physical systems (2006)
10. Golini, R., Landoni, P.: International development projects by non-governmental organizations: an evaluation of the need for specific project management and appraisal tools. Impact Assess. Proj. Apprais. **32**(2), 121–135 (2014)
11. Greene, B.: Agile methods applied to embedded firmware development. In: Agile Development Conference 2004, pp. 71–77 (2004)
12. Helps, R., Mensah, F.N.: Comprehensive design of cyber physical systems. In: 13th Annual Conference on Information Technology Education, pp. 233–238 (2012)

13. Huang, P.M., Darrin, A.G., Knuth, A.: Agile hardware and software system engineering for innovation. In: IEEE Aerospace Conference, pp. 1–10 (2012)
14. Insaurralde, C.C., Petillot, Y.R.: Cyber-physical framework for early integration of autonomous maritime capabilities. In: IEEE International Systems Conference, pp. 559–566 (2013)
15. Jun, D., Rui, L., Yi-min, H.: Software processes improvement and specifications for embedded systems. In: Conference on Software Engineering Research, Management & Applications, pp. 13–18 (2007)
16. Kim, K.D., Kumar, P.R.: Cyber-physical systems: a perspective at the centennial. In: Proceedings of the IEEE 100 (Special Centennial Issue), pp. 1287–1308 (2012)
17. Lattmann, Z., et al.: Towards an analysis-driven rapid design process for cyber-physical systems. In: 2015 International Symposium on Rapid System Prototyping, pp. 90–96 (2015)
18. Lee, E.A.: Cyber physical systems: design challenges. In: 11th IEEE International Symposium on Object Oriented Real-Time Distributed Computing, pp. 363–369 (2008)
19. Lee, E.A., Seshia, S.A.: Introduction to Embedded Systems: A Cyber-Physical Systems Approach. MIT Press, Cambridge (2011)
20. Lee, E.A., Seshia, S.A.: Introduction to Embedded Systems: A Cyber-Physical Systems Approach, 1.5th edn. MIT Press, Cambridge (2014)
21. Lester, A.: Project Management, Planning and Control: Managing Engineering, Construction and Manufacturing Projects to PMI, APM and BSI Standards, 6th edn. Butterworth-Heinemann, Oxford (2006)
22. Lester, A.: Project Management, Planning and Control: Managing Engineering, Construction and Manufacturing Projects to PMI, APM and BSI Standards, 6th edn. Butterworth-Heinemann, Oxford (2014)
23. Madachy, R., Boehm, B., Lane, J.A.: Assessing hybrid incremental processes for SISOS development. Softw. Process Improv. Pract. 12(5), 461–473 (2007)
24. Madachy, R.J.: Cost modeling of distributed team processes for global development and software-intensive systems of systems. Softw. Process Improv. Pract. 13(1), 51–61 (2008)
25. Palma, F.E.S.P., Fantinato, M., Rafferty, L., Hung, P.C.K.: Managing scope, stakeholders and human resources in cyber-physical system development. In: 21st International Conference on International Information System, pp. 36–47 (2019)
26. Pandi-Perumal, S.R., et al.: Project stakeholder management in the clinical research environment: how to do it right. Front. Psychiatry 6, 71 (2015)
27. Parkhomenko, A., Gladkova, O.: Virtual tools and collaborative working environment in embedded system design. In: 11th International Conference on Remote Engineering and Virtual Instrumentation, pp. 90–93 (2014)
28. Penzenstadler, B., Eckhardt, J.: A requirements engineering content model for cyber-physical systems. In: 2nd Workshop on Requirements Engineering for Systems-of-Systems, pp. 20–29 (2012)
29. PMI: Guide to the project management body of knowledge. Proj. Man. Inst. (2013)
30. Rajkumar, R.: A cyber-physical future. Proc. IEEE 100, 1309–1312 (2012)
31. Rajkumar, R.R., Lee, I., Sha, L., Stankovic, J.: Cyber-physical systems: the next computing revolution. In: 47th Design Automation Conference, pp. 731–736 (2010)
32. Reusch, P.J.: Extending project management processes. In: IEEE International Conference on Intelligent Data Acquisition and Advanced Computing Systems: Technology and Applications, pp. 511–514 (2015)

33. Rong, G., Shao, D., Zhang, H., Li, J.: Goal-driven development method for managing embedded system projects: an industrial experience report. In: International Symposium on Empirical Software Engineering and Measurement, pp. 414–423 (2011)
34. Sapienza, G., Crnkovic, I., Potena, P.: Architectural decisions for HW/SW partitioning based on multiple extra-functional properties. In: IEEE/IFIP Conference on Software Architecture, pp. 175–184 (2014)
35. Savio, D., Anitha, P., Iyer, P.P.: Considerations for a requirements engineering process model for the development of systems of systems. In: Workshop on Requirements Engineering for Systems, Services and Systems-of-Systems, pp. 74–76 (2011)
36. Sha, L., Gopalakrishnan, S., Liu, X., Wang, Q.: Cyber-physical systems: a new frontier. In: Tsai, J., Yu, P. (eds.) Machine Learning in Cyber Trust: Security, Privacy, and Reliability, pp. 3–13. Springer, Boston (2009). https://doi.org/10.1007/978-0-387-88735-7_1
37. Shatil, A., Hazzan, O., Dubinsky, Y.: Agility in a large-scale system engineering project: a case-study of an advanced communication system project. In: IEEE International Conference on Software Science, Technology and Engineering, pp. 47–54 (2010)
38. Shen, Y., Tuuli, M.M., Xia, B., Koh, T.Y., Rowlinson, S.: Toward a model for forming psychological safety climate in construction project management. Int. J. Project Manag. **33**(1), 223–235 (2015)
39. Silva, C.M.B.d., Loubach, D.S., Cunha, A.M.d.: An estimation model to measure computer systems development based on hardware and software. In: IEEE/AIAA 28th Digital Avionics Systems Conference, pp. 6.C.2-1–6.C.2-12 (2009)
40. Singh, M.P.: Norms as a basis for governing sociotechnical systems. ACM Trans. Intell. Syst. Technol. **5**(1), 21 (2013)
41. Wolff, C., Gorrochategui, I., Bücker, M.: Managing large HW/SW codesign projects. In: 6th International Conference on Intelligent Data Acquisition and Advanced Computing Systems, pp. 919–922 (2011)
42. Yue, T., Ali, S.: Applying search algorithms for optimizing stakeholders familiarity and balancing workload in requirements assignment. In: 2014 Conference on Genetic and Evolutionary Computation, pp. 1295–1302 (2014)
43. Zhu, J., Mostafavi, A.: Towards a new paradigm for management of complex engineering projects: a system-of-systems framework. In: 8th Annual IEEE System Conference, pp. 213–219 (2014)

Function Point Tree-Based Function Point Analysis: Improving Reproducibility Whilst Maintaining Accuracy in Function Point Counting

Marcos de Freitas Jr.[1(✉)], Marcelo Fantinato[1], Violeta Sun[1],
Lucinéia H. Thom[2], and Vanja Garaj[3]

[1] School of Arts, Sciences and Humanities, University of São Paulo, São Paulo, Brazil
{marcos.freitas,m.fantinato,violeta}@usp.br
[2] Institute of Informatics, Federal University of Rio Grande do Sul,
Porto Alegre, Brazil
lucineia@inf.ufrgs.br
[3] Department of Electronic and Computer Engineering,
Brunel University London, Uxbridge, UK
vanja.garaj@brunel.ac.uk

Abstract. We propose a method to improve reproducibility whilst keeping accuracy for the Function Point Analysis (FPA) method. The proposed method is based on a new artifact model called Function Point Tree (FPT). FPT enables a standardized and systematic collection of all data required for FP counting. The new measurement method is called Function Point Tree-based Function Point Analysis (FPT-FPA). We designed FPT-FPA to comply with the IFPUG's FPA steps. We implemented a prototype tool to show the feasibility of automation of the proposed method as well as to support its evaluation. We conducted an empirical study to evaluate FPT-FPA. Our results show general coefficients of variation lower than the maximum expected for both reproducibility and accuracy when compared to the standard FPA method.

Keywords: Function Point Analysis · Function Points · Business processes · Functional size · Functional size measurement

1 Introduction

Function Point Analysis (FPA) is a standardized measurement method to establish a software size from its functional requirements [5]. FPA results are used as a reference to project cost or effort estimation, benchmarking, contract outsourcing, progress tracking, portfolio size estimation, change negotiation and defect density management [36]. The International Function Point Users Group (IFPUG) is the FPA regulator agency, responsible for the Counting Practices

© Springer Nature Switzerland AG 2020
J. Filipe et al. (Eds.): ICEIS 2019, LNBIP 378, pp. 182–209, 2020.
https://doi.org/10.1007/978-3-030-40783-4_10

Manual (CPM) [21]. IFPUG's FPA[1] is standardized by ISO/IEC 20926:2010. Several cases of FPA application have been reported (e.g., [6, 27, 36]).

Controversies exist regarding FPA on its benefits and drawbacks. As a major criticism, FPA is seen as rather subjective as it requires individual judgment, restricting a standardized use. Kemerer [24] reported variations of 12% for a same product while Kitchenham and Kansala [25] reported variations of 30%, both considering counters in the same organization. Variance reported across organizations is even greater [32]. Others also argue subjectivity is a major problem, besides the fact APF can be costly and time-consuming [1, 8, 31].

Most of the proposals to solve the FPA's subjectivity attempt to reduce human intervention. They propose a measurement procedure that includes mapping rules between artifacts elaborated by software modeling techniques and FPA concepts to derive the functional size [1, 2, 10–12, 15, 16, 20, 26, 28, 30, 33, 35, 37, 38].

Although these approaches aid to improving the measurement reproducibility[2] among different measured quantity values, they overly simplify the rules of the IFPUG's CPM [21]. This simplification occurs as none of the artifacts used is detailed enough for the complete application of the standard FPA method. The correctness and completeness of pre-existing artifact models, such as UML, with respect to FPA are not guaranteed, since these models were built without FPA in mind [30]. Models not specifically conceived to support measurement may not provide the required information [8]. In the worst cases, the FPA steps are not applicable as the artifact model lacks a piece of essential information the rules require [30]. Thus, the existing approaches to improve reproducibility compromise the measurement accuracy in relation to the true quantity value, which refers herein to the expected number of Function Points (FPs) by the correct FPA application. Reproducibility and accuracy are interrelated concepts and refer to verifying consistency and concordance of measurement results got from repeated measurements, by different subjects, under similar or identical conditions when compared to the true quantity value [3, 9].

We propose a new measurement method named Function Point Tree-based Function Point Analysis (FPT-FPA). The goal is to add to the artifact model *function refinement tree*[3] additional information for the FP counting, creating the new artifact model Function Point Tree (FPT). A requirements analyst can collect the additional information at the software lifecycle to maintain all the information necessary to FPA in a single artifact. This procedure reduces the occurrence of individual interpretation caused by lack of specific information. FPT-FPA was designed to conform to the FPA steps. The aim is to improve the reproducibility of different measured quantity values, to reduce the variation among them, whilst ensuring the accuracy of the measured quantity values in relation to the true quantity value, i.e., the value provided by IFPUG.

---

[1] For the sake of simplicity, the term FPA is be used herein to refer to IFPUG's FPA.

[2] Reproducibility is also referred as inter-rater reliability, i.e., the degree of agreement among raters; a score of homogeneity or consensus in ratings given by different raters.

[3] Part of Requirements Engineering-based Conceptual Modeling (REbCM) [22].

Table 1. Techniques/artifacts used as input for counting in related work.

Step	Description
T1	UML's sequence diagram
T2	UML's class diagram
T3	UML's use case diagram
T4	UML's component diagram
T5	Entity-Relationship Diagram (ERD)
T6	Entity-relationship-Data Flow Diagram (ER-DFD)
T7	Source code
T8	Goal and Scenario Based Requirements Text (GSbRT)
T9	Web Modeling Language (WebML)'s Hypertext model
T10	Requirements Engineering-Based Conceptual Modeling
T11	Vienna Development Method - Specification Language (VDM-SL)
T12	Object-oriented Hypermedia (OO-H)'s navigation access dialogue
T13	Function-Point Tree (FPT) *[proposed here]*

Our contributions are: *(i)* establishing a FPA-compliant measurement method so none of its steps is simplified; *(ii)* supporting the systematic and standardized gathering of all information required for FPA in the single artifact FPT; and *(iii)* eliminating the need for an FPA specialist or an FPA-skilled professional. FPT-FPA was introduced in [17] and here we show more details of the proposed method as well as the work involved in your proposal. We also show a much deeper analysis of the results of the experiment conducted for its evaluation.

There are other Functional Software Measurements (FSM) of other ISO/IEC standards, such as COSMIC, FiSMA, Mark-II and NESM. They are not in the scope of this study as each FSM method introduces its own abstraction and functions that map an empirical object into a numerical one [34]. The conceptual differences among the FSM methods can be found in [19].

This paper contains: Sect. 2 with related work; Sect. 3 outlines FPT-FPA; Sects. 4 and 5 detail FPT and the mapping rules to execute the FPT-based counting; Sects. 6 and 7 show the prototype tool and the evaluation results; and Sect. 8 concludes the paper.

2   Related Work

A quasi-systematic literature review was conducted. We included studies proposing an improvement of the FPA reproducibility[4] and excluded studies: *(i)* related to FPA but not concerned with improving reproducibility (e.g., proposing alternative methods, improving only efficiency, comparing with other approaches, converting FPs to other measures and improving the adjusted size calculation);

---

[4] A broader review was published before [18], aiming at any type of FPA improvement.

(ii) limited to a particular technology, such as data warehouse systems; *(iii)* related to similar methods such as COSMIC, FiSMA, Mark-II and NESMA; *(iv)* not electronically available on the web; *(v)* not written in English; *(vi)* published before 2001[5]; and *(vii)* published as secondary studies.

We identified 15 works. Each one was analyzed to identify to which extent they cover the FPA steps. Our analysis considered only the first three most representative stages (from five), totaling 24 steps. For each work, each step was analyzed in depth to test whether it was being explicitly executed (totally or at least partially). The 15 works mention 13 techniques/artifacts in their approaches (cf. Table 1), some of them using more than one technique/artifact. Table 2 shows the comparison of the 15 works. The base technique/artifact used as input for the approach is firstly shown. For each work, the coverage analysis is shown for each main counting step. For the measurement steps (5 to 24), the last two columns show an overview of the coverage for each work: first, the sum of the individual points assigned to each step (0 to 1), totaling up to 20.0 points; then, the percentage corresponding to the related work (5% to 70%).

The approaches in Table 2 contribute at least partially to improving the FPA reproducibility but face limitations on keeping the accuracy of the results when compared to FPA. This accuracy loss occurs because they usually oversimplify the FPA steps, when proposing the mapping rules between the elements of artifacts used and the data and information needed for counting FPs. This oversimplification usually occurs as none of the used artifacts is sufficient on the data and information needed for the complete FPA application. Thus, when applying a given proposed approach, different FPA specialists may achieve equivalent results among them, but different from the true quantity value (i.e., the expected result according to FPA). This issue has been identified by other researchers, e.g., [30], who argue that there is no guarantee these pre-existing artifact models are completely correct and complete on data and information needed for FPA, since these models were not built with FPA in mind.

Per Table 2, the clear majority of proposed approaches cover up to 50% of all steps necessary for counting FPs, except for an approach that reaches a coverage of 70% [30]. However, this approach maintains the dependence of an FPA specialist or at least an FPA-skilled professional. Although their approach is directed at requirements analysts and project managers, these professionals could hardly count FPs by themselves, based on this approach, in a reliable and IFPUG compatible manner without using a certified FPA counter. No previous approach applies all the rules required by FPA to satisfactorily eliminate the lack of reproducibility. Even the one reaching 70% cannot properly address reproducibility and accuracy as 30% of the steps remain uncovered.

On the approaches covering more than 30% of the FPA steps: five use one or more UML artifacts and one uses ERD-DFD artifacts. Although there are advantages in these artifacts as they are well known by professionals, Table 2 shows they are not able to support the execution of all the FPA steps, even

---

[5] The latest CPM version with no major changes is from 2000.

being used together. This occurs because none of them is sufficiently detailed in which is required for the complete application of the standard FPA method.

Step 8 exemplify oversimplification, related to the exclusion of entities classified as *code data*. If an entity has been specified as a requirement only to ensure data quality by a fixed list of valid values to standardize data entry, it should be classified as code data per the FPA steps. This code data entity should be excluded from the counting procedure as it would not contribute to the total number of FPs. However, if this entity is not excluded and incorrectly classified as an ILF, it results in extra FPs. If it is incorrectly considered an FTR for transactional functions, it contributes to the total number of FPs.

In 2013, the Object Management Group (OMG) [34] proposed a method to automate the FPA steps from source code. This method differs from the IFPUG's CPM [21] where subjective judgments must be replaced by rules needed for the automation. However, there are also limitations to maintain accuracy as it also oversimplifies FPA. Per the OMG specification, all outputs and inquiries should be counted as external outputs since the primary intent cannot be assessed by an automated tool. The OMG specification covers only about 25% of all the FPA steps and provides measurement results different from those yielded by FPA [29].

3   Overview of the FPT-FPA Method

The new method was designed to comply with all the FPA steps. Therefore, it avoids calculating an invalid number of FPs when compared to the *true quantity value*[6], which might occur because of the simplification of the FPA steps.

FPA (cf. Fig. 1(a)) start with *requirements engineering*[7] that delivers the *user requirements specification*, in any format, by the *requirements analyst*. The *user requirements specification* is used by the *FPA specialist* to *gather needed information* and the *gathered information* is applied in parallel by the same *FPA specialist* to *count FPs*. Since the *user requirements specification* may come in different formats, the *FPA specialist* usually must interpret this specification to extract the information needed to the counting procedure.

The first task to *gather needed information* (cf. Fig. 1(b)) is to *extract information from user requirements specification*. The *FPA specialist* assesses whether the elementary processes and data functions can be identified, defining whether the *extracted information is minimally suitable for counting procedure*; if not, the procedure is *canceled*. The *FPA specialist* assesses whether the additional information such as DET, FTR, RET and processing logics can be identified, i.e., whether the extracted *information is complete enough to proceed with counting procedure* and whether this subprocess can be completed with all the information *extracted*. If a lack of information is identified, the *FPA specialist* needs to execute one or two of: *(i) make assumptions* to complete the necessary information

---

[6] The correct expected number of FPs achieved by the accurate FPA application.

[7] *Requirements engineering* and *count FPs* subprocesses are not detailed in this paper.

Table 2. Systematic comparison among related work.

Column groups: S1–S4 = *1. Counting planning steps*[a]; S5–S18 = *2. Measuring data functions*[b]; S19–S24 = *3. Measuring trans. functions*[b].

Related work	Base technique/artifact (cf. Table 1)	S1	S2	S3	S4	S5	S6	S7	S8	S9	S10	S11	S12	S13	S14	S15	S16	S17	S18	S19	S20	S21	S22	S23	S24	Total pts.	% coverage
1 [12]	T1	−	−	±	+	0.5	0	0	0	0	0	0.5	0.5	0	0	0	0	0.5	0.5	0	0.5	0.5	0	0.5	0.5	4.5	23%
2 [13]	T7	−	−	±	±	0.5	0	0	0	0	0	0	0.5	0	0	0	0	0.5	0	0	0.5	0	0	0	0.5	2.5	13%
3 [14]	T1/T2/T3	−	−	−	−	0.5	0	0.5	0	0	0	0.5	0.5	0.5	0.5	0	0	0.5	0.5	0	0.5	0.5	0.5	0.5	0.5	6.5	33%
4 [15]	T6	−	−	−	−	1	0	0.5	0	0	0	0.5	0.5	0.5	0	0.5	0	0.5	1	0.5	1	0.5	0.5	1	0.5	9.0	45%
5 [16]	T1/T2	−	−	−	−	1	0	1	0	0	0	0.5	0.5	0	0.5	0.5	0	0.5	1	0	1	0.5	0.5	1	1	9.5	48%
6 [17]	T5/T9	−	−	−	−	0.5	0	0.5	0	0	0	0.5	0.5	0	0	0	0	0.5	0.5	0.5	0.5	0.5	0	0.5	0.5	5.5	28%
7 [18]	T8	−	−	−	+	0.5	1	0	0	0	0	0.5	0.5	0	0	0	0	0.5	0	0.5	0.5	0.5	0.5	0.5	0.5	6.0	30%
8 [19]	T2/T12	−	+	−	−	0.5	0	0.5	0	0	0	0.5	0.5	0.5	0.5	0.5	0	0.5	0	0.5	0.5	0.5	0.5	0.5	0.5	7.0	35%
9 [20]	T1/T2/T3	−	−	−	±	0	0	0	0	0	0	0.5	0	0	0	0	0	0	0	0	0.5	0	0	0	0	1.0	5%
10 [21]	T2	−	−	−	−	0.5	0	0	0	0	0	0.5	0.5	0.5	0	0	0	0.5	0	0.5	0.5	0.5	0	0	0.5	4.0	20%
11 [22]	T1/T2/T3/T4	−	−	−	+	1	1	1	1	1	1	1	0.5	0	1	1	0	0.5	0	0.5	0.5	0.5	1	1	0.5	14	70%
12 [9]	T10	−	+	−	+	0.5	0	0	0	0	0	0.5	0	0	0	0	0	0.5	0	0.5	0.5	0.5	0.5	0	0.5	4.0	20%
13 [23]	T11	−	−	−	−	0.5	0	0	0	0	0	0.5	0.5	0	0	0	0	0.5	0.5	0	0.5	0.5	0	0	0.5	3.5	18%
14 [24]	T7	−	−	−	−	0.5	0	0	0	0	0	0.5	0.5	0	0	0	0	0.5	0	0.5	0.5	0.5	0	0.5	0.5	4.5	23%
15 [25]	T2	−	−	−	−	0.5	1	0	0	0	0	1	0.5	1	0	0	1	0.5	0	1	1	0	0	0	0	7.5	38%
16 This	T13	+	+	+	+	1	1	1	1	1	1	1	1	1	1	1	1	1	1	1	1	1	1	1	1	20.0	100%

[a] Legend for the coverage of the *counting planning steps*:

+: Planning step **fully supported** by the technique/artifact used as the basis of the proposed approach, i.e., the approach explicitly supports the entire planning step.

±: Planning step **partially supported** by the technique/artifact used as the basis of the proposed approach, i.e., the approach explicitly supports only some actions of the planning step. The remainder of the step needs to be performed by means not provided by the approach.

−: Planning step **not directly supported** by the technique/artifact used as the basis of the proposed approach, i.e., the approach does not explicitly support any action of the planning step. The entire step needs to be performed by means not provided by the approach.

[b] Legend and weights for the coverage of the *measuring steps*:

1: Measuring step **fully covered** by the technique/artifact used as the basis of the proposed approach, i.e., the approach fully complies with the corresponding step in an explicit way.

0.5: Measuring step **partially covered** by the technique/artifact used as the basis of the proposed approach, i.e., the approach does not fully comply with the corresponding step, but with extra actions it is possible to execute it. Diverse levels of extra actions may be needed for each partial covered step, ranging from little effort to much effort; however, considering the difficulty in correctly classifying the level of effort required for each step, all similar cases are always classified on average as *partially covered*.

0: Measuring step **not directly covered** by the technique/artifact used as the basis of the proposed approach, i.e., the approach does not comply at all with the corresponding step. In this case, although the technique/artifact used does not provide any support for this step, it is possible to execute it using their own procedures.

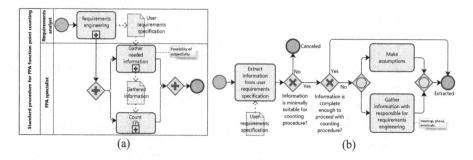

Fig. 1. *(a)* FPA steps, *(b)* Subprocess Gather needed information [17].

or *(ii)* informally *gather information with the responsible for requirements engineering* by meetings, e-mail, phone etc. Both cases can threat reproducibility as they may lead to important variations in the measurement results.

The Function Point Tree-based Function Point Analysis (FPT-FPA) measurement method (cf. Fig. 2) add the subprocess *elaborate FPT* to the FPA steps as part of the *requirements analyst* duties. The need for a formal *FPA specialist* role is then eliminated as the *requirements analyst* executes FPA supported by FPT, which in turn can be aided by a computational tool. Part of the activities that should be performed by an *FPA specialist* is moved to the modeling phase so it can be carried out by the *requirements analyst* and the other part is executed by the standard procedure that can be automated. Since the *requirements analyst* is the role with the best knowledge on software requirements, FPT-FPA improves the whole counting quality. The *requirements analyst* does not need FPA knowledge as the counting is automatically executed based on the FPT available. As a potential drawback for this approach, the *requirements analyst* needs to be a specialist on FPT to be able to elaborate it correctly, but this technique is more related to their usual responsibilities than mastering FPA. The *requirements analyst* does not need to be a specialist on all the FPA steps.

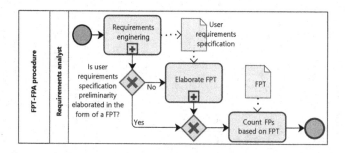

Fig. 2. IFPUG's FPA procedure to count FPs [17].

FPT-FPA also starts with the *requirements engineering*, delivering the *user requirements specification* by the *requirements analyst*. Here, the *user requirements specification* can be firstly produced as an FPT, although not monetarily. If *user requirements specification is preliminarily elaborated as an FPT*, it is directly used to *count FPs based on FPT* (cf. Sect. 5). Otherwise, the *requirements analyst* needs to *elaborate FPT* before proceeding with the counting. The details of the *elaborate FPT* subprocess are shown in Sect. 4 whereas the details of the *count FPs based on FPT* subprocess are shown in Sect. 5. None of these two subprocesses are shown visually due to their complexities.

4   Elaborating the Function Point Tree

An FPT is composed of three levels: root, intermediate and leaf nodes. Figure 3 shows an illustrative example of an FPT, which represents a Human Resources Management System (HRMS). The details are shown as follows.

4.1   Level 1: Tree Root

The root node represents the counting purpose and the counting type. Each root has two types of root markers for: *(i)* the counting purpose, i.e., the purpose for which an organization needs to execute the counting according to the FPA concepts (cf. Fig. 4); and *(ii)* the counting type, which refers to what will be done with the obtained measure (cf. Fig. 5). Exactly one root marker exists for the former case and at least one root marker exists for the latter.

4.2   Level 2: Intermediate Nodes

No change was proposed for this level as originally defined [22].

4.3   Level 3: Leaf Nodes

Leaf nodes represent the software elementary functions and must include: node markers; inclusion dependency connectors (when applicable); and node attributes.

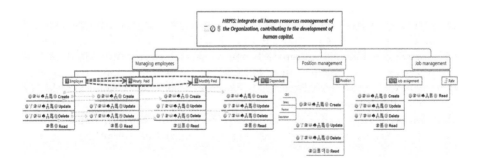

Fig. 3. Example of FPT [17].

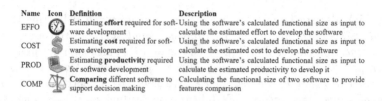

Name	Icon	Definition	Description
EFFO		Estimating **effort** required for software development	Using the software's calculated functional size as input to calculate the estimated effort to develop the software
COST		Estimating **cost** required for software development	Using the software's calculated functional size as input to calculate the estimated cost to develop the software
PROD		Estimating **productivity** required for software development	Using the software's calculated functional size as input to calculate the estimated productivity to develop it
COMP		**Comparing** different software to support decision making	Calculating the functional size of two software to provide features comparison

Fig. 4. Root markers for counting purposes [17].

Name	Icon	Definition	Description
NEW		Representing a **new** software	When the purpose is to get the functional size of a new software to be developed in an organization
EVOL		Representing a software being **evolved**	When the purpose is to get the functional size only of the new user requirements to be added to an existing software that must evolve
EXIS		Representing an **existing** software not undergoing changes	When the purpose is to get the full functional size of a software after first development or evolution

Fig. 5. Root markers for counting types [17].

Node Markers. Node markers refer to the behavior of the elementary functions at the software execution. Whenever an elementary function contains one or more of the behavior properties represented by node markers (cf. Tables 6 and 7), these markers are added to the corresponding leaf node. Figure 6 shows node markers whose corresponding behavior is connected to at least one processing logic. Figure 7 shows extra node markers not connected to any processing logic[8]. PRIM is to represent which marker among MAIN, BEHA and PRES is the main purpose of an elementary function. PRIM is required for a leaf node only when at least two of the other three (MAIN, BEHA, PRES) were selected. For example (cf. Fig. 3), the elementary function *create employee* contains the node markers VALI, PRES, MESS, REFE, COND, MAIN and PRIM; so PRIM was included since PRES and MAIN were previously included. Thus, PRIM is in charge of informing whether the main purpose of this elementary function is PRES or MAIN. Specifically, in this example, the PRIM value is MAIN.

Inclusion Dependency Connector Between Elementary Functions. An inclusion dependency connector shows an inclusion dependency relationship between two elementary functions. It is represented by a yellow arrow (⟶) and is only to connect leaf nodes to each other. It is used when the later elementary function (i.e., after the arrow) does not comply with the user functional requirements if performed alone, but only if the previous elementary function (i.e., contrary to the arrow) is executed first. For example, a user functional requirement might require that, after registering an employee, payment details (monthly or hourly) and dependents have to be registered. Thereby, both following actions do not comply with this user functional requirement: *(i)* registering an employee without sequentially either registering their payment details (monthly or hourly)

---

[8] Only 12 of 13 FPA PLs are used since the last one neither impacts the identification of the type nor contributes to the uniqueness of an elementary process.

Name	Icon	Definition	Example	FPA PL
VALI		Executing data **validation** required by business rules	Validating whether an ID is valid according to rules issued by the responsible agency	1
CALC		Executing at least one **calculation** that complies with a business rule	Calculating interest for overdue payment	2
CONV		Executing format **conversion** for some attribute (maintaining the same information in another format)	Converting attribute *temperature* from unit Celsius degrees to unit Fahrenheit degrees	3
FILT		Executing data **filter** according to some criteria on a data set	Listing employees who *have two children and are more than 40 years old*	4
COND		Depending on some **condition** that, when analyzed, may lead to different results	Displaying on screen different attributes depending on employee's contract type: hourly or monthly paid	5
MAIN		**Maintain** data from at least one entity	Registering a new employee in organization	6
REFE		**Referencing** or retrieving data from at least one entity	Referencing a currency exchange rate to determine sale price of an item	7, 8
DERI		**Deriving** or generating data that characterize additional information from existing data	Generating academic ID by combining part of the name with current year and enrollment day	9
BEHA		Owning attributes that, when updated, change the organization's process **behavior**	Attribute *employee payday*, if updated, causes changes in organization's business processes	10
PRES		**Presenting** information to user	Displaying an organization's list of employees	11
RETR		**Retrieving** information from user	User enters a data set to register a new employee in organization	12

Fig. 6. Node markers for the elementary function behavior (with FPA PL) [17].

Name	Icon	Definition	Example
BATC		Running in **batch** (previously scheduled by the user)	Reporting the company's yearly profits and losses
MESS		Displaying a **message** to the user	Displaying the message *operation not allowed* when user tries to add a duplicated employee
CONS	π	Registering or displaying static, **constant** or domain data, called as *code data* (i.e., a list of valid values)	Displaying a list of states of a country
PRIM		Defining which is the **primary** intention among: MAIN, BEHA or PRES	*Displaying the list of employees* and *creating a new*, when the primary intention is *creating a new employee*

Fig. 7. Additional node markers for the behavior of the elementary functions (without corresponding FPA processing logic) [17].

Name	Icon	Definition	Example
EXTE		Represents a data entity maintained by an **external** software and only referenced by the software being modeled	Data entity *rate* (cf. Fig. 3), maintained by another software and only referenced by HRMS to get the hour value to be paid to an hourly paid employee
TYPE	T	Represents a **type** of data entity that store user's relevant data	Data entity *employee* (cf. Fig. 3)
SUBT	S	Represents a split of a data entity type. A **subtype** inherits all the attributes and relationships of its parent data entity type and may have additional own attributes and relationships	Data entity *hourly paid* (cf. Fig. 3)
ATTR	A T	Represents a data entity type (**attributive**) that complementarily describes one or more properties of another data entity	Data entity *dependent* (cf. Fig. 3)
ASSO	A S	Represents a data entity type (**association**) that describes a many-to-many relationship between two other data entity types	Data entity *job assignment* (cf. Fig. 3)

Fig. 8. Data entity markers to represent the data entity properties [17].

or registering their dependents; and *(ii)* first registering the employee's payment details (monthly or hourly) or first registering the employee's dependents, both without ever having previously registered this employee. Therefore, the leaf nodes *create employee, create hourly paid employee, create monthly paid employee* and *create dependent* are connected by an inclusion dependency connector, starting from *create employee* first and heading toward the other three.

Node Attributes. Node attributes show the information to be displayed to or informed by a user during execution of elementary functions. For each node attribute, it should be informed: if the corresponding information is displayed either in the screen header or footer; if the information is available only for user data reading or also for user data input; and if the information has meaning stand-alone to a business process user or only when combined to another one.

4.4   Relationships Amongst Levels

All intermediate nodes are connected to the tree root (root-intermediate connections); and all leaf nodes are connected to an intermediate node (intermediate-leaf connections). For the latter, the following data accompanies the connections whenever appropriate: data entity labels; data entity markers; exclusion dependency connectors; and data entity attributes.

Data Entity Label. A data entity associated to an intermediate-leaf connection represents a software data entity maintained or referenced by the elementary functions of the corresponding leaf nodes. For example (cf. Fig. 3), the label *position* represents a data entity maintained or referenced by four elementary functions: *create (position)*, *update (position)*, *delete (position)* and *read (position)*. Each informed data entity (represented by a data entity label) is accompanied by the following additional data: data entity markers; exclusion dependency connectors (whenever appropriate); and data entity attributes. Data entities neither maintained nor referenced by elementary functions should not be modeled.

Data Entity Markers. Data entity markers show properties for the corresponding data entity. Whenever a data entity has one or more of the properties in Fig. 8, the corresponding markers are added to it.

Exclusion Dependency Connector Between Data Entities. Exclusion dependency connectors show the existence of an exclusion dependency relationship between two data entities. The relationship is represented by a red arrow (——>) and is to attach two data entities together. The arrow is to connect a data entity with other data entities that compose it so the subsequent data entities (i.e., after the arrow) are parts of the first one (i.e., contrary to the arrow). If the first data entity is deleted, all the data entities connected to it by exclusion dependency connectors are also deleted since they do not exist alone. For example (cf. Fig. 3), if a user functional requirement requires that, by deleting an employee, all the employee's dependents and the employee data (whatever they are hourly or monthly paid) are also deleted; then, the dependent data entities (dependent, hourly paid and monthly paid) have no meaning alone without a connection to an employee. Therefore, *hourly paid*, *monthly paid* and *dependent* are connected via an exclusion dependency connector to *employee*.

Data Entity Attributes. Data entity attributes represent the information stored in a data entity and are maintained or referenced by the elementary functions in the corresponding leaf nodes. For each entity, all data maintained or referenced needed to execute the corresponding functions is informed. For each attribute, it is necessary to inform whether the corresponding information has meaning stand-alone to a business process user or only combined.

5 Executing the Counting Based on FPT-FPA

The data in the FPT is to support the counting procedure ensuring all the FPA steps are met. Mapping rules are used so data modeled on the FPT are used as input to FPA. This section describes the proposed mapping rules following the FPA steps, i.e., according to the defined by the IFPUG's CPM [21].

The counting procedure starts by gathering the software documentation. In FPT-FPA, the only input device needed for counting is the FPT and not all the relevant available artifacts as defined by FPA. The FPT is complete enough and hence the only relevant and necessary artifact. Therefore, the information contained in this artifact is used to support the execution of the five counting stages, as described in the following sections.

We detail only the three first stages as no change is proposed to the last two.

5.1 Defining the Counting Boundary, Scope and Purpose

The counting boundary in FPT-FPA is represented by the tree root (cf. Sect. 4.1), as it defines, as child or grandchild nodes, all the sets of functions and data entities to be addressed during the counting procedure. Any other function or data entity not included in the tree is considered as outside of the counting border. The counting scope is represented by all the elementary functions (represented by leaf nodes) and all data entities of the FPT. The complete set of elementary functions and data entities is considered to belong to the counting scope. The counting purpose is represented by one of the following root markers: EFFO, COST, PROD or COMP (cf. Fig. 4); the marker in the tree and its corresponding meaning are used to define the counting purpose. The counting type is represented by a set of one or more of the following root markers NEW, EVOL and EXIS (cf. Fig. 5); all the markers in the tree and their corresponding meanings are used to define the counting type.

5.2 Measuring Data Functions

Identifying the Data Functions. Each data entity (i.e., a label in the FPT, cf. Sect. 4.3) is mapped to a single data function or as part of a composed data function, unless: *(i) the data entity corresponds to a code data*, i.e., data entities whose associated elementary function (represented by a leaf node) has the node marker CONS (cf. Fig. 7) are discarded; *(ii) the data entity stores only attributes unacknowledged by business process users*, i.e., data entities whose information represented by its data entity attributes with no meaning stand-alone to a business process user (cf. Sect. 4.4.4) are discarded; *(iii) the data entity describes a many-to-many relationship between two other data entity types and contains only foreign keys*, i.e., data entities having the data entity marker ASSO (cf. Fig. 8) and presenting up to two data entity attributes with meaning stand-alone to a business process user (cf. Sect. 4.4.4) are discarded; and *(iv) the data entity stores only one data entity attribute*, i.e., data entities presenting only one data entity attribute with meaning stand-alone to a business process user (cf. Sect. 4.4.4) are discarded. Data entities complying with both constraints are mapped to a single data function or as part of a composed data function depending on whether they are logically dependent or independent among them: *(i) data entities logically independent of all the other data entities*, i.e., those not linked to any other data entity by an exclusion dependency connector (cf. Sect. 4.4.3), are directly mapped to a single data function each one (only data entities having meaning for the business by their own are mapped to single data functions); and *(ii) a set of data entities logically dependent among them*, i.e., linked one to another by exclusion dependency connectors (cf. Sect. 4.4.3), is grouped and mapped to a single data function (data entities with meaning for the business only when combined are mapped together to a single data function).

Classifying the Data Functions. Each data function identified is classified as Internal Logical File (ILF) or External Interface File (EIF). This classification relies on the elementary functions that manipulate the data entities components of the data functions. The following two rules are followed to classify a data function as ILF or EIF: ILF – data functions that comply with the following constraint: at least one of its data entities is associated to an elementary function (represented by a leaf node) that has the node marker MAIN (cf. Fig. 6); EIF – data functions that comply with all the following constraints: *(i)* none of its data entities is associated to any elementary function (represented by a leaf node) that has the node marker MAIN (cf. Fig. 6) and *(ii)* at least one of its data entities has the data entity marker EXTE (cf. Fig. 8).

Determining the Numbers of DET and RET for the Data Functions. To determine the number of DETs for a data function, the number is counted of data entity attributes (associated to its data entities) with meaning stand-alone to a business process user (cf. Sect. 4.4.4). To determine the number of RETs, it is considered the data entity properties (defined by the data entity markers; cf. Fig. 8) of its data entities, based on: *(i)* each data entity marked as SUBT, ATTR or ASSO is counted as a RET of the data function and *(ii)* each data entity marked as TYPE and not linked (by exclusion dependency connector) to any data entity marked as SUBT is counted as a RET of the data function.

Determining Complexity and Contribution for the Data Functions. The complexity (i.e., low, medium or high) of each data function is determined based on the numbers of DET and RET, directly applying the values predefined for FPA. Based on the obtained complexities, the last step is to determine the contribution on functional size of each data function, which is executed by the direct application of the values predefined for FPA.

5.3   Measuring Transactional Functions

Identifying the Elementary Processes. Each elementary function (i.e., a leaf node in the FPT, cf. Sect. 4.2) is mapped to a single elementary process or as part of a composed elementary process, unless: *(i) the elementary function maintains or has references to code data*, i.e., elementary functions presenting the node marker CONS (cf. Fig. 7) are discarded; and *(ii) the elementary function does not process data or control information retrieved from outside the boundary or does not send data or control information to outside the border*, i.e., elementary functions without any node attribute informing availability for user data reading or user data input (cf. Sect. 4.3.3) are discarded. The elementary functions complying with the previous constraints are mapped either to a single elementary process or to a part of a composed elementary process depending whether they are logically dependent or independent among them: *(i) elementary functions logically independent of all the other elementary functions*, i.e., not linked to any other elementary function by an inclusion dependency connector (cf. Sect. 4.3.2), are each one directly mapped to a single elementary function; and *(ii) a set of elementary functions logically dependent among them*, i.e., linked one to another by inclusion dependency connectors (cf. Sect. 4.3.2), is grouped and mapped to a single elementary process. An elementary process maintains software in a consistent state after execution, i.e., it constitutes a complete transaction, is self-contained and is the smallest meaningful unit of activity.

Determining Unique Elementary Processes. Next step is to identify the unique elementary processes representing the transactional functions. Each unique elementary process is identified as a transactional function. Two or more of any elementary processes are identified as a unique elementary process if they have: *(i)* exactly the same node markers representing processing logics (i.e., VALI, CALC, CONV, FILT, COND, MAIN, REFE, DERI, BEHA, PRES and RETR, cf. Fig. 6); *(ii)* exactly the same node attributes representing Data Element Types (DET) (cf. Sect. 5.3.4) for the elementary process (cf. Sect. 4.3.3); and *(iii)* exactly the same data entities representing File Type Reference (FTR) (cf. Sect. 5.3.4) for the associated elementary process (cf. Sect. 4.4.1).

Classifying the Transactional Functions. Each identified transactional function is classified as External Input (EI), External Output (EO) or External Inquiry (EQ), which relies on the primary intention (represented by the node marker PRIM; cf. Fig. 7) of the elementary functions composing the transactional functions. There are three rules to classify a transaction function as EI,

EO or EQ. EI – transactional functions that comply with the following constraint: at least one of its elementary functions has the node marker PRIM (cf. Fig. 7) indicating as the primary intention the node markers MAIN or BEHA (cf. Fig. 6). EO – transactional functions that comply with all the following constraints: *(i)* none of its elementary functions has the node marker PRIM (cf. Fig. 7) indicating as the primary intention the node markers MAIN or BEHA (cf. Fig. 6); *(ii)* at least one of its elementary functions has the node markers CALC, MAIN, BEHA or DERI (cf. Fig. 6); and *(iii)* at least one of its elementary functions marked as CALC, MAIN, BEHA or DERI (cf. Fig. 6) has at least one node attribute informing availability for user data reading (cf. Sect. 4.3.3). EQ – transactional functions that comply with all the following constraints: *(i)* none of its elementary functions has the node marker PRIM (cf. Fig. 7) with primary intention the node markers MAIN or BEHA (cf. Fig. 6); *(ii)* none of its elementary functions has the node markers CALC, MAIN, BEHA and DERI (cf. Fig. 6); and *(iii)* at least one of its elementary functions has one or more node attributes informing availability for user data reading (cf. Sect. 4.3.3).

Determining the Numbers of DET and FTR for the Transactional Functions. To determine the number of DETs for a transactional function, the number is counted of node attributes (associated to its elementary functions) with meaning stand-alone to a business process user (cf. Sect. 4.3.3). Moreover, the following additional rules are followed: *(i)* if the information corresponding to a node attribute is displayed only in the header or in the footer of the screen (cf. Sect. 4.3.3), then this node attribute is discarded for the counting of DETs; *(ii)* if one of the elementary functions has the node marker MESS, it is counted an extra DET for the corresponding transactional function, considering the functional ability to display a message to the user; and *(iii)* if one of the elementary functions does not have the node marker BATC, it is counted one extra DET for the corresponding transactional function, considering the functional ability to initiate some action. To determine the number of FTRs for a transactional function, the data entities related to the elementary functions constituents of this transaction function is considered. Each data entity identified as a data function (or as part of a data function) and associated to the corresponding transactional function is counted as an FTR for this transactional function.

Determining Complexity and Contribution for the Transactional Functions. The complexity (i.e., low, medium or high) of each transactional function is determined based on the numbers of DET and FTR, directly applying the values predefined for FPA. Based on the obtained complexities, the last step is to determine the contribution on functional size of each transactional function, which is executed by the direct application of the values predefined for FPA.

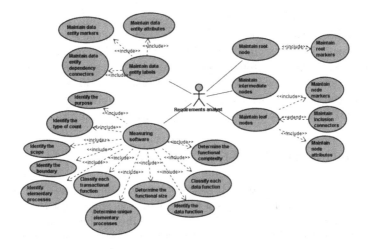

Fig. 9. Use case diagram for the support prototype [17].

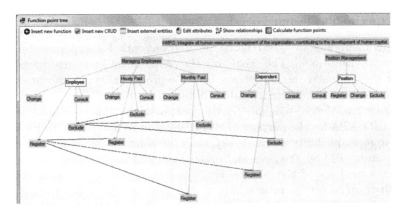

Fig. 10. Screenshot of the developed prototype [17].

6 Support Tool

A prototype tool was developed to support the FP counting based on FPT-FPA. This tool was developed to show the automation feasibility of FPT-FPA and to help verify and validate it, i.e., to be used as a proof of concept. The method evaluation also considered the execution of FPT-FPA without using the tool (cf. Sect. 7) to ensure it is correct regardless of whether the tool is used or not or whether the tool is implemented incorrectly. The development of a full tool for commercial purposes was not the primary goal and, therefore, non-functional requirements such as usability, performance and others were not addressed. As the outcome result, the FPT was simplified on graphic presentation of the elements root markers, nodes and data entity labels as proposed in Fig. 3.

Figure 9 shows a use case diagram representing the functional requirements with five main use cases used by a single actor to whom the system is designed – the requirements analyst. Thus, with FPT-FPA, an FPA specialist would be no longer needed and the requirement analyst would receive some additional tasks.

Figure 10 shows a screenshot of the tool, the part of the FPT shown in Fig. 3, with technical limitations mentioned in the beginning of this section. The complete FPT is not shown in this figure because of readability.

7   Evaluation of FPT-FPA

An empirical study was conducted to evaluate the proposed method regarding reproducibility and accuracy. A quasi-experiment was run to test the hypothesis the proposed method enables a higher reproducibility and accuracy degree than FPA. We used a quasi-experiment as it would be unfeasible to randomly select the subjects due to the study complexity [14, 23].

7.1   Experiment Design

The experiment was designed based on a framework for experimental software engineering [39]. The goal of the experiment was to investigate whether the proposed method shows better reproducibility and accuracy levels when compared to reference values obtained by FPA. Based on the GQM (Goal/Question/Metric) template [7], the goal pursued in this experiment was: to analyze FPT-FPA for the purpose of evaluating it in comparison with FPA with respect to reproducibility and accuracy, from the point of view of the researcher, in the context of M.Sc. students and practitioners measuring FPs.

For the analysis of the results, two different criteria were used. **Reproducibility** (quantitative, ratio scale), as the agreement between the measurement results of different subjects. This study examined the reproducibility of the results calculated by different subjects by FPT-FPA, by comparing the obtained calculation results among subjects. It was expected to get a coefficient of variation for the results with FPT-FPA[9] lower than 17.67%, since this is the average of the coefficients of variation found in related work on reproducibility [13, 24, 25, 32]. Although the only found sources are out-of-date, they can be used as a reference value since FPA can be kept without substantial changes along these years. **Accuracy** (quantitative, ratio scale), as the agreement between the measurement results and the true quantity value. In this case, the study examined the accuracy of the results calculated by different subjects by FPT-FPA, by comparing the obtained results with the official reference value as reported by IFPUG. It was expected to get a coefficient of variation between the results with FPT-FPA[10] and the IFPUG's official value lower than 10.71%

---

[9] Standard deviation (of the values measured with FPTFPA relative to the average of such measured values) divided by the average of the values measured with FPTFPA.

[10] Standard deviation (of the values measured with FPTFPA relative to the IFPUG's value) divided by the IFPUG's value.

since this is the average of the coefficients of variation found in related work on accuracy [1, 4, 15, 16, 28, 33, 38].

For the analysis of these two criteria, the total numbers of measured FPs were considered, i.e., the sum of all Base Functional Components (BFC), from both data functions (ILF and EIF) and transactional functions (EI, EO and EQ). Thus, the reproducibility and accuracy analyses were performed by evaluating the method as a whole and not focusing on specific components. Regardless, some breakdown values are also shown relating to BFCs to help identify where reproducibility and accuracy problems may be located specifically.

A secondary goal was to evaluate the efficiency of applying FPT-FPA aided by the tool. It was expected that the mean time spent by subjects using the tool would be up to 25% of that without using it, representing a considerable gain of automated over manual execution. This value was defined as an initial parameter as no reference value was found in the literature.

The experiment design details are presented here. **Subjects**: 17 individuals with a background education in information systems (or related) were chosen for convenience, most of whom with experience in the IT industry from 1 to 20 years (mainly requirements or systems analysts) and the others from a graduate program. As a single constraint, they should not know FPA to avoid bias when using FPT-FPA. **Variables**: independent variables – the primary independent variable refers to the methods being compared, i.e., FPT-FPA and FPA; the secondary independent variable was the type of execution of FPT-FPA, i.e., manually or automated; and dependent variables – two dependents variables in the study are – reproducibility and accuracy. **Treatment**: the higher-level treatment corresponds to the primary independent variable, i.e., FPT-FPA versus FPA. All the subjects carried out only FPT-FPA. As a lower-level treatment, for the secondary goal, the subjects were randomly assigned to two groups for manual execution (eight subjects) and automated execution (nine subjects). **Instrumentation**: training – all subjects received a presentation on an overview of the experiment and a description of the proposed method, which included none examples; object – a specification of a human resource support software, previously measured by IFPUG via FPA, was chosen for comparison basis; the software has 125 FPs [21]; tool or results form – for the subjects of the automated execution group, the tool was provided; for the manual execution group, a form was provided to fill in the generated data, including the FPT; and characterization form – each subject received a form to report the basic characterization data describing the sample and the total time spent on the experiment. **Hypotheses**: hypothesis A – FPT-FPA shows a reproducibility coefficient of variation lower than 17.67%, i.e., FPT-FPA shows a higher degree of reproducibility than FPA; and hypothesis B – FPT-FPA shows a reproducibility coefficient of variation equal or lower than 17.67%, i.e., FPT-FPA shows a higher degree of reproducibility than FPA.

7.2   Subjects Profile

Figure 11 shows the profile of the subjects, with education background, current position and the length of work experience. All 17 subjects held at least a

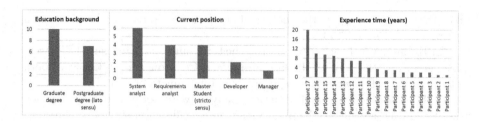

Fig. 11. Selected subjects profile [17].

Table 3. Measurement results obtained (data and transactional functions totalized).
Ref. = Reference value = IFPUG's value [17].

	Ref.	P1	P2	P3	P4	P5	P6	P7	P8	P9	P10	P11	P12	P13	P14	P15	P16	P17	Mean
Total # of FPs	125	104	109	88	110	111	102	101	124	124	122	124	118	124	128	128	122	130	115.8
Exec. time (h)		1.7	2.5	2.6	1.1	2.3	2.1	4.5	2.8	3.5	4.2	3.8	3.2	3.0	5.0	8.0	7.5	2.1	3.52
Exec. type		A	A	A	A	A	A	A	A	M	M	M	M	M	M	M	M	M	–

graduate degree in information systems or related areas and seven of them also
held a postgraduate degree. 13 of them were working in industry, with the majority being system or requirements analysts, one developer and one manager. Some
of these 13 subjects working in industry were also enrolled in a Master of Science Graduate Program in Information Systems. The remaining four subjects to
complete 17 were fully enrolled in the same master program; with some previous
experience in industry. The work experience ranges from 1 to 20 years.

7.3   Results Achieved

Table 3 shows the results breakdown by subject, including the number of FPs
measured, the time spent and the type of execution (manual or automated).

Table 4 shows the mean values for the FPs measured by FPT-FPA and other
values derived from the means needed to evaluate reproducibility and accuracy,
for both automated and manual executions. Table 5 shows the mean time spent
by the subjects, considering both those who used the support tool and those
who performed the counting manually and the relation between both groups.

Table 6 shows the breakdown by different Base Functional Components
(BFC). The execution time was not recorded by each component as the subjects could share their time across all of them according to their preferences.
For Table 6, cells containing values, measured by any subject, different from the
expected value (cf. column *Ref.*) are highlighted in **bold**. Finally, the partial
measurement results from Table 6 are consolidated in Table 7, which shows data
similarly to Table 4. Table 7 repeats the expected coefficient of variation (cf.
Table 4) for reproducibility and accuracy analysis, but only for reference purposes, since these values cannot be directly applied in this context as they were
defined to evaluate only the total number of FPs.

Table 4. Consolidated results on reproducibility and accuracy with breakdown by manual and automated (data functions and transactional functions totalized) [17].

Perspective of analysis	Function points						
	Mean of the measured values	Relative to the mean (reproducibility)			Relative to the true quantity value – IFPUG's value (Accuracy)		
		Standard deviation	Coef. of variation		Standard deviation	Coef. of variation	
			Obtained	Expected		Obtained	Expected
All subjects (man+aut)	115.82	11.57	9.99%	<17,67%	14.76	11.81%	<10.71%
Only manually	124.44	3.50	2.81%		3.54	2.83%	
Only automated	106.13	9.64	9.08%		21.19	16.95%	

Table 5. Time spent by the subjects.

Perspective of analysis	Execution time (hours)		
	Automated (mean)	Manually (mean)	Automated/Manually
All subjects (manually+automated)	2.45	4.48	55%

7.4   Analysis of Results

Reproducibility Analysis. For the reproducibility analysis, the coefficient of variation, relative to the mean (to measure reproducibility), calculated as 9.99%, when observing the measurement results for all subjects (cf. Table 4) is nearly half the maximum value defined as the study goal in comparison to the related work (i.e., 17.67%). This value shows that, on reproducibility, the proposed method is on average substantially better than other approaches present in literature. Evaluating this data considering different perspectives, the results allow for a better understanding of the performance of the proposed method. For the manual execution of the proposed method (cf. Table 4), the calculated coefficient of variation is 2.81%. This value is much lower than the maximum value defined as the study goal (i.e., 17.67%). On the other hand, the calculated coefficient of variation for the subjects who executed the method with the support of the tool is 9.08%, which is similar to the coefficient obtained for all the subjects (i.e., 9.99%). Although these findings show satisfactory results for the proposed method in achieving better reproducibility, it can be inferred the tool seems to have been an obstacle as the best results were obtained using the proposed method manually. Nevertheless, even when using the tool, the achieve results can still be considered better than FPA. A preliminary hypothesis for this behavior is the tool needs further improvements whether it is to become truly useful to the user. It is likely the tool faces many usability issues, which can be observed, for example, comparing the intended design of the FPT (cf. Fig. 3) with the provided by the developed tool (cf. Fig. 10). Moreover, if the reproducibility data is analyzed considering different Base Functional Components (BFC) (cf. Table 7), some additional findings can be observed. Both perspectives, i.e., data functions and transactional functions, show coefficients of variation (11.22% and 14.42%,

Table 6. Partial measurement results for data functions and transactional functions (values not conforming to the true quantity value are highlighted in **bold**).

BFC	Ref	P1	P2	P3	P4	P5	P6	P7	P8	P9	P10	P11	P12	P13	P14	P15	P16	P17	Mean
ILF	21	21	21	21	21	21	**14**	21	21	21	21	21	21	21	21	21	21	**14**	20.18
EIF	10	10	10	10	10	10	10	10	10	10	10	10	10	10	**0**	**14**	10	10	9.65
ILF+EIF	31	31	31	31	31	31	**24**	31	31	31	31	31	31	31	**21**	**35**	31	**24**	29.82
EI	**43**	36	36	15	46	38	38	40	43	43	42	43	43	**42**	**54**	43	40	**52**	40.82
EO	**32**	27	26	28	26	26	27	17	31	31	31	31	31	32	**33**	32	32	**35**	29.18
EQ	**19**	10	16	14	7	16	13	13	19	19	18	19	13	19	**20**	18	19	19	16.00
EI+EO+EQ	**94**	73	78	57	79	80	78	70	93	93	91	93	87	93	**107**	93	91	**106**	86.00

Table 7. Partial consolidated results on reproducibility and accuracy – Breakdown by Data Functions (DFs) and Transactional Functions (TFs).

Perspective of analysis	Function points						
	Mean of the measured values	Relative to the mean (reproducibility)			Relative to the true quantity value – IFPUG's value (Accuracy)		
		Standard deviation	Coef. of variation		Standard deviation	Coef. of variation	
			Obtained	Expected		Obtained	Expected
DFs (ILF+EIF)	29.82	3.35	11.22%	<17,67%	3.55	2.84%	<10,71%
TFs (EI+EO+EQ)	86.00	12.40	14.42%		14.76	11.81%	

respectively) higher than when the method is evaluated as a whole (9.99%). However, both also display a coefficient of variation lower than the maximum (17.67%) expected for reproducibility. The individual parts show higher coefficients of variation because with lower numbers and the same error in absolute terms, a higher standard deviation in percentage is obtained. Consequently, if it was shown a similar analysis for each individual BFC (i.e., ILF, EIF, EI, EO, EQ), the corresponding coefficients of variation would most likely be even higher. Finally, it can be observed, from Table 6, the measured values for the data functions varied less among them than those related to the transactional functions. In addition, for the data functions, there were more variations when the method was manually executed, whereas for the transactional functions, there were more variations when the method was supported by the tool, which shows the tool probably has more usability issues when supporting the counting of transactional functions rather than of data functions.

Accuracy Analysis. For the accuracy analysis, the coefficient of variation, relative to the IFPUG's value, i.e., the true quantity value (to measure accuracy), calculated as 11.81% based on the measurement results for all subjects (cf. Table 4) is slightly higher than the maximum value defined as the study goal in comparison to the related work (i.e., 10.71%). This value shows that, on accuracy, the proposed method is in general less accurate than the found in related work. However, when considering different perspectives, better results are also found, which can again be useful to a better understanding of the performance of the proposed method. For example, when the results are evaluated considering only the subjects who executed the method manually (cf. Table 4), it can also be observed a better coefficient of variation calculated as 2.83%, which is much lower than the maximum value defined as the study goal (i.e., 10.71%). On the other hand, when considering only the subjects who executed the method with the support of the tool (i.e., automated), it can be observed a coefficient of variation of 16.95%, which is still higher than the one obtained with all the subjects (i.e., 11.81%). Although the study goal was achieved for the manual execution, the same issue on the use of the tools was observed when it comes to accuracy: the tool seems to have been an obstacle rather than an aid. The same preliminary hypothesis can be raised again: the tool is not entirely truly useful to the user, because of many usability issues as mentioned in Sect. 7.4.2. If the accuracy data is analyzed for different Base Functional Components (BFC) (cf. Table 7), additional findings are observable. For all cases, the values measured by each subject varied both upwards and downwards relative to the expected correct value. The data functions show a coefficient of variation (2.84%) lower than the method as a whole (11.81%), whereas the transactional functions show a coefficient of variation (11.81%) equal to the method as a whole. Taking the data functions, it can be observed (cf. Table 6), the variations of both components were very low compared to the expected values. As for the transactional functions (cf. Table 6), a higher coefficient of variation was shown, carrying the method as a whole to a coefficient of variation higher than the maximum coefficient of variation (10.71%) expected for accuracy. Still per Table 6, the component EI seems to be the most problematic. Although both the mean (40.82) and the median (42) were very close to the expected value (43 FPs), the standard deviation is quite large, since the measured values ranged from 15 to 54 FPs. Thus, there were considerable errors both upwards and downwards. For the other two components (EO and EQ), the variations were smaller, mainly on errors upwards.

Efficiency Analysis. On efficiency, the results obtained by the support of the tool are higher than the study goal of reducing for up to 25% of the execution time considering the manual execution. The execution time for the automated execution was on average 55% of the time for the manual execution.

7.5 Discussion of Results

In summary, the proposed method showed positive values on reproducibility but not necessarily positive values on accuracy (considering the results initially expected). Although the observed results are not completely positive, they show an improvement trend, since the proposed conceptual method can be considered quite suitable for the proposed goals. By the preliminary results, the current issue with the proposed method on accuracy seems to be exclusively related to the use of the provided tool developed to support it. However, as initially planned, the study goal was only to present a tool to verify the computational feasibility of automating the proposed method. Upon a suitable conceptual basis, improving the computational support is feasible. This issue was found only when evaluating the accuracy of the proposed method by the automated execution; i.e., for the manual execution the accuracy goal was achieved. Moreover, for reproducibility, both manual and automated executions showed results aligned with the initial goals, although the manual execution showed better results.

Exclusively on the automated execution, the tool was useful to maintain different subjects around the same value, i.e., with a fairly narrow standard deviation. However, the automated execution was not really useful to maintain different subjects results close to the expected result, i.e., with a fairly broad standard deviation among the subjects and the true quantity value.

To identify the reasons why there were issues related to the accuracy of the observed results for the automated execution, a detailed analysis was executed of the mistakes of each FPT elaborated. According to this analysis, the occurrence of nine issues was identified (cf. Table 8), sorted by the frequency they occurred. Table 8 is organized considering the two categories of issues: those resulting in missing FPs and those related to extra FPs. The number of occurrences observed for each issue is shown. In addition, the total numbers of FPs not calculated (missing) or over-calculated (extra) because of each corresponding issue are also shown. All these data are shown splitting per automated and manual execution. Finally, some summarized data are shown at the end of this table.

Per Table 8, in relative terms, subjects who followed the automated execution were responsible for more issues than those of the manual one (2.4 versus 1.8 issues/subject). The subjects of the automated execution were also responsible for more missing FPs per issue (17.1 versus 4.3 missing FPs/issue). Some differences can be highlighted. Issue #4 occurred three times, only for the automated execution, responsible for 45 FPs. It shows the tool may have led to the *misuse of the inclusion dependency connector between leaf nodes that are not related to each other*. It is very representative as it represents 15 missing FPs per occurrence and happened only for the automated execution. Issue #6 occurred only once, for manual execution, being responsible for only one missing FP. It is not representative and is probably due to the subject's lack of attention. Issue #1 occurred seven times for the automated execution (about six missing FPs per occurrence) and three times for the manual one (about two missing FPs per occurrence). This issue is rather more representative for the automated execution, on both: number of occurrences and impact of each occurrence on the number of missing FPs. Similarly to issue #4, it shows the use of the tool may have led to the *lack of intermediate-leaf connections along with a data entity label would represent data to be maintained or referenced by the corresponding elementary functions (represented by the leaf nodes*, which was also identified for the manual execution, but on a much smaller scale. Issues #2 and #3 for both automated and manual executions, also with a more representative impact for the automated one. However, the differences between both types are not so representative and hence it is less likely the use of the tool may have led to the occurrences of these issues. Other scenarios may explain these issues as a

Table 8. Errors made by the subjects considering the use of FPT-FPA.

Issue description	Automated			Manual		
	#	Total of FPs		#	Total of FPs	
		Missing	Extra		Missing	Extra
Missing FPs-related issues						
1 Lack of intermediate-leaf connections along with a data entity label would represent data to be maintained or referenced by the corresponding elementary functions (represented by the leaf nodes)	7	45		3	5	
2 Lack of leaf nodes representing some elementary functions of the software specification given to the subjects	5	45		2	9	
3 Lack of the node marker CALC in the leaf nodes representing elementary functions performing functional calculations	5	12		2	2	
4 Misuse of the inclusion dependency connector between leaf nodes that are not actually related to each other	3	45		–	–	
5 Lack of data entity label to represent data entities presented in the software specification provided to the subjects	1	7		2	17	
6 Lack of node attribute on a leaf node	–	–		1	1	
Extra FPs-related issues						
7 Undue inclusion of data entity labels (associated with intermediate-leaf connections) representing data that are neither maintained nor referenced by the corresponding elementary functions	1		3	2		23
8 Lack of the data entity marker EXTE to represent a data entity maintained by an external software and only referenced by the software being modeled	–		–	1		4
9 Assigning extra node attribute to a leaf node	–		–	1		2
Summarization						
Total numbers (occurrences, missing and extra FPs)	22	154	3	14	34	29
Mean per subject (considering nine subjects for the automated execution and eight for the manual execution)	2.4	17.1	0.3	1.8	4.3	3.6

simple subject's lack of attention. Issue #5 occurred only once for the automated execution and twice for the manual execution, with a very similar impact of the occurrences on the number of missing FPs. Therefore, this issue can be also considered as not representative and may have also been caused by both types of problems: tool's poor usability or subject's lack of attention.

As for the over-calculation leading to extra FPs (cf. Table 8), they had more occurrences for the manual execution. However, this aspect is not so representative when compared with the missing FPs, which represent almost 90% of all occurrences and also almost 90% of all the impact of the occurrences on the number of wrong FPs. Only issue #7 should be highlighted as it was responsible for about 12 extra FPs per occurrence for the manual execution, a substantial number. Nevertheless, this issue is probably only a matter of inattentiveness of the subjects, since this problem occurred only twice in the whole experiment, reducing the chances, for example, of being caused by a conceptual error in the proposed method. The same analysis can be carried out for issues #8 and #9.

There is strong evidence the variations observed in the data obtained in this study are not caused by deficiencies in the conceptual rules of the proposed method. Two major sources of issues were identified: potential problems related to the usability of the tool and possible neglect of subjects who incorrectly used the FPT to represent the requirements of the software object of this experiment. It is impossible to rule out the possibility almost all of these issues were caused by subjects' inattention, however, since both the number of occurrences and the occurrences' impact were more representative for the automated execution, it was deduced they should be because of problems related to the tool. As a result, it was concluded some adjusts should be done in the tool to improve its usability. Considering possible problems related to the subjects' negligence, it can be understood these problems may have their root in some conceptual deficiency of the proposed method, since it could be understood the method should maintain the attention and focus of its users. Further studies and analysis should be conducted to find the best adjusts to both method conceptual rules and tool to ensure all functional requirements of a software being measured are completely and correctly included by the technical users in the FPT. These actions are necessary to ensure the results generated have a still higher degree of reproducibility and accuracy, regardless of external factors.

7.6   Threats to Validity

Four types of threats to validity were addressed. **Conclusion validity** – possible validity threats identified to the statistical relationship between treatment and outcome are the small sample size and the non-use of inferential statistics, as only descriptive statistics was applied. **Internal validity** – two threats to the causal relationship between treatment and outcome were identified and addressed: *(1)* the mode of execution (manually or automated) could affect the basic treatment and hence the outcome, then the mode was taken as a secondary independent variable, with its effects investigated; the subjects were randomly assigned to one of the two groups; and *(2)* the difference in profile among subjects could also affect the basic treatment and outcome; however, as the proposed method is designed assuming no experience in measurement methods is required, no impact was expected in the experiment considering the participation of subjects with different levels of experience. **Construct validity** – in terms of the relationship between theory and observation, four actions were taken to ensure the treatment properly reflects the cause construct: *(i)* FPT-FPA was described using exactly the same concepts as FPA; *(ii)* the subjects were offered a training; *(iii)* a standard form was provided to the subjects who manually executed the method for systematization purposes. To ensure the outcome properly reflects the effect construct, the dependent variables used are in accordance to the international vocabulary of metrology [9] and followed in similar works such as by Abrahão, Poels and Pastor [3]. **External validity** – for generalization, we used a representative software requirements specification of a real case provided by IFPUG. However, the awareness exists that, to be able to generalize these results, more empirical studies are needed, using other specifications with distinct levels of complexities and different and larger sets of subjects.

8   Conclusion

FPA has played a key role in organizations. Therefore, it is imperative to get reliable and valid results with its application. However, several issues have been reported on its reproducibility and accuracy. Proposals for improving reproducibility overly simplify the IFPUG's CPM rules [21] and compromise the FPA accuracy. This work proposed a method to solve this issue by providing a better counting standardization through the new artifact model FPT. FPT allows the counting of FPs with better reproducibility whilst maintaining accuracy.

The proposed method was evaluated through an empirical study. The method showed positive values when manually executed, on both reproducibility and accuracy, with scientific conceptual soundness. On the other hand, the prototype still requires adjustments to show a more important technical contribution.

The end users of the proposed method are project and development managers interested in measuring functional sizes based on FPA. These managers could use the proposed method to get more reliable measurements while reorganizing the roles involved since an FPA specialist would no longer be necessary. The proposed method could be used either manually or by implementing a more appropriate tool. However, the method is not yet fully validated and ready for use. In the short term, these results should attract mainly other researchers.

Future work may revise the method steps and tool to ensure better reproducibility and accuracy. More empirical studies should evaluate the method considering a larger number of subjects and more control over external variables.

References

1. Abrahão, S., Insfrán, E.: A metamodeling approach to estimate software size from requirements specifications. In: 34th Euromicro Conference on Software Engineering and Advanced Applications, pp. 465–475 (2008)
2. Abrahão, S., Mendes, E., Gomez, J., Insfran, E.: A model-driven measurement procedure for sizing web applications: design, automation and validation. In: Engels, G., Opdyke, B., Schmidt, D.C., Weil, F. (eds.) MODELS 2007. LNCS, vol. 4735, pp. 467–481. Springer, Heidelberg (2007). https://doi.org/10.1007/978-3-540-75209-7_32
3. Abrahão, S., Poels, G., Pastor, O.: Assessing the reproducibility and accuracy of functional size measurement methods through experimentation. In: International Symposium on Empirical Software Engineering, pp. 189–198 (2004)
4. Adem, N.A.Z., Kasirun, Z.M.: Automating function points analysis based on functional and non functional requirements text. In: 2nd International Conference on Computer and Automation Engineering, pp. 664–669 (2010)
5. Albrecht, A.J.: Measuring application development productivity. In: Joint Share, Guide, and IBM Application Development Symposium, pp. 83–92 (1979)

6. Alves, L.M., Oliveira, S., Ribeiro, P., Machado, R.J.: An empirical study on the estimation of size and complexity of software applications with function points analysis. In: 6th International Workshop on Tools and Techniques in Software Development Process, pp. 27–34 (2014)

7. Basili, V.R., Rombach, H.D.: The TAME project: towards improvement-oriented software environments. IEEE Trans. Software Eng. **14**(6), 758–773 (1998)

8. del Bianco, V., Lavazza, L., Morasca, S.: A proposal for simplified model-based cost estimation models. In: Dieste, O., Jedlitschka, A., Juristo, N. (eds.) PROFES 2012. LNCS, vol. 7343, pp. 59–73. Springer, Heidelberg (2012). https://doi.org/10. 1007/978-3-642-31063-8_6

9. BIPM: International vocabulary of metrology - basic and general concepts and associated terms (VIM). Bureau International des Poids et Mesures, Joint Commit. for Guides in Metrology, 3 edn. (2012). http://www.bipm.org/en/publications/ guides/vim.html

10. Cantone, G., Pace, D., Calavaro, G.: Applying function point to unified modeling language: conversion model and pilot study. In: 10th International Symposium on Software Metrics, pp. 280–291 (2004)

11. Chamundeswari, A., Babu, C.: An extended function point approach for size estimation of object-oriented software. In: 3rd India Software Engineering Conference, pp. 139–145 (2008)

12. Choi, S., Park, S., Sugumaran, V.: Function point extraction method from goal and scenario based requirements text. In: Kop, C., Fliedl, G., Mayr, H.C., Métais, E. (eds.) NLDB 2006. LNCS, vol. 3999, pp. 12–24. Springer, Heidelberg (2006). https://doi.org/10.1007/11765448_2

13. Connolley, M.J.: An Empirical Study of Function Point Analysis Reliability. MIT, Cambridge (1990)

14. Easterbrook, S., Singer, J., Storey, M.A., Damian, D.: Selecting empirical methods for software engineering research. In: Shull, F., Singer, J., Sjøberg, D.I.K. (eds.) Guide to Advanced Empirical Software Engineering, pp. 285–311. Springer, London (2008). https://doi.org/10.1007/978-1-84800-044-5_11

15. Edagawa, T., Akaike, T., Higo, Y., Kusumoto, S., Hanabusa, S., Shibamoto, T.: Function point measurement from web application source code based on screen transitions and database accesses. J. Syt. Softw. **84**(6), 976–984 (2011)

16. Fraternali, P., Tisi, M., Bongio, A.: Automating function point analysis with model driven development. In: 16th Conference of the Center for Advanced Studies on Collaborative Research, p. 18 (2006)

17. Freitas-Jr., M.D., Fantinato, M., Sun, V., Thom, L.H., Garaj, V.: Improving reproducibility whilst maintaining accuracy in function point analysis. In: 21st International Conference on Enterprise Information Systems, pp. 61–72 (2019)

18. de Freitas Junior, M., Fantinato, M., Sun, V.: Improvements to the function point analysis method: a systematic literature review. IEEE Trans. Eng. Manag. **62**(4), 495–506 (2015)

19. Gencel, Ç., Demirörs, O.: Conceptual differences among functional size measurement methods. In: 1st International Symposium on Empirical Software Engineering and Measurement, pp. 305–313 (2007)

20. Harput, V., Kaindl, H., Kramer, S.: Extending function point analysis of object-oriented requirements specifications. In: 11th International Software Metrics Symposium, p. 39 (2005)

21. IFPUG: Function Point Counting Practices Manual, release 4.3.1. Int. Function Point Users Group, Westerville, Ohio (2010)

22. Insfrán, E., Pastor, O., Wieringa, R.: Requirements engineering-based conceptual modelling. Requirements Eng. **7**(2), 61–72 (2002)
23. Kampenesa, V.B., Dybåa, T., Hannaya, J.E., Sjøberga, D.I.K.: A systematic review of quasi-experiments in software engineering. Inf. Softw. Technol. **51**(1), 71–82 (2009)
24. Kemerer, C.F.: Reliability of function points measurement: a field experiment. Commun. ACM **36**(2), 85–97 (1993)
25. Kitchenham, B.A., Känsälä, K.: Inter-item correlations among function points. In: 15th International Conference on Software Engineering, pp. 477–480 (1993)
26. Klusener, S.: Source code based function point analysis for enhancement projects. In: 29th International Conference on Software Maintenance, pp. 373–376 (2003)
27. Lagerström, R., Würtemberg, L.M., Holm, H., Luczak, O.: Identifying factors affecting software development cost and productivity. Softw. Qual. J. **20**(2), 395–417 (2012)
28. Lamma, E.: A system for measuring function points from an ER-DFD specification. Comput. J. **47**(3), 358–372 (2004)
29. Lavazza, L.: Automated function points: critical evaluation and discussion. In: IEEE/ACM 6th International Workshop on Emerging Trends in Software Metrics, pp. 25–43 (2015)
30. Lavazza, L.A., del Bianco, V., Garavaglia, C.: Model-based functional size measurement. In: 2nd International Symposium on Empirical Software Engineering and Measurement, pp. 100–109 (2008)
31. Lavazza, L.A., Morasca, S., Robiolo, G.: Towards a simplified definition of function points. Inf. Softw. Technol. **55**(10), 1796–1809 (2013)
32. Low, G.C., Jeffery, D.R.: Function points in the estimation and evaluation of the software process. IEEE Trans. Software Eng. **16**(1), 64–71 (1990)
33. Miyawaki, T., Iijima, J., Ho, S.: Measuring function points from VDM-SL specifications. In: 5th International Conference on Service Systems and Service Management, pp. 1–6 (2008)
34. OMG: Automated function points. Object Management Group, OMG Document Number PTC/2013-02-01 (2013). http://www.omg.org/spec/AFP/1.0
35. Pow-Sang, J.A., Villanueva, D., Flores, L., Rusu, C.: A conversion model and a tool to identify function point logic files using UML analysis class diagrams. In: Joint Conference of the 23rd International Workshop on Software Measurement and the 8th International Conference on Software Process and Product Measurement, pp. 126–134 (2013)
36. Quesada-López, C., Jenkins, M.: Function point structure and applicability: a replicated study. J. Object Technol. **15**(3), 2:1–26 (2016)
37. Rao, K.K., Nagaraj, S., Ahuja, J., Apparao, G., Kumar, J.R., Raju, G.S.V.P.: Measuring the function points from the points of relationships of UML. In: 1st International Confernece on Computer and Electrical Engineering, pp. 748–752 (2008)
38. Uemura, T., Kusumoto, S., Inoue, K.: Function-point analysis using design specifications based on the Unified Modelling Language. J. of Softw. Maint. Res. Pract. **13**(4), 223–243 (2001)
39. Wohlin, C., Runeson, P., Höst, M., Ohlsson, M.C., Regnell, B., Wesslén, A.: Experimentation in Software Engineering, 1st edn. Springer, Heidelberg (2012). https://doi.org/10.1007/978-3-642-29044-2

A Canonical Data Model for Records Management in the Portuguese Public Administration

Catarina Viegas[1], André Vasconcelos[1,2]([✉]) [iD], José Borbinha[1] [iD], and Zaida Chora[2]

[1] INESC-ID, Instituto Superior Técnico, Lisbon University, Avenida Rovisco Pais 1, Lisbon, Portugal
cativiegas@gmail.com,
{andre.vasconcelos,jlb}@tecnico.ulisboa.pt
[2] Administrative Modernization Agency, Rua de Santa Marta 55, Lisbon, Portugal
zaida.m.chora@ama.pt
https://tecnico.ulisboa.pt/, https://www.ama.gov.pt

Abstract. The Portuguese public administration is a highly regulated environment, where business processes are subject to strong requirements for records management. Therefore business metadata must be produced and maintained along with the regular business objects, to enable effective information exchange. In that sense, when entities of this domain engage in exchanges of information, it is helpful for those involved if also the metadata produced can be exchanged, which requires it to be commonly understood. This research proposes a Canonical Data Model that supports semantic interoperability in the Portuguese public administration, by defining a set of metadata elements for describing records. The proposed solution is compared against other related data models, and its qualities are assessed using the Bruce-Hillman metadata quality framework. Furthermore, the analysis of the proposed solution reveals the proposed model promotes semantic interoperability within the Portuguese public administration, by ensuring the information exchanged retains its original business context meaning.

Keywords: Information management · Public administration · Interoperability · Records management metadata · Canonical Data Model

1 Introduction

Organizations within the same public administration, or others that interact with these organizations, exchange information, frequently, among them. While in the past this exchange was done primarily in the form of paper-based documents, with the advent of digital information systems, these interactions are currently carried out in the form of business objects. These business objects need to be

© Springer Nature Switzerland AG 2020
J. Filipe et al. (Eds.): ICEIS 2019, LNBIP 378, pp. 210–249, 2020.
https://doi.org/10.1007/978-3-030-40783-4_11

kept as records in the records management systems of the sender and recipient organizations, as evidences of business processes.

In the context of interacting multi-organizations it is of paramount importance the definition of a common data schema that defines the data formats and associated metadata of the business objects exchanged. Such a common data model is expected to promote interoperability among systems, facilitating a wide range of system-level tasks such as verification and validation of business or transaction audits for subsequent analyses.

The Portuguese Public Administration comprised multiple entities, of what each is expected to manage their business records according to specific regulations and requirements, while complying with a common general legal framework. Therefore, entities are expected to either have Record Management Systems (RMS), specifically conceived to capture, store and manage records, or to have business systems with that capability.

The collaborative work performed by these organizations results, frequently, in the production of documents and exchange of these as information objects. This exchange of documents is currently done still in large part still via surface mail or e-mail, in any of the cases requiring human action. This is an inadequate, and more importantly, error-prone way to carry out these interactions, potentially leading to an ineffective records management, with important documents never been acknowledge to have been received, resulting in ineffectiveness and even possible legal repercussions. But even when the processes are already automated, usually the capture of metadata for business records is inefficiently made manually.

In April of 2017, the Resolution from the Portuguese Council of Ministers (RCM) no. 51/2017 [26] was enacted with the goal of establishing the initiative "Zero Paper" ("Papel Zero", in Portuguese), whose main objective is the dematerialization of all the exchanges of information among public entities, through the use of information systems and digital platforms obeying to a common set of interoperability principles.

Interoperability is not a new concept in the Portuguese public administration. Solutions in several domains have been developed reacting four viewpoints or interoperability: legal, semantic, technical and organizational. The promotion of measures by the Portuguese government led to the development of an interoperability project with the aim of enabling information objects exchanges among different business systems with records management capability, allowing the automation of business processes and, consequently, reduction of costs and increase of efficiency.

The problem addressed in this research is scoped in that project, addressing of interoperability among public organizations in the Portuguese public administration, specifically, among their RMS (o business systems with records management capabilities).

The Portuguese government has promoted, for the generic purpose of interoperability, the definition of a data model for metadata [3] and a centralized platform [1], to be used by all public entities, ensuring the existence of a common interoperability agreement across all the public administration.

Regardless of these common requirements, the correct solution to achieve interoperability will always depend on the organization's specific requirements and regulations. However, the fact that it already exists an interoperability infrastructure for the integration of information systems for the Portuguese public administration, and also that common requirements for records management have been successfully emerging, motivates the hypothesis of this research of providing a tool capable of supporting information object sharing, embedded in the existing common infrastructure. These information objects are, in this scope, document files and metadata records that describe the documents exchanged among entities, allowing the creation of local copies of the records of the sender entity, in the recipient organization's RMS.

This research proposes a solution to the challenge of exchanging document files and their metadata among public entities of the Portuguese public administration, considering existing Portuguese public administration interoperability measures. The proposed solution aims at promoting an exchange of documents with minimal effort, by ensuring that the metadata records that define the exchanged documents are interpreted equally by every RMS, a goal supported by the employment of Web services and a Canonical Data Model (CDM). The implementation of the proposed solution is expected to expand the efficiency of public administration and to reduce the costs associated with this exchange of documents.

Next this paper presents the state of art of the current interoperability measures in the PPA, and an overview of the techniques for ensuring systems interoperability. These techniques are the basis for the development of the solution, which is presented in Sect. 3. Section 4 provides a demonstration of the solution proposed, applied to a common use case of the Portuguese public administration, and presents the results of the evaluation methods chosen to assess the validity of the Canonical Data Model. The conclusions and future work are presented in last section of the paper.

2   Interoperability in Public Administrations

According to MoReq2010, **Interoperability** is *"the ability of one system to be able to operate using the data and information provided by another system"* [6]. In the context of European public services, according to Decision no. 922/2009/EC of the European Parliament and the Council [11], interoperability is the capability of two or more diverse organizations within public administrations to interact, by sharing information and knowledge through the exchange of data between their Information and communications technology systems. The European Interoperability Framework for European Public Services describes four levels of interoperability [9]:

- **Legal Interoperability:** since laws and policies can differ from different countries, legal interoperability ensures that the legal validity of the information exchanged between systems is maintained;

- **Organizational Interoperability:** this level covers the capability of organizations to cooperate by aligning business processes, motivations and other elements to achieve mutually agreed goals;
- **Semantic Interoperability:** this level of interoperability is achieved through the creation of semantic interoperability assets such as data structures and data elements. These assets ensure that the precise meaning of the information exchanged is preserved and can be unambiguously interpreted by any other system;
- **Technical Interoperability:** this level covers the technical aspects of linking different systems such as the definition of interface specifications, data integration services, etc.

This section is divided into three subsections. Subsect. 2.1 introduces the strategy for achieving interoperability among European public administration. Subsects. 2.2 and 2.3 present the current measures of semantic and technical interoperability in the Portuguese public administration, respectively.

2.1 Europe 2020 Strategy

According to [21], *"interoperability has become a keyword in the Portuguese Public Administration"*. This structural change in the public administration reflects in the way public entities are expected to be capable of exchanging information, through the adoption of interoperable information systems. This new perspective of public administrations has been encouraged by the EU, which developed the European Interoperability Strategy (EIS) and the European Interoperability Framework (EIF), under the ISA programme, in order to establish norms and standards when it comes to develop and implement information exchange and services integration solutions [21].

In Decision No. 922/2009/EC [11], it is agreed the creation of a *"community programme on interoperability solution for European public administrations"* – the ISA Programme. This programme was created with the intention of providing common and shared interoperability solutions for a period of five years (2010–2015) and, consequently, facilitate the efficient and effective electronic interaction between European public administrations [8].

Under the ISA programme, the European Commission presented to the European Parliament two key elements that promote interoperability among EU Member States' public administrations. The EIS and the EIF set a common and coherent approach to interoperability in public administrations. The EIS offers a set of directions that should be taken into consideration when creating public administration solutions, to improve the exchanging of records and information across sectors. The EIF provides this guidance to EU Member States by defining 12 principles that summarize the expectations of public administrations and other stakeholders regarding the delivery of public services, and presents four levels of interoperability: legal, organizational, semantic and technical. It is expected by the EU Member States to take EIF into account when setting up public services and national interoperability frameworks.

ISA2 is an active programme, running for a period of 5 years (2016–2020), following up the results from ISA. The main objectives of this new programme are the revision of EIF and EIS, the elaboration of an Interoperability Architecture and a Cartography of solutions, as well as the development of interoperability solutions for public administration regarding businesses' and citizens' needs [7].

2.2   Semantic Interoperability

Semantic interoperability is the capability of two or more information systems to exchange information while guaranteeing that the information's original meaning and context is maintained after the exchange, in the recipient system. Without a semantic agreement, two systems can communicate but the information exchanged becomes meaningless to the counter part. The exchange of data across different information systems can encounter multiple barriers such as the lack of a commonly agreed metadata set to characterize the information or the divergent interpretation of the data exchanged [10]. Therefore, the establishment of a common reference for every organization, is the key to achieve interoperability in public administrations. The definition of a metadata schema, used by every organization within the Portuguese public administration, facilitates the correct sharing of metadata records every time two RMS engage in a transaction. A **metadata record** is shared when sent to another RMS, and reused by the receiver to create a local record.

MIP [3] is the current Portuguese metadata schema produced to be applied by public administration entities to their records. However, as discussed next, the use of this metadata schema is only a recommendation and not legally mandatory. MEF/LC [13,16] is also a semantic interoperability measure developed to provide the public entities with a classification model to be applied to their RMS.

PAEIS - Portuguese Semantic Interoperability Programme. Following EU interoperability recommendations, DGLAB - Direcao-Geral do Livro, dos Arquivos e das Bibliotecas, the entity that has the role of national archive in Portugal, developed, in 2012, PAEIS (Portuguese Semantic Interoperability Programme), a programme whose aim was to promote an electronic administration through the development of tools that promoted semantic interoperability in the Portuguese public administration [14].

The development of this programme was driven by the need to create new structural measures that would allow the gradual transformation of organizations, such as the increase of transparency and effectiveness in administrative processes. PAEIS promotes a Business-to-Business (B2B) perspective, where it is expected of organizations to integrate and share information and services among them, to improve process' effectiveness [15].

To achieve this communication among different organizations, their different systems must "speak the same language" and comprehend the information exchanged, to integrate it into their systems. To meet this requirement, DGLAB developed MIP, an interoperable metadata schema, and MEF, a normalized functional semantic 2-level classification macrostrucure that represents Administration's functions and subfunctions.

According to PAEIS' regulation [14], any Public Administration entity can join the programme voluntarily, and if it does so, is compelled to:

- Apply MIP and MEF to its RMS in the following two years;
- Follow MEF's norms and rules to represent State functions when implementing RMS;
- Actively contribute for the development of the Program through the promotion, implementation and participation in the improvement process of its tools.

MEF/LC - Classification Model of the Portuguese Public Administration. MEF was developed under the PAEIS programme with the goal of establishing a classification macrostructure common to all the entities of the Public Administration, promoting semantic interoperability [13], and to be used as a referential in the development of functional business classification schemes by public organizations [21].

This hierarchical macrostructure is a conceptual representation of the functions performed by public sector organizations and presents two levels of classification. The first level instances represent the State functions and the second level, the subfunctions in which level 1 instances can be divided [13].

MEF was developed to promote normalization of record classification across the public administration. By collecting the functions developed by public entities, and associating each function with an unique code, MEF provides to organizations a common model to classify their records. This normalization allows the classification of all the records of the Portuguese public administration to be perform under the same referential, therefore, ensuring that if two or more organizations use MEF to classify their records, the recipient organization's RMS recognizes immediately the functional area of the record, independent of the organization's area of intervention.

After the development of MEF, which provided 2 levels of classification, DGLAB recognized the advantages that a more comprehensive classification model would bring, for a clearer description of the records, and consequently, for establishing interoperability across the public administration. The ASIA project was created to determine guidelines for the identification and assessment of the business processes responsible for business objects that can be integrated into RMS, performed by public administration's organizations [20].

DGLAB identified the business processes common to various member organizations and, considering the connection among public administration's functions and subfunctions and the business processes, created a conceptual map that explained how each third level instance was identified [22]. This conceptual map is expected to be used by PAEIS' compliant organizations to define their own third level classes, which are subsequently included in LC, the result of the ASIA project, and from then on managed by DGLAB.

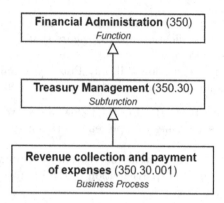

Fig. 1. Classification code from MEF/LC explained.

Lista Consolidada para a Classificação e Avaliação da Informação Pública (MEF/LC), the merge of MEF and LC, is a 3 to 4-level classification macrostructure that integrates the business processes identified by public organizations into MEF's functional structure. This catalogue has an incremental feature [20], allowing the integration of new business processes by new organizations that join the PAEIS programme, and presents a hierarchical structure that contemplates 3 levels classes (4 when needed). The 1st and 2nd level classes represent the functions and subfunctions of the Portuguese public administration, respectively, a result of the MEF project. The 3rd level class represents the business processes performed by public entities, resultant of the ASIA project. Figure 1 depicts the hierarchical architecture of MEF/LC, through the deconstruction of code 350.30.001. Code 350 represents function "Financial Administration" ("Administração Financeira", in the original [13]), performed by public organizations. "Treasury Management" ("Gestão de Tesouraria" [13]), represented by code 350.30, is a subfunction performed under function 350, achieved through the execution of business process 350.30.001, "Revenue collection and payment of expenses" ("Cobrança de receitas e pagamento de despesas" [16]). The first three levels are managed by DGLAB. A 4th level class can be defined by each organization if it is necessary to apply different deadlines and final destinations to the information objects of different stages of the business processes, and represents the subdivision of business processes.

MEF/LC is meant to be used as a foundation for organizations to define their own business classification scheme, guaranteeing semantic interoperability up to level 3 to all MEF/LC compliant organizations [16]. However, MEF/LC is not used by all the entities of the Portuguese public administration. The classification model proposed by DGLAB is only a recommendation, to be used by the different organizations when establishing their own classification scheme. The fact that it is just a recommendation and not mandatory, raises a problem in guaranteeing semantic interoperability across the different systems in the public administration, since there is not an agreement regarding record classification, due to many of the Portuguese public organizations not considering MEF/LC when establishing their own classification scheme.

The ASIA project also contributed for the definition of guidelines for the rightful identification of disposal schedules and destination of the public administration's organizations records, facilitating the elimination of superfluous information and the preservation of important information. The main objectives of these guidelines are (1) the determination of what information should be preserved and for how long, from a global point of view and not only within each entity; (2) the identification of the actors of each business process and who retains the information, (3) the introduction of solutions that avoid the preservation of duplicate information and (4) the elimination of disposable information in a timely manner.

MIP - Metadata for Interoperability. Similar to MEF/LC, Meta Informação para a Interoperabilidade (MIP) is one of DGLAB's initiatives to promote semantic interoperability within the Public Administration. MIP is a data model that gathers a set of basic attributes, capable of identifying and describing, in a non-exhaustive way, any record produced, acquired or maintained by public organizations, using a schema of normalized descriptive elements.

MIP is a metadata schema comprising 17 metadata elements, defined to ensure semantic interoperability in the Portuguese public administration. The goal was to provide the Portuguese public administration with a common metadata schema to describe the records of public entities. This would facilitate the creation and integration of local records, created in the recipient RMS, based on the metadata records received. Thus, with a shared metadata structure, the record could be created with minimal effort and integrated easily in a new system.

The creation of MIP had into consideration three principles [12]: (1) Inclusiveness, by creating a schema abstract enough to be applied to every organization's record but with enough detail to still provide useful information; (2) Logic, by selecting metadata elements able to respond to questions regarding the identity of the record; (3) Simplicity of use, by creating a schema with clearly defined elements in order to reduce ambiguity in the understanding of each element, which is always a risk where semantics is involved.

To determine which metadata elements were important while defining the schema, DGLAB considered the requirements from standards such as the ISO 15849:2016 norm [18] and MoReq2010 [6], which state the metadata elements records that should be defined by, to guarantee the record's authenticity and reliability [3]. Inspired by what is stated by MoReq2010 [6] about metadata, MIP is constituted by two types of elements: required elements, which are necessary to ensure semantic interoperability, considering they are recognized by every organization (always presented in the metadata record) and optional elements, similar to MoReq2010's idea of contextual metadata, but with the difference that the elements are already defined by MIP, only the organizations can decide to add values to those elements or not, according to the record. Metadata elements can be generic or specific, and can have subelements. Every MIP element, following MoReq2010's recommendation, has a metadata element definition, which can be consulted in [3], that describes the attributes of an element, including:

- **designation:** the name of the element;
- **definition:** what the element represents and what the element consists of;
- **objective:** the objectives the presence of this element aims to achieve;
- **obligation:** states if an element is required or optional. When an element is mandatory, it needs to be present; when it is mandatory if applicable, it can or not be used but if it is, it must be present from that moment on; when it is optional can or not be present, according to the organization's needs;
- **repeatability:** indicates if an element has one or multiple instances;
- **equivalences:** international metadata schemas where the element also appears;
- **application notes:** ways to apply the element;
- **representation schemas:** suggested standards or normalization for representing the element;
- **examples:** examples of how the element can be used;
- **subelements:** if an element has associated subelements, they are specified in this attribute.

Nevertheless, the use of this metadata model in public organizations' RMS is not mandatory, being only a recommendation to be considered when establishing the metadata model for each public entity RMS. This influences the lack of normalization in the RMS of the Portuguese public administration, regarding metadata structure. If this normalization could be established, semantic interoperability would be easy to achieve. Since there are multiple data models, achieving interoperability requires connecting all of the different data models in an unified view.

2.3   Technical Interoperability

Technical interoperability is the level of interoperability concerning hardware and software components required to establish a machine-to-machine communication. Nowadays, with the development of the Web, technical interoperability does not represent an issue regarding the exchange of data across multiple information systems. Since the introduction of TCP/IP, organizations are now presented with a multitude of options respecting the exchange of data [19]. This level of interoperability is fulfilled in the Portuguese Public Administration by iAP, the Portuguese interoperability framework.

iAP - Interoperability Framework for the Portuguese Public Administration. The Interoperability Framework for the Portuguese Public Administration (iAP) was developed by AMA with the intention of providing an interoperability platform to the Portuguese public administration. This platform was developed to simplify the communication among organizations and business partners by streamlining business processes and developing services, minimizing the costs and effort of developing new business processes [1].

The Portuguese interoperability platform has four main components [1], shown in Fig. 2: Integration Platform, Authentication Provider, Public Administration Payments Platform and Public Administration SMS Gateway. This research examines, only, the functionalities provided by the Integration Platform, developed as a state-wide Service Oriented Architecture (SOA), providing an expendable catalogue of services published and consumed by organizations of the Portuguese public administration. As shown in Fig. 2, the Integration Platform provides a *Web Interface*, enabling users to monitor their services, and a *Service Management* component, that allows the configuration of the services by service providers [1]. The *Identity Federation* component assures that the services' users remain anonymous to the counter parts, through the conversion of relevant identifiers to non-significant identifiers, and the *Message Engine* component supports the management of execution messages [1]. The *Transaction Engine* ensures the data transformation of the messages received by the platform, and the *Services Directory* accommodates the services published in the platform by iAP-compliant organizations [1]. The *Process Workflow and Services Orchestration* component of the platform, responsible for coordinating the services exposed in the platform, is achieved through the use of an Enterprise Service Bus (ESB) applied to the Portuguese interoperability platform [1].

Among the services exposed in iAP, several allow the transmission of data from one information system to another. However, none of the information currently exchanged through these services is record defining data, capable of being understood and managed by a RMS.

One of the objectives of this research is to provide iAP with a new service layer, which allows the sharing of metadata records and document files among

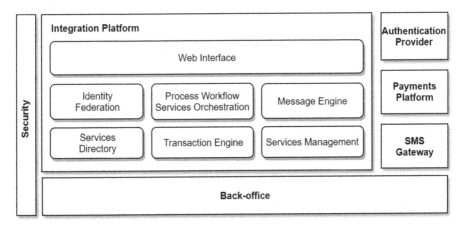

Fig. 2. Logical architecture of the Portuguese interoperability platform.

different RMS. This new layer will ensure that, when these information objects are received by a RMS, the system is capable of generating a local copy of the record, based on the metadata record and the document file. However, this exchange is only successful, if a semantic agreement regarding the schema of that metadata is established between systems.

3   A Canonical Data Model for Records Management

This section presents, in detail, the solution proposed to solve the problem referred in the introductory section of the paper, guided by the drivers presented in Subsect. 3.1. As stated in Sect. 2, the EU considers four levels of interoperability for European public administrations: legal, organizational, semantic and technical. Although there are four levels, this research focused only on developing a technical interoperability solution, presented in Subsect. 3.2, and a semantic interoperability solution, described in Subsect. 3.3. These complementary measures aim at solving the interoperability problem of the Portuguese public administration.

3.1   Solution Drivers

This research proposes a solution, based on a central ESB, that provides a set of services capable of delivering document files and the metadata records associated, every time a transaction is established between two RMS. Each record within its RMS is defined by a metadata record, containing the descriptive information of the record, and a document file, with the contents of the record. A successful transaction of both of these information objects allows the recipient RMS to create a new local record, copy of the record described by the metadata and managed by the sender RMS.

The development of the solution here presented took into consideration a set of drivers ought to be followed. The proposed solution considers the following drivers and requirements:

- Ensure the unique identity of a record;
- Consider previous state-wide interoperability measures such as iAP (see Sect. 2.3), MIP (see Sect. 2.2) and MEF/LC (see Sect. 2.2);
- Be universal to any organization of the public administration;
- Be accessible and easy to apply to already established RMS of public organizations;
- Promote the process automation of the capture of metadata records and creation of new local records in recipient RMS.

According to [17], *"defining a canonical data model is often the first step to resolving cases of semantic dissonance between applications"*. A Canonical Data Model ensures that different systems, with different data models, are capable of sharing data among them and comprehend the information exchanged through the use of data mappings. The definition of a Canonical Data Model is expected to be applied to a set of services published in the central interoperability infrastructure, already implemented in the Portuguese public administration.

The work presented was performed in close proximity with governmental agency AMA, in a pilot project in the Portuguese Public Administration. This pilot project promoted by AMA is an ambitious project that aims to respond to the demand of the Portuguese government of reducing the use of paper-based correspondence among organizations within the public administration, by implementing a state-wide distributed electronic solution for sharing documents, while promoting records management.

3.2 Interoperability Services

One of the goals of the proposed solution is the use of state-wide interoperability measures, such as the Portuguese public administration central ESB, iAP. As stated in Sect. 2.3, iAP is the interoperability platform of the Portuguese public administration, providing services that can be consumed by any iAP-compliant organization. As the platform is already successful in establishing data exchanges among different systems, it was decided that, to solve the problem proposed, services that allow the exchange of documents and associated metadata would be implemented and published in the interoperability platform.

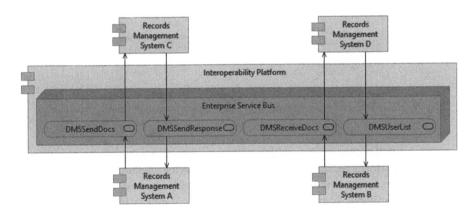

Fig. 3. Static view of the Portuguese interoperability platform

The development and employment of Web services allow RMS to publish and consume the services in the interoperability platform, and, consequently, share information objects, thus guaranteeing an easy access to the solution proposed. The use of Web services removes also any type of inter-institutional dependencies, with the organization being the sole responsible for establishing the connecting between iAP and its RMS, leaving to iAP the task of mediating the communications through an ESB.

Depicted in Fig. 3 are the four Web services implemented in the Portuguese interoperability platform to achieve the main goal of this research. This simplified view includes only the Web services relevant for this research. DMSSendDocs is a Web service developed and published in the interoperability platform, whose purpose is sharing metadata records and document files among RMS. The service invocation parameters are defined by its XSD, defined according to the Canonical Data Model proposed, presented in detail, in Subsect. 3.3. To provide the service with the capability of transporting document files, DMSSendDocs is complemented with a LargeFiles feature, ensured by iAP. The LargeFiles feature supports the platform, and the service, with the capability of exchanging files. To implement this feature into the service, element AttachContext, comprising of subelements TTL, which indicates the "Time to Live", i.e., the time the file is available for download, and FileGuid, which indicates the download identifier of the file, was added to the service interface. This element is repeatable, meaning that more than one file can be sent simultaneously.

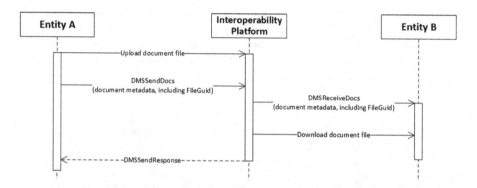

Fig. 4. UML sequence diagram for the Portuguese interoperability platform.

Service DMSSendResponse, which sends a status message from the interoperability platform to the service client, and service DMSReceiveDocs, which sends to the recipient system the metadata provided, were developed to assist service DMSSendDocs. Figure 4 depicts the expected operation of the services between two entities, Entity A and Entity B. Entity A sends a document to Entity B, by uploading the document file to the platform, through address <Handler_URL>/upload.aspx, and invoking service DMSSendDocs, whose parameters hold the metadata values that describe the document sent. The interoperability platform invokes service DMSReceiveDocs in Entity B and sends the information received from Entity A. The metadata sent to Entity B includes subelement FileGuid, which contains the download identifier used by the Entity B to download the file uploaded by Entity A, available <Handler_URL>/download.aspx.

Represented in Fig. 3 is also Web service `DMSUserList`, developed to allow the attainment of the set of users and groups within a specific organization's RMS. Each participant organization is responsible for providing this information when requested via iAP.

3.3 Canonical Data Model Proposed

The metadata of the document is sent through service `DMSSendDocs` (introduced in Subsect. 3.2), and received by the recipient RMS through the SOAP message, structured accordingly to the XSD of the service. To guarantee that the metadata received retains its original meaning, the service's XSD must present an appropriate data structure, that enables the sharing of the metadata values.

As mentioned previously, iAP mediates the communication among systems through the use of an ESB. It is also known that a Canonical Data Model is a data integration pattern to assist in the communication among applications with divergent data formats, by establishing a commonly understood data model. The development of a Canonical Data Model, structured accordingly to the record description requirements, was the approach chosen for this research.

The use of a CDM ensures that different systems, with different data models, are capable of sharing data among them and comprehend the information provided by the data.

By defining a CDM and applying it to the service, the universality of the solution is guaranteed. Both the service and the CDM are free of dependencies and restrictions of specific organizations. The CDM also ensures that the data shared can be received and comprehended by any system, independent of the discrepancies between the data models defined in each RMS.

While applying the CDM to the service, MIP and MEF/LC, two state-wide interoperability measures, were considered. It was important to considered both of these measures, specially MIP, when developing the CDM, since the metadata requested by the CDM must align with the data models used by the organizations. Even though the Canonical Data Model approach allows different data formats, a common ground, regarding the description of records, among the data models used by organizations and the CDM, is critical for a successful data integration. Although MIP is not mandatory, it is the only data model approved by the Portuguese government for describing records and, consequently, the only guidance concerning this topic in the Portuguese public administration. Considering this, the CDM proposed in this research is based on the already established data model for the Portuguese public administration, MIP, avoiding the development of a data model from scratch. The development phase of the proposed model considered MIP as a guideline, maintaining the information provided by MIP, whilst accommodating changes required to attain the goals projected.

The main goal of this research is to develop a common data structure, known by any participant organization, capable of holding the metadata associated with the document file sent through iAP, promoting the automatic creation of a local record from the information objects provided, in the recipient RMS. However, the CDM guarantees the identity of the record, only if the data is structurally capable of providing an appropriate description of the document. Therefore, the urgency of following MIP's guidelines whilst developing the new CDM.

The challenge of developing the CDM was in establishing a balance between maintaining the information offered by MIP elements and the implementation of necessary changes to guarantee the automation of processes in the recipient RMS. The CDM provides a data structure that assists in the interpretation and handling of the data, by the systems, through normalization of data values and element structure.

XML is the language chosen to represent the CDM. XML is a programming language that promotes interoperability by simplifying the sharing of information among systems and applications, due to its basic syntax [27]. XML is used to structure data meant to be passed to other systems, generally through the Web. To structure the XML message to be sent through the service, containing the metadata of the document, an XSD of the service was developed. The combination of XML and a Canonical Data Model manages application's dependencies, with XML capable of removing dependencies on any application-specific data types, and the Canonical Data Model solving dependencies on the application's data formats [17].

The solution proposed was the result of the work developed by a work group from AMA. This work group included members of every organization involved in the AMA pilot project and members from DGLAB, the governmental organization responsible for MIP and MEF/LC.

The XSD file developed defines the structure of the SOAP message sent when the service is invoked, containing the metadata of the document exchanged. All the decisions made while developing the CDM are exemplified, throughout this section, by excerpts of the XSD file or by UML diagrams.

As stated previously, MIP was used as a starting point for the development of the CDM proposed. MIP is an approved standard for the characterization of the records within the Portuguese public administration, and provides effective definitions for the elements of the data model of this domain. The proposed solution is presented in Fig. 5 according to the changes performed in MIP elements in the development of the CDM.

From the 17 main metadata elements presented in MIP, 15 of them are still represented as main elements in the CDM, with 4 maintaining the same subelements and structure defined in MIP. The remaining 11 elements suffered necessary changes to achieve the goals of this research. There was also a need to include 4 new elements, resulting in a total of 19 elements in the CDM, as shown in Fig. 5.

Figure 5 illustrates the UML diagram of the main elements of the CDM. Each class represents a main element of the CDM. Represented are also the obligation and repeatability features of each element in the CDM. If an element is mandatory but non-repeatable, then the element must only appear once in the SOAP message generated, represented in the UML diagram as an association with a multiplicity value of 1; if the element is mandatory and repeatable, it has a multiplicity value of 1..*, meaning that the element must appear at least once;

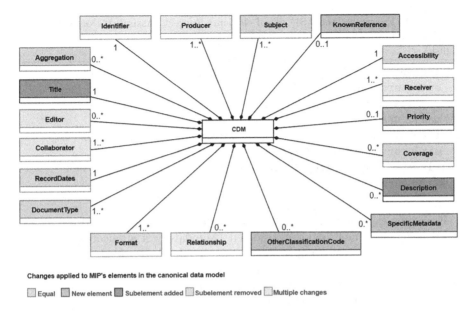

Fig. 5. UML diagram of the 19 main classes of the CDM (translated to English). (Color figure online)

an optional and repeatable element has an association with a multiplicity value of 0..*, meaning it does not have to be present but it can be, multiple times; and an element that is optional and non-repeatable has multiplicity value of 0..1, meaning that the element does not have to appear but, if it does, it can only appear once. As presented in Fig. 5, from the 19 elements in the CDM, all the relevant and mandatory elements from MIP were maintained, either in its original form or with required changes. The UML depicted illustrates only the main elements of the CDM, which are, in vast majority, comprised subelements, presented next in detail.

Equivalent Element Definition. MIP elements *Assunto* (*Subject*, in English), *Cobertura* (*Coverage*), *TipoDocumental* (*DocumentType*) and *Agregacao* (*Aggregation*), marked in yellow in Fig. 5, remain the same in the CDM. Of the elements mentioned, only *TipoDocumental* (*DocumentType*) is mandatory in MIP, which still remains true in the CDM. To define if an element is mandatory in the XSD, a constraint is applied, through the use of the minOccurs attribute in the XML schema, which specifies the minimum of times an element has to appear in the schema. If set to any value greater than 0, then the element is required and value(s) must be provided to the element. If set to 0, then the element is optional. In the CDM, a mandatory element is represented by minOccurs = 1, meaning that the element has to appear at least once in the SOAP Message, as shown in Listing 1.1.

Listing 1.1. Excerpt of the XSD file of elements Subject (Assunto), DocumentType (TipoDocumental), Coverage (Cobertura) and Aggregation (Agregacao) (translated to English).

```
<xs:element name="Subject" type="xs:string" minOccurs="1"
    maxOccurs="unbounded"/>
<xs:element name="DocumentType" type="xs:int" minOccurs="1"
    maxOccurs="unbounded"/>
<xs:element name="Coverage" type="Cobertura" minOccurs="0"
    maxOccurs="unbounded"/>
<xs:element name="Aggregation" type="xs:string" minOccurs="0"
    maxOccurs="unbounded"/>
```

Regarding their obligation, in MIP, *Assunto* is defined as the subject of the record being described, and is considered "Mandatory if applicable", i.e., the element is optional right up until the moment a value is provided. This concept does not exist in the domain of information systems, where a data element is either mandatory or optional. Considering this, it was decided that the metadata element *Assunto* (Subject) would be considered mandatory in the CDM, owing to the fact that, when sharing a metadata record between systems, identifying the subject and context of the document is important to expedite the document recognition in the target application, just like an e-mail allows users of identifying the subject matter, for easier interpretation.

The repeatability of the elements is represented in the XSD by maxOccurs = unbounded. By setting this attribute to unbounded, it implies that the element can appear as many times as required in the SOAP message. Since the default value of maxOccurs is of 1, maxOccurs is not given any value for non-repeatable elements. The application of this attribute is also depicted in Listing 1.1.

Addition of New Subelements. CDM elements *Titulo* (*Title*) and *Descricao* (*Description*), represented in red in Fig. 5, maintain all the subelements described in MIP, and were extended with a new subelement each. Element *Titulo* (Title) contains new subelement, *TituloFormal* (*FormalTitle*), which identifies the legal title of a record, in addition to *TituloAlternativo* (*AlternativeTitle*) and *TituloAtribuido* (*GivenTitle*), subelements instituted by MIP. This addition was necessary to ensure that the CDM is up to date with the new version of MIP that is currently being developed by DGLAB.

Elements with subelements are represented in the XSD as complexTypes, composed by a sequence of simpleType elements that represent their subelements, as shown in Listing 1.2.

Listing 1.2. Excerpt of the XSD file of element Title (Titulo) (translated to English).

```
<xs:element name="Titulo" type="Titulo" minOccurs="1"/>
    <xs:complexType name="Title">
        <xs:sequence>
            <xs:element name="FormalTitle"
                type="xs:string" minOccurs="0"/>
            <xs:element name="AlternativeTitle"
                type="xs:string" minOccurs="0"
                maxOccurs="unbounded"/>
            <xs:element name="GivenTitle"
                type="xs:string" minOccurs="0"/>
        </xs:sequence>
    </xs:complexType>
```

Element *Titulo* (Title) and subelement *TituloAtribuido* (GivenTitle) are described as "Mandatory if applicable" in MIP, meaning that the title of the record is only mandatory from the moment it is introduced in its metadata. Since this is not possible to represent in the CDM, as mentioned previously, element *Titulo* (Title) was defined as mandatory with optional subelements. This implies that at least one subelement of element *Titulo* (Title) has to be presented, to provide any type of title to the document, when sent through iAP. However, when suggested by DGLAB, it was decided that, in case the record owns a legal title, subelement *TituloFormal* (FormalTitle) must contain that value, above all other subelements. This is a norm users agree with when applying the CDM, as it is stated in the CDM application profile. An application profile is a set of metadata elements, and guidelines and policies associated that display how the metadata elements are to be applied to objects.

The same rules apply to element **Descricao** (*Description*). In the CDM, this element continues to include subelements **Idioma** (*Language*) and **Descritores** (*Tags*), and a new subelement **AmbitoeConteudo** (*ScopeAndContent*), also an added feature to the new version of MIP, currently in development. Just as element *Titulo* (Title), element *Descricao* (Description) is a complexType defined by its subelements. Subelement *Idioma* accepts values of type string, which are validated by iAP based on a controlled vocabulary created for the CDM. According to the OCLC, a controlled vocabulary is *"a list of valid terms that can appear in metadata fields"*, whose existence helps ensure the celerity and consistency in the metadata entry process [23]. The obligation and the repeatability of element *Descricao* and subelements *Idioma* (Language), *Descritores* (Tags) and *AmbitoeConteudo* (ScopeAndContent) is the same as stated in MIP.

Deprecated Elements and Subelements. MIP provides a complete list of the required elements to describe records within the Portuguese public administration domain. The CDM was developed based on this list, and the large majority of the elements remain available. However, there are elements and subelements whose presence in the CDM is not required, due to the risk of creating irrelevant or redundant information.

MIP element "Avaliação" (Evaluation) is not represented directly in the CDM, since it is indirectly represented by the classification code provided by MEF/LC, in element *CodigoClassificacao*, as described in Sect. 3.3. MIP element "Avaliação" (Evaluation) is comprised of two subelements, "Prazo de conservação" (Disposal Schedule) and "Destino final" (Final destination). As stated in Sect. 2.2, the ASIA project contributed for the definition of the disposal schedules and final destinations of records, according to their classification codes in MEF/LC. As the use of MEF/LC is implicit in the CDM, as shown further in Sect. 3.3, the existence of an evaluation element would duplicate the information already provided by the MEF/LC classification code of the record. If both elements existed in the same system, there was a risk of two divergent values coexisting in the same metadata record, leading to a potential malfunction of the system, due to not understanding the information provided and which action is meant to perform. For organizations who do not apply MEF/LC, the information about the disposal schedule and final destination of the record, must be presented in the metadata, through the use of element *MetadadoEspecifico* (SpecificMetadataElement), whose functionality is to append extra information to the metadata, as explained in Sect. 3.3.

MIP element "Disponibilidade" (Availability) and its subelements "Custo/preço" (Price) and "Localização" (Location), were also not considered when defining the CDM. The two subelements do not fall under the scope of this work, since the sharing of information objects has no associated transaction costs and the location of the original record is stated by other elements of the CDM, such as *IDOrganismoGerador* (*GeneratorOrganizationID*), as described in Sect. 3.3.

For CDM elements **DatasRecurso** (*RecordDates*) ("Data" (Date) in MIP), **Formato** (*Format*) and **Acessibilidade** (*Accessibility*), represented in green in Fig. 5, the only difference between MIP and the CDM is the deprecation of some of their subelements, irrelevant for this research.

Element *DatasRecurso* (*RecordDates*) defines the dates associated to the record, each type represented by a different subelement: **DataCriacao** (*CreationDate*), which provides information regarding the production date of the record, **DataRegisto** (*RegistrationDate*), which specifies the date of when the record was integrated into a RMS, and **DataAquisicao** (*AcquisitionDate*), which provides the date of when the document was received by the recipient RMS. These subelements are represented in the XSD as type `dateTime`, as shown in Listing 1.3, which specifies the date and time in format *YYYYMMDDTHH:MM:SS*.

Listing 1.3. Excerpt of the XSD file of element RecordDates (DatasRecurso) (translated to English).

```
<xs:element name="RecordDates" type="DatasRecurso" minOccurs="1"/>
<xs:complexType name="RecordDates">
        <xs:sequence>
                <xs:element name="CreationDate" type="xs:dateTime"
                        minOccurs="0"/>
                <xs:element name="RegistrationDate"
                        type="xs:dateTime" minOccurs="1"/>
                <xs:element name="AcquisitionDate"
                        type="xs:dateTime" minOccurs="0"/>
        </xs:sequence>
</xs:complexType>
```

The other subelements of element "Data" in MIP, "Data de Disponibilidade" (Availability date), "Data de Abertura" (Opening date) and "Data de Encerramento" (Closure date), are not represented in the CDM, due to their irrelevance in the scope of this research. "Data de Disponibilidade" (Availability date) is described by MIP as the date the document became publicly accessible; "Data de Abertura" (Opening date) is defined as the date the business process that produced the document was initiated; and "Data de Encerramento" (Closure date) provides the date from when on changes cannot be made to the document [3]. Considering that the document, in this scope, will only be defined by the CDM if an organization sends the document file and its metadata to another, the information provided by element "Data de Disponibilidade" (Availability date) would specify the same information as element *DataAquisicao* (AcquisitionDate), and elements "Data de Abertura" and "Data de Encerramento" (Closure date) provide the same information as element *DataCriacao* (CreationDate).

Element **Formato** (Format) specifies the data format of the document. In MIP, this element is defined by three subelements: "Formato de Dados" (Data Format), "Dimensão" (Size) and "Suporte" (Support). In the CDM, element **Formato** (Format) is defined by subelements **FormatoDados** (*DataFormat*) and **Dimensao** (*Size*), maintained from MIP. Subelement "Suporte" (Support) is not represented in the CDM, since every document is digital and not supported by any physical carrier. The obligation and repeatability of element *Formato* (Format) and its subelements remain the same as stated in MIP.

Element **Acessibilidade** (*Accessibility*) is comprised of eight subelements in MIP. Six of these subelements are represented in the CDM, excluding MIP subelements "Autenticação de assinatura electrónica" (Digital signature authentication) and "Lista de circulação" (Circulation list). Subelement "Lista de circulação" (Circulation list) is defined by MIP as the registration of the organizations that have had access to the record. This registration is handled in the CDM by element **Colaborador** (*Collaborator*), as explained in Sect. 3.3. Subelement "Autenticação de assinatura electrónica" (Digital signature authentication) is defined in MIP as the element that provides the information concerning the digital signature of the record. The existence of this subelement in the CDM is unnecessary, since the records are expected to be digitally [2].

The remainder of MIP subelements of element *Acessibilidade* (*Accessibility*) are represented in the CDM, with changes in MIP subelement "Classificação de Segurança" (Security Classification), due to the type of documents involved in this scope. According to MIP [3], element "Classificação de Segurança" (Security Classification) is used to classify the records based on its security requirements, using four categories: Without Access Restrictions; Reserved, Secret and Top Secret. These categories define the level of access to the record and its contents, following the levels suggested by SEGNAC 4 [24], a Portuguese standard for national security, safeguarding and protection of classified material and computer security. However, RCM no. 42/2015 [25] states that iAP cannot handle confidential information, thus the levels suggested by SEGNAC 4 are not useful in this case, since all information objects sent through iAP would be classified as "Without Access Restrictions". Consequently, it was decided that "Classificação de Segurança" (Security Classification) would be represented by element **NivelAcesso** (*AccessLevel*) in the CDM. This subelement introduces two levels of classification, according to the record's distribution level. The record is either **Publico** *(Public)*, meaning that the all of the record's content is public or that its diffusion will cause no harm to the owner organization; or **Restrito** *(Restricted)*, meaning that the record is only to be accessible by the owner organization and authorized organizations. The values of this subelement will be validated by iAP.

Regarding their obligation, all the subelements classified as "Mandatory if applicable" in MIP, were considered optional in the CDM. In regards to the elements' repeatability, the elements are repeatable in MIP but not in the CDM, considering there can only be one **NivelAcesso** (*AccessLevel*) associated with each record.

Redefinition of Subelements and New Elements. Represented in blue in Fig. 5 are elements who have suffered multiple changes, particularly in their structure, and in orange the new elements included in the CDM.

Element "Identificador" *(Identifier)* is described, in MIP, as a group of subelements that identify uniquely the record. In MIP, this element is comprised of 4 subelements: "Tipo de identificador" (Type of Identifier), "Identificador de recurso" (Record Identifier), "Código de classificação" (Classification Code) and "Versão" (Version). In the CDM, these subelements were modified to better suit the goal of the research. CDM element **Identificador** (*Identifier*) is now composed by 5 subelements, as represented by the UML in Fig. 6.

Subelements **Versao** (*Version*) and **TipoIdentificador** (*IdentifierType*), of element *Identificador* (Identifier), retain their MIP definition and are represented in the CDM as type **string** elements. The values of subelement *Versao* (version) must be represented in a 999.99 format, common for representing versions, and subelement *TipoIdentificador* (IdentifierType) has the constant value of "MDC-iAP" for this project.

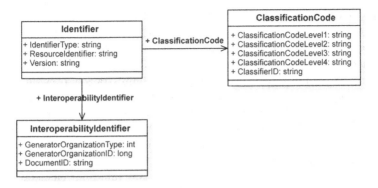

Fig. 6. UML diagram for element *Identificador* in the CDM (translated to English).

IdentificadorInteroperabilidade (*InteroperabilityIdentifier*) is a new subelement of element *Identificador*, implemented in the CDM with the purpose of providing an unique identifier to a document, within a transaction. This subelement is defined by three subelements: ***TipoOrganismoGerador*** (*GeneratorOrganizationType*), ***IDOrganismoGerador*** (*GeneratorOrganizationID*), and ***IDDocumento*** (*DocumentID*), as shown in Fig. 6. This new subelement provides the document with an unique identity in a transaction between two RMS, guaranteeing that two or more documents do not have the same identifier. The addition of this new element was required, considering the possibility of existing two documents with the same identifier in a transaction, if a normalized structure and values to identify the document were not provided. Supposing that two organizations, Entity A and Entity B, want to inform one another. Entity A record's identifier is DOC1. Entity B has a different record registered in its system whose identifier is also DOC1. Entity A sends DOC1 and its metadata to Entity B, via iAP. Entity B captures the information sent and generates, automatically, a new local record. This new record is a copy of record DOC1 of Entity A, meaning that Entity B now has two different records with the same identifier (DOC1).

MoReq2010-compliant RMS have the capability of indexing and retrieving records. The record retrieval can be done through the use of keywords while searching, but simpler RMS only provide search by the record's unique identifier. If two different records have the same identifier within a RMS, this identifier is no longer unique. This can lead to efficiency problems, with the retrieval of the record being difficult, or even legal problems, since RMS have to provide to the organization a simple way of retrieving records to be used as proof in a legal context.

The unique identification of an information object in a transaction is obtain by the CDM through the combination of the three subelements. Subelement *TipoOrganismoGerador* (*GeneratorOrganizationType*) identifies the type of generator organization. A generator organization is the first organization to send the document file and metadata record through iAP. This organization can be public, i.e., part of the Portuguese public administration, or non-public. Public organizations are identified with the value of 1, and non-public organizations with the value of 2. In the CDM, it was decided that public organizations would be identified by an unique SIOE code. SIOE is the authentic source that manages the organizations of the Portuguese public administration, providing to each organization an unique code. SIOE offers a set of Web services, consumed by iAP, that allow the retrieval of these unique codes. To represent non-public iAP-compliant organizations, not covered by SIOE, AMA provides a numeric code to each, in similarity with SIOE. This codification is managed by AMA and can be incremented. To represent this solution in the XSD, attribute `restriction` was applied, as shown in Listing 1.4, accepting only two values for element *TipoOrganismoGerador* (GeneratorOrganizationType), value of 1 or value of 2. The unique code assigned to the organization is hold by element *IDOrganismoGerador (GeneratorOrganizationID)*.

Listing 1.4. Excerpt of the XSD file of subelement GeneratorOrganizationType (translated to English).

```
<xs:element name="GeneratorOrganizationType" minOccurs="1">
    <xs:simpleType>
        <xs:restriction base="xs:int">
            <xs:enumeration value="1"/>
            <xs:enumeration value="2"/>
        </xs:restriction>
    </xs:simpleType>
</xs:element>
```

Subelement *IDDocumento (DocumentID)* (DocumentID) contains the identifier of the record within the generator organization. The combination of these three subelements ensures the unique identifier of a document in a transaction, considering the *IDDocumento* (DocumentID) of each record is different within an organization, as is the code of each organization, in subelement *IDOrganismoGerador* (GeneratorOrganizationID). Therefore, if two organizations have records with the same identifier - DOC1, and SIOE codes 1111 and 2222, the records will have a different *IdentificadorInteroperabilidade* (InteroperabilityIdentifier).

Although subelement *IdentificadorInteroperabilidade* (InteroperabilityIdentifier) was introduced in the CDM to provide the record with an unique identifier, MIP subelement "Identificador de recurso" was still preserved in the CDM as subelement ***IdentificadorRecurso*** (ResourceIdentifier). Subelement *IdentificadorInteroperabilidade* (InteroperabilityIdentifier) possesses subelement *IDDocument* (DocumentID), which specifies the unique identifier of the record, within its generator organization. However, this unique identifier is often the GUID provided by the RMS, and not the identifier by which the document is recognized by the employees of an organization. Although the main goal of this work is for the metadata to be handled, automatically, by the systems, the data must still be human-readable. Therefore, element *IdentificadorRecurso* was included in the CDM to specify the identifier by which the document is recognized by the employees in its generator organization. This addition is specially useful in the handling of response documents, sent back to the generator organization.

In MIP, "Código de Classificação" (Classification Code) is a subelement of element "Identificador" (Identifier). In the CDM, this subelement is represented by *CodigoClassificacao* (*ClassificationCode*).

For classifying records, MIP suggests the use of MEF/LC by every organization. If every organization applied the same classification model to their RMS, all systems could be programmed to interpret the same values, expediting the creation of new local records from the information received, and achieving semantic interoperability across the Portuguese public administration. However, the use of this standard is not mandatory, and organizations are not required to apply this classification model to their records.

In the development phase of the CDM, the need of establishing semantic interoperability across the Portuguese public administration, resulted in the decision of restructuring subelement *CodigoClassificacao* (ClassificationCode) to promote the use of MEF/LC. Element *CodigoClassificacao* (Classification-Code) has five subelements in the CDM. Subelements *CodigoClassificador-Nivel1* (*ClassificationCodeLevel1*), *CodigoClassificadorNivel2* (*Classification-CodeLevel2*), *CodigoClassificadorNivel3* (*ClassificationCodeLevel3*), represent the three classification levels presented in MEF/LC, whereas *Codigo-ClassificadorNivel4* (*ClassificationCodeLevel4*), represents the fourth classification level, to be defined by the organization, if needed. The decomposition of the MEF/LC code into different subelements promotes the automation of the metadata capture and record creation processes. The metadata capture and record creation processes are the processes in which the metadata is received by the system, either manually, through human input or automatically, through rule-based indexing [5], and a new local record is created, according to the information transmitted by the metadata captured, respectively. *CodigoClassi-ficadorNivel4* (*ClassificationCodeLevel4*) is the only subelement of this set of four that is not mandatory, considering not every organization's business processes need to be represented up to level 4. Subelement *IDClassificador* (*ClassifierID*) is mandatory and holds the classification code exactly as it is presented in MEF/LC.

Nevertheless, as stated, the use of this classification model is not mandatory and it would only harm the success of this research if organizations, in order to participate in the project, had to change their classification model drastically. To avoid that, a new element, *OutroCodigoClassificacao* (*OtherClassificationCode*), was implemented in the CDM, allowing organizations of identifying other classification models used and, consequently, the classification code associated to the record. Although this alternative still provides organizations the freedom catered by MIP, the use of MEF/LC is highly promoted by the CDM, which requests organizations with other classification models, to provide an equivalent MEF/LC code, if possible. If not, considering the obligation of element *CodigoClassifica-cao* (ClassificationCode) and its subelements, code 999.99.999 was reserved, in MEF/LC, to be used in these special cases.

Element ***OutroCodigoClassificacao*** (*OtherClassificationCode*) was introduce in the CDM to enable the identification of the classification model used,
if not MEF/LC. This element is composed by two subelements, ***Classificador***
(*Classifier*), which identifies the classification model used by the organization,
and ***CodigoOutroClassificador*** (*OtherClassifierCode*), which holds the classification code of the record, according to the model chosen by the organization.
Although these subelements are mandatory, element *CodigoOutroClassificador*
is not, and can be repeated as many times as required.

Element ***Produtor*** (*Producer*) identifies the organization that produced the
record. In MIP, "Produtor" is defined by four subelements, all represented in
the CDM. Subelement "Sector" is ***TipoOrganismoProdutor*** (*ProducerOrganizationType*) in the CDM, and specifies the type of organization that produced
the record, presenting a similar structure to subelement *TipoOrganismoGerador*
(GeneratorOrganizationType). For this subelement, there are three defined values, represented in the XML schema by the `restriction` and `enumeration`
attributes, as shown in Listing 1.5. If the organization is registered in SIOE, the
subelement holds the value of 1; if it is not represented in SIOE but is iAP-
compliant, holds the value of 2; value of 3 represents non-participant producer
organizations. This situation can occur if a compliant entity sends a document
that was produced by a non-compliant entity. In this case, element *TipoOrganismoProdutor* (ProducerOrganizationType) would hold the value of 3 and ***IDProdutor*** (*ProducerID*) would not hold any value. Considering this, ***IDProdutor***,
in the CDM, is optional. Element *Produtor* (*Producer*) is repeatable, maintaining
its definition provided by MIP.

Listing 1.5. Excerpt of the XSD file of subelement ProducerOrganizationType (translated to English).

```
<xs:element name="ProducerOrganizationType" minOccurs="1">
        <xs:simpleType>
                <xs:restriction base="xs:int">
                        <xs:enumeration value="1"/>
                        <xs:enumeration value="2"/>
                        <xs:enumeration value="3"/>
                </xs:restriction>
        </xs:simpleType>
</xs:element>
```

Colaborador (*Collaborator*) is defined by MIP as the element that provides
information about the organization(s) who have contributed for the elaboration of the document. In MIP, this element is composed by four subelements,
and is optional and repeatable. In the CDM, element *Colaborador* retains the
same MIP subelements and its repeatability, but not its obligation. CDM element *Colaborador* (*Collaborator*) is mandatory in the metadata, due to the
need of registering the organizations who made any type of change to the document, replacing deprecated MIP element "Lista de Circulação" (Circulation list).
The four subelements of this element are ***TipoOrganismodoColaborabor***

(*CollaboratorOrganizationType*), **IDOrganismodoColaborador** (*Collaborator OrganizationID*), **DesignacaoColaborador** (*CollaboratorDesignation*) and **TipoColaborador** (*CollaboratorType*). The approach used for *TipoOrganismodoColaborabor* (*CollaboratorOrganizationType*) and *IDOrganismodoColaborador* (*CollaboratorOrganizationID*) is the same used for subelements *TipoOrganismoGerador* (GeneratorOrganizationType) and *IDOrganismoGerador* (GeneratorOrganizationID). Subelement *TipoColaborador* (CollaboratorType) defines the role of the collaborator organization, and subelement *DesignacaoColaborador* (CollaboratorDesignation) specifies the designation of the collaborator organization.

MIP element Editor is composed by subelements "ID do Editor" (Editor ID), "Designação do Editor" (Editor Designation) and "Tipo" (Type). In the CDM, subelements of element **Editor**, **DesignacaoEditor** (*EditorDesignation*) and **TipoEditor** (*EditorType*) are optional and repeatable, in similarity with MIP. Subelement "ID do Editor" was not considered for the CDM, since there is no simple way of identifying uniquely the editor of a record. The only approach would be the creation of a database that would provide an identifier for every person of the Portuguese public administration that could be an editor, which would be unmanageable. Considering subelement *DesignacaoEditor* can provide information about who edited the record, this option is sufficient, since there is no real need to identify the user uniquely as it does not affect the interpretation of the metadata by the recipient RMS.

MIP element "Destinatário" (Receiver) identifies the organization that will be receiving the document and metadata record, and is composed by four subelements. This element is optional in MIP, however, considering the scope of this research, the information about the recipient organization is a necessity. In the CDM, element **Destinatario** (Receiver) maintains the original four subelements, with minimal adjustments, and includes two more, necessary to guarantee that the document and metadata reach the target system, where a local record can be created, considering the metadata provided. Following the approach stated previously, *Destinatario* (Receiver) has subelements **TipoOrganismoDestinatario** (*ReceiverOrganizationType*) and **IDDestinatario** (*ReceiverID*). *TipoOrganismoDestinatario* (*ReceiverOrganizationType*) can hold two values: value of 1, if the organization is represented in SIOE, or value of 2, if it is iAP-compliant but it is not represented in SIOE. *IDDestinatario* (*ReceiverID*) defines the identifier of the receiver organization, according to its type, provided by subelement *TipoOrganismoDestinatario* (*ReceiverOrganizationType*). **DesignacaoDestinatario** (*ReceiverDesignation*) and **TipoDestinatario** (*ReceiverType*) preserve the functionality stated in MIP. *TipoDestinatario* specifies if the value in subelement *DesignacaoDestinatario* represents an individual person or a group of people, and their role in the receiver organization. **AoCuidadoDe** (*CareOf*) is a new subelement of the element *Destinatario* and expresses whom, within the receiver organization, is the document address to. Other new subelement is **EnderecoDestinatario** (*ReceiverAddress*), which states the group of users to whom the record is directed to. This information is provided by organizations and accessed through service DMSUserList, referred to in Subsect. 3.2.

Element **Priority** (*Prioridade*) was added to the CDM, to provide information regarding the handling priority of the documents received. The addition of this element is a necessity when dealing with the reception of documents, to ensure that urgent cases are dealt with first. There are three valid values for this element: value of 1, for documents whose handling priority is normal; value of 2, for urgent documents; and value of 3, for very urgent documents, represented in the XSD by the `restriction` attribute, as shown previously.

The development of the CDM aimed to achieve the maximum level of abstraction, while still ensuring that the information required to define a record is presented and in compliance with MIP. As a result, specific elements were not considered in the development phase, but are still relevant for particular cases. To tackle the need for representing these missing elements, element **Metadado Específico** *(SpecificMetadataElement)* allows organizations to add information to the metadata record. This element is composed by three subelements, which ensure the rightful identification of these information. Subelements **Designacao Metadado Específico** (*SpecificMetadataDesignation*), **TipoMetadado Específico** (*SpecificMetadataType*) and **Conteudo Metadata Específico** (*SpecificMetadataContent*) specify the name of the new temporary metadata element, its data format and the data provided by the element, respectively. This element is repeatable, which means that the organizations are able to add as many specific metadata elements as required.

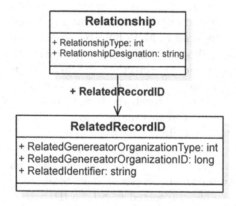

Fig. 7. UML diagram for element *Relationship* in the CDM (translated to English).

Element **Relacao** (*Relationship*) in the CDM, "Relação" in MIP, allows the recognition of the records that are related to the document sent. Since not every document has related records, this element is optional, in MIP and in the CDM. This element is defined by three subelements, maintaining the subelements defined by MIP, in the CDM. Figure 7 depicts an UML diagram of element *Relacao* in the CDM. As shown, subelement **IDRecursoRelacionado** (*RelatedRecordID*) is comprised by a group of three subelements, whose propose is to identify uniquely the related record, through the identification of its generator organization and identifier, with subelements **TipoOrganismoGeradorRelacionado** (*RelatedGenereatorOrganizationType*), which accepts values of 1 or of 2, and **IDOrganismoGeradorRelacionado** (*RelatedGeneratorOrgnaizationID*), which holds the unique identifier of the organization, according to its type, using the structure proposed by the CDM to identify organizations, explained previously. **IdentificadorRelacionado** (*RelatedIdentifier*) is the third subelement and specifies the identifier of the related record.

To identify the type of relationship established, MIP presents a list of subelements of subelement "Tipo de Relação" (Relationship Type), with each subelement representing a different type of relationship. This structure was not maintained in the CDM, since it would require a great effort by the recipient RMS to identify the type of relationship and the related record. To simplify the streaming of this information in the CDM, element **TipoRelacao** (Relationship Type) holds a numeric code, from 1 to 12, each representative of a type of relationship, as shown in Listing 1.6. To implement this restriction in the XSD, attributes `minInclusive` and `maxInclusive` define the limit of accepted values, as shown in Listing 1.6. Subelement **DescricaoRelacao** (*RelationshipDesignation*) is present in the CDM, as it is in MIP, and provides a description of the relationship established.

The presence of this element in the CDM is important to ensure that the recipient RMS is capable of establishing a connection between the local record created, from the metadata record captured, and other records already managed by the system.

Listing 1.6. Excerpt of the XSD file of subelement RelationshipType.

```
<xs:element name="RelationshipType" minOccurs="1">
        <xs:simpleType>
                <xs:restriction base="xs:int">
                        <xs:minInclusive value="1"/>
                        <xs:maxInclusive value="12"/>
                </xs:restriction>
        </xs:simpleType>
</xs:element>
```

Many of the documents exchanged among public organization are responses to other documents. The relationship established between an information object and its response, can be identified by element *Relacao* (Relationship). However, if a document has established a high number of relationships, the automatic handling of the information provided can evolve into a complex task. Consider an example where Entity B produces document D2 as a response to record D1, produced by Entity A. Entity B sends D2, and its metadata, to Entity A, via iAP, with a response to what was proposed by D1. Entity A has to identify that document D2 received is a response to its record D1. Suppose that D2 has 10 other related records, all records produced by Entity A and, consequently in Entity A's RMS. The problem in this scenario is that element

Relacao (Relationship) is not comprehensive enough to indicate which of the 10 related records triggered response D2, hampering the task of identifying D1 as the responsible for the response, and not any of the other 10 related record from Entity A. The more related records identified in a metadata record, the more complex is the automatic treatment of the information.

To simplify this process, and promote the automatic treatment of responses to records, considering that responses are a large part of the information flow among organizations, element **VossaReferencia** (*KnownReference*) was introduced in the CDM. This element has the same goal as element **Relacao**, of identifying the related records, but is reserved for responses, to expedite the process of identifying the record who triggered the response received. *VossaReferencia* (*KnownReference*) is composed by 3 subelements, **TipoOrganismo VossaReferencia** (*KnownReferenceOrganizationType*), **IDOrganismo VossaReferencia** (*KnownReferenceOrganizationID*) and **Identificador-VossaReferencia** (*KnownReferenceIdentifier*), that indicate the type of organization, the organization identifier and the related record's identifier, respectively, following the structure already presented for identifying organizations and records in an unique way.

4   Results Assessment

To evaluate the proposed CDM, two methods were employed: (1) a comparison between MIP and the proposed CDM, to determine and analyze the importance of the CDM and the improvements presented by the model, regarding MIP; and (2) an assessment of the qualities possessed by the CDM developed, according to the Bruce-Hillman Framework [4].

4.1   Comparing MIP and CDM

The comparison between MIP and the CDM developed consisted on the application of the two data models as metadata schemas of iAP's service, in the same scenario. By applying MIP as the metadata schema, two types of problems were identified: (1) Lack of rigid norms of application (Problem A) and (2) Structural problems (Problem B). The CDM presents solutions for these faults that are assessed in this section.

Problem A is summarized by the lack of controlled vocabularies and limits to the range of values of the elements in MIP. Controlled vocabularies are a set of accepted values that metadata elements can hold [23]. MIP documentation provides examples of the values elements can possess. However, this is not enough to guarantee interoperability, because it is not certain that every organization will use and understand the values equally. With MIP, every organization can apply any value they deem fit whilst, to ensure semantic interoperability among different systems, every organization must apply the same set of values defined. This lack of common values also hinders the automation process. The CDM proposed introduces a set of controlled vocabularies to provide organizations with a limit set of valid values for the elements proposed.

Problem B arises from the structural problems of MIP. These structural problems were found in three crucial MIP elements. MIP element "Identificador de recurso" (Record Identifier) is responsible for identifying uniquely a record. The problem with this element is the way it is structured in MIP, which does not ensure the uniqueness of the identifier of a record within an interoperability process. MIP element "Relação" (*Relationship*) also has structural problems in subelement "Tipo de Relação" (Relationship type), which contains multiple subelements, one for each type of relationship the record may established with another. This structure is not efficient since most of the subelements would be left blank. MIP element "Código de classificação"'s (Classification code) structure constitutes a problem, with users not being able to identify the classification model used to classify the record and, consequently, hindering the interpretation of the record's class by the receiver system.

For a better understanding of the origin of these problems and how the CDM provides solutions for them, an example is next presented.

As illustrated by Fig. 8, suppose that Entity A wants to inform Entity B. Upon receiving the document file and metadata (represented in Fig. 8 as an unique entity for a simple understanding), a local record is created in the RMS of Entity B, from the information received. After analyzing the received information, Entity B develops a response document, registers the related information in its RMS and sends the response to Entity A. Without the solution proposed, entities would send the document via e-mail or letter, which would lead to unnecessary costs and time spent, and could potentially lead to an ineffective management of records, since there is no guarantee that a new record would be locally created in the RMS of Entity A upon receiving the document.

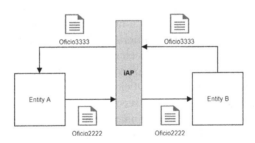

Fig. 8. Example of flow of documents through iAP [28].

As stated, the use of MIP AS-IS as the canonical data model of the service would lead to multiple faults. The way records are identified using MIP would generate a problem if used to identify records in the context of this work. MIP offers only one element to hold the value identifier of the record. This element in MIP does not have any special structure to ensure that the identifier of the record, which must be unique, remains unique when shared with multiple organizations within the same interoperability process. To solve this issue, CDM introduces a new structure for the identifier element, with three subelements. Subelements *GeneratorOrganizationType* and *GeneratorOrganizationID* provide information about the organization that identifies the record, while *DocumentID* holds the identification code provided by said organization. This way, even if two entities have different records with the same identifier, as each organization is identified with an unique code, the set of the three subelements maintains the record's unique identifier.

To identify the classification model used, MIP uses one single element, which can hold any value the organization deems appropriate, without restrictions, since MEF/LC is not of mandatory use. However, the key for success resides on the receiver organizations identifying correctly the class of the record. Without knowing which classification model is used, that is not possible. Thus, when developing the CDM, an extra element (*OtherClassificationCode*) was introduced, to provide non MEF/LC compliant organizations of informing the receiver system of which classification model is being used. However, the use of MEF/LC is promoted by the CDM, through the restructuring of element *ClassificationCode*.

The use of MIP in this context generates a problem in the way organizations are identified in the metadata. In its documentation, MIP provides examples of values for identifying organizations. The problem is that these examples are considered as a suggestion only, and not as a norm, leaving to organizations the responsibility of using any method they deem fit for identifying organizations, not guaranteeing a semantic agreement across all organizations. Thus, in the CDM, it was defined that every entity would be identified using SIOE or, if not present in SIOE, other code that is on a database controlled by AMA.

To identify the relationships established with the record, MIP provides element "Tipo de Relacao" (Relationship type), which contains 11 subelements, each one responsible for identifying a different type of relationship. As stated, this is not efficient. The CDM provides a new structure for identify the relationship type, assigning to each type a numeric code, to populate subelement *RelationshipType*. The CDM also introduces element *KnownReference*, to identify the record who triggered a response. As shown in Fig. 8, Entity A sends to Entity B an information object with identifier Oficio2222 through iAP. Entity B receives this information and generates a local record in its RMS. As a response to Oficio2222, Entity B produces a new information object and sends it to Entity A as a reply (Oficio3333). To establish this relationship between information objects in the metadata, Entity B indicates in element *KnownReference* Oficio2222 as the object to whom Oficio3333 is a response to.

The results of this comparison helped identify the need to develop a new data model and the reason why MIP was not chosen to be applied directly to the service. MIP provides the elements required in a Portuguese metadata schema to correctly identify the records, but it does not provide a well-formed structure to be applied digitally. MIP was developed focusing more on how to identifying records within an organization and less in how these records would be interpreted if their metadata was shared with a different organization.

4.2 Assessment of the CDM Qualities

The Bruce-Hillman Framework (BHF) is a technique used to assess the qualities of metadata schemas [4], defining seven qualities: completeness, provenance, accuracy, conformance to expectations, logical consistency and coherence, timeliness and accessibility. Each quality is associated with questions whose answers provide a narrative score, as depicted in Fig. 9.

According to the BHF, *Completeness* is the capability of the metadata schema to describe the object as completely as possible, considering the project's resources. To measure this quality, the BHF presents two questions. As shown in Fig. 9, the first question can be answered affirmatively, considering that the CDM was developed under the influence of MIP. As concluded in Subsect. 4.1, MIP was not designed to be applied to records that are meant to be exported to other systems, since it does not ensure that the identity of the record is maintained when exported. However, MIP was developed as a measure for describing records metadata correctly. Even if the way MIP is structured is not ideal and would not generate adequate results if applied in this context, it is a fundamental reference for CDM. This way, we can sustain that CDM supports effectively the creation of the local record, since it follows the requirements from MIP. When developing the CDM, and in similarity with MIP, there was a consciousness that not every element is always required, since many just provide extra information that helps to identify the record, but is not necessary seeing as other elements are capable of providing enough. However, every element that is considered important to describe the record is present and is mandatory, meaning that the information provided by those elements is always transmitted, without exception. With this in consideration, the second question proposed by the BHF, shown in Fig. 9 is positive, presenting two examples, in column "Compliance indicator", of elements important to define the record's identity.

Provenance, as a quality, is defined as the capability the metadata has of providing information about its origins and changes throughout time. To assess that, three questions are proposed, as in Fig. 9. The first question assesses if the element set provides information about the responsible for creating the metadata. The CDM is capable of providing this information, considering that the responsible for keying the metadata of the record is the generator organization. The next two questions analyze if the metadata provides information of how the metadata was created and if the metadata has suffered any transformations since its creation. The CDM does not provide any information about these issues. The CDM only registers information regarding the version of the record but not changes in its metadata.

Another quality promoted by BHF is *Accuracy*. Bruce and Hillman state that a metadata schema should be accurate in the way it describes the data object, by providing *"correct and factual"* [4] information. To assess this, the BHF proposes three questions. As mentioned previously, when developing the CDM, there was a concern in ensuring that the information provided by MIP was maintained by the new elements of the CDM.

Quality Measure	Quality Criteria	Narrative Score	Compliance Indicator
Completeness	Does the element set completely describe the objects?	Yes, the CDM describes the record, providing the required information stated by an approved standard (MIP)	MIP and CDM comparison
	Are all relevant element used for each object?	Yes, all the elements considered relevant and important to ensure the record's identity are mandatory	Elements *Identifier* and *DocumentType*
Provenance	Who is responsible for creating, extracting, or transforming the metadata?	The CDM provides this information through one of its elements	Element *GeneratorOrganizationID*
	How was the metadata created or extracted?	The CDM doesn't provide this information	
	What transformations have been done on the data since its creation?	The CDM is not capable of registering which transformations the data has suffered since its creation	
Accuracy	Have accepted methods been used for creation or extraction?	Yes, the CDM was developed to maintain the elements presented by MIP, while introducing necessary changes to achieve the research's goal	MIP and CDM comparison
	What has been done to ensure valid values and structure?	To ensure this, the work group responsible for the development was composed by different professionals with different visions, to cover al the necessities for valid values and structure	Application profile
	Are default values appropriate, and have they been appropriately used?	*The information available is not enough to answer this question*	
Conformance to expectations	Does metadata describe what it claims to?	Yes, the CDM describes the record as correctly as it claims, since its elements provide information based on MIP	MIP and CDM comparison
	Are controlled vocabularies aligned with the audience characteristics and understanding of the objects?	Yes, when developing controlled vocabularies, users' necessities were considered	Element *DocumentType*
	Are compromises documented and in line with the community expectation?	Yes, all the compromises made during the development phase are documented	Internal documentations; Meeting minutes
Logical consistency and coherence	Is data in elements consistent throughout?	Yes, elements with similar functions have a similar structure throughout the CDM	Elements *XOrganizationType* and *XOrganizationID*
	How does it compare with other data within the community?	The CDM allows a bigger data consistency than MIP	MIP and CDM comparison
Timeliness	Is metadata regularly updated as the resources change?	*The information available is not enough to answer this question*	
	Are controlled vocabularies updated when relevant?	*The information available is not enough to answer this question*	
Accessibility	Is an appropriate element set for audience and community being used?	Yes, considering it provides the same information as MIP, an approved schema within the community	MIP and CDM comparison
	Is it affordable to use and maintain?	Yes, it is affordable due to the flexibility of the language used	Documentation and calculations
	Does it permit further value-adds?	Yes, the CDM allows the temporary addition of elements and due to the language, it was develop in, a permanent element is easily added	Element *SpecificMetadata* and use of XML

Fig. 9. Bruce-Hillman framework applied to the CDM [28].

Considering this, the first question, shown in Fig. 9, can be answered affirmatively, seeing as MIP is an accepted method and was used for the creation of the CDM. The second question inquiries about what has been done to ensure valid values and structure for elements of the metadata schema. While developing the CDM, a great deal of importance was given to the structure of the elements, since this was the main factor why MIP was not apt to be used, as shown in Subsect. 4.1. For defining the CDM, a set of professionals, from different areas within the community, that would bring different ideas and perspectives to the table, were selected to help evaluate which values were needed for each element and what structure the elements should adopt to achieve the goals of the research. Since the CDM has yet to be used by organizations within the PA, the third question cannot be answered due to the lack of information regarding its application.

A metadata schema is in *Conformance to expectations* if it is able to respond to the users necessities, by including elements that the community expects to find, while remaining realistic about what is and is not important to be included. To evaluate this quality, BHF proposes three questions. The first, shown in Fig. 9, can be answered affirmatively. The definition of the CDM was driven by the need to guarantee that a record would be described correctly whilst ensuring that this information would not be lose its meaning when received by another system. Considering that CDM elements provide the same information as MIP elements, an accepted standard for defining records within the PPA, it can be said that the CDM describes what it claims. The second question inquiries about the use of controlled vocabularies and if they are aligned with the needs of users and records. When developing the controlled vocabulary for element *DocumentType*, a survey was performed to understand which types of documents were more frequent within the organizations of the PPA. With this information, it was possible to define a controlled vocabulary with 38 types of documents to be used as values for the element. This serves as an example of how users' needs were taken into account when establishing controlled vocabularies for each element. The third question refers to the compromises made throughout the implementation phase, and their registration. To elaborate the CDM, different opinions of archivists and information systems professionals had to be balanced, requiring multiple compromises, documented in meeting minutes and other internal documentation produced during the development phase of the CDM.

Logical consistency and coherence are qualities of a metadata schema with a consistent structure throughout its definition and associated application profile. An application profile is a set of metadata elements with guidelines and policies associated that indicate how the metadata elements are to be applied to the objects. In this case, the CDM proposed is thoroughly explained in its application profile, exposing to the users the accepted values and utilization norms of every element. As shown in Fig. 9, two questions are associated to this quality. The first, inquieres if the data in elements is consistent throughout. For this assessment, it is possible to evaluate what the CDM offers, to ensure that the data will be consistent throughout. This metadata schema is consistent in the way it describes different elements that have the same functionality in the schema, even if used in different contexts. Elements of type *XOrganizationType* and *XOrganizationID* have the same functionality of identifying organizations, present the same structure and accept the same type of values, but can be applied to different types of organizations and their different roles for the record.

Even if there is not, yet, a set of data that can be assessed for its consistency, the CDM has provided all the tools to ensure this consistency. To answer the second question proposed, shown in Fig. 9, taking into consideration the lack of application of the CDM, it is only possible to compare the architecture of the CDM with the architecture of MIP, and how consistent the data provided by both data models would be. As stated in Subsect. 4.1, MIP does not provide rigid rules for the data as the CDM does. Although the MIP provides multiple examples of values to assign to each element, nothing prevents users of applying different rules in the same metadata object. Consequently, this does not ensure that the data will be consistent throughout.

According to the BHF, *Accessibility* is the capability a metadata set has to be viewed and comprehended. This quality is assessed by three questions. The first, assesses the appropriateness of the element set for the community. As stated previously, MIP was used as the basis for developing the CDM. Considering this, the CDM proposed is appropriate for the community, taking into consideration the concerns from multiple perspectives and providing a solution for them. The second question inquiries about the costs of maintenance of the element set. Considering the use of XML and the results from cost estimation calculations, it was concluded that maintenance is affordable and even preferable to the costs of correspondence, nowadays, in the PA. The last question audits the ease of adding further elements to the set. The CDM provides element *SpecificMetadata*, which allows the temporary addition of data to the metadata. A more permanent addition to the CDM is also easy to achieve due to the flexibility of XML, the language used for implementing the CDM.

4.3   Results Discussion

This research presents a solution for achieving technical and semantic interoperability across RMS in the Portuguese public administration. Technical interoperability was guaranteed in this research by the Portuguese interoperability platform, already implemented and used by public organizations, through the definition of new Web services that supported the exchange of document files and metadata records across the platform.

Guaranteeing semantic interoperability among multiple RMS required the implementation of a Canonical Data Model (CDM) capable of ensuring that the identity of the document exchanged was maintained in systems with divergent architectures and policies.

The proposed CDM was validated from two different perspectives. The first evaluation method presented compares the CDM to MIP, disclosing the similarities and variations of both data models, whereas the second evaluation method assesses the validity of the CDM in the scope of this research.

The comparison between CDM and MIP evaluated CDM's capability of describing records and automating metadata capture and record creation processes, whilst considering MIP, the current data model, developed by DGLAB to describe records in the Portuguese public administration. The experiment was divided into two phases. In phase one MIP was used as the data model of the service implemented to exchange documents, whereas in phase two the CDM was the data model of the service, as proposed by this research. The application of both data models to the same document, lead to conclude that MIP does not support the main goals of this research, as it does not guarantee semantic interoperability and process automation.

This first evaluation method showed that MIP is not equipped to be applied AS-IS to the service and, consequently, not equipped to ensure semantic interoperability across RMS. Even though MIP is capable of describing records within an organization, it fails when applied in a situation where this description needs to be understood by another RMS, with no previous knowledge of which methods were used to generate the metadata. This conclusion encouraged the development of a new data model, the CDM, that provided the same information stated by MIP, while ensuring semantic interoperability and promoting the automation of processes among RMS, through the restructuring and deprecation of MIP elements, addition of new elements and application of rigid values.

The second evaluation method assesses the validity of the CDM, according to seven qualities proposed by the Bruce-Hillman Framework. The application of this framework concluded that the CDM provides a complete description of the document exchanged (Completeness); is accurate in its description of the documents within the Portuguese public administration (Accuracy); considers the needs of the users (Conformance to Expectation); guarantees that the data is coherent and consistent (Logical consistency and coherence); and is accessible to use (Accessibility). Considering this, it can be stated that the CDM is a valid model for the Portuguese public administration.

5   Conclusions and Future Work

This section presents the conclusions of this research in Subsect. 5.1 and the future work suggested, in Subsect. 5.2.

5.1   Conclusions

This research proposes an interoperability solution for the Portuguese public administration, capable of establishing interoperability among different information systems with records management capability, thus allowing the effective and efficient electronic exchange of document files and metadata records among organizations.

The success of the proposed solution depended, mostly, on the implementation of two levels of interoperability, namely technical interoperability and semantic interoperability, the latter the main focus of this work. Technical interoperability was achieved with minimal effort, through the implementation of Web services capable of delivering document files and their metadata, in the Portuguese interoperability platform, developed by AMA and consumed by public organizations. Semantic interoperability is attained if the information exchanged retains its original meaning in every system. To guarantee this level of interoperability, this research propose a Canonical Data Model (CDM), to be applied to the services developed. This CDM guarantees that the information exchanged is equally interpreted by every system, independently of each system's specific data format.

Using a pilot project currently in development at AMA as the case study, this research defined a canonical data model that considered MIP, a data model developed by DGLAB for describing records within organizations of the Portuguese public administration. In this context, the current interoperability measures of the Portuguese public administration, such as MIP and MEF/LC, a record classification model, also developed by DGLAB, were analyzed critically throughout this work.

The CDM presented can be seen as an extension of MIP. Through the analysis of which elements are necessary and which ones are not, the new data model was developed to accommodate the metadata of each document sent, allowing the automatic creation of a local record, at the recipient RMS or business system, in accordance with the information and document file received. The Canonical Data Model approach ensures that organizations apply the same data structure to define the metadata of the documents exchanged, guaranteeing semantic interoperability, as the information provided by the metadata can be recognized and interpreted equally by every RMS, being the system's only responsibility the definition of a translation between the CDM and its own data format.

The capability of automating metadata capture and record creation was promoted by this research. The metadata capture process is the set of activities in which metadata is entered into the system, either manually or automatically, whereas the record creation process consists on creating a local record from the document file and metadata captured. The automation of these processes is achieved through the normalization of data structures and values received, guaranteeing that the system establishes system automation rules to handle each of the values expected.

The biggest challenge faced by this research was the reconciliation between guaranteeing the solution's needs for process automation and semantic interoperability, and preserving MIP's guidelines for describing records within the Portuguese public administration. This balance was achieved by guaranteeing that the changes performed on MIP elements, in the CDM, had no impact on the information provided by the elements, thus ensuring that the document exchanged was described according to an approved standard, without jeopardizing the success of this work.

The CDM presented was evaluated from two different angles. First, the CDM was directly compared with MIP, allowing the analysis of their similarities and discrepancies. This experiment concluded MIP's incapacity of ensuring semantic interoperability in an electronic exchange of documents, and CDM's capability to provide a solution to MIP's faults, particularly MIP's element structure and values' normalization. Second, the validity of the CDM as a data model in the domain of this research was assessed, by applying the Bruce-Hillman Framework.

Although the lack of available information, concerning the application of the CDM in a real setting, hampered the assessment of certain metrics, the use of this framework determined that the proposed CDM is valid within the scope of this research, guaranteeing five out of seven qualities, namely Completeness, Accuracy, Conformance to expectations, Logical consistency and coherence and Accessibility.

This research was also able to provide answers to the research challenges presented in Sect. 1. The defined interoperability measures, specifically MIP, cannot ensure semantic interoperability in an electronic exchange of documents, as MIP does not provide enough tools to guarantee that the original meaning of the information exchanged is preserved. The chosen technique for achieving semantic interoperability across RMS of the public administration was the development of a Canonical Data Model. The use of a Canonical Data Model promotes the application of the same data structure, by public organizations, to describe the documents exchanged, ensuring that the information provided by the data is interpreted equally by every system.

Although this research is specific to the Portuguese public administration and its records management requirements, it can still be seen as an example for achieving interoperability among multiple distributed records management systems. This research presents and analyzes the development of a new data model capable of describing records and promoting process automation, and the practices employed can be applied to other similar projects, for public administrations worldwide.

5.2   Future Work

Several future developments for the solution proposed are possible. A logical next step of this research includes the evaluation of the CDM in more scenarios. The evaluation performed by this research concluded the need for a new data model, to achieve the goals proposed, and its validity in the domain of the Portuguese public administration. Still, the application of the CDM in more real document transaction between two business systems would determine if automation is, in fact, possible, as desired, and if documents retain their provenance and business trail across business contexts.

Other future work would also explore the expansion of new elements in the CDM beyond the elements defined. These additions can be performed with minimal effort, due to the flexibility of the solution proposed in this research.

References

1. Administrative Modernization Agency (AMA): Interoperabilidade na Administração Pública, Procedimentos para Adesão à iAP (Interoperability in the Public Administration, iAP Adhesion Guidelines), Version 3.0 (2011). (in Portuguese)
2. Vasconcelos, A.: Identificação Electrónica (Electronic Identification). Administrative Modernization Agency (AMA) (2018). https://www.ama.gov.pt/documents/24077/198481/Identifica%C3%A7%C3%A3o+eletronica.pdf. Accessed 14 Sept 2019. (in Portuguese)

3. Barbedo, F., Corujo, L.: MIP: Metainformação para Interoperabilidade (MIP: Metadata for Interoperability), Version 1.0c. General Directorate for Book, Archives and Libraries (DGLAB), October 2012. (in Portuguese)
4. Bruce, T.R., Hillmann, D.I.: The continuum of metadata quality: defining, expressing, exploiting. ALA editions (2004)
5. Directorate General of Administration and Directorate of Information Technology: Council of Europe Metadata Policy (DGA/DIT/IMD(2012) 08). Council of Europe, December 2012. https://rm.coe.int/16800602ec. Accessed 07 Aug 2018
6. DLM Forum Foundation: MoReq2010: Modular Requirements for Record Systems, Volume 1, Core Services & Plug-in Modules, Version 1.1 (2010, 2011)
7. European Commission: ISA^2 - "About ISA^2 ", https://ec.europa.eu/isa2/isa2_en. Accessed 14 Sept 2019
8. European Commission: ISA Programme - "About ISA". http://ec.europa.eu/archives/isa/about-isa/index_en.htm. Accessed 14 Sept 2019
9. European Commission: COM (2010) 744 final, Annex 2 to the Communication from the Commission to the European Parliament, the Council, the European Economic and Social Committee and the Committee of Regions: "Toward interoperability for European public services", European Interoperability Framework (EIF) for European public services, December 2010
10. European Commission: Improving semantic interoperability in European eGovernment systems. https://ec.europa.eu/isa2/action/improving-semantic-interoperability-european-egovernment-systems_en. Accessed 19 Dec 2017
11. European Parliament and of the Council: Decision No. 922/2009/EC of the European Parliament and of the Council on interoperability solutions for European public administrations (ISA), September 2009
12. General Directorate for Book, Archives and Libraries (DGLAB): Governo Electrónico e Interoperabilidade: documento metodológico para a elaboração de um esquema de metainformação para a interoperabilidade e de uma macroestrutura funcional (E-Government and Interoperability), Lisbon, February 2008. (in Portuguese)
13. General Directorate for Book, Archives and Libraries (DGLAB): Macroestrutura Funcional (MEF) (Functional Macrostructure (MEF)), Version 2.0 (2013). (in Portuguese)
14. General Directorate for Book, Archives and Libraries (DGLAB): Regulamento do Programa "Administração Eletrónica e Interoperabilidade Semântica" (Regulation of the programme "Electronic Administrative and Semantic Interoperability"), Lisbon, May 2017. (in Portuguese)
15. General Directorate for Book, Archives and Libraries (DGLAB): Programa "Administração Eletrónica e Interoperabilidade Semântica (PAEIS)" ("Electronic Administrative and Semantic Interoperability programme (PAEIS)"). http://arquivos.dglab.gov.pt/programas-e-projectos/modernizacao-administrativa/macroestrutura-funcional-mef/. Accessed 14 Sept 2019. (in Portuguese)
16. General Directorate for Book, Archives and Libraries (DGLAB): Lista Consolidada: 3°s níveis em planos de classificação conformes à MEF ("Lista Consolidada": 3rd levels in business classification schemes according to MEF), December 2014. (in Portuguese)
17. Hohpe, G., Woolf, B., Brown, K.: Enterprise Integration Patterns: Designing, Building, and Deploying Messaging Solutions. Addison-Wesley, Reading (2004). A Martin Fowler Signature Book
18. ISO 15489–1:2016: Information and documentation - Records management - Part 1: Concepts and principles (2016)

19. Kubicek, H., Cimander, R., Scholl, H.J.: Organizational Interoperability in E-Government: Lessons from 77 European Good-Practice Cases, 1st edn. Springer, Heidelberg (2011)
20. Lourenço, A., Penteado, P.: A caminho da ASIA - Avaliação Suprainstitucional da Informação Arquivística (On the way to ASIA - Suprainstitutional Evaluation of Archivist Information). In: BAD National Congress, no. 12, October 2015. (in Portuguese)
21. Lourenço, A., Penteado, P., Henriques, C.: O desafio da interoperabilidade na gestão dos arquivos da Administração: propostas do órgão de coordenação nacional de arquivos (The challenge of interoperability in Administration's archive management: Proposals from the national coordination archives association). In: BAD National Congress, no. 11, October 2012. (in Portuguese)
22. Lourenço, A., et al.: Orientações básicas para o desenvolvimento dos 3°s níveis de planos de classificação conformes à Macroestrutura funcional (Basic Orientations for the development of 3rd levels in business classification schemes according to the functional macrostructure). General Directorate for Book, Archives and Libraries (DGLAB), Lisbon (2013). (in Portuguese)
23. Online Computer Library Center: Using a Controlled Vocabulary (2013). https://www.oclc.org/content/dam/training/CONTENTdm/pdf/Tutorials/Metadata/Controlled%20Vocabulary.pdf. Accessed 14 Sept 2019
24. Presidência do Conselho de Ministros: Resolução do Conselho de Ministros (Resolution from the Portuguese Council of Ministers) no. 5/1990. Official Gazette of Portugal, 1st serie, no. 49, February 1990. (in Portuguese)
25. Presidência do Conselho de Ministros: Resolução do Conselho de Ministros (Resolution from the Portuguese Council of Ministers) no. 42/2015. Official Gazette of Portugal, 1st serie, no. 118, June 2015. (in Portuguese)
26. Presidência do Conselho de Ministros: Resolução do Conselho de Ministros (Resolution from the Portuguese Council of Ministers) no. 51/2017. Official Gazette of Portugal, 1st series, no. 77, April 2017. (in Portuguese)
27. St. Laurent, S.: Why XML? (1998). http://www.simonstl.com/articles/whyxml.htm. Accessed 14 Sept 2019
28. Viegas, C., Vasconcelos, A., Borbinha, J., Chora, Z.: Records management support in the interoperability framework for the Portuguese public administration. In: 21st International Conference on Enterprise Information Systems (ICEIS 2019), Crete, Greece, May 2019

An Analysis of Automated Technical Debt Measurement

Ilya Khomyakov, Zufar Makhmutov, Ruzilya Mirgalimova,
and Alberto Sillitti[✉]

Innopolis University, Innopolis, Russian Federation
{i.khomyakov,z.makhmutov,r.mirgalimova,a.sillitti}@innopolis.ru

Abstract. *Background*: Measuring and understanding Technical Debt (TD) is quite complex since there are a number of different definitions and techniques that have been proposed in the last few years and it is not clear which ones should be used in which conditions. The approaches proposed are almost never based on the existing ones and their validation is often performed in a very limited number of projects. For this reasons, practitioners are confused and find difficult to apply such approaches in their projects.

Goals: This paper investigates the available techniques for evaluating TD using automated tools aiming at helping practitioners and researcher in understanding the available options and apply them correctly.

Method: The study has been performed as a Systematic Literature Review (SLR) applied to 835 studies obtained from the three largest digital libraries and databases.

Results: After applying all filtering stages, 38 papers out of 835 have been selected and analyzed in depth. Almost all of them propose novel approaches to measure TD using different criteria and they do not extend or validate existing approaches.

Conclusions: The area is not mature and it lacks independent evaluations of the models proposed. Authors focus on proposing new approaches and no consolidation can be identified. Moreover, almost all the approaches proposed are automated only partially and through prototype tools designed just to support the studies analyzed in the paper in which the approach is proposed and rarely maintained. These facts makes difficult the application of such methods by practitioners.

Keywords: Technical debt · Measurement · Literature review · Tools

1 Introduction

TD is one of the most recent concepts that has been introduced in software engineering. It acknowledges the trade-off between code quality and the need to meet market expectations (e.g., low costs, short time-to-market, etc.). This is a typical situation for startup companies that have strict requirements to produce a Minimum Viable Product (MVP) to test the market and get funding

© Springer Nature Switzerland AG 2020
J. Filipe et al. (Eds.): ICEIS 2019, LNBIP 378, pp. 250–273, 2020.
https://doi.org/10.1007/978-3-030-40783-4_12

to survive. In such contexts, the sub-optimal decisions that decrease the quality of the system leading to the creation of strategic TD [72] could be a key strategy to achieve success. In any case, companies should understand that such sub-optimal decisions require additional effort to fix the product in the long run [20,21]. However, creating TD could be a valuable strategy to push products on the market knowing that the debt needs to be payed (with interests) in the future.

This phenomenon was originally described by Ward Cunningham in 1992 [22] introducing the concept of TD. There are many more sources of TD that have been investigated recently that involve communication, collaboration among team members, documentation, and individual attitudes [37,72].

Since TD is a way of measuring the effort needed to achieve top quality in a software system compared to the current status, it is of paramount importance being able of measuring (or estimating) it. The importance of such an activity is proved by the simple fact that most of the software projects have some TD [25]. Being able to estimate TD allows development teams and managers to plan the work properly.

It may also happen that TD is too high to be payed [18], requiring different approaches to address it (e.g., rewriting the system). However, knowing that and how the system reached that condition could help in the identification of mistakes and improve the development process.

Frequent changes of software artifacts (mainly in the source code) without corresponding quality assurance measures quickly leads to a decrease in software quality, with an increase in the costs for further development and evolution due to the increase TD [19]. Moreover, the evaluation of TD should be performed automatically to avoid increasing the load of the developers and being able to monitor that continuously during any phase of the development. This is particularly useful in conjunction with the usage of Agile approaches since their delivery-oriented nature and continuous adaptation to the needs of the customer can be more prone to generate TD compared to traditional software development. However, they are also more prone to pay TD through the a proper implementation of refactoring.

For all these reasons, being able of measuring TD automatically is of paramount importance to support the daily work of developers. There are many different approaches to TD in literature and this paper provides an extensive analysis pointing out the current status of the research extending the work the same authors in [33]. In this paper, we have enhanced the analysis including a wider number of primary studies.

The paper is organized as follows: Sect. 2 describes the adopted methodology; Sect. 3 discusses the findings; Sect. 4 investigates the related work; Sect. 5 analyzes the threats to validity; finally, Sect. 6 draws the conclusions and introduces future work.

2   Methodology

The protocol adopted for this Systematic Literature Review (SLR) is the one introduced by Kitchenham and Charters [34] for performing such reviews in the software engineering area.

The main goal of this work is to review the existing studies and highlight the aspects related to TD measurement, therefore we have defined the following research questions:

- RQ1: Which are the existing techniques for measuring TD?
- RQ2: Which are the tools that support the automation of the measurement of TD?
- RQ3: Are there any empirical studies able to demonstrate the usefulness of the identified techniques?
- RQ4: Are there any empirical studies able to demonstrate the usefulness of the tools identified?

To answer the research questions, we have searched for papers using the three largest digital libraries: ACM Digital Library, IEEE Xplore, and Google Scholar.

Since only studies focusing on TD as main topic are interesting for our purpose, we suppose that their title or abstract include the key words *technical debt measurement*. Consequently, we used appropriate queries for each library:

- ACM Digital Library:(+technical +debt +measurement) OR recordAbstract: (+technical +debt +measurement)
- IEEE Xplore: (("Document Title":technical debt measurement) OR "Abstract": technical debt measurement)
- Google Scholar: "technical debt measurement"

The data have been extracted in two stages: in August 2018, when the initial version of the study started and in September 2019 to extend the study with the latest research available.

Only certain papers should be included to the final result: containing abstracts, considering TD as a main topic, written in English. No year constraint was specified, since we aimed at collecting all appropriate data despite of the date.

Many publications found in the digital libraries were not appropriate for our study since we were interested in primary studies published in referred workshops, conferences, and journals. Therefore, we excluded documents such as: summaries of workshops, tutorials, introductory descriptions of conferences, research plans, presentations, not primary studies, and technical reports. Therefore, we excluded all the documents that were not proper research papers.

Finally, we manually excluded all the papers not related to our research that passed the previous filters but still included in the list. The selection was performed after reading the entire content of the papers.

3   Results

We found 1,063 papers distributed as follows: ACM Digital Library (211), IEEE Xplore (317), and Google Scholar (535).

As expected, there was a significant overlap in the papers found in the different libraries. Therefore, the first step was merging the results and removing duplicates. Finally, at the end of the process, we selected 46 papers. The overall selection process is summarized in Fig. 1 (the numbers on the arrows show the amount of papers that passed each phase):

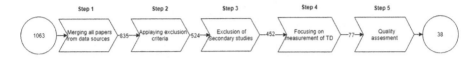

Fig. 1. Steps of the selection process.

- **Step 1: Merging All Papers from Data Sources.** The initial list included 1,063 papers but many duplicates were present. The identification of the duplicates was performed manually to avoid problems with minor character differences in the titles and in the author names. At the end, we had a list of 835 unique papers.
- **Step 2: Applying Exclusion Criteria.** At this stage, we applied the exclusion criteria resulting in a selection of 524 papers. At this stage we still kept in the list the secondary studies.
- **Step 3: Excluding not Primary Studies.** At this stage, we identified the secondary studies (e.g., systematic reviews, systematic mappings, etc.) that were removed from the list and analyzed in Sect. 4. The secondary studies identified are 10 and the list is reduced to 452 papers.
- **Step 4: Considering Studies Related to Measurement of TD.** Reading the title and the abstract of the 452 papers, we identified the studies related to the measurement of TD. We identified 38 papers distributed between 2011 and 2019 as described in Fig. 2.
- **Step 5: Quality Assessment.** We read the 77 papers identified and we excluded 39 of them since they were not dealing with the measurement of the technical debt even if from the title or the abstract they appeared appropriate for our investigation.

3.1   RQ1: Which Are the Existing Techniques for Measuring TD

The identified studies have been analyzed in terms of proposed techniques, their requirements about input data needed for the calculation of TD, the resulting information, advantages and disadvantages of the approach. Table 5 summarises

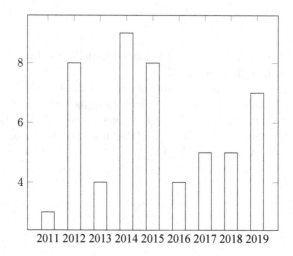

Fig. 2. Distribution of papers related to TD measurement over the years.

Table 1. Input of TD measurement techniques.

Technique (method)	Target quality level	Debt-estimating model	Number of should-fix violations	The hours to fix each violation	The cost of labor	Source code	Output data from static code analyzers	Candidate cloud-based mobile service	Past changes in the history of the system	Developer activity data
SQALE	✓	✓	-	-	-	-	-	-	-	-
CAST	-	-	✓	✓	✓	-	-	-	-	-
SIG	✓	-	-	-	✓	✓	-	-	-	-
A benchmarking-based model	✓	-	-	-	✓	✓	✓	-	-	-
A fluctuation-based modelling approach	-	-	-	-	-	-	-	✓	-	-
Breaking Point for TD	-	-	✓	✓	✓	-	-	-	✓	-
LOC and Fan-In to Quantify the Interest of SATD	-	-	-	-	-	✓	-	-	-	-
A framework for design level TD	-	-	-	-	-	✓	-	-	-	-
A framework for estimating interest on TD	-	-	-	-	-	-	-	-	-	✓
Modularity metrics for ATD	-	-	-	-	-	✓	-	-	✓	-
Detecting and quantifying SATD	-	-	-	-	-	✓	-	-	-	-
Pre-trained word embedding word2vec model	-	-	-	-	-	✓	-	-	-	-
Code metrics for TD	-	-	-	-	-	✓	-	-	-	-
Convolutional Neural Network	-	-	-	-	-	✓	-	-	-	-

the techniques identified while Table 1 compares the input required by the different techniques and Table 2 the output generated.

Letouzey [40] proposed a method for TD evaluation named Software Quality Assessment Based on Lifecycle Expectations (SQALE), which is described as an answer to the need for an objective and standardized open-source method with low false positives. At the official website of the method[1], there is a list of several tools able to analyze the code written in different languages.

The method defines how to formulate and organize non-functional requirements that can affect code quality defining a herarchical structure of characteristics and sub-characteristics similar to the ISO quality model. SQALE has been developed to be automated and considers several properties of the code but two main aspects are not taken into account. The first one is that non-conformities

---

[1] http://www.sqale.org/.

for business or operations are not considered important by any index of SQALE (considering version 1.0 [41]). The second one is that there is no definition of the level of implementation of the requirements.

CAST [23] presents a formula with flexible parameters to measure TD. That flexibility implies the possibility of adjusting the parameters to the specificity of a particular organization. The approach defines five Health Factors that have a different impact on the overall TD: Changeability (30%), Transferability (40%), Robustness (18%), Security (7%), Performance Efficiency (5%).

Violations in each area are rated according to their severity and a formula is applied for calculating the final value of the debt. The approach has been evaluated on 745 business applications containing more than 10 KLOC using the CAST proprietary Application Intelligence Platform.

The SIG/TUViT approach [52] is based on a sound and quantitative approach for measuring software quality from source code. Moreover, the estimation of TD is based on empirical data using a model that is quite simple.

Mayr *et al.* [49] define a model that provides a combination of the benefits of the flexible approaches to quality changes and the simplicity of the SIG model. The approach requires only information from static code analysis. The output is simple as well, being the hours of work required to pay the debt.

Skourletopoulos *et al.* [68] developed a fluctuation-based modelling approach to TD. It measures the amount of profit not earned due to the under-usage of a given service and considering the probability of over-usage of the selected service that would lead to accumulated TD. The hypothesis is that service capacity affects to service choice, which is made with respect to the predicted fluctuations in the number of users over some time and the way TD is gradually paid off. Consequently, formulas for predicting appearance of TD were developed, as well as tools for validating them.

Chatzigeorgiou *et al.* [18] provide an estimation of a breaking point, that is when debt becomes too large to be paid off. The source code is initially assessed by fitness function based on the Entity Placement metric quantifying coupling and cohesion. The approach is based on the identification of the best design for a system. The cost of reaching that best system with necessary refactorings is calculated as well as number of versions leading to the breaking point. However, the authors point out some issues to be considered:

- only coupling and cohesion dimensions exist for the method, but TD has many other aspects
- maintenance effort means not just adding lines of code, but deleting and modifying them
- future maintenance effort cannot be predicted solely on the basis of past maintenance tasks

Kamei *et al.* [32] propose measuring the self-admitted TD interest with code metrics like LOC (because it well correlates with code complexity metrics) and Fan-In (showing how much one piece of code affects another one). They have validated the approach on the Apache JMeter project.

Marinescu [46] proposes a framework exploring TD symptoms at design level. The construction of such framework includes four steps:

1. definition of the principles for finding design defects
2. identification of a set of relevant design defects
3. estimation of the impact of each defect
4. the overall design quality is calculated

The framework also includes:

- a coarse-grain approach to monitor the evolution of TD over time
- a more detailed approach that enables locating and understanding individual flaws, which can lead to a systematic refactoring

The approach has been applied in a case study including 63 releases of two well known Eclipse projects (JDT and EMF). However, the conclusions of the case study cannot be generalized, considering the restricted number of systems analyzed and the limited number of design flaws that were included in the actual instantiation of the framework.

In the framework proposed by Singh *et al.* [66], TD estimation is based on measures of code maintainability obtained via static analysis and interest estimation based on activity data obtained by monitoring developer actions in the IDE. Main contribution of the framework is the integration of a developer activity data with code metrics and to improve the understanding of developer comprehension effort resulting in an improved accuracy of the estimation.

Although the Architectural Technical Debt (ATD) is difficult to measure, the Average Number of Modified Components per Commit (ANMCC) is a metric proposed in [43]. However, commit records may not exist anymore, therefore the authors suggest to use Index of Package Changing Impact (IPCI) and Index of Package Goal Focus (IPGF) instead of ANMCC. The advantage of using such two new metrics is the possibility of obtaining them directly from the source code. Then validation of correlation of that metrics with ANMCC is performed. However, the weakness of whole study is relying only on results of projects developed in C#.

Martini *et al.* [47] conducted a multiple embedded case study in seven sites at five large companies to investigate the current causes for the accumulation of Architectural TD (ATD). The authors investigated two research questions: (i) factors cause the accumulation of ATD, and (ii) current trends in practice in the accumulation and recovery of ATD over time. The authors provided a taxonomy of causes and their influence in the accumulation of ATD.

Maldonado *et al.* [45] examined code comments to identify and evaluate Self-admitted Architectural Debt (SATD). The strength of the approach is the usage of heuristics to eliminate comments which are not likely to affect TD. In addition, the method classify comments to different types of SATD.

Besker *et al.* [12] show critical results for SATD management, such as the fact that monitoring and evaluating ATD using accurate metrics is a key issue and it is not fully supported by any currently available tool.

Table 2. Output of TD measurement techniques.

Technique (method)	Design symptoms of TD	Remediation cost	Non-remediation cost	Relative amount of TD	Breaking point	Number of comments
SQALE	✓	–	–	–	–	–
CAST	–	✓	–	–	–	–
SIG	–	✓	✓	–	–	–
A benchmarking-based model	–	✓	–	–	–	–
A fluctuation-based modelling approach	–	–	–	✓	–	–
Breaking Point for TD	–	✓	✓	–	✓	–
LOC and Fan-In to Quantify the Interest of SATD	–	–	✓	–	–	–
A framework for design level TD	✓	–	–	–	–	–
A framework for estimating interest on TD	–	–	✓	–	–	–
Modularity metrics for ATD	–	–	–	✓	–	–
Detecting and quantifying SATD	–	–	–	–	–	✓
Code metrics for TD	–	–	–	✓	–	✓
Convolutional Neural Network	–	–	–	✓	–	✓
Pre-trained word embedding word2vec model	–	–	–	–	–	✓

Flisar and Podgorelec [26] developed a new SATD identification method which takes advantage of a large corpus of unlabeled code comments. The proposed feature enhancement method was used with the three most common feature selection methods (CHI, IG, and MI) and three well-known text classification algorithms (NB, SVM, and ME). It was tested on ten open source projects achieving 82% of correct predictions of SATD. The proposed method seems to be a good candidate to be adopted in practice.

Lenarduzzi et al. [38] applied the SZZ algorithm to label the fault-inducing commits and used 8 machine Learning techniques: Linear Regression, Random Forest, Gradient Boost, Extra Trees, Decision Trees, Bagging, AdaBoost, and SVM to show that the accuracy of TD can be improved. Authors found that among the 202 violations defined for Java by SonarQube, only 26 have a relatively low fault-proneness.

Pecorelli et al. [56] have reported on a large-scale empirical comparison between five different balancing techniques for ML-based code smell detection. The results suggest that ML models relying on SMOTE (Synthetic Minority Over-sampling Technique) realize the best performance. However, its training phase is not always feasible in practice. Furthermore, avoiding balancing does not dramatically impact the performance. Existing data balancing techniques are therefore inadequate for code smell detection. This hinders the feasibility of the current ML-based approaches.

Capitan and Vogel-Heuser [16] proposed metrics for identifying TD which based on IEC 61311-3 programming languages and adapted for the languages and cycle processing (Halstead's and McCabe's as examples).

Kumar *et al.* [35] proposed a novel approach for identifying TD in service composition in SaaS cloud. The approach combines time series forecasting and a newly proposed TD model to estimate the future debt and utility in the service composition. Through a real world case study, they demonstrate that the approach can successfully identify both the good and bad debts, while producing satisfactory accuracy on estimating the TD in the service composition in SaaS cloud.

Ciolkowski *et al.* [19] developed a prototype and a prediction model for forecasting potential savings based on proposed refactoring of key drivers of TD identified by the machine-learning model.

Verdecchia *et al.* [76] presented a novel approach to identify ATD of Android apps based on architectural guidelines extraction and modeling, architecture reverse engineering, and compliance checking.

Lavazza *et al.* [36] proposed a formal and executable model that supports the simulation of various scenarios in time-boxed software development and maintenance processes. The model is usable to show the effects that TD have on relevant issues such as productivity and quality, depending on how TD is managed, with special reference on how much effort is dedicated to TD repayment and when such effort is allocated.

TD visualizations were designed to improve stakeholder communication to support the business decision-making process at different levels of the organization. [53] concluded that the TD visualization contributes to improve the communication in the decision-making processes associated with the software lifecycle.

[61] addresses the problem of SATD (Self-Admitted Technical Debt) classification using a Convolutional Neural Network, which takes as input the source code comments and predicts as output whether the comment is a SATD comment or not.

Tsintzira *et al.* [74] used an established method for quantifying TD, namely FITTED, to measure the TD of an industrial software product and compare it to the perception of the software engineers.

3.2   RQ2: Which Are the Tools that Support the Automation of the Measurement of TD?

TD measurement techniques often require a large number of input data that require a large amount of effort to be extracted. Therefore, tools are of paramount importance to support development teams in the integration of TD measurement in their daily work. Table 3 provides a summary of the available tools and the methodology they implement.

SonarQube [27] implements the SQALE method of TD evaluation. It is used for continuous inspection of code quality to perform automatic reviews with

Table 3. Tools able to support the automation of the measurement of TD.

Technique (method)	Ref	Tool	Tool URL	Open source
SQALE	[40]	SonarQube	https://www.sonarqube.org/	Yes
		MIND	https://sourceforge.net/ projects/mindyourdebt/	Yes
		FindBugs	http://findbugs.sourceforge. net/	Yes
Breaking Point for TD	[18]	JCaliper	http://se.uom.gr/index.php/ projects/jcaliper/	Yes
A framework for design level TD	[46]	inFusion	https://chocolatey.org/ packages/infusion/	No
A framework for estimating interest on TD	[66]	Blaze monitoring tool	https://sites.google.com/ site/blazedemosite/home/ about	No
A framework for the prioritization of technical	[2]	Tracy	–	No
A tool for auto identification and interactive monitoring of the evolution TD	[50]	VisminerTD	https://visminer.github.io	No
A tool for managing TD	[55]	DeepSourse	https://deepsource.io/	Yes
A tool to prevent mostly invisible technical debt	[7]	Debtgrep	–	No
A tool for automatic architectural smells detection for C/C++ projects	[13]	Arcan tool	http://www.essere.disco. unimib.it/wiki/arcan/	Yes
A tool calculates the presence of a set of code smells and calculates an Intensity index	[38]	JCodeOdor	http://www.essere.disco. unimib.it/jcodeodor/	Yes
A tool for detecting code smells from Java code and prioritizing technical debt based on the smells	[38]	JSpiRIT	–	No
A domain specific static code analysis tool	[14]	PLC software	–	No
A Tool for the strategic planning of TD in Agile Software Projects	[19]	ProDebt	–	No
A programming environment	[70]	EXA2PRO	–	No
Modularity metrics for ATD	[43]	TortoiseSVN	https://tortoisesvn.net/	Yes
LOC and Fan-In to Quantify the Interest of SATD	[32]	Understand	https://scitools.com/	No
		JDeodorant	https://github.com/ tsantalis/JDeodorant	Yes
Detecting and quantifying SATD	[45]	SLOCCount	https://www.dwheeler.com/ sloccount/sloccount.html	Yes

static analysis of code to detect bugs, code smells and security vulnerabilities in several programming languages.

MIND (ManagIng techNical Debt) is an open source tool which is, to the best of our knowledge, the first tool supporting the quantification and visualization of the interest [24]. Basically, it is a plug-in for SonarQube. MIND uses a few metrics to count the interest:

- Defect Proneness
- Maximum Defects per 100 LOC Touched
- Extra Defect Proneness
- Maximum Extra Defects per 100 LOC Touched

- Relative Extra Defect Proneness
- Average Relative Extra Defect Proneness
- Violation Density
- Linkage
- Estimation Error

JCaliper [18] was designed to find the placement of entities that minimizes the Entity Placement metric as a search-space exploration problem. It automatically extracts the number, type and sequence of refactoring activities required to obtain the design without TD.

Blaze is a monitoring tool [69] recording temporal sequence of developer actions, including code navigation actions and edit actions. The log produced is subsequently analysed to figure out class relationships and effort spent by a developer to understand program elements.

TortoiseSVN allows extracting commit records from standard SVN servers and any code repositories supporting Subversion, such as GitHub. That records are used by Li et al. [43] to perform ANMCC metric checking.

JDeodorant [73] is used in [32] for performing source code parsing. In particular, the ability to extract a comment and map it to its corresponding method is interesting. Later in the paper, to calculate the interest that is incurred over time, 16 code metrics were extracted using the Understand tool [1]. JDeodorant [73] is also used in [45] to parse the source code and extract the code comments. However, before that, the SLOCCount tool [77] is applied to calculate SLOC in Java files.

EXA2PRO [70] is a programming environment which integrates a set of tools and methodologies that allow to systematically address many exascale computing challenges, including performance, portability, programmability, abstraction and reusability, fault tolerance, and TD.

[60] presented a process framework for managing TD in commercial software product development. The framework integrates processes required for TD management with existing software quality management processes prescribed by the project management body of knowledge (PMBOK) (https://www.pmi.org/pmbok-guide-standards), and organizes the different processes for TD management in three steps: (1) make TD visible, (2) perform cost-benefit analysis, and (3) control TD. To implement the processes, they introduced a new artifact, the TD register, which stores the principal and the associated interest estimated for the TD related to an asset.

[7] introduced debtgrep, a tool to prevent from growing dependency violations, violation of naming conventions, usage of deprecated API's, and other kinds of mostly invisible TD. They provide some specific examples of use cases for debtgrep.

[67] introduced a tool used for extracting coupling and cohesion metrics at package level to study their impact on TD. The dataset of their study consisted of approximately 1,200 software packages.

[19] introduced the ProDebt tool, a methodology and a software tool to support the strategic planning of TD in the context of agile software development.

[6] proposed a new index for the evaluation of architectural issues as Architectural Smells (AS) and developed a tool to detect AS in Java projects. They focused on AS based on dependency issues, since components that are highly coupled and with a high number of dependencies cost more to maintain and can be considered more critical.

[13] introduces an open source tool for automatic architectural smells detection for C/C++ projects, by creating an abstraction of the project and defining the concept of dependency between elements belonging to the project in order to identify architectural smells.

[48] developed a holistic framework for the semi-automated identification and estimation of ATD in the form of non-modularized components.

[14] presented a static code analysis tool and its usage for identification of TD in IEC 61131-3. The tool supports both bottom-up (study the metric values at individual module and convention violations) as well as top-down analysis (study the call graphs). In addition, the authors provide an extra analysis (horizontally) by making a comparison on the metric results between different demonstrators.

[2] presented Tracy, a decision-making framework that prioritizes TD considering how IT assets support a company's business processes, thus providing a new perspective on TD management.

[50] presented VisminerTD, a tool that allows the automatic identification and interactive monitoring of the evolution of TD items by combining software metrics, code comment analysis, and information visualization. The results provided evidence on the use of the proposed tool, indicating (i) that it can be useful in supporting TD identification and TD monitoring activities and (ii) that it can bring gains in terms of comprehensiveness and efficacy when evaluating the desirable time to identify and monitor different types of debt.

[71] found that the tools used cannot help in identifying many important TD types, involving humans is necessary. Tools could help to identify TD faster or more accurately however, project priorities and current development activities are important to be considered together, along with the values of principal and interest, when deciding to provide a comprehensive evaluation of TD and pay it off.

3.3 RQ3: Are There Any Empirical Studies Able to Demonstrate the Usefulness of the Identified Techniques?

The empirical studies performed to validate the identified techniques are summarized in Table 4.

[28] assessed three methods [23,40,46] to find out if they effectively describe the relationship between the quality of the system and the level of TD.

Izurieta et al. [31] uses Nugroho et al. [52] to exemplify the methodology.

A Benchmarking-based Model of Mayr et al. [49] is closely related to their earlier work on benchmarking-oriented quality assessments. Also it calculates the remediation cost in a way similar to the approach of CAST [23].

Table 4. Identified techniques and the related empirical studies.

Technique (method)	Based on	Ref	Empirical study
SQALE	Previous version [40]	[41]	[28]
CAST	–	[23]	[28]
SIG	SIG quality model [30]	[52]	[31]
A Benchmarking-based Model	Benchmarking-oriented method [29], CAST [23]	[49]	[49]
A Fluctuation-Based Modelling Approach	–	[68]	[68]
Breaking Point for TD	CAST [23], previous version [4]	[18]	[18]
LOC and Fan-In to Quantify the Interest of SATD	–	[32]	–
A framework for design level TD	–	[46]	[28, 46]
A framework for estimating interest on TD	SIG [52]	[66]	[65]
Modularity metrics for ATD	–	[43]	[43]
Detecting and quantifying SATD	Previous version [59]	[45]	–
Convolutional Neural Network	–	[61]	–
Pre-trained word embedding word2vec model	–	[26]	–
A Prodebt Method for the strategic planning of TD in Agile Software Projects	–	[19]	–

Relevant code structure metrics in the framework for estimating interest on TD [66] were selected in such a way that related to maintainability and TD in [52]. Similar to the prior work, static code metrics are used.

[39] conducted an empirical study on 21 well-known mature open-source projects to confirm the hypothesis about the fault-proneness of the SonarQube violations.

[78] selected four different TD identification techniques (code smells, automatic static analysis (ASA) issues, grime buildup, and modularity violations) and applied them to 13 versions of the Apache Hadoop open source software project. The authros showed that different TD techniques are loosely coupled and therefore indicate problems in different locations of the source code. Moreover, their proxy interest indicators (change and defect-proneness) correlate with only a small subset of TD indicators.

[64] surveyed empirical research work in the arising topic of SATD after 2014 and until the compilation of this survey in July of 2018. They compiled the tools and datasets that can be used as a foundation to motivate and facilitate the submission of novel and improved approaches for managing and ultimately, repaying SATD. Simultaneously, authors observed a lack of studies focusing on the repayment and management of SATD, which is of critical importance.

3.4 RQ4: Are There Any Empirical Studies Able to Demonstrate the Usefulness of the Tools Identified?

In [54], TD was measured using two static code analysis tools (Findbugs [8] and SonarQube [27]). The goal was evaluating if the code produced with the Test Driven Development approach has a lower TD than code produced using other techniques. This two tools are widely used in the community for measuring TD.

Other studies tested SonarQube: [44] use it for measuring TD in a particle tracker system; [51] use it for several calculation of TD in the software supply chain; [15] describes a case study in Ericsson, where they had to observe TD measurement tools to use them for evaluation system creation based on ISO standard 15939:2007.

4 Related Work

Investigating the different approaches for measuring TD could be valuable to practitioners and researchers to provide a better understanding of the field and identify research gaps. However, we were not able to identify any secondary study related to the research questions we listed in Sect. 2. Instead, several others deal with TD in general.

The systematic mapping study of Li *et al.* [42] was initiated to find and analyze publications between 1992 and 2013 of TD and its management. After the selection of 92 studies authors classified 10 TD definition, identified 8 TD management activities, and collected 29 tools for the latter.

Another systematic mapping study of TD definitions, Poliakov [58] has performed full review of 159 papers. 107 definitions were separated into keywords. Consequently, the main achievement of the research is built keyword map, supplemented by synonyms and types of TD.

Another literature review has been done by Alves *et al.* [3] based on three research questions. They evaluated 100 studies of 2010–2014 and proposed initial taxonomy of TD types, list of indicators for identifying TD, and existing management strategies.

There is a study considering another aspect of the phenomenon. Ribeiro *et al.* [62] state that the evaluation of appropriate time to pay TD and applying an effective decision-making criteria are an important management goals. Consequently, authors identified 14 such criteria for development teams. Also the results showed gaps where further research can be performed.

Recently, Behutiye *et al.* [9] considered a narrow field of study related to TD, which means that they synthesized the state of the art of TD and its causes, consequences, and management strategies only in the context of agile software development (ASD). In particular, after processing systematic literature review 38 primary studies, out of 346 studies, were identified and analyzed. Then five research areas of interest related to the literature of TD in ASD, as well as 12 strategies for managing it have been found. Authors identified eight categories regarding the causes and five categories regarding the consequences of incurring TD in ASD.

In the case of work performed by Besker *et al.* [11] ATD is considered as affecting to system success and able to cause expensive repercussions, so the goal is to create new knowledge with interest in ATD. Research efforts should be synthesized and compiled for that. The main contributing outcome of the paper is a presentation of a novel descriptive model, providing comprehensive interpretation of ATD phenomenon.

Finally, the last related work focuses on a specific view of TD. Employing a method for syntactic literature review and applying it to seven digital library studies sources Ampatzoglou *et al.* (2016) [5] analyzed financial aspect of TD. Authors conclude that the communication between technical managers and project managers is beneficial, because a vocabulary will be provided, and high-quality goals will be set up. In order to achieve this, they introduced a glossary of terms and a classification scheme for financial approaches.

[63] investigates current state of TD based on 13 secondary studies, dated from 2012 to March 2018, the work shows several interesting conclusions such as coverage of areas (code, test, process, etc.).

[75] investigated the state-of-the-art and examined the major contributions that have been made in the field of TD estimation and forecasting. The authors stated that already existing methods and tools for TD estimation have not reached a satisfactory level of maturity yet, while there is still a large volume of potential metrics and techniques that have not been used and that could potentially increase the completeness of the TD estimation concept. In addition, although there has been extensive research with respect to predicting the evolution of individual software features, quality attributes, and quality properties that are directly or indirectly related to the TD of a software project, no concrete contributions exist in the related literature regarding TD forecasting.

[48] proposed a Strategic Adoption Model for Tracking Technical Debt (SAMTTD) aimed at helping companies to assess their TD management process and make decisions on its improvement.

[10] performed a systematic mapping study to identify and analyzed the empirical studies about TD between 2014 and 2017. The authors presented the most common indicators to identify and evaluate TD and identified thirteen types of TD. They identified forty-eight tools from the selected empirical studies and found that in some empirical studies, there are more than three tools used to investigate TD. Others develop new tools and compared their results to open tools; Also they paid special attention to SATD throughout the code comments and smells as the most applied as indicators of TD.

5   Threats to Validity

The main threats to validity identified are the following:

– Although the applied guideline [34] recommends to consider about seven digital libraries for performing an exhaustive search, in our case only three have been chosen. The reason of it is that other sources contain very few unique papers compared to the ACM and IEEE digital libraries. Moreover, to avoid missing important papers we used Google Scholar that index almost everything.

– Constructing appropriate search string is a tricky task, since the title of some studies we are interested in does not include our key words, we decided to extend the search to the abstracts. Since we are interested in studies focusing on TD, we suppose that the key word is mentioned in the abstract.
– A way of automatically merging the outcome lists from that libraries is risky, since even a single different symbol in title might affect the result. For that reason, duplicates were identified and eliminated manually during the creation of a merged list.
– It may happen that some information has not been considered in our study since some papers could have been accidentally skipped or not present at the time of the query (September 2019).

6 Conclusions and Future Work

TD is a widely used buzzword but having a clear understanding of the available approaches and tools is quite difficult due to the large amount of material spread across a number of sources. This paper aimed at providing to researchers and practitioners an overview of the state of the art about TD focusing on the automated approaches.

According to the review, the research area is new and very active but still not mature. There is a constant presence of new approaches and tools that are not based on the outcomes of previous studies and researchers focus on validating their own approaches without any independent assessments. Moreover, such validations are frequently not replicable due to the usage of proprietary datasets. Therefore, additional effort is needed to identify cross-validated approaches with clear indications about their applicability. This is very important especially for practitioners since it is difficult for them to identify the models to apply in their specific contexts.

The study has also pointed out that where tools are available to support some specific approaches, they are often difficult to use requiring a complex setup and providing a limited support for the wide range of programming languages used in real projects. Moreover, most of the available tools are not able to measure or estimate the overall TD. They usually focus on the *remediation costs* and do not take into consideration the related interests (often named *non-remediation costs*) that are often very important for planning the development process and keep the debt under control over the entire lifecycle of a product.

Appendix

Table 5. Techniques with input, output, and calculation.

Technique	Input	Calculation	Output	Ref
SQALE	1. Target quality level (a list of nonfunctional requirements that define right code) 2. Debt-estimating model (associate each requirement with remediation function turning number of noncompliances into a remediation cost)	Run the code through the analysis tools and use remediation functions to work out remediation costs for each element. TD is the sum of remediation costs for all noncompliances. This debt is called the SQALE quality index (SQI)	Design symptoms of TD (Pyramid - an indicator to represent the specific distribution of TD for eight characteristics)	[41]
CAST	1. Number of should-fix violations in an application 2. The hours to fix each violation 3. The cost of labor	$((\sum$ high-severity violations) x (percentage to be fixed) x (average hours needed to fix) x (\$ per hour)) + $((\sum$ medium-severity violations) x (percentage to be fixed) x (average hours needed to fix) x (\$ per hour)) + $((\sum$ low-severity violations) x (percentage to be fixed) x (average hours needed to fix) x (\$ per hour))	Remediation Cost	[23]
SIG	1. Source code 2. Target quality level 3. The cost of labor	For the extraction of measurement values from source code, the Software Analysis Toolkit of SIG is used. $RE = RF * (SS * TF) * RA$ $ME = \dfrac{MF * (SS * (1 + r)^t * TF)}{2^{(QualityLevel-3)/2}}$	1. Remediation Cost 2. Non-remediation Cost	[52]
A Benchmarking-based Model	1. Static code analyzers output data (reference projects) 2. Source code 3. Target quality level 4. The cost of labor	Tool support is available [57] that facilitates triggering code analysis tools as well as building the benchmark database and benchmark suite 1. the target quality level is specified 2. # of maximum allowed violations is calculated 3. # of violations to be fixed is calculated 4. # of violations to be fixed * the estimated effort for fixing * an hourly cost rate	Remediation Cost	[49]
A Fluctuation-based Modelling Approach	Candidate cloud-based mobile service	Quantifying the TD during the first year $TD_1 = 12*[ppm*(U_{max}-U_{curr})-C_{u/m}*(U_{max}-U_{curr})] = 12*(U_{max}-U_{curr})*(ppm-C_{u/m})$ from the second and onwards $TD_i = 12*[K_{i-2}*[U_{max}-L_{i-2}] - M_{i-2}*[U_{max}-L_{i-2}]] = 12*(U_{max}-L_{i-2})*(K_{i-2}-M_{i-2}), i > 1$	Relative amount of TD	[68]
Breaking Point for TD	1. Number of should-fix violations in an application 2. The hours to fix each violation 3. The cost of labor 4. Past changes in the history of the system (LOC)	TD-Principal is calculated as a function of first 3 input variables. $Interest = addedLOC * (1 - \dfrac{FitnessValue(optimum)}{FitnessValue(actual)})$ $versions = \dfrac{Principal(\$)}{Interest(\$)}$	1. Remediation Cost 2. Non-remediation Cost 3. Breaking point	[18]

(continued)

Table 5. (*continued*)

Technique	Input	Calculation	Output	Ref
LOC and Fan-In to Quantify the Interest of SATD	Source code	1. Extracting comments and mapping them to its corresponding methods 2. Determination of the change over time in these SATD methods 3. Determining metrics measuring interest 4. Calculating the interest per SATD instance	Non-remediation Cost	[32]
A framework for design level TD	Source code	1. Select a set of relevant design flaws 2. Define rules for the detection of each design flaw 3. Measure the negative influence of each detected flaw instance $FlawImpactScore(FIS)_{flaw\_instance} = I_{flaw\_type} * G_{flaw\_type} * S_{flaw\_instance}$ 4. Compute an overall score $DebtSymptomsIndex = \dfrac{\sum FIS_{flaw\_instance}}{KLOC}$	Design symptoms of TD	[46]
A framework for estimating interest on TD	Developer activity data	1. Establishing sessions 2. Calculate metrics related to comprehension effort within a session 3. $Interest(I) = I_{current} - I_{ideal}$ Static metrics show presence of TD in classes Comprehension effort metrics quantify effort to comprehend the classes	Non-remediation Cost	[66]
Modularity metrics for ATD	Past changes in the history of the system (commit records) or Source code	1. Parse the commit records to extract needed data items for ANMCC calculation 2. Filtering out data in commit records 3. $ANMCC = (\sum_{j=1}^{h} NMC(k+j))/h$ A higher ANMCC entails potential increase in ATD or 1. Code map generation (XML) 2. Code map parsing 3. Modularity metrics calculation A higher IPCI or IPGF indicate less ATD	Relative amount of TD	[43]
Detecting and quantifying SATD	Source code	1. Project Data Extraction (release used, the number of classes, the total source lines of code, the total extracted comments and the number of contributors) 2. Parsing the source code and extracting the code comments 3. Filtering comments 4. Manual classification into five different types of SATD	# of comments (number of individual line, block, and Javadoc comments)	[45]
Pre-trained word embedding word2vec model	Source code	The framework is composed of three separated phases: The word embedding phase, the model training phase, and the prediction phase. In the word embedding phase, a word2vec model is built to support the feature enhancement method for the model training phase. In the model training phase, the SATD classifier is built within the next four steps: Comments' prepossessing, feature selection, feature enhancement, and classifier training. In the prediction phase, the built SATD classification model can be used to perform a SATD prediction upon new, previously unseen code comments	# of SATD comments	[26]

(continued)

Table 5. (*continued*)

Technique	Input	Calculation	Output	Ref
Code metrics for Technical Debt	Source code	1. Parsing the source code and extracting the code metrics 2. Based on source code metrics evaluate existence of TD	Using the metrics and proposed in the work rules it could be identified presence or absence of TD	[17]
Convolution Neural Network	Set of source code comments and their corresponding SATD/non-SATD labels	The approach includes four main phases: Model Training, SATD Prediction, Key Phrase Extraction, and SATD Pattern Identification. 1. The trained model is used to predict the SATD/non-SATD label given an unseen source code comment (prediction phase). 2. The trained model is de-convolutioned to extract SATD-indicating key phrases in the input code comments that contribute most to the model's classification decisions, which in turn are summarized into a set of intuitive SATD patterns.	# of comments that are SATD and not-SATD	[61]
A Prodebt method for the strategic planning of TD	Source code	1. Based on coding effort and changes to the source code Productivity are measuring by $P = \dfrac{CodingOutput}{EffortInvested}$ 2. A function introduced $f : q \rightarrow P$, where q is the vector of metrics in the quality model 3. Applied machine learning (a random forest algorithm) to approximate f 4. The saved effort/Approximated TD $e_x = e_o(1 - \dfrac{P_o}{P_x})$	Using the productivity approximator f they computed productivity for a hypothetical quality level, obtained by modifying one quality metric/percent and keeping all other quality metrics at the same level	[19]

References

1. Scientific toolworks, inc. understand 2.6. http://www.scitools.com/
2. de Almeida, R.R., Treude, C., Kulesza, U.: Tracy: a business-driven technical debt prioritization framework. In: 35th International Conference on Software Maintenance and Evolution (ICSME 2019) (2019)
3. Alves, N.S., Mendes, T.S., de Mendonça, M.G., Spínola, R.O., Shull, F., Seaman, C.: Identification and management of technical debt: a systematic mapping study. Inf. Softw. Technol. **70**, 100–121 (2016)
4. Ampatzoglou, A., Ampatzoglou, A., Avgeriou, P., Chatzigeorgiou, A.: Establishing a framework for managing interest in technical debt. In: 5th International Symposium on Business Modeling and Software Design, BMSD (2015)
5. Ampatzoglou, A., Ampatzoglou, A., Chatzigeorgiou, A., Avgeriou, P.: The financial aspect of managing technical debt: a systematic literature review. Inf. Softw. Technol. **64**, 52–73 (2015)
6. Arcelli-Fontana, F., Pigazzini, I., Roveda, R., Tamburri, D., Zanoni, M., Nitto, E.: ARCAN: a tool for architectural smells detection. In: Proceeding of the International Conference on Software Architecture, ICSA 2017, pp. 282–285. IEEE (2017)
7. Arvedahl, S.: Introducing debtgrep, a tool for fighting technical debt in base station software. In: Proceedings of the 2018 International Conference on Technical Debt TechDebt 2018, pp. 51–52. ACM (2018)

8. Ayewah, N., Hovemeyer, D., Morgenthaler, J.D., Penix, J., Pugh, W.: Using static analysis to find bugs. IEEE Softw. **25**(5), 22–29 (2008)
9. Behutiye, W.N., Rodríguez, P., Oivo, M., Tosun, A.: Analyzing the concept of technical debt in the context of agile software development: a systematic literature review. Inf. Softw. Technol. **82**, 139–158 (2017)
10. BenIdris, M., Ammar, H., Dzielski, D.: Investigate, identify and estimate the technical debt: a systematic mapping study. Int. J. Softw. Eng. Appl. **9**(5), 1–14 (2018)
11. Besker, T., Martini, A., Bosch, J.: A systematic literature review and a unified model of ATD. In: 2016 42th Euromicro Conference on Software Engineering and Advanced Applications (SEAA), pp. 189–197. IEEE (2016)
12. Besker, T., Martini, A., Bosch, J.: Managing architectural technical debt: a unified model and systematic literature review. J. Syst. Softw. **135**, 1–16 (2018)
13. Biaggi, A., Arcelli Fontana, F., Roveda, R.: An architectural smells detection tool for C and C++ projects. In: 2018 44th Euromicro Conference on Software Engineering and Advanced Applications (SEAA), pp. 417–420 (2018)
14. Bougouffa, S., Dong, Q.H., Diehm, S., Gemein, F., Vogel-Heuser, B.: Technical debt indication in plc code for automated production systems: Introducing a domain specific static code analysis tool. IFAC-Papers OnLine **51**(10), 70–75 (2018). 3rd IFAC Conference on Embedded Systems, Computational Intelligence and Telematics in Control CESCIT 2018
15. Britsman, E., Tanriverdi, Ö.: Identifying technical debt impact on maintenance effort-an industrial case study (2015). https://gupea.ub.gu.se/handle/2077/40110
16. Capitán, L., Vogel-Heuser, B.: Metrics for software quality in automated production systems as an indicator for technical debt. In: 2017 13th IEEE Conference on Automation Science and Engineering (CASE), pp. 709–716 (2017)
17. Capitán, L., Vogel-Heuser, B.: Metrics for software quality in automated production systems as an indicator for technical debt. In: 2017 13th IEEE Conference on Automation Science and Engineering (CASE), pp. 709–716, August 2017
18. Chatzigeorgiou, A., Ampatzoglou, A., Ampatzoglou, A., Amanatidis, T.: Estimating the breaking point for technical debt. In: 2015 IEEE 7th International Workshop on Managing Technical Debt (MTD), pp. 53–56. IEEE (2015)
19. Ciolkowski, M., Guzmán, L., Trendowicz, A., Salfner, F.: Lessons learned from the ProDebt research project on planning technical debt strategically. In: Felderer, M., Méndez Fernández, D., Turhan, B., Kalinowski, M., Sarro, F., Winkler, D. (eds.) PROFES 2017. LNCS, vol. 10611, pp. 523–534. Springer, Cham (2017). https://doi.org/10.1007/978-3-319-69926-4_42
20. Coman, I.D., Sillitti, A., Succi, G.: Investigating the usefulness of pair-programming in a mature agile team. In: 9th International Conference on eXtreme Programming and Agile Processes in Software Engineering (XP2008), June 2008
21. Corral, L., Sillitti, A., Succi, G.: Software development processes for mobile systems: is agile really taking over the business? In: 1st International Workshop on Mobile-Enabled Systems (MOBS 2013) at ICSE 2013, June 2013
22. Cunningham, W.: The WyCash portfolio management system. In: Addendum to the Proceedings on Object-Oriented Programming Systems, Languages, and Applications (Addendum), OOPSLA 1992, Vancouver, British Columbia, Canada, pp. 29–30. Association for Computing Machinery, New York (1992). https://doi.org/10.1145/157709.157715
23. Curtis, B., Sappidi, J., Szynkarski, A.: Estimating the size, cost, and types of technical debt. In: Proceedings of the Third International Workshop on Managing Technical Debt, pp. 49–53. IEEE Press (2012)

24. Falessi, D., Reichel, A.: Towards an open-source tool for measuring and visualizing the interest of technical debt. In: 2015 IEEE 7th International Workshop on Managing Technical Debt (MTD), pp. 1–8. IEEE (2015)
25. Falessi, D., Shaw, M.A., Shull, F., Mullen, K., Keymind, M.S.: Practical considerations, challenges, and requirements of tool-support for managing technical debt. In: 2013 4th International Workshop on Managing Technical Debt (MTD), pp. 16–19. IEEE (2013)
26. Flisar, J., Podgorelec, V.: Identification of self-admitted technical debt using enhanced feature selection based on word embedding. IEEE Access **7**, 106475–106494 (2019)
27. Gaudin, O.: Evaluate your technical debt with sonar. Sonar, June 2009
28. Griffith, I., Reimanis, D., Izurieta, C., Codabux, Z., Deo, A., Williams, B.: The correspondence between software quality models and technical debt estimation approaches. In: 2014 Sixth International Workshop on Managing Technical Debt (MTD), pp. 19–26. IEEE (2014)
29. Gruber, H., Plösch, R., Saft, M.: On the validity of benchmarking for evaluating code quality. In: IWSM/MENSURA 2010 (2010). https://www.iwsm-mensura.org/2010-conference/
30. Heitlager, I., Kuipers, T., Visser, J.: A practical model for measuring maintainability. In: 6th International Conference on the Quality of Information and Communications Technology, QUATIC 2007, pp. 30–39. IEEE (2007)
31. Izurieta, C., Griffith, I., Reimanis, D., Luhr, R.: On the uncertainty of technical debt measurements. In: 2013 International Conference on Information Science and Applications (ICISA), pp. 1–4. IEEE (2013)
32. Kamei, Y., Maldonado, E.D.S., Shihab, E., Ubayashi, N.: Using analytics to quantify interest of self-admitted technical debt. In: QuASoQ/TDA@ APSEC, pp. 68–71 (2016)
33. Khomyakov, I., Makhmutov, Z., Mirgalimova, R., Sillitti, A.: Automated measurement of technical debt: a systematic literature review. In: 21st International Conference on Enterprise Information Systems (ICEIS 2019), May 2019
34. Kitchenham, B., Charters, S.: Guidelines for performing systematic literature reviews in software engineering (version 2.3). Technical report, Keele University and University of Durham (2007)
35. Kumar, S., Bahsoon, R., Chen, T., Buyya, R.: Identifying and estimating technical debt for service composition in SaaS cloud. In: 2019 IEEE International Conference on Web Services (ICWS), pp. 121–125, July 2019
36. Lavazza, L., Morasca, S., Tosi, D.: A method to optimize technical debt management in timed-boxed processes. In: The Thirteenth International Conference on Software Engineering Advances (ICSEA 2018) (2018)
37. Lenarduzzi, V., Sillitti, A., Taibi, D.: Analyzing forty years of software maintenance models. In: 39th International Conference on Software Engineering (ICSE 2017), May 2017
38. Lenarduzzi, V., Martini, A., Taibi, D., Tamburri, D.A.: Towards surgically-precise technical debt estimation: early results and research roadmap. In: Proceedings of the 3rd ACM SIGSOFT International Workshop on Machine Learning Techniques for Software Quality Evaluation, MaLTeSQuE 2019, pp. 37–42. ACM (2019)
39. Lenarduzzi, V., Saarimäki, N., Taibi, D.: The technical debt dataset. In: Proceedings of the Fifteenth International Conference on Predictive Models and Data Analytics in Software Engineering PROMISE 2019, pp. 2–11. ACM (2019)

40. Letouzey, J.L.: The SQALE method for evaluating technical debt. In: 2012 Third International Workshop on Managing Technical Debt (MTD), pp. 31–36. IEEE (2012)
41. Letouzey, J.L., Ilkiewicz, M.: Managing technical debt with the SQALE method. IEEE Softw. **29**(6), 44–51 (2012)
42. Li, Z., Avgeriou, P., Liang, P.: A systematic mapping study on technical debt and its management. J. Syst. Softw. **101**, 193–220 (2015)
43. Li, Z., Liang, P., Avgeriou, P., Guelfi, N., Ampatzoglou, A.: An empirical investigation of modularity metrics for indicating architectural technical debt. In: Proceedings of the 10th international ACM Sigsoft conference on Quality of Software Architectures, pp. 119–128. ACM (2014)
44. Luhr, R.L., et al.: The application of technical debt mitigation techniques to a multidisciplinary software project. Ph.D. thesis, Montana State University-Bozeman, College of Engineering (2015)
45. Maldonado, E.D.S., Shihab, E.: Detecting and quantifying different types of self-admitted technical debt. In: 2015 IEEE 7th International Workshop on Managing Technical Debt (MTD), pp. 9–15. IEEE (2015)
46. Marinescu, R.: Assessing technical debt by identifying design flaws in software systems. IBM J. Res. Dev. **56**(5), 9–1 (2012)
47. Martini, A., Bosch, J., Chaudron, M.: Architecture technical debt: understanding causes and a qualitative model. In: Proceedings of the 2014 40th EUROMICRO Conference on Software Engineering and Advanced Applications, SEAA 2014, pp. 85–92. IEEE (2014)
48. Martini, A., Sikander, E., Madlani, N.: A semi-automated framework for the identification and estimation of architectural technical debt: a comparative case-study on the modularization of a software component. Inf. Softw. Technol. **93**, 264–279 (2018)
49. Mayr, A., Plösch, R., Körner, C.: A benchmarking-based model for technical debt calculation. In: 2014 14th International Conference on Quality Software (QSIC), pp. 305–314. IEEE (2014)
50. Mendes, T.S., Gomes, F.G.S., Gonçalves, D.P., Mendonça, M.G., Novais, R.L., Spínola, R.O.: VisminerTD: a tool for automatic identification and interactive monitoring of the evolution of technical debt items. J. Brazil. Comput. Soc. **25**(1), 2 (2019)
51. Monteith, J.Y., McGregor, J.D.: Exploring software supply chains from a technical debt perspective. In: Proceedings of the 4th International Workshop on Managing Technical Debt, pp. 32–38. IEEE Press (2013)
52. Nugroho, A., Visser, J., Kuipers, T.: An empirical model of technical debt and interest. In: Proceedings of the 2nd Workshop on Managing Technical Debt, pp. 1–8. ACM (2011)
53. Pacheco, A., Marín-Raventós, G., López, G.: Designing a technical debt visualization tool to improve stakeholder communication in the decision-making process: a case study. In: Tjoa, A.M., Raffai, M., Doucek, P., Novak, N.M. (eds.) CONFENIS 2018. LNBIP, vol. 327, pp. 15–26. Springer, Cham (2018). https://doi.org/10.1007/978-3-319-99040-8_2
54. Parodi, E., Matalonga, S., Macchi, D., Solari, M.: Comparing technical debt in student exercises using test driven development, test last and ad hoc programming. In: 2016 XLII Latin American Computing Conference (CLEI), pp. 1–10. IEEE (2016)
55. Parthiban, D.G.: Examination of tools for managing different dimensions of technical debt. CoRR abs/1904.11062 (2019). http://arxiv.org/abs/1904.11062

56. Pecorelli, F., Di Nucci, D., De Roover, C., De Lucia, A.: On the role of data balancing for machine learning-based code smell detection. In: Proceedings of the 3rd ACM SIGSOFT International Workshop on Machine Learning Techniques for Software Quality Evaluation, MaLTeSQuE 2019, pp. 19–24. ACM (2019)

57. Ploesch, R., Gruber, H., Pomberger, G., Saft, M., Schiffer, S.: Tool support for expert-centred code assessments. In: 2008 1st International Conference on Software Testing, Verification, and Validation, pp. 258–267. IEEE (2008)

58. Poliakov, D., et al.: A systematic mapping study on technical debt definition (2015). https://pdfs.semanticscholar.org/a425/2d6a5d9522a85984379f8ee3bf118df782c1.pdf

59. Potdar, A., Shihab, E.: An exploratory study on self-admitted technical debt. In: 2014 IEEE International Conference on Software Maintenance and Evolution (ICSME), pp. 91–100. IEEE (2014)

60. Ramasubbu, N., Kemerer, C.F.: Integrating technical debt management and software quality management processes: a normative framework and field tests. IEEE Trans. Software Eng. **45**(3), 285–300 (2019)

61. Ren, X., Xing, Z., Xia, X., Lo, D., Wang, X., Grundy, J.: Neural network-based detection of self-admitted technical debt: from performance to explainability. ACM Trans. Softw. Eng. Methodol. **28**(3), 15:1–15:45 (2019)

62. Ribeiro, L.F., de Freitas Farias, M.A., Mendonça, M.G., Spínola, R.O.: Decision criteria for the payment of technical debt in software projects: a systematic mapping study. In: ICEIS, no. 1, pp. 572–579 (2016)

63. Rios, N., de Mendonça Neto, M.G., Spínola, R.O.: A tertiary study on technical debt: types, management strategies, research trends, and base information for practitioners. Inf. Softw. Technol. **102**, 117–145 (2018)

64. Sierra, G., Shihab, E., Kamei, Y.: A survey of self-admitted technical debt. J. Syst. Softw. **152**, 70–82 (2019)

65. Singh, V., Pollock, L.L., Snipes, W., Kraft, N.A.: A case study of program comprehension effort and technical debt estimations. In: 2016 IEEE 24th International Conference on Program Comprehension (ICPC), pp. 1–9. IEEE (2016)

66. Singh, V., Snipes, W., Kraft, N.A.: A framework for estimating interest on technical debt by monitoring developer activity related to code comprehension. In: 2014 Sixth International Workshop on Managing Technical Debt (MTD), pp. 27–30. IEEE (2014)

67. Skiada, P., Ampatzoglou, A., Arvanitou, E., Chatzigeorgiou, A., Stamelos, I.: Exploring the relationship between software modularity and technical debt. In: 2018 44th Euromicro Conference on Software Engineering and Advanced Applications (SEAA), pp. 404–407 (2018)

68. Skourletopoulos, G., Mavromoustakis, C.X., Mastorakis, G., Rodrigues, J.J., Chatzimisios, P., Batalla, J.M.: A fluctuation-based modelling approach to quantification of the technical debt on mobile cloud-based service level. In: 2015 IEEE Globecom Workshops (GC Wkshps), pp. 1–6. IEEE (2015)

69. Snipes, W., Nair, A.R., Murphy-Hill, E.: Experiences gamifying developer adoption of practices and tools. In: Companion Proceedings of the 36th International Conference on Software Engineering, pp. 105–114. ACM (2014)

70. Soudris, D., et al.: Exa2pro programming environment: architecture and applications. In: Proceedings of the 18th International Conference on Embedded Computer Systems: Architectures, Modeling, and Simulation, SAMOS 2018, pp. 202–209. ACM (2018)

71. Spínola, R.O., Zazworka, N., Vetro, A., Shull, F., Seaman, C.: Understanding automated and human-based technical debt identification approaches-a two-phase study. J. Brazil. Comput. Soc. **25**(1), 5 (2019)
72. Tom, E., Aurum, A., Vidgen, R.: An exploration of technical debt. J. Syst. Softw. **86**(6), 1498–1516 (2013)
73. Tsantalis, N., Chaikalis, T., Chatzigeorgiou, A.: Jdeodorant: identification and removal of type-checking bad smells. In: 12th European Conference on Software Maintenance and Reengineering, CSMR 2008, pp. 329–331. IEEE (2008)
74. Tsintzira, A.A., Ampatzoglou, A., Matei, O., Ampatzoglou, A., Chatzigeorgiou, A., Heb, R.: Technical debt quantification through metrics: an industrial validation. In: 15th China-Europe International Symposium on Software Engineering Education (CEISEE 2019). IEEE (2019)
75. Tsoukalas, D., Siavvas, M., Jankovic, M., Kehagias, D., Chatzigeorgiou, A., Tzo-varas, D.: Methods and tools for td estimation and forecasting: a state-of-the-art survey. In: 2018 International Conference on Intelligent Systems (IS), pp. 698–705 (2018)
76. Verdecchia, R.: Identifying architectural technical debt in android applications through automated compliance checking. In: Proceedings of the 5th International Conference on Mobile Software Engineering and Systems, MOBILESoft 2018, pp. 35–36. ACM (2018)
77. Wheeler, D.A.: More than a gigabuck: estimating gnu/linux's size (2001). https://dwheeler.com/sloc/redhat71-v1/redhat71sloc.html
78. Zazworka, N., et al.: Comparing four approaches for technical debt identification. Software Qual. J. **22**(3), 403–426 (2014)

Evaluating Some Heuristics to Find Hyponyms Between Ontologies

Ignacio Huitzil[1]([⊠]), Fernando Bobillo[1,2], Eduardo Mena[1,2], Carlos Bobed[1,3],
and Jesús Bermúdez[4]

[1] University of Zaragoza, Zaragoza, Spain
{ihuitzil,fbobillo,emena,cbobed}@unizar.es
[2] Aragon Institute of Engineering Research (I3A), Zaragoza, Spain
[3] everis/NTT Data, Zaragoza, Spain
[4] University of the Basque Country (UPV/EHU), Donostia-San Sebastián, Spain
jesus.bermudez@ehu.eus

Abstract. The discovery of hyponymy relationships between elements belonging to two different ontologies is a common task when integrating semantic information from different sources. Most of the existing work combines several strategies or criteria to take a global decision (if there is an hyponymy relationship or not) for each pair of entities. However, such heuristics are typically not separately evaluated.

In this paper, we evaluate two techniques used in the discovery of hyponymy relationships based on shared properties and on similar entity names. We also use translation dictionaries to deal with cross-lingual ontology pairs and lexical resources to increase the number of names of an entity. Our experiments make it possible to identify some limitations of ontology sets commonly used as benchmarks and to argue that more complex lexical similarity measures are needed.

Keywords: Ontology alignment · Hyponymy relationships · Semantic web

1 Introduction

In recent years, ontologies have become a standard for knowledge representation. An ontology is an explicit and formal specification of the concepts, individuals, and relationships that exist in some area of interest, created by defining axioms that describe the properties of these entities [2,29]. They have been successfully used in many applications, making knowledge maintenance, addition of semantics to data, information integration, and reuse of components easier.

As each ontology expresses the point of view of a certain group of people about a given knowledge field, different ontologies usually have related semantic terms. *Ontology alignment* consists in using intelligent techniques to find semantic relationships between elements belonging to different ontologies [10,11], so that the integration of the original ontologies becomes easier. For example, it

© Springer Nature Switzerland AG 2020
J. Filipe et al. (Eds.): ICEIS 2019, LNBIP 378, pp. 274–298, 2020.
https://doi.org/10.1007/978-3-030-40783-4_13

is common to look for synonymy, hyponymy, or disjointness relations between a concept from a source ontology and a concept from a target ontology.

Ontology alignment is widely recognized as a very important problem for data integration from different sources. A recent example of application field are *semantic apps*, as using semantic reasoners on mobile devices [4,5] typically needs to integrate the user context (usually represented using an ontology) with more general domain ontologies or, in multiagent scenarios, with ontological knowledge from other users that co-operate to solve complex tasks, e.g., to provide Location-Based Services.

Although there has been a considerable amount of work in the field of ontology alignment, most of the approaches restrict themselves to the problem of finding synonymy relationships (i.e., finding pairs of elements from different ontologies such that are semantically equivalent). In this paper, we will focus on the less studied problem of finding hyponymy relationships (i.e., finding pairs of elements from different ontologies such that one of them is more general than the other). Indeed, synonymy is a very demanding relationship that implies that the two aligned entities have *exactly* the same meaning: two equivalent concepts must have exactly the same individuals in all possible interpretations. On the contrary, in real world domains it is more common to find terms that are quite similar but not exactly the same, as it happens with hyponymy, where two related concepts represent similar semantics but one subsumes the other.

Existing systems implementing the discovery of hyponyms in ontologies combine several heuristics to take a final decision for each pair of ontology entities (i.e., if they have an hyponymy relationship or not). Some heuristics are considered by different systems (for example, two entities with the same name could be similar), but they typically have a different importance in the final value. This makes it possible to perform a global evaluation of different ontology alignment systems (i.e., computing the F1 measure on a dataset) but there is not a separate evaluation of the heuristics. In this paper, we aim at evaluating two common heuristics used in the discovery of hyponymy relationships: a first one based on shared properties, and another one based on entity names.

This paper provides the following contributions:

- We evaluate the impact of the shared properties in the discovery of hyponyms. Based on our experiments, we conjecture that existing benchmarks are not appropriate enough and that new datasets are needed.
- We claim that new lexical measures between ontology entity names are needed, and show the results of an evaluation of a simple heuristic.
- We evaluate the impact on both metrics of using translation dictionaries and lexical resources to extend the heuristics based on lexical measures.

The rest of this paper is organized as follows. Firstly, Sect. 2 recalls the notion of hyponymy in ontologies and some salient properties. Next, Sect. 3 proposes and evaluates a lexical measure on entity names, and Sect. 4 extends it with the use of translation dictionaries and lexical resources. Then, Sect. 5 evaluates empirically the impact of shared properties in hyponymy relationships, and Sect. 6 extends it with the use of translation dictionaries and lexical resources. Finally, Sect. 7

overviews some related work and Sect. 8 sets out some conclusions and ideas for future work.

2 Hyponymys in Ontologies

As in natural language, two synonyms in an ontology have the same meaning. Clearly, synonymy is a reflexive, symmetric and transitive relation.

A common definition of hyponym in natural language is that of a word with a more specific meaning than a general or superordinate term called hypernym. We can see how this almost directly maps to the notion of subsumption between two ontological terms E_h and E_H, which might belong to the same ontology O or two different ontologies. Note that if two terms have a hyponymy relationship, they cannot be synonyms.

Hyponymy is irreflexive and asymmetric relation: a term is never a hyponym of itself, and if E_h is a hyponym of E_H, E_H is not a hyponym of E_h. Hyponymy is also a subproperty of subsumption. If E_h is an hyponym of E_H then E_h is a subclass of E_H. Indeed, in any interpretation model $\mathcal{I}$ we have that $E_h^{\mathcal{I}} \subseteq E_H^{\mathcal{I}}$. The converse of the previous property does not hold in general because subsumption is not asymmetric: it is possible to have two classes such that each of them is a subclass of the other one. Note that the approaches in [6,34] sometimes use the term subsumption relationships when they actually mean hyponymy relationships.

Definition 1. E_h is a direct hyponym of the term E_H if E_h is a hyponym of the term E_H and there is not a term T such that E_h is a hyponym of T and T is a hyponym of E_H.

In the following, we will restrict to direct hyponymy relationships. From a linguistic point of view, one could also be interested in computing the transitive closure of this relation to obtain indirect hyponymy relationships, but we will not address this case further. Thus, from now on, we will write hyponyms to mean direct hyponyms.

As in Description Logic languages or OWL language there is not usually syntactic sugar to define strict subclasses ($C_h \sqsubset C_H$), in practice it is usual to encode hyponymy relationships as subclass relationships [6,34]. However, when doing so, one is implicitly excluding that the two classes are synonyms because otherwise a synonymy relationship would be encoded by stating that the two classes are equivalent ($C_h \equiv C_H$). To be precise, we should also add the axiom

$$\top \sqsubseteq \exists U.(C_H \sqcap \neg C_h), \tag{1}$$

where U denotes a universal role (`owl:topObjectProperty`). This axiom states that the set of individuals that belong to the hypernym and do not belong to the hyponym is not empty, i.e., there should be examples that justify specializing concept C_H.

Equation 1 is not necessary if the ontology already contains instances of $C_H \sqcap \neg C_h$, i.e., if $O \models i : C_H$ and $O \models i : \neg C_h$ holds. Note also that Eq. 1 cannot be expressed in some inexpressive languages such as RDF-S or OWL 2 EL. A similar situation raises when trying to encode hyponymy relationships between properties. In this case, however, Eq. 1 cannot be expressed in OWL 2 DL.

3 On Entity Names in Hyponymy Discovery

In this section we study a lexical measure that seems particularly useful in the discovery of hyponyms. For our purpose, the name of an entity is only the fragment identifier of its URI, e.g., hasEndTime is the name of <http://sweet. jpl.nasa.gov/2.0/time.owl#hasEndTime>.

In ontology alignment, it is usual to consider similarity between the names of a pair of entities as a heuristics to identify relationships between the entities. There are many well-known string similarity metrics (the interested reader can find a good overview in [8]), but we argue that they are mostly appropriate when looking for synonymy relationships. Because we find it reasonable to assume that the confidences on two entities having a synonymy or a hyponymy relationship are somehow contradictory, we think that hyponym and hypernym usually have a similar name but not an equivalent one. If two entities have a similar *name*, our confidence in the existence of a hyponymy relationship usually increases except if the name is exactly the same one: in this case our confidence in the existence of a synonymy relationship increases. Thus, we are interested in metrics that penalize a perfect similarity.

In particular, we observed that the name of the hyponym is sometimes a specification of the name of its hypernym, which is an affix substring. Clearly, this is just a heuristic that does not need to hold in general.

Definition 2. *Given a pair of entities (two concepts or two properties) e_1 and e_2, we say that e_1 is an affix substring of e_2 if the name of e_2, denoted $name(e_2)$, has either a prefix or a suffix relationship with the name of e_1. That is, $name(e_2)$ has one of the following forms: $name(e_1) \circ S$ or $S \circ name(e_1)$, where S is a non-empty string and $\circ$ denotes string concatenation. If e_1 is an affix substring of e_2, e_2 is an affix superstring of e_1.*

That is, e_1 is an affix substring of e_2 if e_2 contains the name of e_1 as a prefix (i.e., at the beginning of the string) or as a suffix (i.e., at the end of the string), and the name of e_1 is different from the name of e_2. Note that we do not look for arbitrary substrings but we look for indications of compound names. For example, Student is an affix substring of its hyponym PhDStudent.

Research Questions. Given a dataset, we are interested in computing[1]:

(e) What is the proportion of hyponymy relationships that involve a hypernym with a name being an affix substring of the hyponym?
(f) What is the proportion of hyponymy relationships that involve a hypernym with the same name as the hyponym?

---

[1] The numbering of the cases (e)–(g) is kept for historical reasons [15].

(g) How many different pairs of concepts/properties are there such that one of them has a name being an affix substring of the other one, but they do not have a hyponymy relationship?

One would expect (e) to be as high as possible, whereas the other cases should be as small as possible. One could also think that the case (f) does not make sense if we are using a single ontology. Apparently, two different entities cannot have the same name if they have different URIs, but it is possible if we only consider the fragment, as shown in Example 1.

Both (e), (f), and (g) can be measured not only for concepts but also for properties (both object an data properties). This will be interesting for the ORE 2015 dataset, as the other datasets do not contain subproperty alignments.

Example 1. Examples of case (e) are pairs with a hyponymy relationship where the hyponym is an affix superstring of the hypernym, such as the object properties hasEndTime and hasEnd, the data properties number_or_volume and volume, and the classes SweetWine and Wine.

Examples of case (f) are pairs with a hyponymy relationship and the same name. This happens with the object properties <http://sweet.jpl. nasa.gov/2.0/time.owl#hasBeginning> and <http://www.w3.org/2006/time# hasBeginning>, the data properties <http://www.fao.org/aims/aos/fi/eez# hasMeta> and <http://www.fao.org/aims/aos/fi/water#hasMeta>, and the classes <http://purl.org/olia/emille.owl#Noun> and <http://purl.org/olia/ olia.owl#Noun>.

Examples of (g) are pairs where an entity is an affix substring of the other one but it is not its hypernym. This happens in the object properties hasTimeReference and hasTime, and in the data properties hasNameEN and hasName.   □

Next, we will discuss an evaluation of the previous claims on several datasets.

Technical Details. All experiments were performed on a desktop computer with Intel Core i5-2320 3.0 GHz, 16 GB RAM (12 GB were allocated for the JVM in the experiments) under Windows 7 64-bits. We used Java 1.8, OWL API to manage the ontologies, and the ontology reasoner HermiT 1.3.8 [13][2] to retrieve implicit axioms. We selected HermiT because it provides a simple method to retrieve directly the direct domain and range of object and data properties, even if they are not explicitly represented in the ontology (methods getObjectPropertyDomains and getObjectPropertyRanges, respectively); to the best of our knowledge, a similar method is not available in other reasoners such as Pellet [27] or Konclude [30]. We also use the reasoner when dealing with the range of an object property P to check if the inverse property of P exists (method getInverseObjectProperties); otherwise we create a new inverse property called InverseOf(P). All the methods above that we use belong to the Reasoner class (org.semanticweb.HermiT.Reasoner).

---

[2] http://www.hermit-reasoner.com.

Datasets. The Ontology Alignment Evaluation Initiative (OAEI)[3] has been organizing (annually since 2004) a benchmark of ontology alignment systems, mainly focused on synonymy relationships, and only two of these editions (2009[4] and 2011[5]) included an "oriented matching" track dedicated to subclass relationships. Firstly, we have considered OAEI 2009 and OAEI 2011 oriented track benchmarks. They provide reference alignments (or official results) between ontology pairs formed by a fixed source ontology and several target ones. The results include equivalence and subclass relationships. As discussed in Sect. 2, we assume that such subclass relationships actually denote hyponymy relationships. Furthermore, we will restrict to those direct relationships explicitly represented in the ontology (recall that one could also consider the transitive closure). Let us now discuss these datasets in detail.

The **OAEI 2009** dataset includes 30 pairs of ontologies about bibliographic references. Ontologies are part of the regular benchmark used in OAEI 2006, but the alignments are different and, in particular, include hyponymy relationships between concepts. Each ontology pair is formed by a fixed ontology (called 101) and a variable ontology (names from 102 to 304[6]). Unfortunately, 7 pairs of ontologies (23%) of the OAEI 2009 had to be discarded because HermiT reasoner could not support them. We also define a subset of this dataset, called **OAEI 2009***, including 3 ontologies where the entity names are not in English.

The **OAEI 2011** dataset includes 12 pairs of ontologies that can be classified in two categories: *Academia* and *Course catalogs*. Academia involves bibliographic references and includes 6 ontology pairs obtained after some modifications of 4 ontologies in the OAEI 2006 dataset (from 301 to 304). Course catalogs involves description of courses in the universities of Cornell and Washington and also includes 6 ontology pairs obtained by modifying 4 real ontologies. For each pair of ontologies, reference alignments include subsumption mappings between concepts. In this case, 3 pairs (25%) could not be processed successfully by the semantic reasoner. Since some of the ontologies in the OAEI 2011 dataset do not include any property, we have identified a fragment, denoted **OAEI 2011***, restricted to ontologies with some (object or data) property.

More recently, Vennesland developed a small dataset to evaluate his work in [33].[7] The dataset contains 3 pairs of ontologies; 4 ontologies from the Conference track of OAEI 2016, another one from the Benchmark track of OAEI 2016, and the well-known Bibo ontology.[8] We will call it **OAEI 2016** dataset.

So far, the number of ontologies was small and there were some limitations (for example, there were no subproperty relationships in the reference alignments). Thus, we additionally considered the **ORE 2015**[9] ontology set, with

---

[3] http://oaei.ontologymatching.org.

[4] http://oaei.ontologymatching.org/2009/oriented.

[5] http://oaei.ontologymatching.org/2011/oriented.

[6] Not each number in the interval corresponds to an ontology, there are only 30 pairs.

[7] http://github.com/audunve/COMPOSE-ReferenceAlignments.

[8] http://bibliontology.com.

[9] http://mowlrepo.cs.manchester.ac.uk/datasets/ore-2015-reasoner-competition-dataset.

1920 ontologies although not oriented to ontology alignment. To this dataset we have added the well-known Wine ontology.[10] It is a general ontology only used for didactic purposes, but it will be useful for us to show very illustrative examples of our metrics. In this case, we consider intra-ontology subclass relationships between entities of one ontology (and, again, we will assume that they denote hyponymy relationships), so we do not consider ontology pairs. We also define a subset of this dataset, called **ORE 2015***, including 6 ontologies where the entity names are not in English.

During our experiments (to be described in the next sections), we set a timeout of 15 min for each ontology to complete our experiments (it only had an effect on ORE 2015 dataset). Because of that, we discarded 848 ontologies (44%) that reached the timeout, 47 ontologies (2.4%) that were found to be inconsistent and 12 ontologies (0.6%) that were not supported by the reasoner.

Table 1. Statistics of the datasets.

Dataset	TOT	OK	C	sub C	pairs C	OOP	OP	ODP	DP	sub OP	pairs OP	sub DP	pairs DP
OAEI 2009	30	23	77	48	1424	23	52	23	89	0	0	0	0
OAEI 2009*	3	3	72	33	1259	3	51	3	92	0	0	0	0
OAEI 2011	12	9	154	84	6006	3	17	3	14	0	0	0	0
OAEI 2011*	6	3	56	18	597	3	52	3	43	0	0	0	0
OAEI 2016	3	3	101	11	2619	3	73	3	51	0	0	0	0
ORE 2015	1920	1013	792	857	1834180	925	44	375	9	25	6600	3	1373
ORE 2015*	6	6	78	88	6772	6	57	4	19	28	4237	0.5	604

Results. In this section, we summarize the results of our experiments. The detailed results can be found online.[11] Firstly, Table 1 shows some statistical data of each dataset considered in our experiments: TOTal number of examples in the dataset (TOT), examples correctly processed within a timeout (OK), average number of Classes (C), average number of subClasses (sub C), average number of pairs of Classes (pairs C), number of ontologies with Object Properties (OOP), average number of Object Properties (OP), number of ontologies with Data Properties (ODP), average number of Data Properties (DP), average number of subObjectProperties (sub OP), average number of subDataProperties (sub DP), average number of pairs of Object Properties (pairs OP), and average number of pairs of Data Properties (pairs DP). In ORE 2015 and ORE 2015*, OK is the number of ontologies; in the other datasets it is the number of ontology pairs. Compared to OAEI 2009, OAEI 2011 has a smaller number of ontologies with a smaller average number of properties but a higher average number of classes. This table is slightly different to the table in [15], as in this version we were able to support more ontologies of the original datasets.

---

[10] http://www.w3.org/TR/owl-guide/wine.rdf.

[11] http://webdiis.unizar.es/~ihvdis/evaluationHyponyms_Results.htm.

Table 2 shows the result of our measures from (e) to (g) for pairs of Object Properties (OP), Data Properties (DP) and Concept Names (C). For each dataset, we show the total number of examples found (Sum), the total number of ontologies with at least one example (#Onts), and the average percentage of examples (Mean%). These values are always shown for classes (C). Note that the denominator of Mean% is not the same in the three criteria e.g., it is the total number of hyponym pairs in cases (e) and (f), and the total number of (possibly non-hyponym) pairs in case (g). Note that the results are slightly different than the results in [15, Table 3].

Because sometimes one of these metrics can behave well in some ontologies and bad in others, the last two columns compare case (e) versus g. #e> denotes the number of ontologies with more positive examples than negative ones, whereas Dif denotes the difference between the number of ontologies with more positive examples than negative ones and vice versa (the number of ontologies with more negative examples). Thus, a positive value indicates that there are more ontologies with more positive examples than the other way around.

Discussion. The percentage of (e) was very low for properties, smaller than 1% in ORE 2015 (the only dataset where there are computed). Percentages are usually higher for classes, reaching 48% in OAEI 2016, where it is applied in all (3) pairs of ontologies. Note that the absolute number of positive examples is significant in ORE 2015, 34863.

Values of (f) are surprisingly high. For properties, the number of hypernyms with the same name than the hyponym is even higher than the number of hypernyms with an affix substring.

The total number of cases (g) is higher than the number of (e). Nevertheless, in OAEI 2011 and ORE 2015 there is a (small) class of ontologies where the value of (e) is greater than the number of counter-examples (g), with 1 and 124 ontologies, respectively. As in the case of shared properties, further studies to identify those ontologies are needed, as in all datasets there are more ontologies where our heuristics gives more false positives than positives than the other way around, as the Dif column shows.

We expected a small number of positives (we are just proposing a simple heuristic), but not such a high number of counter-examples. We think that cases (f) are modeling mistakes: the same name should not designate two different things. Let us now discuss some reasons of the small number of positives.

- Some of the entity names in the datasets are intentionally unreadable, so that ontology alignments approaches cannot take advantage of lexical measures. Any lexical measure, and not only ours, performs poorly on these scenarios. This happens for example in 7 ontologies of OAEI 2009.
- Another example where our measure fails are pairs of ontologies with entity names written in different languages. As it is well known, cross-lingual ontology alignment requires specific techniques [14]. As we will discuss in Sect. 4, This happens for example in 3 ontology pairs of OAEI 2009.

Table 2. Metrics for string affixes on each dataset.

Dataset	Item	Criteria			e vs. g	
		e	f	g	#e>	Dif
OAEI 2009 (C)	Sum	47	2	190	0	−23
	#Onts	15	2	23		
	Mean %	4.3	0.2	1		
OAEI 2009* (C)	Sum	0	0	15	0	−3
	#Onts	0	0	3		
	Mean %	0	0	3		
OAEI 2011 (C)	Sum	74	0	218	1	−6
	#Onts	8	0	9		
	Mean %	10	0	0.4		
OAEI 2011* (C)	Sum	6	0	15	0	−3
	#Onts	2	0	3		
	Mean %	11	0	1		
OAEI 2016 (C)	Sum	16	0	68	0	−3
	#Onts	3	0	3		
	Mean %	48	0	0.87		
ORE 2015 (C)	Sum	34863	403	186357	124	−410
	#Onts	486	43	667		
	Mean %	4	0.05	0.01		
ORE 2015 (OP)	Sum	29	119	4851	0	−491
	#Onts	28	42	491		
	Mean %	0.1	0.46	0.07		
ORE 2015 (DP)	Sum	1	11	1118	0	178
	#Onts	1	3	178		
	Mean %	0.03	0.37	0.01		
ORE 2015* (C)	Sum	39	0	49	1	−4
	#Onts	5	0	6		
	Mean %	7.4	0	0.12		
ORE 2015* (OP)	Sum	0	0	37	0	−6
	#Onts	0	0	6		
	Mean %	0	0	0.15		
ORE 2015* (DP)	Sum	0	0	8	0	−3
	#Onts	0	0	3		
	Mean %	0	0	0.2		

– It can be the case that it is the hypernym the one specializing the name of the hyponym, as it happens in aggregated concepts. This shows that more sophisticated techniques are needed.

- Sometimes, an affix substring implies a meronymy (part-whole) relationship.

Example 2. Let us illustrate the above reasons for the small number of cases (e):

- Concept Chapter (in ontology 101) is an hypernym of sqdsopq (in 101).
- Ontology 210 is written in French. So, for example, one would have to find that TechReport is a subclass of Raport.
- SemillonOrSauvignonBlanc is an hypernym of Semillon.
- BookPart (in ontology 222) is a meronym of Book, not a hyponym.   □

4 Combining Translation, WordNet and Entity Names

Since in Sect. 3 we mentioned some common problems that reduce the applicability of the heuristics based on the entity names, in this section we will discuss more sophisticated techniques. Firstly, we will consider the use of automatic translators, to deal with ontology pairs written in different languages (for example, one in English and another one in French). Secondly, we will consider not only the name of an entity but also the names of its synonyms, retrieved using lexical resources (more precisely, WordNet).

Now, we will detail these extensions and provide some motivating examples. Then, we will reformulate our research questions and discuss our evaluation.

Translation Dictionaries. Let us start with an example to illustrate the usefulness of using translation dictionaries.

Example 3. In order to find that concept Book (from ontology 101, in English) is an hyperonym of Livre (from ontology 206, in French), Livre is translated as the set of terms {*book, british pound, cypriot pound, egyptian pound, record, script, syrian pound*}. Note that this includes both bibliographical and numismatic terms, which in some cases could lead to incorrect deductions.   □

We use two third-party translation dictionaries, namely *ConceptNet*[12] and *Yandex*[13]. ConceptNet can only translate single words but it can provide as a result a list of words in the target language. Yandex can also translate terms with more than one word, but the result is always unique.

In the general case, one needs to find out the language of each ontology entity. If the entity has a label using the annotation property `xml:lang` this is trivial, but we have noticed that it is not widely used in the considered datasets. Otherwise, one could use a third-party service to automatically detect the language for each entity, which can be expensive in large ontologies [7]. To simplify, we assume that all entities in an ontology use a single language, although there are some counter-examples (e.g., in ORE 2015 dataset, ontology 16274 mixes English and Spanish, and ontology 7893 mixes German and English). Once we know the language, we apply a basic preprocessing to each entity name (e.g., to remove non-alphabetical characters) and translate it into English, obtaining a *set of translations* which is stored in a lookup table to avoid future searches.

---

[12] http://conceptnet.io.

[13] http://translate.yandex.com.

Lexical Dictionary. WordNet[14] is a lexical database for the English language [22]. It groups nouns, verbs, adjectives and adverbs into sets of cognitive synonyms (named *synsets*) which each one expresses a different concept. Synsets are related through semantic relations, composing a semantic network of concepts designated by various synonym words (actually, word senses). In our tests, we use JWI 2.4.0 API (Java WordNet Interface)[15].

The idea now is to replace a specific word with a *set of synonyms* obtained with the method `getSynset()`. This list is also stored in a lookup table to avoid future queries. The original word can be an entity name (if the original term was in English) or each of the terms in its set of translations (for other languages).

Example 4. Consider again Example 3. Using WordNet to find the synonyms of the translations of Livre, we end up with the set {*account book, al qur'an, bible, book of account, book, british pound, christian bible, criminal record, cypriot pound, disc, disk, egyptian pound, enter, good book, hand, handwriting, hold, holy scripture, holy writ, koran, ledger, leger, phonograph record, phonograph recording, platter, playscript, put down, quran, read, record book, record, register, reserve, rule book, script, scripture, show, syrian pound, tape, track record, volume, word of god, word*}. Now, we can see that Book is an affix substring of *rule book*.

Note that starting from one term (Livre) we have ended up with a set of 43 terms. Furthermore, some of them are clearly not synonyms (i.e., account book should be a hyponym of book). It is thus not surprising that the use of translation dictionaries and WordNet does not always work well.   □

Table 3. Statistics about the entity names of the datasets.

Dataset	Number of ontologies	Not in English	Alphanumeric or unreadable
OAEI 2009	30	3	7
OAEI 2009*	0	3	0
OAEI 2011	12	0	0
OAEI 2011*	3	0	0
ORE 2015	1013	6	491
ORE 2015*	0	6	0
OAEI 2016	3	0	0

Datasets. We will consider the same datasets described in the previous section, but it is worth to add further information about them. Some datasets include cross-lingual ontology pairs or ontologies with unreadable names (this is intentional to limit the applicability of ontology alignment systems with an excessive dependence on the entity names), as shown in Table 3. In OAEI 2009 there are

---

[14] http://wordnet.princeton.edu.
[15] http://projects.csail.mit.edu/jwi.

3 ontologies written in French (namely 206, 207, 210) and 7 ontologies with unreadable names (namely, 201, 202, and 249–259). ORE 2015 contains 516 ontologies in English language, 6 ontologies in other languages (2 in Portuguese, 2 in German, 1 in French, and 1 in Italian), and 491 ontologies with numeric, alphanumeric, unreadable names, or multilingual (for example, ontology 16274 has 12 object properties: 9 in Spanish and 3 in English).

Research Questions. We are still interested in computing cases (e)–(g). However, in cases (e) and (g), we do not check if the names of two entities have an affix substring relationship, but if there is a pair of terms in their set of synonyms that have it. Furthermore, in case (f), we check *(i)* if some of the terms in the set of synonyms of the first entity is equal to some of the terms in the set of synonyms of the other one, and *(ii)* if both entities do not have an affix substring relationship as described for (e) and (g).

Note that the numbers of cases (e) and (g) cannot decrease: we can find more extended affix substring matches, but those already found using the entity name remain. The number of cases (f) can increase (if we find two terms with the same name) or decrease (if we find an extended affix substring matches).

Next, Example 5 shows how using translation dictionaries and WordNet behaves correctly to identify a case (e) when aligning ontologies 101 (in English) and 210 (in French) from OAEI 2009. Then, Examples 6 and 7 show two counter-examples (f) and (g), respectively, taken from the same pair of ontologies.

Example 5. Revisiting Example 2, we want to discover that TechReport is a subclass of Raport. Note firstly that "raport" is not a correct French word; it is the result of mistyping "rapport". For this reason, one of the dictionaries (ConceptNet) cannot return any translations, but the other one translates it as {*report*}. This shows the usefulness of using two dictionaries rather than a single one. Then, the set of translations is expanded using WordNet into a set of 14 synonyms including report, which is an affix substring of TechReport. □

Example 6. The concept Partie is a hyponym of Reference. There is a common match in their set of synonym terms (*character*) and there is not any pair such that the synonym term of the hypernym is an affix substring of a synonym term of the hyponym. More precisely, the set of translations of Partie is {*game, part, partially, party, plot, region, section, side, subset, symmetry*} and is expanded to the set of 89 synonyms including *character*, and for Reference we obtain a set of 20 synonyms including *character* and *character reference*. As a curiosity, it is possible to find a pair of synonym terms such that the hyponym is an affix substring of a the hyperonym (the pair *character* and *character reference*), but not the other way around. □

Example 7. A curious example of case (g) involves the pairs of concepts Part and Person. Although they do not have an hyponymy relationship, we found an affix substring relationship. Indeed, one of the synonym terms of Part is *persona* (in the sense of "an actor's portrayal of someone in a play", according to WordNet), which clearly has an affix substring relationship with *person*. □

Results and Discussion. Table 4 shows the results of our metrics for string affixes properties combined with Translation dictionaries (T), WordNet (W), or both (TW). Translation is only used in the datasets that only include multilingual ontologies (OAEI 2009* and ORE 2015*); in those ontologies we do not use WordNet without a translation because it only accepts English terms as inputs. Using translation in cross-lingual ontology pairs does not always help: there are 4 more cases (e) in OAEI 2009* and 1 (e) in ORE 2015* for data properties, but there are no changes in ORE 2015* for concepts or object properties. Using WordNet does not usually increase the number of cases (e), except in OAEI 2009* (2 more cases). This suggests that translation is sometimes useless (so WordNet cannot be used) and sometimes enough (as it retrieves a set of translated terms). In the other datasets, cases (e) always increase when using WordNet.

However, this comes with a price: the increase in counter-examples (g) is always higher than the increase in (e), or equal if both are zero. Still, the number of ontologies with more cases (e) and than (g) is usually the same as in Table 2, and it only decreases in ORE 2015* for concepts. Using the translation does not increase the number of counter-examples (f), but using WordNet usually does. This suggests that this extension improves the recall but reduces the precision, so it should only be applied in ontologies where there are more cases (e) than (g).

5   On Shared Properties in Hyponymy Discovery

In this section we discuss how to use the set of shared properties in hyponymy discovery. Clearly, a hyponym concept should include all the properties of its hypernym concept, but we argue that in most of the cases it should also have some additional properties of its own. That is, when an ontology designer decides to specialize a concept by defining a more specific one, his/her decision will be based very often on the existence of some attribute that characterizes such concept. Thus, the existence of new properties increases our confidence in the existence of a hyponymy relationship. Unfortunately, these new properties are sometimes not included explicitly due to modeling decisions, as we will see.

Definition 3. *Let O be an ontology, $C \in O$ a concept name, $R \in O$ a (data or object) property, and $dom(O, R) = \{D$ is a concept name $\in O \mid O \models \{\exists R.\top \sqsubseteq D\}\}$. Now:*

- *C defines R if C is one of the direct domains of R, i.e., $C \in dom(O, R)$ and $\not\exists D \in dom(O, R)$ such that $O \models \{D \sqsubseteq C\}$ and $O \not\models \{D \equiv C\}$.*
- *C has R if a concept name $D \in O$ defines R and $C \sqsubseteq D$.*

We can see that C has a property R if C defines R or if it inherits it from an ancestor in the concept hierarchy that defines it, as the following example shows.

Example 8. Let O be the Wine ontology. $dom(O, \mathsf{hasWineDescriptor})$ includes Wine and their superclasses, such as ConsumableThing, because $O \models \{\exists \mathsf{hasWine}$ $\mathsf{Descriptor}.\top \sqsubseteq \mathsf{Wine}\}$ and $O \models \{\exists \mathsf{hasWineDescriptor}.\top \sqsubseteq \mathsf{ConsumableThing}\}$ hold. Thus, Wine *defines* (and *has*) hasWineDescriptor. Any subclass of Wine, such as SweetWine, *has* (but does not define) hasWineDescriptor.   □

Table 4. Metrics for string affixes combined with translation and WordNet.

Dataset	Item	Criteria			e vs. g	
		e	f	g	#e>	Dif
OAEI 2009 (C) W	Sum	51	20	452	0	−23
	#Onts	15	12	23		
	Mean %	5	2	1.4		
OAEI 2009* (C) T	Sum	4	0	48	0	−3
	#Onts	2	0	3		
	Mean %	4	0	1.3		
OAEI 2009* (C) TW	Sum	6	2	211	0	−3
	#Onts	2	2	3		
	Mean %	6	2	5.7		
OAEI 2011 (C) W	Sum	77	0	242	1	−6
	#Onts	8	0	9		
	Mean %	10	0	0.5		
OAEI 2011* (C) W	Sum	9	0	27	0	−3
	#Onts	2	0	3		
	Mean %	17	0	1.5		
OAEI 2016 (C) W	Sum	17	1	146	0	−3
	#Onts	3	1	3		
	Mean %	52	3	2		
ORE 2015 (C) W	Sum	37802	795	816510	69	−538
	#Onts	495	103	680		
	Mean %	4.3	0.1	0.04		
ORE 2015 (OP) W	Sum	50	141	11715	0	−518
	#Onts	49	46	518		
	Mean %	0.2	0.6	0.2		
ORE 2015 (DP) W	Sum	6	11	2393	0	−203
	#Onts	6	3	203		
	Mean %	0.20	0.37	0.2		
ORE 2015* (C) T	Sum	39	0	49	1	−4
	#Onts	5	0	6		
	Mean %	7.4	0	0.12		
ORE 2015* (C) TW	Sum	39	1	70	1	−4
	#Onts	5	1	6		
	Mean %	7.4	0.2	0.2		
ORE 2015* (OP) T	Sum	0	0	40	0	−6
	#Onts	0	0	6		
	Mean %	0	0	0.16		
ORE 2015* (OP) TW	Sum	0	0	183	0	−6
	#Onts	0	0	6		
	Mean %	0	0	0.8		
ORE 2015* (DP) T	Sum	1	0	22	0	−3
	#Onts	1	0	3		
	Mean %	33	0	0.6		
ORE 2015* (DP) TW	Sum	1	0	129	0	−4
	#Onts	1	0	4		
	Mean %	33	0	3.6		

To be precise, the semantics of Description Logic-based ontologies states that if, for example, the domain of hasWineDescriptor is Wine, then anything with a wine descriptor must be a wine. Instead, we assume that hasWineDescriptor is a characteristic feature of the class Wine, as common in frames or object orientation design.

The properties that a concept has/defines must be computed by a semantic reasoner, as they could not be implicitly represented in the ontology. Please note that range restrictions must be taken into account at this point. For example, if the range of an object property R is C, then C defines the inverse of R, even if the inverse property is not explicitly represented in the ontology.

Our claims regarding the set of shared properties is based on some intuitive ideas such as the duck test, the opposite duck test, and the weak duck test [34]:

- *Duck test*: if it looks like a duck, swims like a duck, and quacks like a duck, then it probably is a duck. In our setting, this implies for example that the hyponymy degree is proportional to the percentage of shared properties.
- *Opposite duck test*: if it does not look like a duck, does not swim like a duck, and does not quack like a duck, then it probably is not a duck. For example, if there are no shared properties, the hyponymy degree is inversely proportional to the number of properties.
- *Weak duck test*: if it looks like a duck and quacks like a duck, then it is probably a kind of duck, although we are not sure that it swims like a duck. In this case, shared properties should have a higher impact in the hyponymy degree than non-shared properties.

Research Questions. Now, we want to answer the following questions:

(a) What is the proportion of hyponymy relationships where the hyponym has all the properties of its hypernym?
(b) What is the proportion of hyponymy relationships such that the hyponym defines some property that its hypernym does not have?
(c) What is the proportion of hyponymy relationships such that the hyponym defines no properties or defines some properties that its hypernym also has?
(d) How many pairs of concepts C, D are there such that C has all the properties of D plus some new defined properties, and C is not a hyponym of D?

To do so, we will compute the precision (percentage of positive examples) and the number of false positives or counter-examples.

One would expect (a) and (b) to be as high as possible, whereas the other cases should be as small as possible. Note also that in cases (b) and (d) we are interested in properties that are actually defined by the hyponym, excluding properties defined by a different ancestor, which could happen in multiple inheritance scenarios.

When considering intra-ontology relationships, a semantic reasoner is used to decide if two properties are equivalent and correspond to the same entity. In the case of inter-ontology relationships, we would need a reference alignment or an alignment software defining synonymy relationships. Because existing benchmarks do not provide such information (they only provide alignments between concepts, but not between properties), we assume that two properties from different ontologies denote the same entity if and only if they have the same name (fragment) and they are of the same type (object and data properties).

Example 9. Let us illustrate the measures that we are computing by providing some examples, taken from the Wine ontology, that appeared in our experiments.

An example of case (b) are the pair of classes WineGrape and Grape which have a hyponymy relationship. Both of them have the same properties (hasMaker, locatedIn, madeFromFruit, inverse of madeFromFruit, and producesWine). Wine-Grape is an hyponym of Grape and defines a new property called madeIntoWine that Grape does not have.

As an example of case (c), AmericanWine class is a hyponym of Wine. Both of them have the same properties (hasBody, hasColor, hasFlavor, hasMaker, has-Sugar, hasWineDescriptor, locatedIn, madeFromFruit, madeFromGrape and producesWine). However, AmericanWine defines itself no new property.

An example of case (d) are Vintage and Winery, two classes without a hyponymy relationship. Vintage has all the properties of Winery (namely, has-Maker, locatedIn, and producesWine) but also a new one (hasVintageYear).   □

Results and Discussion. Table 5 shows the result of the measures related to shared properties, from (a) to (d). Sum, #Onts, Mean%, #e>, and Dif have the same meaning as in Table 2. Similarly, the last four columns compare case (b) versus (c), and (b) versus (d). At the risk of being repetitive, let us mention once again than the results are slightly different than those in [15, Table 3].

Firstly, note that we obtain the same absolute values in Sum and #Ont for OAEI 2011 and OAEI 2011* except for case (c), but the percentages are different because so are the dataset sizes.

Regarding case (a), as expected, we obtained a 100% in the case of intra-ontology relationships (ORE 2015). For inter-ontology relationships, much smaller values are obtained. In some of the datasets we obtained a surprising result of 0%. For example, in OAEI 2011 only 3 ontology pairs involved properties, and none of the properties of an hyponym matched a property of the hypernym. This clearly shows that there is a lot of missing information in the ontologies.

Case (b) only produces reasonably good results in OAEI 2009 and OAEI 2016 (47% and 36%, respectively); in other datasets the percentage are 0.3% or 2%. Note that the absolute number of positive examples is quite significant in ORE 2015 (17273), but the high total number of subclass axioms produces a small percentage. Again, the small value obtained in OAEI 2011 can be partially explained by the low number of ontology pairs with properties.

The number of counter-examples (c) is higher than (b) except in OAEI 2009*. Also, the number of counter-examples (d) is higher than (b) in OAEI 2009, ORE 2015, and ORE 2015*. However, in all datasets there is a (sometimes small) class of ontologies where the value is greater than the number of counter-examples. In OAEI 2009 and OAEI 2015, the number of ontologies with more positive cases (b) than negative cases (c) or (d) ranges between 14 and 123. In OAEI 2016, 33% and 100% of the ontology pairs have more positive cases (b) than (c) or (d), respectively. Nevertheless, one should not be too optimistic to apply this idea to every ontology. In general, there are more ontologies with negative cases (c) than positive cases (b), except in OAEI 2009 and OAEI 2009* datasets, but only in datasets ORE 2015 and ORE 2015* there are more ontologies with negative cases (d) than positive cases (b). This suggests that further work is needed to identify that class of ontologies where our claim about shared properties provides good results.

Since we strongly think that our claim about shared properties is reasonable, the somehow disappointing results make us question the benchmark itself, and we think that the datasets are incomplete (small number of properties and subproperty alignments) and contain an unnatural modeling.

In ontology modeling it is common to pay much more attention to classes than properties. Historically, ontology languages have indeed supported more expressivity for concepts than for properties. Because the ontologies in the datasets include much more concepts than properties (a big quantity of the ontologies do not have any properties at all), heuristics based on properties are penalized. Indeed, in OAEI 2009, OAEI 2011, and OAEI 2016 there were no examples of property hyponymy. Furthermore, ORE 2015 dataset is more useful for object property hyponymy than for data property hyponymy. Although the average number of subproperty axioms is 25, 47.2% of the ontologies do not have any.

Example 10. WineBody, WineFlavor, and WineSugar could be subproperties of WineDescriptor, but this is not represented in the Wine ontology. □

Regarding the unnatural modeling, there is often a rather different representation of the reality in the two ontology pairs: sometimes one of them uses an object property and the other one a data property, sometimes properties are assigned to concepts with different granularity levels, etc.

Example 11. Class Entry in ontology 301 is a hyponym of class Resource in ontology 302. One of the data properties of Entry is has author, but Resource does not have a similar data property. Instead, Publication is a subclass of Resource in the same ontology 302 with two object properties Resource author and Resource first author. Thus, there are notable differences in the modeling. □

We claim that in many cases the fact that a hyponym does not specialize the hypernym with a new property is a modeling error, as the hyponym needs to have some feature that justifies the existence of a subclass. For example, a database developer does not create a new table if there are not any additional attributes. In the case of ontologies, it makes sense to create a subclass without adding a new property: for example, one can restrict the range of possible values, or increase the minimal cardinality. However, in several cases, we think that a new property should be added.

Example 12. RedWine could define a tannin level (although all wines have tannins, they have a stronger impact in red wines) or SweetWine could define a fermentation procedure (as it is different in a naturally sweet wine and in a natural sweet wine or vin doux naturel). □

Table 5. Metrics for shared properties on each dataset.

Dataset	Item	Criteria				b vs. c		b vs. d	
		a	b	c	d	#b>	Dif	#b>	Dif
OAEI 2009 (C)	Sum	346	519	581	2188	15	8	14	6
	#Onts	8	22	22	8				
	Mean %	31	47	53	7				
OAEI 2009* (C)	Sum	0	52	48	0	2	2	2	2
	#Onts	0	2	2	0				
	Mean %	0	52	48	0				
OAEI 2011 (C)	Sum	0	2	762	0	0	−8	2	2
	#Onts	0	2	9	0				
	Mean %	0	0.3	99.7	0				
OAEI 2011* (C)	Sum	0	2	51	0	0	−3	2	2
	#Onts	0	2	3	0				
	Mean %	0	4	96	0				
OAEI 2016 (C)	Sum	0	12	21	0	1	−1	3	3
	#Onts	0	3	3	0				
	Mean %	0	36	64	0				
ORE 2015 (C)	Sum	867810	17273	850537	1327113	123	−706	85	−352
	#Onts	1013	504	938	454				
	Mean %	100	2	98	0.1				
ORE 2015* (C)	Sum	0	68	461	1571	1	−4	0	−6
	#Onts	0	6	6	6				
	Mean %	0	13	87	3.9				

We also observed that too many properties do not have a domain and/or a range axioms, so we infer that they are the Thing class. Enriching ontologies with those axioms will make it possible to identify properties that a class has or defines, and thus to improve the applicability of our heuristic for shared properties. Another finding is that some properties might have a different interpretation in different concepts (the evaluated datasets do not provide enough formal or informal information about the semantics of the terms to be completely sure). Of course, such polysemic properties make discovering hyponyms harder.

Example 13. In the Wine ontology, producesWine property is related to Wine-Grape and Winery classes, but with different semantics (a winery produces a specific wine brand, while a grape is used to produce a general wine type).   □

6   Combining Translation, WordNet and Shared Roles

In this section we will revisit the metrics proposed in the previous section but considering translation dictionaries and lexical resources as well. So far, our heuristics based on shared roles check if pairs of properties have the same name.

In this section, the idea is to replace the property name with a set of synonyms (possibly computed from a set of translations), as the following example shows.

Example 14. The class Adresse (in ontology 207, in French) has 5 properties: état, inverseOf(adresse), inverseOf(localisation), pays, and ville. Each property is translated, e.g., ville leads to the set of translations {*city, new york, town*}. For each translation, we use WordNet to retrieve the set of synonyms {*city, empire state, greater new york, ithiel town, metropolis, n.y., new york city, new york state, new york, ny, town, townsfolk, township, townspeople, urban center*}. This could work well for some synonym terms (*city*) but not for other ones: ConceptNet wrongly translates ville as *new york*, and WordNet wrongly retrieves *empire state* as a synonym of *new york*.   □

Research Questions. Similarly as in Sect. 4, we are still interested in computing cases (a)–(d), but considering sets of synonyms rather than just property names. That is, a hyponym has a property of its hyperonym if there is a pair of terms in their set of synonyms that match. We think that this should only apply to inter-ontology relationships: in a single ontology, if a subclass defines a property that the superclass does not have, we argue that a property name matching one of the property names of its superclass is not enough to consider them as they same property, as the fact that the ontology developer decided to specialize the subclass with a new property is a stronger reason to think that they are not equivalent.

The number of cases (a) and (c) cannot decrease, as we can only find more properties that the hypernym has. The number of cases (b) cannot increase (we can only find out that the hypernym has a property, so the number of properties that the hypernym does not have decreases). Finally, the number of cases (d) can increase (if one of the properties that C has is found to be a property of D) and decrease (if one of the properties that C defines is found to be a property of D).

In the following, we will show some examples of the implications of this change. Firstly, we will show a positive example, where this change helps to avoid a counter-example of case (d).

Example 15. Concepts Academic and Report from ontologies 101 and 103 (both in English) do not have an hyponymy relationship, but Report has all (44) properties of Academic and apparently defines a new one, namely *institution*. However, one of the terms in the synonym set of *institution* is *establishment*, which is also one of the terms in the synonym set of *organization* (a property that both Report and Academic have). Therefore, Report does not define any new property and thus this case is correctly not considered as a case (d).   □

Next, we will show a negative example, where this extension is not enough to detect a case (a), where a hyponym has all the properties of its hypernym.

Example 16. Publisher (from ontology 101, in English) is a subclass of Institution (from ontology 210, in French). Publisher has 14 properties (with English names) and Institution has 12 properties (with French names). After translating and expanding the synonyms, it is possible to match 11 of the 12 properties of Institution. However, the twelfth property cannot be matched. Publisher has a property InverseOf(isPartOf) and Institution has a property InverseOf(partieDe). Clearly, their names are equivalent but the automatic translation does not make it possible to discover it, as *partieDe* is automatically translated as *partOf* rather than *isPartOf*. □

Results and Discussion. Table 6 shows the results of our metrics for shared properties combined with Translation dictionaries (T), WordNet (W), or both (TW). Translation dictionaries are only used in OAEI 2009*, the dataset that only includes cross-lingual ontology pairs. Furthermore, ORE 2015 and ORE 2015* are not evaluated as they only consider intra-ontology relationships.

Compared with Table 5, using translation in OAEI 2009* keeps the number of examples (a), decreases the number of examples (b), and increases the number of counter-examples (c). The numbers are even worse after using WordNet. In OAEI 2011, OAEI 2011*, and OAEI 2016 there are no changes, except 1 more case (d) in OAEI 2016. OAEI 2009 is the only dataset where the extensions has some benefits, increasing (a) and decreasing (d), although it also decreases (b) and increases (c). But even here, the number of ontologies with more examples (b) than counter-examples (c) or (d) decreases, reducing the applicability.

7   Related Work

This section recaps some related work on the discovery of subsumption relationships in ontologies. Most of the work in ontology alignment is focused on the discovery of synonymy relationships, and only a few works consider the discovery of subsumption relationships. Among them, some authors have addressed the discovery of subsumption intra-ontology relationships (see e.g., [21]), but we will focus here on the discovery inter-ontology subsumption relationships.

Some of the previous works are based on the extraction of subsumption relationships on shared instances, but do not take schema information into account [9,18,32,35]. Some of these works also assume that ontology instances are annotated with phrases of text [9].

Previous approaches extracting relationships at the schema level include the systems MOMIS [3], SCARLET [26], RepOSE [19,20], and CSR [28]. The alignments that MOMIS and SCARLET can find must already exist in third-party sources (WordNet and other ontologies, respectively), whereas RepOSE finds missing is-a relationships that are derivable from a set of an ontology network (a set of ontologies). CSR uses machine learning techniques so it requires a previous training step. The authors of CSR recognize that not all the ontologies are suitable for the training step.

STROMA system uses a two-step approach [1], using any matching system to retrieve a list of mappings between ontology terms, and a second step using some heuristics to determine the type of relationships (i.e., synonymy or hyponymy).

Table 6. Metrics for shared properties combined with translation and WordNet.

Dataset	Item	Criteria				b vs. c		b vs. d	
		a	b	c	d	#b>	Dif	#b>	Dif
OAEI 2009 (C) W	Sum	354	460	640	1989	3	−14	12	2
	#Onts	10	22	22	10				
	Mean %	32	42	58	6				
OAEI 2009* (C) T	Sum	0	50	50	0	0	0	2	2
	#Onts	0	2	2	0				
	Mean %	0	50	50	0				
OAEI 2009* (C) TW	Sum	0	42	58	0	0	−2	2	2
	#Onts	0	2	2	0				
	Mean %	0	42	58	0				
OAEI 2011 (C) W	Sum	0	2	762	0	0	−8	2	2
	#Onts	0	2	9	0				
	Mean %	0	0.3	99.7	0				
OAEI 2011* (C) W	Sum	0	2	51	0	0	−3	2	2
	#Onts	0	2	3	0				
	Mean %	0	4	96	0				
OAEI 2016 (C) W	Sum	0	12	21	1	1	−1	3	3
	#Onts	0	3	3	1				
	Mean %	0	36	64	0.01				

More generally, [33] supports having several matchers (e.g., a structural one and a lexical one), and studies how to choose them and how to combine their results, but the automatic combination in different domains is complicated.

Other authors have proposed the use of Natural Language Processing (NLP) tools. The work [16] finds subsumption relations across ontologies using background knowledge from BabelNet [24]. In particular, the authors take into account synonyms (synsets) of the terms to be aligned. One of the problems of BabelNet is that it limits the number of queries per day. Instead, we propose to combine WordNet [22] with a free translation software. In a more recent work, the same authors propose to discover hypernymy relationships from ontology annotations using NLP techniques [17]. Unfortunately, most of the ontologies in our datasets do not contain annotations to apply those techniques.

Other works are not appropriate for general ontology alignment. In [25], the authors build an alignment between two ontologies, DOLCE and SUMO. Such alignment includes subsumption relationships across the two ontologies but they were built by humans, for this specific case. Thus, no general methodology to discover subsumption relationships across two general ontologies is provided. The resulting ontology, called SmartSumo, is not publicly available. In [12,23], the authors use machine learning and NLP, respectively, to find hyponymy relationships in build a light-weight ontology. However, both works do not consider ontology alignment, but only relationships between two low-level terms.

We must also cite some previous work developed in our research group. The present paper studies and evaluates some of the techniques used in the system in [34], including heuristics based on shared properties and entity names, among others. The need to extend this system to take into account cross-lingual information was proposed in [6]. This paper extends an initial evaluation of the heuristics performed in [15] with more ontologies and external resources.

8   Conclusions and Future Work

This paper has discussed several issues related to the automatic discovery of hyponymy relationships across ontology elements. We hope that this will contribute to an increase in the interest in such a kind of relationships, which have received much less attention than synonymy relationships.

Firstly, we claimed that new lexical measures between ontology entities are needed. Indeed, we argue that if two entities have the same name, our confidence in a possible hyponymy relationship should decrease, as they are more likely to be synonyms. As a first step towards lexical measures that penalize a perfect similarity, we studied a simple heuristic based on the fact that the name of the hyponym is sometimes a specialization of the name of its hypernym, which is an affix substring. An empirical evaluation shows that this heuristic is much more useful for classes than for properties, and the existence of ontologies where this idea leads to more positive examples than counter-examples. We also analyzed some cases where our measure fails and provided some justifications and concrete examples, such as having entities with unreadable or multilingual names.

Then, we discussed the impact on shared properties on the discovery of hyponymy relationships. A hyponym concept should include all the properties of its hypernym concept, and we also argue that it is very likely to specialize it with some additional properties. An empirical evaluation over 4 datasets (the only three existing sets considering inter-ontology relationships and an additional one considering intra-ontology relationships) shows that there is a significant amount of examples confirming our claim but there are also a notable number of exceptions. In particular, there is usually a class of ontologies where the number of examples is greater than the number of counter-examples.

The number of counter-examples made us question the benchmark itself, and we conclude that the datasets are incomplete and contain often an unnatural modeling. On the one hand, existing benchmarks are restricted to hyponymy relationships between concepts and exclude the case of properties. Moreover, they have strong limitations in terms of size and number of properties and axioms (in particular, subproperty, domain, and range axioms). This penalizes very much heuristics based on properties as ours. On the other hand, we were able to identify several reasons to explain cases where our measures did not perform well and illustrated them by providing concrete examples.

We have also investigated more sophisticated techniques than simply using the entity names. In particular, we use two translation dictionaries to deal with cross-lingual ontology pairs (or ontologies written in languages other than English), and WordNet lexical database to provide set of synonyms for a given entity. Unfortunately, it turns out that although the number of examples where our metrics are useful, the number of counter-examples is higher in general, thus limiting to scenarios where the recall is important but not the precision. We carefully analyzed the results and proposed some possible reasons, showing examples where one of the dictionaries provides wrong translations, or where WordNet provides a wrong set of synonyms (including terms which should rather be hyponyms). We also noticed that in cross-lingual pairs using two dictionaries is enough, and using WordNet as well does not improve the quality of the results.

Future Work. There are many directions for our future research. Our main priority is to develop a more general system computing at the same time both synonymy and hyponymy relationships (extensible to other semantic relationships). The key idea is that our confidence in a synonymy relationship should decrease our confidence in a hyponymy relationship and vice versa. This idea, and the fact that our algorithm to compute hyponymy relationship assumes some synonymy relationships could create a chicken-egg problem that needs to be properly addressed. To evaluate such approach, we could use external RDF triple stores to measure the confidence in the discovered axioms [31].

As we have already mentioned, further research is needed to identify the class of ontologies where our measures provide good results. Lexical measures across entity names also require more sophisticated techniques than those presented here, such as using word stemming and NLP techniques to compare entity names. Moreover, although we have used WordNet to provide semantic relationships between terms, more sophisticated techniques or alternative resources could be used to improve the poor results. For example, using word2vec to compute word embeddings and restrict to the closest synonyms. Furthermore, hyponyms can not only add a property but also restrict the values of an inherited property.

Finally, the identified limitations of existing datasets lead us to consider developing a new benchmark. Needless to say, it is important to develop a benchmark which is not biased to benefit our specific heuristics, so the contributions of the community will be extremely important.

Acknowledgment. We were partially supported by the projects TIN2016-78011-C4-3-R (AEI/ FEDER, UE), JIUZ-2018-TEC-02 (Fundación Ibercaja y Universidad de Zaragoza), and DGA/FEDER. I. Huitzil was partially funded by Universidad de Zaragoza - Santander Universidades (Ayudas de Movilidad para Latinoamericanos - Estudios de Doctorado). We are also grateful to Miguel Bolsa for some help with the implementation of the interface with the dictionaries and WordNet.

References

1. Arnold, P., Rahm, E.: Enriching ontology mappings with semantic relations. Data Knowl. Eng. **93**, 1–18 (2014)

2. Baader, F., Horrocks, I., Lutz, C., Sattler, U.: An Introduction to Description Logic. Cambridge University Press, Cambridge (2017)

3. Beneventano, D., et al.: Information integration: the MOMIS project demonstration. In: Proceedings of the 26th International Conference on Very Large Data Bases (VLDB 2000), pp. 611–614 (2000)

4. Bobed, C., Bobillo, F., Mena, E., Pan, J.Z.: On serializable incremental semantic reasoners. In: Proceedings of the 9th International Conference on Knowledge Capture (K-CAP 2017), pp. 187–190. ACM (2017)

5. Bobed, C., Yus, R., Bobillo, F., Mena, E.: Semantic reasoning on mobile devices: do androids dream of efficient reasoners? J. Web Semant. **35**(4), 167–183 (2015)

6. Bobillo, F., Bobed, C., Mena, E.: On the generalization of the discovery of subsumption relationships to the fuzzy case. In: Proceedings of the 26th IEEE International Conference on Fuzzy Systems (FUZZ-IEEE 2017), pp. 1–6 (2017)

7. Bolsa-Marquina, M.: An intelligent system for the discovery of synonymy and hyponymy relationships across ontologies. Undergraduate thesis project, University of Zaragoza (2019)

8. Cheatham, M., Hitzler, P.: String similarity metrics for ontology alignment. In: Alani, H., et al. (eds.) ISWC 2013, Part II. LNCS, vol. 8219, pp. 294–309. Springer, Heidelberg (2013). https://doi.org/10.1007/978-3-642-41338-4_19

9. Chua, W.W.K., Kim, J.J.: Discovering cross-ontology subsumption relationships by using ontological annotations on biomedical literature. In: Proceedings of the 3rd International Conference on Biomedical Ontology (ICBO 2012), CEUR Workshop Proceedings, vol. 897 (2012)

10. Ehrig, M.: Ontology Alignment: Bridging the Semantic Gap. Semantic Web and Beyond, vol. 4. Springer, New York (2007). https://doi.org/10.1007/978-0-387-36501-5

11. Euzenat, J., Shvaiko, P.: Ontology Matching, 2nd edn. Springer, Heidelberg (2013). https://doi.org/10.1007/978-3-642-38721-0

12. Evans, M.C., Bhatia, J., Wadkar, S., Breaux, T.D.: An evaluation of constituency-based hyponymy extraction from privacy policies. In: Proceedings of the 25th IEEE International Requirements Engineering Conference (RE 2017), pp. 312–321 (2017)

13. Glimm, B., Horrocks, I., Motik, B., Stoilos, G., Wang, Z.: HermiT: an OWL 2 reasoner. J. Autom. Reason. **53**(3), 245–269 (2014)

14. Gracia, J., Asooja, K.: Monolingual and cross-lingual ontology matching with CIDER-CL: evaluation report for OAEI 2013. In: Proceedings of the 8th International Workshop on Ontology Matching (OM 2013), CEUR Workshop Proceedings, vol. 1111, pp. 109–116 (2013)

15. Huitzil, I., Bobillo, F., Mena, E., Bobed, C., Bermúdez, J.: Some reflections on the discovery of hyponyms between ontologies. In: Proceedings of the 21st International Conference on Enterprise Information Systems (ICEIS 2019), vol. 2, pp. 130–140. SCITEPRESS (2019)

16. Kamel, M., Schmidt, D., Trojahn, C., Vieira, R.: Exploiting BabelNet for generating subsumption. In: Proceedings of the 13th International Workshop on Ontology Matching (OM 2018), CEUR-WS: Workshop Proceedings, vol. 2288, pp. 216–217 (2018)

17. Kamel, M., Schmidt, D., Trojahn, C., Vieira, R.: Hypernym relation extraction for establishing subsumptions: preliminary results on matching foundational ontologies. In: Proceedings of the 14th International Workshop on Ontology Matching (OM 2019) (2019)

18. Kang, D., Lu, J., Xu, B., Wang, P., Li, Y.: A framework of checking subsumption relations between composite concepts in different ontologies. In: Khosla, R., Howlett, R.J., Jain, L.C. (eds.) KES 2005. LNCS (LNAI), vol. 3681, pp. 953–959. Springer, Heidelberg (2005). https://doi.org/10.1007/11552413_136

19. Lambrix, P., Ivanova, V.: A unified approach for debugging is-a structure and mappings in networked taxonomies. J. Biomed. Semant. **4**, 10 (2013)

20. Lambrix, P., Liu, Q.: Debugging the missing is-a structure within taxonomies networked by partial reference alignments. Data Knowl. Eng. **86**, 179–205 (2013)

21. Lambrix, P., Wei-Kleiner, F., Dragisic, Z.: Completing the is-a structure in lightweight ontologies. J. Biomed. Semant. **6**, 12 (2015)

22. Miller, G., Beckwith, R., Fellbaum, C., Gross, D., Miller, K.: WordNet: an online lexical database. Int. J. Lexicogr. **3**, 235–244 (1990)

23. Movshovitz-Attias, D., Whang, S.E., Noy, N., Halevy, A.: Discovering subsumption relationships for web-based ontologies. In: Proceedings of the 18th International Workshop on Web and Databases (WebDB 2015), pp. 62–69 (2015). https://doi.org/10.1145/2767109.2767111

24. Navigli, R., Ponzetto, S.P.: BabelNet: the automatic construction, evaluation and application of a wide-coverage multilingual semantic network. Artif. Intell. **193**, 217–250 (2012)

25. Oberle, D., et al.: DOLCE ergo SUMO: on foundational and domain models in SWIntO (smartweb integrated ontology) (2007)

26. Sabou, M., d'Aquin, M., Motta, E.: SCARLET: semantic relation discovery by harvesting online ontologies. In: Bechhofer, S., Hauswirth, M., Hoffmann, J., Koubarakis, M. (eds.) ESWC 2008. LNCS, vol. 5021, pp. 854–858. Springer, Heidelberg (2008). https://doi.org/10.1007/978-3-540-68234-9_72

27. Sirin, E., Parsia, B., Cuenca-Grau, B., Kalyanpur, A., Katz, Y.: Pellet: a practical OWL-DL reasoner. J. Web Semant. **5**(2), 51–53 (2007)

28. Spiliopoulos, V., Valarakos, A.G., Vouros, G.A.: *CSR*: discovering subsumption relations for the alignment of ontologies. In: Bechhofer, S., Hauswirth, M., Hoffmann, J., Koubarakis, M. (eds.) ESWC 2008. LNCS, vol. 5021, pp. 418–431. Springer, Heidelberg (2008). https://doi.org/10.1007/978-3-540-68234-9_32

29. Staab, S., Studer, R. (eds.): Handbook on Ontologies. IHIS, 2nd edn. Springer, Heidelberg (2009). https://doi.org/10.1007/978-3-540-92673-3

30. Steigmiller, A., Liebig, T., Glimm, B.: Konclude: system description. J. Web Semant. **27–28**, 78–85 (2014)

31. Tettamanzi, A.G.B., Faron-Zucker, C., Gandon, F.: Possibilistic testing of OWL axioms against RDF data. Int. J. Approximate Reasoning **91**, 114–130 (2017)

32. Tournaire, R., Petit, J., Rousset, M., Termier, A.: Discovery of probabilistic mappings between taxonomies: principles and experiments. J. Data Semant. **15**, 66–101 (2011)

33. Vennesland, A.: Matcher composition for identification of subsumption relations in ontology matching. In: Proceedings of the 2017 International Conference on Web Intelligence (WI 2017), pp. 154–161. ACM (2017)

34. Yus, R., Mena, E., Solano-Bes, E.: Generic rules for the discovery of subsumption relationships based on ontological contexts. In: Proceedings of the 2015 IEEE/WIC/ACM International Joint Conference on Web Intelligence and Intelligent Agent Technology (WI-IAT 2015), vol. I, pp. 309–312. IEEE (2015)

35. Zong, N., Nam, S., Eom, J.H., Ahn, J., Joe, H., Kim, H.G.: Aligning ontologies with subsumption and equivalence relations in linked data. Knowl.-Based Syst. **76**, 30–41 (2015)

Towards Design Principles for Visualizing Business Ecosystems

Anne Faber[1(✉)] and Sven-Volker Rehm[2]

[1] Technical University of Munich, Boltzmannstrasse 3, 85748 Garching, Germany
anne.faber@tum.de
[2] EM Strasbourg Business School, Université de Strasbourg,
HuManiS EA 7308, 67000 Strasbourg, France
sven.rehm@em-strasbourg.eu

Abstract. Business ecosystems have recently gained relevance as a reference frame in which firms entertain diverse relationships to develop, produce, and distribute services and products. Only little research however has looked at how to visualize business ecosystems—although visualizations might provide a helpful instrument for firms to position themselves and manage their interactions within their ecosystem. We report from a systematic mapping study that identified 17 types of visualizations used in the business ecosystem context. On basis of this study, we derive requirements and design principles for Visual Analytic Systems (VAS). We discuss some limitations of current VAS with respect to the question how VAS can support management tasks related to business ecosystems, and we provide an outlook on the role of VAS in supporting business ecosystem governance.

Keywords: Business ecosystem · Visualization · Visual analytic system · Business network · Ecosystem governance · Systematic mapping study

1 Introduction

Business ecosystems have recently gained relevance as a reference frame in which firms entertain diverse relationships to develop, produce, and distribute services and products [11, 24]. The business ecosystem concept captures the complex business environment that comprises institutionalized business partnerships such as supply chains and various types of alliances—and extends these by the fabric of further personal and business ties that might involve various other entities such as public institutions, start-ups or non-profit organizations. This way it builds a reference frame marking the holistic environment of a company. This allows firms to position themselves in the fabric of relationships of current and potential future business partners, which constitutes a prerequisite to form

This paper is an extension of the conference paper entitled "Visualizing Business Ecosystems: Results of a Systematic Mapping Study" by Faber, A., Riemhofer, M., Huth, D., Matthes, F., published in the conference proceedings of ICEIS 2019: Proceedings of the 21st International Conference on Enterprise Information Systems.

© Springer Nature Switzerland AG 2020
J. Filipe et al. (Eds.): ICEIS 2019, LNBIP 378, pp. 299–319, 2020.
https://doi.org/10.1007/978-3-030-40783-4_14

effective business networks with relevant customers, suppliers, competitors, regulatory institutions, innovative start-ups and others more [45, 46]. As entities continuously enter and leave this fabric of relationships, business ecosystems are deemed to exhibit a high dynamic [10, 41, 45].

Various types of business ecosystems have been identified and discussed in literature, including for instance *innovation* ecosystems [1, 12], *platform* ecosystems [52, 55] or *software* ecosystems [43, 57]. These different types of ecosystems build different reference frames to capture the diverse *roles* that firms assume within the ecosystem in focus [27, 39] as well as the structures that capture the relevant *characteristics* and *business objectives* of different contexts as they appear e.g., around marketplaces like alibaba.com [51], or in smart cities [59].

In order to collect, illustrate and analyze these ecosystem characteristics, often visualizations have been used. Visual Analytic Systems (VAS) have been proposed and evaluated to leverage related benefits [17, 40]. VAS allow capturing the needs and demands of diverse user groups through different views and types of visualizations, commonly termed 'layouts'. Visualizations have been shown to deliver insights about the entities and their relations within business ecosystems; and interactive visualizations have been proven to support decision-makers in their ecosystem-related tasks [6, 13, 26]. Considering the effort to collect and analyze the regularly high amounts of data and information required to adequately describe the relationships existing in an ecosystem, visualizations can also help to derive value by spotting anomalies, identifying keystone and niche players, or recognizing change patterns and trends [58].

While some progress has been made in conceptualizing business ecosystems in research, in practice firms still face the challenge *to position themselves* advantageously within their ecosystems [2]. Research on business ecosystems has primarily focused on strategic aspects [2, 31, 32, 53, 61]; yet to a lesser extent on how the assumed ecosystem's potential can be practically leveraged. Remarkably few suggestions have been made by extant research with respect to designing instruments and VAS that *support management tasks* related to business ecosystems, and that contribute to governing business ecosystems.

In this chapter, we embark on two aspects related to the visualization of business ecosystems. First, we report from a systematic mapping study we conducted and that exemplifies *types of visualizations* used in extant business ecosystem literature. Second, we identify requirements for Visual Analytic Systems (VAS), from which we derive a set of design principles for VAS with a view on the advancement of management instruments in the business ecosystem context.

As this chapter is an extended version of a conference article [18], alongside several smaller enhancements its major additions are the formulation of design principles, and a more comprehensive rationale and discussion of the role of VAS in the business ecosystem context.

Section 2 presents related research on business ecosystems and highlights previous work in visualizing ecosystems. Here we also showcase prior literature studies on business ecosystems and particularly, emphasize earlier findings on business ecosystem types to show this concept's value as a reference frame for value creating activities. Section 3 introduces to our systematic mapping study and the process of identifying engineering requirements and design principles. Section 4 presents the spectrum of business ecosystems visualizations along with an overview of requirements and design principles as major findings. Section 5 gives a short summary and interpretation of findings and discusses aspects concerning how VAS can support management tasks related to business ecosystems. We point out some limitations and future requirements on business ecosystem visualization before giving a short conclusion.

2 Related Research

2.1 Business Ecosystems

The term business ecosystem was introduced in management literature in the mid-1990s, defining it as a network of companies interacting across adjacent layers of core business, extended business, and business ecosystem [39]. Pointing at the business ecosystem concept's idea as reference frame for the holistic environment of a firm, business ecosystems convey a raison d'être – and undergo a life cycle along several phases [10]. These phases include birth/pioneering, expansion, leadership/authority and self-renewal/death [38, 39].

The first phase denotes the genesis of a core idea or main objective of the ecosystem as its raison d'être, which – as we will illustrate later on – has led to the conception of various types of ecosystems in literature [14]. Towards this objective, firms explore and pioneer in generating innovations, partnerships or technical solutions for existing or new markets. For instance, *innovation* ecosystems often help building consortia that target new technological innovations [3] while *platform* ecosystems center around one platform firm that provides a digital platform as a central hub to which other entities connect [22]. The second phase links to the generation of market structures and evolving competition within and across the ecosystem, which often involves the emergence of network-centric leadership roles by focal firms, or network patterns around digital platforms [53, 54]. The third phase sees the accomplishment of either constant innovation and adaption of the ecosystem's objectives and members, or the failure of adaption, which leads to the dissolution of the ecosystem (as it is conceived in its holistic and goal-oriented nature).

Each developmental phase involves cooperative and competitive challenges [64]. These particularly concern the roles that firms assume within institutionalized business partnerships, as "suppliers, distributors, outsourcing firms, makers of related products or services, technology providers, and a host of other organizations" [27]. These roles are linked by establishing multiple and at times parallel relationships between ecosystem members, which can be flexibly established and dissolved [10]. Firms might also enter or leave the ecosystem, leading to a dynamic rearrangement of partnerships [41].

Different types of relationships emerge from partnership objectives as they are defined in supply chains or various other types of alliances such as technological alliances (for accessing and expanding R&D knowledge), operation-based alliances (for expanding operational/manufacturing capabilities), market-based alliances (for building or complementing market strengths through gaining access to markets or developing market expertise), managerial alliances (for sharing management expertise, e.g. through coaching), or financial alliances (for executing technology acquisition or commercialization strategies) [21]. Beyond such institutionalized business partnerships, the business ecosystem concept also captures the fabric of further personal and business ties that might exist. This fabric involves social relations between entrepreneurs, managers and firm employees, e.g., in expert networks or communities of practice, which together form the overall business environment that is "interconnected through a complex, global network of relationships" [8].

Three meta-characteristics of business ecosystems have been suggested that contribute to a better distinction of the ecosystem concept from clusters or networks – focusing on its emergence along "value-creating activity, such as entrepreneurship or innovation, rather than an industrial sector" [48]. These characteristics are sustainability of resource usage; self-governance, including definition of rules of competition; and evolution via competition and experimentation [48]. This view puts the focus on firms that *actively build business networks* with "resources operating as an interdependent system" [48], allowing to collectively compete against other ecosystems and business networks.

2.2 Visualizing Business Ecosystems

Visualizing the entities and relationships existing in business ecosystems has been proven beneficial for the decision-making of ecosystem stakeholders [7, 13, 26]. Visual Analytic Systems (VAS) have been proposed to enable and support management-tasks related to business ecosystems [15, 40, 44]. They can be used for instance to evaluate a firm's strategic positioning, to identify potential value creation partners, or to recognize newly emerging business opportunities. VAS system architecture generally facilitates user interaction, visual analysis and reporting [40].

VAS use *ecosystem data* in order to provide diverse user groups with different views and types of visualizations (layouts). The availability of data about the ecosystem is an essential requirement for visualizing ecosystems [15, 40]. Apart from data collected from firm-internal sources, ecosystem data generally comprises data sets collected from commercial databases (business and economic data) or from social and business media [6, 8]. Major challenges in collecting ecosystem data concern the high amounts of data and information, the difficulty to distinguish relevant data, the time-consuming nature of manual data search, and the difficulty to find appropriate ways to document information [19].

Various VAS have been developed and described in extant literature. The VAS "dotlink360" supports ecosystem stakeholders in understanding inter-firm relationships in business ecosystems by providing interactive visualizations [5]. It uses six layouts to support visualizing *mobile ecosystems*, involving entities such as mobile network providers, platform providers, or device manufacturers:[1] Scrollable list of entities; composition view (viewing entity detail); temporal view (depicting when relationships were formed and how active an entity is in forming relations); geographical view (location of entities); segment view (chord diagram/network graph); and scatter plot (financial metrics) [5].

---

[1] We will introduce visuals of the mentioned layouts in our *Findings* section.

In context of Supply Network Management, Park et al. [40] present a VAS that uses five layouts "to highlight different structural aspects", including force-directed, circular, treemap, matrix, and substrate-based layouts.

The VAS "ecoxight" was developed in context of visualizing API ecosystems (API…application programming interface) [9]. It draws on data from ProgrammableWeb and Crunchbase[2] and uses five layouts: path view (node-link diagram); category view (chord diagram/network graph); geography view; scatter-net view (scatter plot); and temporal view.

In our own research, we have developed the VAS "Business Ecosystem Explorer (BEEx)" in order to model and visualize "smart city" business ecosystems [15]. BEEx uses a wiki-based approach for collection of ecosystem data and offers collaborative modelling features [20]. It includes five layouts: list; adjacency matrix; force layout; treemap; and chord diagram. In addition, a detail view for each entity is available.

For setting up VAS in practice, diverse stakeholder groups ought to become part of modelling activities [44]. Ecosystem analysts, experts and data scientists together collect ecosystem data and engage in evaluating and interpreting visualizations [14, 18].

Data collection and analysis generally follow four iterative steps [19, 28]: (1) Determining industry structure, i.e., identifying value chain and value propositions; (2) Identifying ecosystem members, i.e., collecting data about organizations and their relevant attributes; (3) Modelling ecosystem elements, i.e., specifying semantics and visual encodings of nodes, edges and dependencies; and (4) Visualize – analyze – interpret, i.e., formulating and refining insights about firms or clusters in key network positions, finding counterintuitive patterns, and identifying eventually missing entities.

2.3 Extant Literature Reviews on Business Ecosystems

As to the increased sensitivity towards the business ecosystem concept, our mapping study is not the first literature review addressing business ecosystems-related research. In Table 1, we briefly summarize four extant literature reviews we have identified. While none of the four reviews directly addresses the issue of visualizing business ecosystems, each of them points towards some requirements for VAS. The studies' insights overall thus provide an impetus to further scrutinize requirements for VAS. In the table, we therefore also point out some basic consequences they have for visualizing business ecosystems. In the following, we discuss how each study informs the positioning of *visualization* in research on business ecosystems.

The study of Mäkinen and Dedehayir [35] looks at ecosystem evolution and strategy. Their focus on the dynamic nature of business ecosystems highlights that the positioning of firms changes over time. As a resulting requirement, VAS need to enable a review of these changes and the influencing factors.

The concept of innovation ecosystems is examined in the study of de Vasconceles Gomes et al. [12]. They identify and discuss six related research streams, which emphasizes that there are diverse "use cases" that should be supported by VAS. As the parameters to describe the use cases overlap, VAS need to provide flexibility for configuring and adapting the model they use for generating visualizations and analytic features.

---

[2] See https://www.programmableweb.com/; https://www.crunchbase.com/.

Table 1. Extant literature reviews on business ecosystems.

Authors/focus and scope	Study outcomes and → *Consequences for visualizing business ecosystems*
Mäkinen and Dedehayir [35]: BE evolution and strategy; 68 articles	- Business ecosystem members and their roles - Factors that influence the evolution of business ecosystems - Dynamics of ecosystem change - Strategic considerations of firms positioned in ecosystems → *The positioning of firms changes over time. VAS need to enable a review of these changes and the influencing factors*
de Vasconceles Gomes et al. [12]: Innovation ecosystems; 193 articles	- Identification of six research streams related to innovation ecosystems: (1) industry platform x innovation ecosystem; (2) innovation ecosystem strategy, strategic management, value creation and business model; (3) innovation management; (4) managing partners; (5) the innovation ecosystem life cycle; (6) innovation ecosystems and new venture creation → *There are diverse "use cases" that should be supported by VAS. The parameters to describe the use cases overlap. VAS thus need to provide flexibility for model configuration and adaptation*
Järvi and Kortelainen [30]: BE analytic framework; 72 articles	- Identification of three units of analysis: (1) the individual actor (typically a firm); (2) the relationship between the actors; (3) the business ecosystem - *Individual actors* occupy different *positions* in ecosystems, such as a hub or niche position by assuming different *roles* such as customer, delivery channel, seller of complementary products and services, supplier, or policy maker etc. - *Relationships* in the ecosystem comprise (a) interaction, (b) interdependence and (c) substitution as well as (d) focal firm—complementor relationship - *Ecosystem* aspects comprise (a) collective and collaborative value creation, (b) competition between ecosystems, (c) ecosystem clockspeed, i.e., to assess the rate of change of an industry (d) ecosystem life cycle, (e) network structure and (f) transition from supply or value chain management to ecosystem management → *VAS need to enable a description of business ecosystem on different interconnected levels, and an analysis from different angles (units of analysis). Various data sources might be required to populate models*
Scaringella and Radziwon [49]: Ecosystem types; 104 articles	- Identification of four main types of ecosystems: (1) business ecosystem; (2) innovation ecosystem; (3) entrepreneurial ecosystem; (4) knowledge ecosystem - Definition of *ecosystem invariants*, such as territory, values, stakeholders, to describe similarities, differences, and complementarities of these four ecosystem types - Overview of *existing territorial approach theories*, which differentiate and describe ecosystems based on the spatial agglomeration, e.g., Italian industrial district or regional innovation systems - Proposal of a research framework for future empirical research → *VAS need to visualize inter-firm connectivity based on various parameters and multiplex relations*
Faber et al. [14]: Ecosystem types; 136 articles	- Identification of 12 business ecosystem types → *VAS need to enable a synthesis of layouts related to the use case (type of business ecosystem considered) and consequently, a case-specific terminology in models*

An analytic framework is formulated by Järvi and Kortelainen [30]. The authors identify individual actors (firms), actor relationships and the business ecosystem overall as central units of analysis. This affords that VAS need to enable a description of business ecosystems on different interconnected levels, and an analysis from different angles (i.e., units of analysis). In addition, it accentuates the fact that various data sources are often required to populate models.

Scaringella and Radziwon [49] identify four major types of business ecosystems. Their findings suggest that VAS need to visualize inter-firm connectivity based on various parameters and multiplex relations.

Our own research [14] brings forward twelve types of business ecosystems, and describes their diverse objectives and underlying structures—which all however might overlap in a given use case. We draw from this the particular requirement that VAS need to enable a synthesis of layouts related to the use case (i.e., the type of business ecosystem considered) and consequently, must allow for a case-specific terminology in models.

In a cross-study perspective, we can constitute that while extant studies consider determining factors of business ecosystems and their analytical value and the like, the tie-in to the *management tasks* appearing in practice – and that afford a visual representation of the ecosystem in focus – stills lacks consideration.

2.4   Ecosystems as Reference Frame for Value Creating Activities

As extant literature on business ecosystems showcases, each identified *type of ecosystem* features distinct constitutive characteristics and relationships that express its overall nature and raison-d'être. In previous research, we have identified and characterized several types of business ecosystems [14]. We identified 12 ecosystem types, which we describe in Table 2. As to our analysis, two perspectives define the central *type of linkage* that drives the conceptualization of business ecosystems (BE); organizational perspective and value perspective. The organizational perspective considers ecosystems as *stakeholder-driven* entities, comprising *Entrepreneurial BE* and *Family Spin-off BE* as well as (to some extent) *Software BE*. The value perspective reflects the *value-driven* nature of ecosystems, i.e., actuated by ideas as well as innovations of products, services and value assets. The most prominent ones in literature involve *Platform BE, Digital BE* and *Innovation BE*.

The diversity of conceptions that have been formulated in order to characterize business ecosystem types suggests that there is a multiplicity and plurality evident in the relationships that substantiate *what we conceive* and study as business ecosystem. In other words, business ecosystems are conceived as *reference frame for various forms of value creating activities and relationships*, whereby the exact conception is delimited to the distinct perspective taken. This notion of a pluralistic nature of the business ecosystem concept as we can observe it empirically motivates our study of ways to visualize the intricate relationships and instantiations involved. On another take, the insight that the pluralistic nature of business ecosystems leads to the *de-facto instantiation of various types of ecosystems* – as networks of organizations, services, resources and the like – points us to scrutinize also the *nature of these networks* that eventually lead to synergetic value creation. (We will touch upon this aspect in the *Discussion* section).

Table 2. Business ecosystem types (based on [14]).

Business ecosystem (BE) type	Definition and selected references
Entrepreneurial BE	An *Entrepreneurial BE* consists of start-up related organizations, such as entrepreneurs, investors or end-users, who collaborate to form a new start-up [48]
Family Spin-off BE	A *Family Spin-off BE* is created in case a spin-off of a family company splits up from the parent company [34]
Platform BE	A *Platform BE* incorporates a platform as the "keystone entity" [22], i.e., a central hub to which other entities connect
Innovation BE	An *Innovation BE* forms around an innovation [12, 56], which occurs when the market demands change or new technologies disrupt the markets [3]
Software BE	A *Software BE* is "a set of businesses functioning as a unit and interacting with a shared market for software and services, together with the relationships among them" [29]
Knowledge BE	A *Knowledge BE* is located around a university, focusing on knowledge generation and is usually geographically localized with close proximity [49]
Digital BE	A *Digital BE* (a term coined by the European Union) essentially is a *Platform BE*
Mobility BE	A *Mobility BE* is a subtype of the *Innovation BE* and includes, e.g., ride sharing, connected cars, and driver-less transportation [48]
IoT BE	An *IoT BE* "is comprised of the community of interacting companies and individuals along with their socio-economic environment, where the companies are competing and cooperating by utilizing a common set of core assets related to the interconnection of the physical world of things with the virtual world of Internet" [37]
Internet BE	An *Internet BE* is the ecosystem around the Internet as the core asset of innovations [4]
Mobile Internet BE	A *Mobile Internet BE* is a subtype of the *Internet BE* [4]
Customer-centric BE	A *Customer-centric BE* focuses on customers in a keystone position, who are involved in the idea generation and product/service development [22, 23]

3   Method

Our research aimed at understanding how, and to what extent, visualizations and VAS are currently being used in the business ecosystems context. To this end, we conducted a study of extant academic literature [33, 42]. More precisely, we undertook a systematic mapping study as proposed by Wendler [63], as we aimed at a general overview that (a) determines the coverage of visualizations/VAS in the field, (b) helps building a classification scheme for visualizations, (c) shows overall occurrences of layouts, and that allows us to (d) combine our results to draw conclusions on the further development of VAS to support design of management instruments in the ecosystem context. After an initial literature study, for the latter aspect (d), in a second step we interpreted our analysis in order to derive requirements for VAS design. These requirements are then categorized to form design principles [50], which we offer to research and practice.

Two research questions guided our inquiry of literature: What visualizations and VAS are reported in literature to illustrate business ecosystems and the overall business ecosystem concept (RQ1)? And, which requirements for VAS have been formulated (RQ2)? The rational of RQ1 is to identify visualization types, such as network or chord diagrams, used within business ecosystem research. RQ2 aims at synthesizing existing VAS requirements to provide visualizations that primarily target the *dynamic* changes of business ecosystem entities and their relations.

3.1 Systematic Mapping Study

A systematic mapping study generally "aims at reviewing a relatively broad topic by identifying, analyzing, and structuring the goals, methods, and contents of conducted primary studies. Therefore, the state-of-the-art research, research gaps, or matured subareas can be identified and explicated" [63, p. 1318]. To accomplish this objective, during our mapping study, we followed eight process steps as visualized in Fig. 1. The following paragraphs describe how we conducted our process steps of searching, selecting, and analyzing.

Selection of Data Sources and Search Strategy. For the selection of suitable databases, we identified computer science, information systems, and management theory as relevant domains to our study focus of VAS and business ecosystems. We limited our search on electronic databases and in a first step selected the databases Association for Computing Machinery (ACM), Electrical and Electronics Engineers (IEEE), ScienceDirect, Scopus, SpringerLink, and Web of Science, as these databases cover publications of the previously identified research domains to a reasonable extent.

We conducted our search in September and October 2018, using the search string "business ecosystem" and consequently analyzed (within the initial search) only titles, abstracts, and keywords of the identified records. If at least one of these three contained the term 'business ecosystem,' we considered the record as relevant; resulting in overall 1,842 records after the initial search.

Inclusion and Exclusion Criteria. In the next process steps, we included relevant articles to the "pool of papers" [63] and excluded irrelevant papers. Irrelevant papers comprise those with a lack of business focus, i.e., not describing interactions of multiple business actors, but that rather described technical aspects or architectural descriptions of business, or biological ecosystems. Records were included in case they were written in English and the scope was related to business ecosystems. In case a record was labeled with a "notice of violation" or "notice of retraction" note, the according record was excluded as well, in order to maintain quality standards of analyzed literature. After reading title, abstract, and keywords, we labeled 382 articles as relevant; from which 124

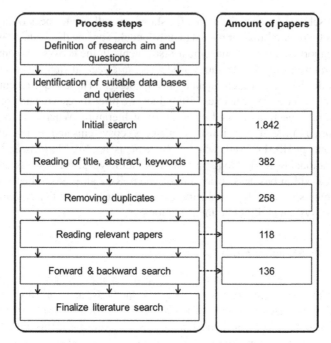

Fig. 1. Search process following Wendler [63].

duplicates were removed, leaving 258 relevant papers. For these remaining papers, we created a *content mapping matrix*, which consisted of the business ecosystem characteristics *definition, roles, phases, types, visualizations, applications,* and *examples.* Table 3 below provides a short characterization of each analytic characteristic.

Applying the content mapping matrix led to 118 relevant records, i.e., records discussing at least one of the seven characteristics. In a final process step, we applied forward and backward citation search on these records as described by Webster and Watson [62], through which we identified 18 additional records. Overall, we analyzed 136 papers in our systematic mapping study. While we made use of this data to undertake other interpretations (e.g., [14]), here we will only present results related to business ecosystem visualizations and VAS.

3.2 Conceptualizing Design Principles

Beyond our efforts to map the field of visualizations and VAS, we intended to draw conclusions on the design of VAS and their use in the ecosystem context. To this end, we carried out an interpretation of the resulting articles, looking at their suggestions for handling visual information, which permitted us to formulate *engineering requirements* for VAS. A consequent categorization of these requirements allowed us to synthesize *design principles* for VAS design. Design Principles are the principal beliefs, philosophies or guidelines that should be interpreted "to enable practitioners and researchers to create further (application software) ...in different organizational setting and environments" [36, 50, 60].

Table 3. Mapping matrix and analytic characteristics used in our mapping study.

Business ecosystem characteristic	Description of characteristic	Number of identified records
Definition	Either a new definition of business ecosystem is established, it adds to an existing definition, sums up different definitions, or com- pares existing definitions	58
Roles	The different roles ecosystem actors incorporate are described, a new descriptive metaphor is established for these roles or different roles are compared	70
Phases	The paper establishes a business ecosystem life cycle, describes at least one state of a business ecosystem, or it compares different life cycle models	29
Types	The paper describes at least one type of business ecosystem or compares multiple types	42
Visualization	The article contains at least one business ecosystem visualization, describes how a business ecosystem can be visualized, develops or uses a modelling or visualization tool	43
Application	Applications of the business ecosystem concept both in research and practice	58
Example	Paper demonstrating a specific example of a business ecosystem in a real-world context, e.g., for Walmart or Alibaba	49

While we identified design principles by studying the existing literature, we also got inspired through our own research (e.g., [25]). Our design principles' validity thus relates to—and is limited by—the cross-case cogency of these references.

We formulate our design principles in a way to delineate the boundary conditions, elements and processes that facilitate application and valuable use of a VAS. For each design principle (DP) we thus formulate those aspects that—to our interpretation—*facilitate* valuable use, i.e. using terms such as 'enable', 'ensure', 'support', 'provide', and the like.

4 Findings

4.1 The Present Spectrum of Business Ecosystems Visualizations

In our mapping study we identified 43 records that include business ecosystem visualizations. Either they use visualizations to describe a business ecosystem, or they discuss how a business ecosystem *can* be visualized. All of these records include at least one visual to depict an actual, simplified, or sample business ecosystem.

In Table 4 we provide an overview of the types of business ecosystem visualizations we identified in our literature study. We group them by their underlying explanatory objective, e.g., whether they are used to showcase geographical dispersion (A. Geographical Map), hierarchies (G.), temporal changes (B.) and others more. Table 4 also indicates the occurrence of instances counted per category. Not surprisingly, with 56 mentions, layouts that explain connections (H.), both static and as flow diagram, comprising matrix, node network, chord diagram and directed network layouts, were the largest group reported. Groupings and hierarchies (G.) constitute the second largest group of

Table 4. Types of business ecosystem visualizations identified in our literature study (adapted from [18]).

Explanatory objective*	Layout type*	Exemplary layout
A. Geographical Map (2)	*A1* Connection Map (1) *A2* Dot Map (1)	
B. Progression (time) (4)	*B1* Timeline (4)	
C. Correlation (5)	*C1* Bubble chart (2) *C2* Scatter plot (3)	
D. Ranking (5)	*D1* Bar chart (5)	
E. Listing (7)	*E1* List (7)	

(continued)

Table 4. *(continued)*

Explanatory objective*	Layout type*	Exemplary layout
F. Progression (any value) (8)	*F1* Line chart (8)	F1
G. Grouping (parts and wholes; hierarchies) (15)	*G1* Moore Framework (4) *G2* Venn diagram (2) *G3* Hyperbolic tree (1) *G4* Sunburst diagram (3) *G5* Tree map (5)	G1 G2 G3 G4 G5
H. Connection (Static) and Flow (56)	*H1* Matrix (7) *H2* Node network (28) *H3* Chord diagram (4) *H4* Directed network (17)	H1 H2 H3 H4

*The numbers in brackets indicate the instances counted per category.

layouts with 15 mentions. This indicates that the navigation within the networked relationships (presumably across different types of network-like structures) as well as the hierarchical, top-down (and vice versa) exploration of these networked structures takes significant space in the analytical use of visualizations.

4.2 Requirements and Design Principles for Visualizing Business Ecosystems

Extending on our discussion reported in Faber et al. [18], in the following section we give an overview of how we synthesized requirements and design principles for VAS in the business ecosystem context. Table 5 summarizes our suggested four design principles and 18 requirements. Our synthesis bases on three major pillars; first, the requirements *explicitly proposed* in articles included in our literature study, particularly from Basole et al. [5], Park et al. [40], Hernandez-Mendez et al. [25], Reschenhofer [47] and Basole et al. [9]; second, our interpretation of further articles from the study; and third, our

insights basing on previous research conducted in close cooperation with business partners as users of VAS in contexts of urban mobility, passenger vehicle innovation, and
publishing business ecosystems [19].

Table 5. Requirements and design principles for VAS in the business ecosystem context (based
on [18]).

Requirements for VAS ordered by Design Principles (DP)	Reference sources
DP 1: Facilitate navigation for analysis of business ecosystems	
- Top-down and bottom-up hierarchical examination of BEs; providing flexible navigation across higher-level overviews and individual details	[5]
- Supporting definition of a case-specific terminology displayed in the GUI in order to facilitate user-specific wording	[5]
- Preferring visual interaction to prompt/query-based user interfaces; providing filters to customize queries	[9, 40]
- Providing configurability for ease-of-use in GUI and model/query design	[9]
- Enable navigation through different layouts	[19, 40]
DP2: Enable flexibility in data and model adaptation	
- Defining multiple attributes for each relation	[19, 47]
- Enabling run-time modification of BE model and visualizations (layouts)	[25, 47]
- Providing role-based GUIs for different stakeholder roles	[25]
- Using web-based technologies, such as JavaScript libraries for building user interfaces	[25]
- Support integration (e.g., through APIs) of different data sources	[19]
DP3: Enable visualizations of BE models and data	
- Capturing and displaying inter-firm connectivity and composition (BE model)	[5]
- Providing multiple layouts to enable comparative perspectives on similar data and contexts	[5, 9]
- Allowing for synthesized layouts that capture higher-level summaries and link to case details	[5]
- Providing interactive features (clicking, dragging, hovering, filtering) for analysis	[19]
DP4: Provide features for analytical use	
- Supporting semi- and non-structured underlying BE data	[25]
- Capturing and displaying temporality of inter-firm connectivity and composition	[5, 9]
- Defining and displaying multiplex relations between entities	[9]
- Enable binding of data and view model, i.e., data and view model should be linked to ensure elements of the data model are visualized at any time	[19, 40]

From our interpretation, we see four groups of requirements emerging as themes that eventually lead to the formulation of four design principles (DPs). These concern requirements towards, the use of VAS to navigate BE visualizations (DP1); the adaptability of the ecosystem data and the VAS model used to create layouts (DP2); the interactive VAS features linked with the layouts (DP3); and VAS features for analytical use (DP4).

Design Principle 1 expresses the need to *"Facilitate navigation for analysis of business ecosystems"*. It captures requirements that concern navigating the complex relationship structures in order to reach a decent impression of the business ecosystem in focus. This involves also the possibility to define case-specific terminology, and to enable visual interactions with the models.

Design Principle 2, *"Enable flexibility in data and model adaptation"* concerns the ecosystem data and how the VAS uses this data to form models. Here, features such as run-time modification of BE model and visualizations, or the option to include different data sources are originating from the necessity to integrate a generally abundant amount of ecosystem data along an intensive and iterative agile modelling process [15].

Design Principle 3 calls for VAS features that *"Enable visualizations of BE models and data"*. This involves requirements on interactive VAS features linked with the layouts, e.g., provision of multiple layouts that offer interactive features for analysis like clicking, dragging, hovering, or filtering.

Design Principle 4 is to *"Provide features for analytical use"*. Both, manual visual analysis as well as automated analysis can potentially be supported by VAS, e.g., automated sensitivity analysis (as reported in [40]). Here, attention must be given to the handling of temporality, or the definition of multiplex relationships between entities.

5   Discussion

5.1   Summary of Findings of the Systematic Mapping Study

Our mapping study covered databases that contain articles holding perspectives from engineering, management and information systems. As we find layouts reappear across these fields, we believe that the found set of layouts (Table 4) provides a decent overview of the current state of play regarding VAS for business ecosystems. We also observe that the requirements for visualizing and analyzing entity distributions, relationships and their networked structures, resurface across different studies and use cases (Table 5).

Among the 17 layouts identified, *network-type visualizations* such as node network layout or directed network layout that emphasize connections as static, transitive or indicating flow, are the most frequently applied visualizations. In addition, the prevalent use of layouts like hyperbolic tree, which accentuate *how* a business ecosystem is conceptualized as hierarchy or in groupings – and *how entities are distributed* within this pattern of relationships (e.g., sunburst diagram) – indicates that VAS are indeed used as instruments that help identifying, navigating and refining relationship structures as *tailored for a given task*.

These impressions have been reinforced by our collection and interpretation of engineering requirements for VAS as they are discussed by us and other authors. We identify 18 requirements on VAS [18], which can be grouped into four design principles. From a high-level perspective, these principles span aspects of usability (DP1), adaptivity (DP2), interactivity (DP3), and analytical readiness (DP4), pointing at the roles of VAS as analytic tool, as data management system, and as management instrument for diverse stakeholders. These findings all speak to the base assumption that each instantiation of a business ecosystem visualization must involve and explicate a *unique set of characteristics* constitutive for both, the ecosystem as it is conceived, and the management task for which the VAS has been set up.

5.2 Making Business Ecosystem Visualizations Actionable: The Missing Design Principle

Particularly striking about business ecosystems' literature is the fact that it mirrors quite a variety of "types of ecosystem" and resulting from that, a diversity of relationships and characteristics that constitute a specific ecosystem conception. This circumstance is particularly important for our exploration of VAS for business ecosystems. The task of a VAS will ultimately be, to help identifying, modelling and analyzing the particular constitutive characteristics as well as those predominant relationships and interrelations that are material to fulfil a task related to managing an organization's positioning in the ecosystem, or related to overall ecosystem governance.

However, the tie-in between ecosystem visualization and the management tasks has not yet been made. Primary management tasks related to business ecosystems include the positioning of a firm in its specific ecosystem environment, and the configuration of effective business networks from the reference frame that the ecosystem conception provides. Both of these tasks base on an *exploration and understanding of the ecosystem's formation rationale*, or raison d'être. VAS in this vein need to help explicating factors that drive the evolution of the ecosystem, and that support the formation of effective business networks along value creation processes or strategies.

This latter aspect provides for a missing Design Principle, which refers to the task of building, i.e., designing and implementing, the infrastructures of business networks, or *"Facilitating business infrastructuring"*. This design principle involves supporting the process along which ecosystem stakeholders turn the *potential* that the ecosystem conception entails, into *effective* business networks.

For forming business networks, firstly, ecosystem stakeholders navigate the ecosystem with help of strategic analyses to identify promising new partnerships or business opportunities. Secondly, business network members ally to design, implement and coordinate their relationships on basis of an actionable infrastructure. Such infrastructures serve as the network's shared asset and allow for establishing performative constellations of value creating activities (as shown in [46]).

For VAS to become a material instrument in the related management tasks, will require to extend the current conception of VAS towards (a) synthesizing network configurations on basis of predefined or learned relationship patterns, as well as (b) orchestrating the set of potential and effectively arranged relationships within defined value creation processes. This latter point is also a prerequisite for the use of VAS as instrument in business ecosystem governance, because it expedites the role of VAS as mediator between platforms and their stakeholders (as exemplified in [44]).

5.3   Limitations and Future Requirements on Business Ecosystem Visualization

In this sense, the set of layouts identified in the mapping study should not be understood as a converging set of visualizations. On the contrary, we believe that in the future more sophisticated layouts will be developed that make use of larger sets of data – as well as of data changing as dynamically as do business ecosystems and their conceptions.

As to our interpretation of the set of design principles and requirements, in particular DP4 will presumably see considerable extension in future applications as it is the basis for an automated analysis of ecosystem data. Given the size and complexity of ecosystems, features for automated data gathering or machine learning-based systems that are able to identify and present data relevant to a specific user of a VAS might bring about a significant extension of applicability and usability of VAS as strategic tool for management tasks related to business ecosystems.

In addition, regarding the handling of ecosystem data, sustainable approaches for collecting ecosystem data and modelling are required. In context of smart city ecosystems for instance, the instantiation of an 'ecosystem editorial office' has been suggested that supervises data collection alongside crowd-based approaches that allow leveraging domain experts as well as citizens [16, 44]. However, how ecosystem analysis can be institutionalized has not been studied so far.

6   Conclusion

VAS for visualizing business ecosystems today provide a sound set of layouts to capture relevant network structures and relationships, as our systematic mapping study shows. The insights reported from extant studies suggest a comprehensive set of engineering requirements for VAS, which can be grouped into four design principles. Together they respond to the dynamic nature of the business ecosystem context including the criticality of handling ecosystem data, navigating and interacting with visualizations, and adapting VAS models and layouts for different stakeholders as VAS users. However, the tie-in to critical management tasks related to business ecosystems has not yet been made. More efforts are required in research and practice to enhance VAS towards management instruments, which facilitate business infrastructuring in order to turn the potential that the ecosystem conception entails into effective business networks.

References

1. Adner, R., Kapoor, R.: Value creation in innovation ecosystems: how the structure of technological interdependence affects firm performance in new technology generations. Strateg. Manage. J. **31**(3), 306–333 (2010)
2. Adner, R.: Ecosystem as structure. J. Manage. **43**(1), 39–58 (2017). https://doi.org/10.1177/0149206316678451
3. Annanperä, E., Liukkunen, K., Markkula, J.: Innovation in evolving business ecosystem: a case study of information technology-based future health and exercise service. Int. J. Innov. Technol. Manage. **12**(4), 1–19 (2015)
4. Bai, B., Guo, Z.: Dynamic complexity of mobile internet business ecosystem. In: 4th International Conference on Systems and Informatics Proceedings, Hangzhou, China, pp. 502–506. IEEE (2018)

5. Basole, R.C., Clear, T., Hu, M., Mehrotra, H., Stasko, J.: Understanding interfirm relationships in business ecosystems with interactive visualization. IEEE Trans. Vis. Comput. Graph. **19**(12), 2526–2535 (2013)
6. Basole, R.C., Hu, M., Patel, P., Stasko, J.T.: Visual analytics for converging-business-ecosystem intelligence. IEEE Comput. Graph. Appl. **32**(1), 92–96 (2012)
7. Basole, R.C., Huhtamäki, J., Still, K., Russell, M.G.: Visual decision support for business ecosystem analysis. Expert Syst. Appl. **65**, 271–282 (2016)
8. Basole, R.C., Russell, M.G., Huhtamäki, J., Rubens, N., Still, K., Park, H.: Understanding business ecosystem dynamics: a data-driven approach. ACM Trans. Manage. Inf. Syst. **6**(2), 6:1–6:32 (2015). https://doi.org/10.1145/2724730
9. Basole, R.C., Srinivasan, A., Park, H., Patel, S.: ecoxight: Discovery, exploration, and analysis of business ecosystems using interactive visualization. ACM Trans. Manage. Inf. Syst. **9**(2), 6:1–6:26 (2018)
10. Bell, S.J., Tracey, P., Heide, J.B.N.: The organization of regional clusters. Acad. Manage. Rev. **34**(4), 623–642 (2009)
11. Bosch, J.: Speed, data, and ecosystems: the future of software engineering. IEEE Softw. **33**(1), 82–88 (2016)
12. de Vasconceles Gomes, L.A., Facin, A.L.F., Salerno, M.S., Ikenami, R.K.: Unpacking the innovation ecosystem construct: Evolution, gaps and trends. Technol. Forecast. Soc. Change **138**, 30–48 (2016)
13. Evans, P.C., Basole, R.C.: Revealing the API ecosystem and enterprise strategy via visual analytics. Commun. ACM **59**(2), 26–28 (2016)
14. Faber, A., Riemhofer, M., Rehm, S.-V., Bondel, G.: A systematic mapping study on business ecosystem types. In: 25th Americas Conference on Information Systems - New Frontiers in Digital Convergence Proceedings. Association for Information Systems, Cancún, Mexico (2019)
15. Faber, A., Hernandez-Mendez, A., Rehm, S.-V., Matthes, F.: An agile framework for modeling smart city business ecosystems. In: 20th International Conference on Enterprise Information Systems Proceedings, pp. 39–50. SciTePress, Madeira, Portugal (2018). https://doi.org/10.5220/0006696400390050
16. Faber, A., Rehm, S.-V., Hernandez-Mendez, A., Matthes, F.: Collectively constructing the business ecosystem: towards crowd-based modeling for platforms and infrastructures. In: Hammoudi, S., Śmiałek, M., Camp, O., Filipe, J. (eds.) ICEIS 2018. LNBIP, vol. 363, pp. 158–172. Springer, Cham (2019). https://doi.org/10.1007/978-3-030-26169-6_8
17. Faber, A., Rehm, S.-V., Hernandez-Mendez, A., Matthes, F.: Modeling and visualizing smart city mobility business ecosystems: insights from a case study. Information **9**(11), 270 (2018). https://doi.org/10.3390/info9110270
18. Faber, A., Riemhofer, M., Huth, D., Matthes, F.: Visualizing business ecosystems: results of a systematic mapping study. In: 21th International Conference on Enterprise Information Systems Proceedings, pp. 357–364. SciTePress, Crete, Greece (2019)
19. Faber, A.: Collaborative Modeling and Visualizing of Business Ecosystems. Unpublished doctoral dissertation, Technical University of Munich, Garching, Germany (2019, forthcoming)
20. Faber, A.: Towards a visual language approach for modeling business ecosystems. In: CEUR Workshop Proceedings (2027), pp. 1–8. PoEM Doctoral Consortium, Leuven, Belgium (2017)
21. Forrest, J.E., Martin, M.J.C.: Strategic alliances between large and small research intensive organizations: experiences in the biotechnology industry. R&D Manage. **22**(1), 41–54 (1992). https://doi.org/10.1111/j.1467-9310.1992.tb00787.x

22. Fragidis, G., Koumpis, A., Tarabanis, K.: The impact of customer participation on business ecosystems. In: Camarinha-Matos, L.M., Afsarmanesh, H., Novais, P., Analide, C. (eds.) PRO-VE 2007. ITIFIP, vol. 243, pp. 399–406. Springer, Boston, MA (2007). https://doi.org/10.1007/978-0-387-73798-0_42

23. Fragidis, G., Tarabanis, K., Koumpis, A.: Conceptual and business models for customer-centric business ecosystems. In: 2007 Inaugural IEEE-IES Digital EcoSystems and Technologies Conference Proceedings, pp. 94–99. IEEE (2007)

24. Guittard, C., Schenk, E., Burger-Helmchen, T.: Crowdsourcing and the evolution of a business ecosystem. In: Garrigos-Simon, F.J., Gil-Pechuán, I., Estelles-Miguel, S. (eds.) Advances in Crowdsourcing, pp. 49–62. Springer, Cham (2015). https://doi.org/10.1007/978-3-319-18341-1_4

25. Hernandez-Mendez, A., Faber, A., Matthes, F.: Towards a data science environment for modeling business ecosystems: the connected mobility case. In: Kirikova, M., et al. (eds.) ADBIS 2017. CCIS, vol. 767, pp. 324–330. Springer, Cham (2017). https://doi.org/10.1007/978-3-319-67162-8_32

26. Huhtamaki, J., Rubens, N.: Exploring innovation ecosystems as networks: four European cases. In: 49th Hawaii International Conference on System Sciences Proceedings, pp. 4505–4514. Association for Information Systems, Hawaii (2016)

27. Iansiti, M., Levien, R.: Strategy as ecology. Harvard Bus. Rev. **82**(3), 68–78 (2004)

28. Iyer, B.R., Basole, R.C.: Visualization to understand ecosystems. Commun. ACM **59**(11), 27–30 (2016)

29. Jansen, S., Finkelstein, A., Brinkkemper, S.: A sense of community: a research agenda for software ecosystems. In: 31st International Conference on Software Engineering Proceedings, Vancouver, BC, pp. 187–190. IEEE (2009)

30. Järvi, K., Kortelainen, S.: Taking stock of empirical research on business ecosystems: a literature review. Int. J. Bus. Syst. Res. **11**(3), 215–228 (2017)

31. Kapoor, R., Agarwal, S.: Sustaining superior performance in business ecosystems: evidence from application software developers in the iOS and Android smartphone ecosystems. Organ. Sci. **28**(3), 531–551 (2017). https://doi.org/10.1287/orsc.2017.1122

32. Kapoor, R., Lee, J.M.: Coordinating and competing in ecosystems: how organizational forms shape new technology investments. Strateg. Manage. J. **34**(3), 274–296 (2013). https://doi.org/10.1002/smj.2010

33. Kitchenham, B., Budgen, D., Breretom, O.P.: Using mapping studies as the basis for further research - a participant-observer case study. Inf. Softw. Technol. **53**(6), 638–651 (2011)

34. Lozano, M.: Ecosystem for the emergence of spin-offs from the family business. Acad. Rev. Latinoam. de Administracion **30**(3), 290–311 (2017)

35. Mäkinen, S.J., Dedehayir, O.: Business ecosystem evolution and strategic considerations: a literature review. In: 18th International Conference on Engineering, Technology and Innovation Proceedings, Munich, pp. 1–10. IEEE (2012)

36. Markus, M.L., Majchrzak, A., Gasser, L.: A design theory for systems that support emergent knowledge processes. MIS Q. **26**(3), 179–212 (2002)

37. Mazhelis, O., Luoma, E., Warma, H.: Defining an internet-of-things ecosystem. In: Andreev, S., Balandin, S., Koucheryavy, Y. (eds.) NEW2AN/ruSMART -2012. LNCS, vol. 7469, pp. 1–14. Springer, Heidelberg (2012). https://doi.org/10.1007/978-3-642-32686-8_1

38. Moore, J.F.: Predators and prey: a new ecology of competition. Harvard Bus. Rev. **71**(3), 75–86 (1993)

39. Moore, J.F.: The Death of Competition: Leadership and Strategy in the Age of Business Ecosystems. Harper Business, New York (1996)

40. Park, H., Bellamy, M.A., Basole, R.C.: Visual analytics for supply network management: system design and evaluation. Decis. Support Syst. **91**, 89–102 (2016)

41. Peltoniemi, M., Vuori, E.: Business ecosystem as the new approach to complex adaptive business environments. In: eBusiness Research Forum Proceedings, pp. 267–281. e-Business Research Center, Tampere, Finland (2004)
42. Petersen, K., Feldt, R., Mujtaba, S., Mattsson, M.: Systematic mapping studies in software engineering. In: 12th International Conference on Evaluation and Assessment in Software Engineering Proceedings, pp. 68–77. BCS Learning & Development Ltd. Swindon, UK (2008)
43. Popp, K.M.: Goals of software vendors for partner ecosystems – a practitioner′s view. In: Tyrväinen, P., Jansen, S., Cusumano, M.A. (eds.) ICSOB 2010. LNBIP, vol. 51, pp. 181–186. Springer, Heidelberg (2010). https://doi.org/10.1007/978-3-642-13633-7_17
44. Rehm, S.-V., Faber, A., Goel, L.: Visualizing platform hubs of smart city mobility business ecosystems. In: 38th International Conference on Information Systems Proceedings, Association for Information Systems, South Korea (2017)
45. Rehm, S.-V., Goel, L.: Using information systems to achieve complementarity in SME innovation networks. Inf. Manage. 54(4), 438–451 (2017). https://doi.org/10.1016/j.im.2016.10.003
46. Rehm, S.-V., Goel, L., Junglas, I.: Using information systems in innovation networks: uncovering network resources. J. Assoc. Inf. Syst. 18(8), 577–604 (2017). http://aisel.aisnet.org/jais/vol18/iss8/2
47. Reschenhofer, T.: Empowering End-users to Collaboratively Analyze Evolving Complex Linked Data. Ph.D. thesis, Technical University of Munich, Munich, Germany (2017)
48. Sako, M.: Business ecosystems: how do they matter for innovation? Commun. ACM 61(4), 20–22 (2018)
49. Scaringella, L., Radziwon, A.: Innovation, entrepreneurial, knowledge, and business ecosystems: old wine in new bottles? Technol. Forecast. Soc. Change 136(September), 59–87 (2018)
50. Schacht, S., Morana, S., Maedche, A.: The evolution of design principles enabling knowledge reuse for projects: an action design research project. J. Inf. Technol. Theory Appl. 16(3), 5–36 (2015). https://aisel.aisnet.org/jitta/vol16/iss3/2
51. Tan, B., Pan, S.L., Lu, X., Huang, L.: Leveraging digital business ecosystems for enterprise agility: The tri-logic development strategy of alibaba.com. In: 30th International Conference on Information Systems, vol. 171. Association for Information Systems, Phoenix, Arizona, USA (2009)
52. Teece, D.J.: Dynamic capabilities and (digital) platform lifecycles. Adv. Strateg. Manage. 37, 211–225 (2017)
53. Tiwana, A., Konsynski, B., Bush, A.A.: Platform evolution: coevolution of platform architecture, governance, and environmental dynamics. Inf. Syst. Res. 21(4), 675–687 (2010). https://doi.org/10.1287/isre.1100.0323
54. Tiwana, A.: Platform synergy: architectural origins and competitive consequences. Inf. Syst. Res. 29(4), 829–848 (2018). https://doi.org/10.1287/isre.2017.0739
55. Toivanen, T., Mazhelis, O., Luoma, E.: Network analysis of platform ecosystems: the case of internet of things ecosystem. In: Fernandes, J.M., Machado, R.J., Wnuk, K. (eds.) ICSOB 2015. LNBIP, vol. 210, pp. 30–44. Springer, Cham (2015). https://doi.org/10.1007/978-3-319-19593-3_3
56. Valkokari, K.: Business, innovation, and knowledge ecosystems: how they differ and how to survive and thrive within them. Technol. Innov. Manage. Rev. 5, 17–24 (2015)
57. van den Berk, I.M., Jansen, S., Luinenburg, L.: Software ecosystems: a software ecosystem strategy assessment model. In: 4th European Conference on Software Architecture, pp. 127–134. ACM, New York (2010)
58. Vartak, M., Huang, S., Siddiqui, T., Madden, S., Parameswaran, A.: Towards visualization recommendation systems. ACM SIGMOD Rec. 45(4), 34–39 (2016). https://doi.org/10.1145/3092931.3092937

59. Visnjic, I., Neely, A., Cennamo, C., Visnjic, N.: Governing the city: unleashing value from the business ecosystem. Calif. Manage. Rev. **59**(1), 109–140 (2016). https://doi.org/10.1177/0008125616683955
60. Walls, J.G., Widmeyer, G.R., El Sawy, O.A.: Building an information system design theory for vigilant EIS. Inf. Syst. Res. **3**(1), 36–59 (1992)
61. Wareham, J., Fox, P.B., Cano Giner, J.L.: Technology ecosystem governance. Organ. Sci. **25**(4), 1195–1215 (2014). https://doi.org/10.1287/orsc.2014.0895
62. Webster, J., Watson, R.T.: Analyzing the past to prepare for the future: writing a literature review. MIS Q. **26**(2), xiii–xxiii (2002)
63. Wendler, R.: The maturity of maturity model research: a systematic mapping study. Inf. Softw. Technol. **54**(12), 1317–1339 (2012)
64. Zhang, Q., Wang, Y.: Struggling towards virtuous coevolution: Institutional and strategic works of Alibaba in building the Taobao e-commerce ecosystem. Asian Bus. Manage. **17**(3), 208–242 (2018)

HCI and SE: Integration Experiences Between Theory and Practice from a SE Program

Alessandra C. S. Dutra[✉] and Milene S. Silveira[✉]

School of Technology, Pontifícia Universidade Católica (PUCRS),
Porto Alegre, Rio Grande do Sul, Brazil
{alessandra.dutra,milene.silveira}@pucrs.br

Abstract. The Software Engineering education faces the challenge of engaging and qualifying professionals with competence to work in an interdisciplinary way and in teams, with flexibility to perform different roles and capable of adapting to change. This study present an experience of integration between theory and practice in a Software Engineering Program, focusing on the application of methods studied in a course from the Human-Computer Interaction (HCI) area. We discuss the lessons learned, challenges, and perspectives of change in those involved courses, bringing the students' opinions, who have highlighted, among other points, the importance of such integration to bring theory closer to their real universe of action.

Keywords: Integration of theory and practice · Interdisciplinarity · Software Engineering program · Human-Computer Interaction

1 Introduction

The Software Engineering education faces, in Brazil and world, the challenge of meeting a growing need for professionals with the ability to produce robust and quality software in a systematic and efficient manner. The characteristics of the area increasingly demand resourcefulness to work in teams and in an interdisciplinary manner, and the integration is a key aspect of our current teaching and learning process.

Integrating theory and practice based on knowledge from different courses and even from different programs is fundamental and strategic so that students can better understand not only their specific fields of study and work but also how they relate in broader research and market contexts.

In this context, we present an experience of integration between theory and practice in the Software Engineering Program from Pontifícia Universidade Católica do Rio Grande do Sul (PUCRS). This Program is associated with a Software Engineering Experiential Agency (AGES), where the students have the opportunity to practice the studied concepts and methods.

The projects developed in AGES provide many integration opportunities. In this paper we focus on the integration between AGES and an Human-Computer Interaction (HCI) course, discussing the lessons learned, challenges, perspectives, and the

© Springer Nature Switzerland AG 2020
J. Filipe et al. (Eds.): ICEIS 2019, LNBIP 378, pp. 320–333, 2020.
https://doi.org/10.1007/978-3-030-40783-4_15

importance of such integration to bring theory closer to the students real universe of action.

To better understand the scenario in which this work is inserted, the next section will address some background and related works. In Sect. 3, the implementation context of these integration experiences is presented, describing the program, the environment where the practical developments are carried out and the HCI course in question. Section 4 presents four different integration experiences encountered in the HCI course throughout the Program's implementation, followed by our final considerations about our study, supported by the references used for its construction.

2 Background and Related Work

In the following sections, we will briefly present the areas related to this work as well as some related work.

2.1 Software Engineering

Software Engineering (SE) began to be discussed as a discipline in 1968 [34] and currently is part of the curriculum of several courses such as Computer Science, Computer Engineering, Information Systems, and Automation Control Engineering. We also have specific Software Engineering courses.

Software Engineering is related with all software production aspects, from the initial stage to its maintenance, involving not only technical development processes, but also project management activities and tools, methods and theories that support its production [23]. Therefore, SE goes beyond programming code creation; it tries to discipline development and brings to software development principles, techniques and knowledge to discuss quality questions, deadlines and economic factors [35].

2.2 Software Engineering Processes

The software engineering process consists of activities for managing the creation of software, including requirement collection, analysis, design, coding, testing, and maintenance [23]. Software engineering methods are just different ways of approaching software development and delivery [23]. Considering the existing methods, Agile methods were born from the need to smooth the heavyweight plan-based methods used in large-scale software-development projects [1]. Many agile methods are available in the literature, popular approaches are Scrum [20], Rapid Application Development (RAD) [14], Feature-Driven Development (FDD) [16], and eXtreme Programming (XP) [15].

2.3 Human-Computer Interaction

The area of Human-Computer Interaction (HCI) studies the interactions and the relationships between humans and computers. According to Helander et al. [12], HCI is more than user interfaces, it is a multidisciplinary field covering many areas. In the first ten to fifteen years of its history, HCI has focused on interfaces (particularly on the possibilities and design criteria for graphical user interfaces (GUIs) using windows, icons, menus, and pointing devices (WIMPs) to create more usable systems. According to Fischer [11], HCI research objectives are concerned not just with interfaces, but with tasks, justifications, with shared understanding, and with explanations, and argumentation about actions. The new essential challenges are improving the way people use computers to work, think, communicate, learn, critique, explain, argue, debate, observe, decide, calculate, simulate, and design.

2.4 Related Work

Among the related works, we can highlight different perspectives about this integration. In a more traditional way, we find the use of techniques from one area to another, as a Web Design Usability Evaluation (Web DUE) technique that aims to allow the evaluation of low-fidelity prototypes (or mockups) during the design of the application [18]. Or the game iThink, that takes advantage of the association between "gamification" concepts and the six hats of thinking method for collecting both new requirements and feedback about existing ones and for presenting the requirement elicitation process in a form of a collaborative game [9].

Rivero et al. [19] presented an empirical study evaluating if the Design Usability Evaluation technologies are able to aid development teams in the quality improvement of mobile Web applications [24], and another work shows the investigation of the impact of Scrum adoption on customer satisfaction [8], as well as an article that proposes a technique for creating personas to support the development of mobile web applications [10].

Other published works have observed requirements such as accessibility and usability in the design and evaluation of interactive computer technologies [4–6].

Considering a more interdisciplinary point of view, in an exploratory research conducted in 2012 with the Brazilian community, both teaching-practice integration and interdisciplinarity were highlighted as challenges regarding the teaching of HCI in the country [2]. Silva [21] also emphasized this lack of integration among areas, particularly considering HCI, as a major issue in computing education.

Taking this context into account, we found several initiatives, arising from the HCI community to try to foster integration and interdisciplinarity.

Bim [3] presented an integration experience among HCI, SE, and Database courses, highlighting the potential of such integration not only for the experimentation, in practice, of the concepts from each area, but also for professors to better understand the role of each course in a systems development project.

Zaina and Alvaro [26], in turn, analyzed the perspectives of working with interdisciplinary projects and, through Project and System Development and Human-Computer Interface courses, proposed, in 2012, a model for conducting those courses that would integrate the concepts studied in both of them into a practical project with the objective of creating entrepreneurial solutions.

In another approach conducted by Silva [21], articulation and integration happened by means of conceptualizing interaction as a communication process, analogous to other fundamental activities of the software development process: requirements engineering, software design, and programming.

Furthermore, Britto [7] provided an experience report on the integration of HCI concepts and techniques in the Design Patterns and Software Engineering courses, corroborated by the research carried out with students, indicating positive indicators about the approach being used.

These initiative examples help to illustrate the community concerns regarding such important issues and how much we can work to improve this context.

3 Work Context

In the following sections, we will present some details about the Program in which the study described here is inserted, the environment in which the practical developments are carried out, and the concerned HCI course.

3.1 The Software Engineering Program

The main objective of the Software Engineering Program from Pontifícia Universidade Católica do Rio Grande do Sul (PUCRS), is to prepare professionals with solid training in Computer Science, Mathematics, and Software Production processes, specializing in the development of applications from information and communication technologies [17]. Focused primarily on software solutions aligned to business, these professionals will have in-depth knowledge of software architecture, technology, and development processes, so as to be able to produce robust, high-quality software in a systematic and efficient way. Their performance will be buoyed by a humanistic and solidary formation, according to the educational principles that guide the actions of the University.

Being innovative in its design, it was created from the context of regional and national industry, in which large software companies require this kind of professionals.

The pedagogical practices in the Software Engineering course seek to create situations similar to those found in the daily work of the future professional, seeking to create conditions for the reflection of the object of study to go beyond the pedagogical models and be elements of potential association to the reality of the job market and its challenges.

This program started in March 2015, having its first group graduating at the end of 2018.

3.2 Program the AGES - Software Engineering Experiential Agency

At the Software Engineering Experiential Agency, undergraduate students have a practical learning environment, which was designed for the following purposes [25]:

a. provide students with the experience of real project situations in an environment that focuses on learning through real projects and clients;
b. enable the interdisciplinary integration of contents from the Software Engineering Program;
c. integrate teaching, research, and extension;

d. allow contact with organizations and companies whenever this contact adds elements for the background of the alumni profile;
e. build with the students their project portfolio through the projects executed by them in the Agency.

In addition, AGES follows the academic guidelines:

- Development of skills in the Software Engineering course, particularly focused on teamwork, respecting individualities;
- Strong link with the contents of the course subjects and teachers;
- Autonomy from ongoing classes;
- Carrying out activities with predictability, but without the urgency of deadline;
- Focus on learning.

At the Agency, the practice courses are developed, being a curricular component of the program. The courses are composed of four modules: Practice in Experiential Agency I, II, III, and IV, each with 120 h (60 h in the classroom (4 credits) and 60 outside the classroom). Table 1 presents the competencies related to each module developed in the Agency, as well as the prerequisites for each module, according to the curricular matrix of the program.

As for the projects executed inside the Agency, they come from:

a. Demands from other University Units;
b. Demands from students;
c. Demands from professors;
d. Open call for project selection;
e. Demands from Companies;
f. University incentive programs to support entrepreneurship and the development of startups.

Regarding the incentive programs (item f), the Agency rewards the top performers with the execution – within the Agency– of their projects.

The Figs. 1 and 2, shows the environments of AGES and some teams working.

Fig. 1. Superior environment.

Fig. 2. Ground floor.

Table 1. Set of evaluative assignments [22].

	Related competencies	Curricular matrix requisites
I	– Programming – Unit testing – Debugging	– Object-Oriented Programming (co-requisite) – Introduction to Software Engineering (special requisite)
II	– Database Project – Requirements Analysis – Development	– Database Modeling and Design (special requisite) – Object-Oriented Programming (prerequisite)
III	– Testing and Verification – Software project – Software Architecture	– Verification and Validation II (special requisite) – Software Architecture and Design (prerequisite)
IV	– Project Management – Deepening of other competencies developed in the program – Senior project portfolio	– Software Project Management (prerequisite)

AGES has an important role in the integration of higher education course subjects, and the goal of AGES is to interact in an interdisciplinary manner with as many course subjects as possible. Within the projects developed over the semesters, we sought to work interdisciplinarity with the disciplines of IHC Fundamentals, Requirements Engineering, Database Modeling and Design, Interaction Design, Software Verification and Validation I, Software Configuration Management and Object Oriented Programming.

Integrations with disciplines can be done before or after a project has been developed. As an example, we can mention the case of the Requirements Engineering discipline, where students raised the requirements and defined the user stories that were later implemented in AGES.

Disciplines such as Software Verification and Validation I and Software Configuration Management have systematically used AGES projects to apply their contents. The IHC course used AGES projects in internal usability projects with students.

3.3 The Course

The HCI area includes two courses from the program: Fundamentals of HCI, a 4-credit mandatory course offered in the 3rd semester, and Interaction Design, a 2-credit course which is also compulsory, offered in the 4th semester. In this article, our focus is on the first course.

The course, Fundamentals of HCI, aims at introducing the HCI area, its main concepts and theories, as well as different evaluation methods on quality of use and the principles of the interaction design process.

The course has several of its topics deepened through the practical application of the methods discussed in class. In addition to various exercises and activities throughout the semester, a set of four evaluative assignments is carried out: the first three dealing with the evaluation of the quality of use of interactive systems (one with the application of collecting users' opinion, another with the application of evaluation methods by inspection, and the last one through usage observation), and the fourth on elicitation and analysis of user data, as presented in Table 2.

Table 2. Set of evaluative assignments [22].

	Focus	Used methods
T1.1	– Collecting Users' opinions	– Surveys – Interviews – Focus Groups
T1.2	– Inspection	– Heuristic Evaluation
T1.3	– Usage Observation	– Usability Evaluation – Communicability Evaluation
T2	– Elicitation and analysis of user data	– Surveys – Interviews – Focus Groups – Personas – Scenarios

The main focus of these assignments relies on real projects, especially those under development at the Agency itself. This way, students may analyze real cases, with the opportunity to interact with their stakeholders, with their project and development team, as well as with their future users. Moreover, all results obtained from the projects are forwarded to the Agency, so that they can be used as inputs for new design and development stages.

The course's first class was in 2016/1 and, in the last semesters, it was possible to analyze a good range of projects. Some of these experiences will be discussed in the next section.

4   Integration Experiences

As mentioned in the previous section, the assignments carried out at Fundamentals of HCI have been mostly applied in real cases under development in the Agency, and, in some cases, in other projects developed within the University.

To better illustrate how these experiences happen, some of these experiences of integration between the course and the Agency will be presented and discussed [22].

4.1   Contact with Stakeholder

One of the projects developed at the Agency met a demand from the University library for bibliographic records by curriculum/program's course, integrated to the consultation of existing titles in the library and allowing the generation of acquisition demands and monitoring of requests. In the previous semester, we had already met a request from the director of the library with the analysis of the library's search system. In this case, focusing on the bibliographic registration system, the focus was on the collection and representation of users' needs (T2), two moments of emphasis on students.

At first, a collective interview was held with the director of the library, who was willing to go during the course and talk to the class, to which the students had prepared themselves from what there had already been in terms of documentation on the project, creating, in small groups, questions to be asked during the interview. They were also responsible for conducting the interview and recording all obtained data.

From the data collected and analyzed, the students created personas representing the system's main users, as well as possible scenarios of interaction with the system. On the work presentation day, the director of the library attended again, discussing the obtained results with the students.

As a highlight, in this specific case, besides the real contact with the main stakeholder of the project, we mention the need of internal organization of the groups, in the definition of who would record the answers, who would ask the questions, and so on, always bearing in mind they were dealing with a professional - the Director of the library - and not a classmate.

4.2   Feedback During Sprints

Generally, feedback from HCI students to the Agency is given at the end of each semester, when the results of each group (for each assignment) are consolidated and sent to be used by the teams. In a particular semester, we were able to align the analysis of a prototype system with one of its delivery sprints and thus provide feedback during the development process.

The project in question was intended for people with visual impairments, with a system that, from the donation of voices, would help in the creation of audiobooks, to be developed by the University Publishing House.

For the assignment of the course (T1.3), students should perform a Communicability Evaluation of the current version of the system, focusing on voice donor users. After planning the evaluation, conducting user observations, and analyzing the data collected, the professor of Fundamentals of HCI and the students representing the class met with the Practice Professor at the Agency and representatives of her students to present and discuss the results obtained.

For the Fundamentals of HCI students, this was a significant opportunity to discuss the evaluation carried out directly with those who would make use of the results for project improvement. As for the Practice students, this was an opportunity to receive feedback about the work developed through an external view, and, based on such feedback, they were able to review the whole project, thus, presenting a new version already with the adjustments for the project client.

4.3 Contact with Potential Users

Getting to know your potential users is fundamental for the development of an interactive system that values the quality of use. One of the Agency's projects focused on developing a game that would help children "take care of their health without knowing they were taking care of their health", *id est*, to support disease prevention.

In order to better understand the problem and the profile of potential users of this type of game (T2), besides studying the project documentation, students researched scientific articles in qualified publications about children, games, disease prevention, among others, and also sought results from demographic research on the subject. After appropriating the subject, in small groups, they developed interview scripts to be carried out with children.

A group of 5 children (children of professors from the program) was invited to participate in one of the classes so that the students could understand this profile and, most importantly, the children's point of view, which would be crucial in an application of this genre.

The class was composed of 32 students and was divided into three large groups. The children - 3 girls and 2 boys, aged between 9 and 13 years old – were also divided into three groups (2 pairs and 1 individual), and were interviewed as a "circuit" (they went through all groups).

Besides the observation of this dynamic by the course professor, the software architect, member of the Agency's technical team, also took part in the lesson, observing the activity.

One of the activity highlights was to "break" some preconceived views students had regarding children in general (many of their "certainties" about children behavior ended up not being confirmed), proving the importance of knowing the users intended to be achieved.

4.4 Self-knowledge

As stated in the previous section, knowing your potential users is critical, but self-knowledge and self-reflection are also key steps in the teaching and learning process. In some cases, HCI students themselves were invited to participate as users, in the scope of users' opinion collection work (T1.1).

In one of the assignments, the focus was on the project of a system directly related to the Agency, to capture ideas of new projects to be executed in it. In this assignment, students, through semi-structured interviews, should collect opinions from students of the Software Engineering program.

In total (in the consolidation of answers from different groups of the class), 42 students from the program were interviewed. In addition to specific points related to the project, the students' knowledge (or not) about the Agency's objective in the Program was emphasized. Some students pointed out that they would have restrictions on sending ideas to the Agency – through the system in question- fearing plagiarism of their ideas, and others stated they expected some sort of bonus for the projects developed in it. These points, more than helping to (re)think the tool in question, help in a refinement of the presentation of the Agency and its objective, which is, as mentioned before, to provide the students with the experience of real project situations in an environment focused on learning, through the development of projects with real clients.

Another example of the students' participation as users during the period of opinion collection, focused on the same project of the game to support children in the prevention of diseases previously mentioned, but in the course that took place in the semester following that of the interview with the children. On this occasion, with a greater understanding of what the project would be (a quiz game), an activity was carried out with the application of usage logs, in which, for a week, the students should use known quiz tools daily (some of which even mentioned by the children in the previous stage), recording their interaction every day. After the recording stage, the students participated in focus groups to define main characteristics, positive and negative points, which were then returned to the game design team.

Another interesting factor worth highlighting in this Agency's project analysis is that sometimes students are in Fundamental courses and developing the Practices at the same time, and can bring feedback from the class to their teams in an immediate way, besides serving as a support point of the class for doubts about the projects as well.

4.5 Participants' Point of View

In order to comprise the students' vision regarding this integration as well, an online survey was conducted, questioning them about their opinion on the use of Agency projects as a basis for the assignments of Fundamentals of HCI. We gathered 16 answers, which, despite not being a high number, shed light on some points for discussion and reflection on the course. Respondents represent students from different semesters of the program, and even two students were attending the course when the survey was applied. Everyone had already taken at least one of the Agency's courses.

As for the experience of working with projects developed (or under development) by the Agency, the use of real projects stands out, as described by P14, "*analyzing a real project was a good experience*" (P14, student from the 4th semester), and by P15, "*I liked it, because it brings a real level of difficulty to the assignments*" (P15, student from the 4th semester). Moreover, the importance for the projects themselves was mentioned: "*It was a great idea because the contents we saw in HCI are perfectly compatible with any project developed in the Agency. This would also benefit project teams, as UX and usability issues are often overlooked by teams. It is important that people understand how important this area is in SE*" (P9, a student from the 3rd semester), and "*The dynamics worked out quite well (...). The cool thing is that many of the stories had not been implemented yet, so investigating criteria and options for using the tool via interviews and surveys made a lot of sense*" (P11, 7th semester).

The benefits for the teams were also highlighted when students were asked about the return of the results to the Agency: "*Great, because this way we can make improvements*" (P7, 7th semester), "*It helped to find no visible problems in the progress of the project*" (P14, 4th semester), and "*it helped to find errors that had gone unnoticed. Not to mention that it helped us make the interface more user-friendly*" (P15, 4th semester).

For one of the students, it was "*Indifferent, because we received feedback only in the project's finish line and we did not have time to evaluate students' suggestions. I believe that the ideal would be to follow-up sprints*" (P10, 4th semester). This is one of the challenges faces by the courses, in the sense of adjusting the calendars of both, which, as previously described, we have achieved in some semesters and have more and more tried to align (Fig. 3).

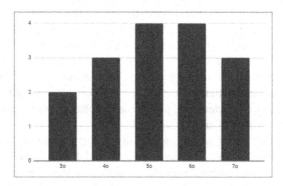

Fig. 3. Respondents' semester (3rd 4th 5th 6th 7th) [22].

Furthermore, still in relation to the return to the Agency, the concepts worked on the course as a whole, and not necessarily the analysis of some specific project, was also highlighted: "*Only in one instance did I see this bridge being made; in my second module, some students were attending the course and, with some fresher concepts in mind, brought improvements to the system*" (P7, 7th semester).

When asked about the contact with real users, the students have emphasized the importance of this point of view to better understand users' needs: "*It was important to know what the users were thinking, we have already had an idea of what the application would be like, but seeing what they thought of it was important*" (P3, 5th semester); "*I found the proposals very nice, and they emphasize the importance of the User's point of view very much, which is a matter that certainly cannot be missing in the HCI course*," (P4, 5th semester); "*Great interaction with the stakeholder to clarify doubts*" (P7, 6th semester); "*Direct involvement with the client and not with the developer, thus being a 'clearer' view of real needs*" (P13, 6th semester).

An interesting point highlighted by a student who is attending the course this semester is that it is *"unfair that only one project is involved. If this is so, only one project will always benefit, because often these things are not done within other projects due to lack of time"*. He suggests to diversify the projects in each semester, not being the same for the whole class, and *"with this, we can benefit all teams, or at least give them a chance"* (P9, 3rd semester). This suggestion was taken into account during the current semester, and the groups were able to choose the projects they would like to analyze, seeking partner teams in the Agency.

Finally, one of the students from the class of possible graduates points out that *"The more courses having a bridge with the Agency the better, because it is within the Agency that students without any market experience have their first notion of this universe, which is totally different from the academic environment"* (P16, 7th semester).

Besides the students' point of view, we also sought the software architect's vision, who is a member of the Agency's technical team and monitors the students' work:

"The Agency's integration with the courses from the Software Engineering program is very enriching for the students' learning. We have been able to achieve great results with the HCI course, as a consequence of the work that has been improving throughout the semesters of existence and development of the Agency. At the end of each semester, we were able to analyze, reflect, and adapt the teaching process for next semester.

In the case of HCI course, at the beginning of each semester, we set up a new schedule and define which Agency projects will be object of study, always with the guidance and endorsement of the responsible professor. The chosen projects may have already been finished or still in progress, depending on the status of each of the Agency's projects.

Throughout the semesters, some students came to me requesting further information on these projects, trying to better understand the decisions made. Some of the questions were, as follows:

- *Why do we use such technology?*
- *Why was a certain functionality made like that?*
- *Where did the "stakeholders" come from?*

There are also dynamics in the classroom that attracted a great deal of interest in the students. I remember one in particular, which was the interview made with children for the project whose objective was the development of a game. The children came up with incredible insights, to which the students were led to think really fast to accompany them.

I can assure the interdisciplinarity between the Agency and the IHC course has been gratifying for both the Agency and our students, and the learning outcomes are excellent."

5   Final Considerations

To Zaina and Alvaro [26], "Interdisciplinarity in undergraduate education is a practice that directly contributes to the development of competencies and skills based on the integrative vision and the constant relationship between theory and practice" [26]. Matos

[13] also highlights that "curriculum integration has been one of the education initiatives so that lessons make sense to students".

In agreement with these authors' perspectives we described one of our interdisciplinary attempts in the Software Engineering Program. Considering the presented case, the integration of HCI practices to the projects developed in AGES, each semester and each new analyzed project bring a new set of learned lessons, challenges, and perspectives for reflection and change. Students deal with schedule changes, the unavailability of users for data collection, problems with the platform used, and the challenges of have to communicate with the projects' stakeholders and to collaborate with their teammates: as what would happen in a project in the industry, the students in class needed to adapt to changes, new demands, and new scopes of work.

Our current goal is to increase integration with other courses from the program, as well as the courses from other programs, like Computer Science and Information of Systems. In this case, we have begun the interaction with the development of applications that are intended to other programs of the University, to which we have the closest stakeholders and users, favoring a quite interesting contact among areas.

References

1. Abran, A., Moore, J.W., Bourque, P., Dupuis, R., Tripp, L.L.: Guide to the Software Engineering Body Of Knowledge: 2004 Version SWEBOK. IEEE Computer Society, Washington, D.C. (2004)
2. Barbosa, S. D. J.: Pesquisa sobre Ensino de IHC no Brasil em 2012: desafios e oportunidades (Research on IHC education in Brazil in 2012: challenges and opportunities). In: WEIHC2012, III Workshop sobre Ensino de IHC. CEUR Workshop Proceedings, vol. 977, pp. 3–5 (2012). (in Portuguese)
3. Bim, S.A.: Uma experiência de integração entre as disciplinas de IHC, Engenharia de Software e Banco de Dados (An experience of integration between the disciplines of HCI, Software Engineering, and Database). In: EIHC2010, Workshop sobre Ensino de IHC (2010). (in Portuguese)
4. Borges, L.C.L.F., Filgueiras, L.V.L., Maciel, C., Pereira, V.C.: Customizing a communication device for a child with cerebral palsy using participatory design practices: contributions towards the PD4CAT method. In: XI IHC, pp. 57–66. SBC (2012)
5. Boscarioli, C., Baqueta, J.J., Salles, C.G., Colling, J.P.: Avaliação e design de interação de jogos voltados ao aprendizado de crianças surdas. In: XI IHC, pp. 25–26. SBC (2012)
6. Braz, P., Raposo, A., Souza, C.S.: Uso de design probes no design de tecnologias para terapeutas de crianças com autismo. In: XIII IHC, pp. 140–149. SBC (2014)
7. Britto, T.C.P.: Como integrar IHC em disciplinas da Especialização em Software Engineering: relato de relato de de experiência (How to integrate IHC in specialization disciplines in Software Engineering: experience report). In: WEIHC2014, V Workshop sobre Ensino de IHC, pp. 20–24. SBC (2014). (in Portuguese)
8. Cartaxo, B., Araujo, A., Barreto, A.S.: The impact of scrum on customer satisfaction: an empirical study. In: XXVII SBES, pp. 129–136. SBC (2013)
9. Fernandes, J., Duarte, D., Ribeiro, C., Farinha, C., Madeiras Pereira, J., da Silva, M.M.: iThink: a game-based approach toward improving collaboration and participation in requirement elicitation. Procedia Comput. Sci. **15**, 66–77 (2012)
10. Ferreira, B., Conte, T., Barbosa, S.D.J.: Eliciting requirements using personas and empathy map to enhance the user experience. In: XXIX SBES, pp. 80–89. SBC (2015)

11. Fischer, G.: Beyond human computer interaction: designing useful and usable computational environments. In: People and Computers VIII: Proceedings of the HCI 1993 Conference, Loughborough, England, pp. 17–31. Cambridge University Press, Cambridge (1993)
12. Helander, M.G., Landauer, T.K., Prabhu, P.V. (eds.): Handbook of Human-Computer Interaction (Second, Completely Revised ed.). Elsevier Science Ltd., Amsterdam (1997)
13. Matos, E.: Integração curricular por meio da prática de ensino interdisciplinar em IHC (Curricular integration through the practice of interdisciplinary teaching in IHC). In: WEIHC 2013, V Workshop sobre Ensino de IHC. CEUR Workshop Proceedings, pp. 25–30 (2013). (in Portuguese)
14. Martin, J.: Rapid Application Development. Macmillan Publishing Co., Inc, New York (1991)
15. Maurer, F., Martel, S.: Extreme programming. Rapid development for web-based applications. IEEE Internet Comput. **6**(1), 86–90 (2002)
16. Palmer, S.R., Felsing, M.: A Practical Guide to Feature-Driven Development. Pearson Education, London (2001)
17. PUCRS, Pontifícia Universidade Católica do RS. http://www.pucrs.br/politecnica/curso/engenharia-de-software/. Accessed June 2018
18. Rivero, L., Conte, T.: Using an empirical study to evaluate the feasibility of a new usability inspection technique for paper based prototypes of web applications. In: XXVI SBES, pp. 81–90. SBC (2012)
19. Rivero, L., Kawakami, G., Conte, T.: Using a controlled experiment to evaluate usability inspection technologies for improving the quality of mobile web applications earlier in their design. In: XXVIII SBES, pp. 161–170. SBC (2014)
20. Schwaber, K., Sutherland, J.: The Scrum Guide, vol. 12. Scrum Alliance, Westminster (2011)
21. Silva, B.: Computadores e Sociedade: uma oportunidade de ensinar conceitos básicos de IHC (Computers and society: an opportunity to teach basic IHC concepts). In: WEIHC 2014, V Workshop sobre Ensino de IIIC, pp. 15–19. SBC (2014). (in Portuguese)
22. Silveira, M., Dutra, A.: Bringing life to the classroom: engaging students through the integration of HCI in SE projects. In: ICEIS 2019, 22a International Conference on Enterprise Information System (2019)
23. Sommerville, I.: Software Engineering, 9th edn. Pearson Prentice Hall, Upper Saddle River (2010)
24. Valentim, N.M.C., Conte, T.: Improving a usability inspection technique based on quantitative and qualitative analysis. In: XXVIII SBES, pp. 171–180. SBC (2014)
25. Yamaguti, H.M., Oliveira, M.F., Trindade, A.W.C., Dutra, C.S.A.: AGES – an interdisciplinary space based on projects for software engineering learning. In: Proceedings of SBES, Fortaleza, CE, Brazil (2017). https://doi.org/10.1145/3131151.3131187. (in Portuguese)
26. Zaina, L., Alvaro, A.: IHC e Empreendedorismo: uma parceria de sucesso no ensino de desenvolvimento de software (IHC and entrepreneurship: a successful partnership in teaching software development). In: WEIHC 2014, V Workshop sobre Ensino de IHC, pp. 15–19. SBC (2014). (in Portuguese)

A Design Process Integrating Human-Data Interaction Guidelines and Semio-Participatory Design

Eliane Zambon Victorelli[1](✉)(iD), Julio Cesar Dos Reis[1](iD),
Antonio Alberto Souza Santos[2](iD), and Denis José Schiozer[2](iD)

[1] Institute of Computing, University of Campinas (UNICAMP), Campinas, Brazil
{eliane.victorelli,jreis}@ic.unicamp.br
[2] Center for Petroleum Studies, University of Campinas (UNICAMP),
Campinas, Brazil
{alberto,denis}@cepetro.unicamp.br

Abstract. Software tools that facilitate human interaction with data play a key role in the understanding of information from large masses of data. Interaction design in the domain of petroleum field exploration is a challenging task, in part because of its complex intrinsic context, and the lack of methodological framework to support design activities. The use of guidelines builds on the expertise of design specialists, but does not leverage the knowledge of the various stakeholders in the problem. In this article, we advocate a more socially comprehensive approach to the design of Human-Data Interaction (HDI) applications, articulating design guidelines with artifacts and methods from Organizational Semiotics and Participatory Design. Our investigation defines a process for the design of visual data analysis tools and conducts a case study in the context of petroleum production strategy with the participation of key stakeholders. We propose practices for each step of our design process. Adapted participatory practices combined with design guidelines were used to clarify the problem, design the solution, and evaluate the prototype. Participants showed satisfaction with the employed design practices and the outcomes.

Keywords: Human-Data Interaction · Participatory design · Visual analytics

1 Introduction

Individuals in different contexts and domains have been overwhelmed by huge and complex data collections that have to be analyzed. Often, they need to discover patterns or outliers to make decisions in crisis situations, or to monitor data sets in real time [18]. This has justified large investments in the automation of data analysis. Although progress has been made in many data analyses situations, fully automated analysis methods only work for well-defined and well-understood problems [17]. There must be a model of the underlying problem to

© Springer Nature Switzerland AG 2020
J. Filipe et al. (Eds.): ICEIS 2019, LNBIP 378, pp. 334–360, 2020.
https://doi.org/10.1007/978-3-030-40783-4_16

support the automated analysis. Even if a model exists, then the results of the automated analyses have to be understood and interpreted by analysts. Therefore, for several situations, it is necessary to combine computational methods of data analysis with good interaction techniques to enable more effective data analyses.

The scenario of increasing production, collection and use of data, with or without the support of automated analysis, has motivated discussions on ways of enabling data interaction and understanding. This gave rise to the term Human-Data Interaction (HDI) as a reference to "human manipulation, analysis and sensemaking of large, unstructured and complex datasets" [11]. The term HDI was also used to denote the "problem of providing customized, context sensitive, and understandable information from large data sets" [7]. The HDI area has investigated how people interact with data in a manner analogous to the Human-Computer Interaction (HCI) area in relation to people and computers [15,19,45]. One of the key aspects addressed by the HDI area is the legibility of data [27]. It states the necessity of understanding data in order to make sense of it.

Intuitive and efficient user interactions are fundamental components which must be supported by any system that upholds data analysis and favors data legibility. This integration of interaction techniques into both visual representations and automatic analysis methods supports the human-information discourse [18]. Visual analysis (VA), the science of analytical reasoning facilitated by interactive visual interfaces, consists of interactive and iterative dialogue between human and computer. The interactive analysis process refers to a sequence of actions by the user and responses by the computer motivated by analytical questions [40,41].

While several VA tools have been developed to support exploration of large amounts of data, they do not yet sufficiently support a good experience of interaction in some complex exploratory analysis scenarios [4]. There is a shortage of support environments where domain specialist and machine work in harmonious and smooth interaction for data exploration. An important step towards achieving the desired results from data analysis is providing a process to facilitate the construction of VA tools that offer a good HDI experience.

In this context, several studies argue that designing VA tools based on guidelines is an important approach to help materialize the knowledge and experience gained by experts in the field [1,13,31,34,36,46]. However, in our view, this approach alone does not favor people affected by the system to participate in the process of building the system.

In this context, the following research questions are raised about design approaches:

– How to facilitate the identification of stakeholders and clarification of their vision on issues that could be resolved through visual data analysis?
– Can the adequate involvement of stakeholders in the VA design process be valuable to improve HDI?
– Is it feasible to design interactions in VA tools combining guidelines and participatory approaches?

In this article, we propose a design process for HDI in decisions supported by VA that combines the advantages of using participatory practices and guidelines. We investigate ways to enable in-depth interactions with data analysis tools, highlighting the importance of considering stakeholders' contributions during the entire development cycle. The novelty of our study is the combination of two complementary approaches.

The successful realization of such processes involves a number of elements that need to work in coordination: (i) identifying key stakeholders and ensuring effective participation during design and selection of solutions; (ii) search for a set of guidelines to consider as a starting point; (iii) selection of relevant guidelines adequate for the context; (iv) finding the best way to unravel, explain and facilitate understanding of the chosen guidelines to the involved participants; (v) definition of practices and adequate flow for the conduction of design activities to ensure their harmonious flow to produce the desired results. This work refers to an original extension of our previous HDI design process proposal [43]. We added the following to the initial proposal: (i) further results of the semio-participatory process, especially about the problem clarification step; (ii) improved process design description; (iii) case study details.

While developing and refining our approach for design process, we were significantly informed by a series of practices carried out in UNISIM at the Center for Petroleum Studies (CEPETRO), University of Campinas. The UNISIM group develops methodologies and tools to support an integrated decision analysis in the development and management of petroleum fields [35]. In this study, the design situation involved a VA tool that supports analytical needs for optimization of oil production strategy. This provided the opportunity to conduct the necessary design workshops for evaluating our proposal.

The methodology initiates with the problem clarification meetings. We rely on the practices and artifacts of Organizational Semiotics [24,39] and Participatory Design [29] to conduct elicitation activities. Storyboard Prototyping and BrainDraw techniques supported the design stage. The results of the design were materialized in a functional prototype and evaluated using conceived practices: participatory HDI design guidelines evaluation and adapted Thinking-aloud. The practices of design and evaluation were performed in an iterative manner. Finally, a questionnaire was answered by the involved participants.

The key contributions of this investigation include: (i) the definition of a design process tailored for HDI design describing the conceived steps to allow future reuse and replication of the dynamics; (ii) The requirements gathering from a case study in a data intensive environment related to oil reservoir management where the process was applied; and (iii) A low fidelity prototype for a VA tool that supports an analysis scenario selected from the case study requirements.

The remainder of this article is organized as follows: Sect. 2 presents the related work. Theoretical and methodological background are shown in Sect. 3. Section 4 reports the proposed process, detailing practices and outcomes involved in each step of the process. Whereas Sect. 5 presents an assessment of the process and discusses the findings and lessons learned, Sect. 6 presents our final considerations and directions for future research.

2   Related Work

The more common alternative approaches to our proposal are purely participatory processes or purely based on guidelines. This section provides a literature analysis by discussing similar alternative studies and their limitations related to our addressed research problem.

The semio-participatory approach for design of interactive systems has been explored in literature. Existing studies have focused on the principles and artifacts of participatory design and Organizational Semiotics to seek design solutions for diversified problems such as: Interactive Digital TV application [6], digital learning scenarios [14], social software [32] or search engines in Social Network Services [10]. The design problems dealt in these studies were unrelated to Visual Analysis and most of them do not mention design guidelines.

The use of principles and guidelines for interaction design in visual analysis applications has been approached in a few investigations. They show how to best design interaction by offering recommendations. A set of guidelines for fluid interaction is presented with the aim of transforming the visual analysis into an efficient and enjoyable experience while helping the user remain within the flow [12]. The author does not address how to incorporate the guidelines into the design process and also does not relate design guidelines to participatory practices.

The proposal for design data practices presented by Churchill [8] attempted to demystify the "genius designer" whose instincts and intuition lead to great design decisions. The work states the need of taking a proactive and critical stance to design, develop, or evaluate products that incorporate capture, storage and data analysis. It lists practical actions to take, but does not propose a design process for tools that deal with data.

A process to describe the context in which the visualization operates was originally proposed by Van Wijk [42]. This process admits being evaluated and measured in terms of efficiency or knowledge gained. There are discussions and evolutions of this process describing the integration of visual and automatic data analysis methods in context of the visual analytics process [17,18]. In short, an initial representation and adequate interactions can be chosen after applying different statistical and mathematical techniques. Then, the process begins a loop in which the user can gain knowledge on the data driving the system towards more adequate analytical techniques. By interacting with the visualization, the user gains a better understanding of his own visualization, specifies different visualizations that helps him/her confirm or reject hypotheses constructed in previous iterations.

The process of visual analytics presented [42] deals with the interactions involved in construction, parameterization and refinement of visualization. The process for developing specific visualization applications or tools is not addressed.

This scenario assumes that the user is an integral part of the process and has the mastery of technology to act in all phases therein. Often, these are called human-in-the-loop process. Our proposal is to include relevant stakeholders in the design process, even those that would normally be excluded from specific phases of process (*e.g.* Specification or Initial Analysis) because they do not master the technology and cannot specify and update views without the support of a context-specific application.

Leman *et al.* [22] studied typical data visualizations which result from linear pipelines that start by characterizing data and end by displaying the data. The goal was to provide users with a natural means to adjust the displays to support good HDI. This method supports a dynamic process for defining visualizations in which users can learn from visualizations and visualizations adjust to the expert's judgement. This proposal differs from ours, mainly because it is a method for the execution time and not a process for the design and development time.

A review of Nielsen's heuristic evaluation method based on participatory concerns including users (work-domain experts) as inspectors was proposed by Muller *et al.* [29]. The authors extended Nielsen's original heuristic set with several process-oriented heuristics. Their evaluation method can help to guide iterative design processes. The online community was the target of a study that combined participatory methods for design with heuristic evaluation, applied iteratively [33]. A specific set of heuristic sociability was added to the Nielsen's heuristics. The set of sociability guidelines was refined by iteratively testing it on online communities. The feedback from the online communities feedback enabled the elaboration of new items for the test and the refinement of the heuristics.

The studies conducted by Muller *et al.* [29] and Preece *et al.* [33] proposed guideline evaluation practices combined with participatory methods similar to the practices proposed in our work. However, the authors dealt with specific extensions of the Nielsen set of heuristics. They do not address HDI and VA issues or propose a design process. These facts highlight the innovation of our proposal for a design process which combines participatory design and HDI guidelines.

3   Theoretical and Methodological Background

Subsection 3.1 introduces design guidelines; Subsect. 3.2 presents the approach of semio-participatory design; and Subsect. 3.3 describes evaluation techniques.

3.1   Guidelines

Design guidelines are recommendations a designer can follow to enhance the interactive properties of the system [9]. Based on their experience gained from various projects, some design experts compile recommendations that can help other designers predict the consequences of their design decisions. Using these recommendations enables less experienced professionals to leverage the expertise of the most experienced to improve their design. One example of a guideline is the information density guideline, which suggests "to provide only necessary and immediately usable data; do not overload your views with irrelevant data" [34].

These design recommendations can be classified according to the level of authority and generality. The authority indicates if the rule is a suggestion or if it must be followed in the design. The generality can be understood as the diversity of design situations in which a usability rule can be applied [9]. Some recommendations apply to any type of project. Recommendations of this type are usually called heuristics. Guidelines are recommendations that apply to a set of projects, to a class of products or systems. In addition, there are specific recommendations for a particular project or product referenced as patterns [9, 25].

In this work, we use the term 'guideline' to discuss design recommendation made by experts and that can be used in the design of other systems in a comprehensive manner, without distinguishing the level of generality or authority. We adopt guidelines as an approach to bring specialists' knowledge to assist in the identification of points for redesign, which favors HDI. Our investigation combines specific recommendations collected from HDI literature to a set of guidelines brought from Visualization and Human-Computer Interaction areas. Our set of heuristics includes, for example, those of Nielsen that refer to general guidelines applicable to all user interfaces [30].

3.2 Semio-Participatory Design

In our view, the use of guidelines should not exclude people's contribution to the design and evaluation of interactive technology. Participatory Design is a democratic design methodology which emphasizes the active involvement of all people who are affected by the project. Participatory Design values the expertise that comes from experience and argues that all actors have important perspectives and can be involved in proposing solutions to different challenges [28]. It is a design approach where professionals with more experience in design methods work together with people with less experience. People from different backgrounds, professions, interests and roles within the workplace are involved in a design process or joint creation.

In Participatory Design for software tools, users must be actively involved throughout the software life cycle. Participatory practices are group activities led by the designer. Muller *et al.* [29] defined a set of 61 participatory practices for various stages of the design process. These practices includes:

- The Storyboard Prototyping practice involves users and other individuals to evaluate and use a prototype that exists only as a series of images, a storyboard. This type of prototype is faster and cheaper to create when compared to programming. Therefore, it is faster to evaluate design iterations [29].
- The BrainDraw practice is a graphical round-robin brainstorming for rapidly creating interface designs. Each participant draws an initial design and passes it on to the next participants for completion [29].

– The Thinking Aloud practice proposes that a participant interacts with a prototype to complete a pre-defined task and describes what he/she is thinking [23].

Our approach explores Organizational Semiotics (OS) artifacts. OS helps in the understanding of the context in which the technical system is inserted and the main forces that direct or indirectly act on the situations [24,39]. It studies the effective use of information in business context and assumes that people achieve organized behavior through the communication and interpretation of signs by others, individually and in groups. OS investigates the organization at different levels of formalization - informal, formal, and technical.

We adopted a semio-participatory approach which articulates the principles and practices of the Participatory Design with OS [3,21]. It includes shared knowledge and mutual commitment to establish communication during the design process. The term 'semio-participatory' is used to refer to the application of principles of participatory design with the support of artefacts from the OS for conducting the workshops. Various artefacts are proposed to mediate this communication and facilitate creative and collaborative design engagement into semio-participatory workshops. They facilitate the interaction and communication of a group with diversified profiles [3].

Semio-participatory workshops are the engine of the model. They move the design process through the different levels of formalization throughout the design life cycle. In the beginning of the design process, the conduction of specific participatory practices helps generate the following artefacts:

– Stakeholder Identification Diagram (SID) [24] refers to a layered structure that facilitates the identification of the involved parties (stakeholders) in a process of new technology conception and introduction. The stakeholders are organized in the following categories: (i) Operation, (ii) Contribution: Actors and Responsible people—contribute directly to the situation or its solution or are directly affected by it; (iii) Source: Clients and Suppliers - use the solution or provide data or are a source of information in the situation or solution; (iv) Market: Partners and Competitors—involved with market aspects related to the design situation; (v) Community: Bystander and Legislator—community representatives in the social context.
– Evaluation Framework (EF) [2] supports the articulation of problems and the initial search for solutions. It informs about specific issues from stakeholders and ideas or solutions envisaged that have potential impact in the design. The evaluation framework extends the stakeholder's identification diagram by considering issues and solutions to the problems for each stakeholder.
– Semiotic Framework (SF) [38] is an artifact from OS that supports the identification and organization of requirements according to six different communication levels. The first are related to technological issues (the physical, empirics, and syntactics), and the others concern the aspects of human information functions (semantics, pragmatics, and social world).

In our work, we explored a semio-participatory approach to guide the conducted workshops, taking advantage of people's participation, starting with conception and elicitation activities (*cf.* Subsect. 4.1).

3.3   Evaluation Techniques

We investigated which evaluation techniques are appropriated for our HDI design process. The evaluation of systems that make use of visual representations is an very complex task. Different from a common user interface, a VA system must be evaluated, not only in terms of the interface, but also for the information that it manages. There are several approaches for this kind of evaluation. Some are based on expert evaluation whereas others involve final user assessment. The VA evaluation methodology can be subdivided: analytical evaluations and empirical evaluations [26].

The analytical type of evaluation is carried out by experts who verify whether a certain system is compliant with a series of heuristics or guidelines. Empirical evaluation methods make use of functioning prototypes of systems and involve the final users. In our participatory approach, it is important to count on stakeholders contribution in the evaluation stage. Therefore, in addition to analytical assessments based on guidelines, we conduct empirical assessments.

One of the usability test techniques known as Thinking-aloud [23] consists in asking users to think aloud about what they are doing while using the system. The expectation is that their thoughts show how users interpret each interface item.

Another set of evaluation techniques relies on asking the users about the interface. Query techniques can be useful in eliciting details on users' view of a system. They can be explored in evaluation with the advantage of obtaining users' viewpoint directly and may reveal issues that have not been considered by the designers. Interviews and questionnaires are the main types of this technique [9].

The techniques mentioned here are not enough to support our study because our approach involves evaluating guidelines by stakeholders that are not design specialists. We need practices that combine some aspects of analytical evaluations with empirical evaluations. Therefore, we propose adaptations to the evaluation practices to engage stakeholders while we aggregate the knowledge and experience acquired by experts through the use of guidelines.

4   Design Process for Human-Data Interaction by Combining Guidelines with Semio-Participatory Techniques

We propose a design process for HDI design which combines guidelines with semio-participatory practices. Our proposal was based on the process originally developed by Victorelli *et al.* [43]. Figure 1 presents the defined flow that drives the main phases and the artifacts that are used and produced in each one.

The proposed process includes four main phases. It starts with problem clarification. Then the design phase itself is performed. After the design phase, pre-evaluation tasks are required. Finally, the evaluation occurs. Each phase consists of several activities, detailed in the following Subsects. 4.1, 4.2, 4.3, and 4.4.

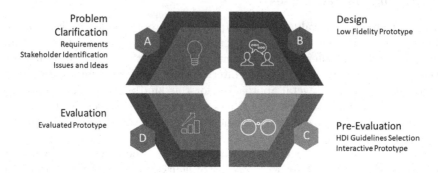

Fig. 1. Process for HDI design combining guidelines with participatory design approaches. The details for Problem Clarification are shown in Fig. 2; further information of the design phase is presented in Fig. 4; Fig. 6 presents the pre-evaluation details and Fig. 7 presents the evaluation.

The proposed process was exercised in the activities conducted at UNISIM. One challenge addressed by UNISIM consists in the investigation of technologies for selection of deterministic optimal production strategy in oil fields [35]. The process of defining the production strategy involves great effort in analysing voluminous data. Specific steps involved in the methodology used may benefit from different types of visualization: production curves in the time, dispersion charts, standard deviation and risk curves for information associated with the strategies.

UNISIM team has developed SEPIA, a VA tool to facilitate the decision analysis process. This case study emphasized the design of the SEPIA environment. The objective was to refine the HDI for some analyses performed during the production strategy selection process.

The participants collaborated in different activities proposed for problem clarification, requirement elicitation, designing as well as creation and refinement of prototypes for the application and its evaluation. The activities of this study were conducted from June to December, 2018 and involved 2 Computer Science researchers and 6–8 participants playing different roles at UNISIM. The application required 7 meetings and workshops of 3 h each, on average. Thus, the entire process was conducted in roughly 21 h of session with 6 participants on average. In addition, a similar effort was made to prepare the presentations and practices for each meeting.

We present the results below for each step. In subsequent sections, we explain the details of each phase of the design process. Additionally, we report the results of the case study obtained in the referred process step.

4.1   Problem Clarification Activities

The process begin with the identification of the stakeholders, followed by investigating their problems and issues and discovering ideas and solutions they see to their problems. This is a semio-participatory approach since, in the clarification phase we draw on Organizational Semiotics [24,39] to understand the problem and how it affects the various stakeholders and the activities are carried out in a participatory manner. Figure 2 presents the clarification activities.

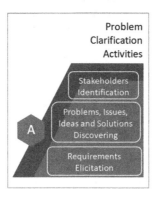

Fig. 2. Detailed activities for clarification phase of the HDI process.

In our proposal, stakeholders are largely involved. They provide and validate information throughout the process and ideally are directly involved in the elaboration of OS artifacts. Occasionally, some stakeholders are not accessible to be directly involved in all meetings. Generally, the time available to meet with experts, for example, is limited. In these cases, it is necessary to adopt strategies to optimize the process by gathering information during business briefing meetings. Artifacts can be completed at a later time based on the information provided by the stakeholders and, whenever necessary, the information and understanding obtained must be confirmed.

Stakeholders' Identification. Initially, it is necessary to identify the stakeholders, understand their concepts, terms and values regarding the design problem [24]. All stakeholders involved must be identified and value discovery activities need to take their interest into account [24].

Stakeholder Identification Diagram (SID) is the supporting artefact for this stage in semio-participatory workshops. It helps thinking beyond traditional participants and focusing attention on different levels of engagement, involving the ones who may direct or indirectly influence or be influenced by the problem being discussed and the solution under design [3].

We created an initial list of stakeholders directly involved with the SEPIA in the context of CEPETRO. There were many stakeholders potentially involved with the SEPIA tool and its support regarding definition of the oil exploration strategy. Initially, the identified stakeholders were the developers, designers, development project manager. Figure 3 presents the diagram with the results of the conducted stakeholder identification activities.

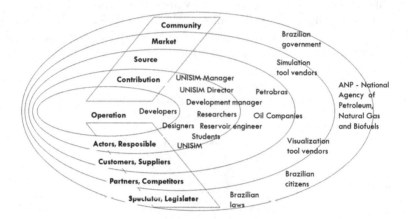

Fig. 3. Stakeholders identified in the clarification phase distributed in different layers of SID.

This initial group of stakeholders was positioned in the inner layers of the stakeholder identification diagram. For example, "Developers", the person that specifies, develops and maintains the SEPIA tool was inserted in the operation layer of stakeholder identification diagram; "Designers" were inserted between the operation and contribution layers. UNISIM and the development project manager, that lead tool development projects, conducting and managing persons involved with software engineering, figured in the contribution layer because they are responsible for the production of the tool. Still in the contribution layer, are the "Engineers" and "Researchers", involved in engineering studies of oil and gas reservoirs, which are very important stakeholders because they are real users of the SEPIA tool. In some cases, they need to codify their own visualizations for their daily activities.

The use of the stakeholder identification diagram enabled the discovery of other relevant stakeholders related with SEPIA. For example, the "Students" who are master's degree students, are involved with researches in petroleum production strategies and use SEPIA tool to support their activities. Technical project managers, who lead research projects, conducting and managing research teams composed of researchers, PhD and Master's students, who are SEPIA users, were also identified during the SID detailing activities.

In the market layer we identified CMG[1], a reservoir simulation software developer, and other tools vendors. In the community layer we inserted the Brazilian regulation agency responsible for the activities that integrate the oil and natural

---

[1] https://www.cmgl.ca/software.

gas and biofuel industries in Brazil, the ANP[2]. Brazilian government, Brazilian citizens and Brazilian laws were also identified as stakeholders due to their importance in the context of the application being developed. After this activity, different stakeholders began to participate in the workshops. They participate very actively during the clarification, design and evaluation workshops.

Problems, Issues, Ideas and Solutions. From the overview obtained with SID, it is important to know the problems and issues as well as the ideas and solutions related to each stakeholder. They can have different perspectives about the subject. The evaluation framework is the artefact used to support this part of the process [3].

We conducted meetings to learn about the main issues and the vision stakeholders had regarding the use of visualization tools in the context of defining oil exploration strategy. The developers, for example, were interested in understanding the way researchers work using the available tools. The developers were also concerned about the technical feasibility of requirements and their impact on the existing tool.

Most issues were found in the contribution layer. The issues of the researchers regarding the visualization tool included conducting their studies quickly and accurately. Some of the main problems emphasized during the activity were the large time involved in data preparation tasks. Researchers were concerned with the difficulties in managing and comparing results due to the large volume of data.

It was not possible to directly involve market stakeholders because they are professionals with low availability and it would be difficult to involve them in a research project. Nevertheless, some participants who knew representatives of this layer well were able to inform their requirements to some extent. Some aspects of the community layer were worked through the citizen's view and knowledge of the legislation of the participants of the other layers.

Requirement Elicitation. We explored the six aspects of the Semiotic Framework [24,37] to obtain the requirements elicitation. In our case study, the specialists made several presentations related to underlying domain concepts so the designers and developers could understand the complex domain of strategies for petroleum exploration. Additionally, to deepen this understanding, a number of individual interviews were conducted. Table 2 presents a selection of the requirements proposed for the SEPIA application gathered in this phase, organized according to the Semiotic Framework (SF) artifact.

It was not possible to address some of the requirements currently proposed due to resource or time limitations. Thus, they were not in the scope of the first version of the prototype by the participants. For example: "Support for geocoded data in map views" and "Interactivity between charts and maps" was not considered because the participants decided that some tests still needed to be performed with the technology platform that would support these requirements. The participants prioritized some requirements resulting from these practices.

---

[2] http://www.anp.gov.br.

Table 1. EF: Examples of problems and issues, ideas and solutions identified during the participatory practices.

Stakeholder	Problems and issues	Ideas and solutions
Operation	Understand the real need of users Technical feasibility of requirements and their impact in the existing tool	Meetings to detail specific scenario and steps often used by engineers Prototype construction integrated with the existing tool
Contribution	Extensive time involved in data preparation activities Difficulty managing and comparing results due to large data volume Flexibility in the tool to perform in-depth studies without having to do programming Facilitate and guarantee the quality of the analysis and decision making activities Meet the user's need and ensure quality development	Define solutions that would facilitate comparisons between the results obtained from the various simulations Support guided or semi-automated functionality for standard user activities that enhance productivity and accelerate training for new team members Allow tool configuration for advanced users
Source	Identify viability and interest of oil field exploration by the company	Develop application according to accepted methodologies for strategy definition Use of publicly available current data
Market	Meet customer needs with different process types	Develop process-configurable software
Community	Brazilian oil reserves must be exploited profitably and sustainably	Observe and respect existing laws and regulations

The comparison between the results of simulations for the production strategy was the requirement selected as the scope to be exercised in the design activities and for construction of interactive prototype (Table 2).

After a number of simulations, it is necessary to perform comparisons to verify the differences in relation to the return of investment and oil volume produced. This is done based on the changes made from one simulation to another. Participants used bar chart visualizations to compare strategy results.

Techniques Used in the Clarification Activities. Several types of activities and techniques can be promoted to allow the scope delimitation for the design project. We proposed the use of techniques such as presentations, group dynamics, interviews, document analysis. In this context, Laddering interview is especially useful, as a type of interview approach that can be carried out with users to understand participants' views and personal values [5]. Discussion begins with concrete aspects and evolves to more abstract level and the topic of conversation evolves naturally. This in-depth interview technique is based on repeating the question: "Why is this important to you?"

We conducted 4 individual interviews with an average duration of one and a half hours based in laddering techniques with the SEPIA users. The users were encouraged to speak about their daily activities, their issues, problems, and possible solutions.

Table 2. SF: Examples of requirements identified in the participatory practice.

Layer	Requirements
Social world	Considering the diversity of users at CEPETRO and Oil and Gas Companies Develop solutions to maximize the return of investment in the field
Pragmatics	Develop applications that motivate users by helping them improve their performance
Semantics	Show application functionality in context appropriate for use Ensure that all possible application functionality are accessible, if necessary Support for visualizations and semiautomatic features or that guide users in activities that are not of interest to their study Support strategy comparison Interactivity between charts and maps Allow user to view and work at a higher level of abstraction of the various datasets that are in files
Syntactics	Separate and make the concepts of production strategy, reservoir model and economic scenario visible in SEPIA Support for geocoded data in map views
Empirics	Develop multi-platform applications that run on clusters, desktops, tablets and mobile devices
Physical world	Develop an application that can process large volumes of data in the shortest time possible

The results of the interviews revealed that one important issue was the execution of several attempts to optimize the strategies and the comparison of the results. Comparisons between the results obtained from the simulation runs were interfered by the time, data volume and number of files involved in these attempts. One user, *e.g.*, often had to perform several simulations by slightly varying the position of a specific well that was part of a particular production strategy. As already mentioned, the support for the comparison between strategies was chosen as the central requirement to be addressed in the design of the prototype, and to evaluate the execution of the process proposed in this investigation.

4.2 Design Activities

The issues, problems, ideas and solutions as well the requirements identified during problem clarification activities are the source for the design activities. In some situations, design may involve people from different hierarchical positions. Specific stakeholders may, even unintentionally, have a disproportionate influence on the design decisions. In the participatory design philosophy, this situation must be avoided through mechanisms that seek to balance the forces. Involving and encouraging the effective participation of all stakeholders in the design activities is primordial. Participants of all hierarchical levels should offer their contributions during participatory design workshops. Techniques such as Storyboard Prototyping and BrainDraw can facilitate the engagement. The main activities of design phase were supported by these techniques (*cf.* Fig. 4).

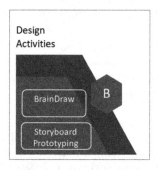

Fig. 4. Detailed activities for design phase of the HDI process.

Storyboard Prototyping. The functionality under design and the various steps involved in its execution need to be well explored. An interaction scenario must be properly defined and tasks performed in the scope of the activity should be well delineated. This definition helps in the understanding of the scenario by all those involved in the design process. Sometimes a verbal or written description is sufficient. However, if the problem involves participants with different profiles, it may be necessary to adopt visual techniques to promote a complete understanding.

In our approach, all stakeholders should be encouraged to contribute to Storyboard Prototyping. A description based on the storyboard can help in the pre-visualization of a digital interface that might support some task. It uses a sequence of stages where each stage shows a moment in time, *e.g.*, an interface state. It visually tells a story. It is useful for participants to interpret how each interface proposal fits into the design problem. After reaching a consensus about the flow, the solution supporting each interface state can be designed.

In our case study, the first participatory design activity was conducted in a meeting with the goal of consolidating the needs reported by users during the interviews. It was necessary to agree on the scope for the following activities.

The optimization of the production strategy, mentioned earlier, requires the performance of many simulations, with some variations among them. After some simulations, it is necessary to perform comparisons to verify the differences in relation to the return of investment and oil volume produced. This is carried out based on the changes made from one simulation to another. Participants used bar chart visualizations to compare strategy results.

SEPIA does not have specific functionalities to support this scenario. In the design phase of this case study, we cover how to evolve HDI in SEPIA to support comparisons between the results of different production strategies. Our proposed design process was applied to this scenario.

A storyboard was conceived as an annotated state transition diagram and illustrated with visual interface prototypes to support the discussion of the execution flow of two current use cases of comparisons. The flow presented by the storyboard was evolved as the design activities progressed. The technique was useful during the entire process to build an agreement concerning the execution flow under discussion.

Figure 5 shows the resulting storyboard. Initially, the user chooses the simulations to compare by selecting sets of models that make up the simulations (*cf.* interfaces 1 and 2 of Fig. 5). Then, the user chooses the chart type and other visualization parameters (*cf.* interface 3 of Fig. 5) and the system displays a dashboard with the specified visualizations (*cf.* interfaces 4 of Fig. 5). Finally, it is possible to save the dashboard and its visualizations. (*cf.* interfaces 5 of Fig. 5).

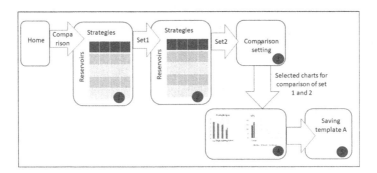

Fig. 5. Storyboard showing the execution flow agreed in participatory design activity (source: [43]).

BrainDraw. It is the technique used to materialize ideas and proposals into low-fidelity interface prototypes for digital applications. In our process, each interface state identified in the storyboard may be the target of a BrainDraw session.

During this activity, all participants are arranged in a circle. Each participant draws its initial idea for the interface that would support the defined task using a sheet of paper and pen. After a predetermined short period of time, the drawing is passed to the next participant who completes it. The exchange of drawings is repeated until each participant received his/her original drawing back. Then, each participant presents his/her proposal to others and the group must agree on a consolidated solution to be adopted.

In our case study, after reaching consensus for the first version of the storyboard, it was possible to identify the goal of each interface involved in the process. BrainDraw sessions were guided by the flow and states defined in the Storyboard Prototyping practice. We performed two BrainDraw sessions, one for each relevant state identified in the storyboard.

In the BrainDraw sessions, each participant was given one minute to draw the screen to achieve the desired goal following the previously detailed procedure for the activity. On average, the BrainDraws were elaborated by six participants and the drawing phase lasted roughly 30 min. This procedure generated several alternatives ideas for each interface. Each idea was presented by the participant who initially proposed the design solution. After the team discussed the ideas, a consolidated interface screen was defined. This process took another 30 to 60 min. In general, the consolidated drawing was a mixture of ideas from several participants.

4.3   Pre-evaluation Activities

In our proposal, the group creates a low fidelity prototype during design activities, without design guideline orientation. The guidelines are introduced in the evaluation phase. The evaluation of the prototype requires certain preparation activities (*cf.* item C of Fig. 1) to allow navigation with the prototype as well as selecting and explaining the guidelines.

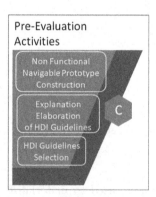

Fig. 6. Detailed activities for pre-evaluation phase of the HDI process.

Construction of a Non-functional Navigable Prototype. We consider it necessary for the prototype to be navigable and facilitate the evaluation of interaction with data. Based on the low fidelity prototypes and the agreed storyboard, a designer can build a navigable prototype.

The low-fidelity paper prototypes obtained in the BrainDraw workshops and the storyboard were transformed into navigable medium-fidelity prototypes using the Marvel[3] tool. A navigable prototype was very useful during the Thinking-aloud activities and helped raise many issues and suggestions.

Selection of HDI Guidelines and Elaboration of Explanation. Designers should define which sets of guidelines are relevant for use in the prototype evaluation. Given the nature and complexity of the problem for facilitating the HDI for VA application, we draw upon previous studies [31] with a compiled set of VA and HCI guidelines and heuristics [1,13,34,36,46]. We also considered a set of recommendations found in the HDI article review [45]. In this work, we call the set that resulted from this merge as the initial set of HDI design guidelines. If there is any set of guidelines for the application domain or standards used by the target organization, these should also be included in the initial set.

In our case study, the designers selected which guidelines from the initial set were related to the scope of the prototype that matter in the context. It was then necessary to find ways to unravel, explain and facilitate understanding of those chosen guidelines to help participants comprehend them and decide on their use. We used examples from different contexts. This turned out to be a good way of explaining the guidelines.

The HDI guidelines found in the literature consisted of high-level recommendations. We detailed the content and adapted them to the scope of the prototype. Examples of guidelines used in this study are: (i) "Consider all stages of the data life-cycle and the relevant stakeholders" [16]; (ii) Provide visual or textual indicators about relevance, usability and quality of search results, such as relevance indicator supported by automatically computed metrics or user-generated reviews and annotations [20].

There was not any known set of guidelines for visualizations in the oil production domain to the best of our knowledge. We included a specific guideline about colors adopted at UNISIM into the set. There is a color standard to differentiate the representation of activities according to the stage of the methodology in which it is executed. One color is used for activities related to reservoir modeling and construction, another for reduction of scenarios (data assimilation) a third color represents long-term production optimization (prediction) and a fourth color represents sort-term production optimization activities for the future.

4.4   Evaluation Activities

The navigable prototype and the selected guidelines support the evaluation activities and enable decisions to improve and refine the prototype. We proposed a participatory approach for the activities of the evaluation phase. All identified points in the evaluation phase need to be organized in a priority order, according to the participants' view, to be treated in a redesign cycle.

---

[3] https://marvelapp.com/.

It is essential to evaluate to which extent users think the prototype might help them accomplish their tasks and how the prototype can be improved. For this stage, we proposed two new participatory evaluation practices: "Participatory Thinking-aloud Evaluation" and "Participatory HDI Design Guidelines Evaluation". These new practices should be associated to a User Evaluation (*cf.* Fig. 7).

Fig. 7. Detailed activities for evaluation phase of the HDI process.

Participatory Thinking-Aloud Evaluation. Our proposed dynamics is an adaptation from the original Thinking-Aloud method [6,23]. A participant is invited to interact with the navigable prototype to complete a use case, conducting a pre-defined task, previously explained to the group. In our proposal, during the interaction, the entire group is stimulated to report their thoughts and impressions about the prototype. All participants in the workshop speak aloud while one participant interacts with the prototype. This activity enables moderators to understand the impression that a prototype caused.

The Thinking-aloud activity was undertaken in groups of five to six people. In the first session, only the designer handled the prototype, because other participants did not want to do it. In the second time, the prototype was more familiar to them, and one of the participants volunteered to navigate in the prototype.

The sessions were long because all the participants contributed extensively. These lasted one and a half hour on average and were very productive to refine the ideas for the redesign of the prototype. Sometimes the expressed thoughts led to low impact modifications such as changing the location of an interface component, *e.g.*, the position of action buttons. However, we could also identify an opportunity of improvement concerning the interaction approach that would demand a high impact change in the flow of execution.

Participatory HDI Design Guidelines Evaluation. We note that the participants should, in the beginning of the design process, propose alternatives freely over worrying about guidelines. In this sense, they can think of creative ways to solve the problem without being biased to adopt a recommendation.

Thus, in each round of the process, the guideline usage starts after the elaboration and consensus of the design activities.

For each guideline, participants are introduced to the recommendation of design with an explanation and previously prepared examples of applications. After the explanation, participants should discuss about how the guideline could be adopted in the prototype, the advantages and the disadvantages and impacts of their adoption. They need to decide if the guideline will be adopted. Finally, a subset of the discussed guidelines which are potentially useful and the associated ideas for redesign can be generated by this activity.

We recommend first performing the Thinking-aloud and then the HDI design guidelines evaluation so participants have the status of the prototype in mind to relate it with the guidelines. Depending on the issues found during the participatory evaluation activities, participants elaborate a list of problems and suggestions for improving the application in a redesign phase.

At this point, the team has the opportunity to decide if they are going to make a redesign activity to adjust the prototype to identified issues. Depending on the group's decision, it may be necessary to return to the Storyboard and BrainDraw sessions or other previous activities. This cycle can be repeated more than once until participants feel that the prototype design is appropriate for their needs.

In our study, the selected guidelines were exposed to the group so they could decide whether changes suggested by the guidelines could benefit the prototype. In general, each selected guideline was explained and discussed at a given time. During the consolidation of the proposal for the visualization interface (*cf.* item 4 of Fig. 5), the participants liked an idea different from the approach currently used in SEPIA. Despite this, they were uncomfortable with the shift in paradigm at the first moment. The following HDI guidelines supported the choice:

– "Shneiderman mantra" [36]: *overview first, zoom and filter, than details on demand.*
– "Information density" [34]: provide only immediately usable data; do not overload views with irrelevant data.
– "Filter the uninteresting" [36]: allow users to control display content and quickly focus on interests by eliminating unwanted items.

Currently in SEPIA, in situations similar to those under design, all graphs of all the wells would be generated and displayed simultaneously, providing an overview of the data. However, it may overload the user's view with irrelevant data and hamper the selection of view with data of the desired well. Considering the prototyped interfaces, only one well graphic view would be shown in each frame with a widget control to quickly focus on the given well and eliminating graphics from other wells. This approach appears to reduce the information density, but eliminates the overview of data that was familiar to users.

After the presentation of the guidelines, the participants considered that the overview guaranteed by the more traditional approach did not provide relevant information to the analysis situation under design. Considering the entire data life-cycle, the overview was necessary only at the beginning of the process. Additionally, users would not like to have to undertake complex activities unnecessarily. Supported by the analyses of the guidelines in the context of the interface under discussion, participants were able to approve the innovative design option more comfortably. The new solution involved the use of coordinated views. This aspect required a redesign cycle [44] based on the design process proposed in this study.

User Evaluation. When the design of the prototype is mature, an user evaluation based in the Query Technique [9] is conducted for all participants asking them about the results directly. This is applied by interview or questionnaire.

In the final stage of this study, the participants were invited to answer a questionnaire and one open question evaluating the resulting prototype from previous activities. The evaluation used a Likert scale from 0 to 3 in which the respondents specified their appraisal of the generated prototype. Notes 2 and 3 were considered positive. Five people answered the questionnaire (all of them had participated in the design and evaluation activities).

The questions attempted to identify users' evaluation of the prototype in general, and specifically, regarding the adequacy of interfaces design, interaction flow and meeting general users' needs. Table 3 presents results for each question, in which Aver. Grade is the average grade for all respondents, %Positive represents the percentage of participants with grades greater than or equal to 2 and %Max. Grade is the percentage of participants whose grades are equal to 3. The overall evaluation was considered positive for 100.0% of the participants and 66.7% of them rated at the maximum grade. The adequacy of the execution flow was the only item that did not achieve 100% of positive reviews. The adequacy of consolidated design to meet the stakeholders' needs was rated with the highest grades.

5   Assessment and Discussion

After the conclusion of design and evaluation activities, all participants were invited to evaluate the process through a questionnaire and an open question. The scale and the criteria to consider a positive opinion was the same used for the prototype evaluation. Five participants answered the questionnaire. Table 4 presents the overall view of the results of the evaluation. The overall evaluation of the process was considered positive for 100.0% of the participants and 33.3% rated them at the maximum grade. For the questions about specific issues regarding the various activities of the process, the item with the worst grade was regarding the time involved, achieving only 40% of positive opinion and 0% of maximum grade. The best aspect considered by the participants was the adequacy of practices used for the objectives with 100% of positive opinion and maximum grade.

Table 3. Prototype evaluation (source [43]).

Question	Aver. Grade	% Positive	% Max. Grade
What is your overall evaluation of the results generated by the workshops	2.5	100.0	66.7
Is the consolidated design suitable for the proposed screens?	2.5	100.0	66.7
Is the flow of the proposed interaction suitable for the comparison functionality?	2.5	75.0	66.7
Does the comparison functionality as prototyped suit your needs as a user?	2.63	100.0	66.7
Does the comparison functionality as prototyped meet the needs of most users?	2.63	100.0	66.7

Table 4. Process evaluation (source [43]).

Question	Aver. Grade	% Positive	% Max. Grade
What is your overall evaluation of the workshops you attended?	2.3	100.0	33.3
What is your opinion about the time involved in the workshops?	1.4	40.0	0.0
Did you feel comfortable expressing your opinions?	2.8	100.0	75.0
Were the practices used in the workshops adequate for the objectives?	3.0	100.0	100.0
Did the activities allow the reconciliation of different points of view?	2.4	100.0	25.0
Did the meetings allow the creation of shared understanding of the problem addressed?	2.2	80.0	25.0
Did the BrainDraw activity help bring about new design solutions?	2.6	100.0	75.0
Was the navigable prototype useful for understanding the solutions being discussed?	2.8	100.0	75.0
Was Thinking-aloud useful for prototype evaluation?	2.8	100.0	75.0
Was the presentation of design guidelines sufficient to understand the recommendation?	2.0	80.0	25.0

We proposed combining the advantages of using guidelines and participatory practices in a design process for HDI in decisions supported by VA. The participatory evaluation practices helped us understand if the generated prototype made sense for stakeholders. We verified to what extent users think the prototype might help them and in what points the prototype can be improved. The evaluation practices also sought to understand relevant aspects about the suitability of the process.

Our achieved results indicate that both the proposed process and the product generated by it (the prototype) had a good acceptance. However, some points of improvement were evidenced by user's feedback. Two main issues found were about the duration of the meetings and understanding of the guidelines.

One of the challenges to ensuring the effective participation of key stakeholders is the time and effort required to participate during the process as a whole. In our case study, many meetings were necessary for understanding, delimiting the scope, designing and approving the solution. The process proved to be somewhat onerous in relation to the number of meetings and their duration. The time spent in meetings and workshops, as detailed in Sect. 4, was perceived by the participants as time consuming. In our case study, extensive time was spent clarifying the problem. We realized that such time spent was directly related to the complexity of the business domain and it is not due to the process used.

One of the consequences generated by the duration of the activities was the inability to guarantee the participation of all experts in all meetings. The strategy used to minimize the effort required was to alternate meetings with and without final users, or at a high level with focus on the domain understanding and low level with focus on practical aspects of the tool.

The time involved in the activities should be considered to enable further applicability of the process. Some participants suggested ways to speed up the meeting with stricter control of the meeting agenda. However, care must be taken that stricter control does not inhibit the participation and creativity of all.

Regarding the moment of the application of guidelines, both the use of guidelines at design or evaluation activities offer their advantages and challenges. In the scenario of this investigation, we had a wide range of potentially useful guidelines. It would not be possible to restrict the number of guidelines to be addressed if we did not have a prototype depicting the participants' initial ideas. If the guidelines were used in the beginning of the design, it would be difficult and time consuming to train the participants in all the guidelines. On the other hand, the guidelines-based evaluation conducted by the design experts would require much effort to train the participants in the application domain, due to the complexity of the subject. Teaching the design guidelines to the participants was challenging, but the training of design specialists on the subjects of oil production strategies domain would be even harder.

Therefore, it would not be possible to include several design specialists in the evaluation process. We involved only two design specialists and prioritized the participation of users in the evaluation phase. More specifically, we found that conducting a participatory evaluation, based on guidelines, after the design phase, enabled the reduction of the number of relevant guidelines that needed to be addressed in the training. It also proved to be advantageous in terms of training effort and the process was viable with good results.

The ease or difficulty for obtaining consensus in the decisions is an interesting point to consider in a participatory process. In a context in which a single participant suggested altering one proposal made individually by another, consensus would probably not be so easy. However, in the process carried out, both the initial ideas and the proposals for change in the prototype came from various participants. The ideas were discussed as soon as they arose. The acceptance of the changes was facilitated, and the entire group adopted solutions in consensus.

Finally, during the participatory practices, the constructive nature of the process allowed us to observe how shared understanding about the problem domain was obtained, different viewpoints were conciliated, different proposals were consolidated, and the application was created. The discussions were fruitful and led to the materialization of the proposed solutions.

In this sense, we found that, although sometimes costly in the design time, it is achievable to take advantages of participatory approaches to design VA tools. In addition, stakeholder involvement in the VA design process can help improve HDI. Advances in HDI design reduce the likelihood of rework after solution development, thus offsetting the additional efforts made with participatory practices.

This investigation demonstrated that the adequate involvement of stakeholders in the VA design process is valuable to improve HDI. Considering the participants' positive assessment of the process and practice, we understand that OS artifacts and participatory design practices have proven to be an effective way to facilitate stakeholder identification, understanding of their needs and identification of the requirements for visual analysis tools. We understand that the success of the clarification step is paramount to ensure a good HDI in the final product. In addition, our findings revealed the feasibility of combining the advantages of designing visualizations and VA tools, based on guidelines and participatory approaches.

As future steps, we plan to identify a small, well-delineated scope so that it is feasible to involve multiple design specialists and conduct a guideline evaluation involving several design specialists. We also seek to investigate other ways to facilitate the understanding of the guidelines. We intend to explore examples from other domains and examples adopted in other visualization tools for the petroleum production strategy domain.

6   Conclusion

VA application design requires a comprehensive and contextual analysis so that the tool makes sense and is effectively used by the various profiles involved in the analysis. In the domain of petroleum fields exploration, participatory design of VA tools is an activity not yet incorporated into its development chain. Therefore, practices are necessary for supporting the collective understanding of the needs involved in the analysis. They must favor the design of applications that make sense to users and that are appropriate for development capacity.

In this paper, we proposed a design process to improve HDI in VA that combines the advantages of both data visualization guidelines and participatory practices. We presented participatory practices with artifacts adapted from Organizational Semiotics to understand a situated context at different levels of abstraction and from different viewpoints to clarify the problem for the construction of a VA tool used in the decision on the oil production strategy. Participatory practices combined with guidelines have been proposed to facilitate application design and evaluation.

Our obtained results indicated users positive evaluation of the prototype generated by the process. Participants demonstrated satisfaction with the practices used and comfort to express their ideas. Our proposal presented good potential for applications in the design of VA solutions involving HDI in high complexity domains. In future work, we plan to investigate how to measure the HDI improvement in addition to test the process in other HDI domains involving a larger number of participants with broader, non-specialized profiles.

Acknowledgments. We thank the support from Petrobras and Energi Simulation inside of the R&D of ANP. We appreciate the involvement of the Research Group of Simulations and Management of Petroleum Reservoirs (UNISIM-UNICAMP) at CEPETRO and Institute of Computing at UNICAMP. This work was supported by the São Paulo Research Foundation (FAPESP) (grant #2017/02325-5)(The opinions expressed in here are not necessarily shared by the financial support agency.)

References

1. Amar, R., Stasko, J.: A knowledge task-based framework for design and evaluation of information visualizations. In: IEEE Symposium on Information Visualization, pp. 143–149 (2004)
2. Baranauskas, M.C.C., Schimiguel, J., Simoni, C.A.C., Medeiros, C.B.: Guiding the process of requirements elicitation with a semiotic-based approach - a case study. In: 11th International Conference on Human-Computer Interaction, pp. 100–111 (2005)
3. Baranauskas, M.C.C., Martins, M.C., Valente, J.A.: Codesign de Redes Digitais: tecnologia e educação a serviço da inclusão social. Penso Editora (2013)
4. Behrisch, M., et al.: Commercial visual analytics systems-advances in the big data analytics field. IEEE Trans. Vis. Comput. Graph. **25**, 1–20 (2018)
5. Bourne, H., Jenkins, M.: Eliciting managers' personal values: an adaptation of the laddering interview method. Organ. Res. Methods **8**(4), 410–428 (2005)
6. Buchdid, S.B., Pereira, R., Baranauskas, M.C.C.: Playing cards and drawing with patterns - situated and participatory practices for designing iDTV applications. In: Proceedings of the 16th International Conference on Enterprise Information Systems (2014)
7. Cafaro, F.: Using embodied allegories to design gesture suites for human-data interaction. In: Proceedings of the 2012 ACM Conference on Ubiquitous Computing, pp. 560–563. ACM (2012)

8. Churchill, E.F.: Designing data practices. Interactions **23**(5), 20–21 (2016)
9. Dix, A., Finlay, J., Abowd, G.D., Beale, R.: Human-Computer Interaction, 3rd edn. Pearson Prentice-Hall, London (2004)
10. Dos Reis, J.C., Bonacin, R., Baranauskas, M.C.C.: Search informed by a semiotic approach in social network services. In: NOTERE 2010 - 10th Annual International Conference on New Technologies of Distributed Systems, pp. 321–326 (2010)
11. Elmqvist, N.: Embodied human-data interaction. In: ACM CHI 2011 Workshop Embodied Interaction: Theory and Practice in HCI, pp. 104–107 (2011)
12. Elmqvist, N., Moere, A.V., Jetter, H.C., Cernea, D., Reiterer, H., Jankun-Kelly, T.J.: Fluid interaction for information visualization. Inf. Vis. **10**(4), 327–340 (2011)
13. Freitas, C.M.D.S., Luzzardi, P.R.G., Cava, R.A., Winckler, M.A.A., Pimenta, M.S., Nedel, L.P.: Evaluating usability of information visualization techniques. In: Proceedings of 5th Symposium on Human Factors in Computer Systems (IHC 2002), pp. 40–51 (2002)
14. Hayashi, E.C., Baranauskas, M.C.C.: Affectibility in educational technologies: a socio-technical perspective for design. J. Educ. Technol. Soc. **16**(1), 57–68 (2013)
15. Holzinger, A.: Extravaganza tutorial on hot ideas for interactive knowledge discovery and data mining in biomedical informatics. In: Ślezak, D., Tan, A.-H., Peters, J.F., Schwabe, L. (eds.) BIH 2014. LNCS (LNAI), vol. 8609, pp. 502–515. Springer, Cham (2014). https://doi.org/10.1007/978-3-319-09891-3_46
16. Hornung, H., Pereira, R., Baranauskas, M.C.C., Liu, K.: Challenges for human-data interaction – a semiotic perspective. In: Kurosu, M. (ed.) HCI 2015. LNCS, vol. 9169, pp. 37–48. Springer, Cham (2015). https://doi.org/10.1007/978-3-319-20901-2_4
17. Keim, D., Andrienko, G., Fekete, J.D., Carsten, G., Kohlhammer, J., Melançon, G.: Visual Analytics: Definition, Process, and Challenges. Information Visualization - Human-Centered Issues and Perspectives, pp. 154–175 (2008)
18. Kerren, A., Schreiber, F.: Toward the role of interaction in visual analytics. In: Proceedings of the 2012 Winter Simulation Conference (2012)
19. Knight, S., Anderson, T.D.: Action-oriented, accountable, and inter(active) learning analytics for learners. CEUR Workshop Proc. **1596**, 47–51 (2016)
20. Koesten, L.M., Kacprzak, E., Tennison, J.F., Simperl, E.: The trials and tribulations of working with structured data:-a study on information seeking behaviour. In: Proceedings of the 2017 CHI Conference on Human Factors in Computing Systems, pp. 1277–1289. ACM (2017)
21. Kuhn, S., Muller, M.: Participatory design. Commun. ACM **36**(6), 24–29 (1993)
22. Leman, S.C., House, L., Maiti, D., Endert, A., North, C.: Visual to parametric interaction (V2PI). PLoS ONE **8**(3), e50474 (2013)
23. Lewis, C.: Using the 'thinking-aloud' method in cognitive interface design. Research Report RC9265, IBM TJ Watson Research Center (1982)
24. Liu, K.: Semiotics in Information Systems Engineering. Cambridge University Press, Cambridge (2008)
25. Martins Netto, O.A.: Heurísticas e guidelines para apresentação de hiperdocumentos multimídia na Web. Ph.D. thesis, Universidade de São Paulo (2002)
26. Mazza, R.: Introduction to Information Visualization. Springer, London (2009). https://doi.org/10.1007/978-1-84800-219-7
27. Mortier, R., Haddadi, H., Henderson, T., McAuley, D., Crowcroft, J.: Human-data interaction: the human face of the data-driven society. SSRN Electron. J. (2014). https://papers.ssrn.com/sol3/papers.cfm?abstract_id=2508051
28. Muller, M., Kuhn, S.: Participatory design. Commun. ACM **36**(6), 24–29 (1993)

29. Muller, M.J., Matheson, L., Page, C., Gallup, R.: Participatory heuristic evaluation. Interactions **5**(5), 13–18 (1998)
30. Nielsen, J.: Usability inspection methods. In: Conference Companion on Human Factors in Computing Systems, pp. 413–414. ACM (1994)
31. de Oliveira, M.R.: Adaptação da Avaliação Heurística para Uso em Visualização de Informação. Master thesis, Universidade Estadual de Campinas (2017)
32. Pereira, R., de Miranda, L.C., Baranauskas, M.C.C., Piccolo, L.S.G., Almeida, L.D.A., Dos Reis, J.C.: Interaction design of social software: clarifying requirements through a culturally aware artifact. In: International Conference on Information Society (i-Society 2011), pp. 293–298. IEEE (2011)
33. Preece, J., Abras, C., Krichmar, D.M.: Designing and evaluating online communities: research speaks to emerging practice. Int. J. Web Based Communities **1**(1), 2 (2004)
34. Scapin, D.L., Bastien, J.M.: Ergonomic criteria for evaluating the ergonomic quality of interactive systems. Behav. Inf. Technol. **16**(4–5), 220–231 (1997)
35. Schiozer, D.J., Santos, A.A.S., Santos, S., Hohendorff Filho, J.: Model-Based Decision Analysis Applied to Petroleum Field Development and Management. Oil —& Gas Science and Technology - Rev. IFP (2019)
36. Shneiderman, B.: The eyes have it: a task by. In: Proceedings of IEEE Symposium on Visual Languages (1996)
37. Stamper, R.: Information in Business and Administrative Systems. Wiley, New York (1973)
38. Stamper, R.: Signs, information, norms and systems. In: Signs of Work: Semiosis and Information Processing in Organisations, pp. 349–397 (1996)
39. Stamper, R., Liu, K., Hafkamp, M., Ades, Y.: Understanding the roles of signs and norms in organizations-a semiotic approach to information systems design. Behav. Inf. Technol. **19**(1), 15–27 (2000)
40. Thomas, J., Cook, K.: Illuminating the path: the research and development agenda for visual analytics. IEEE Computer Society, p. 184 (2005)
41. Turkay, C., Kaya, E., Balcisoy, S., Hauser, H.: Designing progressive and interactive analytics processes for high-dimensional data analysis. IEEE Trans. Vis. Comput. Graph. **23**(1), 131–140 (2017)
42. Van Wijk, J.J.: The value of visualization. In: IEEE Visualization, pp. 79–86 (2005)
43. Victorelli, E., Dos Reis, J.C., Santos, A.A.S., Schiozer, D.J.: Design process for human-data interaction: Combining guidelines with semio-participatory techniques. In: Proceedings of the 21st International Conference on Enterprise Information Systems - Volume 2: ICEIS, pp. 410–421. INSTICC, SciTePress (2019)
44. Victorelli, E.Z., Dos Reis, J.C., Santos, A.A.S., Schiozer, D.J.: Participatory evaluation of human-data interaction design guidelines. In: Lamas, D., Loizides, F., Nacke, L., Petrie, H., Winckler, M., Zaphiris, P. (eds.) INTERACT 2019. LNCS, vol. 11746, pp. 475–494. Springer, Cham (2019). https://doi.org/10.1007/978-3-030-29381-9_30
45. Victorelli, E.Z., Dos Reis, J.C., Hornung, H., Prado, A.B.: Understanding human-data interaction: Literature review and recommendations for design (preprint). Int. J. Hum.-Comput. Stud. **134**, 13–32 (2020)
46. Zuk, T., Carpendale, S.: Theoretical analysis of uncertainty visualizations. In: Proceedings of SPIE - The International Society for Optical Engineering (2006)

Semantic Concept Recommendation for Continuously Evolving Knowledge Graphs

André Pomp[✉], Vadim Kraus, Lucian Poth, and Tobias Meisen

Chair of Technologies and Management of Digital Transformation,
University of Wuppertal, 42119 Wuppertal, Germany
pomp@uni-wuppertal.de
http://www.tmdt.uni-wuppertal.de

Abstract. With the digitalization of many industrial processes and the increasing interconnection of devices, the number of data sources and associated data sets is constantly increasing. Due to the heterogeneity of these large amounts of data sources, finding, accessing and understanding them is a major challenge for data consumers who want to work with the data. In order to make these data sources searchable and understandable, the paradigms of Ontology-Based Data Access (OBDA) or Ontology-Based Data Integration (OBDI) are used today. An important part of these paradigms is the creation of a mapping, such as a semantic model, between a previously defined ontology and the existing data sources. Although there are already many approaches that automate the creation of this mapping by using data-driven or data-structure-driven approaches, none of them focuses on the fact that the underlying ontology evolves over time. However, this is essential in today's age of large amounts of data and ever-growing number of data sources.

In this paper, we propose an approach that allows the recommendation of semantic concepts for data attributes based on a constantly evolving knowledge graph. The approach allows the knowledge graph to learn data-driven representations for any concept that is available in the knowledge graph and that is already mapped to at least one data attribute. Instead of supporting a single method for recommending semantic concepts, we design the approach to be able to learn multiple data representatives per semantic concept, with each representative being trained on a different method, such as machine learning classifiers, rules, or statistical methods. In this way, for example, we are able to distinguish between different data types and data distributions. In order to evaluate our approach, we have trained it on several different publicly available data sets. In comparison to existing approaches, our evaluation shows that the accuracy of the recommendation improves through the use of our flexible and dedicated classification approach.

Keywords: Semantic model · Knowledge graph · Ontologies ·
Machine learning · ESKAPE · Semantic recommendation · Semantic
labeling · Semantic data platform

ⓒ Springer Nature Switzerland AG 2020
J. Filipe et al. (Eds.): ICEIS 2019, LNBIP 378, pp. 361–385, 2020.
https://doi.org/10.1007/978-3-030-40783-4_17

1   Introduction

The increasing digitalization in enterprises leads to an increasing amount of generated data. In order to exploit the potential of machine learning approaches and realize modern adaptive manufacturing, enterprises are beginning to collect and store these data sets. With an increasing number of sensors and applications within a production facility, such modern adaptive manufacturing will result in improved quality management, as goods in the production line will be inspected much faster, easier and more reliably [7].

An established approach, which is often used for the integration of heterogeneous structured and unstructured data and which is advantageous for the application of schema-on-read methods, is the so-called data lake. While this storage approach has the advantage that one does not need a predefined data schema, it also suffers from the drawback that this flexibility leads to the data lake quickly becoming a data swamp. While data lakes allow both grown systems from the brownfield and existing data sinks to be integrated, the possible resulting swamps of data then make it impossible for data scientists to find, understand and process the data sets they need for their daily work. This especially leads to an increased time-to-analytics, which is a key indicator that refers to the total time that elapses between the collection of the data and the time of analysis by the data scientist [14]. In order to solve these issues, different solutions exist. For instance, Terrizzano et al. [19] propose to use a curated data lake where the data does not need to be fully transformed and cleansed before integration, but has a data manager for annotating the data with meta-information to improve the processing steps and make the data valuable. Other solutions rely on applying the paradigms of Ontology-Based Data Access (OBDA) or Ontology-Based Data Integration (OBDI). Therefore, enterprises define knowledge bases in the form of ontologies, business glossaries or knowledge graphs. Subsequently, these knowledge bases are used to establish a mapping between the different data attributes of the data sets that are stored in the data lake and the concepts or terms stored in the knowledge base. This task is often referred to as semantic labeling, semantic modeling or semantic typing.

Since industrial data sets might cover hundreds or thousands of different data attributes and knowledge bases, such as ontologies might get quite large as well, the manual creation of these mappings is a cumbersome task that is very time consuming and requires a lot of domain knowledge. Thus, there already exist various approaches that automate the mapping process by applying different strategies. For instance, data-structure-driven approaches like the one of Paulus et al. [8] focus on recommending semantic concepts by identifying the overall best possible match between concepts and data labels. For that, Paulus et al. [8] use external knowledge databases, like WordNet and BabelNet.

Although Paulus et al. [8] achieve very good results on data sets that have conventional data labels, there always exist cases where data labels are cryptic and do not match any concept within the available knowledge bases. For instance, this happens if the data labels were auto-generated by a database schema generation process. To support the mapping process also in these cases, concepts can be recommended based on a deep analysis of the data instead of the labels. In order to recommend semantic concepts based on data, recent approaches apply different machine learning classifiers and approaches. The most promising approaches in here currently rely on neural networks and multi-class classification. Unfortunately, these approaches have an essential disadvantage. As soon as the underlying knowledge base changes, e.g., by adding or removing a semantic concept, the complete approach has to be re-trained. With an increasing number of concepts and especially data sets within an industrial data lake, this approach is not scalable in practice, especially if the corresponding knowledge bases changes frequently, such as every day.

Thus, in this paper, which is an extended version of our paper [15], we propose an approach that allows the recommendation of semantic concepts for data attributes based on a constantly evolving knowledge graph. For this reason, we are developing a data-driven recommendation approach based on the knowledge graph of the semantic data platform ESKAPE [12] as this platform already provides a model for a continuously evolving knowledge base. Our approach allows to learn different data representations, called *data representatives*, for concepts and is able to use those learned representations to recommend concepts. Instead of learning just one data representative per concept, our approach allows to learn several different representatives per concept. This enables us, for instance, to also cover concepts where the data have different *Data Classes*, such as numerical and textual data values. Since different data classes also have different requirements, we exploit in our work which data-driven approaches, called *classification approaches*, are suitable for different data classes and how those approaches can be used to learn the data representation of semantic concepts. As potential classification approaches, we consider different machine learning methods, a rule-based approach as well as a statistical method. In general, we expect multiple recommendation strategies to achieve different accuracies based on the data class in which a set of values is grouped. In order to analyze the accuracy of our data-driven recommendation approach, we have semantically modeled real data sets and evaluated the quality of the semantic concept recommendation under the conditions of the different data classes.

In summary, this paper provides the following contributions compared to the current state of the art:

1. We provide an incrementally learning approach that makes it possible to learn semantic concept representations for dynamic knowledge bases. This means that the approach needs not to be re-trained on all available data sets if the underlying knowledge base changes or new data are added.
2. We provide an extension for the knowledge graph model proposed by [12] so that we are able to equip knowledge graphs with data representations.
3. We provide an approach that is capable of learning multiple data representatives and classification approaches for a single semantic concept.
4. We provide a more detailed identification of different types of data classes.
5. We show in our evaluation that the performance of the different classification approaches for the identified data classes is comparable with those reached by current state of the art systems.

In comparison to our previous paper [15], this paper provides the following extensions:

1. The evaluation of an additional machine learning classification approach. In addition to the previously used Support Vector Machines (SVMs), we now additionally evaluated the accuracy of Autoencoders.
2. An approach for automatically identifying the data classes.
3. An algorithm for combining the results of the developed data-driven recommendation with the recommendations made by the framework of Paulus et al. [8].

The rest of this paper is organized as follows: Sect. 2 motivates the need to develop a recommendation approach that uses data instances and can handle knowledge bases that are extended at run-time. Afterwards, Sect. 3 discusses the related work and Sect. 4 presents the results of the data classes, which we identified when reviewing real-world data sets. Based on these classes, we present the implementation of our approach and the classification approaches in Sect. 5. In Sect. 6, we subsequently present the evaluation of our approach before we finally conclude with a summary and a short outlook in Sect. 7.

2   Motivating Example

In this section, we present a motivating example that illustrates the need to develop an approach that supports the user in creating semantic models by providing recommendations based not only on data labels but also on data values, and that is capable of dealing with a constantly evolving knowledge base.

In the following scenario, we consider a large global enterprise operating in many different industries with multiple locations in different countries. For example, it develops mobility solutions and consumer goods. The enterprise has a large number of different production processes. As a result of the digitization strategy of the enterprise, the enterprise has already been storing the collected data in its data lake for several years. For each production process, the enterprise plans to set up a digital twin that virtually models the behavior of the machines involved. These digital twins will later be used to optimize the operation and maintenance of the production processes. Since the developers, such as data scientists, who are involved in the construction of the digital twins, have to find and access the required data, the enterprise has established a metadata management solution. This approach uses an enterprise ontology and user-defined semantic models as mappings to better describe the data sources. The semantic models are created by *data providers*, who are employees that are domain experts and know the semantics of the data very well.

Since data sources in industrial environments may contain hundreds of data attributes [8], creating sophisticated semantic models is a complex and time-consuming task. To improve the quality of semantic models, it is therefore important to support the data provider in the creation process. Therefore, we assume in the following that a data provider wants to create a semantic model for the simplified data set in Table 1, which shows a product that has been dried in an oven at a certain temperature and later manually checked for proper functioning by an employee. The data provider selects concepts from the underlying ontology and assigns them to the columns of the table. For example, the *prodID* column would be mapped to the *Identifier* concept and the *tinms* column to the *Timestamp* concept. In addition, the data provider can specify other details, such as the unit *Seconds* in which the timestamp is measured. Later this detailed information will help the developers of the digital twin application to understand the data and implement their application correctly (e.g., considering the correct unit for timestamps).

Table 1. Exemplary data set for which a data provider wants to create a semantic model [15].

prodID	tmp	tinms	e-mail	sta
313-16	856	1476912300	x@cp.com	OK
215-14	857	1476922300	y@cp.com	NOK
513-31	845	1476932300	x@cp.com	OK
...	...	...	...	...

Considering this table and the presented task of the data provider shows that when the data sets become much larger, creating semantic models is a complex and time-consuming task that requires important domain knowledge. Supporting the user with label-based recommendations would already help reliably identifying concepts such as E-Mail for the *e-mail* column, but would fail for all other columns. The analysis of the data instances of the columns raises the suspicion that a recommendation based on the data instances can lead to better results. For example, the *prodID* and *e-mail* columns follow a fixed pattern, while the temperature values in the *temp* column are limited to a certain range (845–857 °C) and the *sta* column consists of only two valid values (OK, NOK). The diversity of the different types of data instances also shows that it is not possible to develop a solution based exclusively on a single classification approach. For example, it is possible to train a machine learning classifier that detects a valid temperature, while the training for the product identifier does not work because each entry is unique. The definition of rules for the product identifier, e.g., by using regular expressions, would, however, lead to a valid data representation for this concept. Nevertheless, the assignment of a single data representative to a semantic concept also leads to incorrect results. Depending on the production process and its context, the data instances for a semantic concept can be different. For example, there might be production processes where the values of the valid temperatures are not between 845–857 °C, but between 12–15 °C. The data instances for a semantic concept may differ depending on the production process and its context. In these cases, it is necessary to learn a different data representation for the same semantic concept.

In addition to these examples, the scenario is also based on a fixed vocabulary provided by the underlying ontology. In this case, one could also try to convert the use case with all its data into a multi-class classification problem, where each data representation for each semantic concept becomes a class. This would be a first solution, but leads to a very static scenario. In cases where the underlying vocabulary of the ontology is extended or new devices with different data representatives are introduced for the same concept, it becomes necessary to re-train the entire machine learning model, which is very time-consuming and unmanageable in a large multi-site enterprise with a diverse product portfolio.

It is therefore necessary to develop an approach that takes into account not only the labels of the data attributes, but also the data instances. In addition, this approach should be independent of the number of available concepts. If new concepts are introduced or data instances with different representation forms are added, these must also be learnable.

3   Related Work

The research areas semantic annotation, labeling or modeling have the goal to assign semantic concepts to the data attributes of structured and semi-structured data sources. In order to facilitate the retrieval, access and storage of data, several attempts have been made to develop strategies for analyzing data sets and subsequently propose concepts that match their properties. In this context, initial approaches focus on the analysis of labels attached to attributes in order to propose concepts. Other approaches take into account the relationships between these labels and current work also focuses on analyzing the instances to which the labels are assigned.

In the context of data-structure-driven analysis, various approaches exist that deal with the suggestion of semantic concepts based on labels of the data attributes or by using the hierarchical structure of the given data set. For instance, Polfliet et al. [11] developed an approach that uses different similarity measures for String comparisons in order to establish a mapping between an ontology and the given data labels. Pinkel et al. [10] propose an approach for mapping relational databases to ontologies by using their developed application *IncMap*. To perform the matching, Pinkel et al. rely on lexical as well as structural similarity. Other approaches, like Syed et al. [18] or Wang et al. [20] include additional external knowledge bases, such as Wikitology or Probase in order to improve the mapping results. This allows, for instance, to also consider hypernyms, hyponyms or synonyms, which might not exist in the knowledge base that is used for mapping. Both approaches already identified that using a single data label may not be sufficient. Thus, Syed et al. [18] as well as Wang et al. [20] additionally examine the data values by also matching them to the external knowledge databases. Another approach that also detected that the usage of single data labels is not sufficient, is presented by Paulus et al. [8]. Instead of using only a single external knowledge database and a single label, they propose an approach that uses multiple external knowledge databases to increase the possible set of candidate mappings. The returned results are then automatically merged and rated with a corresponding algorithm so that they identify the largest subset of concepts which fits best together in the given context.

Although Paulus et al. [8] base their approach solely on the use of data labels, the authors also note that there exist many data sets where a data-structure-based strategy cannot work. Thus, the use of a data-driven strategy is required as well. Again, there exist many different approaches. For instance, Goel et al. [4,5] make use of conditional random fields (CRF) to annotate data attributes with semantic concepts from a pre-defined ontology. Instead of using the plain data values, Goel et al. divide them into tokens. For instance, the value 70 °F is divided into the tokens 70, ° and F. The newly created tokens are combined with the original labels of the data set in order to create a sequence CRF graph. This means that each token receives a token label based on the given data attribute name, such as *TempF*. Based on the received CRF graph, they assign a semantic label to each data value of the data set. The semantic label for the entire data attribute is then exactly the one that occurs most often. In distinction to our work, this approach exploits the same classification strategy (CRF) for each annotation process whereas our approach considers multiple classification approaches per semantic concept.

Another approach relying on machine learning is presented by Ramnandan et al. [16]. In comparison to the approach of Goel et al. who assign semantic labels based on a majority decision of the semantic labels they have obtained for each data value, Ramnandan et al. [16] consider the set of all instances belonging to a data attribute as a whole. For all available data values, they analyze which characteristics describe that attribute. Those characteristics are then linked to semantic concepts of a pre-defined ontology. The authors differentiate between textual and numerical data as they use different analysis techniques on them. To suggest a label for the attribute of a new text document, the *cosine similarity* between all indexed documents and the new document is calculated to present the top k elements with the highest similarity score. For numerical instances, a *statistical hypothesis testing* is used, which is performed between a new data set that should be labeled and every numerical data sample used for training. As a new data set is compared with every already learned characteristic, the system is adoptable to new semantic labels without any effort. In general, the idea of this approach is similar to ours as it is also rather focused on the exploitation of the data instances than the attribute labels. However, the authors only differentiate between text and numerical instances whereas our approach focuses on more fine-granular data classes. In addition, we allow to learn multiple data representations for the same semantic concept.

In [9], Pham et al. present an approach that does not focus on the pure data instances but the similarity of the metadata (respectively similarity metrics) of these instances, whereby their approach becomes independent of the domain the model was trained upon. As similarity metrics, the authors use *Attribute Name Similarity*, *Value Similarity*, *Distribution Similarity* for numerical instances, *Histogram Similarity* for textual instances and *Ratio* for cases where a mixture of numerical and textual instances is available. For every attribute of a set $\{a_1, a_2, ...a_n\}$, a feature vector $f_{ij}(i \neq j)$ is computed. Every similarity metric in dimension k is thereby calculated for itself, with $f[k]$ representing the similarity of a_i and a_j under metric k. Every calculated vector is annotated manually, whether the attributes are semantically similar or not. Based on the identified feature vectors, they train a machine learning classifier. They evaluated their approach for data sets of four different domains under the usage of two different classifiers, respectively Logistic Regression and Random Forest, with Logistic Regression showing the better performance. Compared to our approach, Pham et al. only train one classifier whereas our work permits multiple data representations per concept where each representation can be based on different classification approaches. Similar to our approach, Pham et al. already take the data class into account to calculate similarity metrics differently, but they restrict their differentiation merely to textual and numerical instances, with the classifier handling them similar. The data classes evaluated in our work offer a broader variety and the impact of different classification approaches is evaluated on all data classes.

Beside the approach of Pham et al. [9], which is able to deal with changing ontologies and new data sets, the most recent approaches focus on training multi-class classifiers where each concept of the ontology becomes one class. Examples include the works of Rümmele et al. [17], Chen et al. [1,2] and Hulsebos et al. [6]. While all these approaches yield the most promising results in recommending semantic concepts, they all leverage from the disadvantage of re-training and extending the learned classifiers as soon as new data sets are available or as soon as the ontology changes. If the number of data sources and classes increases, the effort for re-training increases drastically leading to a scalability problem in large real-world data lakes.

Altogether, we summarize that all the current approaches provide good results for extending the recommendation of semantic concepts for data attributes. However, we believe that it is not possible to cover all different concepts with a single approach just as label recommendation, similarity measures or machine learning. Instead, we believe that the quality of the recommendation for data instances depends on the data class the instances belong to.

4   Identification of Data Classes

Since our approach aims at semantic concept suggestions based on concrete data values, we have to consider the basic properties of data values. We have identified a specific categorization that groups these properties into data classes. These classes are later used as an additional characteristic or criterion for selecting the recommendation method. This section provides an overview of the data classes we have identified and discusses their characteristics. The overview is based on a selection of data sets also used by [8], mainly in the domain of publicly available, municipal data sets as well as the data set used by [9] from the domain of soccer and museum. Pham et al. already divided their data sets into textual and numerical values to perform different suggestion algorithms based on the data type, but we expect that further gradations of the data properties might improve the accuracy of suggestion strategies. We do not claim that the following list of properties and classes is exhaustive, however, all assumptions can be validated and they cover the most seen properties. Also, video, picture, sound and any more complex data is not covered by this classification, as the assumption is made that they can be transformed into numerical values for semantic analysis.

4.1 Data Classes

The following data properties were observed. The first defining property of a data point is the **Data Type**. A data type defines the most basic limitation to the expressiveness to one single data value. The observed types range from numbers (discrete and floating) to a sequence of any characters. Other properties are defining the relation between two data points. A **Scale** provides the possibility to interpret the distance between two data points. Scales can be either categorical or numerical, whereby the categorical scale can be divided into nominal or ordinal scales. In a nominal scale there is no relation between the instances, they are comparable to labels. In an ordinal scale, the difference between two values is still not quantifiable or has no specific meaning, however, values can be **Sorted**. Finally, in a numerical scale, even the distance between two values has a meaning. The following data classes are a result of the combination of these properties:

Full Text. This class (*text*-class) is the least restrictive. Many of the reviewed data sets contained attributes whose values consisted of longer texts (e.g., a description or an abstract). As most of the machine learning techniques we use are based on numerical values, their application for values that consist of longer texts is quite challenging. Also, histograms are insufficient as the variety of the texts is too high. One possible solution for this issue is assumed to be a dictionary of n-grams in order to have a look up for certain phrases occurring in longer texts.

Identifier. This class (*id*-class) restricts the first class in two aspects. First, it contains less characters and second, the characters follow a more or less strict pattern. Names are a typical representative of this class. However, determining whether an arbitrary sequence of characters is conceptually a name is hard, as names do not follow any predictable pattern. Same holds true for other identification strings or numbers, which can also occur in a combination of characters and numbers. Other identifiers like an IBAN or ISBN have a fixed pattern by which they are created. Email addresses make up a set in between as they contain an "@", which cannot be used otherwise, but the rest is quite arbitrary.

Bag-of-Words. The next class also consists of limited character sequences, however, in this case the structure of the character sequence is of secondary importance. The defining criteria of this class is that the attributes are composed only from a fixed set of allowed values called a bag-of-words (*bow*). Examples for this are soccer player positions ("Goalkeeper", "Left-back", "Centre midfield", "Striker", ...) or nominal scales ("good", "average", "bad"). A direct transfer from values with a similar semantic meaning but different representations is not possible. For example, a fixed set of words cannot be recognized by the abbreviation of the words (e.g., for soccer "GK", "LB", "CM", "ST") or one nominal scale by another (e.g., English to German grades). The new set has to be attached to the corresponding concept in order to suggest this concept.

Numerical Values. The last class consists of only numbers (discrete or floating point). Numerical values (num-class) occur in any form of measurement or calculated results. The possible values in a data set with real values cannot be grouped with a fixed set as there are arbitrary many valid values. In difference to the identifiers that may also be composed of numbers, real numbers can be put in a relation to each other, which allows different evaluations as they can be placed on numerical scale.

4.2   Automatic Identification of Data Classes

In order to improve the identification of relevant classification approaches we argue that the data class is relevant. However, in typical scenarios this information is not immediately present and has to be extracted or provided. One solution would include a change of the data collection process, i.e., when a data set is obtained, there could be a system in place which would either enable the provider or the consumer to manually enrich the data attributes with the data class property. Considering the industrial target setting of our approach, data sets often contain hundreds of columns. Therefore, manual enrichment steps should be avoided whenever it is possible. Consequently, we consider to automate the recommendation of data classes. Since we follow a data-driven approach when analyzing data values, we also consider this approach for determining the class.

Based on our previous analysis of data classes, we have determined the potential target classes, which serve as labels in a supervised machine learning approach. We are currently evaluating the use of different classification approaches. In this section, we discuss an approach based on the use of Autoencoders. Autoencoders are special types of neuronal networks, which aim to extract characteristics of an input data set and create an encoding, which is able to represent the data more efficiently. This approach is also often used for dimension reduction, as it is building a projection from an input dimension to a defined output dimension. We selected this method based on this premise, as we try to achieve exactly the same with the data classes, i.e., extract a characteristics from the values and project them onto known labels.

For this purpose, we trained models on the museum and soccer data sets. Since Autoencoders require numerical data, we converted each value of each data set with the same transformation function. First, we consider each input to be a string, then we create a sequence of bytes by decoding the string using the ANSI character-set. Since the length of the input varies, we fixed the length of the sequences to 169, considering that average sentences should fit into the sequence. Smaller sequences were appended with zeros and larger ones were cut.

For the training we used convolutional networks. All the data sets were labeled manually with the expected data classes. For the training, we split our data set into three parts. The first set was considered the hold out set, consisting of 20% of each data attribute. The remaining data split into test (24%) and training (56%) sets to be used during the training phase. All data sets were shuffled before selection. We trained one model for each data class. The classification was performed on each data attribute using the hold out part. A prediction for each model was calculated and the mean squared error of the input calculated. The model with the least difference was selected as the predicted data class. We repeated this procedure for a ten fold cross validation.

Current results using this approach yield an average classification precision of about 60%. This result is surely not high enough to fully rely on an automated classification, however, deeper inspection revealed interesting insights, which will help to improve the results. For example, the *id*-class was miss-classified as *bow*-class very frequently. Indicating that the selected byte encoding is not expressive enough to capture the difference between these classes. In contrast, the *num*-class contains almost no miss-classifications.

In summary, these results motivate further research to enable the automated data classification and data class suggestion. Future work in this area also includes a systematic unsupervised analysis of data values. For example, trying to determine new or different data classes based on the data instead of the classes identified by our observations.

5   Implementation of the Data Representatives

In this section, we present our developed approach that we integrated into the semantic data platform ESKAPE [12], which offers Ontology-Based Data Integration (OBDI). The idea of ESKAPE is that data providers publish data sources and describe the additional required and interesting meta-information with semantic models. Based on the semantic models, other users like data scientists, can query and access these data sources later on. In order to support the data provider during the semantic model creation, ESKAPE identifies semantic concept recommendations based on the framework presented by [8]. Data providers can then create the semantic models with the graphical user interface of ESKAPE [13] where they can choose from the recommendations or browse through all existing semantic concepts and relations provided by ESKAPE's underlying knowledge graph, which encourages them to make choices upon that shared terminology. Compared to traditional OBDI or OBDA approaches, users can extend the knowledge graph's vocabulary by introducing new concepts or relations on-demand directly to the knowledge graph to make them available for others. This circumstance is very crucial for the design of our approach as it excludes the possibility of using a multi-class classification approach. If we would use this method, the approach would require re-training after a new semantic concept has been added to the knowledge base. However, this would be very time- and resource-intensive. Hence, the goal of our approach is to enhance each semantic concept with data representatives that capture or describe the characteristics of the data instances that are annotated with this concept.

We therefore identified different approaches, such as statistical methods, regular expressions and machine learning methods that can be used for representing the instances of a semantic concept. The goal of these approaches is to evaluate later on if a number of data instances are valid or invalid representatives of this semantic concept. We call these approaches *classification approaches*. Each semantic concept can be represented by one or more classification approaches. For instance, one could have different machine learning models or statistical methods that are used for identifying if a data value is a representative of this semantic concept. We decided to link a semantic concept to different classification approaches as the instances of data attributes can belong to different data classes. We then integrated our framework into the semantic data platform ESKAPE and modified the semantic modeling approach of ESKAPE. In the following, we give an overview of the identified classification approaches (cf. Sect. 5.1), the modifications that we made for the knowledge graph model provided by ESKAPE (cf. Sect. 5.2) and the process of how the recommendation and training works (cf. Sects. 5.3 and 5.4). Finally, we present how we combine data-structure-driven and data-driven strategies in Sect. 5.5.

5.1 Classification Approaches

Classification approaches represent the idea that we can describe a semantic concept based on the sum of all of its data instances. However, since the same semantic concept can be represented by different kinds of data instances (e.g., as a textual representation or as a number), we identified that it is not possible to solely find a single classification approach that is capable of capturing all characteristics of the semantic concept. Based on the data classes and their characteristics that we identified in Sect. 4, we selected classification approaches which match these. As classification approaches, we chose a rule-based approach based on regular expressions, a histogram approach as statistical method and machine learning approaches in the form of one-class classifiers.

Regular Expression. The analysis of the given data sets showed that certain attributes contain instances, which follow a fixed set of syntactic rules. For example, the attribute *dim* of a data set with information to paintings contain instances like 135.7×55.3 cm, 44.2×55.0 cm and 62.8×81.9 cm. The concept of the attribute is "dimension", which can be described by a representative based on a regular expression (RegEx) as the instances follow a fixed pattern. The RegEx sufficient to characterize this instances would be (\d)*.\d x (\d)*.\dcm. The disadvantage of this approach is that the user has to come up with the RegEx by hand in order to describe the instances. It is also necessary to keep the RegEx as specific as possible in order to prevent it fitting to other concepts. The RegEx .* would also cover the top example, but every other value would also be verified by this pattern.

Histogram. Opposed to the rule-based approach, which takes every value separately into account, the histogram-based method is chosen to use the frequency of every value as metadata. This frequency is intended to provide a better insight into the data set, as it provides an opportunity to distinguish concepts that inherit similar instances, but are semantically different. As a histogram does not consider the order of the instances, a distribution of the instances is not taken into account. As mentioned in Sect. 4, the order of the instances might include further information on a data set if the instances are denoted in a fixed order which is often encoded in the instances of a different attribute. For real numbers, we also consider binning strategies based on a rounding factor. For textual instances, this binning is not implemented (e.g., to group instances with a similar meaning).

One-Class Classifier. In order to detect boundaries between instances that represent one concept and instances representing another one, a one class classifier (OCC) is used. The usage of an OCC provides the advantage over other classification techniques that it is restricted to a training set containing only valid instances. For the classification approaches of the concepts, this is useful as each classification approach becomes independent for the other. New classification approaches can be added without the need for re-training of previously trained models. Currently, we use a support vector machine (SVM) as one-class classifier. We are currently evaluating the use of Autoencoders. Section 6.2 presents the current results using this approach for general concept classification.

5.2   Adaptation of the Knowledge Graph Model

For our implementation, we first extended an existing knowledge graph model provided by the semantic data platform ESKAPE [12] to be capable of linking semantic concepts to data representations.

The original graph model described by [12] describes a basic model for semantic concepts, called Entity Concepts, and the relations between them. To additionally enable the learning of data representations for those Entity Concepts, we extended the graph model. Therefore, we extended each Entity Concept node ec_x with an additional data representation node drn_x. The data representation node drn_x is linked to the different data representatives drc_i that were trained for the entity concept ec_x. We introduce for each new data representative j, a new node drc_j and attach it to the corresponding drn node. Depending on the type of the data representative (Histogram, Regex, OCC, etc.), each of those drn nodes has different properties. For histograms, we save the *data class* for which this histogram was created, a *location* where we store the histogram model and the *rounding*, which describes on how many decimal places we round, or -1 if it is a text-based histogram. For the one class classifier, we store the *location* where the trained model is stored and for which data class it was trained. Finally, for a regular expression, we store the *data class*, the *pattern* and a *fit percentage* which describes the percentage of data instances of the annotated data attributes on which this regular expression matched.

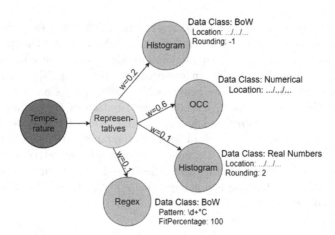

Fig. 1. Example for the concept Temperature. Based on the currently annotated data, four different data representations were created. The weights w show that most of the annotated data attributes were trained with the One Class Classifier [15].

Since the number of possible data representations per semantic concept potentially increases with the number of new data sources, we added a weighting factor w to the edge e_{ij} between the data representation node drn_xi and the corresponding data representative drc_j. This weighting factor describes how many percent of all annotated data attributes were used with this concept to train this data representative. Figure 1 shows an example. For the semantic concept *Temperature*, ten data attributes were annotated with this concept, but only four different data representatives were trained. Two of those representatives are Histograms, one OCC and one regular expression. The weighting factor shows how many data attribute columns were used for the different data representatives. For instance, the 0.6 for the OCC indicates that the instances of six out of ten data attributes were currently used to train the OCC model, whereas for the regular expression representative the instances of only one data attribute were used. In the later recommendation process, the data representatives with the higher weight will be evaluated first.

5.3   Recommendation of Concepts

The recommendation and the training or updating of existing data representatives is done during the schema analysis and the semantic model creation in the ESKAPE platform. During the schema analysis, ESKAPE identifies the best fitting semantic concept for a corresponding data attribute. Previously, this process was based on the recommendation framework provided by [8]. We extended this process to additionally evaluate the already existing data representatives. First, we randomly sample ten percent of the available data instances dv from the data attribute da. For each available concept that has already attached data representatives in the knowledge graph, we check how well this concept

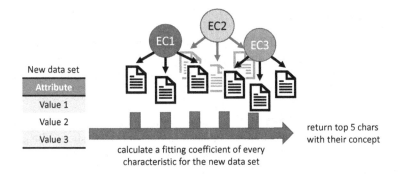

Fig. 2. Model of the concept suggestion based on different classification approaches. The instances of a new data set are analyzed and compared with every existing classification approach and a similarity score is calculated. The concepts with the highest score are returned [15].

represents the data instances. Therefore, we calculate for each data representative drc a similarity score s between the set of randomly extracted data instances and the drc. This similarity score defines how well the data instances fit the current representation of the semantic concept. To speed-up the finding of a match, we first evaluate the data representatives that have a higher weight. If a data representative with a high similarity score, i.e., at least 80%, was identified, the concept is marked as relevant and the other data representatives of this concept are not evaluated anymore. As soon as all semantic concepts were evaluated, the top five concepts with the highest similarity score are returned as recommendations. Figure 2 shows this approach for a small example.

Similarity Score. The calculation of the similarity score depends on the different classification approaches. For the rule-based approach based on regular expressions and for the one class classifier, the strategies are quite similar. In both cases, for every data value of the attribute that is about to be annotated, it is checked whether they fit into the given data representation or not. For the rule-based approach, the RegEx pattern is evaluated on every value and for the OCC-based method every value is classified by the OCC algorithm and the percentage of instances fitting the class is used for evaluation. The higher the percentage of fitting instances is, the more it is assumed that the concept associated with the respective data representation fits to the attribute of the instances. To suggest a concept based on a histogram classification approach, the histogram for the instances of the data set is calculated. The histogram is normalized as the amount of instances should not effect the calculation. Afterwards, the histogram of every available representative is compared with the one from the new data set and the intersection for them is calculated. Due to the normalization, results between 0 and 1 occur with the highest rated intersections being used for the suggestion of their respective concepts.

5.4   Training of Concepts

With each new data set and the corresponding created semantic model, the concept representations are updated and/or extended. For training classification approaches for semantic concepts, we have to differentiate between different cases.

No Representation Available. In this case, we allow the user, who is creating the semantic model, to select a classification approach that should be used for learning the semantic concept. Hence, if the user selects the histogram or one class classification approach, the system will calculate a histogram or train a SVM/autoencoder classifier for the annotated data attribute and store them on the underlying storage system. For the histogram, the user has to additionally define the rounding factor. For the SVM/autoencoder classifier, the user does not have to define anything. Currently, all SVM/autoencoder parameters are set to default. However, in the future we plan to perform an automatic grid search with a different parameter set. With the help of cross-validation, we will then select the best fitting parameters for the available data instances. If the user selects a regular expression, he has to define it and provide it to the system. Subsequently, our approach creates a new data representative for the used semantic concept.

Representation Available but Inappropriate. If a semantic concept has already assigned classification approaches but none of those were valid candidates for the recommendation, then we request the user to define the same information as if no representation would be available. This means a user has to choose a classification approach and has to define the required parameters. Our approach will then create a new data representative for the used semantic concept.

Appropriate Representation Available. If an appropriate representation is available, i.e., the similarity score was larger than 80%, this representation will be extended with the new instances. In case of a regular expression classification approach, the fit percentage value will be updated. In case of histogram, we will create a new histogram and store it. The one class classifier will be re-trained with the old and new data instances.

5.5   Combine Data-Structure-Driven and Data-Driven Recommendation

In order to improve the results of our data-driven strategy, we combine our approach with the data-structure-driven strategy provided by Paulus et al. [8]. The main idea of combining these two approaches is that the approach of Paulus et al. allows us to identify the best combination of labels that are returned by the data-driven strategy by cross-checking them with external knowledge databases.

Let D be a data set and let $a_1...a_n$ be the different data attributes of this data set. Moreover, let $v_1...v_n$ be the values of the corresponding data attributes $a_1...a_n$ and let $l_1...l_n$ be the data labels of the these attributes.

In a first step, we perform our data-driven strategy for each $a \in D$, i.e., we identify the best fitting concepts per data attribute. As a result, we obtain up to four different concepts $c_{i1}...c_{in}$ for each data attribute a_i. Please note that it is also possible to not get any recommendation per data attribute. This happens, for instance, if none of the learned data representatives matches. In a second step, we query the framework of Paulus et al. to identify a combination of concepts for the given set of labels $l_1...l_n$. Again, we receive up to four concepts $p_{i1}...p_{in}$ per data attribute a_i, where the set of these concepts are already fitting together very well. Afterwards, we identify for each data attribute a_i the set of relevant concepts as $c_i \cap p_i$. However, if $c_i \cap p_i = \emptyset$, we define the result as $c_i \cup p_i$. This enables us to receive a greater set of results in cases where both strategies yield different results whereas we receive more specific results in cases where both strategies identify similar concepts. In addition, it also allows us to receive results in cases where one of the strategies did not return any results.

6   Evaluation

This section evaluates the implemented classifications approaches (histogram-based, rule-based and OCC-based approach) and how accurate their suggestions of concepts are compared to manually annotated concepts. All evaluations are conducted with respect to the data classes (cf. Sect. 4). This means that we considered the four identified data classes (bag-of-words (*bow*), Numerical values (*num*), identifiers (*id*) and textual (*text*)). The results are compared with the ones achieved by [9]. To achieve compatibility with Pham et al., we limit our evaluation to the data sets of the domains *museum* and *soccer*. The source data sets museum and soccer can be summarized with following distribution: The museum data set contains 4132 entries over 28 different semantic concepts in total. Most frequently, the *bow* class can be observed with 18 entries. The other concepts are evenly distributed among the other classes. For the soccer data set, the *bow* class and the *numeric* class are the most prominent with 14 and 13 out of 33 respectively. The other classes are also evenly distributed. There are 9443 entries in total in this set. The other domains provided either only ten data values or provided only five attributes.

6.1   Evaluation Method

All measurements are conducted on a knowledge graph, which contains all concepts that are manually assigned to the attributes of the data sets.

Two varieties of hit ranks are measured. The *Mean Reciprocal Rank* (MRR) of the top four elements (MMR4) is evaluated beside the top-rating (T1). The top four elements are evaluated as they are also used by [9] for their evaluation. The MRR is defined by [3] as followed:

Mean Reciprocal Rank. *The Reciprocal Rank (RR) information retrieval measure calculates the reciprocal of the rank at which the first relevant document was retrieved. RR is 1 if a relevant document was retrieved at rank 1,* *if not it is 0.5 if a relevant document was retrieved at rank 2 and so on. When averaged across queries, the measure is called the Mean Reciprocal Rank (MRR). Mathematically described as followed for all queries Q:*

$$\text{MRR} = \frac{1}{|Q|} \sum_{i=1}^{|Q|} \frac{1}{\text{rank}_i}.$$

After the hit rank is evaluated, the current accuracy of the suggestion process is evaluated and a representation that is created based on the values of the current attribute is attached to the manually labeled concept.

Since we propose an evolutionary learning approach, the order in which the data representatives are added might affect the quality of the suggestion. Thus, we perform a ten-fold cross validation using a random shuffle of the attributes.

6.2   Classification Methods

To evaluate which of the classification approaches suits best for which kind of data class, we first compare our suggestions in their basic form on single domains. In the next step, we increase the complexity by considering multiple domains.

Single Domain. Figure 3 (museum data set) and Fig. 4 (soccer data set) show the domain dependent results of the evaluation of which classification approach suits best for which kind of data class, a cross evaluation of all approaches on the data sets from the domain museum and soccer is conducted. As the number of attributes associated with the data class *text* in the soccer domain data sets are too few, they were left out of the evaluation. The data set contained only seven entries, which are all labeled with "date".

For the museum data set, the OCC approach is only evaluated on the data class *num*, since the mapping process from text values to numerical values is too expensive, i.e., the suggestion of a single concept takes on average ten minutes, even if only a few representatives are available. The OCC accuracy is evaluated for the data set from the soccer domain, since the number of data values per attribute is much lower than those for the museum data set. However, the calculation of the OCC approach is still slower than that of the other approaches.

In the museum data, the best results for *numerical* data could be achieved through a rule-based approach with a measured accuracy of T1: 0.9182 (MRR4: 0.9575). For the soccer data set, the OCC-based approach performed better with accuracies of 0.7353 (0.8480), however. While the histogram approach achieves reasonable results for the museum set, it has a very low accuracy in the soccer case 0.3744 (0.3902).

The *bow*-class is similarly well predicted by the histogram- and rule-based approach in the museum case, with accuracies of 0.7137 (0.7640) for the histogram-based and 0.6583 (0.7436) for the rule-based approach. The histogram result can be reproduced in the soccer case 0.7462 (0.7831), however, the rule-based approach performs badly 0.2795 (0.5057).

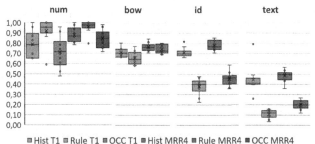

Fig. 3. Box plot diagrams of the measurement series' over the different data classes with different classification approaches on the museum data set [15].

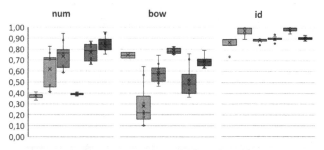

Fig. 4. Box plot diagram for the evaluated accuracy on the soccer data sets. The data class *text* is left out as the amount of attributes associated with that class is too low [15].

The histogram-based approach performed well for the *id*-class and *text*-class, while the *text*-class has generally a bad accuracy for the museum data sets. In the soccer set, the rule-based approach performs best with accuracies of 0.9737 (0.9868), while the histogram-based approach also has reasonably fine and even significantly better results than for the museum case, i.e., 0.8684 (0.8989) vs. 0.7137 (0.7640).

These results show that no single approach is a universal winner, the right approach seems to depend heavily on individual data points.

Mutliple Domains. As the previous tests where restricted to only one domain, the evaluation of this section measured the accuracy for the mixture of soccer and museum based data sets. This enlarges the set of possible concepts that can be suggested to an attribute and creates a broader variety of concepts within one knowledge graph. The results of the evaluation are depicted in the box plot diagram of Fig. 5.

The results of the analysis show that the developed framework holds up the measured accuracy for mostly all combinations of data classes and classification approaches. The only significant drops of quality occurred with the rule-based approach being conducted to the data classes *bow* and *id*. For the *bow*-class, the quality dropped from 0.6583 (0.7436) in the museums domain to 0.4020 (0.5570) in the overall approach. The range of the box plot diagram is also enlarged indicating the importance of the order in which the representatives are added to the concepts. This might be explained with the low quality of the rule-based approach achieved on the soccer domain for data sets that are assigned to the *bow*-class.

One significant improvement of the accuracy could be measured for the combination of the data class *num* and the histogram-based classification approach. The quality was enhanced from 0.2795 (0.5057) in the soccer domain based data sets to 0.7244 (0.7572) in the domain mixed approach. Also the range of the box blot scale shrinks drastically for the histogram-based approach.

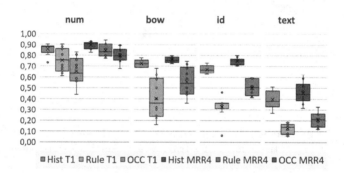

Fig. 5. Box plot diagram for the accuracy measured over all data classes and classification methods with data sets from the museum and soccer domain being included into the knowledge graph and annotated randomly mixed [15].

The results of this test show that the enlargement of the concept variety does not impact the accuracy of the classification methods as long as the boundaries of the added concepts stay disjointed.

Comparison to Pham. This section provides a discussion of the measured results. As the accuracy measured on the data sets from the domains soccer and museum is based on the same data sets as the evaluation of Pham et al. the results will be set into the context of their evaluation (cf. Tables 2 and 3).

As our evaluation was only conducted on the data sets from the domains soccer and museum, only those results are relevant for comparison with the results of Pham et al. Since Pham et al. present the results of a MRR of the top four suggestions, the same measured results are presented in Tables 4 and 5.

The results of this paper are achieved by a different approach than the one used by Pham et al., but show a similar accuracy like the one measured by Pham

Table 2. Results when training on the soccer data set of Pham et al. The results show the MRR scores [15].

	soccer	museum
Logistic Regression	0.814	0.863
Random Forest	0.794	0.799

Table 3. Results when training on the museum data set of Pham et al. The results show the MRR scores [15].

	soccer	museum
Logistic Regression	0.815	0.845
Random Forest	0.820	0.778

et al. Certain combinations of classification approach and data class showed to be more efficient, while other performed worse.

As the provided data sets and number of concepts is not that high, with 12 data sets of soccer and 28 data sets of museum data, the results can be described as equally accurate. Since the actual concepts used by Pham et al. are not all listed in their paper, the same ones could not be annotated to the attributes, evaluated by this paper. As the used concepts are unknown, the variety of annotated concepts is also slightly different. Pham et al. distinguish 20 concepts in the museum domain and 14 in the soccer domain. In this paper, for the museum domain 28 concepts and for the soccer domain 33 concepts have been identified. However, as described in Sect. 4 they are split up into the different data classes in this paper.

Table 4. MRR scores of the classification approaches on soccer. Bold marked values scored higher than the best result of Pham et al. on the soccer data [15].

	bow	num	id	text	average
Histogram	0.783	0.390	**0.899**	**0.954**	0.757
Rule	0.506	0.771	**0.987**	**0.983**	0.812
OCC	0.687	**0.848**	**0.907**	**0.950**	**0.848**

Table 5. MRR scores of the classification approaches on museum. Bold marked values scored higher than the best result of Pham et al. on the museum data [15].

	bow	num	id	text	average
Histogram	0.764	**0.877**	0.793	0.783	0.804
Rule	0.752	**0.974**	0.457	0.200	0.596
OCC		0.843			0.843

Both methods are domain independent but follow different strategies to achieve this goal. The method presented by Pham et al. relies on the training of one ML model, trained to tell whether two attributes can be associated with the same concept based on the metadata of the data instance. While Pham et al. distinguish between textual and numerical values, the here presented method focuses further on the data class a set of values can be described by. Textual data is split into the data class *bow*, *id* and *text* and numerical data is split into the data classes *num*, *bow* and *id*. The numerical values are mapped to the class *bow* or *id* if their semantic meaning does not focus on the numerical comparison of the values, but could be replaced by text (e.g., replace a rating from one to ten in a survey or replace a numerical id by a textual unique identifier). The implementation of this paper offers individual classification approaches for every concept. Similar to the method of Pham et al. the here presented implementation follows the suggestion strategy, which compares the representatives of an attribute that should be annotated with every previously integrated representative.

The results of the comparison between the different data classes and classification approaches show that for certain combinations one or the other is more efficient. While the histogram underperformed on the data class *num* on the data sets of the soccer domain, the rule-based approach showed to be inefficient on the classes *id* and *text* of the museum data.

Evaluation of Autoencoders: Similar to the classification approach for the data classes, presented in Sect. 4.2, we also evaluated the general feasibility of using autoencoders for the suggestion of concepts as another form of OCC.

We trained models for each combination of concept and data class, which was present in the museum and soccer data sets. The training process was performed similarly to the one described before, however, we consider the MMR of the top four suggestions as the evaluation metric.

Based on the knowledge gained from the data class classification approach, we decided to focus on the use of Long short-term memory networks (LSTM), hoping they might be able to better capture the nuances of different concepts of the same data class.

In order to get a baseline, we first trained models for each concept without considering their data classes. Afterwards, we trained with a separation of data classes. The results validate our initial assumption of the importance of data classes, since the results improved for almost each data class by a factor of two. We also trained models using convolutional networks. While the results are only minimally worse compared to the LSTM, our assumption about LSTMs being able to better capture the difference seem to be manifesting very prominently in the *num*-class. Finally, we also evaluated the use of LSTMs on sequences of numerical values of various lengths without the use of the byte array transformation step. In general, the LSTM approach performed the best. Table 6 shows a summary of the results of this evaluation for each data class.

In summary, these results also indicate that the use of a single classification approach for every concept and data class is unreasonable, as for some combinations the precision is very low. However, even if the approach still needs some refinement, we learned from this evaluation that autoencoders in combination

with LSTM networks are a concept worth some future work, especially for the
num-class.

Table 6. MMR4 classification results based on different autoencoder approaches.

	bow	num	id	text	average
LSTM Mixed	0.115	0.289	0.069	0.4116	0.2211
LSTM Separate	0.298	0.70	0.684	0.27	0.488
Conv.	0.272	0.542	0.587	0.2939	0.424
LSTM num		0.5897			

7   Conclusion and Future Work

In this paper, we have presented a novel approach that allows the recommendation of semantic concepts for data attributes based on a constantly evolving
knowledge graph, which is one of the main differences to related work that focuses
exclusively on the recommendation of semantic concepts based on a predefined
ontology. We therefore focused our work mainly on proposing semantic concepts
based on the data instances of a data set whose semantic meaning is encap-
sulated in a classification approach that is added to the concept stored in the
knowledge graph via an additional data representative. We therefore integrated
our approach into the semantic data platform ESKAPE as it already features a
continuously evolving knowledge graph.

In order to use the characteristics of the values as accurately as possible, the
attributes of the values are assigned to different data classes before concepts are
proposed. Compared to our previous work [15], we additionally presented in this
paper a method that allows to automatically determine the data class, which
increases the usability of the approach. As concept classification approaches, we
developed are rule-, histogram- and one-class-classifier-based approach. Thereby,
the set of available classes was determined based on the evaluation of different
real data sets and consists of *bag-of-words*, *numerical*, *identifier* and *full text*.

The main benefit of using multiple different data classes is that it allows us to
distinguish more finely between different representations of an available semantic
concept. Due to this reason, we designed our approach in such a way that it also
allows to learn multiple different representatives per concept. This enables us,
for instance, to also cover concepts where the data have different *Data Classes*,
such as numerical and textual data values. In addition, we provided different
learning strategies, called classification approaches. The main idea behind the
provision of multiple classification approaches is that we believe that not all
semantic concepts and data classes can be represented equally well by a single
classification approach. In a first place, we therefore provided a machine learning
approach based on SVMs, a statistical method in the form of histograms as well
as a ruled-based method based on regular expressions. In addition, we also added
in this paper an additional approach in the form of autoencoders.

For evaluating our approach, we trained the different classification approaches using the data sets provided by Pham et al. [9]. Altogether, the results show that there are significant differences in the accuracy of the classification approaches in context of specific data classes, which confirms our hypothesis that not all semantic concepts and data classes can be represented equally well by a single classification approach. The use of a flexible and dedicated classification of semantic concepts, like we presented in this paper allows for better suggestions and improves the semantic labeling process massively. To further improve our recommendation accuracy, we proposed a concept in this paper that allows to combine the data-structure-driven recommendations returned by the framework of Paulus et al. [8], with our data-driven strategy. Here, we are sure that combining the strategies of both worlds will result in more accurate recommendations in the future.

As further improvements of our approach, we imagine the use of a summarized representatives, i.e., global representatives that aggregate multiple other specialized representatives. This shall improve the look-up strategy so that we do not have to check every concept for suitability. The current state of the autoencoder approach illustrates potential, however, still requires further tuning. Additionally, we will focus on identifying further machine learning methods as potential classification approaches. Currently, our aim is to evaluate different anomaly detection approaches. In addition, we would also like to offer a more user-friendly variant for defining rules, as many users have problems with specifying regular expressions. Finally, we must examine to what extent the results of our approach can be generalized in larger real applications. It will therefore be necessary to perform evaluations with a larger number of data records with similar yet different concepts and data attributes.

References

1. Chen, J., Jiménez-Ruiz, E., Horrocks, I., Sutton, C.: ColNet: embeddingthe semantics of web tables for column type prediction. In: Proceedings of the AAAI Conference on Artificial Intelligence, vol. 33, no. 01, pp. 29–36 (2019). https://doi.org/10.1609/aaai.v33i01.330129, https://aaai.org/ojs/index.php/AAAI/article/view/3765
2. Chen, J., Jiménez-Ruiz, E., Horrocks, I., Sutton, C.: Learning semantic annotations for tabular data. CoRR abs/1906.00781 (2019)
3. Craswell, N.: Mean reciprocal rank. In: Liu, L., Özsu, M.T. (eds.) Encyclopedia of Database Systems, p. 1703. Springer, Boston (2009). https://doi.org/10.1007/978-0-387-39940-9_488
4. Goel, A., Knoblock, C.A., Lerman, K.: Using conditional random fields to exploit token structure and labels for accurate semantic annotation. In: Proceedings of the 25th National Conference on Artificial Intelligence (AAAI 2011), San Francisco, CA (2011)
5. Goel, A., Knoblock, C.A., Lerman, K.: Exploiting structure within data for accurate labeling using conditional random fields. In: Proceedings of the 14th International Conference on Artificial Intelligence (ICAI) (2012)

6. Hulsebos, M., et al.: Sherlock. In: Teredesai, A., Kumar, V., Li, Y., Rosales, R., Terzi, E., Karypis, G. (eds.) Proceedings of the 25th ACM SIGKDD International Conference on Knowledge Discovery & Data Mining - KDD 2019, pp. 1500–1508. ACM Press, New York (2019). https://doi.org/10.1145/3292500.3330993

7. Li, X., Tu, Z., Jia, Q., Man, X., Wang, H., Zhang, X.: Deep-level quality management based on big data analytics with case study. In: Proceedings 2017 Chinese Automation Congress (CAC), Piscataway, NJ, pp. 4921–4926. IEEE (2017). https://doi.org/10.1109/CAC.2017.8243651

8. Paulus, A., Pomp, A., Poth, L., Lipp, J., Meisen, T.: Gathering and combining semantic concepts from multiple knowledge bases. In: Proceedings of the 20th International Conference on Enterprise Information Systems, pp. 69–80. SCITEPRESS - Science and Technology Publications (2018). https://doi.org/10.5220/0006800700690080

9. Pham, M., Alse, S., Knoblock, C.A., Szekely, P.: Semantic labeling: a domain-independent approach. In: Groth, P., et al. (eds.) ISWC 2016. LNCS, vol. 9981, pp. 446–462. Springer, Cham (2016). https://doi.org/10.1007/978-3-319-46523-4_27

10. Pinkel, C., Binnig, C., Kharlamov, E., Haase, P.: IncMap: pay as you go matching of relational schemata to OWL ontologies. In: OM, pp. 37–48 (2013)

11. Polfliet, S., Ichise, R.: Automated mapping generation for converting databases into linked data. In: Proceedings of the 2010 International Conference on Posters & Demonstrations Track, ISWC-PD 2010, Aachen, Germany, Germany, vol. 658. pp. 173–176. CEUR-WS.org (2010). http://dl.acm.org/citation.cfm?id=2878399.2878443

12. Pomp, A., Paulus, A., Jeschke, S., Meisen, T.: ESKAPE: information platform for enabling semantic data processing. In: Proceedings of the 19th International Conference on Enterprise Information. SCITEPRESS - Science and Technology Publications, April 2017

13. Pomp, A., Paulus, A., Klischies, D., Schwier, C., Meisen, T.: A web-based UI to enable semantic modeling for everyone. In: SEMANTiCS 2018–14th International Conference on Semantic Systems (2018)

14. Pomp, A., Paulus, A., Kirmse, A., Kraus, V., Meisen, T.: Applying semantics to reduce the time to analytics within complex heterogeneous infrastructures. Technologies 6(3), 86 (2018)

15. Pomp, A., Poth, L., Kraus, V., Meisen, T.: Enhancing knowledge graphs with data representatives. In: Proceedings of the 21st International Conference on Enterprise Information Systems, pp. 49–60. SCITEPRESS - Science and Technology Publications, 5 March–5 May 2019. https://doi.org/10.5220/0007677400490060

16. Ramnandan, S.K., Mittal, A., Knoblock, C.A., Szekely, P.: Assigning semantic labels to data sources. In: Gandon, F., Sabou, M., Sack, H., d'Amato, C., Cudré-Mauroux, P., Zimmermann, A. (eds.) ESWC 2015. LNCS, vol. 9088, pp. 403–417. Springer, Cham (2015). https://doi.org/10.1007/978-3-319-18818-8_25

17. Rümmele, N., Tyshetskiy, Y., Collins, A.: Evaluating approaches for supervised semantic labeling. CoRR abs/1801.09788 (2018)

18. Syed, Z., Finin, T., Mulwad, V., Joshi, A.: Exploiting a web of semantic data for interpreting tables. In: Proceedings of the Second Web Science Conference, vol. 5 (2010)

19. Terrizzano, I.G., Schwarz, P.M., Roth, M., Colino, J.E.: Data wrangling: the challenging yourney from the wild to the Lake. In: CIDR (2015)

20. Wang, J., Wang, H., Wang, Z., Zhu, K.Q.: Understanding tables on the web. In: Atzeni, P., Cheung, D., Ram, S. (eds.) ER 2012. LNCS, vol. 7532, pp. 141–155. Springer, Heidelberg (2012). https://doi.org/10.1007/978-3-642-34002-4_11

Linear Hashing Implementations for Flash Memory

Andrew Feltham, Nadir Ould-Khessal, Spencer MacBeth, Scott Fazackerley, and Ramon Lawrence(✉)

University of British Columbia, Kelowna, BC V1V 1V7, Canada
{andrew.feltham,spencer.macbeth}@alumni.ubc.ca, nkhessal@okanagan.bc.ca,
{scott.fazackerley,ramon.lawrence}@ubc.ca

Abstract. With flash memory having different performance character-istics, specifically fast random reads, there is an opportunity for indexing techniques based on hashing to have increased usage. Embedded devices have minimal memory and use flash memory for storage, which makes them interesting candidates for hash-based indexing. Linear hashing has constant time operations, and several implementation variants are eval-uated as an index structure for embedded devices. Experimental results show that linear hash implementations are significantly affected by flash memory properties, and performance is hardware dependent.

Keywords: Linear hashing · Embedded · Query · Arduino · Database

1 Introduction

Database performance is directly linked to the physical hardware that stores the data. Throughout history, algorithms and data structures for data access have been modified and optimized to adapt to the hardware. As the underlying storage technology has moved from tape drives, to hard drives, to solid state drives, to in-memory storage and beyond, database algorithms have adapted. Flash memory used in solid state drives (SSDs) has faster read versus write times and indexes have changed to favor reads over writes.

The focus of this paper is indexing on flash memory embedded devices. As more devices are deployed in a variety of Internet of Things [10] applications, there is an increasing focus on being able to store and process data on embed-ded devices rather than sending it over the network. On-device data processing improves response time and battery life and reduces the amount of data sent over the network. Flash-based storage on embedded devices is in many ways more challenging than working with SSDs due to the huge diversity of storage options. Flash-based storage may be achieved using a SD card, with or without using a file system, or by using any of the hundreds of different manufacturer implementations of NOR and NAND memory.

Linear hashing has potential for embedded, flash indexing due to its con-stant time performance and minimal memory usage. Prior work [5] described

© Springer Nature Switzerland AG 2020
J. Filipe et al. (Eds.): ICEIS 2019, LNBIP 378, pp. 386–405, 2020.
https://doi.org/10.1007/978-3-030-40783-4_18

and evaluated one implementation of linear hashing on the Arduino platform that demonstrated good performance suitable for a variety of use cases. The contribution of this work is the development and experimental evaluation of three different implementations of linear hashing for embedded devices. Each implementation makes different tradeoffs related to the flash memory. Experimental results demonstrate that variations with the flash memory technology have an affect on algorithm performance and suitability. A unique contribution is experiments executing on raw flash memory that presents distinctive implementation challenges and opportunities.

The remainder of this paper includes a background on linear hashing and embedded indexing followed by a description of the linear hashing implementation variants. Experimental results are in Sect. 4, and the paper closes with future work and conclusions.

2 Background

Linear hashing was developed by Litwin [12] and expanded by Larson [8,9]. Linear hashing is an expandable hash table with constant time operations. Linear hashing has been implemented in many database systems including PostgreSQL, but B+-trees are more commonly used as they also provide ordered access. Linear hashing is interesting for flash memory as it has the potential to perform fewer writes and its usage of random reads has no penalty in flash memory. It does not require a directory structure for finding bucket locations if buckets are allocated contiguously in storage. The hash table has the capability of dynamically growing or shrinking as the storage utilization (load factor) changes. Collisions are handled by using overflow chains. If the bucket where a record should be placed has no more space, a new block on storage is allocated to place the record and then this block is linked to the bucket. Thus, each bucket consists of a linked list of blocks on storage. Ideally, the number of blocks in each bucket is small if the records are distributed evenly within the hash table.

The key feature of a linear hash table is that expansion occurs one index at a time as needed instead of doubling the table size as in a regular hash table. This is made possible by the hashing function and splitting mechanism. Two hashing functions are used to calculated the table index shown in Eqs. 1 and 2. These equations require the hash table properties N as the initial number of buckets, and L the number of times the hash table has doubled in size. Algorithm 2 is used to calculated the table index for a given key hash. $nextSplit$ in this algorithm is the next bucket that will be split. This algorithm finds the last number of bits in the key hash that is a valid hash table index. Every time the linear hash table doubles in size additional bits in the hash are used to find the table index.

$$H_0(H) = H \bmod (N \times 2^L) \tag{1}$$

$$H_1(H) = H \bmod (N \times 2^{L+1}) \tag{2}$$

Overflows in a bucket are handled by adding a new bucket to a linked list of buckets. Overflow buckets are chained together as needed. An example table is shown in Fig. 1. This figure shows hashed keys inserted into a table with an initial size of 4. This table demonstrates key hashing and overflow chaining.

Algorithm 1. Hashes a key to a table index.

---

if $H_0(H) < nextSplit$ then
    $index \leftarrow H_1(H)$
else
        $index \leftarrow H_0(H)$
end

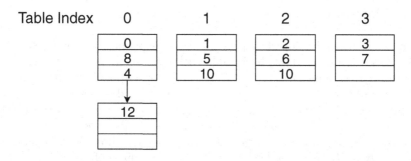

Fig. 1. Example linear hash table with hash keys.

The hash table is dynamically resized when the storage utilization (load factor) increases beyond a set amount. At that point, a new bucket is added to the end of the hash file and records are divided between the new bucket and the current bucket to split in the table. After every insert operation, load factor is calculated using Eq. 3 and compared against the maximum load factor. If it is exceeded then a split operation is triggered.

$$load = \frac{totalRecords}{size * recordsPerBucket} \tag{3}$$

During a split operation the table size is expanded by one and a new bucket is created. The bucket referenced by the *nextSplit* is loaded and split into the newly added bucket. Due to the way the hashing works, all records that should belong in the new table index are inside the buckets at the *nextSplit* index. Records are moved if the H_0 and H_1 functions have different values. Once the split has completed, if the table size has now doubled, the *nextSplit* is reset to the first index otherwise it is incremented by one. An example split is shown in Fig. 2. In this example a new bucket was added to the end of the table and records from table index 0 were split with this new bucket.

Table Index   0   1   2   3   4

0	1	2	3	4
8	5	6	7	12
	10	10		

Fig. 2. Example linear hash table with hash keys after a split.

Linear hashing was extended by Larson [8] using partial expansions. Search performance is increased with a trade-off of the need for buffering and splitting $k + 1$ buckets in memory where k is the number of partial expansions. Adding additional buffers in memory is a concern for embedded devices given the limited amount of memory available. [9] allowed for the primary buckets and overflow buckets to use the same storage file by reserving pre-defined overflow pages at regular intervals in the data file.

Linear hashing has been previously adapted to flash memory by using log buffering to perform fewer writes. The Self-Adaptive Linear Hash [17] buffers logs of successive operations before flushing the result to storage. Buffering decreases the number of write operations and allows them to be executed sequentially. Self-Adaptive Linear Hash also adds higher levels of organization to achieve more coarse-grained writes to improve the bandwidth.

Embedded devices are small, low powered, computer systems. Many embedded devices exist today for use within the open source community. One of the most popular is the Arduino project [15] that produces multiple embedded computers with varying capabilities. This work used an Arduino 2560 Mega as a benchmarking and testing device. This Arduino device has 8 KB of SRAM and a 16 MHz CPU. Developing with so little available RAM produces a challenge for implementing efficient data structures. Flash memory is commonly used in embedded devices as a long term storage. An Ethernet shield with a microSD slot was used for the Arduino 2560 Mega used in this work.

SD cards are rated by their sequential read or write speed and have varying performance depending on their class. In general read speeds are better than write speeds and sequential access is faster than random access. These memory characteristics guided the development into using less writes and potentially favoring sequential over random access.

Prior work has built database libraries and software tools for these embedded devices starting with the sensor-database networks such as TinyDB [13] and COUGAR [2] to database software installed and executing on the device such as Antelope [16], PicoDBMS [1], LittleD [3], and IonDB [4]. [7,11] describe data structures designed for flash-memory.

3   Linear Hash Implementations

Several implementations of a linear hash table were constructed, benchmarked, and compared. This section describes the implementations with their optimizations and intended uses. Since the goal was experimenting with different possibilities for optimization of the linear hash table on flash memory, a basic framework of a linear hash table was created and modified for the different implementations described later in this section.

Implementation decisions are affected by flash memory properties and limited resources of embedded devices. These decisions include the bucket structure and how overflow blocks are chained together, support for deletions and reclaiming free space, and overall memory usage of the data structure. Optimizations were designed to minimize RAM consumed, favor reads over writes, and avoid overwriting the same flash location. Many embedded systems perform logging applications where the device is collecting sensed data over time. For these scenarios, optimizing inserts is the most important with some emphasis on data retrieval. Update and delete operations are relatively rare.

3.1   Common Linear Hash Table Implementation

Due to the shared core functionality of a linear hash table, many of the structures, functions, and logic were identical. This section describes the common structures used in each implementation.

Records. Records are stored in buckets in binary format. Each record contained a key and a value. Separators were not used between the key and value as the keys and values are required to be constant sizes which is set during the linear hash table creation. The linear hash table pre-calculated the record size during initialization.

Buckets. A linear hash table is built around buckets which contain records and metadata describing the bucket and its contents. The same bucket structure is used for top level buckets in each hash table index and overflow buckets that are linked together as a linked list. Each bucket can contain up to a maximum number of records which was calculated using Eq. 4.

$$recordsPerBucket = floor(\frac{blockSize - bucketHeaderSize}{recordSize}) \qquad (4)$$

The bucket object was implemented using a C struct object. This struct contains the hash table index it belongs to, the number of records stored in the bucket, a pointer to the next bucket in the chain, and the remainder of the space was for record data. To optimize file reading and writing performance, each bucket was set to be 512 bytes in size to align to the file system's block boundaries. The header used 12 bytes total leaving 500 bytes for the bucket data. Buckets are loaded from the files using buffers, modified in memory and written out to the file as entire blocks.

Overflow buckets are handled by linking buckets together as a linked list. The overflow_block field in the header points to the logical block in the overflow location (implementation dependent) where the next bucket in the chain exists.

The UINT32_MAX value was used to indicate there the was no overflow bucket for a particular bucket.

Buffers. The buffer structure was used to load a bucket block from a file and keep track of values related to that buffer. Two buffers were allocated for each implementation as a minimum of two are required during a split operation to read a bucket and move records into another bucket. However, most functions required only one buffer. These buffers were allocated when the linear hash table implementation was created. This is the main memory impact of the implementations. Each buffer had to store both the 512 bytes of data plus the additional buffer flags, resulting in 1042 bytes of memory overhead. A dirty flag was used to save some unnecessary writes during splits, deletes, and updates. The buffer contents were written and read only as entire blocks of data.

Hashing. Hashing keys to index values is the key feature of the linear hash table. Several key hashing functions were tested to find a function that offered reasonable distribution and performance for the embedded environment. Using the work done by Fritter et al., the SDBM function was found to offer well rounded performance on the Arduino hardware [6]. This function was implemented as the default key hashing function. A function pointer was added on the linear hash table structure to allow easy replacement of the hashing function. A key was hashed to the hash table index with Algorithm 2. This function was used at the beginning of every operation and was not modified for any of the three implementations. Note that this function is dependent on the linear hash table values *nextSplit* and *initialSize*. These values are modified as the hash table grows during the split operation.

Algorithm 2. Hashes a key to a table index.

Input: The key to hash
Output: The table index where that key should be found
Function getIndex(*key*)
    $hash \leftarrow SDBM(key)$
    $index \leftarrow H_0(hash)$
    if $index < nextSplit$ **then**
        $index \leftarrow H_1(hash)$
    end
    return *index*
Function H_0(*hash*)
    return $hash\&(initialSize - 1)$
Function H_1(*hash*)
    return $hash\&(2 * initialSize - 1)$

3.2   Hash Table Operations

Get. The get or find hash table operation is shown in Algorithm 3. This operation is a linear scan through all the buckets in the bucket chain found at the index for the key. The find operation requires exactly 0 writes as it does not perform any modifications to the hash table. The operation takes minimum $O(1)$ and maximum $O(N)$ reads where N is the number of buckets in the bucket chain at the given index.

Delete. Delete operations are a linear scan through the buckets in an index chain and matching records are removed. Since each bucket is loaded into memory, records are manipulated in place. This operation is outlined in Algorithm 4.

During deletion records are shifted up to maintain a continuous block of records. This saves time during insertion as the insertion spot is at the bottom of the currently used area. To remove a bucket, the previous bucket in the linked list must be loaded and its next bucket pointer updated. This requires an extra read and write. To save writes and memory space, empty buckets were not removed from the overflow chains and records were not shifted between buckets. This can result in partially empty or empty buckets remaining in the bucket chain. Deletion requires a linear scan through the bucket chain which requires N reads and between 0 and N writes depending on the buckets modified.

Split. Splitting was implemented with Algorithm 5. This algorithm ensures that the new bucket chain is continuous with entirely full buckets. A split is triggered when the load of the linear hash table is reached after an insert. This load is configurable on the on the linear hash table structure. Similar to deleting, empty gaps in the splitting chain are filled, empty buckets are not removed, and partially full buckets are not filled. This function is the main reason two buffers are required: one buffer to load the splitting bucket and a second buffer for the new bucket. Splitting requires reading every bucket in the bucket chain for an index (N) and writing every bucket in the chain as well as all newly created buckets. In the worst case where every record must be moved this takes $2N$ writes.

Insert. In general the insert functionality loaded the top level bucket and potentially further buckets as needed until an empty spot was found. If required a new overflow bucket was added. After an insert a split could potentially be performed. This operation was determined to be the operation where optimizations and experiments could be made. Once an insert has been made, the load is checked using Eq. 3, compared to the maximum load set on the table. If the load is larger then the maximum load, a table split is made.

3.3   File Implementation

The file based implementation was built as a simple base implementation of a linear hash table. The goal of this implementation was to provide a performance

Algorithm 3. Get Operation.

> **Input**: The key to find
> **Output**: The value found or an error code
> $index \leftarrow getIndex(key)$
> $bucket \leftarrow loadTopBucket(index)$
> $terminal \leftarrow false$
> **while** $\neg terminal$ **do**
>> **foreach** $record\ in\ bucket.records$ **do**
>>> **if** $record.key = key$ **then**
>>>> **return** $record.value$
>>>
>>> **end**
>>
>> **end**
>> **if** $bucket\ has\ overflow$ **then**
>>> $bucket \leftarrow loadOverflowBucket(bucket.overflow)$
>>
>> **else**
>>> $terminal \leftarrow true$
>>
>> **end**
>
> **end**
> **return** $NotFound$

comparison between a standard linear hash table and further attempts at modifications. This implementation requires two files, data and overflow, to store the linear hash table contents. A third file was used to store the hash table state. The data file was used to contain top level buckets in the linear hash table. Each file block contained a bucket that matched the table index for that bucket. As the table was expanded new buckets were added to the end of the file. Overflow buckets were added to the overflow file. When an overflow block was created, it was always appended to the end of the overflow file and then the previous bucket was linked to the logical file index for that file block.

Get. The get operation functions identically as in Algorithm 3. The only change required is to load the bucket from different files during $loadTopBucket$ and $loadOverflowBucket$.

Delete. The delete operation functions as in Algorithm 4. The only modification required is to load the bucket from different files during $loadTopBucket$ and $loadOverflowBucket$.

Split. The split operation functions as in Algorithm 5. The buckets are tracked if they are a top level or an overflow bucket to write them out to the correct file.

Insert. Inserting into the file based implementation involves finding the index for the key then iterating through the buckets in the bucket chain until a bucket with space is found. If all bucket are full then a new bucket is added to the end

Algorithm 4. Delete Operation.

Input: The key to delete
Output: The number of records deleted
$deleted \leftarrow 0$
$index \leftarrow getIndex(key)$
$bucket \leftarrow loadTopBucket(index)$
$terminal \leftarrow false$
while $\neg terminal$ **do**
    $insert, read \leftarrow firstRecordPointer$
    $count \leftarrow bucket.recordCount$
    for $i \leftarrow 0$ **to** $count$ **do**
        $record \leftarrow recordAtReadPointer$
        if $record.key = key$ **then**
            $bucket.recordCount-=1$
            $deleted+=1$
        else
            if $insert \neq read$ **then**
                copy record at read to insert
            end
            $insert+=recordSize$
        end
        $read+=recordSize$
    end
    write out bucket
    if $bucket$ has overflow **then**
        $bucket \leftarrow loadOverflowBucket(bucket.overflow)$
    else
        $terminal \leftarrow true$
    end
end
return $deleted$

---

of the chain. Note that whenever a bucket is written to storage it is written at the same logical address in the file. The file performance for this function is best case $O(1)$ reads and $O(1)$ writes in the case where the top level block is not full. In the worse case, where a new bucket must be added, it performs N reads where N is the number of buckets in the current bucket chain and 2 writes in order to insert the new bucket and update the previous bucket overflow pointer. Any updates to the bucket chain requires overwriting an existing block in storage.

3.4 Bucket Map

The bucket map implementation was built around the goal of reducing the number of writes and reads required for an insert and removed the extra file needed by the file based implementation. The two data files that were required in the file based implementation were merged by always inserting buckets to the end of the

---

Algorithm 5. Split Operation.

Input: The key to delete
Output: The number of records deleted
$deleted \leftarrow 0\ index \leftarrow getIndex(nextSplit)$
$splittingBucket \leftarrow loadTopBucket(index)$
$newBucket \leftarrow createNewBucket()$
$completed \leftarrow false$
while $\neg completed$ **do**
    $insert, read \leftarrow splittingBucket.firstRecordPointer$
    $count \leftarrow bucket.recordCount$
    for $i \leftarrow 0$ **to** $count$ **do**
        $record \leftarrow recordAtReadPointer$
        $hash \leftarrow SDBM(record.key)$
        if $H_0(hash) \neq H_1(hash)$ **then**
            insert the record into the new bucket
            write out the $newBucket$ if full and create a new overflow
            $splittingBucket.recordCount- = 1$
        else
            if $insert \neq read$ **then**
                copy record at read to insert
            end
            $insert+ = recordSize$
        end
    end
    write out $splittingBucket$
    if $splittingBucket$ has overflow **then**
        $splittingBucket \leftarrow loadOverflowBucket(splittingBucket.overflow)$
    else
        $completed \leftarrow true$
    end
end
write out new bucket
$currentSize$**++**
if $currentSize == 2 \times initalSize$ **then**
    $initialSize \leftarrow 2 \times initalSize$
    $nextSplit \leftarrow 0$
else
    $nextSplit$**++**
end

---

file. To map a hash table index to a top level bucket, an in-memory expandable array was added to the hash table that maps the index to a file block.

Insert. Insertion can now be done in exactly one read and write by inserting an overflow bucket to the top of the bucket chain instead of the bottom and only reading the top bucket before creating an overflow. This process is shown in

Algorithm 6. Inserts a key and value into the hash table.

Input: The key and value to insert
Output: Error or success code
$index \leftarrow getIndex(key)$
$bucket \leftarrow loadBucketFromDataFile(index)$
$completed \leftarrow false$
while $\neg completed$ **do**
    if $bucket$ is not $full$ **then**
        insert record into the bucket
        write out bucket
        $completed \leftarrow true$
    else
        if $bucket$ has $overflow$ **then**
            $bucket \leftarrow loadOverflow(bucket.overflow)$
        else
            $bucket.overflow \leftarrow nextOverflowBlock$
            write out bucket
            $bucket \leftarrow initalizeNewBucket()$
            insert record into the bucket
            write out bucket
            $completed \leftarrow true$
        end
    end
end
$numRecords+ = 1$
if $currentLoad > load$ **then**
    $split()$
end

Algorithm 7. By adding an overflow bucket to the front of the chain, rather than the end of the chain, only 1 write is required, and it is not necessary to overwrite an existing bucket. Overwriting a bucket already on storage at a given logical address is still performed when there was space available in the bucket for the new record. The downside of only reading the top level bucket before expanding is that partially empty buckets further in the chain will never be filled. This can impact the performance of the split, get and delete operations.

Get. Get functions as in Algorithm 3. The only difference is that the file location is retrieved from the bucket map before reading the bucket from the file.

Delete. Delete functions identically as in Algorithm 4. The only difference is that the file location for the top level bucket is read from the bucket map.

Split. The split algorithm was modified to load the splitting bucket using the file location in the bucket map as well as updating the bucket map for the new

Algorithm 7. BucketMap Insert Operation.

Input: The key and value to insert
Output: The error or success code
$index \leftarrow getIndex(key)$
$fileIndex \leftarrow bucketMap[index]$
$bucket \leftarrow loadBucket(fileIndex)$
if *bucket is full* **then**
    $bucket \leftarrow initalizeNewBucket()$
    $bucket.overflow \leftarrow fileIndex$
    insert record into bucket
    $writeBucket(nextFileIndex)$
    $bucketMap[index] \leftarrow nextFileIndex$
    $nextFileIndex+ = 1$
else
    insert record into the bucket
    $writeBucket(fileIndex)$
end
$numRecords+ = 1$
if $currentLoad > load$ **then**
    $split()$
end

---

bucket and its overflows. The new bucket chain is created in the same way as in the insert algorithm.

3.5 Serial Writing

An implementation was created with the goal of taking advantage of the flash memory performance for serial writes. The hash table was modified to always write changed and new buckets to the end of the file. This requires using the bucket map implementation to always know where the top level buckets were located.

Insert. Insertion was a simple modification of Algorithm 7 that wrote out the changed bucket to the next available file location and updated the bucket map.

Split. In order for splitting to work with overflow chains, the splitting bucket chain has to be reversed and rebuilt during the split. This was accomplished by reading the bucket chain top down and then updating both the bucket map and overflow pointers as further blocks were read and written out.

The serial writing implementation is interesting as it never requires overwriting a logical block address. The previous two implementations rely on a flash translation layer (FTL) built into the SD card to translate logical file addresses to physical block locations. The FTL and file level interface of FAT16 running on the SD card hides the issue of overwriting a physical block. When a logical block in a file is overwritten by the algorithm, the FTL and file system select a different physical block to use transparently to the algorithm and thus there is no physical memory overwrites of flash blocks, which are expensive operations.

4   Experimental Results

Benchmarks were performed by inserting random 2-byte keys and random 2-byte values. The linear hash table was configured with the SDBM hashing function and a load of 85%.

4.1   Block Statistics

Writing to flash memory file blocks was tested with three different SD cards. 10000 file blocks were written as random or sequential writes. A file of 10000 blocks was benchmarked with sequential and random reads.

These benchmarks are shown in Fig. 3 and demonstrate the large variability of different SD cards and the general expected performance. In general, read operations are faster than writes, and sequential writes are faster then random writes. Sequential reads took an average of 47% of the time it takes for a sequential write. A random read takes an average of 64% of the time of a random write. There was no performance advantage of a sequential versus random write.

4.2   Insert

Insertion was benchmarked by recording the time to insert records into a hash table. These statistics are an average of five runs and include the time for splitting. Figure 4 shows the time per insert for a range of inserts.

It is obvious from this graph that the serial writing implementation did not perform as expected. This trend continued for all benchmarks and is left out in later figures. The reason is that serial writing resulted in large file sizes on the FAT16 file system. It is known that performing random access in FAT16 is very costly [14], and there was no benefit for avoiding overwriting logical blocks in a file. The FTL is successful in hiding the logical to physical block translation. The result was that it was more efficient to overwrite the same logical block (and have the FTL handle selecting a new physical block to write) rather than explicitly writing a new logical block.

Figure 5 shows the same graph with the non-overwrite removed. It shows that the bucket map is faster as expected until around 70,000 records have been inserted. After this cut off the file based implementation performs better. This performance difference is a result of the time used to expand the bucket map array as well as additional time needed during a split due to increased bucket map chains. Figures 6 and 7 show the block reads and writes for the insert operation benchmarks. As expected the bucket map implementation is less then the file implementation and is around 1 read and write per insert operation.

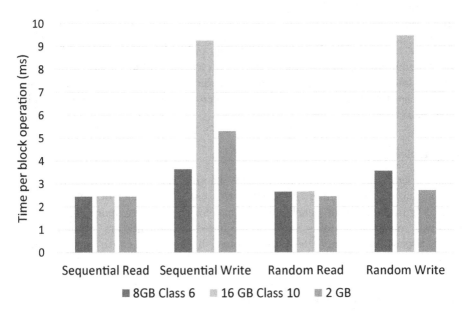

Fig. 3. SD card read/write benchmarks.

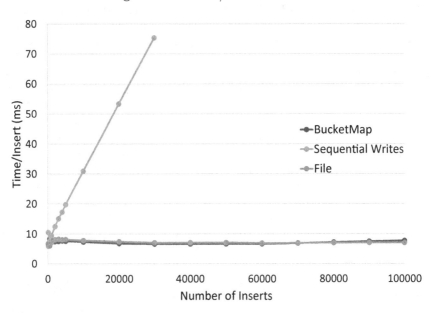

Fig. 4. Time per insert.

4.3 Get

Get operations were benchmarked by getting random keys from a table of varying size. The number of gets was made as half the current table size. Figure 8 shows that the bucket map implementation was variable and consistently slower then the file based implementation. This is expected as a result of larger partially filled bucket chains.

4.4 Delete

Delete operations were benchmarked by deleting random keys from tables of different sizes. The number of deletions was half the number of records in the table. Figure 9 shows the benchmarked times for these delete operations. Bucket map was consistently slower then the file based implementation. Similar to the get statistics this is likely the result of longer bucket chains with partially filled buckets.

4.5 Evaluation on RAW Flash Memory

Linear hashing was evaluated on raw flash memory using the same Arduino Mega 2560 processor with 8 KB SRAM running at 16 MHz. The Arduino is interfaced to a Microchip 64 Mbit SPIFlash SSTV26VF chip. This NOR flash chip is based on Microchip's Super-Flash technology which uses less current to program and has a shorter erase time (Sector/Block Erase: 18 ms (typ), 25 ms (max) Chip Erase: 35 ms (typ), 50 ms (max)). The write size is 256 bytes, and the erase granularity is a 4 KB sector. The data was obtained using the standard SPI interface.

The performance of this memory is reading at 2.06 ms/block and writing at 3.95 ms/block. Reading is about twice as fast as writing (not considering erase time). These times are similar to the read/write performance for the SD card experiments with reading being slightly faster. In both cases, the cost of transmitting the data from the processor to the memory using the SPI interface is a bottleneck in the process.

Implementing an algorithm on raw memory chips has additional challenges as there is no flash translation layer mapping logical file blocks to physical blocks in memory. The file-based and bucket map linear hash implementations that used a file interface for writing buckets are not directly portable to this platform as that would require a flash translation layer. The sequential writing algorithm was adaptable to raw flash memory as the writes are occurring sequentially with no overwrites in the logical address space. A flash translation layer is not required, and the algorithm must only manage when to cycle back to the start of the address space and erase blocks that were previously used.

The performance results were about 6.3 ms/insert and 2.8 ms/get. These results are comparable with the SD card performance but were only achievable by using the sequential writing algorithm that had extremely poor performance on a SD card.

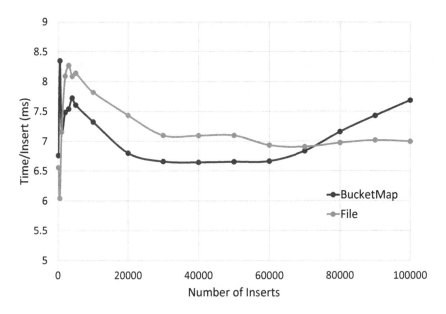

Fig. 5. Time per insert.

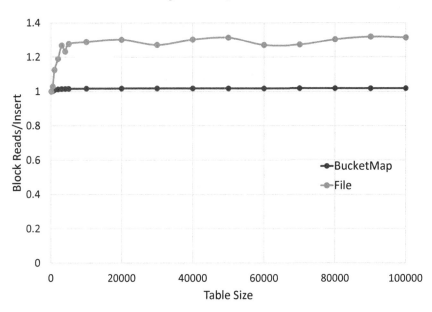

Fig. 6. Block reads per insert.

5   Future Work and Conclusions

The performance of three implementations of a linear hash table were compared on SD cards and raw flash memory. The major result is that algorithm

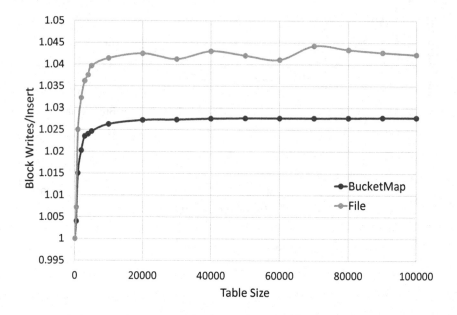

Fig. 7. Block writes per insert.

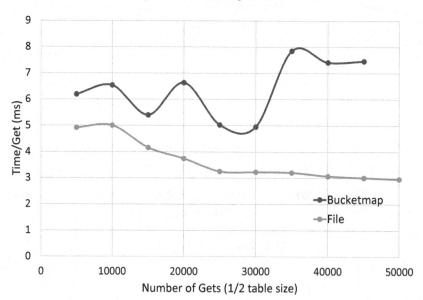

Fig. 8. Time per get operation.

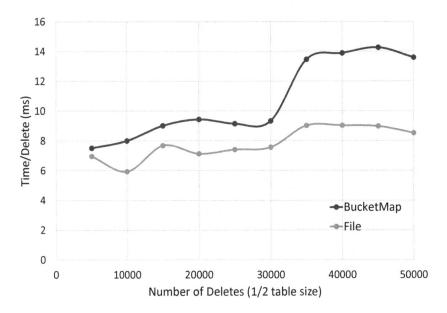

Fig. 9. Time per delete operation.

optimizations are very specific to the underlying hardware. When using SD card for storage with a file system like FAT16, there is minimal benefit to modifying the standard linear hash algorithm to be more flash-aware. The bucket map implementation was optimized for inserts and had higher insert performance in many cases. However, there was a trade-off for all other operations and the insert improvement was not consistently higher. The reason is that the flash translation layer and file system hide the complexity of overwriting physical blocks. The algorithm can operate with logical file blocks with minimal performance impact. Whereas low-level memory optimizations such as block or memory aligned access/writes have been shown to have a beneficial impact in other storage contexts, avoiding overwrites in SD card-based embedded flash memory does not seem to be as significant. Favoring writes over reads is a good strategy, but when the performance difference is not as significant (for SD cards tested no more than two to one) even that is not as crucial.

The results are different when running on raw flash memory. Without the aid of a FTL, the algorithm is responsible for handling low-level details and physical overwriting of blocks is not possible (without erasing first). In this environment, both the standard and bucket-map implementations of linear hash are not executable as they rely on overwriting existing blocks in the file. The sequential writing algorithm avoids overwriting completely and does not have a dependence on a FTL. Performance results show very good performance comparable with the implementations that run on SD cards.

In conclusion, indexing algorithm implementation on flash memory, especially memory without a FTL, require different strategies to achieve good performance.

Future work will examine optimizations for raw flash memory and develop a B+-tree implementation for comparison with linear hashing.

References

1. Anciaux, N., Bouganim, L., Pucheral, P.: Memory requirements for query execution in highly constrained devices. In: VLDB 2003, pp. 694–705. VLDB Endowment (2003). http://dl.acm.org/citation.cfm?id=1315451.1315511
2. Bonnet, P., Gehrke, J., Seshadri, P.: Towards sensor database systems. In: Tan, K.-L., Franklin, M.J., Lui, J.C.-S. (eds.) MDM 2001. LNCS, vol. 1987, pp. 3–14. Springer, Heidelberg (2001). https://doi.org/10.1007/3-540-44498-X_1. http://dl.acm.org/citation.cfm?id=648058.746944
3. Douglas, G., Lawrence, R.: LittleD: a SQL database for sensor nodes and embedded applications. In: Proceedings of the 29th Annual ACM Symposium on Applied Computing, SAC 2014, pp. 827–832. ACM, New York (2014). https://doi.org/10.1145/2554850.2554891
4. Fazackerley, S., Huang, E., Douglas, G., Kudlac, R., Lawrence, R.: Key-value store implementations for Arduino microcontrollers. In: IEEE 28th Canadian Conference on Electrical and Computer Engineering, pp. 158–164, May 2015. https://doi.org/10.1109/CCECE.2015.7129178
5. Feltham, A., MacBeth, S., Fazackerley, S., Lawrence, R.: Adapting linear hashing for flash memory resource-constrained embedded devices. In: Filipe, J., Smialek, M., Brodsky, A., Hammoudi, S. (eds.) Proceedings of the 21st International Conference on Enterprise Information Systems, ICEIS 2019, Heraklion, Crete, Greece, May 3–5, 2019, vol. 1, pp. 176–181. SciTePress (2019). https://doi.org/10.5220/0007709301760181
6. Fritter, M., Ould-Khessal, N., Fazackerley, S., Lawrence, R.: Experimental evaluation of hash function performance on embedded devices. In: 2018 IEEE Canadian Conference on Electrical & Computer Engineering (CCECE). IEEE, May 2018. https://doi.org/10.1109/ccece.2018.8447870
7. Gal, E., Toledo, S.: Algorithms and data sructures for flash memories. ACM Comput. Surv. **37**(2), 138–163 (2005). https://doi.org/10.1145/1089733.1089735
8. Larson, P.A.: Performance analysis of linear hashing with partial expansions. ACM Trans. Database Syst. **7**(4), 566–587 (1982). https://doi.org/10.1145/319758.319763. http://doi.acm.org/10.1145/319758.319763
9. Larson, P.: Linear hashing with overflow-handling by linear probing. ACM Trans. Database Syst. **10**(1), 75–89 (1985). https://doi.org/10.1145/3148.3324. http://doi.acm.org/10.1145/3148.3324
10. Lin, J., Yu, W., Zhang, N., Yang, X., Zhang, H., Zhao, W.: A survey on internet of things: architecture, enabling technologies, security and privacy, and applications. IEEE Internet Things J. **4**(5), 1125–1142 (2017). https://doi.org/10.1109/JIOT.2017.2683200
11. Lin, S., Zeinalipour-Yazti, D., Kalogeraki, V., Gunopulos, D., Najjar, W.A.: Efficient indexing data structures for flash-based sensor devices. Trans. Storage **2**(4), 468–503 (2006). https://doi.org/10.1145/1210596.1210601. http://doi.acm.org/10.1145/1210596.1210601
12. Litwin, W.: Linear hashing: a new tool for file and table addressing. In: 6th International Conference on Very Large Data Bases, pp. 212–223. IEEE Computer Society (1980)

13. Madden, S.R., Franklin, M.J., Hellerstein, J.M., Hong, W.: TinyDB: an acquisitional query processing system for sensor networks. ACM Trans. Database Syst. **30**(1), 122–173 (2005). https://doi.org/10.1145/1061318.1061322. http://doi.acm.org/10.1145/1061318.1061322

14. Penson, W., Fazackerley, S., Lawrence, R.: TEFS: a flash file system for use on memory constrained devices. In: 2016 IEEE Canadian Conference on Electrical and Computer Engineering (CCECE), pp. 1–5, May 2016. https://doi.org/10.1109/CCECE.2016.7726822

15. Severance, C.: Massimo banzi: building arduino. Computer **47**(1), 11–12 (2014). https://doi.org/10.1109/MC.2014.19

16. Tsiftes, N., Dunkels, A.: A database in every sensor. In: SenSys 2011, pp. 316–332. ACM, New York (2011) https://doi.org/10.1145/2070942.2070974, http://doi.acm.org/10.1145/2070942.2070974

17. Yang, C., Jin, P., Yue, L., Zhang, D.: Self-adaptive linear hashing for solid state drives. In: ICDE, pp. 433–444, May 2016. https://doi.org/10.1109/ICDE.2016.7498260

On-Premise or Cloud Enterprise Application Deployment: Fit-Gap Perspective

Jānis Grabis(✉)

Information Technology Institute, Riga Technical University,
Kalku 1, Riga, Latvia
grabis@rtu.lv

Abstract. The fit-gap analysis of enterprise applications allows to identify their customization needs during implementation at a company. The enterprise applications provide a set of customization tools and customization flexibility is affected by a deployment mode. The on-premise deployment requires effort to install the application and its updates while there are a few restrictions on depths and breath of customization. The cloud deployment of Software as a Service applications is easier to setup while there are some restrictions of kind of customizations made. This paper elaborates an optimization model to select an enterprise application customization strategy as a part of the fit-gap analysis in the case of the choice between on-premise and cloud deployment of the enterprise application. The model also takes into account newly released standard features provided by the vendor of the enterprise applications. The model analysis is performed to investigate factors affecting the choice between on-premise and cloud deployment and an impact of company's customization preferences on the gaps resolution strategy. An application example is also provided.

Keywords: Fit-gap analysis · Enterprise applications · Customization roadmap

1 Introduction

Enterprise applications such as Enterprise Resources Planning (ERP) and Customer Relationship Management (CRM) systems are large software applications used by companies to run their business processes. These applications typically are packaged applications implementing so called best practice processes as envisioned by software vendors. Nowadays, many enterprise applications are available for both on-premise and cloud deployment. The applications deployed in the cloud are offered to companies as Software as a Service (SaaS). SaaS applications can be deployed more rapidly than on-premise applications, however, their users do not have full control over these applications [1].

Enterprise applications provide generic functionality not specifically tailored to a particular company implementing the system. However, the enterprise applications have some degree of flexibility and customization capabilities to accommodate specific requirements. Companies aim to select an application best suited for their needs. Packaged application selection methods [2] and fit-gap analysis [3] are employed for these purposes.

© Springer Nature Switzerland AG 2020
J. Filipe et al. (Eds.): ICEIS 2019, LNBIP 378, pp. 406–423, 2020.
https://doi.org/10.1007/978-3-030-40783-4_19

Nevertheless, there are gaps between functionality and capabilities provided and the requirements, and these gaps need to be resolved during implementation of the enterprise applications. The gaps can be resolved by customizing the enterprise application. These applications typically provide a range of customization methods [4]. These methods include custom coding, user interface modification, workflow development and others. Several existing works investigate a choice between customization alternatives [5] and implications of customization on business value and operation of enterprise applications [6].

Customization often is time-consuming and costly and poses various risks [7]. In order to reduce the amount of customization, companies might benefit from software updates released by vendors of enterprise applications. The updates might contain functionality or features requested by the companies. The vendors publish information about forthcoming updates as product development roadmaps. In the case of on-premise deployment introducing new updates might be time-consuming and lead to complex migration from one version to another. In the case of SaaS new updates are applied automatically with a little effort to the company.

Grabis (2019) argues that the fit-gap analysis and selection of customization choices should be synchronized with the vendor's enterprise application development roadmap [8]. In general, the fit-gap analysis should be viewed as a strategically oriented activity creating a plan for staged evolution of the enterprise application. The strategy development includes two major decisions. At first the company needs to choose between on-premise or cloud deployment what is followed by development of the gaps resolution strategy. The gaps resolution strategy specifies selection of customization methods to deal with the gaps, timing of implementation of customizations and possibilities to avoid customization by adopting new features provided by the vendor of the enterprise application. This paper argues that there are interdependencies between the choice of the deployment mode and selection of the customization options.

The objective of the paper is to develop a model for optimization of the gaps resolution strategy to choose between on-premise and cloud deployment. This paper extends the previous research reported in [8] by considering the on-premise and cloud deployment modes. The optimization model balances a trade-off between customization effort and value, and specifically takes into account the standard software evolution roadmap provided by the vendor of the enterprise application. The model allows to evaluate various enterprise applications implementation policies depending on company's preferences and customization circumstances. The specific research questions of the evaluation are: (Q1) what are the factors affecting the choice between on-premise and cloud deployment; and (Q2) what is the impact of company's customization preferences on the gaps resolution strategy. Application of the model is demonstrated using an example of customization of the lead qualification process in a CRM system.

The rest of the paper is organized as follows. Section 2 reviews background information and related work on enterprise applications systems and fit-gap analysis. The optimization model is formulated in Sect. 3. Section 4 provides model analysis results and the application example is explored in Sect. 5. Section 6 concludes.

2 Background

There are several types of enterprise applications and ERP systems represent the most prominent type of these applications. Therefore much of foundational research on enterprise applications is developed by analyzing ERP systems though the results are often applicable to other enterprise applications as well. Similarly, the foundational research including that on the implementation process and fit-gap analysis was created for on-premise applications and is applicable to cloud based systems as well if cloud specific circumstances are taken into account.

2.1 Implementation and Customization of Enterprise Applications

The enterprise application implementation process consists of project planning, design and customization, implementation and maintenance and continuous improvement phases [9]. During the project planning phase, key requirements are identified and a suitable enterprise application is selected. The enterprise application selected provides a set of standard features and customization tools [10]. Detailed analysis of the requirements and functionality of the enterprise applications is performed in the design and customization phase. Companies implementing enterprise applications use either the standard features or customize the applications. The usage of the standard features might result in a need to redesign its business processes. In the case of customization, unique business processes are retained and modification of the enterprise application is undertaken.

Enterprise application customization concerns modification of their standard features using various tools provided. It is performed in the customization and implementation phases and reduces gaps between the required and provided functionality. Aslam et al. [4] summarize several typologies of customizations in ERP systems. They include configuration, bolt-ons, screen masks, reporting, workflow development, interface modification and package code modification. Hustad et al. consider tailoring of reports, interfaces, enhancements, forms, workflows and portals [11]. Similar customization options are also available in SaaS applications [12].

There is no agreement on benefits of customization [4]. Several authors point out that customization is time consuming and complicates system's maintenance, especially, due to added effort to introduce new updates [6]. Research by Parthasarathy and Sharma suggests that customization does not yield expected benefits [13]. Yet, companies have strong desire for customization [14], and Holsapple et al. argue that customization has a major importance on preserving value-adding functions at companies using packaged applications [15]. SaaS applications often lack required functionality and there are customization limitations as well [16]. Cloud based enterprise applications often are not as flexible as on-premise applications and some customizations cannot be implemented or implementation is more complex [17, 18]. Obviously, customization requires some development effort and must have sufficient value or utility for the enterprise to be considered for implementation.

The important part of the implementation process is interplay with software vendor. The software vendor continuously evolves the software and the recent move to software as a service mode of software delivery implies that new features are delivered continuously without the need for upgrading from one version to another. Vendors release new version two to four times a year [19]. The envisioned changes are announced in advance in a form of software development roadmap [20]. The development roadmap includes the expected new features and their estimated release dates. If an appropriate new feature will be released the corresponding customizations might be postponed or averted.

The fit-gap analysis is a part of the planning and design phases of the enterprise application implementation process. Initially, it is performed for the high level requirements to provide input for selection among alternative enterprise applications. The detailed analysis is conducted for the selected application to provide inputs to the implementation phase. The fit-gap analysis yields a set of fits and a set of gaps. The gaps can be resolved either by customizing the enterprise application or adopting the forthcoming standard features as envision in the vendor's application development roadmap.

2.2 Related Work on Fit-Gap Analysis

A number of fit gap analysis methods have been developed. One group of the methods focus on identification of gaps and another group of the methods also consider selection of customization choices to address the gaps.

Identification of gaps is analyzed by Wu et al. [21]. Enterprise requirements are captured in goal, activity and data models, which are compared with the ERP systems to identify the differences. Yen et al. [22] identify misfits at the strategic level and propose their classification framework, where the misfits are categorized as enterprise, industry or country specific.

Sarfaraz et al. [23] proposed to use AHP to evaluate technical customization choices vs process customization choices with respect to degree of customization. Parthasarathy and Daneva develop a requirements prioritization framework and a heuristic algorithm to find a justifiable degree of customization [5]. They consider introduction of new standard features in future releases of the ERP system as one of the evaluation criteria. Pajk and Kovacic describe a detailed fit-gap analysis process including high-level fit-gap analysis, identification of gaps and fits, and gaps resolution [24]. Process adaptation, system adaption, third party solution and workaround are identified as resolution strategies. These and other fit-gap analysis methods are also reviewed by Ancveire [25]. As far as identified there is no work on fit-gap analysis specifically for cloud based enterprise applications.

The proposed model is an optimization model as opposed to heuristic method used in literature and it specifically takes into account dynamics of introduction of new standard features by the ERP vendor what is of particular relevance in the case of cloud deployment.

2.3 Gaps Resolution Strategy

A strategic approach to gaps resolution was proposed in the earlier steps of this research [8]. The gaps resolution strategy defines selection of customization options and their timing to reduce gaps between the required functionality and the functionality provided by the selected enterprise application. It takes into account vendor's application development roadmap.

The conceptual model of the gaps resolution strategy is shown in Fig. 1. It is assumed that the company has identified requirements towards an enterprise application. If the selected application does not meet some of the requirements, corresponding gaps are identified. The strategy is driven by company's preferences concerning customization. The vendor's roadmap indicates timing of the release of new features. The new features might address some of the gaps though there is no guarantee that they will be definitely delivered. The gaps resolution strategy consists of customization choices. The customization choice indicates when and what gaps resolution approaches will be used. The packaged enterprise applications differ from custom-built applications that there is well-defined set of customization options characteristic to a particular application.

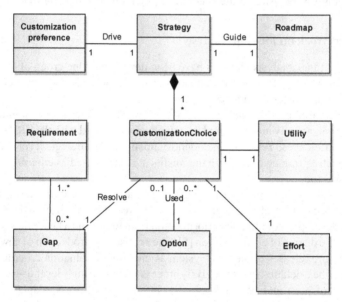

Fig. 1. The conceptual model of the gaps resolution strategy [8].

Every customization choice has its utility and associated implementation effort. The utility and effort are specific to a combination of the gap and its resolution option. The utility characterizes business value achieved by making a specific customization choice. The effort characterizes the implementation effort. The utility does not necessarily outweight the effort.

The process of establishing the gaps resolution strategy is illustrated in Fig. 2. It is assumed that requirements towards the enterprise applications have been elicited and there is sufficient information about available standard features. The application can be deployed either on-premise or in the cloud as SaaS application. Attributes characterizing the deployment modes are identified. That includes quantification of deployment costs in the case of on-premise deployment and identification of customization restriction in the case of cloud deployment. Gaps among the required functionality and available standard features are identified. It is expected that the gaps are similar for both types of deployment though some differences are possible. Utility and effort associated with every customization option are evaluated per gap. Simultaneously, the vendor's roadmap is analyzed and opportunities for using newly released features to resolve the gaps are identified. There is a utility associated with adopting the new features as well.

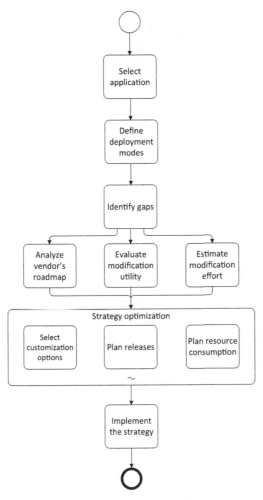

Fig. 2. The gap resolution strategy development process.

The utility and effort estimates, and roadmap are inputs to gaps resolution strategy optimization. The strategy selects either on-premise or cloud deployment mode. It is established for a finite planning horizon and the optimization results are selection of customization options and timing of implementation of the changes bundled as releases. The optimization is performed subject to development resource constraints. Finally, the strategy is implemented. Implementation adjustments might be required because of changes in the vendor's roadmap or adjustment utility and effort estimation. However, the deployment mode selection is a long-term decision fixed in the first round of the strategy development.

3 Optimization Model

The optimization model is elaborated to establish the gaps resolution strategy. The optimization model selects customization choices to maximize the difference between customization utility and effort. It takes into account expected release of new features by the enterprise application vendor and availability of development resources needed for customization. Additionally, the choice between on-premise and cloud deployment is made.

Notation

m — deployment mode, where $m = 1$ refers to on-premise and $m = 2$ refers to cloud deployment

i — gaps index

j — customization options index

t — time period index

TT — planning horizon

G_i — gaps

O_j — implementation options

Y_m — selected deployment mode equals to 1 if on-premise deployment is used and 0 if cloud deployment is used

X_{mijt} — selected implementation option equals to 1 if ith gap is resolved using jth option in tth period and 0 otherwise

τ_i — release time period of new standard feature for ith gap

E_{mij} — implementation effort for gap i using option j in points what might be deployment mode specific

V_{ij} — unadjusted variable implementation utility for gap i using option j in points

V_{ij}^* — unadjusted fixed implementation utility for gap i using option j in points

U_{ij} — variable implementation utility for gap i using option j in points adjusted according to customization preferences

U_{ij}^* — fixed implementation utility for gap i using option j in points adjusted according to customization preferences

R_t — resources available in period t in points

Π_t — resource usage in in period t in points

Q_t — equals to 1 if standard features are applied in tth period in the case of on-premise deployment and 0 otherwise

ϖ — the fixed effort for applying standard features in the case of on-premise deployment

δ — customization preference coefficient

N — large number

Assumptions

The following assumptions are made in the optimization model:

- Gaps are independent;
- Customizations are independent;

- Tasks are small enough to be completed within one period;
- Tasks can be split over two periods if resources are not available in a single period;
- Customizations are rolled-out at the end of every period if any;
- In the case of on-premise deployment adoption of new vendor's releases incurs additional cost;
- Customization effort can be larger for the cloud deployment for some types of customizations;
- Only one customization option can be selected for a gap;
- If a customization option is not suitable for the gap then modification effort is set to a large number.
- Effort, utility and resource capacity are measured in points, which are appropriately scaled.

Objective

The objective function (Eq. 1) selects customization choices that maximize customization gains expected as the difference between customization utility and effort. The utility is divided in two terms, namely, variable and fixed returns. The fixed returns are evaluated over the whole enterprise application life-cycle and are accounted for regardless when the gap is resolved. The variable returns are realized during the strategy's planning horizon starting with the period when the gap is resolved. In the case of on-premise deployment, additional costs are incurred every time newly received standard features are applied. Only one deployment mode can be chosen at a time.

$$
\begin{aligned}
Z = \sum_{i=1}^{I} \sum_{j=1}^{J} \sum_{t=1}^{TT} \left((TT - t)U_{ij} + U_{ij}^* \right) X_{mijt} \\
- \left(\sum_{i=1}^{I} \sum_{j=1}^{J} \sum_{t=1}^{TT} E_{mij} X_{mijt} + \sum_{t=1}^{TT} \varpi Q_t \right) \to \max
\end{aligned}
\tag{1}
$$

Constraints

The optimization is performed subject to:

$$
Y_1 + Y_2 = 1 \tag{2}
$$

$$
\sum_{i=1}^{I} \sum_{j=1}^{J} \sum_{t=1}^{TT} X_{mijt} \le NY_m, m = 1, 2 \tag{3}
$$

$$
\sum_{j=1}^{J} \sum_{t=1}^{TT} X_{mijt} \le 1, \forall i \tag{4}
$$

$$
\Pi_t = \sum_{i=1}^{I} \sum_{j=1}^{J} E_{ij} X_{mijt} \le R_t, t = 1, \ldots, TT \tag{5}
$$

$$
\Pi_t - (R_{t-1} - \Pi_{t-1}) \le R_t, t = 1, \ldots, TT \tag{6}
$$

$$
\sum_{i=1}^{I} \sum_{j=1}^{J} E_{mij} X_{mijt} \le R_t, t = 1 \tag{7}
$$

$$
t \ge \tau_i X_{i1t}, \forall i, t \tag{8}
$$

$$
\sum_{i=1}^{I} X_{1i1t} \le NQ_t, t = 1, \ldots, TT \tag{9}
$$

$$\sum_{t=1}^{TT} Q_t \leq NY_1 \tag{10}$$

$$U_{ij} = \delta V_{ij}, \, U_{ij}^* = \delta V_{ij}^*, \, \forall i, j \tag{11}$$

Equation 2 states that only one deployment mode can be selected. The constraint (3) relates choice of the customization options with the deployment mode. The constraint (4) implies that every gap can be resolved no more than just once (including using just one customization option). The Eq. (5) calculates the resource usage on customization in a given time period. The constraint (6) imposes that the resource usage over the two subsequent periods cannot exceed available resources in every period. The constraint (7) defines resource restrictions for the first period. The constraint (8) states that the vendor's released features cannot be adopted before they are released. The constraint (9) defines that if the standard feature is adopted at the given time period then the vendor's update should be applied to the on-premise deployment. This is applicable only for the on-premise deployment (Eq. 10). The Eq. (11) adjusts the customization utility. If the customization preference coefficient δ is increased the company has stronger incentives to customize system. If the customization preference coefficient is decreased the company prefers usage of standard features and the gaps are resolved by either changing business processes or waiting for appropriate updates to be released by the vendor. Thus, the equation represents company's strategic preference for customization or standardization.

The gap resolution strategy is manifested as a plan of enterprise application customization or adoption of newly released features provided by the application's vendor. The strategy is visualized as a table representing the optimization results (Table 1).

Table 1. Tabular representation of the gap resolution strategy.

m, if $Y_m = 1$		Time periods		
Gap	Option	1	$\cdots$	TT
1	j, if $\exists X_{mijt} = 1$	X_{m1j1}	$\cdots$	X_{m1jTT}
$\cdots$	$\cdots$	$\cdots$	$\cdots$	$\cdots$
I	j, if $\exists X_{mijt} = 1$	X_{mIj1}	$\cdots$	X_{mIjTT}

4   Model Analysis

Experimental studies are conducted with the model. Their objective is to investigate factors affecting the choice between on-premise and cloud deployment and to demonstrate the impact of the customization preferences on the gap resolution strategy. A synthetic data set is used in the studies. It is assumed that 20 gaps are identified and 5 customization options including adoption of newly released standard features. Customization effort varies from 0 (for standard features) to 13 points. In the case of cloud deployment, the effort is larger than for the on-premise deployment for some of the gaps (50% on average in the experiments conducted). The extra effort is represented using the exponential distribution with the mean value $1/\lambda$. The utility is generated as a randomized multiple of the effort and on average is by 20% larger than the effort over the planning horizon. There are 12 periods within the planning horizon, and development capacity for each period is 20 points. The vendor releases new features after every four periods and they are good for resolving 12 gaps although some of the features become available quite late in the planning horizon. In the case of on-premise deployment, the vendor releases new features and it is assumed that installing these new releases take extra effort ϖ. For the experimental purposes, $\varpi = \beta \times \lambda$, where β is the coefficient showing how many times fixed installation effort for the on-premise deployment exceeds premium customization effort of cloud deployment. The experimental results are obtained for ten randomly generated sets of utility values for every treatment.

To answer the first model analysis question, λ is varied from 1 to 1,5 (low value indicates that there is a more significant extra effort of cloud customization) and β is varied from 1 to 10. Figure 3 shows selection of the deployment mode depending on β and λ. The on-premise deployment is favoured if installation of new updates is not expensive or the cloud deployment customization requires more effort. If cloud based applications are flexible enough to have negligible extra customization effort, then the cloud deployment is favoured because new releases can be incorporated easier. In the frontier between two choices the optimization model yields one or another of deployment modes depending on specific values of customization utility. These situations are risky to companies because there is no clear cut decision and the preference for the deployment mode can change over time even though switching between the modes is problematic.

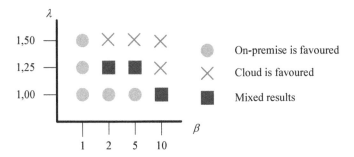

Fig. 3. Selection of the deployment mode depending on β and λ.

Gap resolution choices depending on β and λ are illustrated in Fig. 4. The figure shows how many gaps out of 20 were resolved, how many times newly released standard features were adopted and how many times customizations were made. As expected, the figures show that customizations are made more frequently for the on-premise deployment and standard features are adopted more frequently for the cloud deployment. There is a slight tendency that an increasing number of gaps are resolved as λ increases for the cloud deployment. The appeal of using the standard features decreases if β increases, i.e. installation of new updates takes extra effort. The non-linear dependence of the numbers of standard features used and customizations made on λ is due to the frontier effect as one switches from using the on-premise deployment to the cloud deployment.

To answer the second research question, the customization preference coefficient δ is varied from 0.25 to 2, where the former value resembles company's preference to use standard features while the latter value resembles company's preference to customize. The optimization results (Table 2) show that customization choices significantly depend on the customization preference coefficient. If $\delta = 0.25$ the enterprise opts for changing business processes or using standard features as they become available. If customization utility is high almost all gaps are resolved and there are few incentives to wait for standard features to be delivered. That, however, is also affected by availability of development resources (in this case resource utilization is about 70% for $\delta = 2$). The optimization model clearly allows to identify trade-offs between customization and adoption of standard features depending on customization preferences of the enterprise.

5 Example

Application of the model is demonstrated using an example of implementing a CRM system (the functionality and available customization options are inspired by Microsoft Dynamics 365). More specifically, the lead qualification process [8, 26] is considered

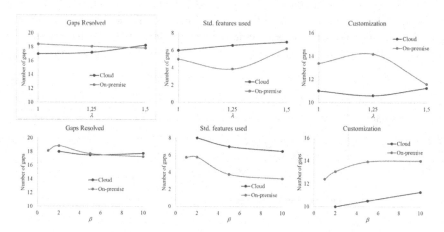

Fig. 4. The gaps resolution depending on λ and β.

Table 2. The impact of customization preferences on the gaps resolution strategy.

δ	Number of gaps resolved by customization	Number of gaps resolved by standard features	Number of gaps unresolved
0,25	2	9,2	8,8
0,5	8,8	7,8	3,4
1	15,2	3,8	1
2	18,3	1	0,6

(Fig. 5). In this process, a lead represents a potential source of sales. Information about lead is registered in the system. Initial information might be incomplete and initial data cleansing is required to identify duplicated records. The leads are contacted by sales representatives to gather additional data and to evaluate sales potential. If potential customers respond positively they are converted into opportunities. If initial contacts are not successful, further activities are planed until the lead is converted into an opportunity or dropped. The number of leads can be substantial and there are many opportunities for process automation.

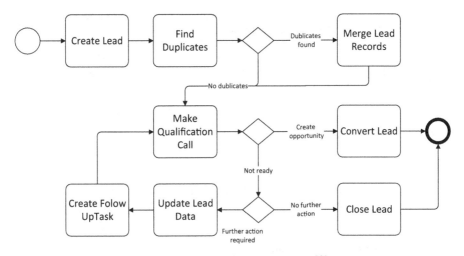

Fig. 5. The lead qualification process [8].

The cloud deployment of the CRM application is considered. Multiple customization options categorized as data view, user interface (UI) modification, custom report, different types of workflows and add-ons are available. The data view customization option provides simple improvements for searching, filtering and performing other data processing operations. The UI customization option modifies the existing UI, for instance, to make data input more efficient. Reports typically provide analytical features. Basic processes provide process execution guidance while workflows support task automation and advanced process execution logics. Add-ons are developed using low-level modification techniques (i.e., custom code development) or purchased from third-parties.

It is assumed that several gaps have been identified (Table 3). The company aims to make process execution more efficient and considers changes ranging from UI modification to introduction of automated processing. The available customization options are also listed (not all options are available for every gap). For instance, the report customization option is suitable for the Update lead data task. Six customizations options are available for gap G2 in the Find Duplicates task. The Data view customization provides a set of filter facilitating manual identification of duplicates. The UI customization emphasis data fields needed for the task. The report customization provides analytical data need for the task. Process defines standard steps to be performed to find duplicates

Table 3. Gaps and available customization options for the lead qualification process [8].

Process tasks	Gap	Customization options
Create lead	G1: The data entry is too time-consuming due to extra navigations steps	Std. feature
		Data view
		UI
		Basic process
		Workflow
Find duplicates	G2: Provided data are not appropriately tailored and a lot of manual work	Data view
		UI
		Report
		Basic process
		Workflow
		Add-on
Make qualification call	G3: The conversation is not scripted	Std. feature
		Basic process
		Workflow
Update lead data	G4: The update is manual and involves extra navigation steps	UI
		Basic process
		Workflow
Create follow up tasks	G5: Not all information to decide on follow up tasks is available	Data view
		UI
		Report
Close lead	G6: Closing is manual	UI
		Basic process
		Workflow
Convert lead	G7: Conversion is manual	UI
		Report
		Basic process Workflow

and the workflow automates some of these tasks. The Add-on provides a classification algorithm for merging lead according to a set of attributes.

The effort and utility of the customization options is determined (Table 4). Generally, it is assumed that user interface modifications are the simplest and development (or procurement) of add-ons require the most effort. Similarly, usage of more advanced and lower level customization options potentially yields more benefits (i.e., higher utility). The values provided are illustrative and their actual values are determined on the case to case basis. These values were also used in the previous work reported in [8].

The planning horizon is six periods and resources are available to implement 15 points worth of customization in each period. The vendor will provide new features for the first three gaps in the third period. Standard features are not expected for other four gaps. The customization preference coefficient δ is varied from 0.25 to 2.

Figure 6 shows the optimization results according to the customization preference coefficient δ. If the company aims to avoid customizations then standard features are

Table 4. Effort and utility per customization choice [8].

Gap	Customization option	Effort	Utility
G1	Std. feature	0	10
	Data view	1	2
	UI	3	3,5
	Basic process	3	3,5
	Workflow	8	10
G2	Std. feature	0	10
	Data view	1	1,5
	UI	3	4
	Report	5	12
	Basic process	3	4
	Workflow	8	10
	Add-on	13	25
G3	Std. feature	0	3
	Basic process	3	3,2
	Workflow	13	20
G4	UI	5	3,3
	Basic process	3	3,2
	Workflow	5	6
G5	Data view	1	1
	UI	1	1
	Report	5	6
G6	UI	3	2
	Basic process	1	2
	Workflow	5	6
G7	UI	3	3,5
	Report	3	4
	Basic process	1	2
	Workflow	8	10

introduced where available and other gaps are unresolved. As the customization preference increases most of the gaps are resolved and customization takes precedence over
the standard features because they tend to have higher utility.

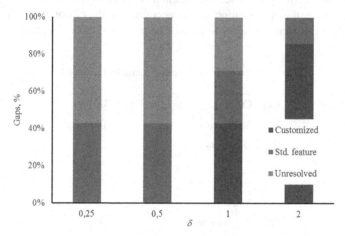

Fig. 6. The gap resolution choice depending on δ.

Figure 7 shows an example of the gap resolution strategy. It shows timing of implementing customizations and adoption of newly released standard features. If the standard
features are adopted they are introduced immediately. Gaps 4 and 5 are left unresolved
because their resolution utility is lower than the effort. The basic process customization option is favoured instead of the workflow customization option because it can be

Gap 7	Basic process						
Gap 6	Basic process						
Gap 5	-						
Gap 4	-						
Gap 3	Std. feature						
Gap 2	Add-on						
Gap 1	Std. feature						
		1	2	3	4	5	6

Fig. 7. A fragment of the sample gap resolution strategy. The second column indicates the customization approach used, green filling indicates periods the customization is implemented and
used, light read indicates availability of new standard features and dark red indicates usage of the
new standard features. (Color figure online)

implemented sooner (due to smaller effort) and business benefits can be realized for the whole planning horizon. The standard feature for Gap 3 becomes available at the third period though it was beneficial to introduce the customization already in the first period because resource restrictions were not significant.

The optimization is also performed without accounting for the vendor's roadmap. As the result, the value of the objective function is by 58% smaller than initially. That indicates that using the vendor's roadmap as an input one can find a better strategy. The comparison was also made with a heuristic method following the greedy principle. The heuristic started with implementation of customization choices with the largest difference between effort and utility as long as resources are sufficient for the period. The obtained value of the objective function was by 87% smaller than the optimal.

6 Conclusion

The new optimization model for resolving gaps in implementation of enterprise applications has been elaborated. It provides dynamic gaps resolution planning with respect to resource availability and vendor's software evolution roadmap in the case of the choice between on-premise and cloud deployment. The model can be used to evaluate various enterprise application implementation policies, for instance, impact of company's preferences for customization or retaining standard features. This analysis is important because there is no consensus on business value of enterprise applications customization and companies have different needs and preferences.

The experimental results show that the cloud deployment is favoured if there is a small extra customization effort and if the on-premise deployment requires significant effort in installing new updates. The cloud based enterprise applications are becoming more flexible and their modification possibilities keep increasing. However, not all customization can be made in cloud based applications. The updates of new standard feature are appealing to companies only of their installation is sufficiently effortless compared to the utility gains.

There is always an effort and utility estimation error and utility can change over time. While there are a number of experimental scenarios when the choice between cloud and on-premise deployments is clear, there are also several scenarios when results are quite sensitive depending on variations in utility. These scenarios would require extra evaluation. The experimental results confirm that companies opt for the cloud deployment and usage of standard features if customization preference is low.

The paper does not consider implementation cost differences between the cloud and on-premise deployment. The choice between the deployment alternatives is considered only from the fit-gap perspective. The paper does not investigate specific methods for estimating utility and effort, and effort estimation by planning poker [27] is adopted for illustrative purposes. The utility can be determined using cost of delay criterion as described by Leffingwell [28].

The optimization model can be extended in various ways. Currently, it assumes that maintenance considerations are captured using the utility measure though more explicit treatment of maintenance could be provided. The model also does not consider relationships among gaps and possibilities to used multiple customization options for a single gap.

Company and vendor relationships also could be explored further. Unfortunately, vendors change their roadmaps frequently and this uncertainty also should be represented in the model. Additionally, vendors charge support fees, which include delivery of new features. The model could be used to evaluate whether (1) these fees are justifiable and (2) features are delivered soon enough or the company is better off with implementing changes on its own.

References

1. Weng, F., Hung, M.C.: Competition and challenge on adopting cloud ERP. Int. J. Innovation Manage. Technol. **5**(4), 309–313 (2014)
2. Jadhav, A.S., Sonar, R.M.: Evaluating and selecting software packages: a review. Inf. Softw. Technol. **51**(3), 555–563 (2009)
3. Gulledge, T.R.: ERP gap-fit analysis from a business process orientation. Int. J. Serv. Stan. **2**(4), 339–348 (2006)
4. Aslam, U., Coombs, C., Doherty, N.F.: Benefits realization from ERP systems: the role of customization. In: ECIS 2012 - Proceedings of the 20th European Conference on Information Systems (2012)
5. Parthasarathy, S., Daneva, M.: An approach to estimation of degree of customization for ERP projects using prioritized requirements. J. Syst. Softw. **117**, 471–487 (2016)
6. Zach, O., Munkvold, B.E.: Identifying reasons for ERP system customization in SMEs: a multiple case study. J. Enterp. Inf. Manage. **25**(5), 462–478 (2012)
7. Kholeif, A.O., Abdel - Kader, M., Sherer, M.: ERP customization failure: institutionalized accounting practices, power relations and mark et forces. J. Account. Organ. Change 3, 250–269 (2007)
8. Grabis, J.: Optimization of gaps resolution strategy in implementation of ERP systems. In: Proceeding of ICEIS, no. 1, pp. 84–92 (2019)
9. Erazo, J., Arboleda, H., Pino, F.J.: Analysis of the software implementation process for ERP systems. In: 12th Colombian Conference on Computing, CCC 2017. Communications in Computer and Information Science, vol. 735, pp. 297–312 (2017)
10. Luo, W., Strong, D.M.: A framework for evaluating ERP implementation choices. IEEE Trans. Eng. Manage. **51**(3), 322–333 (2004)
11. Hustad, E., Haddara, M., Kalvenes, B.: ERP and organizational misfits: an ERP customization journey. Procedia Comput. Sci. **100**, 429–439 (2016)
12. Ali, A.Q., Sultan, A.B.M., Ghani, A.A.A., Zulzalil, H.: Systematic mapping study on the customization solutions of software as a service applications. IEEE Access **7**, 88196–88217 (2019)
13. Parthasarathy, S., Sharma, S.: Efficiency analysis of ERP packages - a customization perspective. Comput. Ind. **82**, 19–27 (2016)
14. Gool, S., Seymour, L.F.: Managing enterprise resource planning system customisation post-implementation: the case of an African petroleum organisation. In: ICEIS 2018 - Proceedings of the 20th International Conference on Enterprise Information Systems, p. 111 (2018)
15. Holsapple, C., Wang, Y., Wu, J.: Empirically testing user characteristics and fitness factors in enterprise resource planning success. Int. J. Hum. Comput. Interact. **19**(3), 325–342 (2005)
16. Abd, M.A., Nasrb, E.S., Geitha, M.H.: Benefits and challenges of cloud ERP systems – a systematic literature review. Future Comput. Inf. J. **1**(1–2), 1–9 (2016)
17. Saeed, I., Juell-Skielse, G., Uppström, E.: Cloud enterprise resource planning adoption: motives & barriers. In: Advances in Enterprise Information Systems, pp. 429–442 (2012)

18. Nowak, D., Kurbel, K.: Understanding the flexibility of cloud ERP software. In: Piazolo, F., Geist, V., Brehm, L., Schmidt, R. (eds.) ERP Future 2016. LNBIP, vol. 285, pp. 135–146. Springer, Cham (2017). https://doi.org/10.1007/978-3-319-58801-8_12

19. Hamerman, P.D.: The SaaS ERP Applications Landscape, Forrester (2015)

20. Keizer, G.: Microsoft puts Dynamics 365 on twice-a-year release cadence, Computerworld, 11 July (2018). https://www.computerworld.com/article/3289388/

21. Wu, J.H., Shin, S.S., Heng, M.S.H.: A methodology for ERP misfit analysis. Inf. Manage. **44**(8), 666–680 (2007)

22. Yen, T.S., Idrus, R., Yusof, U.K.: A framework for classifying misfits between enterprise resource planning (ERP) systems and business strategies. Asian Acad. Manage. J. **16**(2), 53–75 (2011)

23. Sarfaraz, A., Jenab, K., D'Souza, A.C.: Evaluating ERP implementation choices on the basis of customisation using fuzzy AHP. Int. J. Prod. Res. **50**(230), 7057–7067 (2012)

24. Pajk, D., Kovacic, A.: Fit gap analysis – the role of business process reference models. Econ. Bus. Rev. **15**(4), 319–338 (2013)

25. Ancveire, I.: Fit gap analysis methods for ERP systems literature review. In: Proceedings of ISACI 2018 - IEEE 12th International Symposium on Applied Computational Intelligence and Informatics, pp. 161–166 (2018)

26. Monat, J.P.: Industrial sales lead conversion modeling. Market. Intell. Plann. **29**(2), 178–194 (2011)

27. Qureshi, M.R.J.: Agile software development methodology for medium and large projects. IET Softw. **6**(4), 358–363 (2012)

28. Leffingwell, D.: Agile Software Requirements: Lean Requirements Practices for Teams, Programs, and the Enterprise. Addison-Wesley, Upper Saddle (2011)

CoRP: A Pattern-Based Anomaly Detection in Time-Series

Ines Ben Kraiem[1(✉)], Faiza Ghozzi[2(✉)], Andre Peninou[1(✉)], and Olivier Teste[1(✉)]

[1] University of Toulouse, UT2J, IRIT, Toulouse, France
{ines.ben-kraiem,andre.peninou,olivier.teste}@irit.fr
[2] University of Sfax, ISIMS, MIRACL, Sfax, Tunisia
faiza.ghozzi@isims.usf.tn

Abstract. Monitoring and analyzing sensor networks is essential for exploring energy consumption in smart buildings or cities. However, the data generated by sensors are affected by various types of anomalies and this makes the analysis tasks more complex. Anomaly detection has been used to find anomalous observations from data. In this paper, we propose a Pattern-based method, for anomaly detection in sensor networks, entitled CoRP "Composition of Remarkable Point" to simultaneously detect different types of anomalies. Our method detects remarkable points in time series based on patterns. Then, it detects anomalies through pattern compositions. We compare our approach to the methods of literature and evaluate them through a series of experiments based on real data and data from a benchmark.

Keywords: Anomaly detection · Sensor networks · Pattern-based method · Time series

1 Introduction

Today, sensor networks open up promising prospects for energy management systems in buildings or more broadly in campuses or even cities. In fact, they make it possible to monitor the level of operation of the various equipment and to manage buildings as efficiently as possible. Thus, sensor networks allow to send alerts to experts, warn them in case of over-consumption, leaks or potential malfunctions. Based on these systems, experts (e.g., engineers, maintenance technicians) make analyzes by exploring the curves of the data from the sensors. However, incidents in sensor networks cause several anomalies in these data and therefore make the analysis of the experts more complicated and subtler. Various types of anomalies can be observed in real deployments. For example, Fig. 1 illustrate different time series of a calorie sensor of a building. Figure 1(a) depicts a level shift in a time series. Hence, all observations appearing after the anomaly move to a new level. Figure 1(b) includes several peaks representing reading defects. Finally, Fig. 1(c) presents a constant anomalies. Indeed, the sensor reports a constant value due to sensor shutdown or a problem a communication between the supervision devices. All these scenarios can appear separately or simultaneously in time series.

© Springer Nature Switzerland AG 2020
J. Filipe et al. (Eds.): ICEIS 2019, LNBIP 378, pp. 424–442, 2020.
https://doi.org/10.1007/978-3-030-40783-4_20

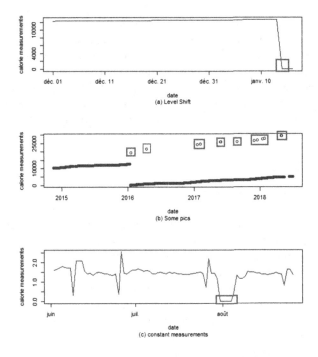

Fig. 1. Example of anomalies observed in real deployments.

In order to do a fine analysis of the buildings, the experts tend to analyze the curves visually by detecting the data points which have an unusual and different behavior compared to the other data points. These points are therefore considered as remarkable points in time series. Moreover, their ultimate goal is to simultaneously detect different types of anomalies observed in real deployments.

To resolve this problem, *anomaly detection* appears to identify and to find patterns in data that do not conform to expected behavior or do not conform to a well defined notion of normal behavior [1]. In addition to sensor networks, anomaly detection is used in several application areas. Among them, we can quote intrusion detection, industrial damage detection, image processing and medical anomaly detection, insurance or health care, textual anomaly detection, habitat monitoring, online transactions and fraud detection etc [1,2,4]. A variety of anomaly detection techniques have been developed in several research communities. However, these techniques cannot always detect different types of anomalies simultaneously and thus real applications are forced to use several methods to accurately detect all existing anomalies.

To solve the problem of detection of multiple types of anomalies at the same time, we proposed a new configurable approach based on patterns entitled CoRP "Composition of Remarkable Point". Our method is based on two steps: the first step is to detect the remarkable points using the patterns created through a regular rules developed through expert analysis. The second step is to create pattern compositions to detect anomalies. We have performed a detailed evaluation in order to compare our work with four different techniques to handle the types of anomalies we seek to detect on our real case data sets and on benchmarks which contains real and synthetic time series.

This paper is organized as follows. The second section reviews the most relevant works that deal with anomaly detection. Section 3 explains our pattern-based method for anomaly detection. Section 4 presents the experimental setup, the case study with the real world data sets and a benchmark data sets, and discussion results. Finally, in Sect. 5, we conclude with the perspectives and ideas for further research.

2   Related Work

Anomaly detection is a topic that had been addressed under various survey and review articles. Chandola et al. [1] have done a detailed survey on existing techniques into different categories based on the fields of application or the types of anomalies to be detected. Omar and et al. [3] presented an overview of research directions for applying supervised and unsupervised methods for managing the problem of anomaly detection. Agrawal [4] provided an overview of data mining techniques for anomaly detection. In fact, he categorizes anomaly detection based on the underlying used methods. For instance, probabilistic models, statistical models, linear models, proximity based models, and anomaly detection in high dimensions [4]. Plenty of anomaly detection techniques exist in research literature including clustering, classification, statistics, nearest neighbors, regression, spectral decomposition, and information theory.

Anomaly Detection in Sensor Network.   In this section, we talk about anomaly detection techniques designed for time series data. Due to the large variety of scenarios and algorithms, anomaly detection problem is categorized in many ways. Some authors have chosen techniques that are appropriate for detecting particular types of anomalies observed in real deployments [6]. They explore and characterize different classes of fault detection methods to detect anomalies observed in real deployment. These anomalies are short, noise and constant anomalies. Hence, they explore four qualitatively different classes of fault detection methods namely: rule-based methods (short, noise, constant rules), least-squares estimation-based method, learning-based methods (HMM) and Time-series-analysis-based methods (ARIMA). However, these methods cannot detect effectively multiple anomalies. To resolve this problem, the authors used hybrid methods, Hybrid(U) and Hybrid(I), to improve their results and reduce the error rate. Hybrid(U) declares a point as an anomaly if at least one of the methods explored (two or more) identified that point as an anomaly, while Hybrid(I) declares a point as an anomaly when all the explored methods identified this point as an anomaly.

Segmented Sequence Analysis (SSA) was proposed in [7]. This is an algorithm to online anomaly detection in measurements collected by sensor systems. It compares the collected measurements against a reference time series and leverages temporal and spatial correlations in sensor measurements. This method also fails to accurately detect existing anomalies. In fact, SSA is able to detect instances of long-duration anomalies but it fails to detect the short duration anomalies. Thus, the authors proposed a hybrid approach to improve the accuracy of SSA. Typically, a combination of SSA with the rule-based method (short and constant rules). They choose rule-based method because it's designed for identification short duration anomalies. Indeed, they start by applying the rule-based method using short rule and constant rule to detect short-term anomalies. Then, they apply SSA to detect the remaining anomalies.

Statistical anomaly detection techniques are most commonly employed to detect anomalies. Statistical techniques fit a statistical model, usually for normal behavior, to the given data and then apply a statistical inference test to determine if an unseen instance belongs to this model or not [1]. Normal data instances locate at high probability area of a model, while anomalies have a low probability. There are parametric and non-parametric techniques for creating the statistical model. The difference between the two techniques is that: Parametric techniques assume knowledge of the underlying distribution and estimate the parameters from the given data while non-parametric do not. An example of parametric technique is Regression Model-Based. For example, Autoregressive Integrated Moving Average (ARIMA) models described in [14]. The major disadvantage of statistical techniques is that anomaly detection depend on the assumption that the data is generated in a particular distribution which is not usually the case.

An overview of the research on Nearest Neighbor Based Anomaly Detection was proposed in [8]. Such techniques are based on the key assumption that Instances of Normal Data occur in dense neighborhoods, while anomalies occur far away from their closest neighbors. these techniques can be grouped into two categories [1]:

(1) Distance to Kth Nearest Neighbor Based: techniques that use the distance of a data instance to its kth nearest neighbors as the anomaly score [8];
(2) Relative Density Based: techniques that compute the relative density of each data instance to compute its anomaly score for example LOF (Local Outlier Factor) algorithm [9].

One of the drawbacks of nearest neighbor based techniques is, that they fail to label data correctly if the data has normal instances that do not have enough close neighbors or if the data has anomalies that have enough close neighbors [1].

Other methods for anomaly detection are using an approximately normal distribution of data such that in Generalized Extreme Studentized Deviate (ESD) test to handle more than one anomaly [10] and Change Point [11, 12] to handle level shift.

ESD is used to detect from 1 to k anomalies in a uni-variate data sets. Given the upper bound, k, the generalized ESD test essentially performs k separate tests: a test for one anomaly, a test for two anomaly, and so on up to k anomalies. The limitation of ESD is that it requires to specify an upper bound for the suspected number of anomalies. This is not possible on all applications and is impossible for online anomaly detection.

Change point detection is the problem of finding abrupt changes in data when a property of the time series changes [11, 12]. Change Point detects distribution changes (e.g., mean, variance, co-variances) in sensor measurements. The disadvantage of this method that it detects each change as an anomaly. Meanwhile, changes may exist in the time series that do not necessarily represent an anomaly and vice versa.

Methods Used for Comparison. Since the methods of the literature fail to simultaneously detect different types of anomalies, we have created an approach based on patterns. To evaluate it, we made a comparison with methods of literature that detect anomalies close to our domain. We have used an existing implementation of these methods and create the rest based on available source. So, this section summarizes the state-of-the-art methods used for comparison with the proposed approach. In fact, we explored five methods that belong to four different techniques to detect the types of anomalies observed in real deployment:

- Rule-based method: We used two rules to detect short anomalies (abnormal change) and constant anomalies [6]. *Short rule* processes the time series by comparing two successive observations each time: an anomaly is detected if the difference between these observations is greater than a given threshold. To automatically determine the detection threshold, we used the histogram-based approach [13]. *Constant rule* calculates the standard deviation for a set of successive observations. If this value is equal to zero, the whole is declared as an anomaly.
- Density-based method: This approach compares the density around a point with the density of its local neighbors. We used the LOF algorithm to detect local and global anomalies. In this method, k-nearest-neighbors set is determined for each instance by computing the distances to all other instances. Indeed, anomaly scores are measured using a local outlier factor, which is the ratio of the local density around this point to the local density around its nearest neighbors. The point whose LOF value is high is declared an anomaly [9].
- Statistics-based method: Firstly, we used the ESD method for the automatic detection of local and global anomalies. Secondly, we used the Change Point method to detect the level shift.
- Time series analysis method: This method uses temporal correlations to model and predict the values of the time series. We used ARIMA model (AutoRegressive Intergrated Moving Average) for the creation of the prediction model according to the approach described by [14]. A sensor measurement is compared to its predicted value to determine if it is an anomaly.

There are open source implementations for algorithms like LOF, ARIMA, S-H-ESD and Change Point that we have used for experiments [10, 12, 15, 16]. On the other hand, we have implemented other approaches (short rule and constant rule) depending on available sources. Hence, we used Short rule, ARIMA, LOF and S-H-ESD algorithms to detect positive and negative peak. Then, we explored Constant rule to detect constant anomalies and finally we used ARIMA and Change Point to detect Level Shift also known in literature by Concept Drift. In this paper we will remain on the terminology of Level Shift.

3   CoRP: Approach for Anomaly Detection in Time Series

3.1   Detection of Anomalies by Experts

In actual operation, the monitoring of sensor networks is done by the experts (e.g., operating engineers, maintenance technicians) by observing the curves to detect points that seem remarkable and that show unusual behavior. Typically, these are the measurements of the sensors of our illustrated case study in Fig. 1. These remarkable points are the unusual variations between the successive points of a time series and which are the indices of possible anomalies. Thus, the experts look around the remarkable points, compare the differences between the values and then deduce one or more points that represent the anomaly. Based on the experience of experts (detection of remarkable points and identification of anomalies), we have created our configurable approach, called CoRP, for anomaly detection. It is based on patterns for the detection of remarkable points and compositions of these points to identify anomalies.

CoRP is built in two phases: The first one is dedicated to detect the points considered as remarkable in the time series. The second phase is dedicated to identify anomalies by using compositions of remarkable points [17].

3.2 Notations

Definition 1. A *time series* is composed of successive observations or points collected sequentially in time at a regular interval. These observations represent the measures that are associated with a timestamp indicating the time of its collection.

Let $Y_i = \{y_1, y_2, y_3....\}$ be a time series representing the sequence of collected sensor measurements for each observation, $i \in \mathbb{N}$.

Definition 2. A *point* is a measure composed of a value and a time stamp. In this paper, we note a measure $y_i = (t_i, v_i)$ such as t_i is the timestamp of y_i (called $t(y_i)$) and v_i is the value of y_i (called $v(y_i)$).

3.3 Detection of Remarkable Points

The detection of remarkable points is made from detection patterns created in cooperation with expert analysts.

Definition 3. A *pattern* is defined by a triple (l, σ_a, σ_b) where l is a label that characterizes the pattern, σ_a and σ_b are two thresholds used to decide if a point is remarkable (or not). A pattern is applied to three successive points of a time series. We denote three successive points y_{j-1}, y_j, y_{j+1} of a time series Y as y_{minus}, y, y_{plus}. σ_a is the difference between $v(y_{minus})$ and $v(y)$ whereas σ_b is the difference between $v(y)$ and $v(y_{plus})$ as shown in the Fig. 2. When a pattern is checked on y_{minus}, y, y_{plus}, the label l of the pattern is used to label the point y.

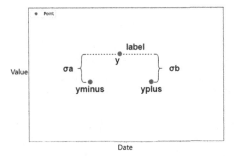

Fig. 2. Labellization of a remarkable point "y" by a pattern [17].

Definition 4. *A labeled time series* is a time series of points on which the labels detected by the patterns are added to each point.

Definition 5. *A point* y_i of a labeled time series is defined by a triple (t_i, v_i, L_i) where t_i is the timestamp, v_i is the value and $L_i = \{l_1, l_2, ...\}$ is a list of labels that characterizes the point as a remarkable point.

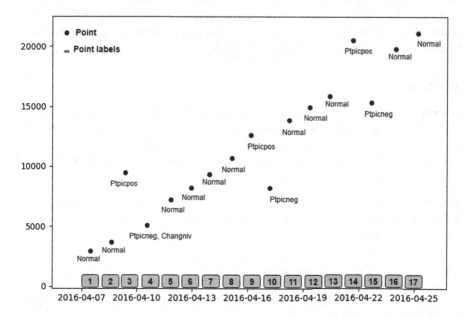

Fig. 3. Labeling a series of remarkable points [17].

The patterns are independently used to detect remarkable points and add them their corresponding label to these points. Thus, the list of labels of a point consists of all the labels of all the different patterns that are triggered on this point. The Fig. 3 illustrates an extract from a labeled time series of index data that tends to grow. This time series represents data, from our case study, used later in the experiments. It presents four examples of labels (Normal, Ptpicpos, Ptpicneg, Changniv). We note that we label all the points of the time series, by default, as 'Normal'. Let us notice the point number 4 which includes two labels (Ptpicneg, Changniv).

Example. Examples of patterns used to label the curve of Fig. 3 are: (i) a remarkable "Positive Peak Point" (Ptpicpos, 100, 100) where Ptpicpos represents the descriptive label of the pattern, $\sigma_a = 100$ and $\sigma_b = 100$; (ii) a remarkable "Negative Peak Point" (Ptpicneg, -100, -100); and (iii) a remarkable "Level Change" (Changniv, -1000, -100).

Algorithm 1, called EvaluatePattern, can evaluate any different pattern using rules. This function takes as input three successive points denoted y_{minus}, y and y_{plus} and the pattern p to be evaluated. It returns the result of the evaluation p en the three points.

Different verification rules are applied according to the signs of σ_a and σ_b. The rules for comparing y_{minus} and y according to σ_a are as follows:

- If $\sigma_a > 0$, the rule is $v(y) >= v(y_{minus}) + \sigma_a$;
- If $\sigma_a < 0$, the rule is $v(y) <= v(y_{minus}) + \sigma_a$;
- If $\sigma_a = 0$, the rule is $v(y) = v(y_{minus})$;

The rules to compare y and y_{plus} according to σ_b are similar (see Algorithm 1 [17]).

Algorithm 2 [17] uses the EvaluatePattern function to process a time series. It takes as input the initial time series and the list of patterns and returns a new labeled time series. The processing consists of browsing the time series and the list of patterns. For each point and for each pattern p, the EvaluatePattern function is called in order to add (or not) the label of p to the evaluated point.

Algorithm 1. Evaluate Pattern [17].

---

function BOOLEAN EVALUATEPATTERN($y_{minus}, y, y_{plus}, p$)
Input $y_{minus}, y, y_{plus}, p = (l_p, \sigma_a, \sigma_b)$
Output Boolean
    if $p.\sigma_a > 0$ **then** leftFlag $\leftarrow$ ($v(y) \geq v(y_{minus}) + p.\sigma_a$? true : false)
    else if $p.\sigma_a < 0$ **then** leftFlag $\leftarrow$ ($v(y) \leq v(y_{minus}) + p.\sigma_a$? true : false)
    else if $p.\sigma_a = 0$ **then** leftFlag $\leftarrow$ ($v(y) = v(y_{minus})$? true : false)
    end if
    if $p.\sigma_b > 0$ **then** rightFlag $\leftarrow$ ($v(y) \geq v(y_{plus}) + p.\sigma_b$? true : false)
    else if $p.\sigma_b < 0$ **then** rightFlag $\leftarrow$ ($v(y) \leq v(y_{plus}) + p.\sigma_b$? true : false)
    else if $p.\sigma_b = 0$ **then** rightFlag $\leftarrow$ ($v(y) = v(y_{plus})$? true : false)
    end if
remarkable= leftFlag and rightFlag
return remarkable
end function

Algorithm 2. Remarkable Point Detection [17].

    Input $Y = \{y_1, y_2, y_3....\}$, $P = \{p_1, p_2, p_3....\}$
    Output Y_L a labeled time serie
for i in range(2..$|Y|$-1) **do**
    for k in range(1..$|P|$) **do**
        if EvaluatePattern($y_{i-1}, y_i, y_{i+1}, p_k$) **then**
            $L_i \leftarrow L_i + p_k.l$
        end if
    end for
end for
    return Y_L

3.4 Composition of Remarkable Points

The result of Algorithm 2 is a time series labeled using patterns. As shown in Fig. 3 (or Fig. 4 also), a point can be labeled with one or more label "through one or more pattern".

From a subset of points of a labeled time series, we can construct by concatenation of labels L_i of these remarkable points, a sequence of labels. This sequences of labels are used to detect anomalies. An anomaly is recognized by a specific composition of labels and the verification of conditions on the values of these points.

Definition 6. *An anomaly* is one or more remarkable points belonging to a subset of points for which are verified: (i) a composition of the labels of these points (ii) and a condition expressed on the values of these points. The anomaly is finally identified on one or more points of the subset specifying the composition.

To define a composition of labels, we propose a grammar, illustrated in Fig. 5, which defines the elements of a composition of labels. The grammar allows to define the possible labels (one or more) on successive points making it possible to recognize a composition of labels. Referring to the Fig. 5, the grammar explanation is = The grammar starts from labels placed on the points (<label>). Labels can be combined on one point with AND, OR, and NOT logical expressions (<label-comp> and <point-label>). NOT means that a point is not labeled with l, l1 and l2 means that a point is labeled with both l2 AND l2, l1 OR l2 means a point is labeled with l1 or l2 or l1 and l2. For example "l1 AND NOT l2 AND l3" designates a point labeled with l1, labeled with l3 and not labeled l2. Each label composition on a single point can be repeated on successive points by quantifiers: ? (0 or 1), + (1 or more) And * (0 or more) (<label-enum>). For example "(l1) +" means that the composition must comprise one or more successive points labeled l1. The final label composition is created through a succession of labels separated by "." (<composition>). For example, "l1. (l2) *. l1 OR l3" means a point

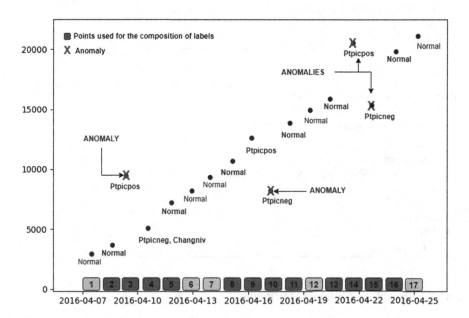

Fig. 4. Result of phase 2 of the CoRP algorithm - Anomaly detection [17]. (Color figure online)

labeled with l1 followed by zero or more points labeled with l2 followed by a point labeled with l1 or l3.

Definition 7. *Composition of labels.* Thus, a composition of labels to recognize an anomaly is composed of three parts:

- *composition*: the composition of the labels on successive points. It is defined according to the grammar presented in Fig. 5;
- *condition*: a condition on the values of the recognized points corresponding to the sequence of the labels of the composition. Indeed, the same label composition on successive points can correspond to different anomalies and the condition allows to identify only one anomaly. This condition on values is a classical condition created using the operators ($<$, $<=$, etc) to compare values and logical operators (and/or/not) to combine comparisons. To avoid the use of $v(y)$ notation, we denote by v_i the value of the ith point recognized by the composition, v_1 the first one and v_n the last one; note that the number of points involved in the composition can be variable;
- *conclusion*: the identified anomaly for which are indicated its type (name of the anomaly) and the list of points where the anomaly is. The list can be enumerative list of points or all if all point are concerned.

```
<composition> ::= <label-enum> ("." <label-enum>)*

<label-enum> ::= <label-comp>
         |        "(" <label-comp> ")" "?"
         |        "(" <label-comp> ")" "*"
         |        "(" <label-comp> ")" "+"

<label-comp> ::= <point-label> ("OR" <point-label>)*
         |        <point-label> ("AND" <point-label>)*
         |        <point-label>

<point-label> ::= <label>
         |         "NOT" <label>

<label> ::= list of words (remarkable points)
              defined by patterns
```

Fig. 5. Grammar for the definition of a composition of labels [17].

We can thus define label compositions to identify anomalies. For example, we give hereafter three examples of anomalies to be detected as presented in the introduction: (i) anomaly of constant values, (ii) anomaly of values in negative peak, (iii) anomaly of values in positive peak; the latter is possibly recognized by 2 label compositions [17].

Label-Composition 1

composition: Normal . Ptpicpos . Ptpicneg . Normal
condition: $v_2 > v_4$ and $v_3 > v_1$
conclusion: positive peak $->v_2$

Label-Composition 2

composition: Normal . Ptpicpos . Ptpicneg . Normal
condition: $v_2 < v_4$ and $v_3 < v_1$
conclusion: negative peak $- > v_3$

Label-Composition 3

composition: Begincstpos . Cst* . Endcstneg
condition: $v_1 == v_2$ and $v_{n-1} == v_n$
conclusion: constant $- >$ all

Label-Composition 4

composition: Normal . Ptpicpos . Ptpicneg AND Changnivneg . Normal
condition: $v_2 > v_4$ and $v_3 > v_1$
conclusion: positive peak $- > v_2$

Example. Consider the subsets of points shown in Fig. 4 in red. The index points 2 to 5 give the following series of labels: (Normal . Ptpicpos . Ptpicneg and Changniv . Normal) detected by the label composition 4 of the example above. This composition therefore makes it possible to detect the positive peak anomaly at 3.

The index points 8 to 11 trigger the label compositions 1 and 2. For Label-Composition 1, the condition is $v_9 > v_{11}$ and $v_{10} > v_8$ which is false so the composition is not valid.

For Label-Composition 2, the condition is $v_9 < v_{11}$ and $v_{10} < v_8$ which is true so the composition is valid and the Negative Pic anomaly is recognized in v_{10}.

Finally, we have implemented an algorithm able to browse a labeled timeseries Y_L and check, from each point, which label compositions apply to identify anomalies (and corresponding points).

4   Experimental Setup

We have evaluated CoRP on our case study and provided a detailed comparison with five anomaly detection methods. Then we have evaluated more these algorithms with benchmarks data. Both synthetic and real time series data from different domains are used for experiments. We will show according to the experiments that our method is more efficient to simultaneously detect different types of anomalies by comparing it with the methods of literature.

4.1   Experimental Setting I: SGE Data Sets

The field of application treated in this paper, is the sensor network of the Management and Exploitation Service (SGE) of Rangueil campus attached to the Rectorate of Toulouse. This department exploits and maintains the distribution network from the data related to the different installations. More than 600 sensors of different types of fluids (calorie, water, compressed air, electricity and gas), which are scattered in several buildings, are managed by the SGE supervision systems.

Data Sets Description. In this paper, we used calorie and electricity sensor data. We processed 25 cal sensors and 10 electricity sensors deployed in different buildings. Calorie measurements are daily data for more than three years (1453 data per sensor or 36325 data points in total). The measurements of these sensors are reassembled at a regular frequency and represent the *indexes* (readings of calorie meters) which are then used to calculate the quantities of energy consumed. We were able to identify the types of anomalies that exist in the calorie data through the knowledge gained from the SGE experts by visually inspecting the data sets. The predominant anomaly in these readings is the constant values, nearly 8578 observations on all the data and this is due to the stopping of the sensors. We also found among these values, several constants with an offset. Typically, a constant with a level shift that begins with a positive or negative peak. Then, there is a lot of abnormal change such as positive or negative peaks, nearly 380. And finally, there are eight level shift due to sensor changes. These time series contain 8966 anomalies in total.

Electricity measurements are collected hourly for 10 months. Each time series contains 226 – 16786 instances which is 43793 in total. These data are irregular and contain several anomalies (e.g., negative and positive peak, constant anomaly, level shift). The total number of anomalies is 664. The time series generated by sensors are uni-variate with a timestamp and a value. Experts have shown us where the anomalies are and types of anomalies that can be found.

Experimentation on Real Case Time Series (Increasing Series). In this part, we explore the different anomaly detection methods described in the related work section. We chose these methods because they can detect the types of anomalies we want to find. As noted above, these techniques have proven effective in detecting anomalies in the sensor data. However, as we will see through the results of the experiments, none of these methods are effective at simultaneously detecting multiple types of anomalies. Thus, we present an evaluation of the following methods: Short rule, Constant rule, LOF, ARIMA, S-H-ESD and Change Point. Since these methods do not detect all types of targeted anomalies, we apply them by category of anomalies.

All the anomaly detection methods in this experimental setting are applied on each time series separately. Average F-scores, recall, are reported for each method to compare and evaluate the results of anomaly detection.

$$F - score = 2 \cdot \frac{Precision \cdot Recall}{Precision + Recall} \tag{1}$$

Parameters of Anomaly Detection Methods. In order to detect the remarkable points using CoRP, we created 14 patterns and 25 label compositions of these patterns to detect the anomalies on calorie and electricity data. Also, we need to select the parameters such as the threshold for the short rule, the neighbor number for LOF or the model type for ARIMA etc as follow:

– The LOF method, which is based on the nearest K neighbors, produces an index, called the score function, which represents the degree of anomaly assumed for the observations. It is then sufficient to define a threshold to qualify the "normal" and "abnormal" results. In our experiments we have varied the choice of K in a range of 30 to 10 in order to evaluate the influence of this parameter on the detection result and we have judged a threshold = 1.5 corresponding to an observation in the standard of distribution scores;

- For the Short rule, we need to set a threshold to compare it with the variation between successive observations. To this end, we used the histogram-based approach. We have plotted the histogram of the sensor reading change between two successive samples for the short rule and then select one of the histogram modes as a threshold;
- For the Constant rule, we have varied the choice of size of sliding window in a range of 30 to 10;
- For S-H-ESD we define the values of the alpha and direction parameters. (i) Alpha: this parameter defines the level of statistical significance with which to accept or reject anomalies. We used three values for this parameter i.e. 0,05, 0,1, and 0,2. (ii) Direction: this parameter defines the direction (positive or negative) of anomalies to be detected. We used 'both', as anomalies can be in any direction in this data sets.

Results. In order to evaluate the performance of these methods we use the number of true positives (true detected anomalies), the number of false positives (false detected anomalies) and the number of false negatives (true undetected anomalies) as evaluation metrics. The results are presented in Fig. 6 as follows: the method based on the Short rule and the method based on the Constant rule are noted SR and CR respectively while the Change Point is noted LS.

Table 1. Evaluation of anomaly detection methods for calorie data sets [17].

Evaluation	Precision	Recall	F-measure
CoRP	1	1	1
SR	0.52	0.17	0.32
CR	1	0.80	0.88
LOF	0.022	0.12	0.022
S-H-ESD	0.34	0.40	0.36
ARIMA	0.30	0.07	0.11
LS	0.29	0.87	0.43

As shown in Fig. 6A and B, we applied methods that are able to detect the abrupt change between two successive samples that could be a positive or negative peak or a small variation. We presented LOF results in a separate chart for more visibility. Based on the results presented in Fig. 6, we make the following observations: LOF is the method that generates the most false positives while ARIMA generated the most false negatives. The S-H-ESD method is the method that can detect the most true positive among them, but on the other hand it causes a lot of false positives and false negatives. Then the method based on the Short rule detects fewer anomalies when compared to S-H-ESD. However, it causes fewer false positives than the other methods.

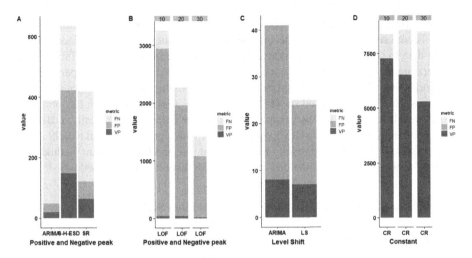

Fig. 6. Evaluation of anomaly detection methods on index data [17].

Table 1 presents the evaluation of anomaly detection methods on calorie sensor data. Based on Fig. 6 and Table 1 we observe that: (i) the efficiency of the Constant rule or the LOF method strongly depends on the choice of the sliding window or the number of neighbors (Fig. 6B and D). (ii) The Change Point method works well when there is actually a true level shift in the time series but however, in the absence of anomaly it has a low accuracy and creates a lot of false positives. (iii) Between the Short rule, ARIMA and S-H-ESD, the Short rule is the most accurate and ARIMA is the least efficient for detecting abnormal change. By comparing with these methods, our CoRP algorithm can detect all types of anomalies with better accuracy and recall. In effect, CoRP works very well on the index data and typically on our real case study.

Table 2. Evaluation of anomaly detection methods for electricity data sets.

Evaluation	Precision	Recall	F-measure
CoRP	0.99	0.93	0.95
SR	0.52	0.36	0.42
CR	1	0.83	0.90
LOF	0.32	0.25	0.28
S-H-ESD	0.47	0.52	0.49
ARIMA	0.30	0.27	0.28
LS	0.60	0.80	0.68

Table 2 presents the evaluation results of the algorithms on electricity data sets. We note that the CoRP's accuracy is less than its accuracy on the calorie data. This is due to the frequency of the data. Indeed, the electricity data are generated hour by hour and the differences between the values of the successive points are sometimes very small. Therefore, Corp fails, in the first phase, using patterns already defined on the calorie data to detect all the remarkable points. Also, it can be seen from Table 2 that the literature algorithms are much more efficient on these data sets by comparing with the calorie data. This is due to the types of existing anomalies and the frequencies of the anomalies. Nevertheless, based on results, we can say that our approach has obtained the best result of F-measure by comparing with other algorithms. Actually, it detects the most of anomalies with the least possible errors with a precision equal to 0,99 and a recall equal to 0.93. Then, the result of the constant rule and Change Point method was close to the best and obtained the best accuracy with respect to rest of methods.

Experimentation on Real Case Time Series (Variable Series). To further evaluate our algorithm and to demonstrate the effectiveness of the anomaly detection methods, we used SGE consumption data. So, we took the measurements that come from 25 calorie sensors. Consumption data are seasonal data and their daily evolution, unlike index data, are somewhat variable. We have manually inspected these data to understand how these data work and to create patterns of anomalies that may exist. The anomalies we have seen in the data are: positive and negative peaks, constant anomalies, constants that start and end with a big peak. Since the data is not stationary, we did not apply the Change Point algorithm because there is no level shift in this data to be detected. Thus we have created 9 patterns to detect remarkable points and 5 label compositions to detect anomalies.

Table 3 shows that the literature algorithms are much more efficient on the consumption data by comparing with the index data. Even with this type of data, our approach has obtained the best result of F-measure by comparing with other algorithms. Actually, it detected the most anomalies with the least possible errors with a precision equal to 1 and a recall equal to 0.98. Then, the result of the rule-based method (SR, CR) and the ARIMA method was close to the best and obtained the best accuracy with respect to LOF and SH-ESD. On the other hand, SH-ESD is the method that was closest to the best result in terms of recall with a value equal to 0.80. But it should be noted, that these algorithms that we evaluated cannot detect all the types of anomalies observed in the data which means that each algorithm is efficient in a specific type. The particularity of our method is that we can set the patterns and the composition of labels according to our needs to detect, with a great precision and efficiency, all the types of anomalies observed in the real deployments [17].

Table 3. Evaluation of anomaly detection methods in consumption data sets [17].

Evaluation	Precision	Recall	F-measure
CoRP	1	0.98	0.98
SR	0.66	0.63	0.64
CR	1	0.72	0.83
LOF	0.39	0.78	0.52
S-H-ESD	0.41	0.80	0.54
ARIMA	0.66	0.25	0.36

4.2 Experimental Setting II: NAB Data Sets

NAB (Numenta Anomaly Benchmark) [18] is a benchmark containing real-world data streams with labeled anomalies. It is comprised of over 58 data files each with 1,000 – 22,000 instances. The majority of the data is real-world from a variety of sources such as AWS server metrics, Twitter volume, advertisement clicking metrics, traffic data, and more. The data sets is labeled either based on the known root cause of an anomaly or as a result of following the defined labeling procedure (described in [18]). We applied the algorithms of literature in 15 NAB time series from different domains. These time series contains 26 anomalies in total. These anomalies are positive peak and negative peaks. These data are ordered, timestamped and single-valued metrics:

- realTraffic: Real time traffic data from the Twin Cities Metro area in Minnesota. Included metrics include occupancy, speed, and travel time from specific sensors;
- realTweets: A collection of Twitter mentions of large publicly-traded companies such as Google and IBM. The metric value represents the number of mentions for a given ticker symbol every 5 min;
- realKnownCause: This category contains different domains. We processed the ambient temperature data in an office setting and Temperature sensor data of an internal component of a large industrial machine.

Table 4. Evaluation of anomaly detection methods in NAB data sets.

Nab data sets	Real traffic			Real tweets			Real known cause		
Algorithm	Evaluation								
	Pre.	Rec.	F-mea.	Pre.	Rec.	F-mea.	Pre.	Rec.	F-mea.
CoRP	0.75	0.50	0.60	0.55	0.4	0.46	0.60	0.63	0.61
ARIMA	0.57	0.30	0.39	0.35	0.27	0.30	0.15	0.20	0.17
LOF	0.11	0.20	0.14	0.33	0.25	0.28	0.11	0.20	0.14
S-H-ESD	0.20	0.20	0.20	0.33	0.25	0.28	0.30	0.10	0.15
SR	0.36	0.26	0.30	0.30	0.15	0.20	0.30	0.12	0.17

We applied 4 time series anomaly detection algorithms in addition to CoRP. The algorithms are evaluated on the basis of precision, recall and F-measure. The evaluated algorithms include ARIMA, LOF, S-H-ESD and SR. We did not apply CR and LS on this data because the existing anomalies do not contain constant anomalies or level changes. We initially labeled the time series, as for previous experiments, with the 'Normal' label. Then we created 2 patterns to detect the remarkable points and 3 pattern compositions for each category of time series. Table 4 shows results of our NAB experiment. It can be observed in this table that CoRP outperforms other algorithms by significant margin. In fact, our algorithm is better than the best performing algorithm for different domains in the NAB data sets.

Table 5. Evaluation of anomaly detection methods in ARIMA data sets [17].

Datasets	HIPC		IPI	
Algorithm	Evaluation			
	Precision	Recall	Precision	Recall
CoRP	1	0.80	0.75	0.75
ARIMA	1	1	1	1
LOF	0.11	0.20	0	0
S-H-ESD	0.20	0.20	0.33	0.25
RC	0	0	0	0
LS	0	0	0	0

4.3   Experimental Setting III: ARIMA Data Sets

In order to evaluate the algorithm in another context, different to our case study, we used the data sets used in the package developed in R and implements ARIMA method [19]. Among this data, we explored the data of HIPC, that represents Harmonised indices of consumer prices in the Euro area. Also, we explored the data of IPI that represents the industrial production indices in the manufacturing sector of European Monetary Union countries [19]. Each of these data sets contains several time series which present monthly data from 1995 to 2013. We tested two time series of these two data sets. Each of them contains 229 measurements with 5 anomalies in HIPC and 4 anomalies in IPI. These anomalies are a mix of AO (Additive Outlier), TC (Temporary Change) or LS (Level Shift).

Thus, we analyzed the characteristics of these data and the curve that represents the time series to be able to specify the patterns. So, we first created a 4 patterns to detect the remarkable points in HIPC and IPI time series. Then we made 5 compositions of these patterns to detect anomalies.

Table 5 is a comparison between the literature algorithms and our algorithm, on the data used in the ARIMA package. We did not test the constant rule in the HIPC and IPI data-sets because the anomalies observed in these data do not contain a constant anomalies. Therefore, we applied CoRP, ARIMA, LOF with a number of neighbors equal to 20, S-H-ESD, Change Point and the Short rule on these data. As we can see, ARIMA has the best results because it is designed to detect these types of anomalies in these time series. The algorithm based on the Short rule and Change Point are the worst among these algorithms, while our algorithm is the best among them and can detect the majority of anomalies observed with few errors.

4.4   Complexity

In this part, we focus on the computing time required by the different methods of the literature and our algorithm. The experiments are performed on machine running windows 10 professional and optimized by an Intel (R) Core (TM) i5 processor and 16 GB of RAM. We used the Python 3.7 Anaconda open source distribution to turn our algorithm and R 3.5 to turn the algorithms of the literature. We calculated the execution time of index data for each algorithm we evaluated to compare it with the execution time of our algorithm. The algorithms according to their run-time performance are as follows: The rule-based method and the S-H-ESD method are the fastest with an execution time of 0.5 s. Then, the LOF method with an execution time equal to 2.5 s. Subsequently our algorithm with 3.50 s of execution time and finally ARIMA with 5.60 s.

5   Conclusion

In this paper, we seek to simultaneously detect several types of anomalies at the same time in uni-variate time series. In this context, we have proposed a new configurable approach based on patterns entitled CoRP. Our method is based on two steps: the first step is to detect the remarkable points using the patterns created through a regular rules developed through expert analysis. The second step is to create pattern compositions to detect anomalies. Our approach requires application domain expertise to be able to efficiently define patterns.

Our case study is based on a real context: sensor data from the SGE (Rangueil campus management and operation service in Toulouse). The evaluation of this method is illustrated by first using calorie and electricity sensor data managed by the SGE and, secondly, by using NAB and ARIMA benchmark. To evaluate our algorithm, we have explored 5 different algorithms (rule-based, S-H-ESD, LOF, ARIMA, and Change Point) and then applied them to real-world and synthetic data sets. Our evaluation study illustrated that our approach is the most accurate and efficient at detecting simultaneously different types of anomalies by minimizing false detection.

Future work includes: (1) use machine learning methods to automatically build patterns and/or label compositions to detect and classify anomalies (e.g., Decision tree, Support Vector Machines, Neural Networks etc), (2) apply our algorithm on data streams to trace alarms as early as possible, and (3) handle multivariate time series.

Acknowledgment. This PhD thesis is financed by the Management and Exploitation Service (SGE) of Rangueil campus attached to the Rectorate of Toulouse and the research is made in the context of neOCampus project (Paul Sabatier University, Toulouse). The authors thank the SGE for providing access to actual sensor data. They also thank the experts who helped to understand this data and identify the anomalies observed during the operation.

References

1. Chandola, V., Banerjee, A., Kumar, V.: Anomaly detection: a survey. ACM Comput. Surv. (CSUR) **41**(3), 15 (2009)
2. Hodge, V., Austin, J.: A survey of outlier detection methodologies. Artif. Intell. Rev. **22**(2), 85–126 (2004)
3. Omar, S., Ngadi, A., Jebur, H.: Machine learning techniques for anomaly detection: an overview. Int. J. Comput. Appl. **79**(2) (2013)
4. Agrawal, S., Agrawal, J.: Survey on anomaly detection using data mining techniques. Procedia Comput. Sci. **60**, 708–713 (2015)

5. Sreevidya, S.S.: A survey on outlier detection methods. IJCSIT Int. J. Comput. Sci. Inf. Technol. **5**(6) (2014)
6. Sharma, A.B., Golubchik, L., Govindan, R.: Sensor faults: detection methods and prevalence in real-world datasets. ACM Trans. Sens. Netw. (TOSN) **6**(3), 23 (2010)
7. Yao, Y., Sharma, A., Golubchik, L., Govindan, R.: Online anomaly detection for sensor systems: a simple and efficient approach. Perform. Eval. **67**(11), 1059–1075 (2010)
8. Upadhyaya, S., Singh, K.: Nearest neighbour based outlier detection techniques. Int. J. Comput. Trends Technol. **3**(2), 299–303 (2012)
9. Breunig, M.M., Kriegel, H.P., Ng, R.T., Sander, J.: LOF: identifying density-based local outliers. In: ACM Sigmod Record, vol. 29, no. 2, pp. 93–104, May 2000
10. Rosner, B.: Percentage points for a generalized ESD many-outlier procedure. Technometrics **25**(2), 165–172 (1983)
11. Basseville, M., Nikiforov, I.V.: Detection of Abrupt Changes: Theory and Application, vol. 104. Prentice Hall, Englewood Cliffs (1993)
12. Aminikhanghahi, S., Cook, D.J.: A survey of methods for time series change point detection. Knowl. Inf. Syst. **51**(2), 339–367 (2017)
13. Ramanathan, N., et al.: Rapid deployment with confidence: calibration and fault detection in environmental sensor networks (2006)
14. Chen, C., Liu, L.M.: Joint estimation of model parameters and outlier effects in time series. J. Am. Stat. Assoc. **88**(421), 284–297 (1993)
15. Hochenbaum, J., Vallis, O.S., Kejariwal, A.: Automatic anomaly detection in the cloud via statistical learning. arXiv preprint arXiv:1704.07706 (2017)
16. Cleveland, R.B., Cleveland, W.S., McRae, J.E., Terpenning, I.: STL: a seasonal-trend decomposition. J. Official Stat. **6**(1), 3–73 (1990)
17. Ben Kraiem, I., Ghozzi, F., Péninou, A., Teste, O.: Pattern-based method for anomaly detection in sensor networks. In: International Conference on Enterprise Information Systems, vol. 1, pp. 104–113, May 2019
18. Lavin, A., Ahmad, S.: Evaluating real-time anomaly detection algorithms-the numenta anomaly benchmark. In: 2015 IEEE 14th International Conference on Machine Learning and Applications (ICMLA), December 2015, pp. 38–44. IEEE (2015)
19. López-de-Lacalle, J.: tsoutliers R package for detection of outliers in time series. CRAN, R Package (2016)

A Tool for Analyzing Academic Genealogy

Gabriel Madeira⬤, Eduardo N. Borges$^{(\boxtimes)}$⬤, Giancarlo Lucca⬤, Helida Santos⬤, and Graçaliz Dimuro⬤

Centro de Ciências Computacionais, Universidade Federal do Rio Grande-FURG, Rio Grande, Brazil
{gabrielmadeira,eduardoborges,giancarlo.lucca,helida, gracaliz}@furg.br

Abstract. Academic genealogy investigates the relationships between student researchers and advisors and has been used as a resource to analyze the spread of scientific knowledge. This work presents the development of a system that creates academic genealogy trees of researchers from the Brazilian library of theses and dissertations. The proposed system allows users to query and track information about researchers available on the database and retrieve their academic trees with the any desirable depth. This paper extends a previous work presenting new analyzes including the temporal distribution of documents and the number of advisors as a function of advising relationships.

Keywords: Academic genealogy · Genealogy trees · Data integration · Information visualization

1 Introduction

Currently, there are a large number of scientific publications and academic papers available in various Web repositories. Each research institution or university publishes the results achieved in its own institutional repository. In this way, scientific publications are cataloged and organized in a dispersed manner. These data altogether contain the major scientific contributions and collaborations among researchers over time. Analyzing the metadata from multiple publications allows one to map and understand how the relationships between researchers affect the advancement of knowledge in several areas of science.

Genealogy is an auxiliary field of history that studies the origin, evolution and spread of family groups [13]. This evolution is often represented using a structured diagram in the form of family trees [5]. Genealogy trees are well-known structures that organize, through kinship ties, the whole history of an individual's ancestors. Using this structure we can analyze the origin and development of a family lineage over time.

Genealogy trees can be used in academia to analyze relationships between professors, students and researchers. Figure 1 [12] shows an example of an academic genealogy tree. Any metadata sets that describe the elements or their relationships can be used.

The drawing of an academic genealogy tree allows one to see who advised a researcher and how this researcher influenced others over time. A forest (set of trees)

© Springer Nature Switzerland AG 2020
J. Filipe et al. (Eds.): ICEIS 2019, LNBIP 378, pp. 443–456, 2020.
https://doi.org/10.1007/978-3-030-40783-4_21

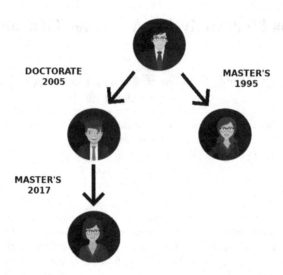

Fig. 1. An academic genealogy tree representing advising relationships in graduate programs. Each edge starts from the advisor and presents the year of master's or doctorate degree [12].

depicts the description a research area using metrics that let, through statistical analyzes and data mining, to extract relevant knowledge for the area under study [3]. Therefore, these structures allow us to analyze how knowledge is spreading across generations of scientists and how these links affect the development of science.

Aiming at visualizing academic genealogy trees created from a set of metadata extracted and integrated from multiple sources, the Information Management Research Group developed at Centro de Ciências Computacionais at Universidade Federal do Rio Grande (FURG) an information system called The Gold Tree [12]. This system allows a researcher to query and track information about his or her advisors and graduate students at any level. A case study was explored to validate the system using data from more than 570 thousand PhD theses and masters dissertations. In addition to including recent related work in the study, this paper extends previous work reporting new data analysis: an overview of the researchers' graph, the temporal distribution of relationships, and the number of advisors as a function of advising relationships.

The rest of this paper is organized as follows. In Sect. 2, we discuss related work. Section 3 presents the methodology to develop the proposed solution. Details on the obtained results are given in Sect. 4. Finally, in Sect. 5, we draw our conclusions and point out some directions for future work.

2   Related Work

In recent years, several studies have explored the visualization of academic collaboration data. While some platforms such as ResearchGate [17], Google Citations, and the Web of Science (WoS) classify registered researchers by citation indexing their articles and papers [1], other tools such as Pajek [2] and PubNet [8] are only concerned with viewing the research networks. Furthermore, we point out that there are also solutions that use specific data sources to extract information and generate knowledge from co-authoring relationships [10, 14]. The following subsections present in details the works used as baseline in the validation of the proposed system.

2.1 Academic Family Tree

Neurotree is a Web database created to document the lineage of academic mentorship in neuroscience [5]. The authors present a temporal analysis of the database growth in a period of seven years. The following metrics were performed: the number of researchers and relationships, the monthly growth rate, the fraction of researchers linked in the main graph, the average distance between researchers, and the average number of connections per researcher. In addition, they report the accuracy of related data in Neurotree with data reported on Web sites of five research groups. Finally, in order to study the relationship between mentorship groups and research areas within neuroscience, they provide a clustering analysis.

This tree exists as a part of the larger Academic Family Tree,[1] which seeks to build a genealogy across multiple academic fields, building a single, interdisciplinary academic genealogy. Figure 2 [12] presents the result of a query by the name of the researcher.

The contents of the database are entirely crowd-sourced. So it is totally dependent on human effort. This feature makes it very susceptible to field fill errors, always presenting incomplete data as well. Any Web user can add information concerning researchers and the connections between them, which can leave the database with a poor quality and/or with false information.

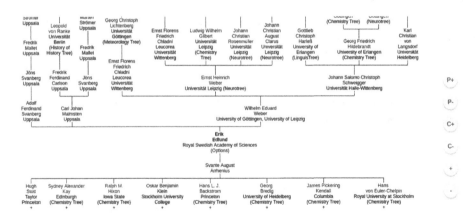

Fig. 2. Result of the query "Erik Edlund" using the Academic Family Tree [12].

---

[1] https://academictree.org.

2.2 Acácia Platform

Acácia Platform[2] [4] is a system created in 2017 for documenting the formal relations of advising in the context of Brazilian graduate programs. The system uses data registered in the Lattes Platform,[3] which is a database of Brazilian researchers' curricula maintained by the Ministry of Science and Technology and Innovation. Currently, Acacia Platform has over 1 million vertices and relationships. Each vertex represents a researcher and each edge an advising relation completed between two researchers (advisor and student). Figure 3 [12] presents the result of a query by the researcher's name. The system shows some bibliometric indexes as the number of direct and indirect descendants and information about the advising relationships.

José Palazzo Moreira de Oliveira

Grande Área[t]: Ciencias Exatas E da Terra
Área[t]: Ciência da Computação
Instituição[t]: Universidade Federal do Rio Grande do Sul
Titulação[t]: Doutorado
Ano de Titulação[t]: 1984
Descendência[t]: 302
Fecundidade[t]: 71
Índice Genealógico[t]: 6

Ascendentes   Descendentes

N ⬍	Nome ⬍	Nível ⬍	Tipo ⬍	Conclusão ⬍
1	Adriana Jouris	Mestrado	Orientador	2011
2	Alencar Machado	Doutorado	Orientador	2015
3	Allomar Mariano Rêgo	Mestrado	Orientador	1990
4	Ana Carla Macedo da Silva	Mestrado	Orientador	2002
...	Ana Mariiza Pernas Fleischmann	Doutorado	Orientador	2012

Fig. 3. Result of the query "José Palazzo Moreira Oliveira" using Acácia Platform. For each relationship, the name, academic degree and year of conclusion are presented [12].

2.3 Science Tree

Created in 2015, the Science Tree[4] application collects metadata of academic genealogy from many countries [6]. The authors are crawling data from a variety of sources, including the Networked Digital Library of Theses and Dissertations (NDLTD), which has more than 4.5 million theses and dissertations from around the world. They developed a framework to extract academic genealogy trees from these data, providing a series of analyses that describe the main properties of the academic genealogy tree. Figure 4 [12] presents the result of a query using the same researcher of Fig. 3.

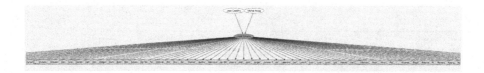

Fig. 4. Result of the query "José Palazzo Moreira Oliveira" using Science Tree [12].

[2] http://plataforma-acacia.org.
[3] http://lattes.cnpq.br.
[4] http://www.sciencetree.net.

2.4   The Brazilian Research Community

Aiming to reconstruct advisor-advisee relationships from records from many institutions around the world and from distinct disciplines, Dores et al. [7] also build academic genealogy trees from the Lattes Platform. In this paper, 222,674 curricula vitae from researchers holding a PhD degree were collected and then processed.

The proposed algorithm, in the first step, orders the curricula by the year of the PhD conclusion. Then, for each researcher with a curriculum on Lattes Platform it is created or updated a vertex which refers to itself on the graph. After that, for each advising relationship (masters and/or PhD) an edge is established between this researcher vertex and the corresponding students' vertices. Thus the relationships between students and advisors can be gradually built. Figure 5 shows the tree of Marcos André Gonçalves, where the node colors represent the tree levels.

Among the reported results, the authors presented 903,183 vertices, 1,144,051 edges, 70,610 trees, and 22,061 distinct components. The average tree size was 40.19 while the average tree width was 3.81. The 10 largest trees have more than 5,000 nodes, although 80% of them have less than 20 nodes. Regarding the distribution of the trees depth, 50% of them had only one level.

They also report that several researchers opt to study abroad. Portugal followed by United States were the countries most chosen by Brazilian researchers to conclude their masters and/or doctorate studies.

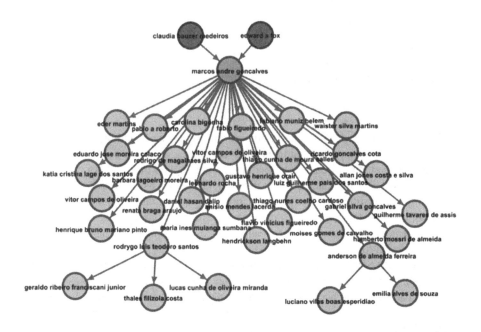

Fig. 5. Example of an academic genealogy tree built from Lattes [7].

3   Methodology

This section presents the methodology adopted in this paper. The proposed approach is divided into the following steps: data source definition, harvesting and pre-processing, data modeling and indexing, web information system construction, and data analysis.

Unlike the Academic Family Tree presented in Sect. 2.1, which is user dependent, we have chosen to collect official data available in digital libraries. These data sources must support some interoperability feature such as the OAI-PMH protocol [11] and the Dublin Core[5] format. This choice solves the problem of cold start and registration of false information.

In order to evaluate the proposed system we use Brazilian Digital Library of Theses and Dissertations[6] (BDTD). It is developed and managed by the Brazilian Institute of Information in Science and Technology (IBICT), and integrates the repositories of educational and research institutions in Brazil, and also stimulates the registration and publication of theses and dissertations electronically. At the time of our harvesting more than 570,000 documents were indexed.

The main metadata fields collected were:

- author;
- advisor;
- name of the educational or research institution;
- acronym of the educational or research institution;
- title;
- topics;
- URL of the document in the original repository;
- PhD thesis or Master's dissertation;
- URL of the author curriculum at Lattes Platform;
- citation;
- year of publication.

After the data selection and harvesting, a set of cleaning operations were applied. Several analyzes were performed to identify anomalies, so errors could be corrected or eliminated. Some transformation operations were applied in the author and advisor fields. The most common ones include: inverting last names based on the comma character, removing institution acronyms, and removing structural prefixes present in the content of a metadata. In addition, duplicate tuples from more than one digital repository were removed. At the end of the cleaning process, the number of theses and dissertations decreased to 465,847.

In Computer Science, trees are data structures widely used to represent elements hierarchically organized. However, the academic genealogy trees are represented by graphs, because a researcher may have more than one ancestor (one for each dissertation or thesis) and because there may be cycles. That is the reason why we transformed the cleaned data to store the complete graph in the relational model. Figure 6 shows the data model [12]. The first table contains all the researchers and their properties. The second

---

[5] http://dublincore.org.

[6] http://bdtd.ibict.br.

keeps M:N directed advising relationships between pairs of academics. The Database Management System (DBMS) used for storage was PostgreSQL. All the process of harvesting and pre-processing were developed in PHP programming language.

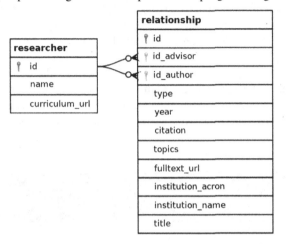

Fig. 6. Relational data model representing the genealogy academic trees [12].

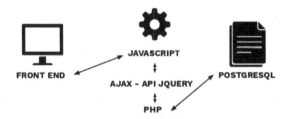

Fig. 7. Data flow between front and back ends [12].

The Web application interface was developed using Javascript, HTML, and CSS. The queries are sent to the back-end using Jquery library [15]. Methods implemented in PHP retrieve the subgraph from data stored in the DBMS. We have used the dagre-d3 library [16] to draw the academic trees with the selected data. Figure 7 shows the data flow between front and back-end [12].

From the developed system we analyze some properties of the genealogy graph, such as the giant component, the advising distribution by year and the advising density.

4   Results

4.1   The Developed Tool

Figure 8 shows the web interface of the proposed system, which is designed to be simple and intuitive. The button *Search Academic* opens a query field that allows the user to search by the name of the researcher.

The architecture presented in Fig. 7 [12] allowed to implement a dynamic search that suggests multiple researchers as the user types in the query field. For each character entered, the results are filtered and displayed on the screen. All substrings of author and advisor names with at least 3 characters have been indexed in the DBMS, so the user does not need to know the full name of a researcher, the order of names nor to complete each name. Figure 9 exemplifies this behavior while the user is querying by "avancini mar" [12].

Next to the button *Search Academic* the user can edit the depth level. The tree expands the number of levels both toward the leaves and toward the root. Thus, he or she can see the advising lineage and the graduated students. Figure 8 shows the result tree setting two levels and selecting "Rita Maria Pereira Avancini" from the five returned researchers.

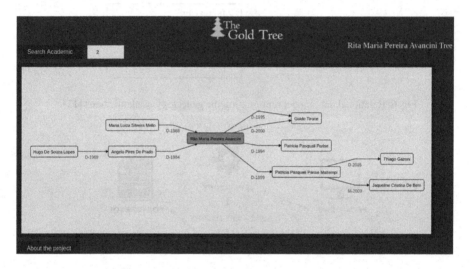

Fig. 8. Web interface of the proposed system showing the result selecting "Rita Maria Pereira Avancini" with 2 levels depth [12]. (Color figure online)

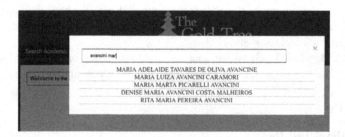

Fig. 9. Example of the dynamic search feature, that suggests multiple researchers as the user types in the query field [12].

Each researcher is represented by a vertex that contains his or her full name. Master's advising relationships are edges with M-YEAR labels in blue. Doctoral advising relationships have D-YEAR labels in red.

The user can freely move the tree in the rectangular area in which it appears and zoom in/out using the mouse controls. By clicking on a relationship, a window opens displaying the information available in the thesis or dissertation metadata (Fig. 10 [12]). Also, when you click on a vertex, a new tree is generated using the selected researcher as the target of the query.

The information system developed is available online.[7]

4.2   An Example Case of Brazilian Academic Genealogy

Figure 11 shows the genealogy of the researcher with the highest number of descendants (274 masters and 159 doctorates, with a total of 433 advising relationships), considering 3 levels of depth. This view contains 3726 vertices and 4192 edges, which represents almost 1% of the BDTD. We have applied the Yifan Hu algorithm [9], named ego network, to organize the vertices and then draw this researcher tree.

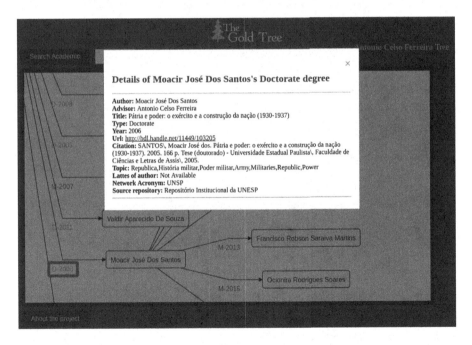

Fig. 10. Metadata describing the thesis or dissertation presented when clicking on an advising relationship [12].

---

[7] http://thegoldtree.c3.furg.br/.

Expanding the ego network to the maximum depth, we found the giant component of the BDTD graph with 305,733 (68.9%) vertices connected by 320,591 (68.8%) edges. These properties are summarized in Table 1.

Table 1. Properties of the Brazilian research network extracted from BDTD.

Property	Value
Vertices	443,654
Edges	465,847
Vertices in the giant component	305,733
Edges in the giant component	320,591

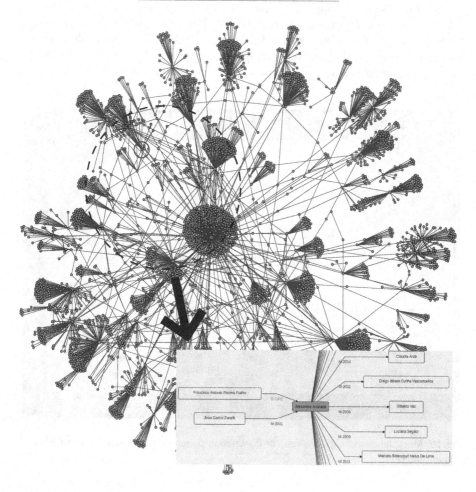

Fig. 11. An ego network of the advisor with the greatest number of descendants.

Analyzing the temporal distribution of the amount of published theses and dissertations (Fig. 12, we can see a constant and timid growth rate up to the year of 2000. The amount increases significantly between 2001 and 2013, not only because of the popularity of the digital institutional repositories, but also due to the expansion of Brazilian universities and graduate programs. However, the publication of documents has been decreasing in recent years.

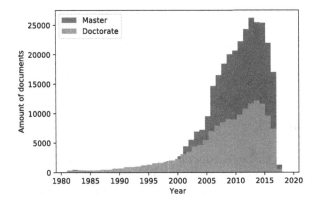

Fig. 12. Distribution of theses and dissertations published over time.

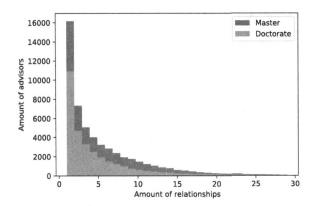

Fig. 13. Distribution of advising relationships.

Figure 13 shows the density of advising relationships. On a logarithmic scale, Fig. 14 shows the equivalent power law. The vast majority of researchers has mentored few master's or doctoral students. Only 396 (1.2%) researchers advised more than 30 students.

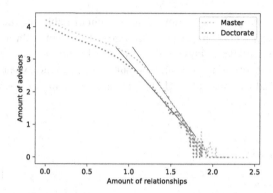

Fig. 14. Distribution of advising relationships in a logarithm scale.

5   Conclusion

This paper carries on studies conducted in a previous work [12], which describes the development of an academic tree visualization system called The Gold Tree. Such tool is based on the Brazilian Digital Library of Theses and Dissertations (BDTD). Despite the results presented in our work used a single database, the data source chosen could be easily replaced by one that publishes the metadata using the Dublin Core standard and the OAI-PHM protocol.

The Gold Tree would aid the study of Brazilian academic genealogy, since it would allow a user to query about a researcher on the database, defining the level of the tree depth in order to visualize the academic tree. The database used could be more understood as some studies of the features of the database were conducted, such as the number of researchers and connections, information on which was the largest component, the distribution of documents (theses and dissertations) per year, and the distribution of the amount of advising relationships.

Compared to related and similar systems, The Gold Tree is able to handle some limitations of others, as described as follows. Our proposed system uses an official source of data unlike Academic Family Tree, which is fed by users with unofficial confirmation. On Acácia Platform, it is not possible to visualize the academic tree. And on Science Tree, there is a limitation on the tree level of depth and also it is not possible to have a dynamic search. Both of these issues are solved in our proposal. Comparing the results obtained previously in [7], while the analysis is done only on the data of the Lattes Platform, in this paper we focus on data extracted from the Brazilian Digital Library of Theses and Dissertations, completing the available information about the Brazilian academic genealogy.

Future work concern on the creation of a recommendation system of advisors, which based on an abstract of a thesis or masters proposal. The system would be able to extract several features from the titles and abstracts of the theses and dissertations of all the descendants of a researcher to set up the advising profile, based on the vector space model. An machine learning approach would rank a list of the most apt academic advisors, using multiple classification algorithms with a high diversity.

Acknowledgment. This study was supported by the Fundação de Amparo à Pesquisa do Estado do RS (FAPERGS) [grant numbers TO 17/2551-0000872-3, TO 19/2551-0001279-9, and TO 19/2551-0001660], Conselho Nacional de Desenvolvimento Científico e Tecnológico (CNPq) [grant number 305882/2016-3], and Coordenação de Aperfeiçoamento de Pessoal de Nível Superior - Brazil (CAPES) [grant number 88887.464880/2019-00].

References

1. Barabâsi, A.L., Jeong, H., Néda, Z., Ravasz, E., Schubert, A., Vicsek, T.: Evolution of the social network of scientific collaborations. Physica A **311**(3–4), 590–614 (2002)
2. Batagelj, V., Mrvar, A.: Pajek—analysis and visualization of large networks. In: Mutzel, P., Jünger, M., Leipert, S. (eds.) GD 2001. LNCS, vol. 2265, pp. 477–478. Springer, Heidelberg (2002). https://doi.org/10.1007/3-540-45848-4_54
3. Chang, S.: Academic Genealogy of Mathematicians. World Scientific, Singapore (2011)
4. Damaceno, R.J.P.; Rossi, L.M.C.J.P.: Identificação do grafo de genealogia acadêmica de pesquisadores: Uma abordagem baseada na plataforma lattes. In: Proceedings of the 32nd Brazilian Symposium on Databases, Uberlândia (2017)
5. David, S.V., Hayden, B.Y.: Neurotree: a collaborative, graphical database of the academic genealogy of neuroscience. PLoS ONE **7**(10), e46608 (2012). https://doi.org/10.1371/journal.pone.0046608
6. Dores, W., Benevenuto, F., Laender, A.H.: Extracting academic genealogy trees from the networked digital library of theses and dissertations. In: Proceedings of the 16th ACM/IEEE-CS on Joint Conference on Digital Libraries, pp. 163–166. ACM, New York (2016). https://doi.org/10.1145/2910896.2910916
7. Dores, W., Soares, E., Benevenuto, F., Laender, A.H.F.: Building the Brazilian academic genealogy tree. In: Kamps, J., Tsakonas, G., Manolopoulos, Y., Iliadis, L., Karydis, I. (eds.) Research and Advanced Technology for Digital Libraries, pp. 537–543. Springer International Publishing, Cham (2017)
8. Douglas, S.M., Montelione, G.T., Gerstein, M.: PubNet: a flexible system for visualizing literature derived networks. Genome Biol. **6**(9), R80 (2005). https://doi.org/10.1186/gb-2005-6-9-r80
9. Hu, Y.: Efficient, high-quality force-directed graph drawing. Math. J. **10**(1), 37–71 (2005)
10. Laender, A., Moro, M., Silva, A., et al.: Ciência brasil-the brazilian portal of science and technology. In: Seminário Integrado de Software e Hardware, pp. 1366–1379. Sociedade Brasileira de Computação (2011)
11. Lagoze, C., Van de Sompel, H.: The open archives initiative: building a low-barrier interoperability framework. In: Proceedings of the 1st ACM/IEEE-CS Joint Conference on Digital libraries, pp. 54–62. ACM, New York (2001). https://doi.org/10.1145/379437.379449
12. Madeira, G., et al.: The gold tree: an information system for analyzing academic genealogy. In: Proceedings of the 21st International Conference on Enterprise Information Systems - Volume 1: ICEIS, INSTICC, pp. 114–120. SciTePress (2019). https://doi.org/10.5220/0007758401140120
13. Malmgren, R.D., Ottino, J.M., Nunes, L.A.: The role of mentorship in protégé performance. Nature Int. J. Sci. **465**. 7298, 622 (2010). https://www.nature.com/articles/nature09040
14. Mena-Chalco, J.P., Cesar-Jr, R.M.: Prospecção de dados acadêmicos de currículos Lattes através de scriptLattes, chap. Bibliometria e Cientometria: reflexões teóricas e interfaces, pp. 109–128. Pedro & João Editores, São Carlos (2013)
15. Osmani, A.: Learning JavaScript Design Patterns: A JavaScript and jQuery Developer's Guide. O'Reilly Media, Inc. (2012)

16. Roeder, L.: Dagre-d3 (2018). https://github.com/dagrejs/dagre-d3
17. Yu, M.C., Wu, Y.C.J., Alhalabi, W., Kao, H.Y., Wu, W.H.: Researchgate: an effective altmetric indicator for active researchers? Comput. Hum. Behav. **55**, 1001–1006 (2016). https://doi.org/10.1016/j.chb.2015.11.007

Improving and Optimizing Verification and Testing Techniques for Distributed Information Systems

Moez Krichen[1,2](✉)

[1] Faculty of CSIT, Al-Baha University, Al-Baha, Kingdom of Saudi Arabia
[2] ReDCAD, ENIS, University of Sfax, Sfax, Tunisia
`moez.krichen@redcad.org`

Abstract. In this paper, we deal with two validation techniques which may be adopted for improving the quality and ensuring the correctness of Distributed Information Systems. These two techniques are Formal Verification and Model Based Techniques. The first one consists in checking the correctness of a mathematical model used to describe the behavior of the considered system before its implementation. The second technique consists in deriving tests suites from the adopted model, executing them and finally deducing verdicts about the correctness of this system under test. In both cases, we need to tackle the explosion state challenge which corresponds to the fact of reaching a very large space of states and consuming a very long time during the validation process. To solve this problem we propose a set of appropriate techniques taken from the literature. We also identify a set of techniques which may be used for the optimization of the test component placement procedure.

Keywords: Distributed · Information systems · Formal verification · Model based testing · Optimization · Test component placement

1 Introduction

During the few last years, information systems have been continuously gaining a larger value as an important component for a large range of computerized systems and advanced technologies. We are interested, more precisely, in distributed information systems [19,38,77] which are decentralized systems composed of sets of software components and physical devices.

In this work, we deal with the so-called *model-based testing (MBT) and formal verification* which may be seen as *formal methods*. The latters are mathematically based techniques used for the specification, development and automatic property checking of different systems. A variety of formal techniques and languages can be used to deal with different kinds of properties at distinct steps of system production. On the other hand, Model Based Testing approaches consist in deriving automatically test scenarios from the mathematical description of the implementation under test.

© Springer Nature Switzerland AG 2020
J. Filipe et al. (Eds.): ICEIS 2019, LNBIP 378, pp. 457–472, 2020.
https://doi.org/10.1007/978-3-030-40783-4_22

Generally, MBT and Formal Verification are likely to face the famous *state explosion challenge*. The latter corresponds to the fact that test generation and system formal verification may need an immense amount of time and a very big space to produce and save the set of test scenarios. The situation may become even more critical when sophisticated and large systems like distributed information systems are considered.

To solve this problem we propose in this paper to adopt a set of methods borrowed from our previous works and from the literature and which aim to diminish the duration, complexity and cost of verification and test generation. Firstly, the methods related to formal verification are: Abstraction; Compositionality and Modularization; Symmetry Identification; Data Independence Identification; Removing Functional Dependencies; Exploiting Reversible Rules. Secondly, the methods dealing with MBT are: Refinement Techniques; Diminishing the Size of Digital Testers; Producing Timed Automata Testers; Upgrading Test Scenarios after System Update; Coverage Techniques; State Identification.

Moreover, we propose a set of techniques inspired from the fog computing field. These techniques may be used for optimizing the test component placement problem. For that purpose, we identify the different types of constraints we may consider, the objectives functions that may be adopted and the possible algorithms to use to solve the corresponding optimization problem.

The rest of this paper in structured as follows. In Sect. 2, we provide some preliminaries about formal methods, model based testing, the timed automaton model and the diff rent kinds of testers. In Sect. 3, we give details about the several techniques that may be adopted to improve formal verification methods. Similarly, details about the techniques to use for improving model based testing techniques are given in Sect. 4. Section 5 provides the necessary ingredients for solving the test component placement problem. Finally Sect. 6 concludes the paper and gives directions for future work.

2   Preliminaries

2.1   Formal Methods

During the last years of the last century, scientists started making computerized systems verification methods more sophisticated and more accurate [15,59]. In fact, with the emergence of mathematical formalisms for the specification of computerized systems [40], the first formal verification methodologies have appeared. There are mainly tow categories of formal verification techniques, namely: model checking [15,59] and automated theorem proving [7,18,56].

2.2   Model Based Testing

Model-Based Testing (MBT) [30,31,34,36,55,70,80] is a methodology where the system of interest is described by a mathematical model which encodes the behavior of the considered system. This methodology consists in using this mathematical model to compute abstract test scenarios. These sequences of abstract actions are then transformed into concrete test sequences which are executed on the considered system under test. The verdict of the this testing activity is provided by comparing the observed outputs from the system with the outputs generated by the model.

2.3 Timed Automata

Timed automata (TA) [1,12,62] are an expressive and simple tool for describing the behavior of computer systems which combine continuous and discrete mechanisms. TA may be represented as finite graphs enriched with a finite set of clocks defined as real entities whose value progresses continuously over time. In Fig. 1 we propose an example of a TA which has five nodes, four transitions, three actions and one clock.

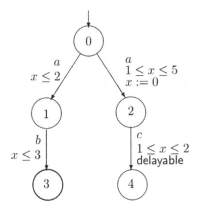

Fig. 1. A TA with 5 states, 4 transitions, 3 actions and 1 clock.

2.4 Different Kinds of Testers

A test case is an interactive scenario between the system under test (SUT) and the tester. The tester provides input actions to the system under test and collects generated corresponding output actions. After that, the tester verifies whether the produced output sequences are acceptable or not and emits correspondingly either Fail or Pass verdicts. Usually, it is possible to define three kinds of testers:

– TA Testers: represented as timed automata (built before test execution).
– On-the-Fly Analog Testers: able to measure time with precision (generated during test execution).
– Digital Testers: measure time with less precision (produced either before or during test execution).

3   Improving Formal Verification Methods

3.1   Abstraction

The authors of In [69] were interested in verifying cyber-physical systems. The basic idea consisted in applying specific transformations to remove details irrelevant to the properties of interest. Likely the authors of [2] came up with a collection of languages for modelling hardware systems. Wide datapaths were abstracted away and low-level details corresponding to the control logic were kept.

3.2   Symmetry Identification

Symmetry identification [16,26,41,57,72] is a method which makes use of symmetries which occur during the execution of the system, for minimizing the considered state space. It allows to compute a mapping between the set of states of the system and the representatives of the classes of equivalences.

3.3   Data Independence Identification

Data independence identification [5,53,61] is an other method which may be adopted for reducing the complexity of formal verification too. This method can be used in the case where the designer of the system under verification identifies the fact that the behaviour of the system in independent of some particular inputs. In this situation, the designer can reduce significantly the size of the model of the considered system.

3.4   Removing Functional Dependencies

In [14] functional dependency is detected using Craig interpolation methods and SAT solving. In [29], the authors detect functional dependencies from transition functions and not from the computation of the reachable states. In [24] the researchers worked on the verification of hardware conception. They identified variables which are functionally dependent for reducing the size of the used data structures.

3.5   Exploiting Reversible Rules

This method [27,28] allows to collapse subgraphs of the state graph into abstract states (named progenitors). This operation is performed by defining generation principles which may be reversed.

4   Improving Testing Methods

4.1   Refinement Techniques

These techniques consist in converting high-level symbols into sequences of lower-level symbols. In [6], the authors came up with a refinement based methodology for testing timed systems. This approach is illustrated in Fig. 2 and an example of such a transformation is illustraterd in Figs. 3 and 4.

4.2   Diminishing the Size of Digital Testers

Digital testers may become very big since they may sometimes contain very long sequences of tick actions. A possible solution to tackle this problem consists in extending testers with more sophisticated variables and data structures [36]. For instance, an example of a (relatively) big tester reduced into two smaller alternative equivalent testers is shown in Fig. 5.

4.3   Producing Timed Automata Testers

In general, one can not transform a non deterministic timed automaton into a deterministic one making use of a finite number of resources (i.e., nodes, transitions, actions, clocks, etc.). Alternatively, it is possible to produce a deterministic approximation of the tester in the form of a timed automaton using appropriate algorithms and heuristics like the ones presented in [8–11, 36, 37]. For instance a timed automaton tester corresponding the specification presented in Fig. 1 is given in Fig. 6.

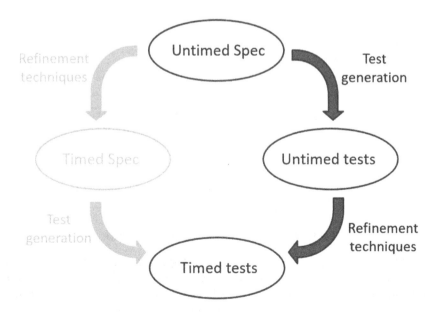

Fig. 2. Refinement technique principle.

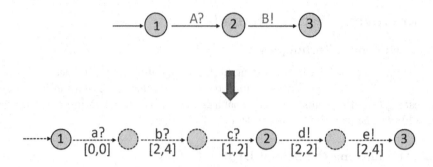

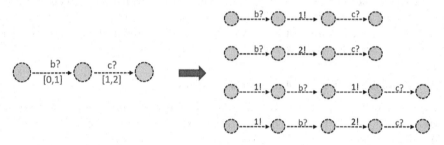

Fig. 3. An untimed model refined into a timed one.

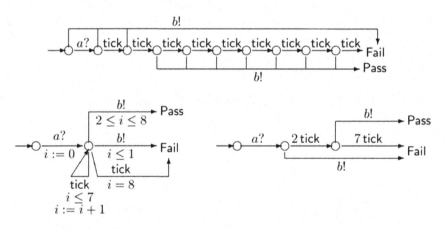

Fig. 4. Digital refinement.

Fig. 5. A digital tester with two possible alternatives for diminishing its size.

4.4 Upgrading Test Scenarios After System Update

This method [42–44] allows to optimize the test synthesis phase when a dynamic evolution of the considered system occurs. The model of the system may change either completely or partially after a behavioral evolution occurs. As a consequence, we have to upgrade the collection of available test scenarios either by producing new test scenarios or updating old ones (Fig. 7).

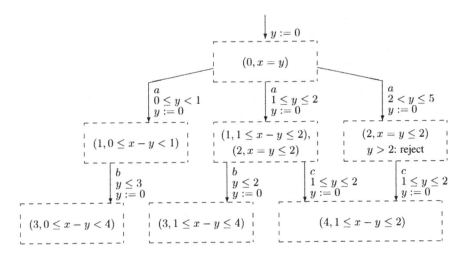

Fig. 6. A TA Tester corresponding to the specification presented in Fig. 1.

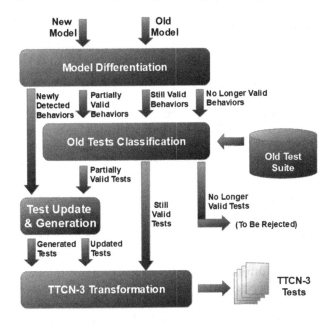

Fig. 7. Behavioral adaptations validation.

4.5 Coverage Techniques

Several coverage techniques can be used in testing field such as statement cover-age and branch coverage [54]. Likely, for timed systems existing methodologies [23,36] can be used for the coverage of specific entities of the considered system in order to diminish significantly the number of generated test cases.

4.6   State Identification

The state identification problems [32,33,35] were initially introduced for the case of finite state machines (FSMs). The solution for this problem consists in identifying either the initial or the final state of the considered machines which in turn makes test generation easier and less time and resource consuming since it allows to reach zones of interest of the state space in an efficient way.

5   Testers Placement Optimization

This problem is inspired by fog computing approaches [4,20,51,67] and by some of our previous contributions [42,45,50]. It consists in allocating the set of testers on the different computational nodes of the SUT in an optimal manner under several types of constraints as mentioned below.

5.1   Different Types of Constraints

Node Constraints. For example, the writers of [76] took into account only storage and the writers of [76] only CPU. In [3], both CPU and storage were taken into account. In [20], the authors considered both CPU, RAM and storage constraints.

Network Constraints. In [51,66] only latency constraint was taken into account. In addition in [22,58], both bandwidth and latency were considered by the authors. Moreover the authors of [3,67] were interested in bandwidth requirement along with hardware constraints.

Energy Constraints. For instance in [4], the fog nodes were characterised with their energy capacities. Moreover, the writers of [65] proposed the notion of energy cells to estimate the energy consumed by the fog nodes.

Application Constraints. In [21], the demand rate of the applications was considered in order to optimize the placement problem. Moreover, the writers of [76] proposed an analysis of the workload generated by every region of the fog and the relations and dependencies between the different application components. In [58], these relations and dependencies were presented as a special graph.

5.2   Objective Functions

Energy. Energy optimisation was taken into account from distinct levels. For example, the authors of [4] considered a linear objective function of the energy cost. Likewise in [25], the adopted goal consisted in diminishing the communication energy cost.

Execution Time and Network Delay. For example this objective function was adopted by the authors of [63,78]. In addition in [75], the response time was optimised in order to augment the number of requests to be served before a chosen deadline. Further in [66], the service execution time of the service was reduced by evaluating the needed time slots.

Migrations. In [58], the migrations number was optimised by reducing the network use without impacting its latency. Likewise in [76], the migrations number was optimised along with latency and resource consumption. Further, the authors of [17] presented a technique to diminish the number of migrating applications between the different computational available nodes.

Cost. In [3] the authors worked on minimizing the overall cost of the deployment of the considered applications by allocating them computational nodes which have minimal costs. Likewise, cost minimisation of each link and device was considered by the authors of [73].

QoS-Assurance. In [51], the chosen QoS requirement corresponded to reaching execution times that are smaller than the applications deadlines. Moreover, the writers of [71] adopted QoS aspects associated with the frequency of executed transactions and requests.

5.3   Algorithms

Search-Based Algorithms. In [22] an algorithm was proposed to find a placement scenario for internet of things applications. In addition in [21], a distributed search method was proposed for similar goals. Moreover in [13], an exhaustive and greedy backtracking algorithm was proposed to deal the placement problem.

Dynamic Programming. In [65] the placement problem was modelled as a multidimensional knapsack problem (MKP). Likewise in [60], the placement problem was modelled as a knapsack instance.

Mathematical Programming. This technique is always adopted to solve optimisation problems by investigating the space of the considered objective functions. Several works [20,66,76] solved the placement problem using this mathematical method.

Game Theory. In [79], the placement problem was encoded as a pair of games. The first one was introduced to calculate the cardinality of the set of necessary execution blocks and the second one was proposed to set prices in order to maximise the corresponding financial profits.

Genetic Algorithms. In [74], the authors proposed parallel genetic algorithms in order to deal with placement problem. Likewise, the authors of [64] came up with a genetic algorithm approach based on iFogSim.

Deep Learning. In [68], the authors exploited modern learning techniques to deal with the placement problem. For that, they proposed a deep learning algorithm to control applications migrations.

Complex Networks. Filiposka et al. [17] used network science theory to study the placement problem. Moreover they adopted a community detection method in order the solve the considered problem.

6 Conclusion and Future Work

The work presented in this paper was an extension of a previous work [38] accepted in ICEIS 2019. Our goal was to identify a set of techniques which may help in solving the state explosion problem that may be encountered when adopting FV and/or MBT techniques during the validation process of distributed information systems. The proposed techniques related to FV were: 1. Abstraction; 2. Compositionality and Modularization; 3. Symmetry Identification; 4. Data Independence Identification; 5. Exploiting Reversible Rules; 6. Removing Functional Dependencies. On the other hand, the techniques related to Model Based Testing were: 1. Refinement Methods; 2. Compacting Digital Testers; 3. Producing TA Testers; 4. Upgrading Test Scenarios after System Update; 5. Coverage Techniques; 6. State Identification. Moreover, we proposed a set of techniques inspired from the fog computing field. These techniques may be exploited for the optimization of the test component placement problem. We identified the different types of constraints to consider, the objectives functions to adopt and the possible algorithms to use to solve the corresponding optimization problem.

In the future, our priority will be to implement the different proposed techniques in order to validate them. Moreover we may need to combine both Load and Functional testing procedures as proposed in [39,46–49,52] in order to take into account the correlation existing between these two types of testing methods.

References

1. Alur, R., Dill, D.: A theory of timed automata. Theor. Comput. Sci. **126**, 183–235 (1994)
2. Andraus, Z.S., Sakallah, K.A.: Automatic abstraction and verification of verilog models. In: Proceedings of the 41st Annual Design Automation Conference. pp. 218–223. DAC 2004, ACM, New York, NY, USA (2004). https://doi.org/10.1145/996566.996629
3. Arkian, H.R., Diyanat, A., Pourkhalili, A.: Mist: fog-based data analytics scheme with cost-efficient resource provisioning for iot crowdsensing applications. J. Netw. Comput. Appl. **82**, 152–165 (2017). https://doi.org/10.1016/j.jnca.2017.01.012. http://www.sciencedirect.com/science/article/pii/S1084804517300188

4. Barcelo, M., Correa, A., Llorca, J., Tulino, A.M., Vicario, J.L., Morell, A.: Iot-cloud service optimization in next generation smart environments. IEEE J. Sel. Areas Commun. **34**(12), 4077–4090 (2016). https://doi.org/10.1109/JSAC.2016.2621398
5. Benalycherif, L., McIsaac, A.: A semantic condition for data independence and applications in hardware verification. Electron. Notes Theor. Comput. Sci. **250**(1), 39–54 (2009). https://doi.org/10.1016/j.entcs.2009.08.004. http://www.sciencedirect.com/science/article/pii/S1571066109003296. Proceedings of the Seventh International Workshop on Automated Verification of Critical Systems (AVoCS 2007)
6. Bensalem, S., Krichen, M., Majdoub, L., Robbana, R., Tripakis, S.: A simplified approach for testing real-time systems based on action refinement. In: ISoLA. Revue des Nouvelles Technologies de l'Information, vol. RNTI-SM-1, pp. 191–202. Cépaduès-Éditions (2007)
7. Bertot, Y., Castran, P.: Interactive Theorem Proving and Program Development: Coq'Art The Calculus of Inductive Constructions, 1st edn. Springer, Incorporated (2010)
8. Bertrand, N., Jéron, T., Stainer, A., Krichen, M.: Off-line test selection with test purposes for non-deterministic timed automata. In: Tools and Algorithms for the Construction and Analysis of Systems - 17th International Conference, TACAS 2011, Held as Part of the Joint European Conferences on Theory and Practice of Software, ETAPS 2011, Saarbrücken, Germany, March 26–April 3, 2011, Proceedings. pp. 96–111 (2011). https://doi.org/10.1007/978-3-642-19835-9_10
9. Bertrand, N., Jéron, T., Stainer, A., Krichen, M.: Off-line test selection with test purposes for non-deterministic timed automata. Logical Meth. Comput. Sci. **8**(4), 1–33 (2012)
10. Bertrand, N., Stainer, A., Jéron, T., Krichen, M.: A game approach to determinize timed automata. In: Hofmann, M. (ed.) FoSSaCS 2011. LNCS, vol. 6604, pp. 245–259. Springer, Heidelberg (2011). https://doi.org/10.1007/978-3-642-19805-2_17
11. Bertrand, N., Stainer, A., Jéron, T., Krichen, M.: A game approach to determinize timed automata. Formal Meth. Syst. Des. **46**(1), 42–80 (2015)
12. Bornot, S., Sifakis, J., Tripakis, S.: Modeling urgency in timed systems. In: de Roever, W.-P., Langmaack, H., Pnueli, A. (eds.) COMPOS 1997. LNCS, vol. 1536, pp. 103–129. Springer, Heidelberg (1998). https://doi.org/10.1007/3-540-49213-5_5
13. Brogi, A., Forti, S.: Qos-aware deployment of iot applications through the fog. IEEE Internet of Things J. **4**(5), 1185–1192 (2017). https://doi.org/10.1109/JIOT.2017.2701408
14. Lee, C.-C., Jiang, J.R., Huang, C.-Y., Mishchenko, A.: Scalable exploration of functional dependency by interpolation and incremental sat solving. In: 2007 IEEE/ACM International Conference on Computer-Aided Design, pp. 227–233, November 2007. https://doi.org/10.1109/ICCAD.2007.4397270
15. Clarke, E.M., Emerson, E.A.: Design and synthesis of synchronization skeletons using branching time temporal logic. In: Kozen, D. (ed.) Logic of Programs 1981. LNCS, vol. 131, pp. 52–71. Springer, Heidelberg (1982). https://doi.org/10.1007/BFb0025774
16. Emerson, E.A., Wahl, T.: Dynamic symmetry reduction. In: Halbwachs, N., Zuck, L.D. (eds.) TACAS 2005. LNCS, vol. 3440, pp. 382–396. Springer, Heidelberg (2005). https://doi.org/10.1007/978-3-540-31980-1_25

17. Filiposka, S., Mishev, A., Gilly, K.: Community-based allocation and migration strategies for fog computing. In: 2018 IEEE Wireless Communications and Networking Conference (WCNC), pp. 1–6, April 2018. https://doi.org/10.1109/WCNC.2018.8377095

18. Gordon, M.J.C., Melham, T.F. (eds.): Introduction to HOL: A Theorem Proving Environment for Higher Order Logic. Cambridge University Press, New York (1993)

19. Grusho, A.A., Grusho, N.A., Timonina, E.E.: Information security architecture synthesis in distributed information computation systems. Autom. Control Comput. Sci. **51**(8), 799–804 (2017). https://doi.org/10.3103/S0146411617080089

20. Gu, L., Zeng, D., Guo, S., Barnawi, A., Xiang, Y.: Cost efficient resource management in fog computing supported medical cyber-physical system. IEEE Trans. Emerg. Topics Comput. **5**(1), 108–119 (2017). https://doi.org/10.1109/TETC.2015.2508382

21. Guerrero, C., Lera, I., Juiz, C.: A lightweight decentralized service placement policy for performance optimization in fog computing. J. Ambient Intell. Humanized Comput. **10**(6), 2435–2452 (2019). https://doi.org/10.1007/s12652-018-0914-0

22. Gupta, H., Dastjerdi, A.V., Ghosh, S.K., Buyya, R.: ifogsim: a toolkit for modeling and simulation of resource management techniques in the internet of things, edge and fog computing environments. Softw. Pract. Exper. **47**(9), 1275–1296 (2017). https://doi.org/10.1002/spe.2509

23. Hessel, A., Larsen, K., Nielsen, B., Pettersson, P., Skou, A.: Time-optimal real-time test case generation using UPPAAL. In: FATES 2003 (2003)

24. Hu, A.J., Dill, D.L.: Reducing BDD size by exploiting functional dependencies. In: 30th ACM/IEEE Design Automation Conference. pp. 266–271, June 1993. https://doi.org/10.1145/157485.164888

25. Huang, Z., Lin, K.J., Yu, S.Y., Jen Hsu, J.Y.: Co-locating services in iot systems to minimize the communication energy cost. J. Innov. Digital Ecosyst. **1**(1), 47–57 (2014). https://doi.org/10.1016/j.jides.2015.02.005

26. Iosif, R.: Symmetry reduction criteria for software model checking. In: Bošnački, D., Leue, S. (eds.) SPIN 2002. LNCS, vol. 2318, pp. 22–41. Springer, Heidelberg (2002). https://doi.org/10.1007/3-540-46017-9_5

27. Norris Ip, C.: Generalized reversible rules. In: Gopalakrishnan, G., Windley, P. (eds.) FMCAD 1998. LNCS, vol. 1522, pp. 403–419. Springer, Heidelberg (1998). https://doi.org/10.1007/3-540-49519-3_26

28. Ip, C.N., Dill, D.L.: State reduction using reversible rules. In: Proceedings of the 33st Conference on Design Automation, Las Vegas, Nevada, USA, Las Vegas Convention Center, June 3–7, 1996, pp. 564–567 (1996). https://doi.org/10.1145/240518.240625

29. Jiang, J.-H.R., Brayton, R.K.: Functional dependency for verification reduction. In: Alur, R., Peled, D.A. (eds.) CAV 2004. LNCS, vol. 3114, pp. 268–280. Springer, Heidelberg (2004). https://doi.org/10.1007/978-3-540-27813-9_21

30. Krichen, M.: A formal framework for black-box conformance testing of distributed real-time systems. IJCCBS **3**(1/2), 26–43 (2012). https://doi.org/10.1504/IJCCBS.2012.045075

31. Krichen, M., Tripakis, S.: Black-box conformance testing for real-time systems. In: Graf, S., Mounier, L. (eds.) SPIN 2004. LNCS, vol. 2989, pp. 109–126. Springer, Heidelberg (2004). https://doi.org/10.1007/978-3-540-24732-6_8

32. Krichen, M., Tripakis, S.: State identification problems for finite-state transducers. Technical report TR-2005-5, Verimag, February 2005

33. Krichen, M., Tripakis, S.: The epistemology of validation and verification testing. In: Khendek, F., Dssouli, R. (eds.) TestCom 2005. LNCS, vol. 3502, pp. 1–8. Springer, Heidelberg (2005). https://doi.org/10.1007/11430230_1

34. Krichen, M., Tripakis, S.: Interesting properties of the conformance relation tioco. In: ICTAC 2006 (2006)

35. Krichen, M., Tripakis, S.: State-identification problems for finite-state transducers. In: Havelund, K., Núñez, M., Roşu, G., Wolff, B. (eds.) FATES/RV -2006. LNCS, vol. 4262, pp. 148–162. Springer, Heidelberg (2006). https://doi.org/10.1007/11940197_10

36. Krichen, M., Tripakis, S.: Conformance testing for real-time systems. Formal Meth. Syst. Des. **34**(3), 238–304 (2009)

37. Krichen, M.: Model-Based Testing for Real-Time Systems. Ph.D. thesis, PhD thesis, University Joseph Fourier, December 2007 (2007)

38. Krichen, M., Alroobaea, R., Lahami, M.: Towards a runtime standard-based testing framework for dynamic distributed information systems. In: Proceedings of the 21st International Conference on Enterprise Information Systems, ICEIS 2019, Heraklion, Crete, Greece, May 3–5, 2019, vol. 1, pp. 121–129 (2019). https://doi.org/10.5220/0007772101210129

39. Krichen, M., Maâlej, A.J., Lahami, M.: A model-based approach to combine conformance and load tests: an ehealth case study. IJCCBS **8**(3/4), 282–310 (2018). https://doi.org/10.1504/IJCCBS.2018.096437

40. Kripke, S.A.: Semantical considerations on modal logic. Acta Philos. Fennica **16**(1963), 83–94 (1963)

41. Kwiatkowska, M., Norman, G., Parker, D.: Symmetry reduction for probabilistic model checking. In: Ball, T., Jones, R.B. (eds.) CAV 2006. LNCS, vol. 4144, pp. 234–248. Springer, Heidelberg (2006). https://doi.org/10.1007/11817963_23

42. Lahami, M., Krichen, M., Jmaïel, M.: Safe and efficient runtime testing framework applied in dynamic and distributed systems. Sci. Comput. Program. (SCP) **122**(C), 1–28 (2016)

43. Lahami, M., Fakhfakh, F., Krichen, M., Jmaïel, M.: Towards a TTCN-3 test system for runtime testing of adaptable and distributed systems. In: Proceedings of the 24th IFIP WG 6.1 International Conference Testing Software and Systems (ICTSS 2012), pp. 71–86 (2012)

44. Lahami, M., Krichen, M., Barhoumi, H., Jmaiel, M.: Selective test generation approach for testing dynamic behavioral adaptations. In: Testing Software and Systems - 27th IFIP WG 6.1 International Conference, ICTSS 2015, Sharjah and Dubai, United Arab Emirates, November 23–25, 2015, Proceedings. pp. 224–239 (2015). https://doi.org/10.1007/978-3-319-25945-1_14

45. Lahami, M., Krichen, M., Bouchakwa, M., Jmaïel, M.: Using knapsack problem model to design a resource aware test architecture for adaptable and distributed systems. In: Proceedings of the 24th IFIP WG 6.1 International Conference Testing Software and Systems (ICTSS 2012), pp. 103–118 (2012)

46. Maâlej, A.J., Hamza, M., Krichen, M., Jmaiel, M.: Automated significant load testing for WS-BPEL compositions. In: Sixth IEEE International Conference on Software Testing, Verification and Validation, ICST 2013 Workshops Proceedings, Luxembourg, Luxembourg, March 18–22, 2013, pp. 144–153 (2013). https://doi.org/10.1109/ICSTW.2013.25

47. Maâlej, A.J., Krichen, M.: A model based approach to combine load and functional tests for service oriented architectures. In: VECoS, pp. 123–140 (2016)

48. Maâlej, A.J., Krichen, M., Jmaiel, M.: Conformance testing of WS-BPEL compositions under various load conditions. In: 36th Annual IEEE Computer Software and Applications Conference, COMPSAC 2012, Izmir, Turkey, July 16–20, 2012, p. 371 (2012). https://doi.org/10.1109/COMPSAC.2012.100

49. Maâlej, A.J., Krichen, M., Jmaiel, M.: Model-based conformance testing of WS-BPEL compositions. In: 36th Annual IEEE Computer Software and Applications Conference Workshops, COMPSAC 2012, Izmir, Turkey, July 16–20, 2012, pp. 452–457 (2012). https://doi.org/10.1109/COMPSACW.2012.86

50. Maâlej, A.J., Lahami, M., Krichen, M., Jmaïel, M.: Distributed and resource-aware load testing of WS-BPEL compositions. In: ICEIS (2). pp. 29–38. SciTePress (2018)

51. Mahmud, R., Ramamohanarao, K., Buyya, R.: Latency-aware application module management for fog computing environments. ACM Trans. Internet Technol. 19(1), 9:1–9:21 (2018). https://doi.org/10.1145/3186592

52. Maâlej, A.J., Krichen, M.: Study on the limitations of WS-BPEL compositions under load conditions. Comput. J. 58(3), 385–402 (2015). https://doi.org/10.1093/comjnl/bxu140

53. Momtahan, L.: Towards a small model theorem for data independent systems in alloy. Electron. Notes Theor. Comput. Sci. 128(6), 37–52 (2005). https://doi.org/10.1016/j.entcs.2005.04.003. http://www.sciencedirect.com/science/article/pii/S1571066105002355. Proceedings of the Fourth International Workshop on Automated Verification of Critical Systems (AVoCS 2004)

54. Myers, G.: The Art of Software Testing. Wiley, Hoboken (1979)

55. Neto, A.C.D., Travassos, G.H.: A picture from the model-based testing area: concepts, techniques, and challenges. Adv. Comput. 80, 45–120 (2010)

56. Nipkow, T., Wenzel, M., Paulson, L.C. (eds.): Isabelle/HOL–A Proof Assistant for Higher-Order Logic. LNCS, vol. 2283. Springer, Heidelberg (2002). https://doi.org/10.1007/3-540-45949-9

57. Norris, C., Dill, D.L.: Better verification through symmetry. Formal Meth. Syst. Des. 9(1), 41–75 (1996). https://doi.org/10.1007/BF00625968

58. Ottenwälder, B., Koldehofe, B., Rothermel, K., Ramachandran, U.: Migcep: operator migration for mobility driven distributed complex event processing. In: Proceedings of the 7th ACM International Conference on Distributed Event-based Systems, pp. 183–194. DEBS 2013, ACM, New York, NY, USA (2013). https://doi.org/10.1145/2488222.2488265

59. Queille, J.P., Sifakis, J.: Specification and verification of concurrent systems in CESAR. In: Dezani-Ciancaglini, M., Montanari, U. (eds.) Programming 1982. LNCS, vol. 137, pp. 337–351. Springer, Heidelberg (1982). https://doi.org/10.1007/3-540-11494-7_22

60. Rahbari, D., Nickray, M.: Scheduling of fog networks with optimized knapsack by symbiotic organisms search. In: 2017 21st Conference of Open Innovations Association (FRUCT), pp. 278–283, November 2017. https://doi.org/10.23919/FRUCT.2017.8250193

61. Roscoe, A.W., Broadfoot, P.J.: Proving security protocols with model checkers by data independence techniques. J. Comput. Secur. 7(1), 147–190 (1999). http://content.iospress.com/articles/journal-of-computer-security/jcs120

62. Sifakis, J., Yovine, S.: Compositional specification of timed systems. In: Puech, C., Reischuk, R. (eds.) STACS 1996. LNCS, vol. 1046, pp. 345–359. Springer, Heidelberg (1996). https://doi.org/10.1007/3-540-60922-9_29

63. Skarlat, O., Schulte, S., Borkowski, M., Leitner, P.: Resource provisioning for iot services in the fog. In: 2016 IEEE 9th International Conference on Service-Oriented Computing and Applications (SOCA), pp. 32–39, November 2016. https://doi.org/10.1109/SOCA.2016.10

64. Skarlat, O., Nardelli, M., Schulte, S., Borkowski, M., Leitner, P.: Optimized iot service placement in the fog. Serv. Oriented Comput. Appl. **11**(4), 427–443 (2017). https://doi.org/10.1007/s11761-017-0219-8

65. Souza, V.B., Masip-Bruin, X., Marin-Tordera, E., Ramirez, W., Sanchez, S.: Towards distributed service allocation in fog-to-cloud (f2c) scenarios. In: 2016 IEEE Global Communications Conference (GLOBECOM), pp. 1–6, December 2016. https://doi.org/10.1109/GLOCOM.2016.7842341

66. Souza, V.B.C., Ramírez, W., Masip-Bruin, X., Marín-Tordera, E., Ren, G., Tashakor, G.: Handling service allocation in combined fog-cloud scenarios. In: 2016 IEEE International Conference on Communications (ICC), pp. 1–5, May 2016. https://doi.org/10.1109/ICC.2016.7511465

67. Taneja, M., Davy, A.: Resource aware placement of iot application modules in fog-cloud computing paradigm. In: 2017 IFIP/IEEE Symposium on Integrated Network and Service Management (IM), pp. 1222–1228, May 2017. https://doi.org/10.23919/INM.2017.7987464

68. Tang, Z., Zhou, X., Zhang, F., Jia, W., Zhao, W.: Migration modeling and learning algorithms for containers in fog computing. IEEE Trans. Serv. Comput. p. 1 (2018). https://doi.org/10.1109/TSC.2018.2827070

69. Thacker, R.A., Jones, K.R., Myers, C.J., Zheng, H.: Automatic abstraction for verification of cyber-physical systems. In: Proceedings of the 1st ACM/IEEE International Conference on Cyber-Physical Systems, pp. 12–21. ICCPS 2010, ACM, New York, NY, USA (2010). https://doi.org/10.1145/1795194.1795197

70. Utting, M., Pretschner, A., Legeard, B.: A taxonomy of model-based testing approaches. Softw. Test. Verif. Reliab. **22**(5), 297–312 (2012). https://doi.org/10.1002/stvr.456

71. Venticinque, S., Amato, A.: A methodology for deployment of iot application in fog. J. Ambient Intell. Humanized Comput. **10**(5), 1955–1976 (2019)

72. Wahl, T., Donaldson, A.: Replication and abstraction: symmetry in automated formal verification. Symmetry **2**(2), 799–847 (2010). https://doi.org/10.3390/sym2020799

73. Wang, S., Zafer, M., Leung, K.K.: Online placement of multi-component applications in edge computing environments. IEEE Access **5**, 2514–2533 (2017). https://doi.org/10.1109/ACCESS.2017.2665971

74. Wen, Z., Yang, R., Garraghan, P., Lin, T., Xu, J., Rovatsos, M.: Fog orchestration for internet of things services. IEEE Internet Comput. **21**(2), 16–24 (2017). https://doi.org/10.1109/MIC.2017.36

75. Xia, Y., Etchevers, X., Letondeur, L., Coupaye, T., Desprez, F.: Combining hardware nodes and software components ordering-based heuristics for optimizing the placement of distributed iot applications in the fog. In: Proceedings of the 33rd Annual ACM Symposium on Applied Computing, pp. 751–760. SAC 2018, ACM, New York, NY, USA (2018). https://doi.org/10.1145/3167132.3167215

76. Yang, L., Cao, J., Liang, G., Han, X.: Cost aware service placement and load dispatching in mobile cloud systems. IEEE Trans. Comput. **65**(5), 1440–1452 (2016). https://doi.org/10.1109/TC.2015.2435781

77. Yesikov, D., Ivutin, A., Larkin, E., Kotov, V.: Multi-agent approach for distributed information systems reliability prediction. Procedia Comput. Sci. **103**, 416–420 (2017). https://doi.org/10.1016/j.procs.2017.01.003. http://www.sciencedirect.com/science/article/pii/S1877050917300042. XII International Symposium Intelligent Systems 2016, INTELS 2016, 5–7 October 2016, Moscow, Russia

78. Zeng, D., Gu, L., Guo, S., Cheng, Z., Yu, S.: Joint optimization of task scheduling and image placement in fog computing supported software-defined embedded system. IEEE Trans. Comput. **65**(12), 3702–3712 (2016). https://doi.org/10.1109/TC.2016.2536019

79. Zhang, H., Xiao, Y., Bu, S., Niyato, D., Yu, F.R., Han, Z.: Computing resource allocation in three-tier iot fog networks: a joint optimization approach combining stackelberg game and matching. IEEE Internet of Things J. **4**(5), 1204–1215 (2017). https://doi.org/10.1109/JIOT.2017.2688925

80. Zhu, H., Belli, F.: Advancing test automation technology to meet the challenges of model-based software testing - guest editors' introduction to the special section of the third IEEE international workshop on automation of software test (AST 2008). Inf. Softw. Technol. **51**(11), 1485–1486 (2009)

Systematizing the Relationship Between Business Processes' and Web Services' Non-functional Requirements

Camila F. Castro Jr.[1], Marcelo Fantinato[1(✉)], Ünal Aksu[2], Hajo A. Reijers[2], and Lucinéia H. Thom[3]

[1] School of Arts, Sciences and Humanities, University of São Paulo, São Paulo, Brazil
{marcos.freitas,m.fantinato}@usp.br
[2] Department of Information and Computer Sciences,
Utrecht University, Utrecht, The Netherlands
{u.aksu,h.a.reijers}@uu.nl
[3] Institute of Informatics, Federal University of Rio Grande do Sul,
Porto Alegre, Brazil
lucineia@inf.ufrgs.br

Abstract. We propose in this paper a conceptual framework for the hierarchical decomposition of Non-Functional Requirements (NFRs) from the business process level to the web service level. This framework seeks to reduce the dependence on a particular IT expert's knowledge by simplifying the dialog between the business and IT areas. The proposed framework relies on a structure of NFRs interdependence. The main reference was the ISO/IEC 25010 Product Quality Model, extended by additional software quality models and particular QoS attributes. This framework is accompanied by an extensive dictionary of non-functional requirements for both business processes and web services that can serve as a reference for researchers and industry practitioners. We assume that orchestrating web services to run business processes requires a rigorous definition of the functional requirements and NFRs of these web services. Web service NFRs are often defined as Quality of Service (QoS) attributes, which is done at the implementation level by IT teams. The definition of QoS attributes should consider the business process NFRs, since misinterpretations of web service NFRs may affect the behavior of the web services and hence achieving the business goals. The approaches proposed so far in the literature are still heavily dependent on an IT expert's knowledge to identify the appropriate QoS attributes required to meet particular business process NFRs. However, defining appropriate QoS attributes without reference to business process-level NFRs may be a costly, time-consuming task.

Keywords: Non-functional Requirements · Service Level Agreements · Quality of Services · Web services

J. Filipe et al. (Eds.): ICEIS 2019, LNBIP 378, pp. 473–497, 2020.
https://doi.org/10.1007/978-3-030-40783-4_23

1   Introduction

Software Engineering has fostered approaches that reuse software components to implement business functionalities to reduce cost, time and effort throughout the software life-cycle. A modern and popular approach is Service-Oriented Architecture (SOA): a framework in which business functionalities are built, deployed and integrated as autonomous services [24]. Services provided and accessed over the web are denominated web services, and their widespread use by organizations has made them the most popular implementation of SOA. Through web services, business processes can be implemented and executed by assembling and coordinating business activities among corresponding web services, using a concept denominated web service composition or orchestration [24]. Web services invoke software code that should execute a corresponding business activity.

To ensure the success of executing a business process through a web service orchestration, functional requirements and Non-functional Requirements (NFRs) of the web services should be considered. Web service NFRs are often defined as Quality of Service (QoS) attributes, which are formalized in Service Level Agreements (SLA) established between web service providers and consumers. QoS attributes defined in SLAs are propagated from specific business goals [24], for instance: a business goal related to agility may require QoS attributes such as adaptability, scalability and extensibility. Therefore, different web services require different QoS attributes, and what attributes are required depends on the business domain, intended use and user requirements [2].

Seeking strategic alignment, the definition of QoS attributes in SLAs should rely on business process NFRs. Business process NFRs can be formalized in Business Level Agreements (BLA), which are should be defined by business or requirements analysts and capture business process-level NFRs useful later for web service provisioning [7,27,28]. However, a decomposition of BLAs into SLAs would depend on an IT expert's knowledge to identify the appropriate QoS attributes required for a web service, based on implicit business process NFRs.

As an illustrative example, Fig. 1 shows a fragment of a business process model for assessing loan against property applications [11]. Once received the customer application form from the *Loan Officer*, the *Financial Officer* needs to check the customer's credit history to assess the loan risk, while the *Property Appraiser* appraises the property. When both of them complete these activities, the *Loan Officer* is able to assess the customer's eligibility for the requested loan. This set of activities is susceptible to some NFRs. For example, the execution of these activities may include BLAs related to: *(i)* security, since private customer data in other institutions should be accessed; *(ii)* performance efficiency, since a rapid response must be sent to the customer so as not to lose this business opportunity; and *(iii)* compliance, as regulatory rules may need to be met. The web services implementing these activities are also susceptible to related NFRs since the effective execution of the business process depends directly on the effective execution of the web services.

Translating the business process NFRs exemplified above into appropriate NFRs to provide web services to support the execution of such a business process

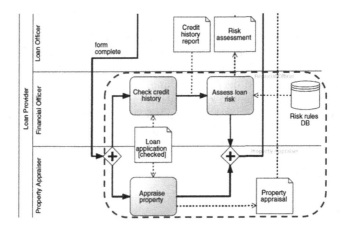

Fig. 1. Fragment of a business process for assessing loan applications [11].

is a challenge. Assuming the business team defines a BLA stating the execution of these three activities together should not exceed 5 min: what QoS properties for which web services should be defined to ensure achieving this business goal? The challenge addressed here is how IT teams can define which SLAs (and for what web services) are needed to meet a BLA defined by business teams.

We present here a conceptual framework to hierarchically decompose NFRs from the business process level to the web service level. This framework relies on the NFR-interdependence among NFRs. Given a business process-level NFR, this framework describes the related NFRs that could be considered at the web service level to meet business goals. This decomposition is not automated, but an approach to help IT teams in breaking down preferences of business process NFRs into more detailed preferences related to web service QoS attributes. Our motivation is the importance of an appropriate web service execution to meet business goals, which requires pertinent QoS attributes based on business needs.

To achieve this goal, we first developed a dictionary of NFRs, including both business process and web service levels. Then, we defined the interdependence among the NFRs at both levels via UML (Unified Modeling Language) class diagrams. The interdependence framework considers the relationships among business process-level NFRs, and between the business process and web service levels in a top-down strategy. The ISO/IEC 25010 Product Quality Model is the main reference, enriched by extra quality models on software and QoS attributes.

A preliminary version of this paper has already been published in [8], which is extended here with the full version of the web services' non-functional requirements dictionary. The main contributions of this work are several:

- Extensive gathering of NFRs related to business processes and technical aspects of web service provisioning, and the definition of their interdependence relationships to support those who want to systematize their decomposition.

- Conceiving a conceptual framework that, while designed primarily for the context of business process automation through web service orchestration, is generic enough to be used or adapted to other areas considering NFRs.
- Presenting an approach that, while not automatic, can be further used to support semi-automated decision making.
- Delivering an unprecedented compilation of NFR for both levels - business process and web services, with a hierarchical view among them, which can be used as a reference by researchers and industry practitioners.

The rest of this paper presents the following sections: underlying concepts, research method, obtained results, related work and concluding remarks.

2   Underlying Concepts

2.1   Business Process Automation

A business process comprises a set of activities executed in a specific order to achieve a common organizational goal [32]. Business Process Management (BPM) refers to overseeing how work is performed in an organization, to ensure consistent outcomes and take advantage of improvement opportunities [11]. The BPM life-cycle involves the identification, analysis, redesign, implementation and monitoring of business processes.

Considering the expected strategic alignment between business and Information Technology (IT) as background, activities of business processes can be outsourced by services provided by business partners, using the SOA-style architecture. A service implements a well-defined piece of business functionality, with a published and discoverable interface [24]. Through SOA, requesters can reuse services to implement business functionalities, and the only part they need to know is the service description, i.e., they can abstract the details of the underlying logic and implementation [24].

The popularity of SOA increased as services become available on the web, giving rise to web services. A web service can be as simple as performing a credit card number check or as complex as dealing with a mortgage application [19].

Using web services to implement business functionalities allows automating the execution of business processes by orchestrating web services, i.e., orchestrating heterogeneous web services to achieve a common business goal [2,12]. A web service orchestration strategy requires the pre-modeling of a business process in terms of both functional requirements and NFRs. This modeling is relevant, considering that the behavior of an individual activity performed through a web service can influence the entire business process and hence the achievement or not of an organizational business or strategic goal.

2.2   Non-functional Requirements

In software engineering, Non-functional Requirements (NFRs) are defined as constraints on services or functionalities offered by a system, including characteristics related to software behavior and constraints imposed by standards [30].

These NFRs are defined based on user needs, budget constraints or external factors, such as regulatory and legislative determinations [30]. Examples are performance, security and availability.

In BPM and SOA, NFRs represent quality aspects expected in the provisioning of services responsible for executing business processes. These quality aspects define guarantee levels which allow comparison among distinct services offering the same functionality [3]. Web service NFRs are often expressed as QoS attributes and their specification is usually made through SLAs.

SLAs refers to a commitment between web service providers and consumers, whereby the exact quality conditions that guide the web service provisioning are systematically defined [27][1]. An SLA could include, for instance, a QoS attribute for availability with a target of 99% and a QoS attribute for response time with a target of 5 ms. In SLAs, penalties and rewards are defined and imposed depending on the breach of pre-defined guarantee terms.

SLA terms are defined by IT considering technical aspects of web service provisioning [7]. However, business aspects should be also considered, mainly in the context of business process automation via web service orchestration [5]. A different type of agreement is then required, what can be done through BLAs.

The structure of a BLA is like of an SLA, including penalties and rewards. The main difference lies in their scopes: while SLAs are associated with web services and consider mainly technical aspects involved in web service provisioning, BLAs are associated with business process activities that will be executed in the form of web services [5,27]. BLAs are defined during business process analysis and modeling whereas SLAs are determined during business process implementation and execution [27].

The differences between BLA and SLA are illustrated by Salles et al. [28] who exemplify a BLA goal with *"the business subprocess starting in the activity [1] and ending in the activity [4] must be concluded within 24 h"* whereas the corresponding SLAs goals are exemplified with *"the web service invoked to execute the activity [1] must be completed within 2 h"* and *"the web service invoked to execute the activity [4] must have 95% of availability"*.

A BLA can be mapped to a set of SLAs, each BLA related to a specific business process activity automated through a set of web services with their SLAs [13]. Assuming that all the guaranteed terms of each SLA are satisfied, the corresponding BLA is expected to be satisfied accordingly.

2.3   Software Quality Models

According to the IEEE Standard Glossary of Software Engineering Terminology [15], software quality means the degree to which a system, component or business process meets specific requirements. Specifying functional requirements

---

[1] In this work, only technical aspects involved in a web service provisioning are considered in SLAs; i.e., IT outsourcing or out-tasking web services for higher-level tasks, including human tasks, are not part of the scope.

and NFRs for software is not a trivial task; a common approach is to use software quality models as a reference to describe and assess software requirements.

Quality models support the identification of relevant quality characteristics to be used as requirements and their corresponding satisfaction criteria and measures [17]. Quality models provide the foundation for software evaluation, providing consistent QoS terminology and supporting software measurement [6].

There are several software quality models proposed in the literature from international standards to several domain and company-specific models. One of the most popular approaches is the ISO/IEC 25010 System and Software Quality Model, which is a part of the ISO/IEC 25000 Software Product Quality Requirements and Evaluation (SQuaRe) model and results from evolving several other standards, especially the ISO/IEC 9126 [17]. ISO/IEC 25010 addresses a set of QoS attributes for software product quality and software quality in use.

Figure 2 shows the structure of ISO/IEC 25010 Product Quality Model, depicting its eight main quality characteristics and 31 related sub-characteristics. Alternative software quality models were proposed [4, 10, 21]. Detailed information about quality models can be found in [22, 29, 31].

Fig. 2. ISO/IEC 25010 Product Quality Model [17].

Regarding BPM and SOA, quality models can be used as a reference to define requirements related to business processes and web services, allowing for the overall quality improvement of SOA-based applications. To the best of our knowledge, there is no general standard accepted as a quality model for web services being orchestrated to automate business processes. However, web services and software modules share the same set of properties; therefore, if software components can be replaced by web services, then the quality requirements of both solutions must be compatible with [1]. As a result, software quality models can also be used to address quality characteristics of web services.

As the ISO/IEC 25010 quality model is a recognized quality standard for any type of software, it can be used to provide QoS attributes for web services [1]. Other quality models used in the context of web services were proposed [2, 23].

3   Research Method

This work was developed following principles of the *design science* research paradigm, which considers the creation and evaluation of artifacts to solve identified organizational problems [14]. These artifacts need to address an unsolved problem or propose an improvement for an existing solution to more significantly contribute with science and practice [14]. In this research, the problem refers to the lack of a systematic structure to support a straightforward decomposition of NFRs, from business to QoS attributes related to web services. However, contrasting the paradigm, this research did not include a validation work to ascertain the results, thus resulting in a theoretical research based on literature analysis. In this context, developing an conceptual interdependence framework for NFRs included two major activities: *(i)* the elaboration of a dictionary of NFRs, considering NFRs for both business process and web service levels; and *(ii)* the definition of interdependence relationships between identified NFRs, taking relationships between NFRs at the same level (for the business process level) and relationships between NFRs at different levels (from the business process level to the lower levels).

Regarding the dictionary of NFRs, an exploratory literature study was conducted to elicit a set of quality characteristics related to business or technical aspects of web service provisioning. The structure of characteristics and sub-characteristics of the ISO/IEC 25010 Product Quality Model was the main reference due to its wide use and acceptance by business and IT practitioners [1]. This base structure was expanded through extra research on software and web services quality models and studies related to SOA and QoS attributes.

The definition of the interdependence relationships among the dictionary's NFRs was based on the studies of McCall, Richards and Walters [21] and Zulzalil et al. [35] which were used as the main references to describe the relationships between the business process-level NFRs. Although these studies predate the publication of the ISO/IEC 25010 Product Quality Model, both share the same evaluated characteristics.

With respect to the relationships between NFRs from the business process level to the web service level and also between NFRs at the web service level, the structure of characteristics and sub-characteristics of the ISO/IEC 25010 Product Quality Model was also used as the main reference. For most of the NFRs got from other references during the elaboration of the dictionary, the corresponding studies already incorporated some hierarchical classification that could be the basis to define the decomposition structure.

Remaining relationships were determined via logical inference based on empirical analysis. The authors conducted iterative brainstorming meetings to discuss potential relationships between the NFRs mapped in the dictionary. The ideas that came up during these meetings were refined resulting on a final set of relationships, which are presented as follows.

4   NFR Decomposition

Considering business processes being automated through web service orchestration, a conceptual NFR decomposition framework is proposed to support a straightforward definition of web service QoS attributes. The definition of QoS attributes is carried out based on constraints determined by business areas at process modeling time. Using this approach, IT teams are given hints of which QoS attributes they can assign to a web service to meet a business demand. Thus, the expected users for this framework are IT teams working on the perspective of a web service provider and hence involved in the definition of web service SLAs to be executed by business units.

The designed NFR decomposition framework is presented below. An explanation of the framework is first given, with details on the dictionary of NFRs and the interdependence diagram, followed by the decomposition diagrams.

4.1   Conceptual Framework Overview

The set of NFRs is organized into a dictionary structure. The dictionary of NFRs is formed by two sections: one for business process NFRs (cf. Table 1) and another for web service NFRs (cf. Tables 2, 3, 4, 5, 6, 7, 8, 9). The structure of both sections comprises four attributes: **ID**, a numerical NFR identification; **Name**, the NFR name; **Definition**, a brief description of the NFR; and **Reference**, the references of the works from which the NFR was extracted from. Synonyms are identified and grouped using a unique ID. Specifically for web service NFRs, there is an extra attribute, **Measurement Unit**, which identifies the primary unit used to measure a quantitative NFR. The measurement unit was filled in the dictionary only when found in the literature.

Table 1. Dictionary of business process NFRs [8].

ID	Name	Definition	Ref.
1	Performance efficiency	Degree to which a business process can efficiently use an amount of resources (such as software, products, hardware and generic materials) under stated conditions	[17]
2	Compatibility	Degree to which a business process can exchange information with other business processes, and/or perform its activities while sharing the computing environment	[17]
3	Usability	Degree to which a business process can be used by specified users to achieve specific goals with effectiveness, efficiency and satisfaction	[17]
4	Reliability	Degree to which a business process performs specified activities under specified conditions for a period	[17]
5	Security	Degree to which a business process can protect information and data from unauthorized access	[17]
6	Maintainability	Degree of effectiveness and efficiency with which the activities of a business process can be modified	[17]
7	Portability	Degree of effectiveness and efficiency with which a business process can be configured in an environment and transferred from one environment to another	[17]
8	Compliance	Degree to which a business process is compliant with internal procedures of an organization and external guidelines	[30]

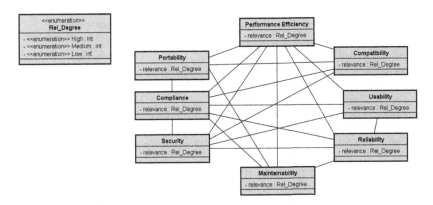

Fig. 3. Interdependence relationships for business process NFRs [8].

Considering the relationships between the NFRs, they are represented through UML class diagrams (cf. Figures 3, 4, 5, 6, 7, 8, 9, 10, 11). Each class in the diagram represents an NFR included in the dictionary. Relationships between NFRs at the same level are represented using the *association* bidirectional connector (e.g., Fig. 6, association between *Confidentiality* and *Access Control*). Relationships between NFRs of different levels are defined through *aggregation* connectors, i.e., lower-level NFRs contribute to those at a higher level, although they exist independently (e.g., Fig. 6, aggregation between *Confidentiality* and *Encryption*).

Each class in the diagram includes a configurable attribute denominated **relevance**, which considers three values: high, medium or low. Business and IT areas should use this attribute to show which NFRs are how likely relevant when creating SLAs in an organization, based on the business domain and previous experiences. As the proposed decomposition framework has been developed to be generic enough to be considered in different organizational contexts, no prior definition of relevance for each NFR is provided. As a result, each organization willing to use this framework should define its own relevance values considering its own context and historical data.

Table 2. Web services' dictionary of NFRs – performance efficiency.

ID	Name	Definition	Meas. Unit	Ref.
1	Capacity	Maximum limits of a service (i.e., concurrent users, stored data etc.) for which performance is guaranteed		[17]
2	Execution time	Time for a service to execute a sequence of activities and process a request	Time	[18]
3	I/O utilization	Measurement of estimated I/O utilization to complete a specified task	Number of buffers	[16]
4	Latency time	Round-Trip Delay (RTD) between the dispatch of a request and receive of a response for a service	Time	[3]
5	Memory utilization	Measurement of the estimated memory size a service will occupy to complete a specified task	Bytes	[16]
6	Resource utilization	Degree to which the amount and type of resources used meet requirements in service provisioning		[17]
7	Response time	Time necessary to complete a certain service request, from the moment it is dispatched until a response is received	Time	[18]
	[Average and maximum response time]	Mean time needed for the packet of control data to get to the provider's server and return to the requester	Time	[3]
	[Execution duration]	Expected delay from the dispatch of a service request until the result is received by the client	Time	[34]
8	Scalability	Degree to which a service operates correctly, without degradation of other quality attributes, when the system is changed in size or in volume in order to meet users' needs		[24]
9	Throughput	Measurement of the number of service requests served in a given time interval	Processed rqts/time	[18]
	[Maximum Throughput]	Maximum number of services that a platform providing services can process for a unit time		[23]
10	Time behavior	Degree to which the response and processing times and throughput rate meet requirements in service provisioning		[17]
11	Timeliness	Degree to which a service meets deadlines, i.e., to process a request in a deterministic and acceptable amount of time		[24]
12	Transaction time	Time that passes while the service is completing one complete transaction. This concept may depend on the definition of a service transaction	Time	[18]
13	Transmission utilization	Estimated amount of transmission resources utilized by a service	Bits/time	[16]

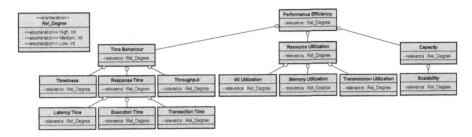

Fig. 4. NFR decomposition diagram – performance efficiency [8].

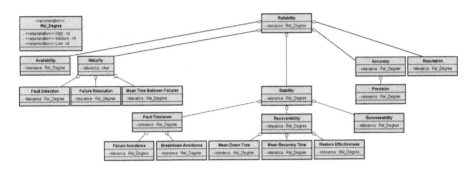

Fig. 5. NFR decomposition diagram – reliability [8].

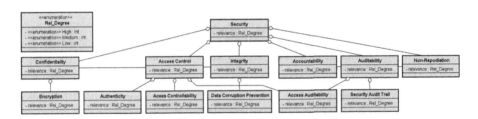

Fig. 6. NFR decomposition diagram – security [8].

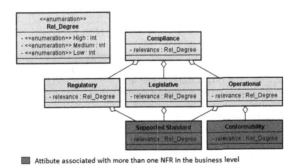

Fig. 7. NFR decomposition diagram – compliance [8].

Table 3. Web services' dictionary of NFRs – reliability.

ID	Name	Definition	Meas. Unit	Ref.
1	Accuracy	Degree of precision to which a service provides right outcomes or effects		[29]
2	Availability	Proportion of total time during which a service is operational and accessible when required for use	Percentage	[17]
3	Breakdown avoidance	Proportion of breakdowns in production environment in comparison to the total number of failures	Percentage	[16]
4	Failure avoidance	Proportion of fault patterns identified by the service to avoid critical and serious failures, considering the number of executed test cases of fault patterns during testing	Percentage	[16]
5	Failure resolution	Proportion of resolved fault conditions that do not recur in relation to the number of failures detected	Percentage	[16]
6	Fault detection	Measurement of failures detected by a service in a certain period of time	Detected failures	[16]
7	Fault tolerance	Degree to which a service operates as intended despite the presence of hardware or software faults		[17]
	[Error tolerance]	Degree to which a service provides continuity of operation under abnormal conditions		[21]
8	Maturity	Degree to which a service meets needs for reliability under normal operation		[17]
9	Mean down time	Mean time a service stays unavailable when a failure occurs before it gradually starts up	Time	[16]
10	Mean recovery time	Mean time a service takes to complete recovery from initial partial recovery	Time	[16]
11	Mean time between failures	Mean time between failures of a service in operation	Time	[16]
12	Precision	Measurement of the frequency to which users encounter results with inadequate precision	Inaccurate results/ Time	[16]
13	Recoverability	Degree to which, in the event of an outage or failure, a service can recover directly affected data and restore the desired operational state		[17]
14	Reputation	Measurement of a service's trustworthiness in terms of service quality, user's satisfaction and reliability on its operation		[20]
15	Restore effectiveness	Proportion of successful restorations meeting the target restore time in comparison to the number of restorations required	Percentage	[16]
16	Stability	Degree to which a service can deliver continuous, consistent and recoverable services despite increased throughput, congestion, system failures, natural disasters and intentional attacks		[23]
17	Sucessability	Degree to which services yield successful results over request messages	Percentage	[23]

Table 4. Web services' dictionary of NFRs – security

ID	Name	Definition	Meas. Unit	Ref.
1	Access auditability	Proportion of user accesses to a service recorded in the access history database	Percentage	[16]
2	Access control	Degree to which a service restricts unauthorized user's access by using services security token or similar approach		[23]
3	Access controllability	Proportion of illegal operations detected by the service, in comparison to the number of illegal operations defined in the specification	Percentage	[16]
4	Accountability	Degree to which the actions of a user can be traced uniquely to the user		[17]
5	Auditability	Degree to which a service keeps sufficiently adequate records in the database to support financial or legal audits		[24]
6	Authenticity	Degree to which the identity of a subject or resource can be proved		[17]
7	Confidentiality	Degree to which a service ensures that its data is accessible only by authorized users		[17]
	[Data confidentiality]	Degree to which a service protects data against unauthorized disclosure		[23]
	[Privacy]	Degree to which access to sensitive data by unauthorized people can be controlled		[21]
8	Data corruption prevention	Measurement of data corruption events identified and prevented by the service	Corruption events	[16]
9	Encryption	Degree to which a service's data is encrypted, making it unreadable without special knowledge		[25]
10	Integrity	Degree to which a service prevents unauthorized access to, or modification of, functions and data		[17]
	[Data integrity]	Degree to which a service ensures that data has not been altered or destroyed in an unauthorized manner		[23]
11	Non-repudiation	Degree to which action or events in a service can be proven to have taken place, so that they cannot be repudiated later		[17]
12	Security audit trail	Degree to which a service records a log of attempted attacks in order to evaluate its vulnerability		[23]

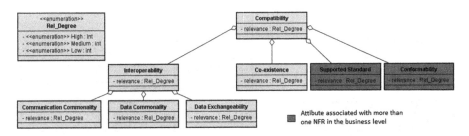

Fig. 8. NFR decomposition diagram – compatibility [8].

Table 5. Web services' dictionary of NFRs – compliance.

ID	Name	Definition	Meas. Unit	Ref.
1	Conformability	Degree to which a service uses the standard technology for services (i.e. SOAP, WSDL e UDDI)		[24]
2	Legislative	Legislative requirements that must be followed to ensure that the service operates within the law		[30]
3	Operational	Operational process requirements that define how a service should be used		[30]
4	Regulatory	Regulatory requirements that set out what must be done for the service to be approved for use by a regulator		[30]
5	Supported standard	Degree to which a service operation complies with standards (e.g. industry specific standards)		[26]

Table 6. Web services' dictionary of NFRs – compatibility.

ID	Name	Definition	Meas. Unit	Ref.
1	Co-existence	Degree to which a service can perform its required functions while sharing environment and resources with other products		[17]
2	Communication commonality	Degree to which a service uses standard protocols and interface routines for communication		[21]
3	Conformability	[as defined for *compliance*]		
4	Data commonality	Degree to which a service uses standard data representations		[21]
5	Data exchangeability	Proportion of successful data transfers between the target service and other services	Percentage	[16]
6	Interoperability	Degree to which two or more components or services can exchange information and use the information that has been exchanged		[17]
	[Integrability]	Degree to which two or more components and services of a system are integrated		[25]
7	Supported standard	[as defined for *compliance*]		

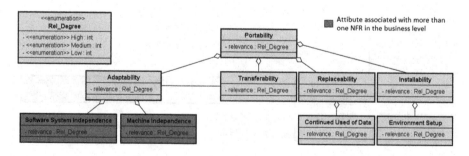

Fig. 9. NFR decomposition diagram – portability [8].

Table 7. Web services' dictionary of NFRs – portability

ID	Name	Definition	Meas. Unit	Ref.
1	Adaptability	Degree to which a service can effectively and efficiently be adapted for different hardware, software or other operational environments		[17]
2	Continued use of data	Proportion of data that can be used in the same way after service migration or replacement, in comparison to the number of total data items required to be used from old services	Percentage	[16]
3	Environment setup	Ease with which a service can be configured to be used in a certain environment		–
4	Installability	Degree of effectiveness and efficiency with which a component of a service can be successfully installed and/or uninstalled in a specified environment		[17]
5	Machine independence	Degree of service dependency on the hardware system		[21]
6	Replaceability	Degree to which a service can replace another for the same purpose in the same environment		[17]
7	Software system independence	Degree of service dependency on the software environment, including operating systems, utilities, input/output routines, etc		[21]
8	Transferability	Ease of moving a computer program from one computing environment to another		[21]

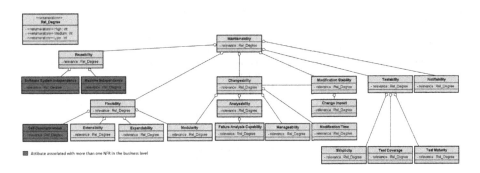

Fig. 10. NFR decomposition diagram – maintainability [8].

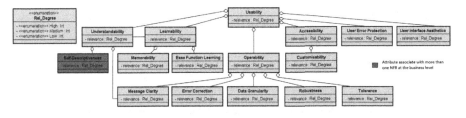

Fig. 11. NFR decomposition diagram – usability [8].

Table 8. Web services' dictionary of NFRs – maintainability.

ID	Name	Definition	Meas. Unit	Ref.
1	Analyzability	Degree of effectiveness and efficiency with which a change in parts of a service is evaluated		[17]
2	Change impact	Proportion of detected adverse impacts after the modification of a service, in comparison to the number of modifications performed	Percentage	[16]
3	Expandability	Degree to which a service can be expanded relative to data or function requirements		[21]
4	Extensibility	Ease with which service features can be extended without affecting other services/systems		[24]
	[Extendibility]	Degree to which a service can be expanded to new specification changes or other domains		[29]
5	Failure analysis capability	Proportion of times a user can identify which operations caused a service to fail considering the total number of failures detected	Percentage	[16]
6	Flexibility	Effort needed to change an operational service		[29]
7	Machine independence	[as defined for *portability*]		
8	Manageability	Degree to which a service lends itself to efficient administration of its components		[21]
9	Changeability	The ease with which a service can be modified		[17, 22]
	[Modifiability]	Degree to which a service can be effectively and efficiently modified without introducing new defects or degrading the product quality		[17]
10	Modification stability	Degree to which a service can avoid unexpected effects from modification of the software		[17, 22]
11	Modification time	Time required to modify a part of a service, from identifying the new requirement or modification to its implementation and validation	Time	[21]
12	Modularity	Degree to which a service is composed of discrete components such that a change to one component has minimal impact on other components		[17]
13	Notifiability	Degree to which service providers notify changes on a service's functions and resources to an external quality manager or any other stakeholder		[23]
14	Reusability	Degree to which an asset can be used in more than one service or to develop other services		[17]
15	Self-Descriptiveness	Ease with which a service's functions and documentation can be understood by humans		[21]
16	Simplicity	Degree to which the functions of a service are implemented in the most understandable manner, avoiding practices that increase complexity		[21]
17	Software system independence	[as defined for *portability*]		
18	Test coverage	Degree to which a service is effectively tested in terms of source code statements executed	Percentage	[30]
19	Test maturity	Proportion of test cases that have been successfully performed during testing in comparison to the total number of test cases	Percentage	[16]
20	Testability	Degree of effectiveness and efficiency with which test criteria can be established for a service and tests can be performed to determine whether those criteria have been met		[17]

Table 9. Web services' dictionary of NFRs – usability.

ID	Name	Definition	Meas. Unit	Ref.
1	Accessibility	Degree to which a service can be used by people with distinctive characteristics and capabilities to achieve a specified goal in a context of use		[17]
2	Customizability	Proportion of operations and procedures of a service that can be customized by the user	Percentage	[16]
3	Data granularity	Granularity of data a service provides in response to user requests		[24]
4	Ease of function learning	Mean time a user takes to learn to use a service function correctly	Time	[16]
5	Error correction	Mean time a user takes to correct an error on a task while using the service	Time	[16]
6	Learnability	Degree to which a service can be used by specific users to achieve specific learning goals with effectiveness, efficiency and satisfaction		[17]
7	Memorability	Degree to which users remember the operations of a service over time	Time	[25]
8	Message clarity	Proportion of messages with clear explanations provided by a service, from the total number of messages implemented	Percentage	[16]
	[Communicativeness]	Degree to which a service provides useful inputs and outputs which can be assimilated by users		[21]
9	Operability	Degree to which a service has attributes that make it easy to operate and control, in conformance with user expectations		[17]
	Ease of use	Degree to which a service is easy for users to operate and control		[16]
10	Robustness	Degree that represents the ability of the service to act properly even if some of the input parameters are missing or incorrect		[3]
	[Exception handling]	Degree that represents how well a service handles exceptions on data inputs		[26]
11	Self-Descriptiveness	[as defined for *maintainability*]		
12	Tolerance	Degree to which a service accepts different forms of the same data as valid or supports some input variation without malfunction or rejection		[21]
13	Understandability	Degree to which a user understands the logical concept of a service and its applicability		[25]
	[Appropriateness Recognizability]	Degree to which users can recognize whether a service is appropriate for their needs		[17]
14	User error protection	Degree to which a system protects users against making errors		[17]
15	User interface aesthetics	Degree to which a user interface enables satisfying interaction for the user, such as the use of color and the nature of the graphical design		[17]

4.2 Decomposition Diagrams

The NFR decomposition framework considers attributes at business process and web service levels, defined by business and IT areas, respectively. For business process NFRs, the first section of the dictionary has eight attributes (cf. Table 1).

To identify the business process-level NFRs, the characteristics proposed in the ISO/IEC 25010 Product Quality Model [17] were considered as describing generic aspects of product quality to be selected by business areas [9]. From eight characteristics in the ISO/IEC 25010 model (cf. Fig. 2), seven were adapted to be added in the dictionary as business process NFRs: *Performance Efficiency, Compatibility, Usability, Reliability, Security, Maintainability* and *Portability*. Only *Functional Suitability* was not considered as it addresses functional requirements and not NFRs which is the purpose of this dictionary.

ISO/IEC 25010 and other related software quality models describe quality characteristics only from the product perspective. Aiming at completeness for the business context, the dictionary of business process NFRs was extended with an attribute addressing regulatory, legislative and operational aspects involved in business process enactment. This NFR is *Compliance*, adapted from the types of NFRs for software systems presented by Sommerville [30].

The attributes in Table 1 relate to each other. For instance, the conversion from standard protocols to ensure compatibility may affect performance efficiency [21], while a fast maintenance implies in higher recoverability in the presence of errors, improving reliability levels. Identifying interdependence relationships between business process NFRs is relevant to recommend a more complete set of web service NFRs to be defined in SLAs. For example, when business areas define a constraint related to compatibility, the IT team could take care of performance NFRs as well. Figure 3 shows the interdependence relationships between the business process NFRs that were identified in this work.

Some relationships shown in Fig. 3, such as *performance efficiency* vs. *compatibility* and *reliability* vs. *maintainability*, were defined based on studies found in the literature [21,35]. Others, such as *reliability* vs. *security* and *compliance* vs. *security*, were defined via logical inference based on an empirical analysis by the authors of this work. Table 10 presents a brief explanation of the meaning of the interdependence relationships shown in Fig. 3.

Regarding the web service NFRs, the characteristics and sub-characteristics proposed in the ISO/IEC 25010 Product Quality Model [17] were considered describing technical aspects of web service provisioning to be defined in SLAs by IT teams. This model was refined by extra works on software quality models and QoS attributes and, as a result, the dictionary of web service NFRs is formed by 93 requirements, each of them related to at least one business process NFR. The dictionary of web service NFRs, with requirements definition, references, measurement unit and additional details regarding its elaboration.

The NFR decomposition framework is split into eight decomposition diagrams offering a better visualization of the relationships between the attributes. Figures 4, 5, 6, 7, 8, 9, 10, 11) show one diagram for each business process NFR (cf. Fig. 3).

Table 10. Details of interdependence relationships between business process NFRs.

NFR1	NFR2	Relationship explanation	Ref.
Perf. Effic.	Compatib.	The conversion from standard protocols to ensure compatibility between web services may affect performance efficiency	[21]
Perf. Effic.	Usability	The additional code and processing required to ease an operator's task or provide more usable output may affect performance efficiency	[21]
Perf. Effic.	Maintain	The need of using modularity, instrumentation and well commented high-level code to increase maintainability may affect performance efficiency	[21]
Perf. Effic.	Security	The additional code and processing required to control the access of a web service or data may affect performance efficiency	[21]
Perf. Effic.	Portability	Using direct code or optimized system software to increase performance may affect web service portability	[21]
Perf. Effic.	Reliability	The implementation of strategies to increase web service's availability may affect performance efficiency	—
Compatib.	Security	Coupled systems or web services can be accessed by different users, increasing the potential for accidental access of sensitive data and thus affecting security requirements	[21]
Compatib.	Portability	The guarantee of the web service's compatibility may affect portability requirements in terms of platform independence	–
Usability	Reliability + Security	The implementation of error prevention functions in a web service's interface may affect its maturity and stability in terms of fault detection and fault tolerance	[35]
Reliability	Maintain	Increasing maintainability usually affects a web service's reliability, as it turns easier for a web service to be maintained in case of breakdown	[35]
Reliability	Security	The security of a web service may affect its reliability in terms of stability and reputation	—
Maintain	Portability	Increasing maintainability can affect the effort to move a web service from one operating environment to another	[35]
Compliance	*	Regulatory, legislative or operational guidelines can be applied to all seven remaining NFRs included in the framework	–

For example, the NFRs shown in Table 2 are related to *performance efficiency*, with which 13 NFRs describing web service's time behavior, resource utilization and capacity are associated. Contrasting the dictionary of business process NFRs (cf. Table 1), the measurement unit is defined here for some web service NFRs. Synonyms from different references are grouped in a unique ID as for *Response time, Average and maximum response time* and *Execution duration.*

Figure 4 shows the decomposition diagram for *performance efficiency*. The NFRs and most of the relationships between them were extracted from works from the literature [3, 16–18, 23, 24]. For instance, the relationships between the attributes related to *resource utilization*. Other relationships were mapped from related studies or defined via logical inference. The attributes *latency time, execution time* and *transaction time*, for instance, are associated with *response time* considering the definition of the latter: "response time is defined as the time required to complete a web service request" [18]. Thus, response time should include the round-trip delay for the network propagation (i.e., the latency time) plus the execution time required to process the request in the provider (i.e., the execution time). In addition, if transactions are processed, it should also consider the time to complete the transaction (i.e., the transaction time).

Figures 5 and 6 show the decomposition diagrams for *reliability* and *security*, respectively. As for reliability, 17 web service NFRs are presented, which are mainly related to web service availability and stability in the presence of failures. The NFRs and most of the relationships were extracted from [16, 17, 21, 23, 29, 34]. For instance, the attributes *fault detection, failure resolution* and *mean time between failures* as associated with *maturity*. Other relationships were defined via logical inference, such as associating *fault tolerance, recoverability* and *successability* in meeting requests as attributes related to web service *stability*.

Regarding security, 12 web service NFRs are presented, which are mainly related to data confidentiality and integrity, access control and traceability. The NFRs and some relationships were extracted from works from the literature [16, 17, 21, 23–25]. Other relationships, such as the bidirectional association between *confidentiality* and *access control*, were defined via logical inference. For the latter, we considered that confidentiality requires that data should be read only by those with access to it, implying in access control. The association between *access control* and *integrity*, on the other hand, was proposed in the literature with a similar argument [21].

Figures 7 and 8 show the decomposition diagrams for *compliance* and *compatibility*, respectively. Regarding *compliance*, the NFRs were extracted from works from the literature [23, 26, 30, 33] and all the relationships were defined via logical inference. On the other hand, the NFRs and most of the relationships for *compatibility* were extracted from works from the literature [16, 17, 21], as the attributes associated with *interoperability*. The attributes *supported standard* and *conformability* were identified by the authors as being related to both *compliance* and *compatibility* and hence are shown in both diagrams in orange color. The definition of this dual association considered a scenario where technical standards must be addressed in web service provisioning, as a demand of regulators, organizations or the government itself. When these standards are related to the communication between systems, this attribute may also be defined in terms of compatibility. Conformability is the degree to which the pre-defined standards are met and hence considered in both cases.

Figures 9, 10 and 11 show the decomposition diagrams for *portability, maintainability* and *usability*, respectively. The NFRs and relationships in these diagrams were mainly extracted from the literature [3,16,17,21–25,29]. The attributes *software system independence* and *machine independence* are related to both *maintainability* and *portability*, and shown in both diagrams in orange color. This dual classification considered that, the more a system is independent of the computational environment, the easier it is to adapt its operation to different environments and reuse its components in different contexts. Likewise, the attribute *self-descriptiveness* is classified as related to both *maintainability* and *usability*, considering that the clearer a web service and its documentation is, the easier it is to maintain and operate it.

4.3 Examples of NFR Decomposition

Using the illustrative example of business process presented in Fig. 1, some NFRs can be defined to the web services that will implement such a process.

Consider the BLA related to *performance efficiency* associated with the set of highlighted activities. Some levels for web service QoS attributes should be pursued in order to ensure that this BLA is met, and the decomposition framework proposed herein can be used for this purpose. Considering that for each activity one or more web services can be used, different QoS attributes can be defined for each web service, depending on the needs identified by the analysts involved. Per Fig. 4, to meet the BLA *performance efficiency* for these three activities, 13 distinct QoS attributes may be associated with the web services that will be used to implement them. For example, for some web services, QoS attributes related to *response time* or *throughput* may be defined, associated with some target values; i.e., the QoS levels. IT teams may also understand that, for some web services, they should use a more specific QoS attribute related to *latency time, execution time* or *transaction time*.

Besides the direct relationships addressed in the previous example, indirect QoS attributes can also be defined as they can also interfere in the performance efficiency of these three activities. For example, according to Fig. 3, *performance efficiency* is related to *reliability*. Thus, web services that implement one or more of the three activities in Fig. 1 may also have QoS attributes associated with *reliability*, as they may also affect the performance efficiency of the business process, as explained in Table 10. An example would be to define a QoS attribute related to *availability* (cf. Fig. 5) because the business process will be delayed if the web service is not available.

Still taking the example in Fig. 1, another BLA associated with the three activities being addressed is related to *security*. Using Fig. 6 as the main reference for the decomposition of security-related NFRs, 12 QoS attributes are suggested as ideas for the IT team to add in the corresponding SLAs. From these 12 QoS attributes, eight are leaf nodes, i.e., the most specific attributes, whereas four are intermediate nodes, i.e., more generic ones. Any attribute level can be used, depending on the needs perceived by the IT team. The business team should provide detailed information related to the security BLA, explaining exactly what the requirement means, so IT teams can choose the most appropriate QoS attributes to be associated with the web services, such as *access control, encryption, auditability* and so on. The information from the business area is also relevant to allow identifying which web services will need QoS attributes or not. Other QoS attributes can be chosen by referring to Figs. 4, 5, 7, 8 and 11 as the attributes related to *performance efficiency, reliability, compliance, compatibility* and *usability* are indirectly related to *security* (cf. Fig. 3).

5   Related Work

Several studies have addressed business process automation with SOA. However, only a few of them discusses the relationship between business process NFRs and web service QoS attributes. Still in 2005, the particularities involved in using quality requirements originally defined as software quality models were discussed for SOA [24]. SOA and underlying concepts were explained in detail, examining their impact on meeting business goals in organizations. A structured list of QoS attributes used in SOA was provided.

In 2008, the ISO/IEC 9126 quality characteristics (ISO/ IEC 25000 predecessor) were investigated to develop web-based applications [35]. Eliciting information from stakeholders with an online survey, interactions between pairs of quality characteristics were identified, considering three possible relationships: positive, negative and independent. This approach enabled to understand how software quality aspects influence each other, contributing to elaborate a quality model that combines individual QoS attributes based on specific relationships.

In 2009, a related approach was proposed to address quality requirements expressed at the level of SOA applications and break them down to the level of components used to create the applications, i.e., at the web service level [1]. The structure used for decomposition considers two ontologies: *(i)* SQuaRE-based SOA Quality Ontology, with 14 high-level quality characteristics extracted from ISO/IEC 25000 SQuaRE quality model and is used by business users; and *(ii)* Semantic Web Service QoS Ontology, with a set of qualitative and quantitative QoS attributes related to web services. This approach supports a more direct decomposition of high-level QoS attributes into detailed preferences, in a task less dependent on an IT expert's knowledge.

Discussions for the business process level were introduced by showing the need for defining functional requirements and NFRs of web service provisioning in a different type of agreement, which is the aforementioned BLA [7].

The Strategic Alignment with BPM (StrAli-BPM) framework was proposed in 2013 to foster the strategic alignment between business and IT, in organizations executing business processes via web service orchestration [27,28]. StrAli-BPM was extended [5] and is formed by four components, one of which is particularly related to the work being presented herein – the BLA2SLA component. BLA2SLA considers a top-down strategy for a generic decomposition of business process NFRs (represented by BLAs) into web service QoS attributes (represented by SLAs). The definition of BLAs and SLAs is supported by meta-models, each including a set of attributes related to the business process and web service levels, respectively. BLA2SLA enables the use of a standardized structure to define NFRs for web services based on business needs.

Many of the related work focuses on only discussing individual quality aspects of software components and web services, regardless of their relationship to NFRs of the business processes being automated. The BLA2SLA [27,28] component is closer to the aim sought in this work but using a loose relationship between the addressed concepts: business areas define a BLA, but IT teams only receive this BLA as a reference and must use their experience to define the SLAs considered more appropriate to address this BLA.

The decomposition model proposed by Abramowicz et al. [2] considers the relationships between high-level and low-level quality characteristics to semi-automate the derivation of QoS attributes. They assume NFRs defined from scratch by business users in the SOA development. This assumption contrasts with our work, which assumes that specific activities of business processes (to be automated through web services) are associated with business goals. Their proposed structure considers mainly product quality characteristics to be selected by business users, disregarding organizational and external requirements (i.e., regulatory and legislative) that might be demanded by business areas in software applications. For some of those characteristics, no related QoS attribute was mapped to be defined at the web service level. Ultimately, the relationships among high-level quality characteristics themselves were not considered, resulting in each characteristic being examined only individually.

In the approach of Zulzalil et al. [35], only the relationships among high-level quality characteristics themselves were explored, disregarding their relationship with web service QoS attributes. Finally, despite presenting an analysis of QoS attributes in SOA, O'Brien, Bass and Merson [24] did also not consider the relationships with business process NFRs.

6   Concluding Remarks

With this paper, we aimed to present a solution that systematically supports IT teams that need to define web service NFRs based on business process NFRs. Our solution is a conceptual framework that drives a breakdown of business process NFRs (which may or may not be formalized into BLAs) into web service NFRs (which may or may not be formalized into SLAs that group QoS attributes). The conceptual framework comprises one high-level decomposition diagram (for business process NFRs) and eight low-level decomposition diagrams (for web services). In addition, the nine decomposition diagrams are accompanied by an extensive dictionary with about 100 NFR attributes. This framework facilitates the decomposition of BLAs into SLAs and can be used to mitigate the dependence on specialized human knowledge about business-IT integration.

As future work, we would like to delve deeper into validating and adjusting the framework being proposed. This includes the relationships between the identified NFRs and an improved definition of each NFR attribute. First, we would like to extend the tool prototype presented in Salles et al. [27,28] to incorporate the decomposition diagrams proposed in this paper so that the interdependence relationships between NFRs are specifically addressed in the context of the StrAli-BPM approach. In terms of validation, other possible actions that can be taken, individually or jointly, are through case studies and interviews with experts in organizations that may be interested in the proposed approach.

References

1. Abramowicz, W., Haniewicz, K., Hofman, R., Kaczmarek, M., Zyskowski, D.: Decomposition of SQuaRE-based requirements for the needs of SOA applications. In: International Conference on Advances in Communication Technologies and Engineering Science, pp. 81–94 (2009)
2. Abramowicz, W., Hofman, R., Suryn, W., Dominik, Z.: SQuaRE based web services quality model. In: International MultiConference of Engineers and Computer Scientists (2008)
3. Abramowicz, W., Kaczmarek, M., Zyskowski, D.: Duality in web services reliability. In: Advanced International Conference on Telecommunications and International Conference on Internet and Web Applications and Services, pp. 165.1–165.6 (2006)
4. Boehm, B.W., Brown, J.R., Kaspar, H., Lipow, M.: Characteristics of Software Quality. TRW Software Technology, Amsterdam (1978)
5. Borges, E.S., Fantinato, M., Aksu, U., Reijers, H.A., Thom, L.H.: Monitoring of non-functional requirements of business processes basedon quality of service attributes of web services. In: 21st International Conference on Enterprise Information Systems (ICEIS) (2019)
6. Botella, P., Burgués, X., Carvallo, J.P., Franch, X., Pastor, J.A., Quer, C.: Towards a quality model for the selection of ERP systems. In: Cechich, A., Piattini, M., Vallecillo, A. (eds.) Component-Based Software Quality. LNCS, vol. 2693, pp. 225–245. Springer, Heidelberg (2003). https://doi.org/10.1007/978-3-540-45064-1_11
7. Bratanis, K., Dranidis, D., Simons, A.J.H.: Towards run-time monitoring of web services conformance to business-level agreements. In: 5th International Academic and Industrial Conference on Practice and Research Techniques, pp. 203–206 (2010)
8. Castro, C.F., Fantinato, M., Aksu, Ü., Reijers, H.A., Thom, L.H.: Towards a conceptual framework for decomposing non-functional requirements of business process into quality of service attributes. In: 21st International Conference on Enterprise Information Systems, pp. 481–492 (2019)
9. de Castro, C.F., Fantinato, M.: Dictionary of non-functional requirements of business process and web services. Technical report 003/2018, Graduate Program on Information Systems, University of São Paulo (2018)
10. Dromey, R.G.: Software product quality: theory, model, and practices. Technical report, Software Quality Institute, Griffith University, Brisbane, Australia (1999)
11. Dumas, M., Rosa, M.L., Mendling, J., Reijers, H.A.: Fundamentals of Business Process Management. 2 edn. (2013)
12. Garcia, D.Z.G., de Toledo, M.B.F.: Quality of service management for web service compositions. In: 11th International Conference on Computer Science and Engineering, pp. 189–196 (2008)
13. Goel, N., Kumar, N.V.N., Shyamasundar, R.K.: SLA monitor: a system for dynamic monitoring of adaptive web services. In: 9th European Conference on Web Services, pp. 109–116 (2011)
14. Hevner, A.R., March, S.T., Park, J., Ram, S.: Design science in information systems research. MIS Q. 28(1), 75–105 (2004)

15. IEEE: IEEE standard glossary of software engineering terminology, IEEE Std 610.12-1990 (1990)
16. ISO/IEC: ISO/IEC 9126 software product quality, IEEE Std 9126:2002 (2002)
17. ISO/IEC: ISO/IEC 25010 system and software quality models (2010)
18. Lee, K., Jeon, J., Lee, W., Jeong, S.H., Park, S.W.: QoS for web services: requirements and possible approaches. Technical report NOTE-ws-qos-20031125, W3C Korea Office (2003)
19. Leymann, F., Roller, D., Schmidt, M.T.: Web services and business process management. IBM Syst. J. **41**(2), 198–211 (2002)
20. Liu, Y., Ngu, A.H., Zeng, L.Z.: QoS computation and policing in dynamic web service selection. In: 13th International WWW Conference, pp. 66–73 (2004)
21. McCall, J.A., Richards, P.K., Walters, G.F.: Factors in software quality. volume-iii. preliminary handbook on software quality for an acquisiton manager. Technical report RADC-TR-77-369, Defense Technical Information Center (1977)
22. Miguel, J.P., Mauricio, D., Rodriguez, G.D.: A review of software quality models for the evaluation of software products. Int. J. Softw. Eng. Appl. **5**(6), 31–54 (2014)
23. OASIS: Quality model for web services (2005). http://www.oasis-open.org/committees/download.php/15910/WSQM-ver-2.0.doc
24. O'Brien, L., Bass, L., Merson, P.: Quality attributes and service-oriented architectures. Technical report CMU/SEI-2005-TN-014, Software Engineering Institute, Carnegie Mellon University (2005)
25. Pettersson, A.: Service-Oriented Architecture (SOA) Quality Attributes - A Research Model. Master's thesis, Department of Informatics, Lunds University, Sweden (2007)
26. Ran, S.: A model for web services discovery with QoS. ACM SIGecom Exch. **4**(1), 1–10 (2003)
27. Salles, G.M.B., Fantinato, M., de Albuquerque, J.P., Nishijima, M.: A contribution to organizational and operational strategic alignment: incorporating business level agreements into business process modeling. In: IEEE International Conference on Service Computing, pp. 17–24 (2013)
28. Salles, G.M.B., Fantinato, M., Barros, V.A., de Albuquerque, J.P.: Evaluation of the strali-bpm approach: strategic alignment with BPM using agreements in different levels. Int. J. Bus. Inf. Syst. **27**(4), 433–465 (2018)
29. Sheoran, K., Sangwan, O.P.: An insight of software quality models applied in predicting software quality attributes: a comparative analysis. In: 4th International Conference on Reliability, Infocom Technologies and Optimization, pp. 1–5 (2015)
30. Sommerville, I.: Software Engineering, 9th edn. Pearson, Addison-Wesley, London (2010)
31. Tomar, A.B., Thakare, V.M.: A systematic study of software quality models. Int. J. Softw. Eng. Appl. **2**(4), 61–70 (2011)
32. Weske, M.: Business Process Management: Concepts, Languages, Architectures. Springer, Heidelberg (2012). https://doi.org/10.1007/978-3-642-28616-2
33. Yoon, S., Kim, D., Han, S.: WS-QDL containing static, dynamic, and statistical factors of web services quality. In: International Conference on Web Services, pp. 808–809 (2004)
34. Zeng, L., Benatallah, B., Dumas, M., Kalagnanam, J., Sheng, Q.Z.: Quality driven web services composition. In: 12th International Conference on WWW, pp. 411–421 (2003)
35. Zulzalil, H., Ghani, A.A.A., Selamat, M.H., Mahmod, R.: A case study to identify quality attributes relationships for web based applications. Int. J. Comput. Sci. Netw. Secur. **8**(11), 215–220 (2008)

A Graph Pattern Based Approach for Automatic Decomposition of IoT Aware Business Processes

Francisco Martins[1,2] , Dulce Domingos[1(✉)] , and Daniel Vitoriano[1]

[1] LASIGE, Faculdade de Ciências, Universidade de Lisboa, Lisbon, Portugal
[2] University of the Azores, Ponta Delgada, Portugal
fmartins@acm.org, mddomingos@ciencias.ulisboa.pt,
daniel.vitoriano@reitoria.ulisboa.pt

Abstract. The context information that business process can get from the Internet of Things (IoT) can be used as a competitive advantage in terms of optimisation and agility. However, the exchange of messages between central systems and IoT devices come with a price, battery consumption, a scarcely resource of such devices. Despite the literature offers many technical proposals to tackle this problem, we take an approach driven by the process definition perspective. We propose to reduce the number of exchanged messages by decentralising process execution, moving parts of the business processes to IoT devices, and taking advantage of their computational capabilities. The first step for decentralisation is decomposition, i.e., the division of processes into parts and identify those that IoT devices can execute.

In this paper, we present an automatic decomposition solution for IoT aware business processes, described using the Business Process Model and Notation (BPMN). We start from a BPMN definition that follows a centralised approach and apply our decomposition method to transfer to the IoT devices the operations that can be performed there. We use a graph based approach and transform a BPMN definition into a directed graph. Thereafter, we identify cuts that define the parts to be transferred to the IoT devices. This decomposition preserves the control and the data dependencies of the original process, reduces the number of exchanged messages as well as the central processing. The code that IoT devices execute is automatically generated from the BPMN process being decentralised.

Keywords: Internet of things · BPMN · Process decomposition

1 Introduction

Internet of things (IoT) aware business processes put together two technologies, and has gained increased attention in the recent years.

Organisations use business processes to automate and optimise their operations by modelling them as flows of activities enriched with events, data flows, and information about resources and participantes, among other perspectives. Business processes are often defined with graphical notations, such as the Business Process Model and Notation (OMG 2011).

© Springer Nature Switzerland AG 2020
J. Filipe et al. (Eds.): ICEIS 2019, LNBIP 378, pp. 498–513, 2020.
https://doi.org/10.1007/978-3-030-40783-4_24

In addition, the IoT makes possible to interconnect everyday physical devices, which can interact with each other and cooperate with their neighbours. These devices are also accessible through the Internet, providing information and functionalities on behalf of physical objects or things. Interconnected small devices pose several challenges, such as energy consumption, the scarcest resource of the IoT; scalability, due to the number of devices that can be quite high; reliability, as network nodes are susceptible to a wide variety of failures; and security, since devices have computational limitations, and, typically, their physical integrity is difficult to assure (Atzori et al. 2010; Lee and Kim 2010; Moreno et al. 2014; Rault et al. 2014; Zorzi et al. 2010).

Business processes can use the IoT to gain competitive advantage in terms of optimisation and agility. Business processes may use the information the IoT provides about what is actually happening in the real world to optimise their execution, and react to new situations in real time (Yousfi et al. 2016). However, in most cases, business processes interact with IoT devices following a request-response or a publish-subscribe scheme to gather information and to trigger actuators. These interaction schemes promote the exchange of messages between IoT devices and the execution engine, which results in a high power consumption profile from the IoT device.

An alternative approach is for business processes to use IoT devices as active participants for executing parts of the business process logic (Haller et al. 2009), taking advantage of their computational and communication capabilities. IoT devices can be used to aggregate and filter data, as well as to make decisions locally, executing local flows, without needing a centralised coordination. Following this approach, it is possible to reduce the number of exchanged messages, increasing battery lifespan, and to promote scalability, by moving parts of the execution of the process from the central engine to IoT devices. We point out that this extra execution consumes power of the IoT device, but the energy consumption of the migrated tasks is much smaller than that used on communication.

Despite the benefits of decentralisation, business processes are still defined following a centralised approach. Our proposal automatically decomposes BPMN business processes, identifying and moving to the IoT parts of the processes that IoT devices can execute, assuring the reduction of the number of exchanged messages, while maintaining data and control dependencies.

Our work is distinct from related work in four main aspects: business process representation; decomposition technique; considered dependencies; and meeting criteria. Some authors represent business processes as generic graphs (Xue et al. 2018), while Nanda et al. (2004) use Web Services Business Process Execution Language (WS-BPEL) (OASIS 2007). Still considering the way these proposals represent business processes, almost all of them only support block structured processes. Xue et al. (2018) supports non-block structured processes, but only deal with processes having regions with one entry point and one exit point (SESE). Decomposition techniques use approaches mainly based on dependency tables (Fdhila et al. 2009) or on generic graphs (Nanda et al. 2004; Xue et al. 2018). While all proposals consider control dependencies, some of them disregard data dependencies (Nanda et al. 2004). Finally, we can find different criteria for decomposition in the literature such as communication cost, delay cost, or confidentiality (Fdhila et al. 2014; Goettelmann et al. 2013; Hoenisch et al. 2016; Povoa et al. 2014).

These proposals cannot be straightforward applied to BPMN business processes. The transformation of a BPMN business process definition to a generic graph poses many challenges, such as the implicit concurrent behaviour introduced by send tasks, and the identification of data dependencies. Furthermore, BPMN business processes can be non-block structured with many entry and exit points.

Our previous work proposes a pattern based approach to decompose IoT aware BPMN business processes (Martins et al. 2019; Domingos et al. 2019). We identify the common scenarios in this kind of processes, where is it possible to reduce the number of exchanged messages between the central engine and IoT devices. In addition, we define the transformation rules to move to the IoT parts of the processes that IoT devices can execute, while maintaining control and data dependencies.

The work we present in this paper goes a step further by adopting a more generic approach based on graph concepts. We transform the BPMN definition into a typed directed graph, where we identify cuts that are used to define the parts that can be transferred to the IoT devices. This decomposition preserves the control and the data dependencies of the original process, reduces the number of exchanged messages as well as the central processing. The code that IoT devices execute is automatically generated from the BPMN process being decentralised.

This paper is organised as follows: the next section discusses related work; Sect. 3 presents the use case we resort to illustrate the proposed decomposition procedure and the patterns we identified in our previous work. The decomposition procedure is detailed in Sect. 4, and Sect. 5 overviews the developed prototype. The last section concludes the paper and discusses future work.

2 Related Work

One of the early works on process decomposition is proposed within the Mentor project (Wodtke et al. 1996). The authors define workflow models by using state and activity diagrams and describe how a centralised model can be partitioned and executed in a distributed setting, maintaining the original semantics and taking into account control and data dependencies.

The growing use of the Web Services Business Process Execution Language (WS-BPEL) (OASIS 2007) justified the development of decomposition proposals of such processes. Nanda et al. (2004) transform a BPEL model into a program dependence graph (PDG). Based on the PDG, they propose an algorithm to create partitions by merging portable nodes with fixed nodes, taking into account control and data dependencies. Each partition has exactly one fixed node and zero or more portable nodes. However, this partitioning technique can only be applied to block structured models.

Fdhila et al. (2009) propose a decomposition technique based on dependency tables. They create a direct control dependency table and a direct data dependency table taking into account control and data dependencies. From the dependency tables, they generate transitive dependency tables with the transitive dependencies between activities invoking the same service. This way, each subprocess represents the control flow between activities invoking the same service.

In Domingos et al. (2015), the authors also use dependency tables to decompose IoT aware business processes, considering control flow as well as data flow. In addition, the activities that IoT devices can execute are identified automatically, taking into account the capabilities of these devices.

A subsequent work by Fdhila et al. (2014) decompose processes based on the collocation and separation constraints that designers can define between pairs of activities. Partitions respect the constraints and optimise communication cost and the Quality of Service (QoS) of services assigned to execute activities. Goettelmann et al. (2013) extend this work by adding security constraints to meet the requirements of distributing the executions of some activities into the cloud.

To make use of the advantages offered by the cloud to execute fragments of business processes, Duipmans et al. (2012) divide business processes into two categories: those that run locally and those that can run in the cloud. With this division, the authors intend to perform the most computationally intensive tasks in the cloud, as long as their data is not confidential. The identification of these tasks is performed manually. Povoa et al. (2014) propose a semi-automatic mechanism to determine the location of activities and their data based on confidentiality policies, monetary costs, and performance metrics. Hoenisch et al. (2016) optimise the distribution of activities taking into account some additional parameters such as the cost associated with delays in the execution of activities and the unused, but paid, time of cloud resources.

Xue et al. (2018) create partial partitions using a graph based technique for process partitioning. They define the business model through a typed direct graph where edges are typed as control or data, to distinguish control from data dependencies, and vertices are typed as fixed or portable. Based on the direct graph, they identify SESE regions (Johnson et al. 1994) of the graph and generate a process structure graph. After that, they apply a set of transformation rules to group together portable vertices with a fixed vertex. Each group corresponds to a partitions. The main difference to previous work is that they support unstructured business models (both control and data dependencies). However, this partition technique disregard the specificities of IoT aware business processes.

Martins et al. (2019) propose a decomposition technique that identifies specific patterns within processes that can be delegated to IoT devices, maintaining the control and the data flows of the original processes. Decomposition follows specific rules according to the identified patterns. This work is further generalised in Domingos et al. (2019), undermining, however, some control flow dependencies.

In this paper we take a step further following a graph-based approach, while assuring data and control dependencies.

3   Use Case Based Decomposition Patterns

This section presents our use case and the patterns that we have identified to reduce the number of communications (message flows) between the central pool and IoT pools (Martins et al. 2019).

3.1   Use Case

We exemplify the application of our proposal through a simplified automatic irrigation system use case. The choice for this use case is justified by the acquired experience in deploying an irrigation controlling system prototype in collaboration with the Lisbon city council. The system controls four electrovalves, managing a total of 40 sprinklers, and is successfully running for almost two years. Furthermore, by selecting a similar use case for illustrating our previous approaches (see, for instance, Martins et al. 2019), it makes it easier to compare them and to showcase our state-of-the-art advances.

This system automatically determines when to irrigate, based on the soil moisture and on the rainfall. The water used for the irrigation comes from tanks, whose water level is also controlled by the system. It is possible to check the water level of the tanks and fill them whenever necessary.

The water level values are stored in a historical record file for future expenses audit. In addition, the system periodically contacts IoT devices to gather rainfall and soil moisture levels. If the levels are below given thresholds, it triggers the irrigation process.

Figure 8 (in the appendix) illustrates the simplified BPMN model of our use case. The two pools define the behaviour of the central system as well as the behaviour of IoT devices (sensors and actuators).

The central pool defines the actions of the central system responsible for executing the irrigation business processes. It contains two execution flows: the top describes tank refilling; the other specifies the irrigation process itself.

The top execution flow is triggered manually (S1 start event) and starts by requesting the tank's water level (SEND T1), sending a message to the IoT pool (SM1). The sensor reads the tank's water level (T11) and forwards this information back to the irrigation process (SEND T12). The Receive Water Level task (RECEIVE T2) blocks until a message arrives. Upon message arrival, it stores the information and forwards it (SEND T3) to the actuator (SM2) that triggers the Refill Water Tank task (T17) to set the tank's water level to the top. Meanwhile, the Save Refill Record task (T4) stores this occurrence by writing it to the Historical Record data store (H1).

The bottom flow executes periodically (ST1), and starts by determining if the rainfall and the soil moisture levels provided by the IoT device are within the acceptable range. For this, it requests the rainfall value (SEND T18) to the IoT pool that starts the process (SM6), reads the rainfall (T21), and sends a message with this information (SEND T22) back to the irrigation process. Then, the process checks this value (IF3) and terminates in case it has recently rained. Otherwise, it gets the soil moisture by sending a request to the IoT pool (SEND T5), which starts process (SM3), reads the soil moisture value (T13), and sends it (SENDT14) back to the irrigation process.

Then, the process checks if it is necessary to start an irrigation cycle. For that, the exclusive gateway Check Moisture Values (IF1) forces the process to follow only one of its paths. If the moisture value is below the defined threshold, it computes the irrigation time based on the moisture level received (T7) and signals the actuators (SENDT8) to start irrigating (T15). The purpose of the irrigation intermediate timer event (ST2) is to wait for the irrigation time before sending a signal (SENDT9) to stop the actuator (T16). Finally, the process records the soil moisture level (T10) into the historical record data store (H2). The purpose of the converging gateway (IF2) is to forward the process to task T10, regardless of the path taken by the process.

This process, despite using IoT devices, takes a centralised approach. In the following sections, we use it to illustrate the various steps of our decomposition procedure.

3.2   Decomposition Patterns

This section presents the patterns that we have identified as ineffective uses of the computational capabilities of IoT devices in Martins et al. (2019). The main concern on the identification of the patterns, and their respective transformations, is to reduce the number of communications between the central process and to preserve the execution flow of the initial business process. This means that the tasks still execute in the original order after the transformations.

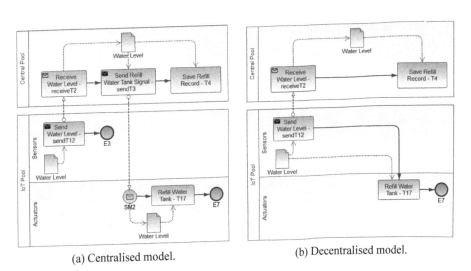

(a) Centralised model.   (b) Decentralised model.

Fig. 1. Pattern 1 example instance taken from the use case - adapted from (Martins et al. 2019).

The first pattern, illustrated in Fig. 1a, is identified by a receive task (RECEIVET2) followed by a send task (SENDT3) in the central pool that are, respectively, preceded and followed by a send (SENDT12) and a receive task or start message event (SM2) belonging to the same IoT pool. This includes an unnecessary communication between the two pools: the transformation eliminates SENDT3 and SM2. To enforce the original control flow, RECEIVET2 is connected to T4 and SENDT12 is connected to T17, as Fig. 1b illustrates.

The second pattern is exemplified in Fig. 2a. The central pool process starts with a timer event (ST1) and is followed by a send task (SENDT18) and a receive task (RECEIVET19), both to and from the same IoT pool. By moving the timer to the IoT pool, we eliminate one communication between SENDT18 and SM6 (typically, IoT devices have timer operations), as Fig. 2b shows.

Figure 3a contains an excerpt of our use case that illustrates the third pattern. Typically, IoT devices have sufficient computational capabilities to perform logical and mathematical operations, so it is possible to transfer gateways to the IoT network, as long as the data for making the decision is available. Also script tasks that compute mathematical expressions can be moved to IoT devices as it is the case for task 7. This pattern is characterised by a message flow from the IoT pool to the central process (in this case, from SENDT14 to RECEIVET6), which, afterwards, branches (IF1 gateway) based on the received data. The goal is to transfer as much tasks as possible to the IoT pool, while preserving control and data flow dependencies. Figure 3b illustrates the application of this pattern to our running example. The message flow from the IoT pool to the central process is postponed as long as the central process has BPMN elements that can be moved to the IoT pool. This set of BPMN elements includes exclusive gateways, script tasks that only compute mathematical expressions, timer events, and send tasks targeted at the IoT pool.

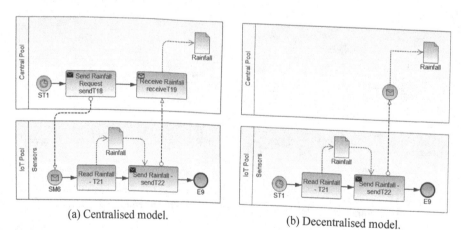

(a) Centralised model.   (b) Decentralised model.

Fig. 2. Pattern 2 example instance taken from the use case - adapted from (Martins et al. 2019).

In Domingos et al. (2019), we generalised the presented patterns making them applicable to additional scenarios, but still relaxing control flow preservation. The result is that the overall meaning of the process remains the same, but some task that might happen in parallel in the original process may happen before others after the transformation, and vice versa. In the work we present in Sect. 4, the decomposed process maintains faithfully both the control flow and the data flow of the original process.

4 Graph Based Decomposition Patterns

Unlike our previous proposals (Martins et al. 2019; Domingos et al. 2019), the work we present here uses a graph based technique to identify which parts of the process IoT devices can execute. Before detailing our technique, this section starts by explaining the transformation from the BPMN business process model to a typed directed graph.

4.1 Defining a BPMN Process as a Typed Directed Graph

The first step to decompose a business process is to represent it as a typed directed graph, where vertices and edges are typed, meaning that we decorate vertices and edges with additional information that is then used by our decomposition algorithm.

Edges can be of two types: control or data. Sequence flows and message flows are converted to control type edges. Data flow dependencies are derived using *def-use path* dependencies (Ammann and Offutt 2016), where a *def* corresponds to a write into a data object or a data store and a *use* represents an access. To identity data dependencies we exclude send and receive tasks, since these tasks are only used to handle the communication between pools.

Tasks, gateways, and events are converted to vertices. The ones that can be executed in either pools (gateways, timers, end events, and script tasks that only include mathematical operations) as well as send tasks and receive tasks are typed as portable. The others are typed with the name of the pool that represents the participant where they have to be executed.

We point out that the send and receive tasks are represented by fork and join vertices, maintaining the semantics of the concurrent behaviour of the executions flows.

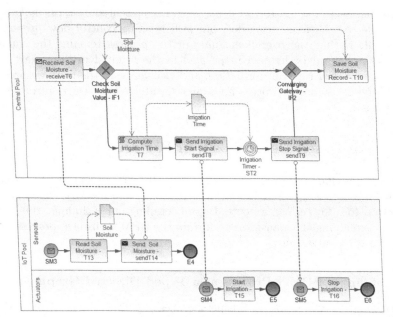

(a) Centralised model.

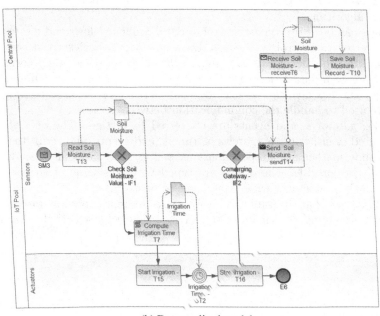

(b) Decentralised model.

Fig. 3. Pattern 3 example instance taken from the use case - adapted from (Martins et al. 2019).

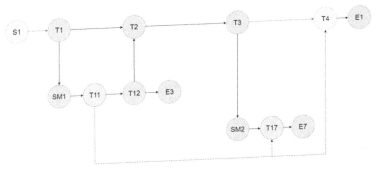

Fig. 4. The digraph of the execution flow that starts with S1. (Color figure online)

Figure 4 presents the typed directed graph that corresponds to the execution flow that begins with start event S1. We use colours to distinguish the type of vertices. Yellow nodes (S1 and T4) represent *Central Pool* vertices, blue nodes (T11 and T17) represent *IoT Pool* vertices, and green nodes represent portable vertices. Dashed and solid lines edges represent data and control types, respectively.

4.2 Decomposition Graph-Based Patterns

To reduce the number of exchanged messages between the central pool and IoT devices, we first identify the scenarios (designed as patterns) where it is possible to reduce messages (from two (or more) to one or from three (or more) to two).

The first scenario occurs when: (1) the graph has a cut, i.e, a partition of the graph into two disjoint subsets; (2) one of the cut sets includes one edge typed as control and zero or more edges typed as data; and (3) one of the subsets includes, at least, two message flows and all its nodes are typed as portable or *IoT Pool*. The rationale behind this scenario is that we can decompose the process, transferring the tasks in the subset satisfying (1), (2), and (3) to the IoT pool. This way, the two or more message flows of the subset are reduced to only one, the one that corresponds to the cut edge that links both subsets.

Figure 5 presents the typed directed graph of the execution flow that starts with ST1 timer event. This graph has four cuts according to the conditions defined for the first scenario. The control cut edge of each of these cuts is identified in pink. When a cut whose subset includes all the other, we select it as it reduces the number of transformations.

To get the final decomposed BPMN process from the graph, fork nodes that represent send tasks in the original process are replaced by diverging parallel gateways, while join nodes that represent receive tasks are replaced by converging parallel gateways. To link both partitions, we add a send task and a receive task (or a message start event) with a message flow. If the cut set also includes data typed edges, this message flow must include the corresponding values.

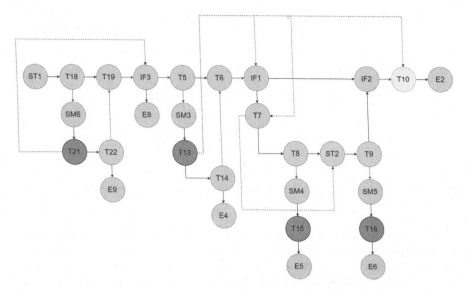

Fig. 5. The digraph of the execution flow that starts with ST1.

Figure 6 presents the decomposed version of the process for the execution flow that starts with ST1 timer event. In future work, we are going to identify and remove the parallel gateways that neither synchronise two or more control flows nor creates two or more parallel flows.

In the second scenario, it is possible to reduce from three (or more) messages to two messages. This scenario occurs when: (1) the graph has a cut; (2) the cut set includes two edges typed as control and zero or more edges typed as data; and (3) one of the subsets includes, at least, three message flows and all its nodes are typed as portable or as *IoT Pool*. The rationale behind this scenario is that we can decompose the process, transferring all subset task to the IoT pool. This way, the process is going to have only two message flows, the ones that correspond to the edges that belong to the cut set, i.e. that link both subsets.

Figure 4 presents the typed directed graph for the execution flow that starts with start event S1. This graph has one cut in the conditions defined for the second scenario. The control edges that belongs to the cut subset are identified in pink.

As we describe for the first scenario, to get the final decomposed BPMN process from the graph, fork nodes that represent send tasks in the original process are replaced by diverging parallel gateways, while join nodes that represent receive tasks are replaced by converging parallel gateways. To link both partitions, we add two send tasks and two receive tasks (or message start events) with message flows. If the cut subset also includes edges typed as data, these message flows must include the corresponding values.

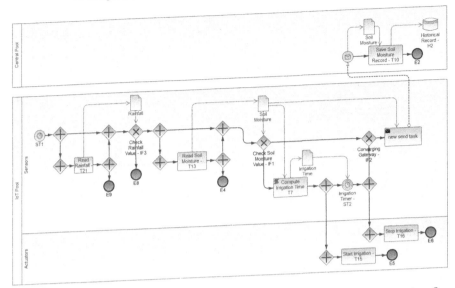

Fig. 6. The decomposed version of the BPMN business process - the execution flow that starts with ST1.

Figure 7 presents the decomposed process for the execution flow that starts with S1 start event.

5 Prototype

We are in the process of conceiving a prototype that performs the decomposition procedure described in the previous section. Our previous prototype tool is available at github (https://github.com/fcmartins/bpmn-decomposition.git).

The tool is being developed in Java and makes use of the following tools:

- jBPM (version 6.3.0);
- Eclipse Luna (version 4.4.2) with BPMN2 Modeller and SonarLint plug-ins;
- Graphviz.

The prototype builds on top of previous tools we developed that translate BPMN into CALLAS (a high-level sensor programming language (Lopes and Martins (2016))) and that automatically transform the BPMN model to communicate with the IoT network either using request-response or publish-subscribe architectures (Domingos and Martins 2017a, 2017b).

jBPM implements the BPMN standard and is associated with the Luna version of Eclipse. BPMN2 Modeller is a BPMN graphical visualisation plug-in and SonarLint a plug-in for enforcing source code quality. Graphviz is a tool for drawing graphs specified in the dot language.

In order to execute the prototype, we provide a BPMN file with the model to be decomposed. This prototype also translates the IoT behaviour into Callas bytecode to support the execution of all the BPMN model, as detailed in (Domingos and Martins (2017b)).

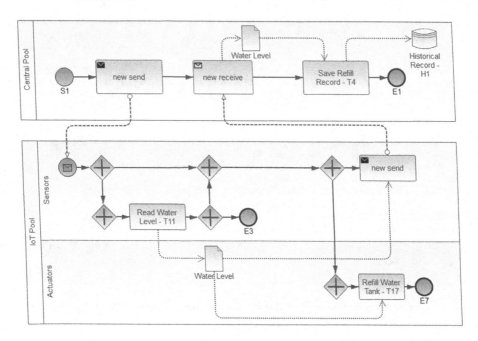

Fig. 7. The decomposed BPMN business process—the execution flow that starts with S1.

6   Conclusions and Future Work

Business processes are increasingly using information made available by IoT devices to provide timely responses according to their context. This is a challenge for IoT devices as they are limited by battery lifespan.

The work we propose in this paper mitigates this problem taking an approach from the business process perspective. The automatic decomposition technique we developed takes advantage of the computational capabilities of IoT devices, identifying the parts of process definitions that IoT devices can execute and transfers them from the central systems. This way, we reduce the number of exchanged messages, increasing the energy autonomy of these devices.

The evaluation of the completeness of our approach as well as its results is not straightforward. As stated before, the results have to be checked manually, being a very time-consuming task.

As for future work, we intend to formalise our approach in order to be able to prove the results. In addition, we plan to evaluate this work by comparing it with an heuristic based approach and using a larger set of processes generated by our process generator tool.

to designing tools that could help the decision makers to successfully innovate their BMs. Some of these works suggest standardized procedures; for example, [4] suggests a procedure to use analogies. Other works [5, 6] suggest using patterns as a help in designing new business models. Patterns can be on the highest level as in [5, or on the level of elements of the business model, as in 6].

Generally, patterns are used to find solutions for common problems and share knowledge about both problem and solutions [7]. In regards to BMI, there are many different kinds of patterns, ranging from patterns for revenue generation to patterns for the ways activities are carried out in an organization. In [8], authors analyzed business models of 250 companies and proposed 55 patterns which can serve as a basis for new business models.

The patterns mentioned above show what can be included in a new business model. In this paper, however, we focus on so-called transformational patterns; a transformational pattern shows how some elements of an old business model can be transformed into the elements of a new business model. Therefore, in our context, we define a BMI pattern as a combination of (a) constructs that can be applied to analyze the current structure of the enterprise and highlight some elements of it and (b) a construct where a new combination of the highlighted elements serves as a basis for a new business model.

In addition, in this paper, we deal only with industry level BMI according to classification from [3]. The industry level BMI amounts to changing the position of the enterprise in the value chain, entering new markets, and/or other types of radical changes. This type of BMI, for example, covers such cases as when a traditional manufacturing company that both designs and manufactures their products decides that they would concentrate only on one aspect of their current business. The company then can become a manufacturer who produces goods based on somebody else's design, or a designer – designing goods to be manufactured by somebody else. The cases of industry level BMI can be found in such companies as LEGO [9] or TSMC [10].

Paper [3] also introduces two other types of BMI: revenue model innovation and enterprise model innovation. The first results in changes in how a company generates revenues, e.g. reconfiguring offerings and/or introducing new pricing models. The second involves innovating the structure of an enterprise, such as enterprise goals, business processes, products and/or services. Both are important, and can accompany the enterprise level BMI, but they remain outside the scope of this work.

In this work, we follow the ideas from [11], which present a way for defining and designing transformational patterns from real-life cases of industry level BMI using enterprise modeling for this end. The idea can be expressed as a sequence of the following steps:

1. Find an interesting example of the industry level BMI
2. Build an enterprise model before the transformation on the needed level of details
3. Build an enterprise model after the transformation, also on the needed level of details
4. Relate elements of these two models showing which elements of the original model have been used in the transformed model and how they have been changed during the transformation
5. Abstract from the details of the given case creating a transformational pattern

This paper is devoted to designing one BMI transformational pattern from a case currently being considered in one of the German companies. Though the transformation has not yet been completed, we have found it quite interesting and realistic to take it as a basis for designing a pattern. The main idea of this pattern can be formulated as "transforming from a manufacturing business to becoming a provider of software services that can predict the needs for maintenance of equipment used in manufacturing lines". The idea of taking over maintenance of somebody else's equipment is not completely new in its nature, as it was used by Rolls Royce in TotalCare [12], where customers responsibilities were taken at the supplier end. However, it is new in the sense that in our case, maintenance does not belong to the core operations of the company.

For the purpose of modeling of the enterprise before and after planned transformation, we follow [11] and use so-called Fractal Enterprise Model described in details in [13]. The choice of modelling technique is personal, as the first co-author of this work is part of the team engaged in FEM development. The question whether other enterprise modeling techniques can be used for the purpose of designing transformational patterns remains outside the scope of this paper.

The rest of the paper is structure in the following way. In Sect. 2, we give an overview of FEM so that the reader does not need to go elsewhere to obtain this knowledge. In Sect. 3, we present the business case as it is and a fragment of FEM that is of interest for the planned business transformation. In Sect. 4, we build a FEM for a business-to-be and compare it with the FEM for the current business. While making the comparison, we discuss which elements of the current structure could be used in the new one, and what needs to be created from scratch. In Sect. 5, we derive a transformational pattern from the models presented in Sect. 3 and 4 using guidelines from [11]. In Sect. 6, we summarize our findings and draw plans for the future.

This paper is based on paper [14] presented at ICEIS 2019. In difference from [14], the focus here is on building a transformational pattern, not on the analysis of the proposed transformation. Therefore, the introduction and conclusion have been totally rewritten to reflect changes in the focus. In addition, Sect. 5, which presents a new transformational pattern, is completely new. Besides, the models presented in the paper are refined and supplied with more technical details related to the business case.

2 Overview of Fractal Enterprise Model

The Fractal Enterprise Model (FEM) includes three types of elements: business processes, assets, and relationships between them, see Fig. 1 in which a fragment of a model is presented. This fragment is related to a business case considered in the next sections. Graphically, a process is represented by an oval; an asset is represented by a rectangle (box), while a relationship between a process and an asset is represented by an arrow. FEM differentiates two types of relationships. One type represents a relationship of a process "using" an asset; in this case, the arrow points from the asset to the process and has a solid line. The other type represents a relationship of a process changing the asset; in this case, the arrow points from the process to the asset and has a dashed line. These two types of relationships allow tying up processes and assets in a directed graph.

In FEM, a label inside an oval names the given process, and a label inside a rectangle names the given asset. Arrows are also labelled to show the types of relationships between the processes and assets. A label on an arrow pointing from an asset to a process identifies the role the given asset plays in the process, for example, *Workforce*, *Infrastructure*, etc. A label on an arrow pointing from a process to an asset identifies the way in which the process affects (i.e. changes) the asset. In FEM, an asset is considered as a pool of entities capable of playing a given role(s) in a given process(es). Labels leading into assets from supporting processes reflect the way the pool is affected, for example, a label *acquire* identifies that the process can/should increase the size of the pool.

Note that the same asset can be used in two different processes playing the same or different roles in them, which is reflected by labels on the corresponding arrows. It is also possible that the same asset can be used for more than one role in the same process; in this case, there can be more than one arrow between the asset and the process, however, with different labels. Similarly, the same process could affect different assets, each in the same or in different ways, which is represented by the corresponding labels on the arrows. Moreover, it is possible that the same process affects the same asset in different ways, which is represented by having two or more arrows from the process to the asset, each with its own label.

In FEM, different styles can be used for shapes to group together different kinds of processes, assets, and/or relationships between them. Such styles can include using dashed or double lines, or lines of different thickness, or colored lines and/or shapes. For example, a diamond start of an arrow from an asset to a process means that the asset is a stakeholder of the process (see the arrows *Workforce* in Fig. 1). Another example, an assets with the dashed border represents a soft-asset, like an opinion of the agents outside the given organization (see an example in Fig. 1).

Labels inside ovals, which represent processes, and rectangles, which represent assets, are not standardized. They can be set according to the terminology accepted in the given domain, or be specific for a given organization. Labels on arrows, which represent the relationships between processes and assets, however, can be standardized. This is done by using a relatively abstract set of relationships, like, *workforce*, *acquire*, etc., which are clarified by the domain- and context-specific labels inside ovals and rectangles. Standardization improves the understandability of the models.

While there are a number of types of relationships that show how an asset is used in a process (see example in Fig. 1), there are only three types of relationships that show how an asset is managed by a process – *Acquire*, *Maintain* and *Retire*.

To make the work of building a fractal model more systematic, FEM uses archetypes (or patterns) for fragments from which a particular model can be built. An archetype is a template defined as a fragment of a model where labels inside ovals (processes) and rectangles (assets) are omitted, but arrows are labelled. Instantiating an archetype means putting the fragment inside the model and labelling ovals and rectangles; it is also possible to add elements absent in the archetype, or omit some elements that are present in the archetype.

FEM has two types of archetypes, process-assets archetypes and an asset-processes archetype. A process-assets archetype represents which kind of assets that can be used in a given category of processes. The asset-processes archetype shows which kinds of processes are aimed at changing the given category of assets.

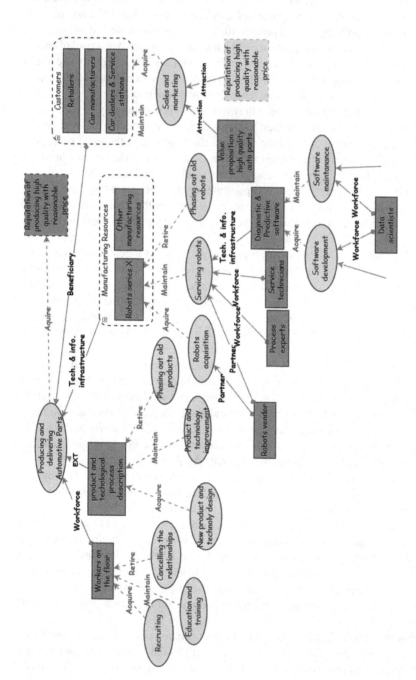

Fig. 1. A fragment of FEM (a modified version of Fig. 1 from [14]). (Color figure online)

3   Business Case

3.1   Overview of the Current State and FEM Model for It

The case considered in this paper concerns Robert Bosch GmbH, Bamberg-plant that manufactures different lines of products for automotive industry like spark plugs, fuel injection and sensors. These products can be bought by companies, retailers or end-consumers for their usage. The company uses different machines for producing the products like laser machines and robots. In this paper, we focus on robots used in manufacturing and referred them as "Robots series X" for simplicity and generic representation.

Figure 1 presents a fragment of a fractal enterprise model of the current business activity. In the root of this model is a primary process of manufacturing and delivering products. Underneath of it, there are various assets that are needed for the process working smart-free. Under smart-free, we mean that instances of this process (production batches) are started with normal frequency. As shown in FEM in Fig. 1, the process requires variety of assets such as workers on the flour (*Workforce*), manufacturing equipment (*Technical and informational infrastructure*) and customers (*Beneficiary*). Note that the FEM fragment in Fig. 1 does not show all assets that are needed to run the primary process, for example, a stock of orders for producing product batches is not presented. The choice of what to present in Fig. 1 has been made based on the most important assets and assets that are of interest for BMI to be considered in the paper.

After the assets of the first level (underneath the primary process) are put in the model, the unfolding of FEM continues by applying the asset-processes archetype, which requires finding processes that manage the identified assets. These processes are connected with the asset(s) by three types of relationships: *Acquire*, *Maintain* and *Retire*. Dependent on the type of assets, the asset managing processes have different nature. For a workforce type of assets, they are hiring, training and retiring. For the infrastructure type of assets, they are acquisition, maintenance, and phasing out. For the execution template (EXT) type of assets, they are develop/design, maintain and phase out.

After the management processes are identified, assets that are needed to run them are identified using process-assets archetypes. For example, the customer asset needs sales and marketing for both acquiring new customers and keeping them attached to the company, so that they continue to add orders to the stock of orders. The equipment asset, e.g. Robots series X, needs a service/maintenance process (see Fig. 1).

The process of unfolding of FEM can continue by applying the asset-processes archetype for newly identified assets. Thus, marketing and sales requires well-defined value proposition and reputation that backs it (see Fig. 1), as well as other assets (not identified in the figure), like sales executives. Note that the reputation is created by the main process itself as shown in Fig. 1 via an arrow labeled acquire between the main process and the reputation. The reputation asset is shown in Fig. 1 twice, once as an asset acquired by the main process, and once as an asset playing role of attraction in the sales process. The second occurrence has a lighter background color than the first one. The lighter background is used to show that this asset is presented in another part of the diagram, thus the new occurrence serves as a ghost of the first one.

Robot series X maintenance requires service technicians, machine process experts, robots providers (partners to provide spare parts, advice, etc.) and diagnostic tools. As machine diagnostic and prediction is in the focus of this work, we will look at this topic in more details in the next sub-section.

3.2 Machine Maintenance

In a manufacturing organization, production equipment - machines are very important resources for production. Different Key Performance Indicators (KPIs) related to manufacturing resources are used to ensure the optimal usage of the machines, such as OEE (Overall Equipment Efficiency) defined in ISO standard [15, 16]. A stoppage in production line due to machine failure costs a lot of money for an organization.

In the context of Industry 4.0, maintenance is an important area that has an enormous potential in terms of cost saving and resource efficiency. There are many use cases that come under the category "maintenance 4.0", like automatic maintenance order generation, notifications to stakeholders (users, other machines and mobile devices), predictive maintenance, flexible manufacturing, and support services (augmented reality).

Normally, in an organization, maintenance is counted as an overhead (however, a mandatory one) on the production. In order to avoid unpredictable costs, machines are serviced in regular intervals (sometimes according to manufacturer specifications). However, despite all regular services, sometimes unplanned maintenance also has to be carried out due to failure in machines or loss of quality in operations carried out by the machines. If a particular machine or its part is situated in a critical position in the line, it has a drastic impact on the whole production, as well as on the quality of products delivered to the customers; thus a failure in such an equipment affects the overall KPIs.

In a manufacturing organization, machines are used as long as they fit for the purpose, no matter how old they become. Several kinds of maintenance are carried out to keep the production lines running. These are briefly described below.

1. *Planned Maintenance.* The planned maintenance is carried out according to a specific plan like after completion of certain number of operating hours (e.g. 20,000 h), or after certain cycles (e.g. 2,000,000 cycles). It is carried out regularly to avoid the unplanned (failure-based) maintenance in order to save costs. However, this planned maintenance is carried out sometime earlier than completion of the operating hours in order to avoid an extra stoppage in production when the production line is stopped for a different reason (like new software updates). However, an earlier planned maintenance has a negative effect on the costs of production for an organization, as shown in Fig. 2.

2. *Condition-based Maintenance.* In this kind of maintenance, certain machine parameters are actively monitored to get information about the health of the machine and to carry out the appropriate actions (reducing speed, load etc.) before situation gets out of control. This also applies to creating maintenance orders if necessary before a planned or unplanned maintenance (in case of a failure or production stoppage) occur.

3. Unplanned (problem-based) maintenance. In unplanned maintenance, as the name suggests, the maintenance is carried out when a problem occurs. In this case, normally, a notification is sent to the service team and a maintenance order is created in case of failure.

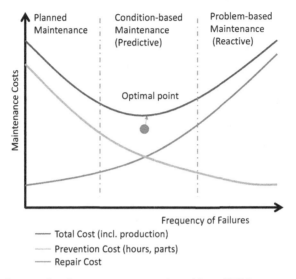

Fig. 2. The impact of maintenance on costs; adapted from [17] (as appeared in [14]).

These three kinds of maintenance are common for all manufacturers. In any kind of maintenance above, in the first place, the internal service team is asked to complete the required service. If they cannot carried out the service, then the external resources are used. The goal of any organization is to avoid unplanned maintenances and run the production as continuously as possible.

3.3 Improving Effectiveness of Maintenance

As was discussed in the previous sub-section, machine maintenance costs, direct and indirect, are quite high. To reduce the cost of maintenance itself, and revenue lost from unexpected breakdowns, organizations look to applying the latest research results in several brunches of Computer Science, e.g. Internet of Things (IoT), data mining, machine learning and Artificial Intelligence, which might improve the maintenance process.

The goal of the project started in Bamberg-plant and considered in this paper, is to develop a tool able to detect in advance when the machine is about to fail and carry out appropriate measures when planning production and maintenance. Several sub-goals are defined to achieve the main goal in a stepwise manner. The sub-goals include introducing monitoring the machine status and its parameters, and in case of deviation from the normal behavior, automatically sending notification to the service technicians. Another sub-goal includes analysis of the historical data and identification of the patterns that cause machine failure, and then using these patterns as a basis for predictive maintenance. The main idea of the project sub-goals is represented in a graphical form in Fig. 3, which is based on material from [18–20]. The direction, the project takes is to handle more complexity and get more business value from the effort.

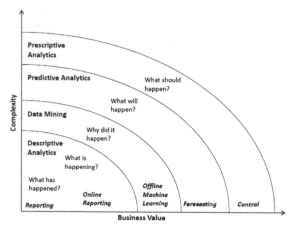

Fig. 3. The goals of the project as a diagram (as appeared in [14]).

3.4 Extending the Scope of Usage

The project described in the previous sub-section was started having a technical goal in mind, i.e. improving the maintenance effectiveness at this plant. However, when under the way, the project spawned the discussion of extending the scope of the usage of its results beyond the given plant and even beyond the whole company. This is understandable considering the costs of the project and the needs of establishing a permanent team that would deal with maintaining and further developing the software produced by the project. The latter is represented in Fig. 1 by the sub-tree starting from the asset node *Diagnostic & Predictive software*. This asset is used as *Technical & Informational infrastructure* for the *Servicing robots* process in Fig. 1.

As any other asset, *Diagnostic & Predictive software* requires its managing processes, two of which, *Acquire* and *Maintain,* are represented in Fig. 1. Continuing unfolding of the FEM structure for the *Diagnostic & Predictive software* node, we will add assets needed for these management processes, such as *Workforce* represented in Fig. 1. Furthermore, the *workforce* asset, i.e. *Data Scientists*, needs its own processes of hiring and training, etc.

As follows from the deliberation above, unfolding node *Diagnostic & Predictive software* reveals quite a complex structure that needs to be in place in order to use the results of the project described in Sect. 3.3 in practice. This explains the desire to extend the goal of the project from just improving the effectiveness of the maintenance in one plant to envisioning new BMs (Business Models) that could generate additional revenues for the company. The current discussion of extending the scope of usage ranges from providing maintenance services to other plants of the firm (remotely) to creating a separate business of licensing the diagnostic software to external companies. The latter example would be exploited in the next section.

4 Building a FEM for a New Business Model

The most radical suggestion for a new business model based on the project was to open a new business of licensing diagnostic software to other manufacturers that uses the same type of robots, including the firm's competitors. To analyze the feasibility of introducing this BM, we drafted a basic FEM related to the new BM as presented in Fig. 4.

The primary process for the new BM becomes *Licensing of Predictive Software*. It needs certain assets to ensure that this process functions smart-free. The central asset for this process is *Diagnostic & Predictive Software* promoted from the old BM; in Fig. 4, the whole tree related to this asset is moved from FEM in Fig. 1. This asset serves as *Technical & information infrastructure* for the primary process (the root of the diagram). Besides this asset, other assets are needed, in particular *Workforce* (*Installation & Configuration Engineers*) and *Beneficiary* (customers).

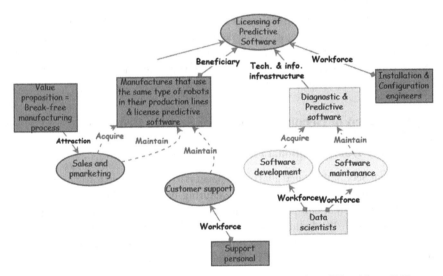

Fig. 4. A FEM fragment for the new BM (a modified version of Fig. 4 from [14]).

While comparing the beneficiary/customer assets in Figs. 1 and 4, it becomes clear that these two assets are completely different. In Fig. 4, asset *Beneficiary* has nothing to do with manufacturing, in difference from Fig. 1. This difference becomes clearer if we compare value propositions for both processes. The difference means that a completely new set of managing processes need to be added to manage the new kind of customers. Two of such processes, Sales and marketing and Customer support are presented in Fig. 4. These processes and assets for them need to be developed separately from the ones that are used in Sales and marketing in the current BM.

To analyze which other existing assets could be used in the new BM, we put two FEM fragments from Figs. 1 and 4 side by side, see Fig. 5, and continue deliberation. To start with, we can decide that process experts and service technicians can serve as installation and configuration engineers on one hand and as customer support staff on the other hand, which is shown by green arrow lines drawn between these assets in Fig. 5. The experience of the process experts and service technicians in using the software would enable them to function in another capacity as well. However, this may help only in the beginning, if the new BM starts producing more customers, more *Workforce* will need to be hired.

The next step would be to use existing reputation on high-level quality as an attraction in the new BM. As many of the new customers will belong to the company's competitors, this reputation can be used in advertising by pointing out that the software to be licensed is used internally in the organization. This gives us a possibility to move asset *Reputation of producing high quality with reasonable price* to the new fragment of FEM in Fig. 5 and mark it with a lighter background color to show that it has already been introduced in the diagram. As the follow up step, we can consider using the robots vendor as a partner for sales and marketing activities, as the vendor has access to all companies who use the machine. In Fig. 5, the machine vendor is moved to the new FEM fragment and also marked with a lighter background color.

The analysis above shows that some existing assets could be used in a new BM, however, introducing it still requires considerable efforts, e.g. in creating different kind of sales and marketing, and support, as well as increasing the size of some existing assets. The latter will mean increasing the capacity of the processes that manage these assets, e.g. hiring and training new members of staff.

5   BMI Pattern of Becoming Software Service Provider

5.1   Deriving a Transformational Pattern from the Example

As follows from Sect. 1, the stated goal of this paper is to design a transformational pattern of the type as "transforming from a manufacturing business to becoming a provider of software services that can predict the needs for maintenance of equipment used in manufacturing lines". We do this based on the models designed in the previous sections and presented in Fig. 5. The main idea of creating a pattern is taking an example and abstracting from the specific details of the case [11]. A transformational pattern built based on this idea from the current case is presented in Fig. 6. We use more or less the same visual representation in the pattern as in the underlying FEM, but with some extensions.

The left-hand side of the pattern in Fig. 6 represents a template that should be applied to the FEM of the current activities of an enterprise. The root is identified just as a main process, meaning that it can be any activity that delivers value to the beneficiaries/customers. This main process employs directly or indirectly complex and expensive equipment of any kind. Directly means that this equipment serves as an infrastructure for the main process, as in the case described in this paper. Indirectly means that it serves as an infrastructure to one of the supporting processes down the line. For example, it can be a piece of equipment employed in research in a high-tech company. The possibility

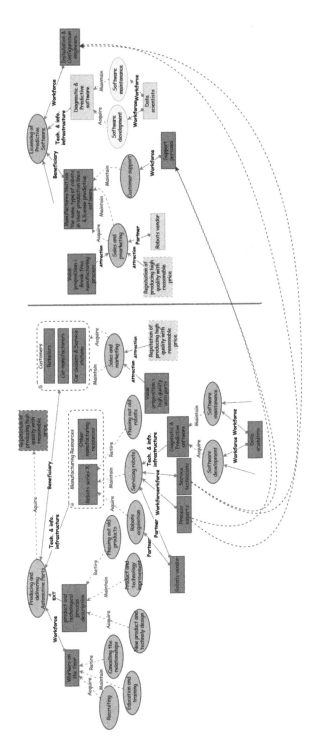

Fig. 5. Comparing two FEM fragments (a modified version of Fig. 5 from [14]). (Color figure online)

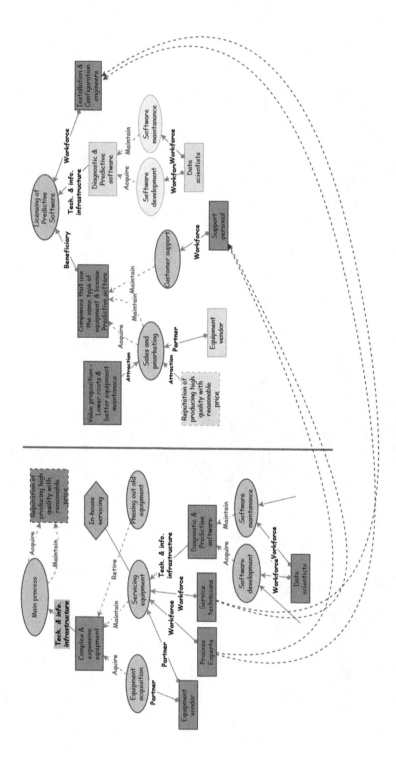

Fig. 6. A pattern derived from the models in Fig. 5. (Color figure online)

of the indirect connection is denoted by having the light gray background on the label between the main process and the equipment asset.

The next level of the business as-is template concerns the equipment that needs to be acquired maintained and discharged. Here, the equipment vendor appears as a partner for delivering new equipment, as well as helping to maintain it via providing spare parts and technicians that can help with reparation. An important process of maintaining equipment is its servicing. In this template we consider that the equipment servicing is done in-house by own people, though help from the third-party, e.g. equipment vendor, in certain situations can be accepted. This is a requirement to be fulfilled in order the pattern becoming applicable to a situation. This requirement is written in a green hexagons, as recommended in [11].

The next important for the template part is the presence of the Diagnostic & Predictive software, which is used to determine the need for service, developed by the company itself. The latter is highlighted by having in-hose supporting processes for developing and maintaining this software. This process require special workforce that is denoted by "data scientists", however, it can be called something else in a business situation that satisfies the left-hand side template.

The right-hand side of Fig. 6 presents a template for business to-be which is an abstraction of the right-hand side of Fig. 5. Left- and right-hand side pictures are connected via the same elements appearing in both. This is identify by the shapes having lighter background colors on the right-hand side of Fig. 6. In addition, green lines show that some assets playing a role in the business as-is can be-used in slightly different roles in the business to-be. Everything else needs to be built from scratch.

5.2 Discussion

The transformational pattern presented in Sect. 5.1 shows how a manufacturer can become a software service provider with the software seemingly not directly connected to the current primary business. Creating a new business does not necessarily results in immediate abandoning the old one. Both can exists in synergy. However, if the new business takes off, the company may consider to expand this business instead of continuing to invest in the old one, and later on deciding on abandoning the old business as less profitable. The needs to abandon the old business may also come from changing business environment, for example, if suddenly, the market for the currently manufactured product collapses. The expansion of the new business may, for example, go in the direction of providing diagnostic and predictive software for other type of equipment, at least in the same class as the current one. This, in turn, may require collaboration with the equipment vendor(s).

Applying the pattern in Fig. 6 to a specific organization does not require having a FEM built in advance. Actually, the template in the left-hand side of Fig. 6 can serve as guidance for building a relevant for the pattern fragment of FEM. One starts with any of the primary processes and tries to figure out if it uses a complex & expensive equipment. One can also start with trying to find out whether such an equipment exists somewhere in the company. After such equipment has been found, the servicing of it becomes in the focus of the study, if the servicing is not done in-house, then there is no match. If the servicing is done in-house, the check is done whether any kind of software is used to control the equipment and predict its breaking down. If such software is used, the check is done whether it was created in-house. If the answer to the last question is yes, the matching is established and one can start with defining a possible transformation that can be analyzed further.

As we can see from Fig. 6, our transformational pattern does not produce a full-fledge business model, e.g. in the form of a Business Model Canvas (BMC) [5]. The goal of a transformational pattern is not to provide all details, but show what new business can be considered, and how the existing elements of the current business can be used in the new one. Everything else needs to be added after the pattern has been applied to the current situation and is considered feasible to explore.

There are a number of decisions to be made when designing a full BM based on the suggested transformation. The first one is to decide in what way the software will be licensed. Will it be in the form of software to download and install on the customer own severs, or a cloud-service fed by customers' equipment constantly sending information from the sensors installed on the equipment? The first solution results in the customer being taught how to use the software. The second solution means that the customer needs to disclose the processes in which the equipment is used. Which decision is taken affects how the supporting processes are defined. For example, in the first case, a customers' education process needs to be created, while the second case requires trust from the customers. The latter may require the company to drop its old business activity, as it might compete with some of the potential customers.

Another decision that needs to be made is payment and pricing. This decision is connected to the first one. The cloud service option gives a better flexibility to device paying schemes. It can be a subscription with regular payment in advance, or payment for the actual usage later or a combination.

Summarizing the above discussion, creating a full BM based on the transformational pattern in Fig. 6 requires adding many concrete details. This can be done by using other types of patterns discussed in the Introduction and partly presented in [6]. Patterns that can help in deciding an approach to delivery, sales and marketing, and payment are of particular interest. In the future, these patterns can be integrated into the transformational pattern suggested in this paper to give the potential users a wider range of options to implement the transformation.

6   Concluding Remarks and Plans for the Future

In this paper, we suggested a BM transformational pattern based on the example of currently discussed transformation in one of the plants of Robert Bosch GmbH. The pattern has been derived based on the recommendations from [11]. Due to the second author engagement in the business case, the detailed information about the case was available, which made it easier to create a pattern.

The authors' long-term plans include creating a library of transformational BM patterns to guide the companies when they need to modify their business model. As the example in this paper shows, each pattern requires some efforts to be build, even when information is available. So this work will take some years. Another long-term plan is to integrate this and other transformational patterns with other types of BM patterns as discussed in the previous section.

One of the important parts of deciding on a specific transformation is analysis of the context. For example, in the case of transformation discussed in this paper, the current competitors of the company need to be considered as potential customers in a new business model. These kind of facts is not represented in the current version of FEM, therefore, introducing the context representation in the model is placed on our short-term agenda. The context information might be important not only for building transformational BM patterns, but for other usages of FEM as well.

Another important issue for both FEM and transformational BM patterns is to have a computerized IT support for both building FEM and matching a pattern. Currently all figures included in this paper were build using InsightMaker [21]. However, at the moment of this writing, we are starting a project of creating a specialized tool based on the ADOxx modeling environment [22].

References

1. Andreini, D., Bettinelli, C.: Systematic Literature Review. Business Model Innovation. ISAMS, pp. 1–23. Springer, Cham (2017). https://doi.org/10.1007/978-3-319-53351-3_1
2. Mangematin, V., Ravarini, A., Sharkey Scott, P.: Special issue: business model innovation. J. Bus. Strategy **38**(2), 3–5 (2017)
3. Giesen, E., Berman, S.J., Bell, R., Blitz, A.: Three ways to successfully innovate your business model. Strategy Leadersh. **35**(6), 27–33 (2007)
4. Rumble, R., Minto, N.A.: How to use analogies for creative business modelling. J. Bus. Strategy **38**(2), 76–82 (2017)
5. Osterwalder, A., Pigneur, Y.: Business Model Generation: A Handbook for Visionaries, Game Changers, and Challengers. Wiley, Hoboken (2014)
6. Echterfeld, J., Gausemeier, J.: How to use business model patterns for exploiting disruptive technologies. In: 24th International Conference on Management of Technology, pp. 2294–2313 (2015)
7. Lodhi, A., Koeppen, V., Wind, S., Saake, G., Turowski, K.: Business process modeling language for performance evaluation. In: HICSS, Waikoloa, pp. 3768–3777 (2014)
8. Gassmann, O., Frankenberger, K., Csik, M.: The business model navigator: 55 Models that will revolutionise your business. Financial Times Pret. (2014)
9. Robertson, D., Hjuler, P.: Innovating a Turnaround at LEGO. Harvard Business Review (September) (2009)
10. Su, Y., Huang, S.: Business Model Innovation with Effective Innovation: An Exploratory Study on TSMC. In: 2006 IEEE International Symposium on Semiconductor Manufacturing, Tokyo, pp. 483–486 (2006)
11. Bider, I., Perjons, E.: Defining Transformational Patterns for Business Model Innovation. In: Zdravkovic, J., Grabis, J., Nurcan, S., Stirna, J. (eds.) BIR 2018. LNBIP, vol. 330, pp. 81–95. Springer, Cham (2018). https://doi.org/10.1007/978-3-319-99951-7_6
12. Rolls Royce: Power by Hour. https://www.rolls-royce.com/media/our-stories/discover/2017/totalcare.aspx. Accessed 2017
13. Bider, I., Perjons, E., Elias, M., Johannesson, P.: A fractal enterprise model and its application for business development. Softw. Syst. Model. **16**(3), 663–689 (2017)
14. Bider, I., Lodhi, A.: Using Enterprise modeling in development of new business models. In: Proceedings of the 21st International Conference on Enterprise Information System (ICEIS) 2019, Heraklion, vol. 2, pp. 525–533 (2019)

15. ISO: ISO 22400-1:2014. Automation systems and integration – Key performance indicators (KPIs) for manufacturing operations management – Part 1: Overview, concepts and terminology. Standard, International Organization for Standardization (2014)
16. ISO: ISO 22400-2:2014. Automation systems and integration – Key performance indicators (KPIs) for manufacturing operations management – Part 2: Definitions and descriptions. Standard, International Organization for Standardization (2014)
17. Etia, M.C., Ogajib, S.O.T., Probertb, S.D.: Reducing the cost of preventive maintenance (PM) through adopting a proactive reliability-focused culture. Appl. Energy **83**(11), 1235–1248 (2006)
18. Davenport, T., Harris, J.: Competing on Analytics: The New Science of Winning. Harvard Business School Press, Brighton (2007)
19. Eckerson, W.: Predictive Analytics. Extending the Value of Your Data Warehousing Investment. Technical report Q1 (2007)
20. Lustig, I., Dietrich, B., Johnson, C., Dziekan, C.: The analytics journey: an IBM view of the structured data analysis landscape: descriptive, predictive and prescriptive analytics. INFORMS Analytics Magazine, November–December, pp. 11–18 (2010)
21. Give Team: Insightmaker. http://insightmaker.com/. Accessed 2014
22. ADOxx.org: ADOxx. https://www.adoxx.org. Accessed 2017

An Architecture Principle Measurement Instrument Tested in Real-Life

Michiel Borgers$^{(\boxtimes)}$ ⓘ and Frank Harmsen ⓘ

School of Business and Economics, Maastricht University,
Tongersestraat 53, Maastricht, The Netherlands
{mac.borgers, f.harmsen}@maastrichtuniversity.nl

Abstract. A high percentage of information system projects still fails due to poor implementation of requirements. Over the years, investigations by numerous scientists suggest that architecture principles are important in the successful implementation of those information systems requirements. However, these investigations are of a theoretical nature; until now, no validation in practice has taken place. Our research stresses this empirical validation: do architecture principles work in real-life situations? To find this evidence, we need an instrument to measure architecture principles, in order to establish the connection between principle and project success. The focus of this paper is such an architecture principle measurement instrument. We describe the results of a literature study, yielding both the definition and the characteristics of the architecture principle. Besides the measurement instrument, we describe the related measurement method, including the test in a real-life case. Based on the outcome of the case study, we extend the instrument with additional architecture principles characteristics and attributes, and we improve the measurement method.

Keywords: Architecture principles · Definition · Description · Characteristics attributes · Measurement instrument · Information system · Case study

1 Introduction

We want information systems[1] to be successful, but we do see projects fail in many cases [1]. So, the implementation of information system requirements is not that straightforward. Architecture principles play, in theory, a key role in guiding the design and the implementation of information system (IS) requirements [2–4]. But the question is: are architecture principles effective in practice, i.e. do they have a – hopefully positive – contribution to the implementation of IS requirements?

To answer this overarching question of our research, we consider in our research the use of architecture principles during the implementation of IS requirements. We measure both the architecture principles and the success of the implementation of the information system requirements, in order to determine some contribution. In this paper we focus on the first part of our research: the measurement of architecture principles.

---

[1] An information system is an system to collect, process, store, and distribute information and includes software, hardware, data, people, and procedures.

© Springer Nature Switzerland AG 2020
J. Filipe et al. (Eds.): ICEIS 2019, LNBIP 378, pp. 531–561, 2020.
https://doi.org/10.1007/978-3-030-40783-4_26

This paper is the result of creating an architecture principle measurement instrument out of theory, challenged in a case study. To do so, we first identified and described architecture principles based on theory. From these results, we created a measurement instrument and tested it in a real-life case. We start this paper with the research methodology in section two. In the next section we describe a definition as well as a framework for identifying and describing architecture principles. Section four provides an architecture principle measurement instrument. The validation results of the measurement instrument, based on a case study, are described in section five. We finish this article with limitations, conclusions and further research.

2   Research Methodology

2.1   Research Questions

Based on the problem analysis described in the introduction, we answer the following main research question:

Main Question: "How to identify and measure architecture principles?"

We answer this research question by splitting the question into two sub research questions. To identify and measure architecture principles we first need to define and describe[2] them. So, the first sub research question will be:

Sub Question 1: "How are, according to literature, architecture principles comprehensively and consistently defined and described?"

In this first sub research question we address two elements. First is the focus on the identification of architecture principles: what kinds of statements are in scope as architecture principles? Secondly, we need a model to describe an architecture principle in a manneer as exhaustive as possible.

After answering sub question 1, we have to challenge the outcome in practice. Are the definition and description of the principles useful in a real-life situation and can we used it for measuring architecture principles? Therefore, we phrased the second sub question as:

Sub Question 2: "How to measure architecture principles in practice?"

To answer this question, we need an measurement instrument. This instrument should be able to identify architecture principles in the first place. Secondly, we have to determine the possible values of the characteristics and attributes of the principles. In determining the characteristics and attributes, it is important that the description is coherent and complete. Though, a measurement instrument in itself is not enough. We also need a method to collect and to analyze the information.

To answer these research questions, we used the approach described below.

---

[2] Definition is an exact statement of the meaning of a subject and description is a listing of all characteristics of a subject [46].

2.2 Research Approach

Obviously, we have chosen a literature study for answering Sub question 1. For Sub question 2 we used the case study approach. There are, in general, two reasons for using the case study approach:

1. Early phases of research: case studies are useful "in early phases of research where there may be no prior hypotheses or previous work of guidance" according to [5], but also stated by [6].
2. Context-related: if a phenomenon is strongly related to its context, case study research "is used to investigate a specific phenomenon through an in-depth limited-scope study" [6]. Yin states that case studies are necessary "when the boundaries between phenomenon and context are not clearly evident" [7].

Architecture principles have been studied since the early 1990's. This would imply that the first reason does not apply to our research. But in [2] we already identified that there is a lack of research about the practical use of architecture principles. And although there is a scientific basis laid out by this theory, we would like to challenge its adequacy, "because they have little empirical substantiation" as Eisenhardt [6] would call it. And, although some of the past publications introduced new definitions and descriptions, they all confirmed the conclusions of previous publications [3]. It is time to juxtaposition theory and practice.

For answering our research question the second reason to choose for the case study approach, is valid as well. In our literature review we cited several authors that "the context in which the architecture principles are used, is important as well, in particular for the effect of a principle." [3]. So, architecture principles are conceptual instruments used by people in the context of the design and implementation process.

2.3 Research Process

For the literature review we used a six-step approach, based on the literature review method of Webster and Watson [8]. This method was also used by Stelzer [9] and Haki [10] and with that, we have equivocality of the research process in this area of research. The six steps were:

1. Defining the boundaries of the literature review;
2. Compiling two models (one for each research question) needed for analyzing the results of the literature review;
3. Identifying and selecting relevant literature;
4. Reviewing the results of the literature review using our models;
5. Answering the sub research questions based on the results of the analysis;
6. Addressing the limitations, discussing the results and presenting implications for further research.

Models Used Supporting Literature Analysis. In step two we defined two models to help us analyzing the results that we found in the selected publications. Our aim is to have an instrument helping to decompose the definitions found. This decomposition helps to identify all elements relevant for describing the essence of the term 'architecture principle' and also to determine which additional elements are not distinctive.

To experience the essence of a subject, the interrogative WH-questions [11] are helpful. We used the 7 most-used interrogative WH questions (what, why, how, with which, who, when, and where) to decompose the definitions. Each element of a definition is attached to one of the questions. After the decomposition of all definitions, we analysed per question the similarities and differences in phrasing. Based on the analysis we formulated a new phrasing for a strengthened definition (see Table 3 in the Appendix) (Fig. 1).

Fig. 1. Decomposing architecture principle definitions with WH-questions [3].

For describing the architecture principle, we used a framework to model the architecture principle. In this framework (see Fig. 2) we distinguish the relevant entities in our research, like architecture principle, design, and strategy. Most of them are artefacts of the development process.

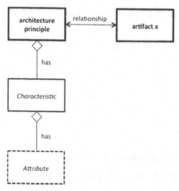

Fig. 2. Framework for modelling the characteristics of an architecture principle [3].

An entity has characteristics, defined as "a feature belonging typically to an architecture principle and serving to identify it". A characteristic, in its turn, has one or more attributes, as "an inherent part of the characteristic". We also address the relationships between the entities and between the entity and its characteristics. In designing the model we used the UML in accordance with [12, 13].

During the literature review we listed each new characteristic or entity we found in a table, including the definition, attributes and relationship. When we did find a synonym, we added that one to the one found earlier. In the end this resulted in a list of unique characteristics, entities and relationships to each other. As a final step, we designed the model describing the architecture principle using the framework.

Search & Selection Criteria. In step three we used the various well-known databases, journals, and search mechanisms (for instance, EBSCO, Google Scholar, AISeL and Research Gate), to find relevant literature. In selecting the right publications, we used the following inclusion and exclusion criteria. First criterion is the selection of English publications only. Secondly, the title or abstract has to contain at least the combination of terms <architecture principle> AND (<Enterprise> OR <IS> OR <IT>). Based on those criteria we obtained a list of publications (see Table 1 in the Appendix).

We analyzed the abstracts of those publications and selected those ones addressing the definition or description of architecture principles in general. We excluded all other literature covering the application of architecture principles. Each of the selected publications was read and analyzed extensively and all relevant information in the publication was structured for analysis.

In some publications we did find citations to prior literature as well. When those publications were addressing specific elements of architecture principles, we added them to our list of publications. In most cases those publications did not satisfy all selection criteria, because they were addressing another (related) subjects.

Case Study Approach. For the case study approach we looked at the steps defined by [6]. She based her steps on literature from authors like [7, 14–16] and experience from authors conducting case studies like [17–19]. We grouped the steps of Eisenhardt in the following three phases (Fig. 3):

Fig. 3. Case study approach [4].

1. *Preparing the Case Study*: in this phase we defined the research question, as described above. Secondly, we selected a case. Because our overall research program is focusing on Dutch government organizations, we chose a case from the Dutch Tax Agency. One reason to choose this case study was, of course, that the project did use architecture principles in the first place. Besides, the chosen project had to be finished: we could see the use of principles during the entire implementation life cycle. We

crafted the instruments and protocols to be used during the case study research. We defined our research team with subject matter experts, defined our survey, and built our measurement instrument and method.

2. *Doing the Research*: this was the iterative phase of data collection, analysis and theory building. We collected the data from documents, surveys, interviews, and a site visit. Based on the results of our desk research, we aimed at specific subjects during our interviews. We added all collected data to the spreadsheets that contained our measurement instrument. During this phase we sharpened our measurement instrument, adding new characteristics and attributes. After all data were collected, the research team evaluated both the measurement instrument and method and made suggestions for improvement.

3. *Closing the Research*: the last phase compared the results with existing literature and to end the case study because there were no new data sources to investigate. We ended the case study after evaluating all possible data sources in our spreadsheet and reporting the results of the case study back to the Dutch Tax Agency. We closed the research by answering the research question.

Because a research approach has to be reliable and valid [20], we used these steps to guarantee the objectivity of the fact finding in this case study approach.

2.4 Boundaries of Research

Our research is focusing on architecture principles to be used for implementing information system requirements. In the initiation of this literature review, however, we found out that there is a lack of architecture principle literature related to the scope of IS specifically. There is, however, literature on enterprise architecture principles and software architecture principles. IS architecture is part of enterprise architecture [21], and therefore it is possible to confine the literature review to the enterprise, which we did. Therefore, all conclusions related to principles used in enterprise architecture can be applied to principles for the IS architecture as well. As a consequence, we scoped our literature search on architecture principles related to Enterprise, Information System, or IT.

Secondly, as mentioned in Sect. 2.2, the context in which architecture principles are used, is relevant. With narrowing the scope to Dutch government organizations, we are scaling down the research scope, resulting in more reliable research results.

3 Defining and Describing Architecture Principles

By describing the results of our literature study, we answer sub question 1. We start with the general research results, and in the two following sub-sections we provide the definition and description of the architecture principles respectively.

3.1 General Literature Study Results

After the search and selection of publications we found 28 publications we rated as most relevant in defining and describing architecture principles (see Table 1 in the Appendix).

Those publications are covering a time span between 1990 and 2017. Some of those publications introduce new definitions and descriptions, while others strengthen existing ones. Many publications confirm and use the conclusions of previous publications.

All authors confirm the importance of architecture principles for the architecture and design of systems. There was only limited practical research about architecture principles. In that research, it turned out that architects state that architecture principles have added value, according to different surveys [22–24].

Of all publications found, most of them are describing architecture principles in general, calling it Enterprise Architecture (EA) principles. Only a few are related to a specific layer of the architecture, such as business, information system, application, or technical infrastructure [25–27]. Specific publications related to architecture principles and information systems are difficult to find. Therefore, as discussed in Sect. 2, we used the more general yet still applicable literature on EA principles instead.

Our research shows, generally speaking, consensus about architecture principle definitions and its characteristics over the previous 27 years. In 2013 Haki already mentioned the increasing consensus on what he was calling "the nature and definition of EA principles" [24]. Since Haki's paper, there were only a few new publications with similar ideas. Nevertheless, between the 28 publications we did find some inaccuracy or incompleteness, which we will elaborate in the next two sections to strengthen both the definition and description of an architecture principle.

3.2 Definition of an Architecture Principle

For defining architecture principles, we first listed all found definitions in literature in a table (see Table 2 in the Appendix). In this overview it is interesting to see that the definitions in later publications are a consolidation of previous definitions and are evolving to more comprehensive ones. In [12, 24] the elaboration of the definitions is quite detailed, which would make it in our terms more a description than a definition. It is noteworthy to see there were no really deviating definition or remarks on prior publications whatsoever.

To give insight in the similarities and differences between those definitions, we decomposed the definition with the WH-questions. During the analysis we were focusing on the essence of an architecture principle, while the definition should be comprehensive and consistent as well. Here we will address the similarities and differences per WH-question as also summarized in Table 3 of the Appendix.

In describing the determining elements of an architecture principle most authors do agree that an architecture principle is a statement, as a type of design principle. In accordance with Haki et al. [24], and Fischer et al. [12] we state that the architecture principle should be "based on business and IT strategy", because with architecture we want to focus on the essential requirements. Although many authors do agree that an architecture principle is a type of design principle, we omit this because we address the design-element later in the definition.

Although defined in many different ways, the purpose of the architecture principle can be summarized as describing restriction to the design. This is consistently formulated by Greefhorst and Proper [26] with "normatively describes a property of the design of an artefact". In our case the artefact is the information system.

In many definitions the objective of the architecture principle is described as "should be met by the architecture" or "justification for decision making throughout an EA". But an architecture in itself has the objective that a system meets its essential requirements. And because architecture is focusing on the 'essential' requirements, we would like to address this in the definition. With that, it is the distinguishing element between design and architecture principles.

Looking for additional elements in describing the essence of an architecture principle, we do not see real distinctive parts. In our analysis of the remaining WH-questions, we only identify elements, which we can link to elements in our definition. E.g., "a rationale is formulated" can be linked to the elements "is based on business and IT strategy" and "its essential requirements". That does not mean that those elements are irrelevant: those elements have to be part of the description of the architecture principle, as we already indicated above. This hypothesis is strengthened by the fact that only four authors are addressing one or more remaining WH-questions in their definition.

By combining all these findings, we define an architecture principle for information systems as:

"An architecture principle is a declarative statement, based on, at least, business and IT strategy. It normatively describes a property of the design of an information system, which is necessary to ensure that the information system meets its essential requirements."

With this analysis we conclude that there is consensus in literature about the definition of an architecture principle. The differences in the definitions found are related to the use of undefined terms or the use of synonyms. Furthermore, we found incomplete or copious definitions, without catching the essence of an architecture principle.

3.3 Description of Architecture Principles

Although the architecture principle now has been defined, it still has to be described as well. As a consequence, we answer the question with which characteristics architecture principles can be described and how architecture principles are related to its environment. In answering this question, we started investigating the different types of principles.

For many years, there were, in general, two types of architecture principle: design principles and representation principles [9, 10, 23]. The latter type refers to the way architectures should be represented, while the first directs the design of a system itself. In literature they were described as having different characteristics and serving different objectives.

Recently Lumor et al. [28] introduced a third type of principle, namely architecture management principles. Those architecture management principles are reflecting the process nature of EA. The idea behind this third type of principles is the fact that in general architecture and its principles might be a product, process, result, etc. [26, 28–30], and an architecture principle should address the process view as well.

In this literature review we take the view that these different types are different perspectives on the same kind of architecture principles. This is in accordance with Lindström [31], who distinguishes syntactic and semantic characteristics. Syntactic characteristics are describing the elements and their interrelationships of a principle. Semantic characteristics describe the quality elements of the principle. Haki posed in [10] that this differentiation is the same kind of subdivision as the differentiation of design and representation principles. So, depending on perspective, the architecture principle has more or less specific characteristics.

We do understand that, with this choice, we will collect all kinds of characteristics, which also might be related to each other. We encountered this consequence already in our previous case study research [32].

In describing architecture principles, we distinguished the characteristics of the architecture principle itself on the one hand and the relationship with entities in its environment on the other. This breakdown is comparable with the definition of Richardson and Aier et al. [12, 23, 33] in a core definition and basic extensions, and helpful to get more transparency in the description of the architecture principle. In literature we found all kinds of characteristics and entities described. Using our framework as described in section two, we listed all these characteristics (see Fig. 4 and Table 4 in the Appendix).

Characteristics. We start with the 'specification' characteristic. There is consensus on the specification of an architecture principle by the attributes 'statement', 'rationale', and 'implications'. All authors naming these three attributes as an inherent part of an architecture principle. We group these three attributes together in one characteristic, because together they specify the architecture principle.

The second characteristic of an architecture principle is called 'measure'. This characteristic describes the level of fulfilment of the principle. To some authors [12, 24, 31], this is a typical characteristic of an architecture principle, because an architecture principle should to some extent be respected.

Hoogervorst [27, 34], endorsed by [13, 23], and Greefhorst and Proper [26], introduced the characteristic 'Key action' as guidelines for implementing the principle. Recently Marosin [35] added the characteristic 'Precondition', which has to be fulfilled by key actions before a principle can be applied. Because both elements are strongly related to each other, we consider them as attributes of one characteristic called 'Prerequisites' of which the principles depend on.

We also introduce the 'meta data' characteristic. This characteristic typifies the architecture principle so it can be managed. Attributes like name, assurance, visualization and generic information are in scope of this characteristic. Many of such attributes are defined by Greefhorst and Proper [26] and till now there is no exhaustive overview of this kind of attributes.

Finally, there are all kinds of quality, or semantic, attributes defined in literature, which the architecture principle should meet. TOGAF [25], Van Bommel [36], Lindström [31], Marosin [35], and Greefhorst [26] all have their own list of quality attributes. A more detailed comparison shows that they only use different terms for the same type of attributes or use a slightly different definition of the quality attribute. Therefore we choose the quality attributes used by Van Bommel [36] and Greefhorst [26]: 'Specific', 'Measurable', 'Achievable', 'Relevant' and 'Time-framed' (SMART). The reason to choose this list of quality attributes, is the fact that they are defined quite detailed in [26] and that they are easy to remember because of the re-use of the SMART criteria for objectives.

Entities in Its Environment. Next to their characteristics listed above, the context in which the architecture principles are used, is important as well [9, 12, 13, 26, 37], in particular for the effect of a principle. The key context of an architecture principle, according to literature, consists of the 'design', 'requirements', 'the architecture', 'the strategy', and 'the architecture principle set'. We describe those relationships one by one (see also Fig. 4).

The most direct relationship an architecture principle has, is with the 'design'. Architecture and therefore also architecture principles restricts the design freedom of a system, according to [26, 27, 34, 38]. As we already have seen in the definition of the architecture principle, that restriction is necessary "to ensure the information system meeting its essential requirements". So, via the design the architecture principle should ensure the information system satisfies the 'requirements'.

In the architecture principle definition, we also have described the statement "...based on business and IT strategy". In our literature review we did not see a clear clarification of the relationship between 'business and IT strategy' and an architecture principle. We consider architecture principles as part of the 'architecture'; the 'strategy' guides this architecture. Because an architecture principle is part of the architecture, it is based on the strategy as well.

And, most of the time, an architecture principle is part of a set of principles. Although in most literature the focus is on individual architecture principles, a principle is only effective if it is part of a set [9, 26, 31, 35, 39]. Because we are interested in the contribution of architecture principles, we have to describe "the architecture principle set" as well. We define an architecture principle set as:

"a group of architecture principles defined and presented as a collection".

Because a set of principles is an entity in itself, it has characteristics and attributes as well. Based on Greefhorst and Proper [26] we define three types of characteristic: 'classification', 'meta data' and 'quality of the set' (see Table 5 in the Appendix).

First, architecture principles are grouped together based on a 'classification'. This 'classification' is based on the type and scope of the architecture principles. The type is related to the architecture layers of an architecture model. There are many definitions of architecture layers in use like TOGAF [25], Zachmann [40], and IAF [41]. In our scope we consider the 'information system' layer and within this layer the subdivisions 'application' and 'infrastructure'. Architecture principles can also be classified based on the (organizational) level of use: for a 'specific solution', a 'division', for 'an entire organization', etc.

Secondly, an architecture principle set can be typified by 'meta data' to manage the principle set, such as 'name', 'release number', 'amount of architecture principles in the set', etc. Some authors do address the point that the amount of principles in the set should be as small as possible [31, 36, 42]. Many attributes may be added to the characteristic 'meta data', and for now there is no complete list available.

And lastly, similar to the individual architecture principle, an architecture principle set meets quality standards: 'quality of the set'. In the case of a set of principles we distinguish the attributes 'representative', 'accessible' and 'consistent'.

Literature Review Results. Based on the literature review we built a model to describe the characteristics of the architecture principle including his environment (see Fig. 4). As discussed in our analysis above, this model is diverging slightly from the meta-model of Aier et al. [12, 13].

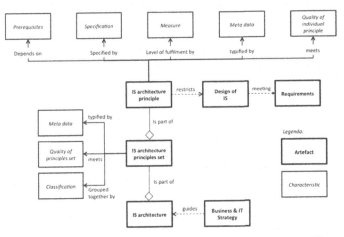

Fig. 4. Model for describing the architecture principle and set [3].

In our literature review we determined consensus on the characteristics. Although we are of the opinion that the different types of architecture principles are perspectives on the same kind of principles, we did not find any contradictions. We added and reorganized some characteristic and attributes. As already addressed in a previous case study research [32], some characteristics were defined relatively subjective in literature, using terms like "significant", "easy", or "obvious". We have strengthened the definitions where possible (see Tables 4 and 5 in the Appendix), while we are aware of the fact that architecture principles are semi structured, informal and written in natural language [21, 35, 39, 43, 44]. Furthermore, we have described the architecture principle set with characteristics and attributes as well, because the contribution of architecture principle is only effective in a set.

4   Measuring Architecture Principles

After the definition and description of architecture principles in theory, we need both a measurement instrument and a corresponding method to be able to measure principles in practice. In section five we will challenge this measurement instrument in a real-life situation.

4.1   Measurement Instrument

To measure architecture principles and related architecture principle sets in practice we need a well-defined measurement instrument. This measurement instrument should be able to:

1. Identify the architecture principles and the architecture principle sets related to them;
2. Describe architecture principle and the architecture principle sets with their characteristics and attributes.

Identification. Based on the literature review as described in section three, we formulated the definition of an architecture principle and set respectively:

> *"An architecture principle is a declarative statement, based on, at least, business and IT strategy. It normatively describes a property of the design of an information system, which is necessary to ensure that the information system meets its essential requirements."*

and

> *"a group of architecture principles defined and presented as a collection"*

We use these definitions to identify the principles and sets, by checking whether or not an architecture principle (set) fulfills all elements of the definition. So, in the measurement instrument we designed a definition check for the elements 'declarative statement', 'based on business and IT strategy', 'normatively', 'describes a property of the design', and 'necessary meeting its essential requirements'. If it is an architecture principle, each of these elements has to be present. And for each element there are explanatory facts as well. For an architecture principle set we do see every group of architecture principles described together as a set, as in the definition has been set.

Description. For describing both the individual architecture principles and the sets of architecture principles we used the model of characteristics and related attributes as described in section three (see Fig. 4). Using this model, we list in our measurement instrument all characteristics and attributes, including their definitions as defined in Table 4 of the Appendix.

Per architecture principle we collect all data related to its characteristics and attributes. In a spreadsheet we record per principle all relevant data found, categorized by source. We use the same approach for describing architecture principle sets.

4.2 Measurement Method

To be able to use the measurement instrument, we also need a reliable and valid measurement method to measure the architecture principles. The measurement method helps with collecting and analyzing the right data and finally with measuring the architecture principles. The measurement method is an iterative three-step approach (see Fig. 5).

Collect Data. The objective of this step is to collect data about architecture principles and the architecture principle set. Therefore, data about the related artefacts are also relevant: IS architectures, IS designs, requirements and business & IT strategies. We use different methods to collect data: desk research, surveys, interviews and site visits.

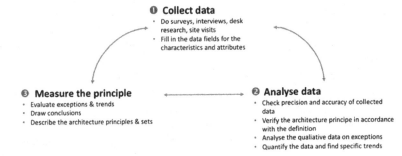

Fig. 5. The measurement method [4].

For the desk research all kind of documents might be useful, like architecture descriptions, requirements specifications, test reports, and so on. All these address elements of the architecture principles and/or the related artefacts. The survey is used to collect data before the interview sessions, to be able to focus on specific items during the interview. The survey consists of open questions based on the characteristics in the framework. The interviews take place with at least two members of the research team. All interviews are recorded, and the minutes of the interview are sent to the interviewee for feedback. Interviewees are architects, software engineers, the test manager, the project leader, and the system owner. Site visits are useful to see the information system running in the daily operation and to consider to what extent the essential requirements are implemented.

We record all relevant data per architecture principle and per source, in order to have different facts about the same characteristic or attribute available. This is useful for the analysis of data, when differences or even conflicts among the data about a specific characteristic or attribute occur.

Analyze Data. In this step we analyze the data to check the precision and accuracy of the data and to find exceptions and trends. For all data collected we check for inconsistencies between sources. If so, we have to go back for data collection to find the right or new data. If, afterwards, data conflicts remain, we have to explain the differences or decide not to use the data.

Secondly, we check whether or not so-called architecture principles are in accordance with the architecture principle definition. We determine if the principle satisfies each element of the definition and write down that reasoning in a spreadsheet. If not, the so-called architecture principle is declared be out of scope.

We then analyze the qualitative data on exceptions. The analysis has to be done per principle, but also between different principles. We look at remarkable differences between attributes or characteristics of a principle or between principles. For instance, the key action cannot be related to the prerequisite of the principle. Or, one architecture principle is fulfilled completely, while another one is not, although those two are strongly related.

The final action is to quantify the data and find specific trends from the quantified data. We simplify the analysis between principles out from different cases. We quantify the data of each principle and set as follows.

- We review the different sources per attribute and set the numerical score;
- The score reflects the level of fulfilment of the definition of the attribute: '0' is no fulfilment, '1' is partly fulfilment and, '2' is complete fulfilment. We call this our code scheme [45]. The reasoning for the score is described in the spreadsheet;
- The score of the characteristic is the average of the score of its attributes;
- Only for the "classification" characteristic of the principle set we use an alternative score: the scores used refer to the specific values the attribute can have. See the appendix for all attribute values of principle sets;
- Finally, we calculate the average score of each characteristic over all principles and sets.

We now are able to make cross-section analyses, to create graphics and to search for trends.

Measure the Principle. This final step is to evaluate the exceptions and trends. We describe the architecture principles and the architecture principle sets, including the overall conclusions about their state. Based on the qualitative and quantified analysis we evaluate the exceptions and trends. We explain those exceptions and trends and draw our conclusions as subject-matter experts. Of course, we add evidence supporting those conclusions.

We end up with describing the architecture principles and the architecture principle sets by describing their characteristics and attributes. In this description we add the qualitative and quantified analysis, including the conclusions.

5 Case Study

We started challenging our measurement instrument with one case study only. Before we use the instruments for many cases simultaneously, we first would like to test to what extent the instrument is useful in practice. Depending on the outcome of the first case study, we can decide how to continue. If there is a big misfit with the instrument itself, we will focus on improving the instrument. If it is working in practice quite well, we can start directly with the research itself and optimize the measurement instrument where necessary.

We used the 'Teruggaaf Dividendbelasting' (TDi), in English: 'Return of Dividend Tax', of the Dutch Tax Agency as case in our research. TDi is an information system supporting the return of tax on dividend payed to legal entities. TDi was rebuilt in an agile project, which we investigated until system release in December 2017. For this case study we reviewed nineteen documents, conducted five interviews with six different stakeholders and examined the TDi system itself during a site visit. These activities were done by our research team consisting of three researchers.

5.1 Architecture Principles of the TDi Case

In the rebuilding of the TDi system 55 potential architecture principles were used. According to our definition (see section four), only 36 architecture principles could be identified as such. In Fig. 6 we see the level of completeness of all those 36 architecture principles together, while the individual scores may differ between the principles.

Looking at the specification characteristic of the architecture principles we did recognize that none of the principles included a rationale, while the statement and implications were worked out well. A reference to the rationale, as they were described in other architecture documents, was missing as well.

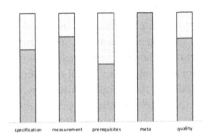

Fig. 6. Level of completeness of the 36 architecture principles [4].

80% of the principles has been fulfilled partly (36%) or fully (44%). Only one principle was not followed ("from object based to subject based working") and in 17% we could not determine whether or not the principles had been fulfilled because of missing resource data (see Fig. 7). Interestingly, developers didn't respect some of the principles as meant to be and implemented parts of the system in other directions.

With respect to the prerequisites, for seven principles specific preconditions were defined, while for all, some overall preconditions were defined. Not all of the preconditions have been fulfilled (completely) at the start or during the project, like "B/CAO building blocks available". Therefore, not all principles could be fulfilled, as we did see. Surprisingly, there were no 'key actions' identified, to get the preconditions fulfilled.

All meta data was in place, so that managing the architecture principles was no issue. Information about author, status, version, users and much more was easy to find.

The architecture principles were meeting the quality attributes as well. The main reason why the overall score of the quality is not 100 percent, is that the rationale was missing. Therefore, we were not able to determine the principle's intention and relevance

Level of fulfilment

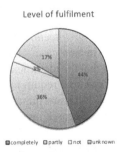

□completely □partly □not □unknown

Fig. 7. Level of fulfilment of the principles [4].

as described in the 'specific' and 'relevant' attribute. All architecture principles, even when they were imposed from outside the project, were translated to the TDi context.

The architecture principles originate from two documents: a High Level Design (HLD) and a Project Start Architecture (PSA). The HLD describes the process, application and technical infrastructure of the TDI system, while the PSA focuses on the application and technical infrastructure only. In the HLD, twelve architecture principles are defined explicitly but most principles are only addressed by referring to other architecture documents. In the PSA, nine ICT principles are described, including directives for using in the TDi system implementation. In both documents many meta data attributes can be found, like authors, administrator, status, target audience, etc.

Given the many architecture principles mentioned in both sets we conclude that the sets are not representative for meeting the essential requirements. There are too many architecture principles adopted from the overall architectures, resulting in overlap. Those principles are not translated to a single principle specific for the TDi system. Although there are many overlapping architecture principles, there are no contradictory principles in the sets. The accessibility of the sets themselves is good, because they were managed by the architects of the TDi project. Because the sets refer to other documents, the accessibility of the original sets of principles is less evident.

5.2 Evaluation of the Measurement Instrument

For evaluating the measurement instrument, we have to test for both the identification and the description of the architecture principles, whether they are complete and coherent. To start with the identification of the architecture principles, the instrument was helpful in determining which of the so-called architecture principles are fulfilling the elements of the definition. As a result, nineteen of the 55 so-called architecture principles did not pass verification. On the other hand, we did not find any other statements, not explicitly called architecture principles, that did fulfil the elements of the definition.

The definition of the architecture principle set was not differentiating enough. There are many ways to present a group of principles together. In our case we analyzed the different kinds of sets to understand the interrelationships between those sets. We did see in this case study that the presentation of the architecture principles was related to other architecture documents, which were already in place. So, the way of presenting the principles is not necessarily related to the system itself but influenced by external factors. Therefore, our case study resulted in a changed definition of the architecture principle set: "*a group of architecture principles defined and presented as a collection based on a similar type or scope of the architecture principles*".

Although we might state that - in this case - the identification of all individual principles was done, we also learned that the identification is also related to the essential requirements. In our case study the essential requirements were defined at a high level, e.g. "the system has to be future-proof", so it was quite easy to link architecture principles to the essential requirements. So, in next cases more in-depth research to the essential requirements is necessary.

The coherence of the architecture principle definition was already theoretically explained in our literature review with the WH-questions approach [3]. During the case study we did not find any inconsistencies between the elements, which might suggest that the elements of the definitions are incorrect.

The second part of the measurement instrument describes the architecture principles. Looking at the completeness of the instrument we found in the case all but two of the attributes defined in the model. The 'rationale' attribute was defined in other documents and, although no 'key actions' were defined, in some interviews necessary key actions to take were brought forward. So, none of the attributes are irrelevant.

In our case study we detected some omissions in the model. The attribute 'degree of acceptance' has to be added to the 'measure' characteristic, because in our case this element was addressed by several sources. It describes an aspect relevant to the fulfilment of the principle and will be defined as: "level of acceptance of the principle by all of its users". The attribute 'preconditions fulfilled', related to the 'prerequisites' characteristic, is also relevant to add. We explicitly saw in the case that, when preconditions were set, it was also relevant to know whether the preconditions were fulfilled. The definition of this attribute can be described as "the level of fulfilment of the preconditions defined".

For the architecture principle set we will add an extra characteristic: 'prerequisites'. We discovered in the case study that some prerequisites were not related to a specific principle, but to a group of principles. Besides the 'precondition' attribute, 'basic assumptions' were described for some sets as well. Basic assumptions are "relevant criteria for successful use of the principle".

In this case we did not find any inconsistencies in the coherence of the description model. Some of the relationships as described in the model, e.g. 'depends on' or 'level of fulfilment', were described explicitly in the documents or way mentioned during the interviews. The amount of information, though, is insufficient to make fact-based statements about the consistency of the coherence. In this case it was clear that there are interrelationships between attributes, e.g. the missing of the rationale and therefore a lower score at quality, as we already described in [32]. More research data is necessary to make clear statements about the coherence.

5.3 Evaluation of the Measurement Method

We evaluate the measurement method by discussing the reliability and validity of the case study results. To challenge the reliability of the results, we want to know to what extent the results would be consistent when doing the case study research again. In the measurement method are different protocols defined to assure the reliability of the outcome: using different kinds of data collections, working with a research team, minutes including feedback, etc. All these mechanisms are important, because this case demonstrates the subjectivity of facts collected. Two architects, for example, were working closely together during the project, but had different opinions about the fulfilment of some of the architecture principles. The research team could, based on all different sources, make an expert judgement about the fulfilment.

Although we used different ways of collection data, in this case study we were lacking some in-depth information about the essential requirements. As a result, it was difficult to see to what extent architecture principles were adding value in meeting the essential requirements. Additional sources related to the essential requirements, e.g. interviewing extra business owners, would help to bridge this gap.

In evaluating the validity of the measurement method, we concluded that the description of the architecture principles reflects the real situation of TDi. Although we found some contradictory data, especially in the interviews, we were able to explain the differences in the data. In this specific case we were not always able to go into details of specific architecture principles. Because the case used quite some principles, 36 in total, it was difficult to address all individual principles. So, in following cases we need mechanisms to get more in-depth information about the individual principles.

6   Limitations, Conclusions and Further Research

6.1   Limitations

Literature Study Limitations. Related to the literature study there are two threats to the validity of our results. The first limitation we have identified is the interpretation of the words that have been used in the definitions and the characteristics. Although semantics of natural language is always an issue in literature study, we encountered in several papers descriptions that were rather vague, and therefore subject to (personal) interpretation and possible wrong conclusions. Because many publications confirm and use the conclusions of previous publications, we judge the risk of misinterpretation low.

The other limitation is the rather broad scope of the literature search by considering architecture principles in the enterprise domain instead of architecture principles in the IS domain. In certain cases, we translated architecture principle characteristics to specific IS ones without knowing whether that would be valid in practice. This is a topic for further research. Because architecture principles can affect multiple architecture domains [26], we consider this as low risk.

To discuss the results of our literature review we also sent our draft paper to a small group of senior experts in this research area. We used their response to eliminate indistinctness in the draft paper. Besides that, the experts addressed some specific remarks related to the paper.

Several experts mentioned that formulating architecture principles is important, but that the use of architecture principle is the real issue in practice. The description of the architecture principle is a precondition, necessary to determine the use and the effectiveness of architecture principles.

The second remark is related to the ordering of the characteristics. As addressed in Sect. 3 we have chosen not to order the characteristics in this part of our research, although there are different perspectives on architecture principles. Two experts suggest to order the characteristics using some framework, for example the dimensions framework defined in Greeforst and Proper [26]. Such frameworks will help in evaluating the relationships between the different characteristics as well.

The last remark was related to the definition of the architecture principle. The original definition suggests that architecture principles are based on business and IT strategy only. We do agree with the experts that business and IT strategy are just two, be it important, sources to formulate architecture principles. So, we reframed the definition by adding 'at least' in the phrasing.

Case Study Limitations. Although the arguments for using the case study approach are still valid, there are some limitations important to address in this case study. We are aware that one case cannot prove the completeness of the measurement instrument. As discussed in section four, the objective of this research is to test to what extent the instrument is useful in practice in the first place. For an extended test on completeness and coherence of the measurement instrument, we need more test cases.

A second limitation might be that the researchers, although all kind of protocols are defined, are biased in searching for characteristics and attributes. The moment we are introducing a model as a description of our research object, we see architecture principles through this model. We tried to avoid this prejudice by avoiding naming of attributes during the survey and interviews. The fact that we identified new attributes and characteristics, shows that we were open for new elements as well.

Finally, we can also note that there is currently no other instrument that measures architectural principles, so we cannot compare this instrument with other instruments. Studies have been done on the added value of architecture in general and we could apply that approach to the same case to assess whether comparable results will be achieved.

6.2 Conclusions

Conclusions for Defining and Describing Principles. In most relevant publications we found 15 different definitions of architecture principles and a large set of characteristics. In a period of 27 years the definition of an architecture principle has been consolidated. Besides, there is consensus about many characteristics. Nevertheless, we did find some inaccuracy or incompleteness in definitions and descriptions, as we addressed in this paper.

First, we found all kinds of definitions in literature, with most of them incomplete or just not striking the essentials of an architecture principle. By decomposing and rephrasing the elements of those definitions we ended up with a more comprehensive and consistent definition.

In describing the architecture principles with characteristics, we defined all types of principles as different perspectives on the same kind of principles. We grouped together the rationale, statement and implication into one characteristic 'specification'. Besides we distinguished 'key action' and 'preconditions' as two separate attributes, combined in the characteristic 'Prerequisites'. We also considered 'Meta data' and 'Quality' as explicit characteristics of an architecture principle, which has not been done in all past literature. Where possible we tried to define the characteristics more objectively – despite the fact that in natural language, interpretations of words are always possible. Altogether, there were no contradictions found in past literature, but we have extended the description of the Architecture principle with new characteristics.

Analyzing the contribution of individual architecture principles without looking at the set of principles is of no use. An architecture principle is only effective in combination with other architecture principles. We therefore also described the characteristics of the architecture principle set: 'Classification', 'Quality' and 'Meta data'. We described the characteristics of both an architecture principle and the architecture principle set into a framework also related to entities in its environment.

Conclusions for Measuring Principles. To answer Sub question 2, we had to describe a measurement instrument and test it in a real-life case study. Based on that experiences from practice we can conclude that the measurement instrument is fit for purpose. Although the instrument can be improved with extra characteristics and attributes. These extensions are 'degree of acceptance' and 'preconditions fulfilled' for describing the individual principle. Besides the characteristic 'prerequisites', including the attributes 'precondition', and 'basic assumption' can be added for the architecture principle set. Although we know that we tested the instrument with one case only, we are beyond doubt that with these add-ons the model has added value in measuring architecture principles and in measuring related architecture principle sets.

Secondly, we had to investigate how to use this measurement instrument in practice. We defined a three-step method to collect, analyze and measure the architecture principle (set). We used this measurement method in our case study, with a description of the architecture principles and principles sets for the TDi case as a result. We have the opinion that the method yields reliable and valid results, although we discovered in this case that more information on the requirements and the individual principles, would strengthen the results of the case study.

6.3 Further Research

In summary, the conclusions and limitations combined confirm that it is feasible to enlarge the number of tests of architecture principle measurements with more cases. With more cases we are able to test the ability to compare architecture principles and principle sets between case studies.

When carrying out new cases, we would prefer the number of cases to be as large as possible. However, substantial scaling up the number of cases requires automatic processing of the data. In our opinion, this is only to a limited extent possible, as compliance with architecture principles always requires some sort of human interpretation.

Secondly, we can use the new case studies to test the completeness and coherence of the measurement instrument and method. We need to investigate whether or not the vision of using architecture principle is a characteristic in itself and we also have to see how we can elaborate on the essential requirements. So, new case studies will give new insights in the use of the instrument and method and help in optimizing them both.

Acknowledgements. Special thanks to the senior experts Saco Bekius (DTA, now M&I Partners), Martin van den Berg (Dutch Central Bank), Danny Greefhorst (ArchiXL), Paul Oude Luttighuis (Le Blanc Advies) and Raymond Slot (Hogeschool Utrecht) for reviewing (parts of) this paper.

We would like to thank Yvette Hoekstra and Henk van den Berg for participating in the research team of the case study and giving all kinds of comments on both the measurement instrument and the case study results. Secondly, we want to thank the Dutch Tax Agency, and Jelco Bosma specifically, for enabling the case study.

Appendix

See Tables 6 and 7.

Table 1. Most relevant publications related to defining and describing architecture principles [3].

Nr.	Title of publication	Author	Year of publication
1	A Principles-Based Enterprise Architecture: Lessons from Texaco and Star Enterprise	G.L. Richardson et al.	1990
2	A Big-Picture Look at Enterprise Architectures	F.J. Armour et al.	1999
3	Enterprise Architecture: Enabling Integration, Agility and Change	J. Hoogervorst	2004
4	Enterprise Architectures – Review on Concepts, Principles and Approaches	D. Chen et al.	2004
5	Giving Meaning to Enterprise Architectures – Architecture Principles with ORM and ORC	P. van Bommel et al.	2006
6	On the Syntax and Semantics of Architectural Principles	Ä. Lindström	2006
7	Impact of principles on Enterprise Engineering	Martin Op 't Land, Erik Proper	2007
8	Architecture principles – A regulative perspective on enterprise architecture	Van Bommel et al.	2007
9, 10	The Open Group Architecture Framework TOGAF^{TM}	The Open Group	2007, 2011
11	Enterprise Architecture Principles: Literature Review and Research Directions	Dirk Stelzer	2009
12	The Roles of Principles in Enterprise Architecture	Erik Proper, Danny Greefhorst	2010
13	What Is an Enterprise Architecture Principle?	Christian Fischer, Robert Winter, Stephan Aier	2010
14	A Conceptual Framework for Enterprise Architecture Design	Sabine Buckl	2010
15	Enterprise Architecture Principles and their impact on the Management of IT Investments	Kalevi Pessi et al.	2011

(*continued*)

Table 1. (*continued*)

Nr.	Title of publication	Author	Year of publication
16	How are Enterprise Architecture Design Principles Used?	Robert Winter, Stephan Aier	2011
17	Construction and Evaluation of a Meta-Model for Enterprise Architecture Design Principles	Stephan Aier, Christian Fischer, Robert Winter	2011
18	Architecture Principles – The Cornerstones of Enterprise Architecture	Danny Greefhorst, Erik Proper	2011
19	New Avenues for Theoretical Contributions in Enterprise Architecture Principles – a Literature Review	Mohammad Kazem Haki, Christine Legner	2012
20	The Dutch State of the Practice of Architecture Principles	Danny Greefhorst, Hendrik Proper, Georgios Plataniotis	2013
21	Enterprise Architecture Principles In Research And Practice: Insights From An Exploratory Analysis	Mohammad Kazem Haki, Christine Legner	2013
22	A Principle-based Goal-oriented Requirements Language (GRL) for Enterprise Architecture	Diana Marosin, Sepideh Ghanavati, Dirk van der Linden	2014
23	Alignment of Enterprise Architecture Principles: A Case Study	Christer Tallberg, Kalevi Pessi et al.	2015
24	Measuring and Managing the Design Restriction of Enterprise Architecture (EA) Principles on EA Models	Diana Marosin, Sepideh Ghanavati	2015
25	The nature and a Process for Development of Enterprise Architecture Principles	Kurt Sandkuhl, Daniel Simon, Matthias Wissotzki, Christoph Starke	2015
26	Do IT architecture principles contribute to IT system's requirements realisation?	Michiel Borgers	2016
27	Case report of identifying and measuring IT architecture principles in the Dutch Tax Agency	Michiel Borgers, Frank Harmsen	2016
28	Formalizing and Modeling Enterprise Architecture (EA) Principles with Goal-oriented Requirements Language (GRL)	Diana Marosin, Marc van Zee, Sepideh Ghanavati	2016

Table 2. Overview of architecture principle definitions by different authors [3].

Nr.	Definition of architecture principle	Author	Year of publication
1	"Principles are an organization's basic philosophies that guide the development of the architecture… Principles provide guidelines and rationales for the constant examination and re-evaluation of technology plans."	G.L. Richardson et al.	1990
2	"… simple, direct statements of how an enterprise wants to use IT. These statements establish a context for architecture design decisions by translating business criteria into language and specifications that technology managers can understand and use. Architecture principles put boundaries around decisions about system architecture."	F.J. Armour et al.	1999
3	"… collectively the design principles are identified as enterprise architecture."	J. Hoogervorst	2004
4	"Architecture principles are rules to use when elaborating enterprise architectures."	D. Chen et al.	2004
5	"Architecture principles define the underlying general rules and guidelines for the use and deployment of all IT resources and assets across the enterprise…."	Ä. Lindström	2006
6	"Principles are general rules and guidelines, intended to be enduring and seldom amended, that inform and support the way in which an organization sets about fulfilling its mission"	TOGAF	2007
7	"Enterprise architecture principles are fundamental propositions that guide the description, construction, and evaluation of enterprise architectures."	Dirk Stelzer	2009
8	"An EA principle constrains and guides the design of the EA and may in turn provide justification for decision-making throughout an EA. In general, principles are self-restraint and not externally obliged, …. by law in terms of compliances."	Sabine Buckl	2010
9	"An EA principle is based on business strategy and IT strategy. Principles can be attributed to different layers. An EA principle is described in a principle statement saying what to improve. For each principle, a rationale is formulated explaining why the principle is meant to help reaching a predefined goal. For each principle, concrete implications or key actions are described explaining how to implement the principle. Measurement is a key issue of EA principles. For every principle, it should be defined how to determine its fulfilment."	Aier et al.	2010
10	"Architectural principles are statements that express how your enterprise needs to design and deploy information systems across the enterprise to connect, share and structure information."	Pessi et al.	2010
11	"A qualitative statement of intent that should be met by the architecture. Has at least a supporting rationale and a measure of importance."	The Open Group	2011
12	"a declarative statement that normatively prescribes a property of the design of an artifact, which is necessary to ensure the artifact meets its essential requirements."	Danny Greefhorst, Erik Proper	2011

(continued)

Table 2. (*continued*)

Nr.	Definition of architecture principle	Author	Year of publication
13	"EA principles can be attributed to different architectural layers, should be based on business and IT strategies, and refer to the construction of an organization. Each EA principle should be described in a principle statement along with a rationale that explains why this principle is helpful in attaining a predetermined goal, as well as implications that describe how to implement this principle. Finally, metrics could be identified for each principle to measure its fulfilment."	Mohammad Kazem Haki, Christine Legner	2013
14	"an enterprise-specific and abstract, yet simple collection of statements, which generally provide a framework for decision making and thus support the transformation process of an enterprise from a current to a target EA."	Kurt Sandkuhl, Daniel Simon, Matthias Wissotzki, Christoph Starke	2015
15	"In EA, principles have been defined as guidelines and rationales for the design and evolution of technology plans. In other words, EA principles can be seen as "rules of conduct" and can be made more precise and operational by formalization."	Diana Marosin	2016

Table 3. Decomposition and consolidation of an architecture principle definition [3].

Interrogative question	Explanation	Definitions in literature	Consolidated description for architecture principle
What	What is an architecture principle? Describing the determining elements	Are organization's basic philosophies [22], are simple, direct statements [19], are design principles [16], are rules [20], defines the underlying general rules and guidelines [23], are general rules and guidelines, intended to be enduring and seldom amended [38], are fundamental propositions [1], are self-restraint and not externally obliged [30], is based on business and IT strategy [17], are statements [39], a qualitative statement of intent [32], a declarative statement [2], should be based on business and IT strategies [14], have been defined as guidelines and rationales [27], can be seen as 'rules of conduct' [27], is described in a principal statement [17], an enterprise-specific and abstract, yet simple collection of statements [24], which generally provide a framework [24]	Is a declarative statement, as a specific type of design principle, based on business and IT strategy
How	How does the principle work? Describing the manner of the principle	Establish a context for architecture design decisions by translating business criteria into language and specifications [19], put boundaries around decisions about system architecture [19], can be attributed to different layers [17], that normatively prescribes a property of the design of an artifact [2], can be attributed to different architectural layers [14], refer to the construction of an organization [14], can be made more precise and operational by formalization [27]	It normatively describes a property of the design of an IS,

(*continued*)

Table 3. (*continued*)

Interrogative question	Explanation	Definitions in literature	Consolidated description for architecture principle
Why	Why is the architecture principle described? Describing the reason(s) or objectives to achieve	That guide the development of the architecture [22], for the constant examination and re-evaluation of technology plans [22], how an enterprise wants to use IT [19], for the use and deployment of all IT resources and assets across the enterprise [23], that inform and support the way in which an organization sets about fulfilling its mission [38], that guide the description, construction, and evaluation of enterprise architectures [1], constrains and guides the design of the EA and may in turn provide justification, for decision making throughout an EA [30], saying what to improve [17], reaching a predefined goal [17], that express how your enterprise needs to design and deploy information systems across the enterprise to connect, share and structure information [39], that should be met by the architecture [32], to ensure the artifact meets its essential requirements [2], why this principle is helpful in attaining a predetermined goal [14], for the design and evolution of technology plans [26], for decision making and thus support of the transformation process of an enterprise from a current to a target EA [24]	Which is necessary to ensure the IS meeting its essential requirements
Which	With which elements is an architecture principle included? Describing the elementary components of an architecture principle	Provide guidelines and rationales [22], a rationale is formulated explaining why the principle is meant to help [17], concrete implications or key actions are described [17], measurement is a key issue of EA principles..it should be defined how to determine its fulfillment [17], has at least a supporting rationale and a measure of importance [32], should be described in a principle statement, along with a rationale….., as well as implications [14], metrics should be identified for each principle to measure its fulfilment [14]	[Not relevant]
Who	Who is using the architecture principle? Describing the personal related to the architecture principle	That technology managers can understand and use [19]	[Not relevant]

(*continued*)

Table 3. (*continued*)

Interrogative question	Explanation	Definitions in literature	Consolidated description for architecture principle
When	When are architecture principles used? Describing the timing of the use	Constant [22], when elaborating enterprise architectures [23]	[Not relevant]
Where	Where is the architecture principle located? An architecture principle should be accessible for people	–	[Not relevant]

Table 4. Characteristics of architecture principles [3].

Characteristic	Attribute	Definition
Specification		
	Statement	Statement
	Rationale	Highlights the business benefits of adhering to the principle
	Implications	Highlights the requirements for carrying out the principle
Measure		Level of the fulfilment of the statement
Prerequisites		
	Precondition	Preconditions and requirements to be fulfilled before the principle can be applied
	Key action	Guidelines for implementing the principle, giving the preconditions
Meta data	Several	Specifications to be able to govern the principle
Quality		
	Specific	The user can understand its intention and its effects to use it in his work
	Measurable	Possible to determine whether or not a given behaviour is in line with architecture principle
	Achievable	The implications of it can all be performed by or adhered to by all those affected
	Relevant	The principle should lead to a improvement of the system meeting the essential requirement
	Time framed	Principle should be stable in context and time

Table 5. Characteristics of architecture principle set [3].

Characteristic	Attribute	Definition
Classification		
	Type	The principles in the set are related to one of the architecture layers
	Scope	Level of use of the principle
Meta Data	Several	Specifications to be able to govern the principle set
Quality		
	Representative	The set covers all relevant requirements in a specific problem domain
	Accessible	Users can find and retrieve the set of principles and they can comprehend the principles
	Consistent	No contradictions between the architecture principles in the set

Table 6. Possible values for the attributes of the classification characteristic [4].

Attribute	Score	Value
Type: The principles in the set are related to one of the architecture layers		
	0	Infrastructure
	1	Application
	2	Information system
Scope: Level of use of the principle		
	0	Part of the target organisation
	1	Full target organisation
	2	More than the target organisation

Table 7. The 36 architecture principles used within the TDi case (translated from Dutch) [4].

Number	Architecture principle
1	Organisational units do specialize
2	Collaboration based on services
3	We share proven services within the Dutch government
4	We communicate digitally with citizen and companies, if possible
5	Data administration is done digitally only
6	Digital workspaces offer customized information

(continued)

Table 7. (*continued*)

Number	Architecture principle
7	We connect with the activities of citizens and companies
8	We develop knowledge about laws and regulations and share them
9	We strengthen the information position of citizens and companies
10	Design modularity carefully
11	Unique management and multiple use of data
12	Design the continuity of business operations completely
13	Use standards
14	Use services available (re-use, before buy, before build)
15	Use ICT products as intended
16	Deliver robust ICT services
17	Take security risks consciously
18	Solve problems at the source
19	Employee centrally, tailor-made information
20	Standard building blocks
21	Client-oriented payment and management of data
22	Establish source data
23	Exchange of information
24	Process characteristics
25	From object-oriented to subject-oriented
26	Maximize compliant behaviour
27	Integral production control
28	Data is used across contexts
29	Event-driven transactions exist alongside periodical transactions
30	The handling time of transactions matches the expectation of the customer
31	We are preparing for settlement of positive and negative claims
32	Advances can be partially paid
33	Operational Excellence is for Customer Intimacy
34	Decoupling of risk detection and determining legal consequences
35	Sensible reuse of process patterns and ICT facilities
36	Where possible, we shift functionality for transaction processing to the interaction process

References

1. Johnson, J., Mulder, H.: CHAOS chronicles, focusing on failures and possible improvements in IT projects. In: 10th International Multi-Conference on Society, Cybernetics and Informatics, IMSCI 2016, July 2016
2. Borgers, M.A.C.: Do IT architecture principles contribute to IT system' s requirements realisation? In: DCEIS 2016 - Doctoral Consortium on Enterprise Information Systems, pp. 3–8 (2016)
3. Borgers, M., Harmsen, F.: Strengthen the architecture principle definition and its characteristics: a survey encompassing 27 years of architecture principle literature. In: ICEIS 2018 - Proceedings of the 20th International Conference on Enterprise Information Systems, vol. 2 (2018)
4. Borgers, M., Harmsen, F.: Measuring architecture principles and their sets in practice. In: ICEIS 2019 - Proceedings of the 21th International Conference on Enterprise Information Systems, vol. 1 (2019)
5. Steenhuis, J., De Bruijn, E.: Building theories from case study research: the progressive case study. J. Chem. Inf. Model. **53**(9), 1689–1699 (2004)
6. Eisenhardt, K.M.: Building theories from case study research. Acad. Manag. Rev. **14**(4), 532–550 (1989)
7. Yin, R.: Case Study Research: Design and Methods. Sage Publications, Beverly Hills (1984)
8. Webster, J., Watson, R.T.: Analyzing the past to prepare for the future: writing a literature review. MIS Q. **26**(2), xiii–xxiii (2002)
9. Stelzer, D.: Enterprise architecture principles: literature review and research directions. In: Dan, A., Gittler, F., Toumani, F. (eds.) ICSOC/ServiceWave -2009. LNCS, vol. 6275, pp. 12–21. Springer, Heidelberg (2010). https://doi.org/10.1007/978-3-642-16132-2_2
10. Haki, M.K., Legner, C.: New avenues for theoretical contributions in enterprise architecture principles - a literature review. In: Aier, S., Ekstedt, M., Matthes, F., Proper, E., Sanz, Jorge L. (eds.) PRET/TEAR -2012. LNBIP, vol. 131, pp. 182–197. Springer, Heidelberg (2012). https://doi.org/10.1007/978-3-642-34163-2_11
11. Chrisholm, W., Milic, L.T., Greppin, J.A.C.: Interrogativity. John Benjamins Publishing, Amsterdam (1982)
12. Fischer, C., Winter, R., Aier, S.: What is an enterprise architecture principle? In: Lee, R. (ed.) Computer and Information Science 2010. Studies in Computational Intelligence, vol. 317, pp. 193–205. Springer, Heidelberg (2010). https://doi.org/10.1007/978-3-642-15405-8_16
13. Aier, S., Fisher, C., Winter, R.: Construction and evaluation of a meta-model for enterprise architecture design principles. In: 10th International Conference on Wirtschaftsinformatik, Zurich, Switz, 16th–18th February 2011, pp. 637–644 (2011)
14. Yin, R.K.: The case study crisis: some answers. Adm. Sci. Q. **26**(1), 58–65 (1981)
15. Strauss, A.L.: Qualitative Analysis for Social Scientist. Cambridge University Press, Cambridge (1987)
16. Miles, M., Huberman, A.M.: Drawing valid meaning from qualitative data: toward a shared craft. Educ. Res. **13**(5), 20–30 (1984)
17. Gersick, C.: Time and transition in work teams: towards a new model of group development. Acad. Manag. J. **31**, 9–41 (1988)
18. Harris, S.G., Sutton, R.I.: Functions of parting ceremonies in dying organizations. Acad. Manag. J. **29**(1), 5–30 (1986)
19. Eisenhardt, K., Bourgeois, L.J.: Politics of strategic decision making in high velocity environments: toward a mid-range theory. Acad. Manag. J. **31**, 737–770 (1988)
20. Babbie, E.: The Practice of Social Research. Cengage Learning, Inc., Boston (2015)

21. Land, M.O., Proper, E., Waage, M., Cloo, J., Steghuis, C.: Enterprise architecture: creating value by informed governance (2008)
22. Greefhorst, D., Proper, E., Plataniotis, G.: The Dutch state of the practice of architecture principles. J. Enterp. Arch., 6 (2013)
23. Winter, R., Aier, S.: How are enterprise architecture design principles used? In: Proceedings of the IEEE International Enterprise Distributed Object Computing Conference Workshops EDOC, September 2016, pp. 314–321 (2011)
24. Haki, M.K., Legner, C.: Enterprise architecture principles in research and practice: insights from an exploratory analysis. In: Ecis, no. 2013, pp. 1–12 (2013)
25. The Open Group: TOGAF® Version 9.1. Van Haren Publishing (2011)
26. Greefhorst, D., Proper, E.: Architecture Principles: The Cornerstones of Enterprise Architecture, vol. 6, no. 3. Springer, Heidelberg (2011)
27. Hoogervorst, J.: Enterprise architecture: enabling integration, agility and change. Int. J. Coop. Inf. Syst. **13**(03), 213–233 (2004)
28. Lumor, T., Chew, E., Gill, A.Q.: Exploring the role of enterprise architecture in IS-enabled OT: an EA principles perspective. In: Enterprise Distributed Object Computing Workshop (2016)
29. Slot, R.: A method for valuing architecture-based business transformation and measuring the value of solutions architecture (2010)
30. Sandkuhl, K., Simon, D., Wißotzki, M., Starke, C.: The nature and a process for development of enterprise architecture principles. In: Abramowicz, W. (ed.) BIS 2015. LNBIP, vol. 208, pp. 260–272. Springer, Cham (2015). https://doi.org/10.1007/978-3-319-19027-3_21
31. Lindström, Å.: On the syntax and semantics of architectural principles. In: Proceedings of the 39th Hawaii International Conference on System Sciences, vol. 00, no. C, pp. 1–10 (2006)
32. Borgers, M., Harmsen, F.: Case report of identifying and measuring IT architecture principles in the Dutch tax agency. In: 2016 IEEE 18th Conference on Business Informatics, pp. 100–110, November 2016
33. Richardson, G.L., Jackson, B.M., Dickson, G.W.: A principles-based enterprise architecture: lessons from Texaco and Star Enterprise. MIS Q. **14**(4), 385–403 (1990)
34. Hoogervorst, J.A.P.: Enterprise governance and enterprise engineering. The Enterprise Engineering Series, p. 428. Springer, Heidelberg (2009). https://doi.org/10.1007/978-3-540-92671-9
35. Marosin, D., van Zee, M., Ghanavati, S.: Formalizing and modeling enterprise architecture (EA) principles with goal-oriented requirements language (GRL). In: Nurcan, S., Soffer, P., Bajec, M., Eder, J. (eds.) CAiSE 2016. LNCS, vol. 9694, pp. 205–220. Springer, Cham (2016). https://doi.org/10.1007/978-3-319-39696-5_13
36. van Bommel, P., Hoppenbrouwers, S.J.B.A., Proper, H.A.(Erik), van der Weide, Th.P.: Giving meaning to enterprise architectures. In: Meersman, R., Tari, Z., Herrero, P. (eds.) OTM 2006. LNCS, vol. 4278, pp. 1138–1147. Springer, Heidelberg (2006). https://doi.org/10.1007/11915072_17
37. Proper, E., Greefhorst, D.: The roles of principles in enterprise architecture. In: Proper, E., Lankhorst, M.M., Schönherr, M., Barjis, J., Overbeek, S. (eds.) TEAR 2010. LNBIP, vol. 70, pp. 57–70. Springer, Heidelberg (2010). https://doi.org/10.1007/978-3-642-16819-2_5
38. Dietz, J.L.G.: Architecture - Building stategy into design. Academic Service, The Hague (2008)
39. Marosin, D., Ghanavati, S.: Measuring and managing the design restriction of enterprise architecture (EA) principles on EA models. In: Proceedings of the 8th International Workshop on Requirements Engineering and Law, RELAW 2015, pp. 37–46 (2015)
40. Zachman, J.A.: A framework for information systems architecture. IBM Syst. J. **26**(3), 276–292 (1987)

41. van't Wout, J., Waage, M., Hartman, H., Stahlecker, M., Hofman, A.: The Integrated Architecture Framework Explained. Why, What, How. Springer, Heidelberg (2010). https://doi.org/10.1007/978-3-642-11518-9
42. Land, M.O., Proper, H.: Impact of principles on enterprise engineering. In: Ecis, no. 2007, pp. 1965–1976 (2007)
43. Marosin, D., Ghanavati, S., Van Der Linden, D.: A principle-based goal-oriented requirements language (GRL) for enterprise architecture. CEUR Workshop Proceedings, vol. 1157 (2014)
44. Buckl, S., Matthes, F., Roth, S., Schulz, C., Schweda, C.M.: A conceptual framework for enterprise architecture design. In: Proper, E., Lankhorst, M.M., Schönherr, M., Barjis, J., Overbeek, S. (eds.) TEAR 2010. LNBIP, vol. 70, pp. 44–56. Springer, Heidelberg (2010). https://doi.org/10.1007/978-3-642-16819-2_4
45. Babbie, E.: The Practice of Social Research (2015)
46. Lyons, J.: Semantics, vol. I. Cambridge University Press, Cambridge (1977)

Author Index